THE MACMILLAN WRITER

Rhetoric and Reader

THE MACMILLAN WRITER

Rhetoric and Reader

SECOND EDITION

Brief Edition

JUDITH NADELL
Rowan College of New Jersey

LINDA McMENIMAN
Rowan College of New Jersey

JOHN LANGAN
Atlantic Community College

MACMILLAN PUBLISHING COMPANY
NEW YORK

EDITOR: Eben W. Ludlow
DEVELOPMENT EDITOR: Nancy Perry
PRODUCTION SUPERVISOR: Katherine Evancie
PRODUCTION MANAGER: Su Levine
TEXT AND COVER DESIGNER: Sheree Goodman
COVER ILLUSTRATION: Jerry McDaniel

This book was set in Palatino, Schneidler, and Weiss by Carlisle Graphics and was printed and bound by R. R. Donnelley/Crawfordsville. The cover was printed by New England Book Components.

Copyright © 1994 by Macmillan Publishing Company, a division of Macmillan, Inc.

Printed in the United States of America

All rights reserved. No part of this book may be reproduced or transmitted in any form or by any means, electronic or mechanical, including photocopying, recording, or any information storage and retrieval system, without permission in writing from the Publisher.

Earlier edition copyright © 1991 by Macmillan Publishing Company.

Macmillan Publishing Company
866 Third Avenue, New York, New York 10022

Macmillan Publishing Company is part of
the Maxwell Communication Group of Companies.

Maxwell Macmillan Canada, Inc.
1200 Eglinton Avenue East, Suite 200
Don Mills, Ontario M3C 3N1

Library of Congress Cataloging-in-Publication Data

Nadell, Judith.
   The Macmillan writer : rhetoric and reader / Judith Nadell.—Brief ed.
     p. cm.
   Includes index.
   ISBN 0-02-386011-1
    1. English language—Rhetoric. 2. College readers.
 I. McMeniman, Linda. II. Langan, John. III. Title.
PE1408.N183 1994
808'.0427—dc20   93-20315
                                                                   CIP

Printing: 1 2 3 4 5 6 7   Year: 4 5 6 7 8 9 0

Acknowledgments begin on page 563, which constitutes an extension of the copyright page.

ABOUT THE AUTHORS

Judith Nadell, formerly Associate Professor of Communication at Rowan College of New Jersey, is now an adjunct professor at the college. During her eighteen-year full-time stint at Rowan, she coordinated the introductory course in the Freshman Writing Sequence and served as Director of the Writing Lab. A Phi Beta Kappa graduate of Tufts University, she received a doctorate from Columbia University. She is the founder of the consulting firm Communication Training Associates and coauthor of *Doing Well in College* (McGraw-Hill) and *The Macmillan Reader.* The recipient of a New Jersey award for excellence in the teaching of writing, Judith Nadell lives with her coauthor husband, John Langan, near Philadelphia.

Linda McMeniman has been a member of the Communication Department at Rowan College of New Jersey for fifteen years. At Rowan, she teaches composition, public speaking, the research process, business writing, and semantics. She also has played a significant role in guiding the college's Freshman Writing Sequence. A Phi Beta Kappa graduate of New York University, she holds a Ph.D. from the University of Pennsylvania. Coauthor of *The Macmillan Reader,* she has also been a free-lance writer and an editorial consultant to several arts and corporate publications. Linda McMeniman lives in Pennsylvania with her husband and family.

John Langan has taught reading and writing courses at Atlantic Community College near the New Jersey shore for the past twenty-one years. He earned advanced degrees in reading at Glassboro State College and in writing at Rutgers University. Coauthor of *The Macmillan Reader* and author of a series of college textbooks on both reading and writing, he has published widely with McGraw-Hill Book Company, Townsend Press, and Macmillan Publishing Company. His books include *English Skills; Reading and Study Skills;* and *College Writing Skills.*

PREFACE

IN our roughly sixty years of combined experience teaching composition, the three of us have gathered ideas from colleagues, journals, books, and conferences. Mindful of shifting trends in composition theory and practice, we've experimented with a variety of instructional methods. We've also risked the deflation of our egos as we've tested numerous hunches of our own. And so, when we started thinking about writing the first edition of this book, we looked as objectively as we could at our classroom experiences. Which approaches, we asked ourselves, had truly helped students become more confident, more skilled, more insightful writers?

Like the original long version, *The Macmillan Writer: Brief Edition* represents a distillation of what we've learned about writing these many years. We adopt an eclectic approach in the book, bringing together the best from often conflicting schools of thought, blending in class-tested strategies of our own. The mix we've come up with works for our students; we think it will for yours, too.

In the book, as in our classes, we try to strike a balance between product and process. Stressing the connection between reading and writing, we describe possible sequences and structures. At the same time, we emphasize that these steps and formats shouldn't be viewed as rigid prescriptions but as strategies for helping students discover what works best for them. This flexibility means that the book can fit a wide range of teaching philosophies and learning styles.

The Macmillan Writer: Brief Edition includes nearly everything that instructors and students need in a one- or two-semester first-year college composition course: a comprehensive *rhetoric*, including chapters on each stage of the writing process, discussions of the exam essay and the literary paper, and an in-depth treatment of the research paper; plus a *reader* with thirty-two *professional selections* and thirteen *student essays* integrated into the rhetoric. The *Brief Edition* thus contains everything that's in the long version *except* for the Handbook. In those classes where students are likely to have purchased a separate English handbook, the short version is especially appropriate.

vii

Throughout the text, we aim for a supportive, conversational tone that inspires students' confidence without being patronizing. Numerous *activities* and *writing assignments—over three hundred in all*—develop awareness of rhetorical choices and encourage students to explore a range of composing strategies.

THE BOOK'S PLAN

Gratified by the warm, enthusiastic reception given the original long version, we decided not to tinker with the book's essential structure. Although the Handbook has been eliminated, the *Brief Edition* is otherwise exactly the same as the long version. The book's format remains as follows.

Part I, "The Reading Process," provides guided practice in a three-step process for reading with close attention and interpretive skill. An activity at the end of Chapter 1, "Becoming a Strong Reader," gives students a chance to put the sequence to use. First, they read Phyllis Theroux's essay "The Worry Factor." Then we show them how to apply the three-step sequence to the selection. Last, they respond to sample questions and writing assignments, all similar to those that accompany the professional selections in Part III. Part I thus does more than just tell students how to sharpen their reading abilities; it guides them through a clearly sequenced plan for developing critical reading skills.

Part II, "The Writing Process," takes students, step by step, through a multistage composing sequence. To make the writing process easier for students to understand, we provide a separate chapter for each of the following stages:

- Chapter 2, "Getting Started Through Prewriting"
- Chapter 3, "Identifying a Thesis"
- Chapter 4, "Supporting the Thesis With Evidence"
- Chapter 5, "Organizing the Evidence"
- Chapter 6, "Writing the Paragraphs in the First Draft"
- Chapter 7, "Revising Overall Meaning, Structure, and Paragraph Development"
- Chapter 8, "Revising Sentences and Words"
- Chapter 9, "Editing and Proofreading"
- Chapter 10, "Writing on a Word Processor"

In Chapter 2, we introduce students to a range of prewriting techniques, including brainstorming, mapping, and journal writing. Stressing the need for students to analyze their purpose and audience, we explain how to limit a broad topic and how to generate raw, preliminary material about the topic. Chapter 2, like the other chapters in Part II, ends with an array of practical activities.

At this point, students are ready for our discussion of thesis statements in Chapter 3. Numerous examples illustrate how to frame an effective thesis and what pitfalls to avoid. The chapter also encourages students to view their first thesis as tentative; they learn that as writing continues, new ideas emerge that may force them to reformulate their initial thesis.

Chapter 4 starts with a description of strategies for gathering evidence to support a thesis. Then we discuss techniques for evaluating the relevance, specificity, accuracy, and persuasiveness of supporting material. Numerous suggestions for organizing evidence are presented in Chapter 5. Besides describing chronological, spatial, and emphatic methods for sequencing material, the chapter illustrates various approaches for preparing effective outlines.

In Chapter 6, students learn how to move from an outline to a first draft. Urging students to view the first draft as work in progress, we describe ways to avoid getting bogged down. Plentiful "before" and "after" examples show how to write unified, specific, and coherent paragraphs and essays. The chapter concludes with techniques for writing strong introductions, conclusions, and titles.

Emphasizing how helpful peer feedback can be, Chapters 7 and 8 introduce students to a multistage revising process. In Chapter 7, students learn to start revision by evaluating an essay's overall content and structure. Once they know how to rework an essay at this level, they are ready to move ahead to Chapter 8. This chapter begins with abundant "before" and "after" examples that illustrate strategies for making sentences clear, concise, and emphatic. The chapter then describes approaches for refining word choice, with extensive examples showing how to make language natural, vigorous, and specific. Rounding out the chapter is a section on nonsexist language. Throughout Chapters 7 and 8, handy checklists make revision more manageable by focusing students on one rewriting stage at a time. And a series of structured activities helps them apply the checklists when they revise their own and other students' papers.

Chapter 9 offers hints for editing and proofreading, while Chapter 10 shows students how to use a word processor during each phase of the composing sequence.

We continually point out in Part II that the stages in the writing process are fluid. Indeed, the case history of an evolving student paper dramatically illustrates just how recursive and individualized the writing process can be. Similarly, we stress that there's no single correct way to write. Focusing on the excitement and sheer fun of exploring ideas on paper, we explain that everyone must tailor the writing process to fit his or her own needs.

Throughout Part II, three instructional devices are used to strengthen students' understanding of the writing process. *Checklists* summarize key concepts and keep students focused on the essentials. Extensive *end-of-chapter activities* also reinforce pivotal skills. Designed to highlight the way invention and revision come into play throughout the writing process, the activities involve students in making rhetorical decisions about such matters as purpose, audience, tone, point of view, organization, paragraph development, and sentence structure. And several *guided exercises* quickly involve students in writing, showing them how to take their papers through successive stages in the composing process.

Finally, to illustrate the link between reading and writing, the chapters in Part II present—from prewriting through revision—the progressive stages of a student essay written in response to Phyllis Theroux's "The Worry Factor" (the professional selection in Part I). In short, *by the end of Part II, the entire reading–writing process has been illustrated,* from reading a selection to writing about it.

Part III, "The Patterns of Development," opens with Chapter 11, which provides a concise overview showing how the patterns enlarge options in every phase of the writing process. The rest of Part III consists of nine chapters, each covering a different pattern: description, narration, illustration, division-classification, process analysis, comparison-contrast, cause-effect, definition, and argumentation-persuasion. The first few chapters address the more personal and expressive patterns of development, while later chapters move to the more public and analytic patterns. However, because they are self-contained, the chapters can be covered in any order. Part III's twenty-eight professional essays are grouped according to the nine patterns of development.

We recognize that some instructors are reluctant to teach the patterns of development as discrete forms; they fear that doing so implies that writers set out to prepare an essay using a specific pattern and that an essay contains only one pattern. Of course, writing usually doesn't work that way at all. So throughout Parts II and III, we provide numerous examples and activities to illustrate that writers select a pattern because it helps them generate material and organize their ideas—that is, it helps serve their rhetorical purposes. We also show that most writing combines two or more patterns, with one pattern usually providing the organizational framework for a piece.

The nine pattern-of-development chapters also illustrate that the multistage composing sequence described in Part II has relevance no matter which pattern or combination of patterns is used in an essay. Each chapter in Part III thus follows the same format:

- A *detailed explanation of the pattern* begins the chapter. The explanation includes these sections: (1) a definition of the pattern, (2) a description of the way the pattern helps writers accommodate their purpose and audience, (3) a Prewriting Checklist to spark creativity and help students get started, (4) step-by-step guidelines for using the pattern, and (5) a Revision Checklist to focus students' efforts when they rework their papers.

    The argumentation-persuasion chapter is even more extensive. Besides the sections described above, it includes a clearly explained section on Toulmin logic, a chart on refutation strategies, and a full discussion of induction, deduction, and logical fallacies.

- Following the explanation of each pattern of development is an *annotated student essay, from prewriting through revision.* Written in response to one of the professional selections in the chapter, each essay clearly illustrates the pattern under discussion. By comparing successive stages of the essay, students come to appreciate the way material is progressively reshaped and refined.

Preface

- *Commentary* after the student essay points out the blend of patterns in the paper, identifies the paper's strengths, and pinpoints areas needing improvement. "First draft" and "revised" versions of one section of the essay reveal how the student writer went about revising, thus illustrating the relationship between the final draft and the steps taken to produce it.
- Next come *extensive prewriting and revising activities.* Together, these two sets of activities help students appreciate the distinctive features of the pattern being studied. The first prewriting activity asks students to generate raw material for an essay and helps them see that the essay may include more than one pattern of development. The last revising activity gives students a chance to rework a paragraph that needs strengthening. Other activities encourage students, working alone or in groups, to examine rhetorical options, to anticipate the consequences of such choices, and to experiment with a variety of composing techniques.
- The *professional selections* follow the activities. Representing a variety of subjects, tones, and points of view, the selections include tried and true classics like George Orwell's "Shooting an Elephant" and E. B. White's "Once More to the Lake." Other selections have rarely, if ever, been included in a composition text. Among these are Meg Greenfield's "Why Nothing Is 'Wrong' Anymore," Beth Johnson Ruth's "Our Drug Problem," and Alice Walker's "Am I Blue?" Of course, each selection clearly illustrates a specific pattern of development or combination of patterns.

  Extensive instructional apparatus accompanies each professional selection:

  1. A *biographical note* gives background on the author and provides a context for the selection.
  2. *Questions for Close Reading* help students dig into and interpret the selection. The first question asks them to identify the selection's thesis; the last provides work on vocabulary development.
  3. *Questions About the Writer's Craft* deal with such matters as purpose, audience, tone, point of view, organization, sentence structure, diction, and figurative language. The first question (labeled "The Pattern") focuses on the distinctive features of the pattern(s) used in the selection. And often there's another question (labeled "Other Patterns") that asks students to analyze the writer's use of additional patterns in the piece.
  4. Next come *four writing assignments,* all prompted by the selection and packed with suggestions on how to proceed. The first two assignments ask students to write an essay using the same pattern(s) as the selection; the last two invite students to discover for themselves which pattern(s) would be most appropriate for an essay. Frequently, the writing assignments are preceded by a special symbol (∞), indicating a cross-reference to another professional selection in the book. By encouraging students to make connections between selections, these assignments broaden students' perspective and give them additional

- material to draw upon when they write. Such paired assignments will be especially welcome to instructors stressing recurring ideas and themes.

- At the end of each pattern-of-development chapter are two sets of Additional Writing Topics: *General Assignments* and *Assignments With a Specific Purpose, Audience, and Point of View.* The first set, new to the second edition, provides open-ended topics that prompt students to discover for themselves the best way to use a specific pattern. The second set, problem-solving in nature, develops students' sensitivity to rhetorical context by asking them to apply the pattern in a real-world setting.

Part IV consists of two chapters on **"The Research Paper."** In this practical, comprehensive guide, we demonstrate how to tailor the multistage composing process described in Part II to the demands of writing a research paper. This section is also filled with hints on using the library, taking notes, introducing quoted material, documenting sources, and avoiding plagiarism. A fully annotated research paper illustrates MLA documentation, while a separate section provides guidelines for using the APA system. Activities at the end of both chapters help ensure mastery of key research skills.

Part V includes two chapters, **"Writing About Literature"** and **"Writing Exam Essays."** Besides showing students how to adapt the composing process to fit the requirements of these highly specific writing situations, each chapter includes a student essay and commentary, as well as helpful end-of-chapter activities.

A comprehensive *Instructor's Manual* for *The Macmillan Writer* includes the following: a thematic table of contents; lists of the book's paired writing assignments and collaborative and/or problem-solving exercises; pointers about using the book; suggested activities; a detailed syllabus; and in-depth responses to the end-of-chapter activities, Questions for Close Reading, and Questions About the Writer's Craft.

WHAT'S NEW

Before beginning work on *The Macmillan Writer: Brief Edition*, we looked closely at the scores of questionnaires completed by instructors using the original long version. The instructors' comments, always discerning and constructive, helped us identify additional material the book might include. Here, then, are the most important new features of *The Macmillan Writer: Brief Edition*.

- *One-quarter of the professional essays are new.* Some of these new readings were suggested by instructors across the country; others were chosen after a thorough search of magazines, nonfiction collections, newspapers, and the like. Whether written by a well-known literary figure like John Ciardi ("Dawn Watch") or a relative newcomer like Nancy Gibbs ("When Is It Rape?"), the new selections are bound to stimulate strong writing on a variety of topics—education, family life, prejudice, friendship, and the mass media, to name just a few. When selecting new readings, we took special care to include pieces dealing with gender, ethnic, and class issues.

- *Chapter 1, "Becoming a Strong Reader," now includes an annotated professional selection.* The annotations exemplify critical reading in action and show how close reading often paves the way to promising writing topics.
- *Part II, "The Writing Process," includes new guided composition activities* that involve students right from the start in the act of writing and revising both paragraphs and first drafts.
- *Chapter 3, "Identifying a Thesis," is more comprehensive.* Textual explanations and several new, highly practical activities show students how to refine a working thesis and how to determine the best place for it in an essay.
- *Chapter 6, "Writing the Paragraphs in the First Draft," illustrates the principle of coherence more fully* and gives a clearer sense of the pitfalls to avoid.
- *Chapter 7, "Revising Overall Meaning, Structure, and Paragraph Development," now covers strategies for responding to instructor feedback.*
- *Chapter 10, "Writing on a Word Processor," includes more nuts-and-bolts suggestions* for using a word processor in every phase of the composing sequence.
- *Chapter 11, "An Overview of the Patterns of Development," reinforces two of the book's key concepts: that the patterns of development come into play throughout the writing process* and *that most writers combine patterns* in their work. The chapter, new to this edition, ends with a checklist that helps students analyze the blend of patterns in the book's selections.
- *Chapter 14, "Illustration," presents additional techniques for making writing specific.*
- *Throughout, there are more writing assignments,* many of them paired thematically. Also, each chapter in Part III now ends with a set of brief, open-ended writing assignments followed by "Assignments With a Specific Purpose, Audience, and Point of View." Numerous assignments engage students in problem solving and collaborative learning.
- *Chapters 21 and 22 on the library and research paper* have been finetuned so that instructions to students *correspond to MLA guidelines.* Also, the two chapters have been reorganized so that *the steps in preparing a research paper parallel more closely the composing stages described in Part II.*
- *Chapter 21 now includes sections on conducting surveys, interpreting statistics, running computerized searches, evaluating conflicting sources, and keeping personal biases in check.*
- *Throughout Chapters 21 and 22, the discussion of plagiarism has been clarified and expanded.*

ACKNOWLEDGMENTS

Throughout our teaching and certainly in writing this book, we've drawn upon the expertise and wisdom of many composition scholars and practitioners. Although we cannot list all those who have influenced us, we owe a special debt to James Britton, Kenneth Bruffee, Frances Christensen, Edward P. J. Corbett, Peter Elbow, Janet Emig, Linda Flower, Donald Hall, Ken Macrorie, James Moffett, Donald Murray, Frank O'Hare, Mina Shaughnessy, Nancy Sommers, and W. Ross Winterowd.

When we first worked on *The Macmillan Writer,* a number of instructors from across the country prepared detailed, thoughtful reviews of draft versions of the manuscript. To those early reviewers, we continue to be grateful: Bruce Coad, Mountain View College; William Dyer, Mankato State University; William Lalicker, Murray State University; Delores Waters, Delgado Community College; Carol Wershoven, Palm Beach Community College; and Gene Young, Morehead State University.

To help us prepare *The Macmillan Writer: Brief Edition,* a good many writing instructors responded to a detailed questionnaire about the original long version. These colleagues' hard-hitting, practical comments guided our work every step of the way. To the following reviewers we are indeed grateful: Thomas G. Beverage, Coastal Carolina Community College; Barry Brunetti, Gulf Coast Community College; Beatrice I. Curry, Columbia State Community College; Juanita Davis, Columbia State Community College; Jo Nell Farrar, San Jacinto College Central; Adam Fischer, Coastal Carolina Community College; Andrea Glebe, University of Nevada, Las Vegas; Linda Hasley, Redlands Community College; M. Jean Jones, Columbia State Community College; Rowena R. Jones, Northern Michigan University; Leela Kapai, University of the District of Columbia; Anne M. Kuhta, Northern Virginia Community College; William Lalicker, Murray State University; Joe Law, Texas Christian University; Carol Owen Lewis, Trident Technical College; James L. Madachy, Gallaudet University; Rita M. Mignacca, State University of New York at Brockport; Betty P. Nelson, Volunteer State Community College; Douglas L. Okey, Spoon River College; Doris Osborn, Northern Oklahoma College; Mack A. Perry, Jackson State Community College; John S. Ramsey, State University of New York at Fredonia; Gladys C. Rosser, Fayetteville Technical Community College; Peggy Ruff, DeVry Institute of Technology; Laura A. Scibona, State University of New York at Brockport; Marilyn Segal, California State University at Northridge; Richard Stoner, Broome Community College; Martha Coultas Strode, Spoon River College; Carole F. Taylor, University of Dayton; Wendy F. Weiner, Northern Virginia Community College; and Stephen Wilhoit, University of Dayton.

At Macmillan, our thanks go to Nancy Perry, Senior Development Editor, for her enthusiastic support, unfailing efficiency, and insightful guidance. Executive Editor Eben Ludlow, who played a key role in helping to shape the book's original long version, kept a watchful eye on the development of the *Brief Edition* and offered perceptive suggestions throughout. We're also indebted to Wendy

Polhemus-Annibell for her scrupulous copyediting and to Sheree Goodman for refining the book's design. And Katherine Evancie, Production Supervisor, deserves thanks for her skillful handling of the complex details in the production process.

Two other individuals, both of whom we've worked with for nearly fifteen years, deserve special thanks. Janet Goldstein, who has extensive experience teaching composition, provided valuable help as we finetuned instructional apparatus. And Dorothy Carroll eased immeasurably the demands of the project by supplying high spirits, impressive word-processing skills, and administrative efficiency.

Of course, much appreciation goes to our families. To both sides of Judy Nadell and John Langan's family go affectionate thanks for being so understanding of our bouts of self-imposed exile. To Linda McMeniman's husband, Larry Schwab, and their children, Laurel, Emily, and Jeremy, much love and thanks for their charm, playfulness, patience, and support.

Finally, we're grateful to our students. Their candid reactions to various drafts of the text sharpened our thinking and kept us honest. We're especially indebted to the thirteen students whose work is included in the book. Their essays illustrate dramatically the potential and the power of student writing.

Judith Nadell
Linda McMeniman
John Langan

BRIEF CONTENTS

PART I: THE READING PROCESS	1
CHAPTER 1: BECOMING A STRONG READER	3

PART II: THE WRITING PROCESS	13
CHAPTER 2: GETTING STARTED THROUGH PREWRITING	15
CHAPTER 3: IDENTIFYING A THESIS	37
CHAPTER 4: SUPPORTING THE THESIS WITH EVIDENCE	44
CHAPTER 5: ORGANIZING THE EVIDENCE	52
CHAPTER 6: WRITING THE PARAGRAPHS IN THE FIRST DRAFT	61
CHAPTER 7: REVISING OVERALL MEANING, STRUCTURE, AND PARAGRAPH DEVELOPMENT	88
CHAPTER 8: REVISING SENTENCES AND WORDS	101
CHAPTER 9: EDITING AND PROOFREADING	133
CHAPTER 10: WRITING ON A WORD PROCESSOR	143

PART III: THE PATTERNS OF DEVELOPMENT — 149

- CHAPTER 11: AN OVERVIEW OF THE PATTERNS OF DEVELOPMENT — 151
- CHAPTER 12: DESCRIPTION — 154
- CHAPTER 13: NARRATION — 185
- CHAPTER 14: ILLUSTRATION — 220
- CHAPTER 15: DIVISION-CLASSIFICATION — 253
- CHAPTER 16: PROCESS ANALYSIS — 284
- CHAPTER 17: COMPARISON-CONTRAST — 315
- CHAPTER 18: CAUSE-EFFECT — 346
- CHAPTER 19: DEFINITION — 379
- CHAPTER 20: ARGUMENTATION-PERSUASION — 408

PART IV: THE RESEARCH PAPER — 455

- CHAPTER 21: SELECTING A SUBJECT, USING THE LIBRARY, AND TAKING NOTES — 457
- CHAPTER 22: WRITING THE RESEARCH PAPER — 494

PART V: THE LITERARY PAPER AND EXAM ESSAY — 529

- CHAPTER 23: WRITING ABOUT LITERATURE — 531
- CHAPTER 24: WRITING EXAM ESSAYS — 552

INDEX — 565

(A Detailed Contents follows this Brief Contents.)

DETAILED CONTENTS

PART I: THE READING PROCESS 1

1 BECOMING A STRONG READER 3
STAGE 1: **Get an Overview of the Selection** 4
STAGE 2: **Deepen Your Sense of the Selection** 5
STAGE 3: **Evaluate the Selection** 5
   Phyllis Theroux, "The Worry Factor" 6

PART II: THE WRITING PROCESS 13

2 GETTING STARTED THROUGH PREWRITING 15
Observations About the Writing Process 15
Use Prewriting to Get Started 17
   Keep a Journal 17
   Understand the Boundaries of the Assignment 19
   Determine Your Purpose, Audience, Tone, and Point of View 19
   Analyzing Your Audience: A Checklist 22
   Discover Your Essay's Limited Subject 24
   Generate Raw Material About Your Limited Subject 27
   Organize the Raw Material 32
Activities: Getting Started Through Prewriting 34

xix

3 IDENTIFYING A THESIS — 37

What Is a Thesis? 37

Finding a Thesis 37

Writing an Effective Thesis 38
- Don't Write a Highly Opinionated Statement 39
- Don't Make an Announcement 39
- Don't Make a Factual Statement 40
- Don't Make a Broad Statement 40

Placing the Thesis in an Essay 41

Activities: Identifying a Thesis 41

4 SUPPORTING THE THESIS WITH EVIDENCE — 44

What Is Evidence? 44

How Do You Find Evidence? 45
- How the Patterns of Development Help Generate Evidence 45

Characteristics of Evidence 46
- The Evidence Is Relevant and Unified 46
- The Evidence Is Specific 47
- The Evidence Is Adequate 48
- The Evidence Is Dramatic 48
- The Evidence Is Accurate 49
- The Evidence Is Representative 49
- Borrowed Evidence Is Documented 49

Activities: Supporting the Thesis with Evidence 50

5 ORGANIZING THE EVIDENCE — 52

Use the Patterns of Development 52

Select an Organizational Approach 53
- Chronological Approach 53
- Spatial Approach 54
- Emphatic Approach 54
- Simple-to-Complex Approach 55

Prepare an Outline 55
- Guidelines for Outlining: A Checklist 56

Activities: Organizing the Evidence 59

6 WRITING THE PARAGRAPHS IN THE FIRST DRAFT — 61

How to Move from Outline to First Draft 61

General Suggestions on How to Proceed 62

If You Get Bogged Down 62

A Suggested Sequence for Writing the First Draft 63

    Write the Supporting Paragraphs 63
    Write Other Paragraphs in the Essay's Body 73
    Write the Introduction 74
    Write the Conclusion 76
    Write the Title 78

Pulling It All Together 78

Sample First Draft 79

    Harriet Davids, "Challenges for Today's Parents" 80
    Commentary 81

Activities: Writing the Paragraphs in the First Draft 82

7 REVISING OVERALL MEANING, STRUCTURE, AND PARAGRAPH DEVELOPMENT 88

Strategies to Make Revision Easier 89

    Set Your First Draft Aside for a While 89
    Work From Typed or Printed Text 90
    Read the Draft Aloud 90
    React to Your Instructor's Comments 90
    Participate in Peer Feedback Sessions 91
    Evaluate and Act on Peer Feedback 92
    View Revision as a Series of Steps 93

Revising Overall Meaning and Structure 94

    Revise Overall Meaning and Structure: A Checklist 94

Revising Paragraph Development 95

    Revise Paragraph Development: A Checklist 96

Sample Student Revision of Overall Meaning, Structure, and Paragraph Development 97

Activities: Revising Overall Meaning, Structure, and Paragraph Development 98

8 REVISING SENTENCES AND WORDS 101

Revising Sentences 101

    Make Sentences Consistent With Your Tone 101
    Make Sentences Economical 102
    Vary Sentence Type 105
    Vary Sentence Length 108
    Vary Sentence Pattern 110
    Make Sentences Emphatic 112
    Revise Sentences: A Checklist 116

Revising Words 116
    Make Words Consistent With Your Tone 117
    Use an Appropriate Level of Diction 117
    Avoid Words That Overstate or Understate 118
    Select Words With Appropriate Connotations 119
    Use Specific Rather Than General Words 120
    Use Concrete Rather Than Abstract Words 121
    Use Strong Verbs 121
    Delete Unnecessary Adverbs 123
    Use Original Figures of Speech 123
    Avoid Sexist Language 125
    Revise Words: A Checklist 127

Sample Student Revision of Sentences and Words 128

Activities: Revising Sentences and Words 129

9 EDITING AND PROOFREADING 133

Edit Carefully 133

Use the Appropriate Manuscript Format 134
    Appropriate Manuscript Format: A Checklist 134

Proofread Closely 136

Student Essay: From Prewriting Through Proofreading 137
    Harriet Davids, "Challenges for Today's Parents" 137
    Commentary 139

Activities: Editing and Proofreading 142

10 WRITING ON A WORD PROCESSOR 143

Some Observations and Hints About Using a Word Processor 144

Prewrite 145

Identify a Thesis 145

Support the Thesis with Evidence 146

Organize the Evidence 146

Write the First Draft 146

Revise Overall Meaning, Structure, and Paragraph Development 147

Revise Sentences and Words 147

Edit and Proofread 148

Detailed Contents xxiii

PART III THE PATTERNS OF DEVELOPMENT 149

11 AN OVERVIEW OF THE PATTERNS OF DEVELOPMENT 151
- The Patterns in Action: During the Writing Process 151
- The Patterns in Action: In an Essay 152
  - Analyzing the Way Writers Combine Patterns: A Checklist 153

12 DESCRIPTION 154
- What Is Description? 154
- How Description Fits Your Purpose and Audience 154
- Prewriting Strategies 156
  - Description: A Prewriting Checklist 156
- Strategies for Using Description in an Essay 157
- Revision Strategies 160
  - Description: A Revision Checklist 160
- Student Essay: From Prewriting Through Revision 161
  - Marie Martinez, "Salt Marsh" 163
  - Commentary 165
- Activities: Description 168
  - Prewriting Activities 168
  - Revising Activities 168
- Professional Selections: Description 170
  - E. B. White, "Once More to the Lake" 170
  - Maxine Hong Kingston, "Photographs of My Parents" 175
  - John Ciardi, "Dawn Watch" 179
- Additional Writing Topics: Description 183

13 NARRATION 185
- What Is Narration? 185
- How Narration Fits Your Purpose and Audience 186
- Prewriting Strategies 186
  - Narration: A Prewriting Checklist 186
- Strategies for Using Narration in an Essay 187
- Revision Strategies 193
  - Narration: A Revision Checklist 193

Student Essay: From Prewriting Through Revision   194
    Paul Monahan, "If Only"   195
    Commentary   197

Activities: Narration   199
  Prewriting Activities   199
  Revising Activities   200

Professional Selections: Narration   201
    George Orwell, "Shooting an Elephant"   201
    Maya Angelou, "Louise Cox"   207
    Alice Walker, "Am I Blue?"   213

Additional Writing Topics: Narration   218

14 ILLUSTRATION   220

What Is Illustration?   220

How Illustration Fits Your Purpose and Audience   221

Prewriting Strategies   223
  Illustration: A Prewriting Checklist   223

Strategies for Using Illustration in an Essay   224

Revision Strategies   227
  Illustration: A Revision Checklist   227

Student Essay: From Prewriting Through Revision   228
    Michael Pagano, "Pursuit of Possessions"   230
    Commentary   232

Activities: Illustration   235
  Prewriting Activities   235
  Revising Activities   236

Professional Selections: Illustration   237
    Anne Morrow Lindbergh, "Channelled Whelk"   237
    Alleen Pace Nilsen, "Sexism and Language"   243
    Bob Greene, "Unwritten Rules Circumscribe Our Lives"   248

Additional Writing Topics: Illustration   251

15 DIVISION-CLASSIFICATION   253

What Is Division-Classification?   253

How Division-Classification Fits Your Purpose and Audience   254

Prewriting Strategies   256
  Division-Classification: A Prewriting Checklist   256

Strategies for Using Division-Classification in an Essay   257

Detailed Contents

Revision Strategies 260
- Division-Classification: A Revision Checklist 260

Student Essay: From Prewriting Through Revision 261
- Gail Oremland, "The Truth About College Teachers" 263
- Commentary 266

Activities: Division-Classification 269
- Prewriting Activities 269
- Revising Activities 270

Professional Selections: Division-Classification 271
- Ann McClintock, "Propaganda Techniques in Today's Advertising" 271
- Russell Baker, "The Plot Against People" 276
- Meg Greenfield, "Why Nothing Is 'Wrong' Anymore" 279

Additional Writing Topics: Division-Classification 282

---

16 PROCESS ANALYSIS 284

What Is Process Analysis? 284

How Process Analysis Fits Your Purpose and Audience 285

Prewriting Strategies 286
- Process Analysis: A Prewriting Checklist 286

Strategies for Using Process Analysis in an Essay 287

Revision Strategies 291
- Process Analysis: A Revision Checklist 291

Student Essay: From Prewriting Through Revision 292
- Robert Barry, "Becoming a Videoholic" 294
- Commentary 297

Activities: Process Analysis 300
- Prewriting Activities 300
- Revising Activities 301

Professional Selections: Process Analysis 303
- Mortimer Adler, "How to Mark a Book" 303
- Malcolm X, "My First Conk" 307
- Carin Quinn, "The Jeaning of America—and the World" 310

Additional Writing Topics: Process Analysis 313

---

17 COMPARISON-CONTRAST 315

What Is Comparison-Contrast? 315

How Comparison-Contrast Fits Your Purpose and Audience 316

    Prewriting Strategies   317
        Comparison-Contrast: A Prewriting Checklist   317
    Strategies for Using Comparison-Contrast in an Essay   318
    Revision Strategies   322
        Comparison-Contrast: A Revision Checklist   322
    Student Essay: From Prewriting Through Revision   323
        Carol Siskin, "The Virtues of Growing Older"   326
        Commentary   328
    Activities: Comparison-Contrast   330
      Prewriting Activities   330
      Revising Activities   331
    Professional Selections: Comparison-Contrast   332
        Suzanne Britt, "Neat People vs. Sloppy People"   332
        Jack Newfield, "Stallone vs. Springsteen"   335
        Joseph H. Suina, "And Then I Went to School"   339
    Additional Writing Topics: Comparison-Contrast   344

18 CAUSE-EFFECT   346

    What Is Cause-Effect?   346
    How Cause-Effect Fits Your Purpose and Audience   347
    Prewriting Strategies   348
        Cause-Effect: A Prewriting Checklist   348
    Strategies for Using Cause-Effect in an Essay   349
    Revision Strategies   354
        Cause-Effect: A Revision Checklist   354
    Student Essay: From Prewriting Through Revision   355
        Carl Novack, "Americans and Food"   357
        Commentary   359
    Activities: Cause-Effect   362
      Prewriting Activities   362
      Revising Activities   363
    Professional Selections: Cause-Effect   364
        George Gallup, Jr., "The Faltering Family"   364
        Jacques Cousteau, "The Bounty of the Sea"   371
        Brent Staples, "Black Men and Public Space"   373
    Additional Writing Topics: Cause-Effect   377

19 DEFINITION — 379

What Is Definition? 379

How Definition Fits Your Purpose and Audience 380

Prewriting Strategies 381
- Definition: A Prewriting Checklist 381

Strategies for Using Definition in an Essay 382

Revision Strategies 385
- Definition: A Revision Checklist 385

Student Essay: From Prewriting Through Revision 386
- Laura Chen, "Physics in Everyday Life" 387
- Commentary 389

Activities: Definition 392
- Prewriting Activities 392
- Revising Activities 393

Professional Selections: Definition 394
- K. C. Cole, "Entropy" 394
- Nancy Gibbs, "When Is It Rape?" 397
- Martin Gottfried, "Rambos of the Road" 403

Additional Writing Topics: Definition 406

20 ARGUMENTATION-PERSUASION — 408

What Is Argumentation-Persuasion? 408

How Argumentation-Persuasion Fits Your Purpose and Audience 409

Prewriting Strategies 412
- Argumentation-Persuasion: A Prewriting Checklist 412

Strategies for Using Argumentation-Persuasion in an Essay 413

Revision Strategies 426
- Argumentation-Persuasion: A Revision Checklist 426

Student Essay: From Prewriting Through Revision 427
- Mark Simmons, "Compulsory National Service" 430
- Commentary 433

Activities: Argumentation-Persuasion 436
- Prewriting Activities 436
- Revising Activities 437

Professional Selections: Argumentation-Persuasion 439
    Fern Kupfer, "Institution Is Not a Dirty Word" 439
    Caryl Rivers, "What Should Be Done About Rock Lyrics?" 443
    Louis Nizer, "Low-Cost Drugs for Addicts?" 446
    Beth Johnson Ruth, "Our Drug Problem" 449

Additional Writing Topics: Argumentation-Persuasion 453

PART IV THE RESEARCH PAPER   455

21 SELECTING A SUBJECT, USING THE LIBRARY, AND TAKING NOTES   457

Some General Comments About the Research Paper 457

Plan the Research 458
    Understand the Paper's Boundaries 458
    Understand Primary Versus Secondary Research 459
    Choose a General Subject 461
    Selecting an Appropriate Subject to Research: A Checklist 462
    Prewrite to Limit the General Subject 463
    Prewrite to Conduct Preliminary Research 463
    Identify a Working Thesis 464
    Make a Schedule 464

Find Sources in the Library 465
    The Computerized Catalog 465
    The Card Catalog 466
    The Reference Section 469
    Periodicals 470

Prepare a Working Bibliography 475

Take Notes to Support the Thesis with Evidence 476
    Why Take Notes? 476
    Before Note-taking: Evaluate Sources 477
    Before Note-taking: Refine Your Working Bibliography 478
    Before Note-taking: Read Your Sources 481
    When Note-taking: What to Select 481
    When Note-taking: How to Record Statistics 481
    When Note-taking: Use Index Cards 482
    Two Other Note-taking Approaches 483
    Kinds of Notes 484

Activities: Selecting a Subject, Using the Library, and Taking Notes 490

22 WRITING THE RESEARCH PAPER — 494

Refine Your Working Thesis 494

Sort the Note Cards 495

Organize the Evidence by Outlining 495

Prepare the Works Cited List: MLA Format 497
- Book Sources 497
- Articles in Periodicals 500
- Nonprint Sources 501

Write the First Draft 502

Presenting the Results of Primary Research 503

Document Borrowed Material: MLA Format 504

How to Avoid Plagiarism 504
- Indicate Author and Page 504
- Special Cases of Authorship 507
- Special Cases of Pagination 508
- More About Quotations 508

Revise, Edit, and Proofread the First Draft 510
- Revising the Research Paper: A Checklist 511

APA Documentation Format 513
- Parenthetic Citations 513
- References List 514

A Note About Other Documentation Systems 515

Student Research Paper: MLA-Style Documentation 515
- Brian Courtney, "America's Homeless: How the Government Can Help" 516
- Commentary 527

Activities: Writing the Research Paper 527

PART V THE LITERARY PAPER AND EXAM ESSAY — 529

23 WRITING ABOUT LITERATURE — 531

Elements of Literary Works 532

How to Read a Literary Work 534
- Read to Form a General Impression 534
- Ask Questions About the Work 534
- Analyzing a Literary Work: A Checklist 534
- Reread and Annotate 535
- Modify Your Annotations 536

Write the Literary Analysis 536
Prewrite 536
Identify Your Thesis 537
Support the Thesis With Evidence 539
Organize the Evidence 539
Write the First Draft 540
Revise Overall Meaning, Structure, and Paragraph Development 541
Revising a Literary Analysis: A Checklist 541
Edit and Proofread 543

Pulling It All Together 543
Read to Form a General Impression 543
Langston Hughes, "Early Autumn" 543
Ask Questions About the Work 544
Reread and Annotate 545

Student Essay 545
Karen Vais, "Stopping to Talk" 545
Commentary 546

Additional Selections and Writing Assignments 547
Elizabeth Bishop, "The Fish" 547
Kate Chopin, "The Story of an Hour" 549

24 WRITING EXAM ESSAYS 552

Three Forms of Written Answers 553
How to Prepare for Exam Essays 554
At the Examination 555
Survey the Entire Test 555
Understand the Essay Question 555

Write the Essay 556
Prewrite 557
Identify Your Thesis 557
Support the Thesis With Evidence 557
Organize the Evidence 557
Write the Draft 558
Revise, Edit, and Proofread 559

Sample Essay Answer 559
Commentary 561

Activity: Writing Exam Essays 561

INDEX 565

THE MACMILLAN WRITER

Rhetoric and Reader

PART I

THE READING PROCESS

1
BECOMING A STRONG READER

MORE than two hundred years ago, essayist Joseph Addison commented, "Of all the diversions of life, there is none so proper to fill up its empty spaces as the reading of useful and entertaining authors." Addison might have added that reading also challenges our beliefs, deepens our awareness, and stimulates our imagination.

Why, then, don't more people delight in reading? After all, most children feel great pleasure and pride when they first learn to read. As children grow older, though, the initially magical world of books is more and more associated with homework, tests, and grades. Reading turns into an anxiety-producing chore. Also, as demands on a person's time accumulate throughout adolescence and adulthood, reading often gets pushed aside in favor of something that takes less effort. It's easier simply to switch on the television and passively view the ready-made images that flash across the screen. In contrast, it's almost impossible to remain passive while reading. Even a slick best-seller requires that the reader decode, visualize, and interpret what's on the page. The more challenging the materials, the more actively involved the reader must be.

The essays we selected for Part III of this book call for active reading. Representing a broad mix of styles and subjects, the essays range from the classic to the contemporary. They contain language that will move you, images that will enlarge your understanding of other people, ideas that will transform your views on complex issues.

The selections in Part III serve other purposes as well. For one thing, they'll help you develop a repertoire of reading skills—abilities that will benefit you throughout life. Second, as you become a better reader, your own writing style will become more insightful and polished. Increasingly, you'll be able to draw on the ideas presented in the selections and employ the techniques that professional writers use to express such ideas. As novelist Saul Bellow has observed, "A writer is a reader moved to emulation."

In the pages ahead, we outline a three-stage approach for getting the most out of this book's selections. Our suggestions will enhance your understanding of the book's essays, as well as help you read other material with greater ease and assurance.

STAGE 1: GET AN OVERVIEW OF THE SELECTION

Ideally, you should get settled in a quiet place that encourages concentration. If you can focus your attention while sprawled on a bed or curled up in a chair, that's fine. But if you find that being very comfortable is more conducive to daydreaming and dozing off than it is to studying, avoid getting too relaxed.

Once you're settled, it's time to read the selection. To ensure a good first reading, try the following hints:

- Get an overview of the essay and its author. Start by reading the biographical note that precedes the selection. By providing background information about the author, the note helps you evaluate the writer's credibility as well as his or her slant on the subject. For example, if you know that George Gallup, Jr., is president of a well-known research firm that measures public opinion, you can better assess whether he is a credible source for the analysis he presents in his essay "The Faltering Family" (reprinted in Chapter 18).

- Consider the selection's title. A good title often expresses the essay's main idea, giving you insight into the selection even before you read it. For example, the title of Louis Nizer's essay, "Low-Cost Drugs for Addicts?" (Chapter 20), suggests that the piece may examine the pros and cons of legalizing drugs. A title may also hint at a selection's tone. The title of Suzanne Britt's piece, "Neat People vs. Sloppy People" (Chapter 17), points to an essay that's light in spirit, whereas George Orwell's "Shooting an Elephant" (Chapter 13) suggests a piece with a serious mood.

- Read the selection straight through purely for pleasure. Allow yourself to be drawn into the world the author has created. Just as you first see a painting from the doorway of a room and form an overall impression without perceiving the details, you can have a preliminary, subjective feeling about a reading selection. Moreover, because you bring your own experiences and viewpoints to the piece, your reading will be unique. As Emerson said, "Take the book, my friend, and read your eyes out; you will never find there what I find."

- After this initial reading of the selection, focus your first impressions by asking yourself whether you like the selection. In your own words, briefly describe the piece and your reaction to it.

Becoming a Strong Reader

STAGE 2: DEEPEN YOUR SENSE OF THE SELECTION

At this point, you're ready to move further into the selection. A second reading will help you identify the specific features that triggered your initial reaction. Here are some suggestions on how to proceed:

- Mark off the selection's main idea, or thesis, often found near the beginning or end. If the thesis isn't stated explicitly, write down your own version of the selection's main idea.
- Locate the main supporting evidence used to develop the thesis. You may even want to number in the margin each key supporting point.
- Take a minute to write "Yes" or "No" beside points with which you strongly agree or disagree. Your reaction to these points often explains your feelings about the aptness of the selection's ideas.
- Return to any unclear passages you encountered during the first reading. The feeling you now have for the piece as a whole will probably help you make sense of initially confusing spots. However, this second reading may also reveal that, in places, the writer's thinking isn't as clear as it could be.
- Use your dictionary to check the meanings of any unfamiliar words.
- Ask yourself if your initial impression of the selection has changed in any way as a result of this second reading. If your feelings *have* changed, try to determine why you reacted differently on this reading.

STAGE 3: EVALUATE THE SELECTION

Now that you have a good grasp of the selection, you may want to read it a third time, especially if the piece is long or complex. This time, your goal is to make judgments about the essay's effectiveness. Keep in mind, though, that you shouldn't evaluate the selection until after you have a strong hold on it. A negative, even a positive reaction is valid only if it's based on an accurate reading.

At first, you may feel uncomfortable about evaluating the work of a professional writer. But remember: Written material set in type only *seems* perfect; all writing can be finetuned. By identifying what does and doesn't work in others' writing, you're taking an important first step toward developing your own power as a writer. You might find it helpful at this point to get together with other students to discuss the selection. Comparing viewpoints often opens up a piece, enabling you to gain a clearer perspective on the selection and the author's approach.

To evaluate the essay, ask yourself the following questions:

Questions for Evaluating a Selection

1. *Where does support for the selection's thesis seem logical and sufficient? Where does support seem weak?* Which of the author's supporting facts, arguments, and examples seem pertinent and convincing? Which don't?

2. *Is the selection unified? If not, why not?* Where does something in the selection not seem relevant? Where are there any unnecessary digressions or detours?
3. *How does the writing make the selection move smoothly from beginning to end?* How does the writer create an easy flow between ideas? Are any parts of the essay abrupt and jarring? Which ones?
4. *Which stylistic devices are used to good effect in the selection?* Which pattern of development or combination of patterns does the writer use to develop the piece? Why do you think those patterns were selected? How do paragraph development, sentence structure, and word choice (diction) contribute to the piece's overall effect? What tone does the writer adopt? Where does the writer use figures of speech effectively? (The terms *patterns of development, sentence structure, diction,* and the like are explained in Chapter 2.)
5. *How does the selection encourage further thought?* What new perspective on an issue does the writer provide? What ideas has the selection prompted you to explore in an essay of your own?

It takes some work to follow the three-stage approach just described, but the selections in Part III make it worth the effort. Bear in mind that none of the selections you'll read in Part III sprang full-blown from the pen of its author. Rather, each essay is the result of hours of work—hours of thinking, writing, rethinking, and revising. As a reader, you should show the same willingness to work with the selections, to read them carefully and thoughtfully. Henry David Thoreau, an avid reader and prolific writer, emphasized the importance of this kind of attentive reading when he advised that "books must be read as deliberately and unreservedly as they were written."

To illustrate the multistage reading process, we've annotated the professional essay that follows: "The Worry Factor" by Phyllis Theroux. Note that annotations are provided in the margin of the essay as well as at the end of the essay. As you read Theroux's essay, try applying the three-stage sequence. You can measure your ability to dig into the selection by making your own annotations on Theroux's essay and then comparing them to ours. You can also see how well you evaluated the piece by answering the preceding five questions and then comparing your responses to ours on pages 9–10.

PHYLLIS THEROUX

A frequent contributor to the *Washington Post, McCall's,* and *Reader's Digest,* Phyllis Theroux (1939–) won special recognition for a series of pieces she wrote for the *New York Times*'s "Hers" column. Theroux's essays, often about the complex relationship between child and parent, combine wry humor with keen insight. Theroux has collected her work in three books: *California and Other States of Grace: A Memoir* (1980), *Peripheral Visions* (1982), and *Night Lights* (1987), from which the following selection is taken.

Becoming a Strong Reader

THE WORRY FACTOR

1   It is commonly acknowledged that the organ that gives us the most pain in life is our brain—or somebody else's in close proximity. And, according to the "EST" training* I have so far managed to avoid, a great many heads are badly "wired" and can electrocute us with worries that the human being is not rubberized to withstand.

— Relevant?

— Drops this idea.

2   Why we like to worry is another question, as is the difference between feckless and fertile worrying, which can produce ulcers or symphonies. But once, while moving half-witted with worry around the kitchen, I stopped, mentally pushed everything that I couldn't do anything about at that moment out of my head, and then, regrounded, looked around to see who was sharing that moment with me. My eyes fell upon my eleven-year-old daughter. Her eyes were full of tears.

— Means "ineffective"

— Awkward transition (like "And" in ¶1)

— Theroux also a worrier

3   She needed to talk. We went into the living room and sat down. She felt terrible, she said. It became clear, as she explained herself, that she had a lot of worries on her mind.

— Narrative to support thesis starts here.

— Smoother transitions

4   For one thing, she was not very pretty. For another, she was not very smart. She was not rich, didn't have clothes as nice as everyone else's, her brother was oftentimes mean to her, and her best friend, to quote her exactly, "totally hates my guts."

— Paragraph gives examples of the daughter's worries.

5   There were other deprivations, deeper and therefore deserving of a curtain of privacy that I will now draw across the rods. But it was a fairly devastating list of liabilities, many of them not of her own making, and I let her spread them all out in their full horror without jumping in like some kind of Red Cross worker to tell her that her worries were only in her mind. Of course, that's where they were!

— Sounds like a child talking; essay has chatty tone.

— Figure of speech shows that Theroux realizes her efforts are probably futile. (See ¶s 8, 10, 11.)

6   Without necessarily agreeing with her on every point, I talked about people who had more than she did, and people who had less. Some rich girls are ugly. Some pretty girls are poor. I felt compelled to add that, inexplicably, some rich girls are also pretty, which is a mystery and nothing we can truly understand.

---

*A self-help program, especially popular during the 1970s.

> Advice doesn't help.

But it seemed to me, I said, that one could look at the world in a couple of ways: as an imperfect place that makes us miserable or as a place that is imperfect and gives us something positive to do.

"You know," I explained, "like when you see a little boy crying in the playground. You can either say, 'How awful, he is so sad,' or go up and ask him what's the matter and try to fix it up."

> Touching image
> Like "Red Cross worker" in ¶5

My daughter of the heart-shaped face didn't quite understand this friendly-carpenter approach to existence. In her mind, at that moment, she was the kid crying on the playground and her chief worry was who (or Who) would *fix her up*.

"I used to ask God to please, please give me a nice day. But it never worked, so I stopped asking."

> Feels daughter's pain

"Maybe," I suggested (telling my heart to stop twitching), "you could turn the question around and ask God to please let you give the day something nice."

> Again, advice doesn't work.
> "As" shows time passing.

Maybe yes, but maybe no. Maybe I hadn't heard her the first time when she listed her problems, and as we walked upstairs to her bedroom, she repeated them for me again. As I watched her climb into bed I observed, "You know, if all you were were your worries, you wouldn't even exist. You'd be a minus."

Hiding under the quilt that all too soon she would be forced to throw off the next morning, my daughter tried to understand this.

> Part of implied thesis

"You can wreck the day you're still in," I continued, "worrying about the day that hasn't even arrived."

> What many people think!

"But you *have* to worry!" she exclaimed, and the look on her face poking over the quilt was incredulous that someone my age did not know that this was one of the first facts and obligations of life.

> Part of implied thesis

"You do?" I answered. "But doesn't worrying just make you more tense by the time tomorrow finally comes?"

A small but hopeful expression flickered across her features. Perhaps, she conceded, there was something to this line of thinking. She smiled, nodded her head and yawned.

"Why don't you take all your worries," I said, bending down to kiss her goodnight, "and shove them right out the window where they belong."

Then, in a final bit of dialogue that reminded me that two heads in close proximity can produce something a great deal more significant than pain, she changed the subject.

Becoming a Strong Reader

19   "This doesn't have anything to do with what we're talking about," she said, "but why is it that when I cry my nose gets stuffy?"   *Dialog here and earlier conveys mother-daughter relationship.*

20   "I don't know," I answered. "Maybe there are just too many tears to fit in your eyes."

21   "My tears are salty."

22   "That's because you have salt in your body."

23   "Mom," she asked, "can you taste my forehead and tell me if it's salty?"

24   I gave it a taste and said, "No, actually it isn't."

25   "Oh, good!" she exclaimed, her face breaking into a wide, relieved smile. "That means I don't have cystic fibrosis."   *Surprise ending—the girl has been worrying about this, too.*

Thesis (implied): We know that worrying is a waste of time, but that doesn't keep us from worrying.

First Reading: Humorous and fun to read but also touching. Easy to relate to. Nicely captures what worry warts we can be.

Second and Third Readings:

1. Uses narration and examples of the daughter's worries to show the negative effect of worrying (thesis).
2. Not everything works (awkward transitions and reference to EST), but overall the essay succeeds.
3. Unexpected ending holds up even after additional readings. Shows how endless and groundless our worries can be. Creates sympathy for the young girl but also pokes gentle fun at her.
4. Possible essay topics: A humorous paper on how to avoid worrying about something (school, social life) or a serious paper on the positive aspects of worrying (it encourages action, we can anticipate and avoid problems, and so on).

The following answers to the questions on pages 5–6 will help crystallize your reactions to Theroux's essay.

1. Where does support for the selection's thesis seem logical and sufficient? Where does support seem weak? The most explicit statement of Theroux's thesis lies in her comments to her daughter: "You can wreck the day you're still in worrying about the day that hasn't even arrived" (paragraph 13), and "But doesn't worrying just make you more tense by the time tomorrow finally comes?" (paragraph 15). But these two remarks aren't the most complete statement of Theroux's main idea: They don't mention the essay's central paradox—that although Theroux tries to allay her daughter's anxieties, she herself is also a worrier. Stating the thesis in your own words may be best: Worrying is a painful waste of energy, yet knowing this does not necessarily help us resist it.

Theroux dramatizes her thesis with a single, strong example—a conversation in which she attempts to allay her daughter's numerous worries. The author provides several examples of what a parent might say to reduce a child's anxiety. Although these reassurances don't entirely console her daughter, they do offer some relief.

2. *Is the selection unified? If not, why not?* The introductory paragraph contains a somewhat distracting reference to "EST" training, and the second paragraph raises an issue—"Why we like to worry"—that is then dropped. From the end of the second paragraph on, however, the essay focuses tightly on a single conversation between Theroux and her daughter. While some of Theroux's suggestions fail to help her daughter (for example, the suggestion in paragraph 10 that her daughter do something positive), these unsuccessful efforts belong in the essay because they illustrate how hard it is to make someone else's worries go away. The concluding bit of conversation turns out be anything but a change of subject: It reveals that the daughter has been worrying about cystic fibrosis, as well as about her looks, her clothes, her popularity, and almost everything else.

3. *How does the writer make the selection move smoothly from beginning to end?* Theroux's first two paragraphs aren't as smooth as one might like. The second sentence begins with the word "And" even though the point Theroux makes in the sentence isn't a continuation of the first sentence. Similarly, in the second paragraph, the phrase "But once" that she uses to lead into the conversation doesn't contrast (as the "But" implies) with the idea expressed in the preceding paragraph. From this point on, however, Theroux writes sharply focused paragraphs and provides clear signals that guide the reader through the conversation with her daughter. For example, she signals her daughter's worries using "For one thing" and "For another" (paragraph 4). She also supplies cues indicating the passage of time: "*as* we walked," "*As* I watched" (paragraph 11), and "*Then*" (paragraph 18).

4. *Which stylistic devices are used to good effect in the selection?* Theroux uses several patterns of development in her essay. The selection as a whole shows the *effect* of useless worry; paragraphs 2 and 7–25 are developed through *narration;* paragraphs 4, 6, and 7 use *examples. Short dramatic sentences* highlight her daughter's strong emotions ("She needed to talk") and punctuate Theroux's own ideas ("Some rich girls are ugly," "Some pretty girls are poor"). The first-person point of view contributes to Theroux's *informal tone* ("I talked about," "I explained," "I felt compelled"). Lively dialog, including colloquial language ("totally hates my guts," "You'd be a minus"), as well as a fragment ("Maybe yes, but maybe no") adds to the essay's conversational feeling. *Figurative language* in paragraphs 1 ("a great many heads are badly 'wired' "), 5 ("some kind of Red Cross worker"), and 8 ("friendly-carpenter approach to existence") further enlivens the essay. Finally, although Theroux is concerned about the corrosive effect of worrying, she leavens her essay with dashes of humor. Certainly, her decision to include the final bit of conversation ("That means I don't have cystic fibrosis") shows how laughable our self-imposed anxieties can be.

5. *How does the selection encourage further thought?* Theroux's essay treats a broad issue that affects all of us—the tendency to worry and thus cause

ourselves pain. Her specific concern is the difficulties parents face trying to divert children from needless fretting. Although Theroux offers no solutions, her personal account sharpens our awareness and prompts us to reexamine what is and is not worth worrying about.

If, for each essay you read in this book, you consider the preceding questions, you'll be able to respond thoughtfully to the *Questions for Close Reading* and *Questions About the Writer's Craft* presented after each selection. Your responses will, in turn, prepare you for the writing assignments that follow the questions. Interesting and varied, the assignments invite you to examine issues raised by the selections and encourage you to experiment with various writing styles and organizational patterns.

Following are some sample questions and writing assignments based on the Theroux essay; all are similar to the sort that appear later in this book. Note that the final writing assignment paves the way for the successive stages of a student essay presented in Part II, "The Writing Process." (The final version of the essay appears on pages 137–139.)

QUESTIONS FOR CLOSE READING

1. How do you know that Theroux is herself a worrier? How does she handle her anxieties?
2. Why do you suppose Theroux's daughter restates her problems as she goes up to bed? What kind of response does she most likely want from her mother?

QUESTIONS ABOUT THE WRITER'S CRAFT

1. The last sentence in paragraph 4 tumbles along in a somewhat rambling fashion. Why might Theroux have decided to write the sentence this way?
2. Why do you think Theroux ends the essay with her daughter's comment, rather than with her own response to that comment?

WRITING ASSIGNMENTS

1. Theroux has difficulty allaying her daughter's worries. Write an essay explaining the steps that you think parents and/or schools should take to minimize children's anxieties about a specific present-day danger—perhaps AIDS, sexual abuse, or divorce.
2. Because the contemporary world is a difficult, even dangerous place, parents understandably worry about their children. Write an essay supporting the idea that today's world is, in many ways, hostile—particularly to children.

The benefits of active reading are many. Books in general and the selections in Part III in particular will bring you face to face with issues that concern all of us. If you study the selections and the questions that follow them, you'll be on your way to discovering ideas for you own papers. Part II offers practical suggestions for turning those ideas into well-organized, thoughtful essays.

PART II

THE WRITING PROCESS

2
GETTING STARTED THROUGH PREWRITING

OBSERVATIONS ABOUT THE WRITING PROCESS

NOT many people retire at age thirty-eight. But Michel Montaigne, a sixteenth-century French attorney, did exactly that. Montaigne retired at a young age because he wanted to read, think, and write about all the subjects that interested him. After spending years getting his ideas down on paper, Montaigne finally published his short prose pieces. He called them "essais"—French for "trials" or "attempts."

In fact, all writing is an attempt to transform ideas into words, thus giving order and meaning to life. By using the term *essais,* Montaigne acknowledged that a written piece is never really finished. Of course, writers have to stop at some point, especially if they have deadlines to meet. But, as all experienced writers know, even after they dot the final *i,* cross the final *t,* and say "That's it," there's always something that could have been explored further or expressed a little better.

When we read a piece of writing, we see only the finished product. Not being privy to the writer's effort to convey meaning, we may hold a romanticized notion of what it means to be a writer. We may imagine the writer transported by flashes of creativity, polished prose appearing —as if by magic—on the page. In practice, though, most writers do anything but pour out well-formed thoughts.

Rather, they stare into space, dash off a few pages, crumple them up, and start all over. Even E. B. White, the American essayist celebrated for his eloquent, seemingly effortless prose, confessed, "Writing ... is a hell of a chore for me, closely related to acid indigestion."

If White, who made his living as a writer, admitted such anxiety, you shouldn't be surprised if you feel some apprehension when it's time to write a paper. Your uneasiness may stem in part from your belief that some people are born writers, others are not—and that you're one of the latter. Some people *do* seem to be born with a gift for language, just as some people seem to be born with a gift for athletics or music. But with practice, just about anyone can learn to play a solid game of tennis or to sing on key. And that's what most of us are aiming for—not to be the Martina Navratilovas, the Pavarottis, or the E. B. Whites of the world, but to perform skillfully and confidently.

As with singing or playing tennis, learning to write well is a challenge. Shaky starts and changes in direction aren't uncommon. Although there's no way to eliminate the work needed to write effectively, certain approaches can make the process more manageable and rewarding. In Chapters 2–9, we describe a sequence of steps for writing essays. Familiarity with a specific sequence develops your awareness of strategies and choices, making you feel more confident when it comes time to write. You're less likely to look at a blank piece of paper and think, "Help! Now what do I do?" During the sequence, you do the following:

- Prewrite
- Identify your thesis
- Support the thesis with evidence
- Organize the evidence
- Write the paragraphs of the first draft
- Revise meaning, structure, and paragraph development
- Revise sentences and words
- Edit and proofread

Even though we present the sequence as a series of steps, it's not a rigid formula that you must follow step by unchanging step. Somewhere in school we were taught that a straight line is the shortest distance between two points. But writing isn't as simple or tidy as that. Most people develop personalized approaches to the writing process. Some writers mull over a topic in their heads, then move quickly into a promising first draft; others outline their essays in detail before beginning to write. Between these two extremes are any number of effective approaches.

Most of us tend to be creatures of habit; we feel secure and comfortable doing things the way we always have. You've probably approached writing in much the same way for many years. At first, you may be reluctant to try the techniques we describe here and in the following chapters. That's understandable. But we urge you to experiment with the strategies we present. Try them, use what works, discard what doesn't. And always feel free to streamline or alter the steps

Getting Started Through Prewriting

in the sequence to suit your individual needs and the requirements of specific writing assignments.

USE PREWRITING TO GET STARTED

Prewriting refers to strategies you can use to generate ideas *before* starting the first draft of a paper. Prewriting techniques are like the warm-ups you do before going out to jog—they loosen you up, get you moving, and help you to develop a sense of well-being and confidence. Since prewriting techniques encourage imaginative exploration, they also help you discover what interests you most about your subject. Having such a focus early in the writing process keeps you from plunging into your initial draft without first giving some thought to what you want to say. Prewriting thus saves you time in the long run by keeping you on course.

Prewriting can help in other ways, too. When we write, we often sabotage our ability to generate material because we continually critique what we put down on paper. "This makes no sense," "This is stupid," "I can't say that," and other critical thoughts pop into our minds. Such negative, self-critical comments stop the flow of our thoughts and reinforce the fear that we have nothing to say and aren't very good at writing. During prewriting, you deliberately ignore your internal critic. Your purpose is simply to get ideas down on paper *without evaluating* their effectiveness. Writing without immediately judging what you produce can be liberating. Once you feel less pressure, you'll probably find that you can generate a good deal of material. And that can make your confidence soar.

One final advantage of prewriting: The random associations typical of prewriting tap the mind's ability to make unusual connections. When you prewrite, you're like an archaeologist going on a dig. On the one hand, you may not unearth anything; on the other hand, you may stumble upon one interesting find after another. Prewriting helps you appreciate—right from the start—this element of surprise in the writing process.

Keep a Journal

Of all the prewriting techniques, keeping a **journal** (daily or almost daily) is the one most likely to make writing a part of your life. If you prefer keeping a handwritten journal, consider using a small notebook that you can carry with you for on-the-spot writing. If you feel more comfortable working at a typewriter or word processor, keep your typed pages or printouts in a loose-leaf notebook. No matter how you proceed, be sure to date all entries.

Some journal entries focus on a single theme; others wander from topic to topic. Your starting point may be a dream, a snippet of overheard conversation, a video on MTV, a political cartoon, an issue raised in class or in your reading— anything that surprises, interests, angers, depresses, confuses, or amuses you. You may also use a journal to experiment with your writing style—say, to vary your sentence structure if you tend to use predictable patterns.

Here is a fairly focused excerpt from a student's journal:

> Today I had to show Paul around school. He and Mom got here by 9. I didn't let on that this was the earliest I've gotten up all semester! He got out of the car looking kind of nervous. Maybe he thought his big brother would be different after a couple of months of college. I walked him around part of the campus and then he went with me to Am. Civ. and then to lunch. He met Greg and some other guys. Everyone seemed to like him. He's got a nice, quiet sense of humor. When I went to Bio., I told him that he could walk around on his own since he wasn't crazy about sitting in on a science class. But he said "I'd rather stick with you." Was he flattering me or was he just scared? Anyway it made me feel good. Later when he was leaving, he told me he's definitely going to apply. I guess that'd be kind of nice, having him here. Mom thinks it's great and she's pushing it. I don't know. I feel kind of like it would invade my privacy. I found this school and have made a life for myself here. Let him find his own school! But it could be great having my kid brother here. I guess this is a classic case of what my psych teacher calls ambivalence. Part of me wants him to come, and part of me doesn't. (November 10)

The journal is a place for you to get in touch with the writer inside you. Although some instructors collect students' journals, you needn't be overly concerned with spelling, grammar, sentence structure, or organization. While journal writing is typically more structured than freewriting (see page 27), you don't have to strive for entries that read like mini-essays. You may leave loose ends, drift to new topics, and evoke the personal and private without fully explaining or describing. The most important thing is to let your journal writing prompt reflection and insights.

Writing openly and fluently doesn't happen overnight; you need to keep at it. Try to complete a page-long journal entry three to five times a week. It's also a good idea to reread each week's entries to identify recurring themes and concerns. Keep a list of these issues at the back of your journal, under a heading like "Possible Essay Subjects." Here, for instance, are a few topics suggested by the preceding journal entry: deciding which college to attend, leaving home, sibling rivalry. Each of these topics could be developed in a full-length essay.

Using the journal to identify potential essay subjects helps you see that everyday life can be the source of meaningful writing. Most of us have become so accustomed to the routines of our lives that we cannot see the interesting in the ordinary. In *Walden*, a collection of journal entries, Henry David Thoreau wrote that our lives would be enriched immeasurably if we "employ[ed] a certain portion of each day looking back upon the time which has passed and in writing down ... [our] thoughts and feelings." Keeping a journal does indeed foster an awareness of our own lives. It prevents us from thinking of ourselves as dull, dreary people to whom nothing happens. And it provides a wealth of material to draw on in our writing.

Getting Started Through Prewriting

Journal writing stimulates thinking in a loose, unstructured way. But when you have a specific piece to write, you should approach prewriting in a purposeful, focused manner. You need to:

- Understand the boundaries of the assignment.
- Determine your purpose, audience, tone, and point of view.
- Discover your essay's limited subject.
- Generate raw material about your limited subject.
- Organize the raw material.

We'll discuss each of these steps in turn. But first, here's a practical tip: If you don't use a word processor during the prewriting stage, try using a pencil and scrap paper. They're less intimidating than pen, typewriter, and "official" paper; they also reinforce the notion that prewriting is tentative and exploratory. If you do use a computer when prewriting, you will find the tips on page 145 helpful.

Understand the Boundaries of the Assignment

Most likely, you'll find considerable variety in your college writing assignments. Sometimes a professor will indicate that you can write on a topic of your own choosing; other times you may be given a highly specific assignment. Most assignments, though, will fit somewhere in between. In any case, you shouldn't start writing a paper until you know what's expected. First, clarify the *kind of paper* the instructor has in mind. Assume the instructor asks you to discuss the key ideas in an assigned reading. What exactly does the instructor want you to do? Should you include a brief summary of the selection? Should you compare the author's ideas with your own view of the subject? Should you determine if the author's view is supported by valid evidence? If you're not sure about an assignment, ask your instructor—not the student next to you, who may be as confused as you—to make the requirements clear. Most instructors are more than willing to provide an explanation. They would rather take a few minutes of class time to explain the assignment than spend hours reading dozens of student essays that miss the mark.

Second, find out *how long* the paper is expected to be. Many instructors will indicate the approximate length of the papers they assign. If no length requirements are provided, discuss with the instructor what you plan to cover and indicate how long you think your paper will be. The instructor will either give you the go-ahead or help you refine the direction and scope of your work.

Determine Your Purpose, Audience, Tone, and Point of View

Once you understand the requirements for a writing assignment, you're ready to begin thinking about the essay. What is its *purpose*? For what *audience* will it be written? What *tone* and *point of view* will you use? Later on, you may modify your decisions about these issues. That's fine. But you need to understand the way these considerations influence your work in the early phases of the writing process.

Purpose

Start by clarifying to yourself the essay's broad **purpose.** What do you want the essay to accomplish? The papers you write in college are usually meant to *inform* or *explain,* to *convince* or *persuade,* and sometimes to *entertain.*

In practice, writing often combines purposes. You might, for example, write an essay trying to *convince* people to support a new trash recycling program in your community. But before you win readers over, you most likely would have to *explain* something about current waste-disposal technology.

When purposes blend in this way, the predominant one influences the essay's content, organization, pattern of development, emphasis, and language. Assume you're writing about a political campaign. If your primary goal is to *entertain,* to take a gentle poke at two candidates, you might use the comparison-contrast pattern to organize your essay. You might, for example, start with several accounts of one candidate's "foot-in-mouth disease" and then describe the attempts of the other candidate, a multimillionaire, to portray himself as an average Joe. Your language, full of exaggeration, would reflect your objective. But if your primary purpose is to *persuade* readers that the candidates are incompetent and shouldn't be elected, you might adopt a serious, straightforward style. Selecting the argumentation-persuasion pattern to structure the essay, you might use one candidate's gaffes and the other's posturings to build a case that neither is worthy of public office.

Audience

Writing is a social act and thus implies a reader or an **audience.** To write effectively, you need to identify who your readers are and to take their expectations and needs into account. An essay about the artificial preservatives in the food served by the campus cafeteria would take one form if submitted to your chemistry professor and a very different form if written for the college newspaper. The chemistry paper would probably be formal and technical, complete with chemical formulations and scientific data: "Distillation revealed sodium benzoate particles suspended in a gelatinous medium." But such technical material would be inappropriate in a newspaper column intended for general readers. In this case, you might provide specific examples of cafeteria foods loaded with additives—"Those deliciously smoky cold cuts are loaded with nitrates and nitrites, both known to cause cancer in laboratory animals"—and suggest ways to eat more healthfully—"Pass by the deli counter and fill up instead on vegetarian pizza and fruit juices."

If you forget your readers, your essay can run into problems. Consider what happened when one student, Roger Salucci, submitted a draft of his essay to his instructor for feedback. The assignment was to write about an experience that demonstrated the value of education. Here's the opening paragraph from Roger's first draft:

When I received my first page as an EMT, I realized pretty quickly that all the weeks of KED and CPR training paid off. At first, when the call came in, it was nerve city for this guy, I can tell you. When the heat is on, my mind tends to go as blank as a TV screen at 2:00 a.m. in the morning. But I beat it to the van right away. After a couple of false turns, my partner and I finally got the right house and found a woman fibrillating and suffering severe myocardial arrhythmia. Despite our anxiety, our heads were on straight; we knew exactly what to do.

Roger's instructor found his essay unclear because she knew nothing about being an EMT (Emergency Medical Technician). When writing the essay, Roger neglected to consider his audience; specifically, he forgot that college instructors are no more knowledgeable than anyone else about subjects outside their specialty. Roger's instructor also commented that she was thrown off guard by the paper's casual, slangy approach ("It was nerve city for this guy, I can tell you"; "I beat it to the van right away"). Roger used a breezy, colloquial style—almost as though he were chatting about the experience with friends—but the instructor had expected a more formal approach.

The more you know about your readers, the more you can adapt your writing to fit their needs and expectations. The accompanying checklist will help you analyze your audience.

☑ ANALYZING YOUR AUDIENCE: A CHECKLIST

- What are my readers' age, sex, and educational level? How do these factors affect what I need to tell and don't need to tell my readers?
- What are my readers' political, religious, and other beliefs? How do these beliefs influence their attitudes and actions?
- What interests and needs motivate my audience?
- How much do my readers already know about my subject? Do they have any misconceptions?
- What biases do they have about me, my subject, and my opinion?
- How do my readers expect me to relate to them?
- What values do I share with my readers that will help me communicate with them?

Tone

Just as your voice may project a range of feelings, your writing can convey one or more **tones**, or emotional states: enthusiasm, anger, resignation, and so on.

Tone isn't a decorative adornment tacked on as an afterthought. Rather, tone is integral to meaning. It permeates writing and reflects your attitude toward yourself, your purpose, your subject, and your readers.

In everyday conversation, vocal inflections, facial expressions, and body gestures help convey tone. In writing, how do you project tone without these aids? You pay close attention to *sentence structure* and *word choice*. In Chapter 8, we present detailed strategies for finetuning sentences and words during the revision stage. Here we simply want to help you see that determining your tone should come early in the writing process because the tone you select influences the sentences and words you use later.

Sentence structure refers to the way sentences are shaped. Although the two paragraphs that follow deal with exactly the same subject, note how differences in sentence structure create sharply dissimilar tones:

> During the 1960s, many inner-city minorities considered the police an occupying force and an oppressive agent of control. As a result, violence grew against police in poorer neighborhoods, as did the number of residents killed by police.

> An occupying force. An agent of control. An oppressor. That's how many inner-city minorities in the '60s viewed the police. Violence against police soared. Police killings of residents mounted.

Informative in its approach, the first paragraph projects a neutral, almost dispassionate tone. The sentences are fairly long, and clear transitions ("During the 1960s"; "As a result") mark the progression of thought. But the second paragraph, with its dramatic, almost alarmist tone, seems intended to elicit a strong emotional response; its short sentences, fragments, and abrupt transitions reflect the turbulence of earlier times.

Word choice also plays a role in establishing the tone of an essay. Words have **denotations,** neutral dictionary meanings, as well as **connotations,** emotional associations that go beyond the literal meaning. The word *beach,* for instance, is defined in the dictionary as "a nearly level stretch of pebbles and sand beside a body of water." This definition, however, doesn't capture individual responses to the word. For some, *beach* suggests warmth and relaxation; for others, it calls up images of hospital waste and sewage washed up on a once-clean stretch of shoreline.

Since tone and meaning are tightly bound, you must be sensitive to the emotional nuances of words. Think about some of the terms denoting *adult human female: woman, fox, broad, member of the fair sex*. While all of these words denote the same thing, their connotations—the pictures they call up—are sharply different. Similarly, in a respectful essay about police officers, you wouldn't refer to *cops, narcs,* or *flatfoots;* such terms convey a contempt inconsistent with the tone intended. Your words must also convey tone clearly; otherwise, meaning is lost. Suppose you're writing a satirical piece criticizing a local beauty pageant. Dubbing the participants "livestock on view" leaves no question about your tone. But if you simply referred to the participants as "attractive young women," readers might be unsure of your attitude. Remember, readers can't read your mind, only your paper.

Point of View

When you write, you speak to your audience as a unique individual. **Point of view** reveals the person you decide to be as you write. Like tone, point of view is closely tied to your purpose, audience, and subject. Imagine you want to convey to students in your composition class the way your grandfather's death—on your eighth birthday—impressed you with life's fragility. To capture that day's impact on you, you might tell what happened from the point of view of a child: "Today is my birthday. I'm eight. Grandpa died an hour before I was supposed to have my party." Or you might choose instead to recount the event speaking as the adult you are today: "My grandfather died an hour before my eighth birthday party." Your point of view will obviously affect the essay's content and organization.

The most strongly individualized point of view is the **first person** (*I, me, mine, we, us, our*). Because it focuses on the writer, the first-person point of view is appropriate in narrative and descriptive essays based on personal experience. It also suits other types of essays (for example, causal analyses and process analyses) when the bulk of evidence presented consists of personal observation. In such essays, avoiding the first person often leads to stilted sentences like "There was strong parental opposition to the decision" or "Although Organic Chemistry had been dreaded, it became a passion." In contrast, the sentences sound much more natural when the first person is used: "*Our* parents strongly opposed the decision" and "Although *I* had dreaded Organic Chemistry, it became *my* passion."

Like many students, you may feel that a lightning bolt will strike you if you use the first person when writing. Indeed, in high school, you may have been warned away from (even forbidden to use) the first person. And it does have its dangers. For one thing, in essays voicing an opinion, most first-person expressions ("I believe that . . ." and "In my opinion . . .") are unnecessary; the point of view stated is assumed to be the writer's unless another source is indicated. Second, in a paper intended to be an objective presentation of an issue, the first person distracts from the issue by drawing unwarranted attention to the writer: "I think it's important to realize that most violent crime in this country is directly related to substance abuse." By way of contrast, note how the matter under discussion is clearly highlighted when the first person is omitted: "Most violent crime in this country is directly related to substance abuse."

In some situations, writers use the **second person** (*you, your, yours*), alone or in combination with the first person. In fact, we frequently use forms of *you* in this book. For instance, we write, "If *you're* the kind of person who doodles while thinking, *you* may want to try mapping . . ." rather than "If a *writer* is the kind of person who doodles while thinking, *he or she* may want to try mapping. . . ." As you can see, the second person simplifies style and involves the reader in a more personal way. You'll also find that the *imperative* form of the verb ("*Send* letters of protest to the television networks") engages readers in much the same way. The implied *you* speaks to the audience directly and lends immediacy to the directions. Despite these advantages, the second person point of view often isn't appropriate in many college courses where more formal, less conversational writing is called for.

The **third-person** point of view is by far the most common in academic writing. The third person gets its name from the stance it conveys—that of an outsider or "third person" observing and reporting on matters of primarily public rather than private importance: "The international team of negotiators failed to resolve the border dispute between the two nations." In discussions of historical events, scientific phenomena, works of art, and the like, the third-person point of view conveys a feeling of distance and objectivity. When you write in the third person, though, don't adopt such a detached stance that you end up using a stiff, artificial style: "On this campus, approximately two-thirds of the student body is dependent on bicycles as the primary mode of transportation to class." Aim instead for a more natural and personable quality: "Two-thirds of the students on campus ride their bikes to class." (For a more detailed discussion of levels of formality, see pages 117–18 in Chapter 8.)

Discover Your Essay's Limited Subject

Once you have a firm grasp of the assignment's boundaries and have determined your purpose, audience, tone, and point of view, you're ready to focus on a **limited subject** of the general assignment. Because too broad a subject can result in a diffuse, rambling essay, be sure to restrict your general subject before starting to write.

The following examples show the difference between general subjects that are too broad for an essay and limited subjects that are appropriate and workable. The examples, of course, represent only a few among many possibilities.

General Subject	Less General	Limited Subject
Education	Computers in education	Computers in elementary school arithmetic classes
	High school education	High school electives
Transportation	Low-cost travel	Hitchhiking
	Getting around a metropolitan area	The transit system in a nearby city
Work	Planning for a career	College internships
	Women in the work force	Women's success as managers

How do you move from a general to a narrow subject? Imagine that you're asked to prepare a straightforward, informative essay for your writing class. The assignment, prompted by Phyllis Theroux's essay "The Worry Factor" (page 7), is as follows:

Assignment

Because the contemporary world is a difficult, even dangerous place, parents understandably worry about their children. Write an essay supporting the idea that today's world is, in many ways, hostile—particularly to children.

Getting Started Through Prewriting

You might feel unsure about how to proceed. But two techniques can help you limit such a general assignment. Keeping your purpose, audience, tone, and point of view in mind, you may **question** or **brainstorm** the general subject. These two techniques have a paradoxical effect. Although they encourage you to roam freely over a subject, they also help restrict the discussion by revealing which aspects of the subject interest you most.

Question the General Subject

One way to narrow a subject is to ask a series of *who, how, why, where, when,* and *what* questions. The following example shows how one student, Harriet Davids, used this technique to limit the Theroux assignment. A thirty-eight-year-old college student and mother of two teenagers, Harriet was understandably intrigued by the assignment. She started by asking a number of pointed questions about the general topic. As she proceeded, she was aware that the same questions could have led to different limited subjects—just as other questions would have.

General Assignment: We live in a world that is difficult, even dangerous for children.

Question	Limited Subject
<u>Who</u> is to blame for the difficult conditions under which children grow up?	Parents' casual attitude toward childrearing
<u>How</u> have schools contributed to the problems children face?	Not enough counseling programs for kids in distress
<u>Why</u> do children feel frightened?	Divorce
<u>Where</u> do kids go to escape?	Television, which makes the world seem even more dangerous
<u>When</u> are children most vulnerable?	The special problems of adolescents
<u>What</u> dangers or fears should parents discuss with their children?	AIDS, drugs, alcohol, war, terrorism

Brainstorm the General Subject

Another way to focus on a limited subject is to list quickly everything about the general topic that pops into your mind. Working vertically down the page, jot down brief words, phrases, and abbreviations to capture your free-floating thoughts. Writing in complete sentences will slow you down. Don't try to organize or censor your ideas. Even the most fleeting, random, or seemingly outrageous thoughts can be productive.

Here's an example of the brainstorming that Harriet Davids decided to do in an effort to gather even more material for the Theroux assignment:

General Subject: We live in a world that is difficult, even dangerous for children.

Too many divorces

Parents squabbling over material goods in settlements

Money too important

Kids feel unimportant

Child abuse growing

Families move a lot

I moved in fourth grade--hated it

Rootless feeling

Nobody graduates from high school in same district they went to kindergarten in

Drug abuse all over, in little kids' schools

Pop music glorifies drugs

Kids not innocent--know too much

TV shows--corrupt politicians, sex, pollution, violence

Kids babysat by TV

Not enough guidance from parents

Kids raise selves

Single-parent homes

Day-care problems

Abuse of little children in day care

TV coverage of abuse--frightens kids

Unrealistic, perfect families on TV make kids feel inadequate

As you can see, questioning and brainstorming suggest many possible limited subjects. To identify especially promising ones, reread your material with pen or pencil in hand. What arouses your interest, anger, or curiosity? What themes seem to dominate and cut to the heart of the matter? Star or circle ideas with potential. Be sure to pay close attention to material generated at the end of your questioning and brainstorming. Often your mind takes a few minutes to warm up, with the best ideas popping out last.

After marking the material, write several phrases or sentences summarizing the most promising limited subjects. These, for example, are just a few that emerged from Harriet Davids's questioning and brainstorming the Theroux assignment:

TV partly to blame for children having such a hard time

Relocation stressful to children

Schools also at fault

The special problems that parents face raising children today

Harriet decided to write on the last of these limited subjects. This topic, in turn, is the focus of our discussion on the pages ahead.

Generate Raw Material About Your Limited Subject

When a limited subject strikes you as having possibilities, your next step is to begin generating material about that topic. If you do this now, in the prewriting stage, you'll find it easier to write the paper later on. Since you'll already have amassed much of the material for your essay, you'll be able to concentrate on other matters—say, finding just the right words to convey your ideas. Taking the time to sound out your limited subject during the prewriting stage also means you won't find yourself halfway through the first draft without much to say.

To generate raw material, you may use *freewriting, brainstorming, mapping,* and other techniques.

Freewrite on Your Limited Subject

Although freewriting can help you narrow a general subject, it's more valuable once you have limited your topic. **Freewriting** means jotting down in rough sentences or phrases everything that comes to mind. Although freewriting looks like regular prose because it is recorded horizontally, from margin to margin, it's much more fragmented. As you freewrite, you get swept along and go wherever your thoughts take you. You may skip back and forth between ideas, taking off in a more focused manner when you stumble across something interesting.

To capture this continuous stream of thought, write nonstop for ten minutes or more. Don't censor anything; put down whatever pops into your head. Don't reread, edit, or pay attention to organization, spelling, or grammar. If your mind goes blank, repeat words until another thought emerges.

Consider part of the freewriting that Harriet Davids generated about her limited subject, "The special problems that parents face raising children today":

> Parents today have tough problems to face. Lots of dangers. Drugs and alcohol for one thing. Also crimes of violence against kids. Parents also have to keep up with cost of living, everything costs more, kids want and expect more. Television? Another thing is Playboy, Penthouse. Sexy ads on TV, movies deal with sex. Kids grow up too fast, too fast. Drugs. Little kids can't handle knowing too much at an early age. Both parents at work much of the day.

Finding good day care a real problem. Lots of latchkey kids. Another problem is getting kids to do homework, lots of other things to do. Especially like going to the mall! When I was young, we did homework after dinner, no excuses accepted by my parents.

Brainstorm Your Limited Subject

Let your mind wander freely, as you did when narrowing your general subject. This time, though, list every idea, fact, and example that occurs to you about your limited subject. Use brief words and phrases, so you don't get bogged down writing full sentences. For now, don't worry whether ideas fit together or whether the points listed make sense.

To gather additional material on her limited subject for the Theroux assignment ("The special problems that parents face raising children today"), Harriet brainstormed the following list:

Trying to raise kids when both parents work

Prices of everything outrageous, even when both parents work

Commercials make everyone want <u>more</u> of everything

Clothes so important

Day care not always the answer--cases of abuse

Day care very expensive

Sex everywhere--TV, movies, magazines

Sexy clothes on little kids. Absurd!

Sexual abuse of kids

Violence against kids

Violence against kids when parents abuse drugs

Cocaine, crack, AIDS

Schools have to teach kids about these things

Schools doing too much--not as good as they used to be

Not enough homework assigned--kids unprepared

Distractions from homework--malls, TV, phones, stereos, MTV

Use Group Brainstorming

Brainstorming can also be conducted as a group activity. Thrashing out ideas with other people stretches the imagination, revealing possibilities you may not have considered on your own. Group brainstorming doesn't have to be con-

Getting Started Through Prewriting   29

ducted in a formal classroom situation. You can bounce ideas around with friends and family anywhere—over lunch, at the student center, and so on.

Map Out the Limited Subject

If you're the kind of person who doodles while thinking, you may want to try **mapping,** sometimes called **diagraming** or **clustering.** Like other prewriting techniques, mapping proceeds rapidly and encourages the free flow of ideas.

Begin by expressing your limited subject in a crisp phrase and placing it in the center of a blank sheet of paper. As ideas come to you, put them along lines or in boxes or circles around the limited subject. Draw arrows and lines to show the relationships among ideas. Don't stop there, however. Focus on each idea; as subpoints and details come to you, connect them to their source idea, again using boxes, lines, circles, or arrows to clarify how everything relates. Here's an example of the kind of map that Harriet Davids could have drawn to generate material for her limited subject based on the Theroux assignment.

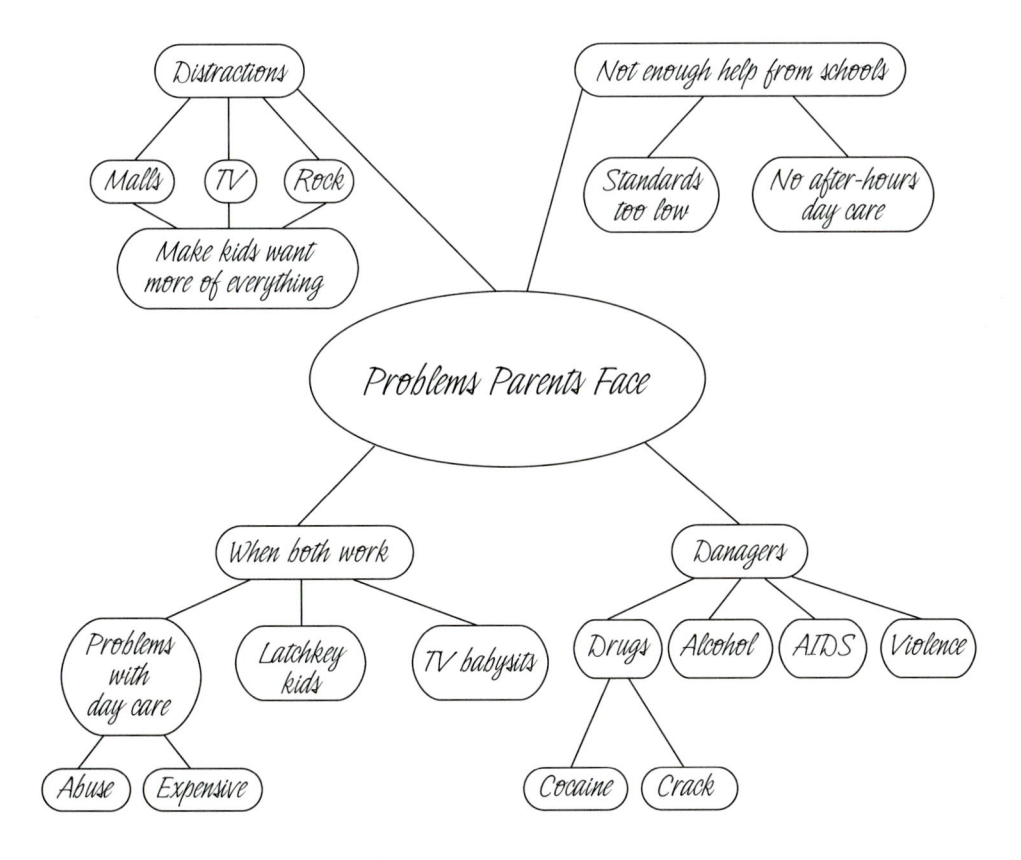

There's no right or wrong way to do mapping. Sometimes you'll move from the limited subject to a key related idea and all the details it prompts before moving to the next key idea; other times you'll map all the major divisions of a limited subject before mapping the details of any one idea.

Use the Patterns of Development

Throughout this book, we show how writers use various **patterns of development,** singly or in combination, to develop and organize their ideas. Because each pattern has its own distinctive logic, the patterns encourage you to think about a limited subject in surprising, new ways.

The various patterns of development are discussed in detail in Chapters 11–20 of Part III. At this point, though, you should find the following chart helpful. It not only summarizes the broad purpose of each pattern but also shows the way each pattern could generate different raw material for the limited subject of Harriet Davids's essay:

Limited Subject: The special problems that parents face raising children today.

Pattern of Development	Purpose	Raw Material
Description	To detail what a person, place, or object is like	Detail the sights and sounds of a glitzy mall that attracts lots of kids
Narration	To relate an event	Recount what happened when neighbors tried to forbid their kids from going to a rock concert
Illustration	To provide specific instances or examples	Offer examples of family arguments nowadays: Can a friend known to use drugs visit? Will permission be given to go to a party where alcohol will be served? Can parents outlaw MTV?
Division-classification	To divide something into parts or to group related things in categories	Identify the components of a TV commercial that distorts kids' values Classify the kinds of commercials that make it difficult to teach kids values
Process analysis	To explain how something happens or how something is done	Explain step by step how family life can disintegrate when parents have to work all the time to make ends meet
Comparison-contrast	To point out similarities and/or dissimilarities	Contrast families today with those of a generation ago

Getting Started Through Prewriting

Pattern of Development	Purpose	Raw Material
Cause-effect	To analyze reasons and consequences	Explain why parents are not around to be with their kids: industry's failure to provide day care and its inflexibility about granting time off for parents with sick kids Explain the consequences of absentee parents: Kids feel unloved; they turn to TV for role models; they're undisciplined; they take on adult responsibility too early
Definition	To explain the meaning of a term or concept	What is meant by "tough love"
Argumentation-persuasion	To win people over to a point of view	Convince parents that they must work with the schools to develop programs that make kids feel more safe and secure

(For more on ways to use the patterns of development in different phases of the writing process, see pages 39, 45–46, 52–53, 65, and Chapter 11.)

Conduct Research

Some limited subjects (for example, "Industry's day-care policies") can be developed only if you do some research. You may conduct **primary research,** in which you interview experts, conduct your own studies, compile your own statistics, and the like. Or you may conduct **secondary research,** in which you visit the library and look for books and articles about your limited subject in the card catalog, the *Readers' Guide to Periodical Literature,* or a computerized reference system. (See pages 461–76 in Part IV on how to conduct research.) At this point, you don't need to read closely the material you find. Just skim and perhaps take a few brief notes on ideas and points that could be useful.

If researching the Theroux assignment, for instance, Harriet Davids could look under the following headings and subheadings:

Day care
Drug abuse
Family
Parent-child relationship
    Child abuse
    Children of divorced parents
    Children of working mothers
School and home

Organize the Raw Material

Some students prefer to wait until after they have formulated a thesis to shape their prewriting material. (For information on thesis statements, see Chapter 3.) But if you find that imposing a preliminary order on your prewriting provides the focus needed to devise an effective thesis, you'll probably want to prepare a **scratch list** or **outline** at this point. In Chapter 5, we talk about the more formal outline you may need later on in the writing process (pages 55–58). Here we show how a rough outline or scratch list can help shape the tentative ideas generated during prewriting.

As you reread your exploratory thoughts about the limited subject, keep the following questions in mind: What *purpose* have you decided on? What are the characteristics of your *audience*? What *tone* will be effective in achieving your purpose with your audience? What *point of view* will you adopt? Record your responses to these questions at the top of your prewriting material.

Now go to work on the raw material itself. Cross out anything not appropriate for your purpose, audience, tone, and point of view; add points that didn't originally occur to you. Star or circle compelling items that warrant further development. Then draw arrows between related items, your goal being to group such material under a common heading. Finally, determine what seems to be the best order for the headings.

By giving you a sense of the way your free-form material might fit together, a scratch outline makes the writing process more manageable. You're less likely to feel overwhelmed once you actually start writing because you'll already have some idea about how to shape your material into a meaningful statement. Remember, though, the scratch outline can, and most likely will, be modified along the way.

Harriet Davids's handwritten annotations on her brainstormed list (page 28) illustrate the way Harriet began shaping her raw prewriting material:

Purpose: To inform

Audience: Instructor as well as class members, most of whom are 18-20 years old

Tone: Serious and straightforward

Point of view: Third person (mother of two teenage girls)

Limited subject: The special problems that parents face raising children today

(1) Day care

Trying to raise kids when both parents work

~~Prices of everything outrageous, even when both parents work~~

~~Commercials make everyone want more of everything~~

~~Clothes so important~~

Day care ~~not always the answer--cases of abuse~~ *problems--before and after school*

Day care very expensive

Getting Started Through Prewriting

> Sex everywhere--TV, movies, magazines
> ~~Sexy clothes on little kids. Absurd!~~
> ~~Sexual abuse of kids~~

③ *Sexual material everywhere*

> Violence against kids
> Violence against kids when parents abuse drugs
> Cocaine, crack, AIDS—*also drinking*
> ~~Schools have to teach kids about these things~~
> ~~Schools doing too much--not as good as they used to be~~
> Not enough homework assigned--kids unprepared

④ *Dangers*

> Distractions from homework--malls, TV, phones, stereos, MTV, *video arcades, rock concerts*

② *Homework distractions*

The scratch outline that starts below and continues on the next page shows how Harriet translated the annotations on her prewriting into a more organized format. (If you'd like to see Harriet's more formal outline and her first draft, turn to pages 57–58 and 80–81.)

Purpose: To inform

Audience: Instructor as well as class members, most of whom are 18-20 years old

Tone: Serious and straightforward

Point of view: Third person (mother of two teenage girls)

Limited subject: The special problems that parents face raising children today

1. Day care for two-career families
   - Expensive
   - Before-school problems
   - After-school problems
2. Distractions from homework
   - Stereos, televisions in room at home
   - Places to go--malls, video arcades, fast-food restaurants, rock concerts
3. Sexually explicit materials
   - Magazines and books
   - Television shows
   - MTV

- Movies
- Rock posters
4. Life-threatening dangers
   - AIDS
   - Drugs
   - Drinking
   - Violence against children (by sitters, in day care, etc.)

(For hints about using a word processor to organize raw material, see page 146.)

The prewriting strategies described in this chapter provide a solid foundation for the next stages of your work. But invention and imaginative exploration don't end when prewriting is completed. As you'll see, remaining open to new ideas is crucial during all phases of the writing process.

ACTIVITIES: GETTING STARTED THROUGH PREWRITING

1. Number the items in each set from 1 (*broadest subject*) to 5 (*most limited subject*):

Set A	Set B
Abortion	Business majors
Controversial social issue	Students' majors
Cutting state abortion funds	College students
Federal funding of abortions	Kinds of students on campus
Social issues	Why students major in business

2. Which of the following topics are too broad for an essay of two to five typewritten pages: soap operas' appeal to college students; day care; trying to "kick" junk food; male and female relationships; international terrorism?

3. Assume you're writing essays on two of the topics on the next page. For each one, explain how you might adapt your purpose, tone, and point of view to the audiences indicated in parentheses. (You may find it helpful to work with others on this activity.)

Getting Started Through Prewriting

a. Overcoming shyness (ten-year-olds; teachers of ten-year-olds; young singles living in large apartment buildings)
b. Telephone solicitations (people training for a job in this field; homeowners; readers of a humorous magazine)
c. Smoking (people who have quit; smokers; elementary school children)

4. Choose one of the following general topics for a roughly five-hundred-word essay. Then use the prewriting technique indicated in parentheses to identify several limited topics. Next, with the help of one or more patterns of development, generate raw material on the limited subject you consider most interesting.

a. Friendship (*journal writing*)
b. Malls (*mapping*)
c. Leisure (*freewriting*)
d. Television (*brainstorming*)
e. Required courses (*group brainstorming*)
f. Manners (*questioning*)

5. For each set of limited subjects and purposes that follows, determine which pattern(s) of development would be most useful. (Save this material so you can work with it further after reading the next chapter.)

a. The failure of recycling efforts on campus

  Purpose: to explain why students and faculty tend to disregard recycling guidelines

b. The worst personality trait that a teacher, parent, boss, or friend can have

  Purpose: to poke fun at this personality trait

c. The importance of being knowledgeable about national affairs

  Purpose: to convince students to stay informed about current events

6. Select *one* of the following limited subjects. Then, given the purpose and audience indicated, draft a paragraph using the first-, second-, or third-person point of view. Next, rewrite the paragraph two more times, each time using a different point of view. What differences do you see in the three versions? Which version do you prefer? Why?

a. American action movies like *The Terminator* and *Lethal Weapon*

  Purpose: to defend the enjoyment of such films
  Audience: those who like foreign "art" films

b. Senioritis

  Purpose: to explain why high school seniors lose interest in school
  Audience: parents and teachers

c. Television commercials aimed at teens and young adults

   Purpose: to make fun of the commercials' persuasive appeals

   Audience: advertising executives

7. Select *one* of the following general subjects. Keeping in mind the indicated purpose, audience, tone, and point of view, use a prewriting technique to limit the subject. Next, by means of another prewriting strategy, generate relevant information about the restricted topic. Finally, shape your raw material into a scratch outline—crossing out, combining, and adding ideas as needed. (Save your scratch outline so you can work with it further after reading the next chapter.)

   a. Rock music

   Purpose: to explain its attraction
   Audience: classical music fans
   Tone: playful
   Writer's point of view: a rock fan

   b. Becoming a volunteer

   Purpose: to recruit
   Audience: ambitious young professionals
   Tone: straightforward
   Writer's point of view: head of a volunteer organization

   c. Sexist attitudes in music videos

   Purpose: to inform
   Audience: teenagers of both sexes
   Tone: objective but with some emotion
   Writer's point of view: a teenage male

   d. Major problems in high school education

   Purpose: to create awareness of the problems
   Audience: teachers
   Tone: serious and concerned
   Writer's point of view: a former high school student

3
IDENTIFYING A THESIS

THE process of prewriting—discovering a limited subject and generating ideas about it—prepares you for the next stage in writing an essay: identifying the paper's *thesis*, or controlling idea.

WHAT IS A THESIS?

Presenting your opinion on a subject, the **thesis** should focus on an interesting and significant issue, one that engages your energies and merits your consideration. You may think of the thesis as the essay's hub—the central point around which all the other material revolves. Your thesis determines what does and does not belong in the essay. The thesis, especially when it occurs early in an essay, also helps focus the reader on the piece's central point and thus helps you achieve your writing purpose.

FINDING A THESIS

Sometimes the thesis emerges early in the prewriting stage, particularly if a special angle on your limited topic sparks your interest or becomes readily apparent. Often, though, you'll need to do some work to determine your thesis. For some topics, you may need to do some library research. For other subjects, the best way to identify a promising thesis is to look through your prewriting and ask yourself questions like these: "What statement does all this prewriting support? What aspect of the limited subject is covered in most detail? What is the focus of the most provocative material?"

For a look at the process of finding the thesis within prewriting material, glance back in Chapter 2 at the annotated brainstorming (pages 32–33) and the resulting scratch outline (pages 33–34) that Harriet Davids prepared for her limited subject, "The special problems that parents face raising children today." Harriet devised the following thesis to capture the focus of her prewriting: "Being a parent today is much more difficult than it was a generation ago." (The full outline for Harriet's paper appears on pages 57–58; the first draft on pages 80–81; and the final draft on pages 137–39.)

Sometimes, though, the thesis won't be as easy to pinpoint as it was for Harriet. Indeed, you may find that you need to refocus your thesis as you move through the stages of the writing process. To see how this progressive clarification might work, imagine you're writing a paper about adjusting to the academic demands of college life. After looking over your prewriting, you might identify this preliminary thesis: "Many college students flounder the first semester because they have trouble adjusting to the amount of work required by their professors." However, once you start writing the essay, you might realize that students' increased personal freedom, not their increased workload, is the primary problem. You would revise your thesis accordingly: "Many college students flounder the first semester because they become so distracted by new freedoms in their personal lives that they don't give enough attention to academics." (For hints about using a word processor to find a thesis, see page 145.)

WRITING AN EFFECTIVE THESIS

What makes a thesis effective? Generally expressed in one or two sentences, a thesis statement often has two parts. One part presents your paper's *limited subject;* the other presents your *point of view,* or *attitude,* about that subject. Here are some examples of the way you might move from general subject to limited subject to thesis statement. In each thesis statement, the limited subject is underlined once and the attitude twice.

General Subject	**Limited Subject**	**Thesis Statement**
Education	Computers in elementary school arithmetic classes	Computer programs in arithmetic can individualize instruction more effectively than the average elementary school teacher can.
Transportation	A metropolitan transit system	Although the city's transit system still has problems, it has become safer and more efficient in the last two years.

Identifying a Thesis

General Subject	Limited Subject	Thesis Statement
Work	College internships	The college internship program has had positive consequences for students.
Sports	Salaries in basketball	The high salaries paid super-star basketball players seriously compromise the integrity of the game.

An effective thesis establishes a tone and point of view suitable for a given purpose and audience. If you're writing an essay arguing that multi-media equipment can never replace a live teacher in the classroom, you need to frame a thesis that matches your and your readers' concerns about the subject. Instead of breezily writing, "Parents, schoolboards, principals: ditch the boob tube and the cutesy interactive computer and put the bucks where it counts—in teachers," you would aim for a more thoughtful and serious tone: "Education won't be improved by purchasing more electronic teaching tools but by allocating more money to hire and develop good teachers."

Another point about writing a strong thesis: On page 20, we show how an essay's purpose may suggest a pattern of development. In the same way, an effective thesis may point the way to a pattern of development that would be appropriate for developing the essay. Consider the thesis statements in the preceding list. The first thesis might use *comparison-contrast*; the second *illustration*; the third *cause-effect*; and the fourth *argumentation-persuasion*. (For more information about the relationship between an essay's purpose and its pattern of development, see the chart on pages 30–31.)

Because preparing an effective thesis is such a critical step in writing a sharply focused essay, you need to avoid the following four common problems.

1. Don't Write a Highly Opinionated Statement

Although your thesis should express your attitude toward your subject, don't go overboard and write a dogmatic, overstated thesis: "With characteristic clumsiness, campus officials bumbled their way through the recent budget crisis." A more moderate thesis can make the same point, *without alienating readers:* "Campus officials had trouble managing the recent budget crisis effectively."

2. Don't Make an Announcement

Some writers use the thesis statement merely to announce the limited subject of their paper and forget to indicate their attitude toward the subject. Such statements are announcements of intent, not thesis statements.

Compare the following three announcements with the thesis statements beside them:

Announcement	Thesis Statement
My essay will discuss whether a student pub should exist on campus.	This college should not allow a student pub on campus.
Handgun legislation is the subject of this paper.	Banning handguns is the first step toward controlling crime in America.
I want to discuss cable television.	Cable television has not delivered on its promise to provide an alternative to network programming.

3. Don't Make a Factual Statement

Your thesis and thus your essay should focus on an issue capable of being developed. If a fact is used as a thesis, you have no place to go; a fact generally doesn't invite much discussion.

Notice the difference between the following factual statements and thesis statements:

Factual Statement	Thesis Statement
Many businesses pollute the environment.	Tax penalties should be levied against businesses that pollute the environment.
Many movies today are violent.	Movie violence provides a healthy outlet for aggression.
America's population is growing older.	The aging of the American population will eventually create a crisis in the delivery of health-care services.

4. Don't Make a Broad Statement

Avoid stating your thesis in vague, general, or sweeping terms. Broad statements make it difficult for readers to grasp your essay's point. Moreover, if you start with a broad thesis, you're saddled with the impossible task of trying to develop a book-length idea with an essay that runs only several pages.

The following examples contrast thesis statements that are too broad with effectively focused statements:

Broad Statement	Thesis Statement
Nowadays, high school education is often meaningless.	High school diplomas have been devalued by grade inflation.
Newspapers cater to the taste of the American public.	The success of *USA Today* indicates that people want newspapers that are easy to read and entertaining.
The computer revolution is not all that we have been led to believe it is.	Home computers are still an impractical purchase for many people.

Identifying a Thesis

PLACING THE THESIS IN AN ESSAY

The thesis is often located in the middle or at the end of the introduction. But considerations about audience, purpose, and tone should always guide your decision about its placement. You may, for example, choose to delay the thesis if you feel that background information needs to be provided before readers can fully understand your key point—especially if the concept is complex and best taken in slowly. Similarly, if you sense your audience is resistant to your thesis, you may wish to lead readers to it gradually. Conversely, if you feel that readers would appreciate a direct, forthright approach, you might place the thesis early in the essay—perhaps even at the very beginning of the introduction.

Sometimes the thesis is reiterated—using fresh words—in the essay's conclusion or elsewhere. If done well, this repetition keeps readers focused on the essay's key point. You may even leave the thesis implied, relying on strong support, tone, and style to convey the essay's central idea.

One final point: Once you start writing your first draft, some feelings, thoughts, and examples may emerge that modify, even contradict your initial thesis. Don't resist these new ideas. Keep them in mind as you revise the thesis and—in the process—move toward a more valid and richer view of your subject.

ACTIVITIES: IDENTIFYING A THESIS

1. For each of the following limited subjects, four possible thesis statements are given. Indicate whether each thesis is an announcement (A), a factual statement (FS), too broad a statement (TB), or an acceptable thesis (OK). Revise the flawed statements. Then, for the acceptable thesis statements, identify a possible purpose, audience, tone, and point of view.

   a. *Limited subject:* The ethics of treating severely handicapped infants

   - Some babies born with severe handicaps have been allowed to die.
   - There are many serious issues involved in the treatment of handicapped newborns.
   - The government should pass legislation requiring medical treatment for handicapped newborns.

- This essay will analyze the controversy surrounding the treatment of severely handicapped babies who would die without medical care.

   b. *Limited subject:* Privacy and computerized records

   - Computers raise some significant questions for all of us.
   - Computerized records keep track of consumer spending habits, credit records, travel patterns, and other personal information.
   - Computerized records have turned our private lives into public property.
   - In this paper, the relationship between computerized records and the right to privacy will be discussed.

2. Turn back to activity 5 on page 35. For each set of limited subjects listed there, develop an effective thesis. Select *one* of the thesis statements. Then, keeping in mind the purpose indicated and the pattern of development you identified earlier, draft a paragraph developing the point expressed in the thesis. (Save the paragraph so you can work with it further after reading the next chapter.)

3. Following are four pairs of general and limited subjects. Generate an appropriate thesis for each pair. Select one of the thesis statements, and determine which pattern of development would support the thesis most effectively. Use that pattern to draft a paragraph developing the thesis. (Save the paragraph so you can work with it further after reading the next chapter.)

General Subject	**Limited Subject**
Psychology	The power struggles in a classroom
Health	Doctors' attitudes toward patients
The elderly	Television's depiction of the elderly
Work	Minimum-wage jobs for young people

4. Each set that follows lists the key points for an essay. Based on the information provided, prepare a possible thesis for each essay. Then propose a possible purpose, audience, tone, and point of view.

Set A

- One evidence of this growing conservatism is the re-emerging popularity of fraternities and sororities.
- Beauty contests, ROTC training, and corporate recruiting—once rejected by students on many campuses—are again popular.
- Most importantly, many students no longer choose possibly risky careers that enable them to contribute to society but instead select safe fields with money-making potential.

Set B

- We do not know how engineering new forms of life might affect the earth's delicate ecological balance.

- Another danger of genetic research is its potential for unleashing new forms of disease.
- Even beneficial attempts to eliminate genetic defects could contribute to the dangerous idea that only perfect individuals are entitled to live.

5. Keep a journal for several weeks. Then reread a number of entries, identifying two or three recurring themes or subjects. Narrow the subjects and, for each one, generate possible thesis statements. Finally, using an appropriate pattern of development, draft a paragraph for one of the thesis statements. (Save the paragraph so you can work with it further after reading the next chapter.)

6. Select a broad topic—either your own or one of the following: animals, popularity, the homeless, money, fashion trends, race relations, parties. Working with a partner, use a prewriting technique to narrow the topic so that it's suitable for an essay of two to five typed pages. Using another prewriting strategy, generate details on the limited topic. Next, examine the material and identify at least two possible thesis statements. Then, for each thesis, reshape your prewriting, determining which items are appropriate, which are not, and where more material is needed.

7. Return to the scratch outline you prepared in response to activity 7 on page 36. After examining the outline, identify a thesis that conveys the central idea behind most of the raw material. Then, ask others to evaluate your thesis in light of the material in your scratch outline. Finally, keeping the thesis—as well as your purpose, audience, and tone—in mind, refine the scratch outline by deleting inappropriate items, adding relevant ones, and indicating where more material is needed. (Save your refined scratch outline and thesis so you can work with them further after reading the next chapter.)

4
SUPPORTING THE THESIS WITH EVIDENCE

AFTER identifying a preliminary thesis, you should develop the evidence needed to support that central idea. This supporting material grounds your essay, showing readers you have good reason for feeling as you do about your subject. Your evidence also adds interest and color to your writing.

In college essays of 500 to 1,500 words, you usually need at least three major points of evidence to develop your thesis. These major points—each focusing on related but separate aspects of the thesis—eventually become the supporting paragraphs (see pages 63–73) in the body of the essay.

WHAT IS EVIDENCE?

By **evidence,** we mean a number of different kinds of support. *Reasons* are just one option. To develop your thesis, you might also include *examples, facts, details, statistics, personal observation* or *experience, anecdotes,* and *expert opinions* and *quotations* (gathered from books, articles, interviews, documentaries, and the like). Imagine you're writing an essay with the thesis, "People normally unconcerned about the environment can be galvanized to constructive action if they feel personally affected by an environmental problem." You could support this thesis with any combination of the following types of evidence:

- *Reasons* why people become involved in the environmental movement: they believe the situation endangers the health of their families; they fear the value of their homes will plummet; they feel deceived by officials' assurances that there's nothing to worry about.
- *Examples* of neighborhood recycling efforts succeeding in communities once plagued by trash-disposal problems.
- *Facts* about residents' efforts to preserve the quality of well water in a community undergoing widespread industrial development.
- *Details* about the specific steps the average person can take to get involved in environmental issues.
- *Statistics* showing the growing number of Americans concerned about the environment.
- A *personal experience* about the way you became involved in an effort to stop a local business from dumping waste in a neighborhood stream.
- An *anecdote* about an ordinarily apathetic friend who protested the commercial development of a wooded area where he jogs.
- A *quotation* from a well-known scientist about the considerable impact that well-organized, well-informed citizens can have on environmental legislation.

HOW DO YOU FIND EVIDENCE?

Where do you find the examples, anecdotes, details, and other types of evidence needed to support your thesis? As you saw when you followed Harriet Davids's strategies for gathering material for an essay (pages 25–34), a good deal of information is generated during the prewriting stage. In this phase of the writing process, you tap into your personal experiences, draw upon other people's observations, perhaps interview a person with special knowledge about your subject. The library, with its abundant material, is another rich source of supporting evidence. (For information on using the library, see Chapter 21.) In addition, the various patterns of development are a valuable source of evidence.

How the Patterns of Development Help Generate Evidence

In Chapter 2, we discussed how the patterns of development could help generate material about Harriet Davids's limited subject (pages 30–31). The same patterns also help develop support for a thesis. Consider the way they generate evidence for this thesis: "To those who haven't done it, babysitting looks easy. In practice, though, babysitting can be difficult, frightening, even dangerous."

Pattern of Development	Evidence Generated
Description	Details about a child who, while being babysat, was badly hurt playing on a backyard swing.
Narration	Story about the time a friend babysat a child who became seriously ill and whose condition was worsened by the babysitter's remedies.
Illustration	Examples of potential babysitting problems: an infant who rolls off a changing table; a toddler who sticks objects in an electric outlet; a school-age child who is bitten by a neighborhood dog.
Division-classification	A typical babysitting evening divided into stages: playing with the kids; putting them to bed; dealing with their nighttime fears once they're in bed. Classify kids' nighttime fears: of monsters under their beds; of bad dreams; of being abandoned by their parents.
Process analysis	Step-by-step account of what a babysitter should do if a child becomes ill or injured.
Comparison-contrast	Contrast between two babysitters: one well-prepared, the other unprepared.
Cause-effect	Why children have temper tantrums; the effect of such tantrums on an unskilled babysitter.
Definition	What is meant by a *skilled* babysitter?
Argumentation-persuasion	A proposal for a babysitting training program to be offered by the local community center.

(For further discussion of ways to use the patterns of development in different phases of the writing process, see pages 30–31, 39, 52–53, 65, and Chapter 11.)

CHARACTERISTICS OF EVIDENCE

No matter how it is generated, all types of supporting evidence share the characteristics described in the following sections. You should keep these characteristics in mind as you review your thesis and scratch list. That way, you can make the changes needed to strengthen the evidence gathered earlier. As you'll see shortly, Harriet Davids focused on many of these issues as she worked with the evidence she collected during the prewriting phase.

The Evidence Is Relevant and Unified

All the evidence in an essay must clearly support the thesis. It makes no difference how riveting material might be; if it doesn't *relate directly* to the essay's central point, the evidence should be eliminated. Irrelevant material can weaken your position by implying that no relevant support exists. It also distracts readers from your controlling idea, thus disrupting the paper's overall unity.

Suppose you want to write an essay with the thesis "Fairly fought arguments can strengthen relationships." To support your thesis, you could adapt prewriting material about an argument you had with a friend: how the disagreement started, how you and your friend worked out your differences, how your friendship deepened because of what you learned about each other. Also to the point would be statements from your sister who found, after reading a book on conflict management, that her relationship with her co-workers improved significantly. Similarly relevant would be an account of a conflict-ridden family whose tensions eased once a counselor taught them how to air their differences. It would *not* serve your thesis, however, to include details about the way negotiating strategies can backfire. This material wouldn't be appropriate because it contradicts the point you want to make.

Early in the writing process, Harriet Davids was aware of the importance of relevant evidence. Take a moment to review Harriet's annotated brainstorming (pages 32–33). Even though Harriet hadn't yet identified her thesis, she realized she should delete a number of items on the reshaped version of her brainstormed list—for example, the second and last items ("prices of everything outrageous . . ." and "schools doing too much already . . ."). Harriet eliminated these points because they weren't consistent with the focus of her limited subject.

The Evidence Is Specific

When evidence is vague and general, readers lose interest in what you're saying, become skeptical of your ideas' validity, and feel puzzled about your meaning. In contrast, *specific, concrete evidence* provides sharp *word pictures* that engage your readers, persuade them that your thinking is sound, and clarify meaning.

Consider a paper with this thesis: "College students should not automatically dismiss working in fast-food restaurants; such jobs can provide valuable learning experiences." Here's how you might go wrong trying to support the thesis: Suppose you begin with the broad claim that these admittedly lackluster jobs can teach students a good deal about themselves. In a similarly abstract fashion, you go on to say that such jobs can affect students' self-concepts in positive ways. You end by declaring that such changes in self-perception lead to greater maturity.

To prevent readers from thinking "Who cares?" or "Who says?" you need to replace these vague generalities with specific, concrete evidence. For example, focusing on your own experience working at a fast-food restaurant, you might start by describing how you learned to control your sarcasm; such an attitude, you discovered, alienated co-workers and almost caused your boss to fire you. You could also recount the time you administered the Heimlich maneuver to a choking customer; your quick thinking and failure to panic increased your self-esteem. Finally, you could explain that the job encouraged you to question some of your values; you became close friends with a bookish, introspective co-worker—the kind of person you used to spurn. This specific, particularized evidence would support your thesis and help readers "see" the point you're making. (Pages 67–68 describe strategies for making evidence specific.)

At this point, it will be helpful to look once again at the annotations that Harriet Davids entered on her brainstormed list (pages 32–33). Note the way she jotted down new details to make her prewriting more specific. For example, to the item "Distractions from homework," she added the additional examples "video arcades" and "rock concerts." And, as you'll see when you read Harriet's first and final drafts (pages 80–81 and 137–39), she added many more vigorous specifics during later stages of the writing process.

The Evidence Is Adequate

Readers won't automatically accept your thesis; you need to provide *enough specific evidence* to support your viewpoint. On occasion, a single extended example will suffice. Generally, though, you'll need a variety of evidence: facts, examples, reasons, personal observations, expert opinion, and so on.

Assume you want to write an essay arguing that "college students living on campus should register and vote where they attend school." Hoping the essay will be published in the campus newspaper, you write it in the form of an open letter to the student body. One reason in support of your thesis strikes you immediately: that eighteen-year-olds should act as the adults they are and become involved in the electoral process. You also present as evidence a description of how good you felt during the last election when you walked into the voting booth set up in the student center. If this is all the support you provide, students probably won't be convinced; you haven't offered *sufficient* evidence. You need to present additional material—statistics on the shockingly low number of students registered to vote at your school; an account of a voter-registration drive at a nearby university that got students involved in the community and thus reduced traditional "town-gown" tensions; quotations from several students who voted against an anti-student housing ordinance and saw the ordinance defeated; an explanation of how easy it is to register.

Now take a final look at Harriet Davids's annotated brainstorming (pages 32–33). You'll see that Harriet realized she needed more than one block of supporting material to develop her limited subject; that's why she identified four separate blocks of evidence (day care, homework distractions, sexual material, and dangers). When Harriet prepared her first and final drafts (pages 80–81 and 137–39), she decided to eliminate the material about day care. But she added so many more specific and dramatic details that her evidence was more than sufficient.

The Evidence Is Dramatic

The most effective evidence enlarges the reader's experience by *dramatizing reality.* Say you plan to write an essay with the thesis "People who affirm the value of life refuse to wear fur coats." If, as support, you state only that most animals killed for their fur are caught in leg-hold traps, your readers will have little sense of the suffering involved. But if you write that steel-jaw, leg-hold traps snap shut on an animal's limb, crushing tissue and bone and leaving the animal to die, in severe pain, from exposure or starvation, your readers can better envision the animal's plight.

The Evidence Is Accurate

Make your evidence as dramatic as you can, but be sure it is *accurate*. When you have a strong belief and want readers to see things your way, you may be tempted to overstate or downplay facts, disregard information, misquote, or make up details. Suppose you plan to write an essay making the point that dormitory security is lax. You begin supporting your thesis by narrating the time you were nearly mugged in your dorm hallway. Realizing the essay would be more persuasive if you also mentioned other episodes, you decide to invent some material. Perhaps you describe several supposed burglaries on your dorm floor or exaggerate the amount of time it took campus security to respond to an emergency call from a residence hall. Yes, you've supported your point—but at the expense of truth.

The Evidence Is Representative

Using representative evidence means that you rely on the typical, the usual, to show that your point is valid. Contrary to the maxim, exceptions don't prove the rule. Perhaps you plan to write an essay contending that the value of seat belts has been exaggerated. To support your position, you mention a friend who survived a head-on collision without wearing a seat belt. Such an example isn't representative because the facts and figures on accidents suggest your friend's survival was a fluke.

Borrowed Evidence Is Documented

If you include evidence from outside sources (books, articles, interviews), you need to acknowledge where that information comes from. If you don't, readers may consider your evidence nothing more than your point of view, or they may regard as dishonest your failure to cite your indebtedness to others for ideas that obviously aren't your own.

The rules for crediting sources in informal writing are less established than they are for formal research. Follow any guidelines your instructor provides, and try to keep your notations, like those that follow, as simple as possible.

Time (July 3, 1989) reports that corporate wrongdoing has led to a rash of consumer protests.

Environmental scientist Natalie Angier believes that private zoos may be the only hope for some endangered species.

In formal research, you need to provide much more detailed documentation of sources. For information on formal documentation, see Chapter 22.

Strong supporting evidence is at the heart of effective writing. Without it, essays lack energy and fail to project the writer's voice and perspective. Such lifeless writing is also more apt to put readers to sleep than to engage their interest and convince them that the points being made are valid. Taking the time to accumulate solid supporting material is, then, a critical step in the writing process. (If you'd like to read more about the characteristics of strong evidence, see pages 66–73. If you'd like suggestions for organizing an essay's evidence, see the diagram on page 79.)

ACTIVITIES: SUPPORTING THE THESIS WITH EVIDENCE

1. Imagine you're writing an essay with the following thesis in mind. Which of the statements in the list support the thesis? Label each statement acceptable (OK), irrelevant (IR), inaccurate (IA), or too general (TG).

Thesis: Colleges should put less emphasis on sports.

    a. High-powered athletic programs can encourage grade fixing.
    b. Too much value is attached to college sports.
    c. Athletics have no educational value.
    d. Competitive athletics can lead to extensive and expensive injuries.
    e. Athletes can spend too much time on the field and not enough on their studies.
    f. Good athletic programs create a strong following among former undergraduates.

2. For each of the following thesis statements, list at least three supporting points that convey vivid word pictures.

    a. Rude behavior in movie theaters seems to be on the rise.
    b. Recent television commercials portray men as incompetent creatures.
    c. The local library fails to meet the public's needs.
    d. People often abuse public parks.

3. Turn back to the paragraphs you prepared in response to activity 2, activity 3, or activity 5 in Chapter 3 (pages 42–43). Select one paragraph and strengthen its evidence, using the guidelines presented in this chapter.

Supporting the Thesis With Evidence   51

4. Choose one of the following thesis statements. Then identify an appropriate purpose, audience, tone, and point of view for an essay with this thesis. Using freewriting, mapping, or the questioning technique, generate at least three supporting points for the thesis. Last, write a paragraph about one of the points, making sure your evidence reflects the characteristics discussed in this chapter. Alternatively, you may go ahead and prepare the first draft of an essay having the selected thesis. (If you choose the second option, you may want to turn to page 79 to see a diagram showing how to organize a first draft.) Save whatever you prepare so you can work with it further after reading the next chapter.

   a. Winning the lottery may not always be a blessing.
   b. All of us can take steps to reduce the country's trash crisis.
   c. Drug education programs in public schools are (or are not) effective.

5. Select one of the following thesis statements. Then determine your purpose, audience, tone, and point of view for an essay with this thesis. Next, use the patterns of development to generate at least three supporting points for the thesis. Finally, write a paragraph about one of the points, making sure that your evidence demonstrates the characteristics discussed in this chapter. Alternatively, you may go ahead and prepare a first draft of an essay having the thesis selected. (If you choose the latter option, you may want to turn to page 79 to see a diagram showing how to organize a first draft.) Save whatever you prepare so you can work with it further after reading the next chapter.

   a. Teenagers should (or should not) be able to obtain birth-control devices without their parents' permission.
   b. The college's system for awarding student loans needs to be overhauled.
   c. VCRs have changed for the worse (or the better) the way Americans entertain themselves.

6. Look at the thesis and refined scratch outline you prepared in response to activity 7 in Chapter 3 (page 43). Where do you see gaps in the support for your thesis? By brainstorming with others, generate material to fill these gaps. If some of the new points generated suggest that you should modify your thesis, make the appropriate changes now. (Save this material so you can work with it further after reading the next chapter.)

   (For more activities on generating evidence, see pages 83–85 in Chapter 6 as well as page 131 in Chapter 8.)

5
ORGANIZING THE EVIDENCE

Once you've generated supporting evidence, you're ready to *organize* that material. Even highly compelling evidence won't illustrate the validity of your thesis or achieve your purpose if it isn't organized properly. Some writers can move quickly from generating support to writing a clearly structured first draft. (They usually say they have sequenced their ideas in their heads.) Most, however, need to spend some time sorting out their thoughts on paper before starting the first draft; otherwise, they tend to lose their way in a tangle of ideas.

When moving to the organizing stage, you should have in front of you your scratch list (see pages 32–33) and thesis, plus any supporting material you've accumulated since you did your prewriting. To find a logical framework for all this material, you'll need to (1) determine which pattern of development is implied in your evidence, (2) select one of four basic approaches for organizing your evidence, and (3) outline your evidence. These issues are discussed in the following sections. (For hints about using a word processor to organize evidence, turn to page 146.)

USE THE PATTERNS OF DEVELOPMENT

As you saw on pages 30–31, and 45–46, the patterns of development (definition, narration, process analysis, and others) can help you develop prewriting material and generate evidence for a thesis. In the organizing stage, the patterns provide frameworks for presenting the evidence in an orderly, accessible way. Here's how.

Each pattern of development has its own internal logic that makes it appropriate for some writing purposes but not for others. (You may find it helpful at this point to turn to pages 30–31 so you can review the broad purpose of each pattern.) Imagine that you want to write an essay *explaining why* some students drop out of college during the first semester. If your essay consisted only of a lengthy *narrative* of two friends floundering through the first month of college, you wouldn't achieve your purpose. A condensed version of the narrative might be appropriate at some point in the essay, but—to meet your objective—most of the paper would have to focus on *causes* and *effects*.

Once you see which pattern (or combination of patterns) is implied by your purpose, you can block out your paper's general structure. For instance, in the preceding example, you might organize the essay around a three-part discussion of the key reasons that students have difficulty adjusting to college: (1) they miss friends and family, (2) they take inappropriate courses, and (3) they experience conflicts with roommates. As you can see, your choice of pattern of development significantly influences your essay's content and organization.

Some essays follow a single pattern, but most blend them, with a predominant pattern providing the piece's organizational framework. In our example essay, you might include a brief *description* of an overwhelmed first-year college student; you might *define* the psychological term *separation anxiety*; you might end the paper by briefly explaining a *process* for making students' adjustment to college easier. Still, the essay's overall organizational pattern would be *cause-effect* because the paper's primary purpose is to explain why students drop out of college. (See page 65 and Chapter 11 for more information on the way patterns often mix.)

Although writers often combine the patterns of development, your composition instructor may ask you to write an essay organized according to a single pattern. Such an assignment helps you understand a particular pattern's unique demands. Keep in mind, though, that most writing begins not with a specific pattern but with a specific *purpose*. The pattern or combination of patterns used to develop and organize an essay evolves out of that purpose.

SELECT AN ORGANIZATIONAL APPROACH

No matter which pattern(s) of development you select, you need to know four general approaches for organizing the supporting evidence in an essay: chronological, spatial, emphatic, and simple-to-complex.

Chronological Approach

When an essay is organized **chronologically,** supporting material is arranged in a clear time sequence, usually starting with what happened first and ending with what happened last. Occasionally, chronological arrangements can be resequenced to create flashback or flashforward effects, two techniques discussed in Chapter 13 on narration.

Essays using narration (for example, an experience with prejudice) or process analysis (for instance, how to deliver an effective speech) are most likely to be organized chronologically. The paper on public speaking might use a time sequence to present its points: how to prepare a few days before the presentation is due; what to do right before the speech; what to concentrate on during the speech itself. (For examples of chronologically arranged student essays, turn to pages 195–97 in Chapter 13 and pages 294–97 in Chapter 16.)

Spatial Approach

When you arrange supporting evidence **spatially,** you discuss details as they occur in space, or from certain locations. This strategy is particularly appropriate for description. Imagine that you plan to write an essay describing the joyous times you spent as a child playing by a towering old oak tree in the neighborhood park. Using spatial organization, you start by describing the rich animal life (the plump earthworms, swarming anthills, and numerous animal tracks) you observed while hunkered down *at the base* of the tree. Next, you re-create the contented feeling you experienced sitting on a branch *in the middle* of the tree. Finally, you describe the glorious view of the world you had *from the top* of the tree.

Although spatial arrangement is flexible (you could, for instance, start with a description from the top of the tree), you should always proceed systematically. And once you select a particular spatial order, you should usually maintain that sequence throughout the essay; otherwise, readers may get lost along the way. (A spatially arranged student essay appears in Chapter 12 on pages 163–65.)

Emphatic Approach

In **emphatic** order, the most compelling evidence is saved for last. This arrangement is based on the psychological principle that people remember best what they experience last. Emphatic order has built-in momentum because it starts with the least important point and builds to the most significant. This method is especially effective in argumentation-persuasion essays, in papers developed through examples, and in pieces involving comparison-contrast, division-classification, or causal analysis.

Consider an essay analyzing the negative effect that workaholic parents can have on their children. The paper might start with a brief discussion of relatively minor effects, such as the family's eating mostly frozen or take-out foods. Paragraphs on more serious effects might follow: children get no parental help with homework; they try to resolve personal problems without parental advice. Finally, the essay might close with a detailed discussion of the most significant effect—children's lack of self-esteem because they feel unimportant in their parents' lives. (The student essays on pages 230–31 in Chapter 14, pages 326–27 in Chapter 17, and pages 430–32 in Chapter 19 all use an emphatic arrangement.)

Simple-to-Complex-Approach

A final way to organize an essay is to proceed with relatively **simple** concepts to more **complex** ones. By starting with easy-to-grasp, generally accepted evidence, you establish rapport with your readers and assure them that the essay is firmly grounded in shared experience. In contrast, if you open with difficult or highly technical material, you risk confusing and alienating your audience.

Assume you plan to write a paper arguing that your college has endangered students' health by not making an all-out effort to remove asbestos from dormitories and classroom buildings. It probably wouldn't be a good idea to begin with a medically sophisticated explanation of precisely how asbestos damages lung tissue. Instead, you might start with an observation that is likely to be familiar to your readers—one that is part of their everyday experience. You could, for example, open with a description of asbestos—as readers might see it—wrapped around air ducts and furnaces or used as electrical insulation and fireproofing material. Having provided a basic, easy-to-visualize description, you could then go on to explain the complicated process by which asbestos can cause chronic lung inflammation. (See pages 357–59 in Chapter 18 for an example of a student essay using the simple-to-complex arrangement.)

Depending on your purpose, any one of these four organizational approaches might be appropriate. For example, assume you want to develop this thesis: "Being a parent today is much more difficult than it was a generation ago." To emphasize that the various stages in children's lives present parents with different difficulties, you'd probably select a *chronological* sequence. To show that the challenges parents face vary depending on whether children are at home, at school, or in the world at large, you'd probably choose a *spatial* sequence. To stress the range of problems that parents face (from less to more serious), you'd probably use an *emphatic* sequence. Finally, to illustrate today's confusing array of theories for raising children, you might take a *simple-to-complex* approach, moving from the basic to the most sophisticated theory.

PREPARE AN OUTLINE

Do you, like many students, react with fear and loathing to the dreaded word *outline*? Do you, if asked to submit an outline, prepare it *after* you've written the essay? If you do, we hope to convince you that having an outline—a skeletal version of your paper—*before* you begin the first draft makes the writing process much more manageable. The outline helps you organize your thoughts beforehand, and it guides your writing as you work on the draft. Even though ideas continue to evolve during the draft, an outline clarifies how ideas fit together, which points are major, which should come first, and so on. An outline may also reveal places where evidence is weak, prompting you to eliminate the material altogether, retain it in an unemphatic position, or do more prewriting to generate additional support.

Like previous stages in the writing process, outlining is individualized. Some people prepare highly structured, detailed outlines; others make only a few informal jottings. Sometimes outlining will go quickly, with points falling easily into place; at other times you'll have to work hard to figure out how points are related. If that happens, be glad you caught the problem while outlining, rather than while writing or revising.

To prepare an effective outline, you should reread and evaluate your scratch list and thesis as well as any other evidence you've generated since the prewriting stage. Then decide which pattern of development (description, cause-effect, and so on) seems to be suggested by your evidence. Also determine whether your evidence lends itself to a chronological, a spatial, an emphatic, or a simple-to-complex order. Having done all that, you're ready to identify and sequence your main and supporting points.

The amount of detail in an outline will vary according to the paper's length and the instructor's requirements. A scratch outline consisting of words or phrases (such as the one on pages 33–34 in Chapter 2) is often sufficient, but for longer papers, you'll probably need a more detailed and formal outline. In such cases, the suggestions in the accompanying checklist will help you develop a sound plan. Feel free to modify these guidelines to suit your needs.

✔ GUIDELINES FOR OUTLINING: A CHECKLIST

- Write your purpose, audience, tone, point of view, and thesis at the top of the outlining page.
- Below the thesis, enter the pattern of development that seems to be implied by the evidence you've accumulated.
- Also record which of the four organizational approaches would be most effective in sequencing your evidence.
- Reevaluate your supporting material. Delete anything that doesn't develop the thesis or that isn't appropriate for your purpose, audience, tone, and point of view.
- Add any new points or material.
- Group related items together. Give each group a heading that represents a main topic in support of your thesis.
- Label these main topics with roman numerals (I, II, III, and so on). Let the order of the numerals indicate the best sequence.
- Identify subtopics and group them under the appropriate main topics. Indent and label these subtopics with capital letters (A, B, C, and so on). Let the order of the letters indicate the best sequence.

Organizing the Evidence

> - Identify supporting points (often reasons and examples) and group them under the appropriate subtopics. Indent and label these supporting points with arabic numbers (1, 2, 3, and so on). Let the numbers indicate the best sequence.
> - Identify specific details (secondary examples, facts, statistics, expert opinions, quotations) and group them under the appropriate supporting points. Indent and label these specific details with lower-case letters (a, b, c, and so on). Let the letters indicate the best sequence.
> - Examine your outline, looking for places where evidence is weak. Where appropriate, add new evidence.
> - Doublecheck that all main topics, subtopics, supporting points, and specific details develop some aspect of the thesis. Also confirm that all items are arranged in the most logical order.

The sample outline that starts below and continues on the next page develops the thesis "Being a parent today is much more difficult than it was a generation ago." You may remember that this is the thesis that Harriet Davids devised for the essay she planned to write in response to the assignment on page 24. Harriet's scratch list appears in Chapter 2 on pages 33–34. When you compare Harriet's scratch list and outline, you'll find some differences. On the whole, the outline contains more specifics, but it doesn't include all the material in the scratch list. For example, after reconsidering her purpose, audience, tone, point of view, and thesis, Harriet decided to omit from her outline the section on day care and the points about AIDS and rock posters.

Harriet's outline is called a **topic outline** because it uses phrases, or topics, for each entry. (See pages 293–94, 325, and 429 for other examples of topic outlines.) For a more complex paper, a **sentence outline** might be more appropriate (see pages 229 and 517–18). You could also mix phrases and sentences (see pages 356–57), as long as you were consistent about where you used each.

In Harriet's outline, note that indentations signal the relationships among the essay's points and that the same grammatical form is used to begin each entry on a particular level. For instance, since a noun phrase ("Distractions from homework") follows roman numeral *I*, noun phrases also follow subsequent roman numerals. Such consistency helps writers see if items at a particular level are comparable.

Purpose: To inform

Audience: Instructor as well as class members, most of whom are 18-20 years old

Tone: Serious and straightforward

Point of view: Third person (mother of two teenage girls)

Thesis: Being a parent today is much more difficult than it was a generation ago.

Pattern of development: Illustration

Organizational approach: Emphatic order

I. Distractions from homework
   A. At home
      1. Stereos, radios, tapes
      2. Television
   B. Outside home
      1. Malls
      2. Video arcades
      3. Fast-food restaurants
II. Sexually explicit materials
   A. In print
      1. Sex magazines
         a. Hustler
         b. Penthouse
      2. Pornographic books
   B. In movies
      1. Seduction scenes
      2. Casual sex
   C. On television
      1. Soap operas
      2. R-rated comedians
      3. R-rated movies on cable
III. Increased dangers
   A. Drugs
   B. Alcohol
   C. Violent crimes against children

If you'd like to see the first draft that resulted from Harriet's outline, turn to pages 80–81. Hints for moving from an outline to a first draft appear on pages 61–62. For additional suggestions on organizing a first draft, see the diagram on page 79.

Before starting to write your first draft, show your outline to several people (your instructor, friends, classmates). Their reactions will indicate whether your proposed organization is appropriate for your thesis, purpose, audience, tone, and point of view. Their comments can also highlight areas needing additional work. After making whatever changes are needed, you're in a good position to go ahead and write the first draft of your essay.

ACTIVITIES: ORGANIZING THE EVIDENCE

1. The following thesis statement is accompanied by a scrambled list of supporting points. Prepare a topic outline for a potential essay, being sure to distinguish between major and secondary points.

Thesis: Our schools, now in crisis, could be improved in several ways.

Certificate requirements for teachers

Schedules

Teachers

Longer school year

Merit pay for outstanding teachers

Curriculum

Better textbooks

Longer school days

More challenging course content

2. For each of the following thesis statements, there are two purposes given. Determine whether each purpose suggests an emphatic, chronological, spatial, or simple-to-complex approach. Note the way the approach varies as the purpose changes.

a. *Thesis:* Traveling in a large city can be an unexpected education.

Purpose 1: To explain, in a humorous way, the stages in learning to cope with the city's cab system

Purpose 2: To describe, in a serious manner, the vastly different sections of the city as viewed from a cab

b. *Thesis:* The student government seems determined to improve its relations with the college administration.

Purpose 1: To inform readers by describing efforts that student leaders took, month by month, to win administrative support

Purpose 2: To convince readers by explaining straightforward as well as intricate pro-administration resolutions that student leaders passed

c. *Thesis:* Supermarkets use sophisticated marketing techniques to prod consumers into buying more than they need

Purpose 1: To inform readers that positioning products in certain locations encourages impulse buying

Purpose 2: To persuade readers not to patronize those chains using especially objectionable sales strategies

3. Return to the paragraph or first draft you prepared in response to activity 4 or activity 5 in Chapter 4. Applying the principles discussed in Chapter 5, strengthen the organization of the evidence you generated. (If you rework a first draft, save the draft so you can refine it further after reading the next chapter.)

4. Each of the following brief essay outlines consists of a thesis and several points of support. Which pattern of development would you probably use to develop the overall organizational framework for each essay? Which pattern(s) would you use to develop each point of support? Why?

a. *Thesis:* Friends of the opposite sex fall into one of several categories: the pal, the confidante, or the pest.

Points of Support

- Frequently, an opposite-sex friend is simply a "pal."
- Sometimes, though, a pal turns, step by step, into a confidante.
- If a confidante begins to have romantic thoughts, he or she may become a pest, thus disrupting the friendship.

b. *Thesis:* What happens when a child gets sick in a two-income household? Numerous problems occur.

Points of Support

- Parents often encounter difficulties as they take steps to locate a babysitter or make other child-care arrangements.
- If no child-care helper can be found, a couple must decide which parent will stay at home—a decision that may create conflict between husband and wife.
- No matter what they do, parents inevitably will incur at least one of several kinds of expenses.

5. For one of the thesis statements given in activity 4, identify a possible purpose, audience, tone, and point of view. Then, use one or more patterns to generate material to develop the points of support listed. Get together with someone else to review the generated material, deleting, adding, combining, and arranging ideas in logical order. Finally, make an outline for the body of the essay. (Save your outline. After reading the next chapter, you can use it to write the essay's first draft.)

6. Look again at the thesis and scratch outline you refined and elaborated in response to activity 6 in Chapter 4. Reevaluate this material by deleting, adding, combining, and rearranging ideas as needed. Then, in preparation for writing an essay, outline your ideas. Consider whether an emphatic, chronological, spatial, or simple-to-complex approach will be most appropriate. Finally, ask at least one other person to evaluate your organizational plan. (Save your outline. After reading the next chapter, you can use it to write the essay's first draft.)

6
WRITING THE PARAGRAPHS IN THE FIRST DRAFT

AFTER prewriting, deciding on a thesis, and developing and organizing evidence, you're ready to write a first draft—a rough, provisional version of your essay. Working quickly, you should concentrate on providing paragraphs that support your thesis. Also try to include all relevant examples, facts, and opinions, sequencing this material as effectively as you can.

Because of your work in the preceding stages, the first draft may flow quite smoothly. But don't be discouraged if it doesn't. You may find that your thesis has to be reshaped, that a point no longer fits, that you need to return to a prewriting activity to generate additional material. Such stopping and starting is to be expected. Writing the first draft is a process of discovery, involving the continual clarification and refining of ideas.

HOW TO MOVE FROM OUTLINE TO FIRST DRAFT

There's no single right way to prepare a first draft. With experience, you'll undoubtedly find your own basic approach, adapting it to suit each paper's length, the time available, and the instructor's requirements. Some writers rely on their scratch lists or outlines heavily; others glance at them only occasionally. Some people write the first draft in longhand; others use a typewriter or computer. (For hints on using a word processor, see Chapter 10.)

However you choose to proceed, consider the following general suggestions when moving from an outline or scratch list to a first draft:

- Make the outline's *main topics* (I, II, III) the *topic sentences* of the essay's supporting paragraphs. (Topic sentences are discussed later in this chapter.)
- Make the outline's *subtopics* (A, B, C) the *subpoints* in each paragraph.
- Make the outline's *supporting points* (1, 2, 3) the *key examples* and *reasons* in each paragraph.
- Make the outline's *specific details* (a, b, c) the *secondary examples,* facts, statistics, expert opinion, and quotations in each paragraph.

(To see how one student, Harriet Davids, moved from outline to first draft, turn to pages 79–81.)

GENERAL SUGGESTIONS ON HOW TO PROCEED

Although outlines and lists are valuable for guiding your work, don't be so dependent on them that you shy away from new ideas that surface during your writing of the first draft. It's during this time that promising new thoughts often pop up; as they do, jot them down. Then, at the appropriate point, go back and evaluate them: Do they support your thesis? Are they appropriate for your essay's purpose, audience, tone, and point of view? If so, go ahead and include the material in your draft.

It's easy to get stuck while preparing the first draft if you try to edit as you write. Remember: A draft isn't intended to be perfect. For the time being, adopt a relaxed, noncritical attitude. Working as quickly as you can, don't stop to check spelling, correct grammar, or refine sentence structure. Save these tasks for later. One good way to help remind you that the first draft is tentative is to prepare it in longhand, using scrap paper and pencil. Writing on alternate lines also underscores your intention to revise later on, when the extra space will make it easier to add and delete material. Similarly, writing on only one side of the paper can prove helpful if, during revision, you decide to move a section to another part of the paper. (See pages 146–47 in Chapter 10 for hints on writing a draft with a word processor.)

IF YOU GET BOGGED DOWN

All writers get bogged down now and then. The best thing to do is accept that sooner or later it will happen to you. When it does, keep calm and try to write something—no matter how awkward or imprecise it may seem. Just jot a reminder to yourself in the margin ("Fix this," "Redo," or "Ugh!") to finetune the section later. Or leave a blank space to hold a spot for the right words when they finally break loose. It may also help to reread—out loud is best—what you've already written. Regaining a sense of the larger context is often enough to get you moving again. You might also try talking your way through a troublesome section. Like most people, you probably speak more easily than you write; by speaking aloud, you tap this oral fluency and put it to work in your writing.

If a section of the essay strikes you as particularly difficult, don't spend time struggling with it. Move on to an easier section, write that, and then return to the challenging part. If you're still getting nowhere, take a break. Watch television, listen to music, talk with friends. While you're relaxing, your thoughts may loosen up and untangle the knotty section. If, on the other hand, an obligation such as a class or an appointment forces you to stop writing when the draft is going well, jot down a few notes in the margin to remind yourself of your train of thought. The notes will keep you from getting stuck when you pick up the draft later.

A SUGGESTED SEQUENCE FOR WRITING THE FIRST DRAFT

Because you read essays from beginning to end, you may assume that writers work the same way, starting with the introduction and going straight through to the conclusion. Often, however, this isn't the case. In fact, since an introduction depends so heavily on everything that follows, it's usually best to write the introduction *after* the essay's body.

When preparing your first draft, you may find it helpful to follow this sequence:

1. Write the essay's supporting paragraphs.
2. Write the other paragraphs in the essay's body.
3. Write the introduction.
4. Write the conclusion.

Write the Supporting Paragraphs

Before starting to write the essay's **supporting paragraphs,** enter your thesis at the top of the page, perhaps underlining key words to keep yourself focused. Remember, though, that writing leads to new ideas; you may have to refine the thesis as the draft unfolds.

Drawn from the main sections in your outline or scratch list, each supporting paragraph should develop an aspect of your essay's thesis. Although there are no hard-and-fast rules, strong supporting paragraphs are (1) often focused by topic sentences, (2) organized around one or more patterns of development, (3) unified, (4) specific, (5) adequately supported, and (6) coherent. Aim for as many of these qualities as you can in the first draft. The material on the following pages will help keep you focused on your goal. But don't expect the draft paragraphs to be perfect; you'll have the chance to revise them later on.

Use Topic Sentences

Frequently, each supporting paragraph in an essay is focused by a **topic sentence.** This sentence usually states a main point in support of the thesis. In a formal outline, such a point customarily appears, often in abbreviated form, as a *main topic* marked with a roman numeral (I, II, III).

The transformation of an outline's main topic to a paragraph's topic sentence is often a matter of stating your attitude toward the outline topic. When changing from main outline topic to topic sentence, you may also add details that make the topic sentence more specific and concrete. Compare, for example, the outline on pages 57–58 with the first draft on pages 80–81. You'll see that the outline entry "I. Distractions from homework" turned into the topic sentence "Parents have to control all the new distractions/temptations that turn kids away from school-work" (paragraph 2). The difference between the outline topic and the topic sentence is thus twofold: The topic sentence has an *element of opinion* ("have to control"), and it is focused by *added details* (in this case, the people involved—parents and children).

The topic sentence functions as a kind of mini-thesis for the paragraph. Generally one or two sentences in length, the topic sentence usually appears at or near the beginning of the paragraph. However, it may also appear at the end, in the middle, or—with varied wording—several times within the paragraph. In still other cases, a single topic sentence may state an idea developed in more than one paragraph. When a paragraph is intended primarily to clarify or inform, you may want to place its topic sentence at the beginning; that way, readers are prepared to view everything that follows in light of that main idea. If, though, you intend a paragraph to heighten suspense or to convey a feeling of discovery, you may prefer to delay the topic sentence until the end.

Regardless of its length or location, the topic sentence states the paragraph's main idea. The other sentences in the paragraph provide support for this central point in the form of examples, facts, expert opinion, and so on. Like a thesis statement, the topic sentence *signals the paragraph's subject* and frequently *indicates the writer's attitude* toward that subject. In the topic sentences that follow, the subject of the paragraph is underlined once and the attitude toward that subject is underlined twice:

Topic Sentences

Some students select a particular field of study for the wrong reasons.

The ocean dumping of radioactive waste is a ticking time bomb.

Several contemporary rock groups show unexpected sensitivity to social issues.

Political candidates are sold like slickly packaged products.

As you work on the first draft, you may find yourself writing paragraphs without paying too much attention to topic sentences. That's fine, as long as you remember to evaluate the paragraphs later on. When revising, you can provide a topic sentence for a paragraph that needs a sharper focus, recast a topic sentence for a paragraph that ended up taking an unexpected turn, even eliminate a topic sentence altogether if a paragraph's content is sufficiently unified to imply its point.

With experience, you'll develop an instinct for writing focused paragraphs without having to pay such close attention to topic sentences. A good way to develop such an instinct is to note how the writers in this book use topic

Writing the Paragraphs in the First Draft 65

sentences to shape paragraphs and clarify meaning. (If you'd like some practice in identifying topic sentences, see pages 82–83.)

Use the Patterns of Development

As you saw on pages 52–53, an entire essay can be organized around one or more patterns of development. These patterns can also provide the organizational framework for an essay's supporting paragraphs. Assume you're writing an article for your town newspaper with the thesis "Year-round residents of an ocean community must take an active role in safeguarding the seashore environment." As the following examples indicate, your supporting paragraphs could develop this thesis through a variety of patterns, with each paragraph's topic sentence suggesting a specific pattern or combination of patterns.

Topic Sentence	Possible Pattern of Development
In a nearby ocean community, signs of environmental damage are everywhere.	*Description* of a seaside town with polluted waters, blighted trees, and diseased marine life
Typically, residents blame industry or tourists for such damage.	*Narration* of a conversation among seaside residents
Residents' careless behavior is also to blame, however.	*Illustrations* of residents' littering the beach, injuring marine life while motor boating, walking over fragile sand dunes
Even environmentally concerned residents may contribute to the problem.	*Cause-effect* explanation of the way styrofoam packaging and plastic food wrap, even when properly disposed of in a trash can, can harm scavenging seagulls
Fortunately, not all seaside towns are plagued by such environmental problems.	*Comparison-contrast* of one troubled shore community with another more ecologically sound one
It's clear that shore residents must become "environmental activists."	*Definition* of an *environmental activist*
Residents can get involved in a variety of pro-environmental activities.	*Division-classification* of activities at the neighborhood, town, and municipal levels
Moreover, getting involved is an easy matter.	*Process analysis* of the steps for getting involved at the various levels
Such activism yields significant rewards.	A final *argumentation-persuasion* pitch showing residents the benefits of responsible action

Of course, each supporting paragraph in an essay doesn't have to be organized according to a different pattern of development; several paragraphs may use the same pattern. Nor is it necessary for any one paragraph to be restricted to a single pattern; supporting paragraphs often combine patterns. For example, the topic sentence "Fortunately, not all seaside towns are plagued by such environmental problems" might be developed primarily through *comparison-contrast*, but the paragraph would need a fair amount of *description* to clarify the differences between towns. (For more on the way the patterns of development come into play throughout the writing process, see pages 30–31, 39, 45–46, 52–53, and Chapter 11.)

Make the Paragraphs Unified

Just as overall evidence must support an essay's thesis (pages 46–47), the facts, opinions, and examples in each supporting paragraph must have *direct bearing* on the paragraph's topic sentence. If the paragraph has no topic sentence, the supporting material must be *consistent* with the paragraph's *implied focus*. A paragraph is **unified** when it meets these requirements.

Consider the following sample paragraph, taken from an essay illustrating recent changes in Americans' television-viewing habits. The paragraph focuses on people's reasons for switching from network to cable television. As you'll see, though, the paragraph lacks unity because it contains points (underlined) unrelated to its main idea. Specifically, the criticism of cable's foul language contradicts the paragraph's topic sentence—"Many people consider cable TV an improvement over network television." To present a balanced view of cable versus network television, the writer should discuss these points, but *in another paragraph*.

Nonunified Support

Many people consider cable TV an improvement over network television. For one thing, viewers usually prefer the movies on cable. Unlike network films, cable movies are often only months old, they have not been edited by censors, and they are not interrupted by commercials. Growing numbers of people also feel that cable specials are superior to the ones the networks grind out. Cable viewers may enjoy such pop stars as Bruce Springsteen, Tina Turner, or Eddie Murphy in concert, whereas the networks continue to broadcast tired Bob Hope variety shows and boring awards ceremonies. <u>There is, however, one problem with cable comedians. The foul language many of them use makes it hard to watch these cable specials with children. The networks, in contrast, generally present "clean" shows that parents and children can watch together.</u> Then, too, cable TV offers viewers more flexibility since it schedules shows at various times over the month. People working night shifts or attending evening classes can see movies in the afternoon, and viewers missing the first twenty minutes of a show can always catch them later. It's not surprising that cable viewership is growing while network ratings have taken a plunge.

Make the Paragraphs Specific

If your supporting paragraphs are vague, readers will lose interest, remain unconvinced of your thesis, even have trouble deciphering your meaning. In contrast, paragraphs filled with **concrete, specific details** engage readers, lend force to ideas, and clarify meaning.

Following are two versions of a paragraph from an essay about trends in the business community. Although both paragraphs focus on one such trend—flexible working hours—note how the first version's vague generalities leave meaning unclear. *What,* for example, is meant by "flex-time scheduling"? *Which* companies have tried it? *Where,* specifically, are these companies located? *How,* exactly, does flex-time increase productivity, lessen conflict, and reduce accidents? The second paragraph answers these questions with specifics and, as a result, is more informative and interesting.

Nonspecific Support

More and more companies have begun to realize that flex-time scheduling offers advantages. Several companies outside Boston have tried flex-time scheduling and are pleased with the way the system reduces the difficulties their employees face getting to work. Studies show that flex-time scheduling also increases productivity, reduces on-the-job conflict, and minimizes work-related accidents.

Specific Support

More and more companies have begun to realize that flex-time scheduling offers advantages over a rigid 9-to-5 routine. Along suburban Boston's Route 128, such companies as Compugraphics and Consolidated Paper now permit employees to come to work any time between 6 a.m. and 11 a.m. The corporations report that rush-hour jams and accidents have been dramatically reduced, so that employees arrive at work free from traffic-induced stress. Studies sponsored by the journal Business Quarterly show that this relaxed state of mind benefits corporations. Stress-free employees increase productivity by working harder and taking fewer days off. Also, the more relaxed the employee, the more quickly conflicts with co-workers and customers are resolved. Perhaps most importantly, employees arriving at work relatively free of tension are less susceptible to on-the-job accidents, such as injuries resulting from a fall or improper handling of dangerous equipment. Flex-time improves employee well-being, and as well-being rises, so do company profits.

Five Strategies for Making Paragraphs Specific. How can you make the evidence in your paragraphs specific? The following techniques should help.

1. Provide examples that answer *who, which, what,* and similar questions. In contrast to the vague generalities in the first paragraph on flex-time scheduling, the second paragraph provides examples that answer a series of basic questions. For instance, the general comment "Several companies outside of Boston" (*which* companies?) is replaced by "Compugraphics and Consolidated Paper." The vague phrase "difficulties their employees face getting to work" (*what* difficulties?) is dramatized with the examples "rush-hour jams and accidents." Similarly, "work-related accidents" (*which* accidents?) is illustrated with "injuries resulting from a fall or improper handling of dangerous equipment."

2. Replace general nouns and adjectives with precise ones. In the following sentences, note how much sharper images become when exact nouns and adjectives replace imprecise ones:

General	More Specific	Most Specific
A *man* struggled to lift the *box* out of the *old* car.	A *young man, out of shape,* struggled to lift the *heavy crate* out of the *beat-up sports car.*	*Joe, only twenty years old but more than fifty pounds overweight,* struggled to lift the *heavy wooden crate* out of the *rusty* and *dented Corvette.*

3. Replace abstract words with concrete ones. Notice the way the example on the right, firmly grounded in the physical, clarifies the intangible concepts in the example on the left:

Abstract	Concrete
The fall day had great *beauty,* despite its *dreariness.*	*Red, yellow,* and *orange* leaves *gleamed wetly* through the *gray mist.*

(For more on making abstract language concrete, see pages 120–21 in Chapter 8.)

4. Use words that appeal to the five senses (sight, touch, taste, smell, sound). The sentence on the left lacks impact because it fails to convey any sensory impressions; the sentence on the right, though, gains power through the use of sensory details:

Without Sensory Images	With Sensory Images
The computer room is eerie.	In the computer room, keys *click* and printers *grate* while row after row of students stare into screens that *glow without shedding any light.* (sound and sight)

(For more on sensory language, see pages 120–21 in Chapter 8 and 159 in Chapter 12.)

5. Use vigorous verbs. Linking verbs (such as *seem* and *appear*) and *to be* verbs (such as *is* and *were*) paint no pictures. Strong verbs, however, create sharp visual images. Compare the following examples:

Weak Verbs	Strong Verbs
The spectators *seemed* pleased and *were* enthusiastic when the wheelchair marathoners *went* by.	The spectators *cheered* and *whistled* when the wheelchair marathoners *whizzed* by.

(For more on strong verbs, see pages 121–23 in Chapter 8.)

Writing the Paragraphs in the First Draft

Provide Adequate Support

Each supporting paragraph should also have **adequate support** so that your readers can see clearly the validity of the topic sentence. At times, a single extended example is sufficient; generally, however, an assortment of examples, facts, personal observations, and so forth is more effective.

Following are two versions of a paragraph from a paper showing how difficult it is to get personal, attentive service nowadays at gas stations, supermarkets, and department stores. Both paragraphs focus on the problem at gas stations, but one paragraph is much more effective. As you'll see, the first paragraph starts with good specific support, yet fails to provide enough of it. The second paragraph offers additional examples, descriptive details, and dialog—all of which make the writing stronger and more convincing.

Inadequate Support

Gas stations are a good example of this impersonal attitude. At many stations, attendants have even stopped pumping gas. Motorists pull up to a combination convenience store and gas island where an attendant is enclosed in a glass booth with a tray for taking money. The driver must get out of the car, pump the gas, and walk over to the booth to pay. That's a real inconvenience, especially when compared with the way service stations used to be run.

Adequate Support

Gas stations are a good example of this impersonal attitude. At many stations, attendants have even stopped pumping gas. Motorists pull up to a combination convenience store and gas island where an attendant is enclosed in a glass booth with a tray for taking money. The driver must get out of the car, pump the gas, and walk over to the booth to pay. Even at stations that still have "pump jockeys," employees seldom ask, "Check your oil?" or wash windshields, although they may grudgingly point out the location of the bucket and squeegee. And customers with a balky engine or a nonfunctioning heater are usually out of luck. Why? Many gas stations have eliminated on-duty mechanics. The skillful mechanic who could replace a belt or fix a tire in a few minutes has been replaced by a teenager in a jumpsuit who doesn't know a carburetor from a charge card and couldn't care less.

Make the Paragraphs Coherent

A jigsaw puzzle with all the pieces heaped on a table remains a baffling jumble unless it's clear how the pieces fit together. Similarly, paragraphs can be unified, specific, and adequately supported, yet—if internally disjointed or inadequately connected to each other—leave readers feeling confused. Readers need to be able to follow with ease the progression of thought within and between paragraphs. One idea must flow smoothly and logically into the next; that is, your writing must be **coherent**.

The following paragraph lacks coherence for two main reasons. First, it sequences ideas improperly. (The idea about toll attendants' being cut off from co-workers is introduced, dropped, then picked up again. References to motorists are similarly scattered throughout the paragraph.) Second, it doesn't indicate how individual ideas are related. (What, for example, is the connection between drivers who pass by without saying anything and attendants who have to work at night?)

Incoherent Support

Collecting tolls on the turnpike must be one of the loneliest jobs in the world. Each toll attendant sits in his or her booth, cut off from other attendants. Many drivers pass by each booth. None stays long enough for a brief "hello." Most don't acknowledge the attendant at all. Many toll attendants work at night, pushing them "out of synch" with the rest of the world. And sometimes the attendants have to deal with rude drivers who treat them like non-people, swearing at them for the long lines at the tollgate. Attendants also dislike how cut off they feel from their co-workers. Except for infrequent breaks, they have little chance to chat with each other and swap horror stories--small pleasures that would make their otherwise routine jobs bearable.

Coherent Support

Collecting tolls on the turnpike must be one of the loneliest jobs in the world. First of all, although many drivers pass by the attendants, none stays long enough for more than a brief "hello." Most drivers, in fact, don't acknowledge the toll collectors at all, with the exception of those rude drivers who treat the attendants like non-people, swearing at them for the long lines at the tollgate. Then, too, many toll attendants work at night, pushing them further "out of synch" with the rest of the world. Worst of all, attendants say, is how isolated they feel from their co-workers. Each attendant sits in his or her booth, cut off from other attendants. Except for infrequent breaks, they have little chance to chat with each other and swap horror stories--small pleasures that would make their otherwise routine jobs bearable.

To avoid the kinds of problems found in the incoherent paragraph, use—as the revised version does—two key strategies: (1) Select a clearly *chronological, spatial,* or *emphatic order* ("*Worst of all,* the attendants say . . .") and (2) use *signal devices* ("*First of all,* although many drivers pass by . . .") to show how ideas are connected. The following sections discuss these two strategies.

Chronological, Spatial, and Emphatic Order. As you learned in Chapter 5, an entire essay can be organized using chronological, spatial, or emphatic order (pages 53–54). These strategies can also be used to make a paragraph coherent.

Imagine you plan to write an essay showing the difficulties many immigrants face when they first come to this country. Let's consider how you might structure the essay's supporting paragraphs, particularly the way each paragraph's organizational approach can help you arrange ideas in a logical, easy-to-follow sequence.

One paragraph, focused by the topic sentence "The everyday life of a typical immigrant family is arduous," might be developed through a **chronological** account of the family's daily routine: purchasing, before dawn, fruits and vegetables for their produce stand; setting up the stand early in the morning; working there for ten hours; attending English class at night. Another paragraph might develop its topic sentence—"Many immigrant families get along without the technology that others take for granted"—through **spatial** order, taking readers on a brief tour of an immigrant family's rented home: the kitchen lacks a dishwasher or microwave; the living room has no stereo or VCR, only a small black-and-white TV; the basement has just a washtub and clothesline instead of a washer and dryer. Finally, a third paragraph with the topic sentence "A number of worries typically beset immigrant families" might use an **emphatic** sequence, moving from less significant concerns (having to wear old, unfashionable clothes) to more critical issues (having to deal with isolation and discrimination).

Signal Devices. Once you determine a logical sequence for your points, you need to make sure that readers can follow the progression of those points within and between paragraphs. **Signal devices** provide readers with cues, reminding them where they have been and indicating where they are going.

Try to include some signals—however awkward or temporary—in your first draft. If you find you *can't*, that's probably a warning that your ideas may not be arranged logically—in which case, it's better to find that out now rather than later on.

Useful signal devices include *transitions, bridging sentences, repeated words, synonyms,* and *pronouns.* Keep in mind, though, that a light touch should be your goal with such signals. Too many call attention to themselves, making the essay mechanical and plodding.

1. Transitions. Words and phrases that ease readers from one idea to another are called **transitions.** Among such signals are the following:

Time	Space	Addition	Examples
first	above	moreover	for instance
next	below	also	for example
during	next to	furthermore	to illustrate
finally	behind	in addition	specifically

Contrast	Comparison	Summary
but	similarly	therefore
however	also	thus
in contrast	likewise	in short
on the one/ other hand	too	in conclusion

Note how the underlined transitions in the following paragraph provide clear cues to readers showing how ideas fit together:

> Although the effect of air pollution on the human body is distressing, its effect on global ecology is even more troubling. In the Bavarian, French, and Italian Alps, <u>for example</u>, once magnificent forests are slowly being destroyed by air pollution. Trees dying from pollution lose their leaves or needles, allowing sunlight to reach the forest floor. <u>During</u> this process, grass prospers in the increased light and pushes out the native plants and moss that help hold rainwater. The soil <u>thus</u> loses absorbency and becomes hard, causing rain and snow to slide over the ground instead of sinking into it. This, <u>in turn</u>, leads to erosion of the soil. <u>After</u> a heavy rain, the eroded land <u>finally</u> falls away in giant rockslides and avalanches, destroying entire villages and causing life-threatening floods.

2. Bridging sentences. Although **bridging sentences** may be used within a paragraph, they are more often used to move readers from one paragraph to the next. Look again at the first sentence in the preceding paragraph on pollution. Note that the sentence consists of two parts: The first part reminds readers that the previous discussion focused on techniques for generating evidence; the second part tells readers that the focus will now be the organization of such evidence.

3. Repeated words, synonyms, and pronouns. The **repetition** of important words maintains continuity, reassures readers that they are on the right track, and highlights key ideas. **Synonyms**—words similar in meaning to key words or phrases—also provide coherence, while making it possible to avoid unimaginative and tedious repetitions. Finally, **pronouns** (*he, she, it, they, this, that*) enhance coherence by causing readers to think back to the original word (antecedent) the pronoun replaces. When using pronouns, however, be sure there is no ambiguity about antecedents.

The following paragraph uses repeated words (underlined once), synonyms (underlined twice), and pronouns (underlined three times) to integrate ideas:

> <u>Studies</u> have shown that color is also an important part of the way people experience food. In one <u>study</u>, individuals fed a rich red tomato sauce didn't notice it had no flavor until they were nearly finished eating. Similarly,

in another experiment, people were offered strangely colored foods: gray pork chops, lavender mashed potatoes, dark blue peas, dessert topped with yellow whipped cream. Not one of the subjects would eat the strange-looking food, even though it smelled and tasted normal.

Write Other Paragraphs in the Essay's Body

Paragraphs supporting the thesis are not necessarily the only kind in the body of an essay. You may also include paragraphs that give background information or provide transitions.

Background Paragraphs

Usually found near the essay's beginning, **background paragraphs** provide information that doesn't directly support the thesis but that helps the reader understand or accept the discussion that follows. Such paragraphs may consist of a definition, brief historical overview, or short description. For example, in the student essay "Salt Marsh" on pages 163–65, the paragraph following the introduction defines a salt marsh and summarizes some of its features. This background information serves as a lead-in to the detailed description that makes up the rest of the essay.

Because you don't want to distract readers from your essay's main point, background paragraphs should be kept as brief as possible. In a paper outlining a program that you believe your college should adopt to beautify its grounds, you would probably need a background paragraph describing typical campus eyesores. Too lengthy a description, though, would detract from the presentation of your step-by-step program.

Transitional Paragraphs

Another kind of paragraph, generally one to three sentences long, may appear between supporting paragraphs to help readers keep track of your discussion. Like the bridging sentences discussed earlier in the chapter, **transitional paragraphs** usually sum up what has been discussed so far and then indicate the direction the essay will take next.

Although too many transitional paragraphs make writing stiff and mechanical, they can be effective when used sparingly, especially in essays with sharp turns in direction. For example, in a paper showing how to purchase a car, you might start by explaining the research a potential buyer should do beforehand: Consult publications like *Consumer Reports*; check performance records published by the automotive industry; call several dealerships for price information. Then, as a transition to the next section—how to negotiate at the dealership—you might provide the following paragraph:

Once you have armed yourself with the necessary information, you are ready to meet with a salesperson at the showroom. Your experience at the dealership should not be intimidating as long as you follow the guidelines below.

Write the Introduction

Many writers don't prepare an **introduction** until they have started to revise; others feel more comfortable if their first draft includes in basic form all parts of the final essay. If that's how you feel, you'll probably write the introduction as you complete your first draft. No matter when you prepare it, keep in mind how crucial the introduction is to your essay's success. First impressions count heavily. More specifically, the introduction serves three distinct functions: It arouses readers' interest, introduces your subject, and presents your thesis.

Introductions are difficult to write—so difficult, in fact, that you may be tempted to take the easy way out and use a stale beginning like "According to Webster...." Equally yawn-inducing are sweeping generalizations that sound grand but say little: "Throughout human history, people have waged war" or "Affection is important in all our lives." Don't, however, go too far in the other direction and come up with a gimmicky opening: "I don't know about you, but in my life, love is the next best thing to being there. Where? Heaven, that's where!" Contrived and coy, such introductions are bound to be inconsistent with your essay's purpose, tone, and point of view. Remember, the introduction's style and content should flow into the rest of the essay.

The length of your introduction will vary according to your paper's scope and purpose. Most essays you write, however, will be served best by a one- or two-paragraph beginning. To write an effective introduction, use any of the following methods, singly or in combination. The thesis statement in each sample introduction is underlined.

Broad Statement Narrowing to a Limited Subject

For generations, morality has been molded primarily by parents, religion, and schools. Children traditionally acquired their ideas about what is right and wrong, which goals are important in life, and how others should be treated from these three sources. But now there is another powerful force influencing youngsters. <u>Television is implanting in children negative values about sex, work, and family life.</u>

Brief Anecdote

At a local high school recently, students in a psychology course were given a hint of what it is like to be the parents of a newborn. Each "parent" had to carry a raw egg around at all times to symbolize the responsibilities of parenthood. The egg could not be left alone; it limited the "parents' " activities; it placed a full-time emotional burden on "Mom" and "Dad." This class exercise illustrates a common problem facing the majority of new mothers and fathers. <u>Most people receive little preparation for the job of being parents.</u>

Writing the Paragraphs in the First Draft

Idea That Is the Opposite of the One Actually Developed

We hear a great deal about divorce's disastrous impact on children. We are deluged with advice on ways to make divorce as painless as possible for youngsters; we listen to heartbreaking stories about the confused, grieving children of divorced parents. Little attention has been paid, however, to a different kind of effect that divorce may have on children. <u>Children from divorced families may become skilled manipulators, playing off one parent against the other, worsening an already painful situation.</u>

Series of Short Questions

What happens if a child is caught vandalizing school property? What happens if a child goes for a joyride in a stolen car and accidentally hits a pedestrian? Should parents be liable for their children's mistakes? Should parents have to pay what might be hundreds of thousands of dollars in damages? Adults have begun to think seriously about such questions because the laws concerning the limits of parental responsibility are changing rapidly. <u>With unfortunate frequency, courts have begun to hold parents legally and financially responsible for their children's misbehavior.</u>

Quotation

Educator Neil Postman believes that television has blurred the line between childhood and adulthood. According to Postman, "All the secrets that a print culture kept from children . . . are revealed all at once by media that do not, and cannot, exclude any audience." <u>This media barrage of information, once intended only for adults, has changed childhood for the worse.</u>

Brief Background on the Topic

For a long time, adults believed that "children should be seen, not heard." On special occasions, youngsters were dressed up and told to sit quietly while adults socialized. Even when they were alone with their parents, children were not supposed to bother adults with their concerns. However, beginning with psychologist Arnold Gesell in the 1940s, childraising experts began to question the wisdom of an approach that blocked communication. In 1965, Haim Ginott's ground-breaking book *Between Parent and Child* stressed the importance of conversing with children. More recently, two of Ginott's disciples, Adele Sager and Elaine Mazlich, wrote a book on this subject: *How to Talk So Children Will Listen and Listen So Children Will Talk.* <u>These</u>

days, experts agree, successful parents are those who encourage their children to share their thoughts and concerns.

Refutation of a Common Belief

Adolescents care only about material things; their lives revolve around brand-name sneakers, designer jeans, the latest fad in stereo equipment. They resist education, don't read, barely know who is president, mainline rock 'n' roll, experiment with drugs, and exist on a steady diet of Ring-Dings, nachos, and beer. This is what many adults, including parents, seem to believe about the young. The reality is, however, that young people today show more maturity and common sense than most adults give them credit for.

Dramatic Fact or Statistic

Seventy percent of the respondents in a poll conducted by columnist Ann Landers stated that, if they could live their lives over, they would choose not to have children. This startling statistic makes one wonder what these people believed parenthood would be like. Most parents, it seems, have unrealistic expectations about their children. Parents want their children to accept their values, follow their paths, and succeed where they failed.

Introductory paragraphs sometimes end with a *plan of development:* a brief preview of the essay's major points in the order in which those points will be discussed. The plan of development may be part of the thesis (as in the first sample introduction) or it may immediately follow the thesis (as in the last sample introduction). Because the plan of development outlines the essay's organizational structure, it helps prepare the reader for the essay's progression of ideas. In a brief essay, readers can often keep track of the ideas without this extra help. In a longer paper, though, a plan of development can be an effective unifying device since it highlights the main ideas the essay will develop.

Write the Conclusion

You may have come across essays that ended with jarring abruptness because they had no conclusions at all. Other papers may have had conclusions, but they sputtered to a weak close, a sure sign that the writers had run out of steam and wanted to finish as quickly as possible. Just as satisfying closes are an important part of everyday life (we feel cheated if dinner doesn't end with dessert or if a friend leaves without saying goodbye), a strong **conclusion** is an important part of an effective essay.

However important conclusions may be, they're often difficult to write. When it comes time to write one, you may feel you've said all there is to say. To prevent such an impasse, you can try saving a compelling statistic, quotation, or detail for the end. Just make sure that this interesting item fits in the conclusion and that the essay's body contains sufficient support without it.

Occasionally, an essay doesn't need a separate conclusion. This is often the case with narration or description. For instance, in a narrative showing how a crisis can strengthen a faltering friendship, your point will probably be made with sufficient force without a final "this is what the narrative is all about" paragraph.

Usually, though, a conclusion is necessary. Generally one or two paragraphs in length, the conclusion should give the reader a feeling of completeness and finality. One way to achieve this sense of "rounding off" is to return to an image, idea, or anecdote from the introduction.

Because people tend to remember most clearly the points they read last, the conclusion is also a good place to remind readers of your thesis, phrasing this central idea somewhat differently than you did earlier in the essay. You may also use the conclusion to make a final point about your subject. This way, you leave your readers with something to mull over. Be careful, though, not to open an entirely new line of thought at the essay's close. If you do, readers may feel puzzled and frustrated, wishing you had provided evidence for your final point. And, of course, always be sure that concluding material fits your thesis and is consistent with your purpose, tone, and point of view.

In your conclusion, it's best to steer away from stock phrases like "In sum," "In conclusion," and "This paper has shown that. . . ." Also avoid lengthy conclusions. As in everyday life, prolonged farewells are tedious.

Following are examples of some of the techniques you can use to write effective conclusions. These strategies may be used singly or in combination. The first strategy, the *summary conclusion,* can be especially helpful in long, complex essays since readers may appreciate a review of your points. Tacked onto a short essay, though, a summary conclusion often seems boring and mechanical.

Summary

Contrary to what many adults think, most adolescents are not only aware of the important issues of the times but also deeply concerned about them. They are sensitive to the plight of the homeless, the destruction of the environment, and the pitfalls of rampant materialism. Indeed, today's young people are not less mature and sensible than their parents were. If anything, they are more so.

Prediction

The growing tendency on the part of the judicial system to hold parents responsible for the actions of their delinquent children can have a disturbing impact on all of us. Parents will feel bitter toward their own children and cynical about a system that holds them accountable for the actions of minors. Children, continuing to escape the consequences of their actions, will become even more lawless and destructive. Society cannot afford two such possibilities.

Quotation

The comic W. C. Fields is reputed to have said, "Anyone who hates children and dogs can't be all bad." Most people do not share Fields's cynicism. Viewing childhood as a time of purity, they are alarmed at the way television exposes children to the seamy side of life, stripping youngsters of their innocence and giving them a glib sophistication that is a poor substitute for wisdom.

Statistic

Granted, divorce may, in some cases, be the best thing for families torn apart by parents battling one another. However, in longitudinal studies of children from divorced families, psychologist Judith Wallerstein found that only 10 percent of the youngsters felt relief at their parents' divorce; the remaining 90 percent felt devastated. Such statistics surely call into question parents' claims that they are divorcing for their children's sake.

Recommendation or Call for Action

It is a mistake to leave parenting to instinct. Instead, we should make parenting skills a required course in schools. In addition, a nationwide hotline should be established to help parents deal with crises. Such training and continuing support would help adults deal more effectively with many of the problems they face as parents.

Write the Title

Some writers say that they often begin a piece with only a title in mind. But for most, writing the **title** is the finishing touch. Although creating a title is usually one of the last steps in writing an essay, it shouldn't be done haphazardly. It may take time to write an effective title—one that hints at the essay's thesis and snares the reader's interest.

Good titles may make use of the following techniques: *repetition of sounds* ("The Plot Against People"), *humor* ("Neat People vs. Sloppy People"), and *questions* ("Am I Blue?"). More often, though, titles are straightforward phrases derived from the essay's subject or thesis: "Shooting an Elephant" and "Our Drug Problem," for example.

PULLING IT ALL TOGETHER

Now that you know how to prepare a first draft, you might find it helpful to examine the illustration on the next page to see how the different parts of a draft can fit together. Keep in mind that not every essay you write will take this shape. As your purpose, audience, tone, and point of view change, so will your essay's

Introductory Paragraph(s)	Opening comments Thesis statement Plan of development (optional)

	Topic sentence 1 Specific details
Supporting Paragraphs	Topic sentence 2 Specific details
	Topic sentence 3 Specific details

Concluding Paragraph(s)	Closing comments

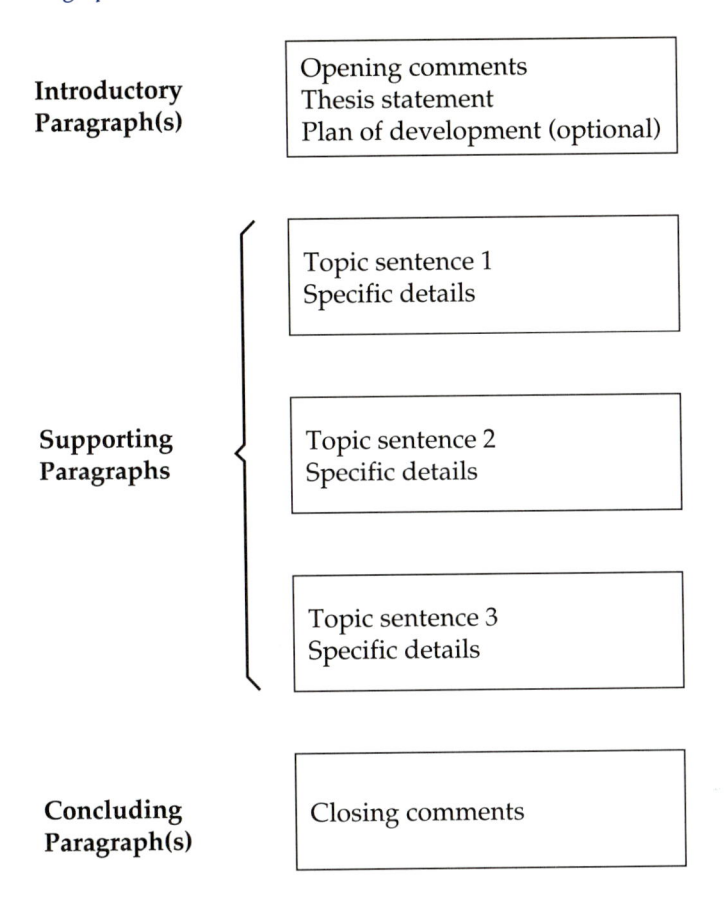

structure. An introduction or conclusion, for instance, may be developed in more than one paragraph; the thesis statement may be implied or delayed until the essay's middle or end; not all paragraphs may have topic sentences; and several supporting paragraphs may be needed to develop a single topic sentence. Even so, the basic format presented here offers a strategy for organizing a variety of writing assignments—from term papers to lab reports. Once you feel comfortable with the structure, you have a foundation on which to base your variations. (This book's student and professional essays illustrate some possibilities.) Even when using a specific format, you always have room to give your spirit and imagination free play. The language you use, the details you select, the perspective you offer are uniquely yours. They are what make your essay different from anyone else's.

SAMPLE FIRST DRAFT

Here is the first draft of Harriet Davids's essay. You saw Harriet's prewriting scratch list on pages 32–33, her thesis on page 38, and so on. Harriet wrote the draft in one sitting. Working at a computer, she started by typing her thesis at the top of the first page. Then, following the guidelines on pages 61–62, she moved the material in her outline (pages 57–58) to her draft. (See page 64 for an explanation of the differences between her outline and draft.) Harriet worked rapidly; she started with the first body paragraph and wrote straight through to the last supporting paragraph.

By moving quickly, Harriet got down her essay's basic text rather easily. Once she felt she had captured in rough form what she wanted to say, she reread her draft to get a sense of how she might open and close the essay. Then she drafted her introduction and conclusion; both appear here, together with the body of the essay. (The commentary following the draft will give you an even clearer sense of how Harriet proceeded.)

Challenges for Today's Parents

by Harriet Davids

Thesis: Being a parent today is much more difficult than it was a generation ago.

Add specifics

Raising children used to be much simpler in the 50s and 60s. I remember TV images from that era showing that parenting involved simply teaching kids to clean their rooms, do their homework, and _____. But being a parent today is much more difficult because nowadays parents have to shield/protect kids from lots of things, like distractions from schoolwork, from sexual material, from dangerous situations.

Parents have to control all the new distractions/temptations that turn kids away from schoolwork. These days many kids have stereos and televisions in their rooms. Certainly, my girls can't resist the urge to listen to MTV, especially if it's time to do homework. Unfortunately, though, kids aren't assigned much homework and what is assigned too often is busywork. And there are even more distractions outside the home. Teens no longer hang out/congregate on the corner where Dad and Mom can yell to them to come home and do homework. Instead they hang out at the mall, in video arcades, and at fast-food restaurants. Obviously, parents and school can't compete with all this.

Weak transition

(Also,) parents have to help kids develop responsible sexual values even though sex is everywhere. Kids see sex magazines and dirty paperbacks in the corner store where they used to get candy and comic books. And instead of the artsy nude shots of the past, kids see ronchey (sp?), explicit shots in <u>Playboy</u> and <u>Hustler</u>. And movies have sexy stuff in them today. Teachers seduce students and people treat sex casually/as a sport. Not exactly traditional values. Even worse is what's on TV. Kids see soap-opera characters in bed and cable shows full of nudity by just flipping the dial. (FIX) The situation has gotten so out of hand that maybe the government should establish guidelines on what's permissible.

Worst of all are the life-threatening dangers that parents must help children fend off over the years. With older kids, drugs fall into place as a main concern (Awk). Peer pressure to try drugs is bigger (wrong word) to kids than their parents' warnings. Other kinds of warnings are common when children are small. Then parents fear violence since news shows constantly report stories of little children being abused (add specifics). And when kids aren't much older, they have to resist the pressure to drink. (Alcohol has always attracted kids, but nowadays they are drinking more and this can be deadly, especially when drinking is combined with driving.) *Redo*

Most adults love their children and want to be good parents. But it's difficult because the world seems stacked against young people. Even Holden Caufield (sp?) had trouble dealing with society's confusing pressures. Parents must give their children some freedom but not so much that the kids lose sight of what's important.

Commentary

As you can see, Harriet's draft is rough. Because she knew she would revise later on (pages 97 and 128), she "zapped out" the draft in an informal, colloquial style. For example, she occasionally expressed her thoughts in fragments ("Not exactly traditional values"), relied heavily on "and" as a transition, and used slangy expressions such as "kids," "dirty paperbacks," and "lots of things." Similarly, rather than finetuning, Harriet simply made marginal or parenthetical notes to herself: "redo" or "fix" to signal awkward sentences; "add specifics" to mark overly general statements; "wrong word" after an imprecise word; "sp" to remind herself to check spelling in the dictionary; "weak trans." to indicate where a stronger signaling device was needed. Note, too, that she used slashes between alternative word choices and left a blank space when wording just wouldn't come. (Harriet's final draft appears on pages 137–38.)

Writing a first draft may seem like quite a challenge, but the tips offered in this chapter should help you proceed with confidence. Indeed, as you work on the draft, you may be surprised how much you enjoy writing. After all, this is your chance to get down on paper something you want to say.

ACTIVITIES: WRITING THE PARAGRAPHS IN THE FIRST DRAFT

1. For each paragraph that follows, determine whether the topic sentence is stated or implied. If the topic sentence is explicit, indicate its location in the paragraph (beginning, end, middle, or both beginning and end). If the topic sentence is implied, state it in your own words.

   a. In 1902, a well-known mathematician wrote an article "proving" that no airplane could ever fly. Just a year later, the Wright brothers made their first flight. In the 1950s, a famed British astronomer said in an interview that the idea of space travel was "utter bilge." Similarly, noted scholars in this country and abroad claimed that automobiles would never replace the trolley car and that the electric light was an impractical gimmick. Clearly, being an expert doesn't guarantee a clear vision of the future.

   b. Motorists in Caracas, Venezuela, must follow an odd/even license-number system for driving their cars on any given day. Cars with license plates ending in even numbers can drive downtown only on even-numbered days. Similarly, in Los Angeles several summers ago, an experimental program required businesses with more than one hundred employees to form "Don't drive to work" programs. Such programs established ride-sharing schedules and offered employees incentives for using mass transportation. Even more extreme is Singapore's method for limiting downtown traffic--most private vehicles are completely banned from central sections of the city.

   c. A small town in Massachusetts that badly needed extra space for grade school classes found it in an unlikely spot. Most of the town's available buildings were too far from the main school or too small. One building, however, was nearby and spacious; it even offered excellent lunchroom and recreation facilities. Despite some objections, the building

Writing the Paragraphs in the First Draft

was chosen--a former saloon, complete with bar, bar stools, cocktail lounge, and pool hall.

d. The physical complaints of neurotics--people who are exceptionally anxious, pessimistic, hostile, or tense--were once largely ignored by physicians. Many doctors believed that neurotics' frequent health complaints simply reflected their emotional distress. New research, though, shows that neurotics are indeed likely to have physical problems. Specifically, researchers have found that neurotics stand a greater chance of suffering from arthritis, asthma, ulcers, headaches, and heart disease. In addition, there is growing evidence that people who were chronically anxious or depressed in their teens and twenties are more likely to become ill, even die, in their forties.

e. Many American companies have learned the hard way that they need to know the language of their foreign customers. When Chevrolet began selling its Nova cars in Latin America, hardly anyone would buy them. The company finally realized that Spanish speakers read the car's name as the Spanish phrase "no va," meaning "doesn't go." When Pepsi-Cola ran its "Pepsi gives you life" ads in China, consumers either laughed or were offended. The company hadn't translated its slogan quite right. In Chinese, the slogan came out "Pepsi brings your ancestors back from the dead."

2. Using the strategies described on pages 67–68, strengthen the following vague paragraphs. Elaborate each one with striking specifics that clarify meaning and add interest. As you provide specifics, you may need to break each paragraph into several.

a. Other students can make studying in the college library difficult. For one thing, they take up so much space that they leave little room for anyone else. By being inconsiderate in other ways, they make it hard to concentrate on the task at hand. Worst of all, they do things that make it almost impossible to find needed books and magazines.

b. Families move to the suburbs for a variety of reasons. Sociologists refer to these causes as "push" and "pull" factors. Some people are pushed to the suburbs because of the difficulties associated with urban life. At the same time, they are pulled toward suburbia because they see a better life for themselves and their children.

c. Some people have dangerous driving habits. They act as though there's no one else on the road. They also seem unsure of where they're going. Changing their minds from second to second, they leave it up to others to figure out what they're going to do. Finally, too many people drive at speeds that are either too slow or too fast, creating dangerous situations for both drivers and pedestrians.

d. Things people used to think were safe are now considered dangerous. This goes for certain foods that are now considered unhealthy. Similarly, some habits people thought were harmless have been found to be risky. Even things in the home, in the workplace, and in the air have been found to cause harm. So much has been discovered in recent years about what is harmful that it makes you wonder: What additional dangers lurk in the environment?

e. Society encourages young people to drink. For one thing, youngsters learn early that alcohol plays a prominent role in family and business celebrations. Children also see that liquor is an important part of adults' celebration of national holidays. But the place where youngsters see alcohol depicted most enticingly is on TV. Prime-time shows and beer commercials imply that alcohol is an essential part of a good life.

3. Using the designations indicated in parentheses, identify the flaw(s) in the development of each of the following paragraphs. The paragraphs may lack one or more of the following: unity (U), specific and sufficient support (S), coherence (C). The paragraphs may also needlessly repeat a point (R). Revise the paragraphs, deleting, combining, and rearranging material. Also, add supporting evidence and signal devices where needed.

a. Studies reveal that individuals' first names can influence other people's perceptions. Some names reflect favorably on individuals. For example, a survey conducted by Opinion Masters, Inc. showed that male business executives thought the names Dorothy and Katherine conveyed competence and professionalism. And participants in a British study reported that names like Richard and Charles commanded respect and sounded "classy." Of course, participants' observations also reflect the fairly rigid stratification of British society. Other names, however, can have a negative impact. In one study, for instance, teachers gave lower grades to essays supposedly written by boys named Hubert and Elmer than to the very same essays when credited to boys with more popular names. Another study found that girls with unpopular names (like Ger-

Writing the Paragraphs in the First Draft 85

trude or <u>Gladys</u>) did worse on tests than girls with more appealing names. Such findings underscore the arbitrary nature of the grading process.

b.   This "me first" attitude is also behind the cheating that seems prevalent nowadays. School is perhaps the first place where widespread cheating occurs, with students devising shrewd strategies to do well--often at the expense of others. And since schools are reluctant to teach morality, children grow up with distorted values. The same exaggerated self-interest often causes people, once they reach adulthood, to cheat their companies and co-workers. It's no wonder American business is in such trouble.

c.   Despite widespread belief to the contrary, brain size within a species has little to do with how intelligent a particular individual is. A human brain can range from 900 cubic centimeters to as much as 2,500 cubic centimeters, but a large brain does not indicate an equally large degree of intelligence. If humans could see the size of other people's brains, they would probably judge each other accordingly, even though brain size has no real significance.

d.   For the 50 percent of adult Americans with high cholesterol, heart disease is a constant threat. Americans can reduce their cholesterol significantly by taking a number of easy steps. Since only foods derived from animals contain cholesterol, eating a strict vegetarian diet is the best way to beat the cholesterol problem. Also, losing weight is known to reduce cholesterol levels--even in those who were as little as ten pounds overweight. Physicians warn, though, that quick weight loss almost always leads to an equally rapid regaining of the lost pounds. For those unwilling to try a vegetarian diet, poultry, fish, and low-fat dairy products can substitute for such high-cholesterol foods as red meat, eggs, cream, and butter. Adding oat bran to the diet has been shown to lower cholesterol. The bran absorbs excess cholesterol in the blood and removes it from the body through waste matter.

4. Strengthen the coherence of the following paragraphs by providing a clear organizational structure and by adding appropriate signal devices. To improve the flow of ideas, you may also need to combine and resequence sentences.

   I was a camp counselor this past summer. I learned that leading young children is different from leading people your own age. I was president of my high school Ecology Club. I ran it democratically. We wanted to bring a speaker to the school. We decided to do a fund-raiser. I solicited ideas from everybody. We had a bull session to figure out which was best. It became obvious which was the most profitable and workable fund-raiser. Everybody got behind the effort. The discussion showed that the idea of a raffle with prizes donated by local merchants was the most profitable.

I learned that little kids operate differently. I had to be more of a boss rather than a democratic leader. I took suggestions from the group on the main activity of the day. Everyone voted for the best suggestion. Some kids got especially upset. There was a problem with kids whose ideas were voted down. I learned to make the suggestions myself. The children could vote on my suggestions. No one was overly attached to any of the suggestions. They felt that the outcome of the voting was fair. Basically, I got to be in charge.

5. For an essay with the thesis shown here, indicate the implied pattern(s) of development for each topic sentence that follows.

Thesis: The college should make community service a requirement for graduation.

Topic Sentences

a. "Mandatory community service" is a fairly new and often misunderstood concept.
b. Certainly, the conditions in many communities signal serious need.
c. Here's the story of one student's community involvement.
d. There are, though, many other kinds of programs in which students can become involved.
e. Indeed, a single program offers students numerous opportunities.
f. Such involvement can have a real impact on students' lives.
g. This is the way mandatory community service might work on this campus.
h. However, the college could adopt two very different approaches—one developed by a university, the other by a community college.
i. In any case, the college should begin exploring the possibility of making community service a graduation requirement.

6. Select one of the topic sentences listed in activity 5. Use individual or group brainstorming to generate support for it. After reviewing your raw material, delete, add, and combine points as needed. Finally, with the thesis in mind, write a rough draft of the paragraph.

7. Imagine you plan to write a serious essay on one of the following thesis statements. The paper will be read by students in your composition class. After determining your point of view, use any prewriting technique(s) you want to

Writing the Paragraphs in the First Draft

identify the essay's major and supporting points. Arrange the points in order and determine where background and/or transitional paragraphs might be helpful.

   a. Society needs stricter laws against noise pollution.
   b. The traditional lecture format used in many large colleges and universities discourages independent thinking.
   c. Public buildings in this town should be redesigned to accommodate the handicapped.
   d. Long-standing discrimination against women in college athletics must stop.

8. Use any of the techniques described on pages 74–78 to revise the opening and closing paragraphs of two of your own papers. When rewriting, don't forget to keep your purpose, audience, tone, and point of view in mind.

9. Reread Harriet Davids's first draft on pages 80–81. Overall, does it support Harriet's thesis? Which topic sentences focus paragraphs effectively? Where is evidence specific, unified, and coherent? Where does Harriet run into some problems? Make a list of the draft's strengths and weaknesses. Save your list for later review. (In the next chapter, you'll be asked to revise Harriet's draft.)

10. Freewrite or write in your journal about a subject that's been on your mind lately. Reread your raw material to see what thesis seems to emerge. What might your purpose, audience, tone, and point of view be if you wrote an essay with this thesis? What primary and secondary points would you cover? Prepare an outline of your ideas. Then draft the essay's body, providing background and transitional paragraphs if appropriate. Finally, write a rough version of the essay's introduction, conclusion, and title. (Save your draft so you can revise it after reading the next chapter.)

11. If you prepared a first draft in response to activity 3 in Chapter 5 (page 60), work with at least one other person to strengthen that early draft by applying the ideas presented in this chapter. (Save this stronger version of your draft so you can refine it further after reading the next chapter.)

12. Referring to the outline you prepared in response to activity 5 or activity 6 in Chapter 5 (page 60), draft the body of an essay. After reviewing the draft, prepare background and transitional paragraphs as needed. Then draft a rough introduction, conclusion, and title. Ask several people to react to what you've prepared, and save your draft so you can work with it further after reading the next chapter.

7
REVISING OVERALL MEANING, STRUCTURE, AND PARAGRAPH DEVELOPMENT

By now, you've probably abandoned any preconceptions you might have had about good writers sitting down and creating a finished product in one easy step. Alexander Pope's comment that "true ease in writing comes from art, not chance" is as true today as it was more than two hundred years ago. Writing that seems effortlessly clear is often the result of sustained work, not of good luck or even inborn talent. And much of this work takes place during the final stage of the writing process, when ideas, paragraphs, sentences, and words are refined and reshaped.

You've most likely seen cartoons picturing writers plugging away at their typewriters, filling their wastebaskets with sheet after sheet of crumpled paper. It's true. Professional writers—novelists, journalists, textbook authors—seldom submit a piece of writing that hasn't been revised. They recognize that rough, unpolished work doesn't do them justice. What's more, they often look forward to revising. Columnist Ellen Goodman puts it this way: "What makes me happy is rewriting.... It's like cleaning house, getting rid of all the junk, getting things in the right order, tightening up."

In a sense, revision occurs throughout the writing process: At some earlier stage, you may have dropped an idea, overhauled your thesis, or shifted paragraph order. What, then, is different about the rewriting that occurs in the revision stage? The answer has to do with the literal meaning of the word *revision*—reseeing, or seeing again. Genuine revision involves casting clear eyes on your work, viewing it as though you're a reader rather than the writer. Revision is not, as some believe, simply touch-up work—changing a sentence here, a word there, eliminating spelling errors, typing a neat final copy. Revision means that you go through your paper looking for trouble, ready to pick a fight with your own writing. And then you must be willing to sit down and make the changes needed for your writing to be as effective as possible.

Throughout this book, we emphasize that everyone approaches early stages in the writing process differently. The same is true for the revision stage. Some people dash off a draft, knowing they'll spend hours reworking it later. Others find that writing the first draft slowly yields such good results that wholesale revision isn't necessary. Some writers revise neatly, while others fill their drafts with messily scribbled changes. Then there are those who find that the more they revise, the more they overcomplicate their writing and rob it of spontaneity. So, for each writer and for each piece of writing, the amount and kind of revision will vary.

Because revision is hard work, you may resist it. After putting the final period in your first draft, you may feel done and have trouble accepting that more work remains. Or, as you read the draft, you may see so many weak spots that you view revision as punishment for not getting things right the first time. And, if you feel shaky about how to proceed, you may be tempted to skip revising altogether.

If all this sounds as though we're talking about you, don't give up. Here are seven strategies to help you get going if you balk at or feel overwhelmed by revising. (For hints on using a word processor when revising, see pages 147–48 in Chapter 10.)

STRATEGIES TO MAKE REVISION EASIER

Keep in mind that the revision strategies discussed here should be adapted to each writing situation. Revising an answer on an essay exam is quite different from revising a paper you've spent several weeks preparing. Other considerations include your professor's requirements and expectations, the time available, and the paper's bearing on your grade. In any case, the following strategies will help you approach revision more confidently.

Set Your First Draft Aside for a While

When you pick up your draft after having set it aside for a time, you'll approach it with a fresh, more objective point of view. How much of an interval to leave depends on the time available to you. In general, though, the more time between finishing the draft and starting to revise, the better.

Work from Typed or Printed Text

Working with an essay in impersonal typewritten form, instead of in your own familiar handwriting, helps you see the paper impartially, as if someone else had written it. Each time you make major changes, try to retype your essay so that you can see it anew. Using a word processor makes it easy to prepare successive copies. If, however, you work from handwritten drafts, don't boldly strike out or erase as you revise. Instead, lightly cross out material, in case you want to retrieve it later on.

Read the Draft Aloud

Hearing how your writing sounds helps you pick up problems that might otherwise go undetected: places where sentences are awkward, meaning is ambiguous, words are imprecise. Even better, have another person read your draft aloud to you. The thought of this probably makes you shudder, but it's worth the risk. Someone else doesn't have—as you do—a vested interest in making your writing sound good. If a reader slows to a crawl over a murky paragraph or trips over a convoluted sentence, you know where you have to do some rewriting.

React to Your Instructor's Comments

Your instructor may use several methods to give feedback on your writing. You may submit a first draft and then meet with the instructor to go over it in conference. At the conference, you may see your instructor's comments recorded on the draft, or the draft may be unmarked because your instructor—thinking you may be distracted by comments—has made notes on a separate piece of paper. Alternatively, your instructor may return your draft accompanied by typed, written, or taped feedback to you to consider before you resubmit the paper for a grade. And, of course, there's the traditional kind of instructor feedback: comments entered in the margin and at the end of the paper, including a grade.

Like many students, you may be tempted to look only briefly at your instructor's comments. Perhaps you've "had it" with the essay and don't want to think about preparing a revised version that reflects the instructor's remarks. And if there's a grade on the essay, you may think that's the only thing that counts. But remember: Although grades are important, comments are even more so. They can help you *improve* your writing—if not in this paper, then in the next one. So, if you're reading or listening to your instructor's feedback, pay close attention and take notes. Then use a modified version of the feedback chart or a system of marginal annotations (see pages 92–93) to help you evaluate and react to the instructor's comments. If you don't understand or don't agree with the instructor's observations, don't hesitate to request a conference. Getting together gives both you and the instructor a chance to clarify your respective points of view.

Participate in Peer Feedback Sessions

Writing is social and interactive; it promotes dialog. For this reason, many instructors include peer feedback sessions as a regular part of a composition course. Or, if you like, you can set up feedback sessions on your own, adapting the suggestions in this and the following section to fit your needs.

Perhaps the idea of receiving (and giving) peer feedback seems strange to you. After all, what can "mere" students learn from each other? But collaborative feedback can be invaluable. For one thing, it increases your writing options by showing you how other students handle the same assignment. Peer feedback also reinforces the importance of audience analysis by reminding you that your instructor isn't your only reader. Finally, collaborative feedback encourages you to take a conscientious approach to your writing. Your classmates' comments can help you strengthen your writing before it undergoes your instructor's scrutiny. This fact alone will motivate you to put forth your best, most serious effort.

If you do set up your own peer feedback sessions, *select readers* who are *critical* (not a love-struck admirer or a doting grandparent) and who are *skilled* enough to provide useful commentary: other students taking similar courses, friends or family members who write on the job, staff in your college writing lab. To ensure that you leave feedback sessions with specific observations about what does and doesn't work in your writing, give your readers a clear sense of what you want from them. If you simply ask, "How's this?" you'll probably receive vague comments like "It's good" or "It's not very effective." What you want are *concrete observations and suggestions:* "I'm confused because what you say in the fifth sentence contradicts what you say in the second" or "You make the same point in the second and fourth paragraphs. Shouldn't the paragraphs be combined?"

To promote such specific responses, ask your readers *targeted questions:* "My introduction seems bland. What ideas do you have for perking it up?" or "I'm having trouble moving from my second to my third point. How can I make the transition smoother?" Questions like these require more than "yes" or "no" responses; they encourage readers to dig into your writing where you sense it needs work. You may develop your own questions or adapt the revision checklists in this and the following chapter.

If you're most concerned about your draft's overall meaning (pages 94–95), your readers don't necessarily need a copy of your essay. The draft can be read aloud so everyone can hear it. However, if you want feedback on individual paragraphs (pages 95–97) or on specific sentences and words (see Chapter 8), you must supply readers with copies of your draft.

Evaluate and Act on Peer Feedback

Accepting criticism isn't easy (even if you asked for it), and not all readers will be tactful. Even so, try to listen to others with an open mind and take notes on their observations. When everyone is finished commenting, reread your notes. Which remarks seem valid? Which recommendations are workable? Which are not? In addition, try using a feedback chart or a system of marginal annotations to help you evaluate and remedy any perceived weaknesses in your draft.

Here's how to use a three-column **feedback chart.** In the first column, list the major problems you and your readers see in the draft. Next, rank the problems, designating the most critical as 1. Then, in the second column, jot down possible solutions—your own as well as your readers'. Finally, in the third column, briefly describe what action you'll take to correct each problem. Here is a sample chart:

	Problems	Suggestions	Decisions
④	Informal expressions in paragraph 3 seem out of keeping with the rest of the essay.	Lighten language elsewhere. Make the language in paragraph 3 less slangy.	Make language in paragraph 3 a bit more formal. Also make overall language less stiff, especially in paragraphs 2 and 5.
①	Thesis in introduction contradicted by paragraph 2.	Delete paragraph 2. Qualify the thesis so that there's no contradiction.	Qualify thesis.
②	Chronological order used until paragraph 4. That background paragraph breaks the flow.	Delete background paragraph. Move paragraph to beginning. Add transition so paragraph fits more easily.	Delete background paragraph--not needed, except for definition, which can be added to introduction.
③	Too many long sentences	Eliminate some prepositional phrases. Break up long sentences into shorter ones.	Take out some prepositional phrases.

If you don't use a feedback chart, be sure to enter **marginal annotations** on your draft before revising it. In the margins, jot down any major problems, numbered in order of importance, along with possible remedies. Marking your draft this way, much as an instructor might, helps you view your paper as though it were written by someone else. Then, keeping the draft's problems in mind, start revising. You may make changes directly above the appropriate line, or, when necessary, rework sections on a separate sheet of paper. To see how such marginal annotations work, turn to page 97 or look at the sample first drafts of student essays in Chapters 12–20.

View Revision as a Series of Steps

The six revision techniques described so far will help you approach revision with more confidence. We've saved for last, though, the strategy we consider most critical: dividing revision into steps.

You can overcome a bad case of revision jitters simply by viewing revision as a process. Instead of trying to tackle all of a draft's problems at once, proceed step by step. (The feedback chart and annotation system will help you do just that.) If time allows, read your essay several times. Move from a broad overview (the *macro* level) to an up-close look at mechanics (the *micro* level). With each reading, focus on different issues and ask different questions about the draft. Here is a recommended series of revision steps:

First step: Revise overall meaning and structure.

Second step: Revise paragraph development.

Third step: Revise sentences and words.

At first, the prospect of reading and rewriting a paper several times may seem to make revision more, not less, overwhelming. Eventually, though, you'll become accustomed to revision as a process, and you'll appreciate the way such an approach improves your writing.

Ernest Hemingway once told an interviewer that he had revised the last page of one of his novels thirty-nine times. When the interviewer asked, "What was it that had you stumped?" Hemingway answered, "Getting the words right." We don't expect you to revise your paper thirty-nine times. Whenever possible, though, you should aim for three readings. Resist the impulse to tinker with, say, an unclear sentence until you're sure the essay as a whole makes its point clearly. After all, it can be difficult to rephrase a muddy sentence until you have the essay's overall meaning well in hand.

Remember, though: There are no hard-and-fast rules about the revision steps. For one thing, there are bound to be occasions when you have time for, at best, only one quick pass over a draft. Moreover, as you gain experience revising, you'll probably streamline the process or shift the steps around. Assume, for example, that you get bogged down trying to recast the thesis so it more accurately reflects the draft's overall meaning (the first step). You might take a break by fastforwarding to the final stage and use the dictionary to check the spelling of several words. Or, while reorganizing a paragraph (the second step), you might realize you need to rephrase some sentences (the third step).

The remainder of this chapter discusses the first and second steps in the revision process—revising overall meaning and structure and paragraph development. Chapter 8 focuses on the third step—revising sentences and words.

REVISING OVERALL MEANING AND STRUCTURE

During this first step in the revision process, you (and any readers you may have) should read the draft quickly to assess its *general effect* and *clarity*. Does the draft accomplish what you set out to do? Does it develop a central point clearly and logically? Does it merit and hold the reader's attention?

It's not uncommon when revising at this stage to find that the draft doesn't fully convey what you had in mind. Perhaps your intended thesis ends up being overshadowed by another idea. (If that happens, you have two options: (1) you may pursue the new line of thought as your revised thesis, or (2) you may bring the paper back into line with your original thesis by deleting extraneous material.) Another problem might be that readers miss a key point. Perhaps you initially believed the point could be implied, but you now realize it needs to be stated explicitly.

Preparing a *brief outline* of a draft can help evaluate the essay's overall structure. Either you or another reader can prepare the outline. In either case, your thesis, reflecting any changes made during the first draft, should be written at the top of the outline page. Then you or your readers jot down in brief outline form the paper's basic structure. With the draft pared down to its essentials, you can see more easily how parts contribute to the whole and how points do or do not fit together. This bare-bones rendering often reveals the changes needed to remedy any fuzziness or illogic in the development of the draft's central idea and key supporting points.

The following checklist is designed to help you and your readers evaluate a draft's overall meaning and structure. As with other checklists in the book, you may either use all the checklist questions or focus only on those especially relevant to a particular essay. (Activities at the end of the chapter will refer you to this checklist when you revise several essays.) To see how one student used the checklist when revising, turn to page 97.

> ✔ **REVISE OVERALL MEANING AND STRUCTURE: A CHECKLIST**
>
> ☐ What is your initial reaction to the draft? What do you like and dislike?
>
> ☐ What audience does the essay address? How suited to this audience are the essay's purpose, tone, and point of view?
>
> ☐ What is the essay's thesis? Is it explicitly stated or implied? If the perceived thesis isn't what was intended, what changes need to be made?

> - What are the essay's main points? If any stray from or contradict the thesis, what changes need to be made?
> - According to what organizing principle(s)—spatial, chronological, emphatic, simple to complex—are the main points arranged? How does this organizational scheme reinforce the thesis?
> - Which patterns of development (narration, description, comparison-contrast, and so on) help shape the draft? How do these patterns reinforce the thesis?
> - Where would background information, definition of terms, or additional material clarify meaning?

You are now ready to focus on the second step in the revising process.

REVISING PARAGRAPH DEVELOPMENT

After you use feedback to refine the paper's fundamental meaning and structure, it's time to look closely at the essay's paragraphs. At this point, you and those giving you feedback should read the draft more slowly. How can the essay's paragraphs be made more unified (see page 66) and more specific (pages 66–68)? Which paragraphs seem to lack sufficient support (page 69)? Which would profit from more attention to coherence (pages 69–73)?

At this stage, you may find that a paragraph needs more examples to make its point or that a paragraph should be deleted because it doesn't develop the thesis. Or perhaps you realize that a paragraph should be placed earlier in the essay because it defines a term that readers need to understand from the outset.

Here's a strategy to help assess your paragraphs' effectiveness. In the margin next to each paragraph, make a brief notation that answers these two questions: (1) What is the paragraph's *purpose?* and (2) What is its *content?* Then skim the marginal notes to see if each paragraph does what you intended.

During this stage, you should also examine the *length of your paragraphs.* Here's why.

You know how boring it can be to travel long stretches of unvarying highway. Without interesting twists and turns, sweeping views, and occasional rest stops, you struggle to stay awake. The same is true in writing. Paragraphs all the same length dull your readers' response, while variations encourage them to sit up and take notice. (We imagine, for example, that the two-sentence paragraph above got your attention.)

If your paragraphs tend to run long, try breaking some of them into shorter, crisper chunks. Be sure, however, not to break paragraphs just anywhere. To preserve the paragraphs' logic, you may need to reshape and add material, always keeping in mind that each paragraph should have a clear and distinctive focus.

However, don't go overboard and break up all your paragraphs. Too many short paragraphs become as predictable as too many long ones. An abundance of brief paragraphs also makes it difficult for readers to see how points are related. (In such cases, you might combine short paragraphs containing similar ideas.) Furthermore, overreliance on short paragraphs may mean that you haven't provided sufficient evidence for your ideas. Finally, a succession of short paragraphs (as in a newspaper article) encourages readers to skim when, of course, you want them to consider carefully what you have to say. So, use short paragraphs, but save them for places in the essay where you want to introduce variation or achieve emphasis.

The following checklist is designed to help you and your readers evaluate a draft's paragraph development. (Activities at the end of the chapter will refer you to the checklist when you revise several essays.) To see how a student used the checklist when revising, turn to page 97.

> ✔ **REVISE PARAGRAPH DEVELOPMENT: A CHECKLIST**
>
> ☐ In what way does each supporting paragraph develop the essay's thesis? Which paragraphs fail to develop the thesis? Should they be deleted or revised?
>
> ☐ What is each paragraph's central idea? If this idea is expressed in a topic sentence, where is this sentence located? Where does something stray from or contradict the paragraph's main idea? How could the paragraph's focus be sharpened?
>
> ☐ Where in each paragraph does support seem irrelevant, vague, insufficient, inaccurate, nonrepresentative, or disorganized? What could be done to remedy these problems? Where would additional sensory details, examples, facts, statistics, expert authority, and personal observations be appropriate?
>
> ☐ By what organizational principle (spatial, chronological, or emphatic) are each paragraph's ideas arranged? Why is this the most effective order?
>
> ☐ How could paragraph coherence be strengthened? What signal devices are used to relate ideas within and between paragraphs? Where are there too few signals? Too many?
>
> ☐ Where do too many paragraphs of the same length dull interest? Where would a short paragraph be more effective? A long one?
>
> ☐ How could the introduction be strengthened? What striking anecdote, fact, or statistic elsewhere in the essay might be moved to the introduction? How does the introduction establish the essay's purpose, audience, tone, and point of view? What strategy links the introduction to the essay's body?

> □ How could the conclusion be strengthened? What striking anecdote, fact, or statistic elsewhere in the essay might be moved to the conclusion? Would echoing something from the introduction help round off the essay more effectively? How has the conclusion been made an integral part of the essay?

SAMPLE STUDENT REVISION OF OVERALL MEANING, STRUCTURE, AND PARAGRAPH DEVELOPMENT

The introduction to Harriet Davids's first draft that we saw in Chapter 6 (page 80) is reprinted here with Harriet's revisions. In the margin, numbered in order of importance, are the problems with the introduction's meaning, structure, and paragraph development—as noted by Harriet's editing group. (The group used the checklists on pages 94–95 and 96–97 to focus their critique.) The above-line changes show Harriet's first efforts to eliminate these problems through revision.

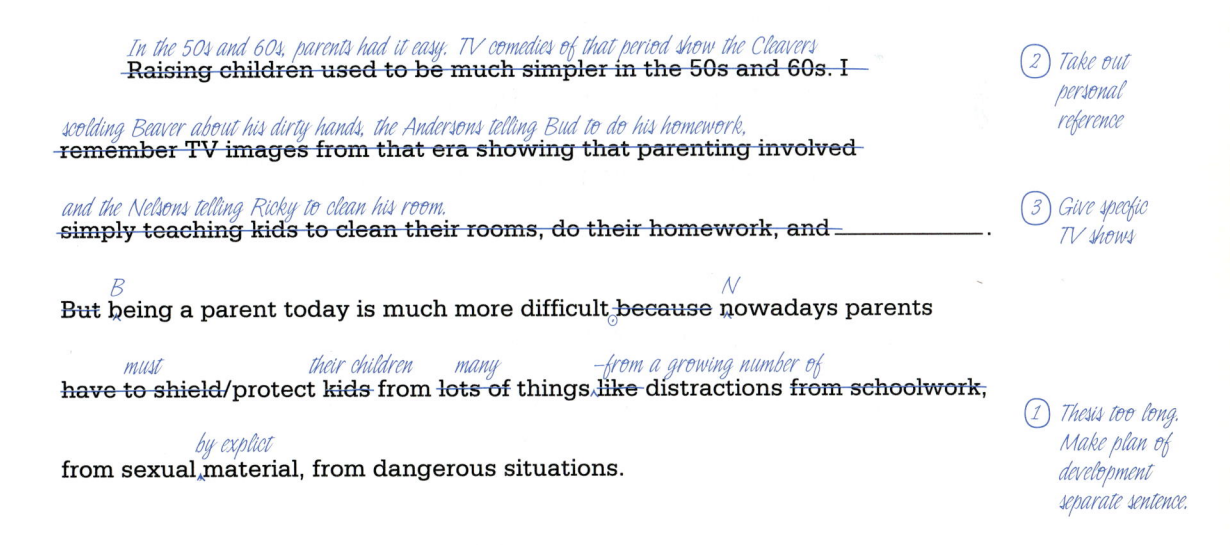

In the 50s and 60s, parents had it easy. TV comedies of that period show the Cleavers ~~Raising children used to be much simpler in the 50s and 60s. I~~ *scolding Beaver about his dirty hands, the Andersons telling Bud to do his homework,* ~~remember TV images from that era showing that parenting involved~~ *and the Nelsons telling Ricky to clean his room.* ~~simply teaching kids to clean their rooms, do their homework, and~~ .

But ʙbeing a parent today is much more difficult ~~because~~ ɴnowadays parents *must* ~~have to~~ shield/protect *their children* ~~kids~~ from *many* ~~lots of~~ things, ~~like~~ *from a growing number of* distractions ~~from schoolwork~~, *by explicit* from sexual ˄material, from dangerous situations.

② *Take out personal reference*

③ *Give specific TV shows*

① *Thesis too long. Make plan of development separate sentence.*

(If you'd like to see Harriet's final draft, turn to page 137.)

There's no doubt about it: As Harriet's reworked introduction shows, revision is challenging. But once you learn how to approach it step by step, you'll have the pleasure of seeing a draft become sharper and more focused. The rather global work you do early in the revision process puts you in a good position to concentrate on sentences and words—our focus in the following chapter.

ACTIVITIES: REVISING OVERALL MEANING, STRUCTURE, AND PARAGRAPH DEVELOPMENT

An important note: When revising essay drafts in activities 1–3, don't worry too much about sentence structure and word choice. However, do save your revisions so you can focus on these matters after you read the next chapter.

1. On page 97, you saw the marginal notes and above-line changes that Harriet Davids added to her first draft introduction. Now look at the draft's other paragraphs on pages 80–81 and identify problems in overall meaning, structure, and paragraph development. Working alone or in a group, start by asking questions like these: "Where does the essay stray from the thesis?" and "Where does a paragraph fail to present points in the most logical and compelling order?" (The critique you prepared for activity 9 in Chapter 6 should help.) For further guidance, refer to the checklists on pages 94–95 and 96–97. Summarize and rank the perceived problems in marginal annotations or on a feedback chart. Then type your changes (into a word processor, if you use one), or enter them between the lines of the draft (work on a newly typed copy, a photocopy, or the textbook pages themselves). Don't forget to save your revision.

2. Retrieve the draft you prepared in response to activity 12 in Chapter 6 (page 87). Outline the draft. Does your outline reveal any problems in the draft's overall meaning and structure? If it does, make whatever changes are needed. The checklists on pages 94–95 and 96–97 will help focus your revising efforts. (Save your refined draft so you can work with it further after reading the next chapter.)

3. On the next page is the first draft of an essay advocating a longer elementary school day. Read it closely. Are tone and point of view consistent throughout? Is the thesis clear? Is the support in each body paragraph relevant, specific, and adequate? Are ideas arranged in the most effective order? Working alone or in a group, use the checklists on pages 94–95 and 96–97 to identify problems with the draft's overall meaning, structure, and paragraph development. Summarize and rank the perceived problems on a feedback chart or in marginal annotations. Then revise the draft by typing a new version or by entering your changes by hand (on a photocopy of the draft, a typed copy, or the textbook pages themselves). Don't forget to save your revision.

The Extended School Day

Imagine a seven-year-old whose parents work until five each night. When she arrives home after school, she is on her own. She's a good girl, but still a lot of things could happen. She could get into trouble just by being curious. Or something could happen through no fault of her own. All over the country, there are many "latchkey" children like this little girl. Some way must be found to deal with the problem. One suggestion is to keep elementary schools open longer than they now are. There are many advantages to this idea.

Parents wouldn't have to be in a state of uneasiness about whether their child is safe and happy at home. They wouldn't get uptight about whether their child's needs are being met. They also wouldn't have to feel guilty because they are not able to help a child with homework. The longer day would make it possible for the teacher to provide such help. Extended school hours would also relieve families of the financial burden of hiring a home sitter. As my family learned, having a sitter can wipe out the budget. And having a sitter doesn't necessarily eliminate all problems. Parents still have the hassle of worrying whether the person will show up and be reliable.

It's a fact of life that many children dislike school, which is a sad commentary on the state of education in this country. Even so, the longer school day would benefit children as well. Obviously, the dangers of their being home alone after school would disappear because by the time the bus dropped them off after the longer school day, at least on parent would be home. The unnameable horrors feared by parents would not have a chance to happen. Instead, the children would be in school, under trained supervision. There, they would have a chance to work on subjects that give them trouble. In contrast, when my younger brother had difficulty with subtraction in second grade, he had to struggle along because there wasn't enough time to give him the help he needed. The longer day would also give children a chance to participate in extracurricular activities. They could join a science club, play on a softball team, sing in a school chorus, take an art class. Because school districts are trying to save money, they often cut back on such extracurricular activities. They don't realize how important such experiences are.

Finally, the longer school day would also benefit teachers. Having more hours in each day would relieve them of a lot of pressure. This longer workday would obviously require schools to increase teachers' pay. The added salary would be an incentive for teachers to stay in the profession.

Implementing an extended school day would be expensive, but I feel that many communities would willingly finance its costs because it provides benefits to parents, children, and even teachers. Young children, home alone, wondering whether to watch another TV show or wander outside to see what's happening, need this longer school day now.

4. Look closely at your instructor's comments on an ungraded draft of one of your essays. Using a feedback chart, summarize and evaluate your instructor's comments. That done, rework the essay. Type your new version, or make your changes by hand. In either case, save the revision so you can work with it further after reading the next chapter.

5. Return to the draft you wrote in response to activity 10 or activity 11 in Chapter 6 (page 87). To identify any problems, meet with several people and request that one of them read the draft aloud. Then ask your listeners focused questions about the areas you sense need work. Alternatively, you may use the checklist on pages 94–95 to focus the group's feedback. In either case, summarize and rank the comments on a feedback chart or in marginal annotations. Then, using the comments as a guide, revise the draft. Either type a new version or do your revising by hand. (Save your revision so you can work with it further after reading the next chapter.)

8
REVISING SENTENCES AND WORDS

REVISING SENTENCES

HAVING refined your essay's overall meaning, structure, and paragraph development, you can concentrate on sharpening individual sentences. Although polishing sentences inevitably involves decisions about individual words, for now focus on each sentence *as a whole;* you can evaluate individual words later. At this point, work to make your sentences

- consistent with your intended tone,
- economical,
- varied in type,
- varied in length,
- varied in pattern, and
- emphatic.

Make Sentences Consistent With Your Tone

In Chapter 2, we saw how integral **tone** is to meaning (pages 21–22). As you revise, be sure each sentence's **content** (its images and ideas) and **style** (its structure and length) reinforce your intended tone: Both *what* you say and *how* you say it should support the essay's overall mood.

Consider the following excerpt from a piece by *Philadelphia Inquirer* columnist Steve Lopez. Having witnessed police curtailment of protest activities at, ironically,

Philadelphia's bicentennial celebration of the U.S. Constitution, Lopez objects to the way police shoved individual protesters and aggressively confiscated their signs. He writes:

> I've listened to explanations from police and park employees for two days now, and they amount, basically, to hogwash. The cops would run a background check if Goofy and Pluto marched in step.

Lopez's tone here is sarcastic; his attitude comes across as critical and mocking. The author establishes this tone partly through sentence content (what he says)—for example, the absurd image of two cartoon characters under investigation. His style (how he says it) also contributes to his overall tone. The first sentence—long and interrupted by a qualifier ("basically") right before its end—suggests that official thinking is ponderous as well as questionable. In short, content and style help express Lopez's attitude toward his subject.

Make Sentences Economical

Besides reinforcing your tone, your sentences should be **economical** rather than wordy. Use as few, not as many, words as possible. Students sometimes pad their writing because they think the longer a paper is, the higher grade it will receive. Most instructors, though, are skilled at spotting wordiness intended only to fill pages. Your sentences won't be wordy if you (1) eliminate redundancy, (2) delete weak phrases, and (3) remove unnecessary *who, which,* and *that* clauses.

Eliminate Redundancy

Redundancy means unnecessary repetition. Sometimes words are repeated exactly; sometimes they are repeated by way of *synonyms,* other words or phrases that mean the same thing. When writing is redundant, words can be trimmed away without sacrificing meaning or effect. Why, for example, write "In the expert opinion of one expert" and needlessly repeat the word *expert?* Similarly, "They found it difficult to get consensus or agreement about the proposal" contains an unnecessary synonym (*agreement*) for *consensus.*

Redundancy isn't the same as repetition for dramatic emphasis. Consider the following excerpt from an address to the United Nations by John F. Kennedy:

> Unconditional war can no longer lead to unconditional victory. It can no longer serve to settle disputes. It can no longer be of concern to great powers alone....

Here the repetition of *unconditional* and *can no longer* drives home the urgency of Kennedy's message. Repetition used, in this way, to underscore the relationship among sentences or ideas is called *parallelism.* (For more on parallelism, see pages 113–14.)

When not used as a stylistic device, however, repetition weakens prose. Take a look at the sentence pairs on the next page. Note how the revised versions are clearer and stronger because the redundancy in the original sentences (italicized) has been eliminated:

Revising Sentences and Words   103

Original   While under the *influence* of alcohol, many people insist they are not under the *influence* and *swear* they are sober.
Revised   While under the influence of alcohol, many people insist they are sober.
Original   *They designed a computer program* that increased sales by 50 percent. The *computer program they designed* showed how the TRS-80 can be *used* and *implemented* in small *businesses* and *firms*.
Revised   Their program, which showed how the TRS-80 computer can be used in small businesses, increased sales by 50 percent.

Delete Weak Phrases

In addition to eliminating redundancy, you can make sentences more economical by **deleting the three types of weak phrases** described here.

1. Empty Phrases. In speaking, we frequently use empty phrases that give us time to think but don't add to our message—expressions such as "Okay?" and "You know what I mean?" In writing, though, we have the chance to eliminate such deadwood. Here are some common culprits—expressions that are needlessly awkward and wordy—along with their one-word alternatives:

Wordy Expressions	Revised
due to the fact that	because
in light of the fact that	since
regardless of the fact that	although
in the event that	if
in many cases	often
in that period	then
at the present time	now
at this point in time	now
in the not-too-distant future	soon
for the purpose of	to
has the ability to	can
be aware of the fact that	know
is necessary that	must

Notice the improvement in the following sentences when wordy, often awkward phrases are replaced with one-word substitutes:

Original   *It is necessary that* the government outlaw the production of carcinogenic pesticides.
Revised   The government *must* outlaw the production of carcinogenic pesticides.
Original   Student leaders were upset by *the fact that* no one in the administration consulted them.
Revised   Student leaders were upset *because* no one in the administration consulted them.

Some phrases don't even call for concise substitutes. Because they add nothing at all to a sentence's meaning, they can simply be deleted. Here are some examples: "shy *type of* child," "*kind of* person," "*field of* communications," "small *in size*." The revised sentence that follows has exactly the same meaning as the original, but the meaning is expressed without the empty phrase *in color*:

Original   The hybrid azaleas were light blue *in color*.
Revised   The hybrid azaleas were light blue.

Other times, to avoid an empty phrase, you may need to recast a sentence slightly:

Original   The midterm assessment is *for the purpose of letting* students know if they are failing a course.
Revised   The midterm assessment *lets* students know if they are failing a course.

***2. Roundabout Openings with* There, It, *and Question Words like* How *and* What.**   At the beginning of a sentence, you're formulating a new thought so you may grope around a bit before pinning down what you want to say. For this reason, the openings of sentences are especially vulnerable to unnecessary phrases. Common culprits include phrases beginning with *There* and *It* (when *It* does not refer to a specific noun), and words like *How* and *What* (when they don't actually ask a question). In the following examples, note that trimming away excess words highlights the subject and verb, thus clarifying meaning:

Original   It was their belief that the problem had been solved.
Revised   They believed the problem had been solved.

Original   There are now computer courses offered by many high schools.
Revised   Many high schools now offer computer courses.

Original   What should be done in this crisis is to transport food to the victims' homes.
Revised   Food must be transported to the victims' homes.

Original   How to simplify the college's registration process should be a priority.
Revised   Simplifying the college's registration process should be a priority.

Of course, feel free to open with *There* or *It* when some other construction would be less clear or effective. For example, don't write "Many reasons can be cited why students avoid art courses" when you can say "There are many reasons why students avoid art courses."

3. Excessive Prepositional Phrases.   Strings of prepositional phrases (word groups beginning with *at*, *on*, and the like) tend to make writing choppy; they weigh sentences down and hide main ideas. Note how much smoother and clearer sentences become when prepositional phrases (italicized in the following examples) are eliminated:

Original   Growth *in the greenhouse effect* may result *in increases in the intensity of hurricanes*.
Revised   The growing greenhouse effect may intensify hurricanes.

Revising Sentences and Words

Original The reassurance *of a neighbor* who was the owner *of a pit bull* that his dog was incapable *of harm* would not be sufficient to prevent most parents *from calling* the authorities if the dog ran loose.
Revised   Despite a neighbor's reassurance that his pit bull was harmless, most parents would call the authorities if the dog ran loose.

These examples show that prepositional phrases can sometimes be eliminated by substituting one strong verb (*intensify*) or by using the possessive form (*neighbor's reassurance, his pit bull*) rather than an *of* phrase.

Remove Unnecessary *Who, Which,* and *That* Clauses

Often *who, which,* or *that* clauses can be removed with no loss of meaning. Consider the tightening possible in these sentences:

Original The townsfolk misunderstood the main point *that the developer made.*
Revised   The townsfolk misunderstood *the developer's main point.*

Original The employees *who protested* the restrictions went on strike, *which was a real surprise to management.*
Revised   The employees *protesting* the restrictions *surprised management* by going on strike.

Vary Sentence Type

Another way to invigorate writing is to **vary sentence type.** Since the predictable soon becomes dull, try to offer a mixture of simple, compound, complex, and compound-complex sentences.

Simple Sentences

A **clause** is a group of words with both a subject and a verb. Clauses can be **independent** (able to stand alone) or **dependent** (unable to stand alone). A **simple sentence** consists of a single independent clause (whose subject and verb are italicized here):

The *president serves* four years.

Marie Curie investigated radioactivity and *died* from its effects.

Unlike most mammals, *birds* and *fish see* color.

Notice that a simple sentence can have more than one verb (sentence 2) or more than one subject (sentence 3). In addition, any number of modifying phrases (such as *Unlike most mammals*) can extend the sentence's length and add information. What distinguishes a simple sentence is its single *subject-verb combination*. Simple sentences can convey dramatic urgency:

Suddenly we heard the screech of brakes. Across the street, a small boy lay sprawled in front of a car. We started to run toward the child. Seeing us, the driver sped away.

Simple sentences are also excellent for singling out a climactic point: "They found the solution." In a series, however, they soon lose their impact and become boring. Also, because simple sentences highlight one idea at a time, they don't clarify the relationships among ideas. Consider these two versions of a passage:

Original

> Many first-year college students are apprehensive. They won't admit it to themselves. They hesitate to confide in their friends. They never find out that everyone else is anxious, too. They are nervous about being disliked and feeling lonely. They fear not "knowing the ropes."

Revised

> Many first-year college students are apprehensive, but they won't admit it to themselves. Because they hesitate to confide in their friends, they never find out that everyone else is anxious, too. Being disliked, feeling lonely, not "knowing the ropes"—these are what beginning college students fear.

In addition to sounding repetitive and childish, the simple sentences in the original version fragment the passage into a series of disconnected ideas. In contrast, the revised version includes a variety of sentence types and patterns, all of which are discussed on the pages ahead. This variety clarifies the relationships among ideas, so that the passage reads more easily.

Compound Sentences

Compound sentences consist of two or more independent clauses. There are four types of compound sentences. The most basic type consists of two simple sentences joined by a *coordinating conjunction* (*and, but, for, nor, or, so,* or *yet*). Here's an example:

> Chimpanzees and gorillas can learn sign language, *and* they have been seen teaching this language to others.

Another type of compound sentence has a semicolon (;), rather than a comma and coordinating conjunction, between the two simple sentences:

> Yesterday, editorials attacked the plan; a week ago, they praised it.

A third type of compound sentence links two simple sentences with a semicolon plus a *conjunctive adverb* such as *however, moreover, nevertheless, therefore,* and *thus:*

> Every year billions of U.S. dollars go to researching AIDS; *however,* recent studies show that a large percentage of the money has been mismanaged.

A final type of compound sentence consists of two simple sentences connected by a *correlative conjunction,* a word pair such as *either . . . or, neither . . . nor,* or *not only . . . but also:*

> *Either* the litigants will win the lawsuit, *or* they will end up in debt from court costs.

Compound sentences help clarify the relationship between ideas. Similarities are signaled by such words as *and* and *moreover,* contrasts by *but* and *however,* cause-effect by *so* and *therefore.* When only a semicolon separates the two parts of a compound sentence, the relationship between those two parts is often a contrast. ("Yesterday, editorials attacked the plan; a week ago, they praised it.")

Complex Sentences

In a **complex sentence,** a dependent (subordinate) clause is joined to an independent clause. Sometimes the dependent clause (italicized in the following examples) is introduced by a subordinating conjunction such as *although, because, if, since,* or *when:*

Since they have relatively small circulations, specialty magazines tend to be expensive.

We knew there had been a power failure *because all the clocks in the building were two hours slow.*

Other dependent clauses are introduced by a relative pronoun such as *that, which,* or *who:*

Several celebrities revealed *that they have been stalked by delusional fans.*

Fame and wealth from his writings had little effect on author J. R. R. Tolkien, *who continued to teach until reaching retirement age.*

As you can see, the order of the dependent and independent clause isn't fixed. The dependent clause may come first, last, or even in the middle of the independent clause, as in this example:

Nurses' uniforms, *although they are no longer the norm,* are still required by some hospitals.

Whether to use a comma between a dependent and an independent clause depends on a number of factors, including the location of the dependent clause and whether it's *restrictive* (essential for identifying the thing it modifies) or *nonrestrictive.*

Because a dependent clause is subordinate to an independent one, complex sentences can clarify the relationships among ideas. Consider the two paragraphs that follow. The first merely strings together a series of simple and compound sentences, all of them carrying roughly the same weight. In contrast, the complex sentences in the revised version use subordination to connect ideas and signal their relative importance.

Original

Are you the "average American"? Then take heed. Here are the results of a time-management survey. You might want to budget your time differently. According to the survey, you spend six years of your life eating. Also, you're likely to spend two years trying to reach people by telephone, so you should convince your friends to get answering machines. Finally, you may be married and expect long conversations with your spouse to occur spontaneously, but you'll have to make a special effort. Ordinarily, your discussions will average only four minutes a day.

Revised

If you're the "average American," take heed. After you hear the results of a time-management survey, you might want to budget your time differently. According to the survey, you spend six years of your life eating. Also, unless you convince your friends to get an answering machine, you're likely to spend two years trying to reach them by telephone. Finally, if you're married, you shouldn't expect long conversations with your spouse to occur spontaneously. Unless you make a special effort, your discussions will average only four minutes a day.

If you find that the original paragraph resembles your writing more than the revised, don't despair. With experience, you'll develop a strong sense of how to connect and rank ideas through subordination. For now, just remember the following: Expressed as a dependent clause, an idea is relegated to a position of secondary importance; expressed as an independent clause, it's emphasized. So, reserve for the independent clause the point you want to highlight.

The following sentences illustrate how meaning shifts depending on what is put in the main clause and what is subordinated:

> Although most fraternities and sororities no longer have hazing, pledging is still a big event on many campuses.
>
> Although pledging is still a big event on many campuses, most fraternities and sororities no longer have hazing.

In the first sentence, the focus is on *pledging;* in the second, it is on the *discontinuation of hazing.*

Compound-Complex Sentences

A **compound-complex sentence** connects one or more dependent clauses to two or more independent clauses. In the following example, the two independent clauses are underscored once and the two dependent clauses twice:

> The Procrastinators' Club, which is based in Philadelphia, issues a small magazine, but it appears infrequently, only when members get around to writing it.

Go easy on the number of compound-complex sentences you use. Because they tend to be long, a string of them is likely to overwhelm the reader and cloud meaning.

Vary Sentence Length

You've probably noticed that simple sentences tend to be short, compound and complex sentences tend to be of medium length, and compound-complex sentences tend to be long. Generally, by varying sentence type, a writer automatically **varies sentence length** as well. However, sentence type doesn't

Revising Sentences and Words

always determine length. In this example, the simple sentence is longer than the complex one:

Simple Sentence

Hot and thirsty, exhausted from the effort of carrying so many groceries, I desired nothing more than an ice-cold glass of lemonade.

Complex Sentence

Because I was hot and thirsty, I craved lemonade.

The difference lies in the number of **modifiers**—words or groups of words used to describe another word or group of words. So, besides considering sentence type, check on sentence length when revising.

Short Sentences

Too many short sentences, like too many simple ones, can sound childish and create a choppy effect that muddies the relationship among ideas. Used wisely, though, a series of short sentences gives writing a staccato rhythm that carries more punch and conveys a faster pace than the same number of words gathered into longer sentences. As you read the two passages that follow, note how the first version's clipped rhythms are more effective for conveying a rush of terrifying events:

Witches bring their faces close. Goblins glare with fiery eyes. Fiendish devils stealthily approach to claw a beloved stuffed bear. The toy recoils in horror. These are among the terrifying happenings in the world of children's nightmares.

Witches bring their faces close as goblins glare, their eyes fiery. Approaching stealthily, fiendish devils come to claw a beloved stuffed bear that recoils in horror. These are among the terrifying happenings in the world of children's nightmares.

Brevity also highlights a sentence, especially when surrounding sentences are longer. Consider the dramatic effect of the final sentence in this paragraph:

Starting in June, millions of Americans pour onto the highways, eager to begin vacation. At the same time, city, state, and federal agencies deploy hundreds, even thousands of workers to repair roads that have, until now, managed to escape bureaucratic attention. Chaos results.

The short sentence "Chaos results" stands out because it's so much shorter than the preceding sentences. The emphasis is appropriate because, in the writer's view, chaos is the dramatic consequence of prolonged bureaucratic inertia.

Long Sentences

Long sentences often convey a leisurely pace and establish a calm tone:

As I look across the lake, I see the steady light of a campfire at the water's edge, the flames tinting to copper an aluminum rowboat tied to the dock, the boat glimmering in the darkness.

However, as with short sentences, don't overdo it. Too many long sentences can be hard to follow. And remember: A sentence stands out most when it differs in length from surrounding sentences. Glance back at the first paragraph on children's nightmares (page 109). The final long sentence stands in contrast to the preceding short ones. The resulting emphasis works because the final sentence is also the paragraph's topic sentence.

Vary Sentence Pattern

While trying to vary sentence type and length, also strive for a graceful blend of **sentence patterns.** A sentence's pattern (often referred to as its **structure**) is the order in which the main subject, its verb, and any modifiers appear. The modifiers may be adjectives, adverbs, phrases, or clauses. On the pages ahead, we describe and illustrate four basic patterns.

Subject-Verb-Modifier Pattern

The most standard pattern in English is that of **subject-verb-modifier,** sometimes called a **cumulative** or **loose sentence** pattern. In such a sentence, the main clause (italicized in the following example) appears at or near the beginning, followed by all or most of the sentence's modifiers:

The school board approved the controversial sex education program, despite teachers' reservations and many parents' objections, creating a stand-off between school officials and the two groups whose cooperation was needed most.

As long as they're not packed with too many modifiers, cumulative sentences offer the clarity of a simple sentence as well as the ability to convey several layers of meaning. However, an uninterrupted string of them weighs writing down and obscures meaning.

Modifiers-First Pattern

The **modifiers-first** pattern is one in which modifiers delay the main subject and its verb. In this pattern, sometimes called a **periodic sentence,** all or most of the modifiers come before the sentence's main clause (italicized here):

After the clean-up crews leave, after environmentalists measure the level of toxic residue in the water, after biologists assess the health of area wildlife—*only then will we know* how much damage the oil spill has caused.

The periodic sentence—like the cumulative sentence—can tighten and strengthen writing. Also, such sentences often create a climactic effect; the modifiers at the start create a momentum that builds toward the main idea at the end.

Since periodic sentences reverse the usual order of sentence elements, use them only occasionally. Too many will make your writing sound contrived.

Embedded-Modifiers Pattern

In the **embedded-modifiers** pattern, some or all of a sentence's modifiers are inserted between the main subject and verb (both italicized in the following example):

> A *nurse*, who looks in on a patient throughout the day, monitoring vital signs, taking the time to chat, *may know* more about the patient's health than the doctor.

Sentences with embedded modifiers may be elegant and economical. They can, however, also be confusing if so many modifiers come between the subject and verb that readers lose sight of the sentence's main idea (italicized here):

> *The long line of refugees*, waiting for food and water, angry at the delay, a delay caused by political in-fighting among competing agencies, *threatened to snap into violence.*

Distributed-Modifiers Pattern

Finally, the **distributed-modifiers** pattern allows you to sprinkle modifiers throughout the sentence. Some are placed before the main subject and verb (both italicized in the following example), others between them, and still others after:

> Able to take numerous business deductions, the *self-employed*, benefiting from recent changes in the tax laws, generally *pay* less in taxes than salaried employees with comparable incomes—a fact that distresses the average worker.

Use the Sentence Patterns to Revise

Now that you're familiar with the four sentence patterns, consider how you might transform the following choppy, repetitive sentences into one richly textured sentence with a number of modifiers:

Original

> The student dragged himself to the front of the room. He smiled tightly. He clutched his note cards with shaky hands. He was afraid that his voice would squeak.

Which sentence pattern you choose depends mainly on your meaning and what you want to emphasize. To give roughly equal weight to the student's reluctant movement to the front of the room and to the way he holds his note cards, you might use a cumulative pattern:

Subject-Verb Modifier

> The student clutched his note cards with shaking hands and dragged himself to the front of the room, smiling tightly, fearing that his voice would squeak.

If, however, you want to give greater emphasis to the picture of the student hauling himself forward, you might use a periodic pattern that builds toward that image:

Modifiers First

> Fearful that his voice would squeak, smiling tightly, note cards clutched in shaking hands, the student dragged himself to the front of the room.

Or, to focus on the student's desperate reliance on his note cards, you might insert modifiers between the subject and verb (both italicized here), thus emphasizing the verb *clutched* by temporarily delaying it:

Embedded Modifiers

> The *student*, dragging himself forward, fearing that his voice would squeak, *clutched* his note cards in shaking hands.

Finally, to single out the risk that a squeaky voice will bring humiliation, you could place modifiers throughout the sentence:

Distributed Modifiers

> Note cards clutched in his shaking hands, the student, smiling tightly, dragged himself forward, fearful that his voice would squeak.

Caution: Don't be so conscientious about varying sentence patterns that you twist sentences out of shape.

Make Sentences Emphatic

The previous section shows how the placement of modifiers affects meaning by highlighting different sentence elements. In addition to such modifier placement, there are a number of other techniques for making sentences **emphatic:** (1) placing key ideas at the beginning or end, (2) setting them in parallel constructions, (3) expressing them as fragments, or (4) expressing them in inverted word order.

Place Key Points at the Beginning or End

A sentence's start and close are its most prominent positions. So, keeping your overall meaning in mind, use those two spots to highlight key ideas.

Let's look first at the **beginning** position. Here are two versions of a sentence; the meanings differ because the openers differ.

> The potentially life-saving drug, developed by junior researchers at the medical school, will be available next month.
>
> Developed by junior researchers at the medical school, the potentially life-saving drug will be available next month.

In the first version, the emphasis is on the life-saving potential of a drug. Reordering the sentence shifts attention to those responsible for discovering the drug.

An even more emphatic position than a sentence's beginning is its **end.** Put at the close of a sentence whatever you want to emphasize:

> Kindergarten is wasted on the young—especially the co-ed naptime.

Revising Sentences and Words

Now look at two versions of another sentence, each with a slightly different meaning because of what's at the end:

Increasingly, overt racism is showing up in—of all places—popular song lyrics.

Popular song lyrics are showing—of all things—increasingly overt racism.

In the first version, the emphasis is on lyrics; in the second, it's on racism.

Be sure, though, that whatever you place in the climactic position merits the emphasis. The following sentence is so anticlimactic that it's unintentionally humorous:

The family, waiting anxiously for the results of the medical tests, sat.

Similarly, don't build toward a strong climax only to defuse it with some less important material:

On the narrow parts of the trail, where jagged cliffs drop steeply from the path, keep your eyes straight ahead and don't look down, toward the town of Belmont in the east.

In the preceding sentence, "toward the town of Belmont in the east" should be deleted. The important point surely isn't Belmont's location but how to avoid an accident.

Use Parallelism

Parallelism occurs when ideas of comparable weight are expressed in the same grammatical form, thus underscoring their equality. Parallel elements may be words, phrases, clauses, or full sentences. Here are some examples:

Parallel Nouns

We bought *pretzels, nachos,* and *candy bars* to feed our pre-exam jitters.

Parallel Adverbs

Smoothly, steadily, quietly, the sails tipped toward the sun.

Parallel Verbs

The guest lecturer *spoke* to the group, *showed* her slides, and then *invited* questions.

Parallel Adjective Phrases

Playful as a kitten but *wise as a street Tom,* the old cat played with the string while keeping a watchful eye on his surroundings.

Parallel Prepositional Phrases

Gloomy predictions came *from political analysts, from the candidate's staff,* and, surprisingly, *from the candidate herself.*

Parallel Dependent Clauses

Since our rivals were in top form, since their top player would soon come up to bat, we knew that all was lost.

As you can see, the repetition of grammatical forms creates a pleasing symmetry that emphasizes the sequenced ideas. Parallel structure also conveys meaning economically. Look at the way the following sentences can be tightened using parallelism:

Nonparallel

Studies show that most women today are different from those in the past. They want to have their own careers. They want to be successful. They also want to enjoy financial independence.

Parallel

Studies show that most women today are different from those in the past. They want to have careers, be successful, and enjoy financial independence.

Parallel constructions are often signaled by word pairs (correlative conjunctions) such as *either . . . or, neither . . . nor,* and *not only . . . but also.* To maintain parallelism, the same grammatical form must follow each half of the word pair.

Either professors are too rigorous, *or* they are too lax.

The company is interested in *neither* financing the project *nor* helping locate other funding sources.

When my roommate argues, she tends to be *not only* totally stubborn *but also* totally wrong.

Parallelism can create elegant and dramatic writing. Too much, though, seems artificial, so use it sparingly. Save it for your most important points.

Use Fragments

A **fragment** is part of a sentence punctuated as if it were a whole sentence—that is, with a period at the end. A sentence fragment consists of words, phrases, and/or dependent clauses, *without an independent clause.* Here are some examples:

Resting quietly.

Except for the trees.

Because they admired her.

A demanding boss who accepted no excuses.

Ordinarily, we advise students to stay clear of fragments. However, like most rules, this one may at times be broken—*if* you do so intentionally and skillfully. To be on the safe side, ask your composition instructor whether an occasional fragment—used as a stylistic device—will be considered acceptable. Here's an

Revising Sentences and Words

example showing the way fragments (underlined) can be used effectively for emphasis:

One of my aunt's eccentricities is her belief that only personally made gifts show the proper amount of love. Her gifts are often strange. <u>Hand-drawn calendars</u>. <u>Home-brewed cologne that smells like jam</u>. <u>Crocheted washcloths</u>. Frankly, I'd rather receive a gift certificate from a department store.

Notice how the three fragments focus attention on the aunt's charmingly offbeat gifts. Remember, though: When overused, fragments lose their effect, so draw on them sparingly.

Use Inverted Word Order

In most English sentences, the subject comes before the verb. When you use **inverted word order,** however, at least part of the verb comes before the subject. The resulting sentence is so atypical that it automatically stands out.

Inverted statements, like those that follow, are used to emphasize an idea:

Normal	My Uncle Bill is a strange man.
Inverted	A strange man is my Uncle Bill.
Normal	Their lies about the test scores were especially brazen.
Inverted	Especially brazen were their lies about the test scores.
Normal	The age-old tree would never again bear fruit.
Inverted	Never again would the age-old tree bear fruit.

A note of caution: Inverted statements should be used infrequently and with special care. Bizarre can they easily sound.

Another form of inversion, the question, also acts as emphasis. A question may be a genuine inquiry, one that focuses attention on the issue at hand, as in the following example:

Since the 1960s, only about half of this country's eligible voters have gone to the polls during national elections. *Why are Americans so apathetic?* Let's look at some of the reasons.

Or a question may be *rhetorical;* that is, one that implies its own answer and encourages the reader to share the writer's view:

Yesterday, there was yet another accident at the intersection of Fairview and Springdale. Given the disproportionately high number of collisions at that crossing, *can anyone question the need for a traffic light?*

The following checklist is designed to help you and your readers evaluate the sentences in a first draft. (Activities at the end of the chapter will refer you to this checklist when you revise several essays.) To see how one student, Harriet Davids, used the checklist when revising, turn to page 128.

> ✔ REVISE SENTENCES: A CHECKLIST
>
> ☐ Which sentences are inconsistent with the essay's intended tone? How could the problem be corrected?
> ☐ Which sentences could be more economical? Where could unnecessary repetition, empty phrases, and weak openings be eliminated? Which prepositional phrases could be deleted? Where are there unnecessary *who*, *which*, and *that* clauses?
> ☐ Where should sentence type be more varied? Where would subordination clarify the connections among ideas? Where would simpler sentences make the writing less inflated and easier to understand?
> ☐ Where does sentence length become monotonous? Which short sentences should be connected to enhance flow and convey a more leisurely pace? Which long sentences would be more effective if broken into crisp, short ones?
> ☐ Where would a different sentence pattern add variety? Better highlight key sentence elements? Seem more natural?
> ☐ Which sentences could be more emphatic? Which strategy would be most effective—expressing the main point at the beginning or end, using parallelism, or rewriting the sentence as a fragment, question, or inverted-word-order statement?

REVISING WORDS

After refining the sentences in your first draft, you're in a good position to look closely at individual words. During this stage, you should aim for

- words consistent with your intended tone,
- an appropriate level of diction,
- words that neither overstate nor understate,
- words with appropriate connotations,
- specific rather than general words,
- concrete rather than abstract words,
- strong verbs,
- no unnecessary adverbs,
- original figures of speech, and
- nonsexist language.

Revising Sentences and Words

Make Words Consistent With Your Tone

Like full sentences, individual words and phrases should also reinforce your intended tone. Consider again the Steve Lopez excerpt on police curtailment of protest activities:

> I've listened to explanations from police and park employees for two days now, and they amount, basically, to hogwash. The cops would run a background check if Goofy and Pluto marched in step.

Earlier we discussed how sentence structure and length contribute to the excerpt's sarcastic tone. Word choice also plays an important role. The slangy term *cops*, with its strong negative overtones, reveals the author's contempt for officially sanctioned misconduct. Similarly, Lopez topples official pretense with the down-to-earth *hogwash*. Such word choices reinforce the overall tone Lopez wants to convey.

Use an Appropriate Level of Diction

Diction refers to the words a writer selects. Those words should be appropriate for the writer's purpose, audience, point of view, and tone. If, for example, you are writing a straightforward, serious piece about on-the-job incompetence, you would be better off saying people "don't concentrate on their work" and they "make frequent errors," rather than saying they "screw up" or "goof off."

There are three broad levels of diction: *formal, popular,* and *informal.* To describe feelings of pervasive sadness, clinical psychologists might use the highly formal term *dysthymia*, while the popular term for such emotions is *depression.* At the other end of the continuum, someone might use the informal phrase *down in the dumps.* Within each level of diction, there are *degrees* of formality and informality: *Down in the dumps* and *bummed out* are both informal, but *bummed out* is the slangier expression.

Formal Diction

Impersonal and distant in tone, **formal diction** is the type of language found in scholarly journals. Contractions are rare; long, specialized, technical words are common. Unfortunately, many people mistakenly equate word length with education: The longer the words, they think, the more impressed readers will be. So, rather than using the familiar and natural words *improve* and *think,* they thumb through a thesaurus (literally or figuratively) for fancy-sounding alternatives *ameliorate* and *conceptualize*. They write "That is the optimum consequence we have the expectation of attaining" rather than "That is the best result we can expect." Remember: It's a word's ability to convey meaning clearly that counts, not its number of syllables.

Similarly, when writing for a general audience, don't show off specialized knowledge by throwing in **jargon,** insiders' terms from a particular area of expertise (say, a term like *authorial omniscience* from literary theory). Such "shop-talk" should be used only when less specialized words would lack the necessary precision. If readers are apt to be unfamiliar with a term, provide a definition.

Some degree of formality is appropriate—when, for example, you write up survey results for a sociology class. In such a case, your instructor may expect you to avoid the pronoun *I* (see page 23). Other instructors may think it's pretentious for a student to refer to himself or herself in the third person ("The writer observed that..."). These instructors may be equally put off by the artificiality of the passive voice (pages 122–23): "It was observed that...." To be safe, find out what your instructors expect. If possible, use *I* when you mean "I." Your writing will be no less objective—unless using *I* tempts you to highly personal remarks and opinions. Even in more formal situations, resist the temptation to dazzle readers by piling up multisyllable words. (For more on avoiding pretentious language, see below.)

Popular Diction

Popular, or **mainstream, diction** is found in most magazines, newspapers, books, and texts (including this one). In such prose, the writer may use the first person and address the reader as "you." Contractions appear frequently; specialized vocabulary is kept to a minimum.

You should aim for popular diction in most of the writing you do—in and out of college. Also keep in mind that an abrupt downshift to slang (*freaked out* instead of *lost control*) or a sudden turn to highly formal language (*myocardial infarction* instead of *heart attack*) will disconcert readers and undermine your credibility.

Informal Diction

Informal diction, which conveys a sense of everyday speech, is friendly and casual. First-person and second-person pronouns are common, as are contractions and fragments. Colloquial expressions (*rub the wrong way*) and slang (*You wimp*) are used freely. Informal diction isn't appropriate for academic papers, except where it is used to indicate *someone else's* speech.

Avoid Words That Overstate or Understate

When revising, be on the lookout for **doublespeak,** language that deliberately *overstates* or *understates* reality. Here's an example of each.

In their correspondence, Public Works Departments often refer to "ground-mounted confirmatory route markers"—a grandiose way of saying "road signs." Other organizations go to the other extreme and use **euphemisms,** words that minimize something's genuine gravity or importance. Hospital officials, for instance, sometimes call deaths resulting from staff negligence "unanticipated therapeutic misadventures." When revising, check that you haven't used words that exaggerate or downplay something's significance.

Select Words With Appropriate Connotations

Mark Twain once said, "The difference between the right word and the almost right word is the difference between lightning and the lightning bug." Even two words listed as synonyms in a dictionary or thesaurus can differ in meaning in important ways.

The dictionary meaning of a word is its **denotation.** The word *motorcycle*, for example, is defined as "a two- or three-wheeled vehicle propelled by an internal-combustion engine that resembles a bicycle, but is usually larger and heavier, and often has two saddles." Yet, how many of us think of a motorcycle in these terms? Certainly, there is more to a word than its denotation. A word also comes surrounded by **connotations**—associated sensations, emotions, images, and ideas. For some, the word *motorcycle* probably calls to mind danger and noise. For motorcyclists themselves, the word most likely summons pleasant memories of high-speed movement through the open air.

Given the wide range of responses that any one word can elicit, you need to be sensitive to each word's shades of meaning, so you can judge when to use it rather than some other word. Examine the following word series to get a better feel for the subtle but often critical differences between similar words:

contribution, donation, handout

quiet, reserved, closemouthed

everyday, common, trite

follower, disciple, groupie

Notice the extent to which words' connotations create different impressions in these two examples:

> The young woman emerged from the interview, her face *aglow*. Moving *briskly* to the coatrack, she *tossed* her raincoat over one arm. After a *carefree* "Thank you" to the receptionist, she *glided* from the room.

> The young woman emerged from the interview, her face *aflame*. Moving *hurriedly* to the coatrack, she *flung* her raincoat over one arm. After a *perfunctory* "Thank you" to the receptionist, she *bolted* from the room.

In the first paragraph, the words *aglow, carefree,* and *glided* have positive connotations, so the reader surmises that the interview was a success. In contrast, the second paragraph contains words loaded with negative connotations: *aflame, perfunctory,* and *bolted.* Reading this paragraph, the reader assumes something went awry.

A thesaurus can help you select words with the right connotations. Just look up any word with which you aren't satisfied, and you'll find a list of synonyms. To be safe, stay away from unfamiliar words. Otherwise, you stand a good chance of using a word incorrectly and creating a howler. Several years ago, one of our students wrote in an essay, "I wanted to *bequeath* the party by midnight."

What he meant was that he wanted to "*leave* the party by midnight." He had, though, already used the word *leave* several times so, looking for a synonym, he turned to the thesaurus where he came across the word *bequeath*. But writing "I wanted to *bequeath* the party by midnight" doesn't work because *bequeath* means to leave property or goods by means of a will. Our advice? Choose only those words whose nuances you understand.

Use Specific Rather Than General Words

Besides carrying the right connotations, words should be **specific** rather than general. That is, they must avoid vagueness and ambiguity by referring to *particular* people, animals, events, objects, and phenomena. If they don't, readers may misinterpret what you mean.

Assume you're writing an essay about the demise of neighborhood movie houses. If, at one point, you refer to the "theaters' poor facilities," readers may imagine you're referring to faulty sound quality and projection. If you mean the theaters' messy physical surroundings, you need specific language to send the right message: wads of gum stuck under the seats, crushed popcorn tubs everywhere, a sticky film coating the floor. Precise words like these eliminate confusion.

Besides clarifying meaning, specific words enliven writing and make it more convincing. Compare these two paragraphs:

Original

Sponsored by a charitable organization, a group of children from a nearby town visited a theme park. The kids had a great time. They went on several rides and ate a variety of foods. Reporters and a TV crew shared in the fun.

Revised

Sponsored by the United Glendale Charities, twenty-five underprivileged Glendale grade-schoolers visited the Universe of Fun Themepark. The kids had a great time. They roller-coastered through a meteor shower on the Space Probe, encountered a giant squid on the Submarine Voyage, and screamed their way past coffins and ghosts in the House of Horrors. At the International Cuisine arcade, they sampled foods ranging from Hawaiian poi to German strudel. Reporters from the *Texas Herald* and a camera crew from WGLD, the Glendale cable station, shared in the fun.

You may have noticed that the specific words in the second paragraph provide answers to "which," "how," and similar questions. In contrast, when reading the first paragraph, you probably wondered, "*Which* charitable organization? *Which* theme park? *Which* rides?" Similarly, you may have asked, "*How* large a group? *How* young were the kids?" Specific language also answers "In what way?" The revised paragraph details *in what way* the children "had a great time." They didn't just eat "a variety of foods." Rather, they "sampled foods ranging from Hawaiian poi to German strudel." So, when you revise, check to make sure that your wording doesn't leave unanswered questions like "How?" "Why?" and "In what way?" (For more on making writing specific, see pages 47–48 and 66–68.)

Revising Sentences and Words 121

Use Concrete Rather Than Abstract Words

Whereas general language fails to bring a clear picture into focus, **abstract words** convey almost no picture at all. **Concrete words,** however, relay strong images and sensations; the reader can almost see, hear, taste, smell, and touch what's being described.

When you revise, provide the most concrete words possible. If you're not sure whether a word is sufficiently concrete, try to figure out where it fits on the *ladder of abstraction:*

Most abstract
Entertainment
Amusement park entertainment
Amusement park ride
Roller-coaster ride
Roller-coaster ride that simulates space flight
The Space Probe ride at Universe of Fun Themepark
Least abstract

In general, try to use words low on the ladder, words that make experience concrete. In particular, beware of empty abstractions that sound important but convey little. *Truth, beauty,* and *justice* are just a few such words. Their meaning, heavily dependent on subjective experience and personal opinion, varies from individual to individual.

Of course, we don't mean that you should never use abstract words. Sometimes they're necessary—especially when your discussion probes just how open such words are to interpretation. Remember, though: Abstract words remain foggy until you provide detailed explanation and concrete examples.

Use Strong Verbs

Because a verb is the source of action in a sentence, it carries more weight than any other element. Replacing weak verbs and nouns with **strong verbs** is, then, another way to tighten and energize language. Consider the following strategies.

Replace *To Be* and Linking Verbs with Action Verbs

Overreliance on *to be* verbs (*is, were, has been,* and so on) tends to stretch sentences, making them flat and wordy. The same is true of motionless **linking verbs** such as *appear, become, sound, feel, look,* and *seem.* Since these verbs don't communicate any action, more words are required to complete their meaning and explain what is happening. Even *to be* verb forms combined with present participles (*is laughing, were running*) are weaker than bare **action verbs** (*laughs, ran*). Similarly, linking verbs combined with adjectives (*becomes shiny, seemed offensive*) aren't as vigorous as the action verb alone (*shines, offended*). Look how much more effective a paragraph becomes when weak verbs are replaced with dynamic ones:

Original

   The waves *were* so high that the boat *was* nearly *tipping* on end. The wind *felt* rough against our faces, and the salt spray *became* so strong that we *felt* our breath *would be* cut off. Suddenly, in the air *was* the sound I had dreaded most—the snap of the rigging. I *felt* panicky.

Revised

   The waves *towered* until the boat nearly *tipped* on end. The wind *lashed* our faces, while the salt spray *filled* our throats and *cut* off our breath. Suddenly, the sound I had dreaded most *splintered* the air—the snap of the rigging. Panic *gripped* me.

The second paragraph is not only less wordy; it's also more vivid.

When you revise, look closely at your verbs. If you find too many *to be* and linking verb forms, ask yourself, "What's happening in the sentence?" Your response will help you substitute stronger verbs that will make your writing more compelling.

Change Passive Verbs to Active Ones

To be verb forms (*is, has been,* and so on) may also be combined with a past participle (*cooked, stung*), resulting in a **passive verb.** A passive verb creates a sentence structure in which the subject is *acted on* and, therefore, is placed in a secondary or passive position. In contrast, the subject of an **active verb** *performs* the action. Consider the following active and passive forms:

Passive	Active
A suggestion was made by the instructor that the project plan be revised by the students.	The instructor suggested that the students revise the project plan.
The employees' grievances will be considered by the union-management team when contract terms are being negotiated.	The union-management team will consider employees' grievances when negotiating contract terms.

Although they're not grammatically incorrect, passive verbs generally weaken writing, making it wordy and stiffly formal. Sometimes, though, it makes sense to use the passive voice. Perhaps you don't know who performed an action. ("When I returned to my car, I noticed the door had been dented.") Or you may want to emphasize an event, not the agent responsible for the event. For example, in an article about academic dishonesty on your campus, you might deliberately use the passive voice: "Every semester, research papers are plagiarized and lab reports falsified."

Unfortunately, corporations, government agencies, and other institutions often use the passive voice to avoid taking responsibility for controversial actions. Notice how easily the passive conceals the agent: "The rabbits were injected with a cancer-causing chemical."

Because the passive voice *is* associated with "official" writing, you may think it sounds scholarly and impressive. It doesn't. Unless you have good reason for de-emphasizing the agent, change passive verbs to active ones.

Replace Weak Verb-Noun Combinations

Just as *to be*, linking, and passive verbs tend to lengthen sentences needlessly, so do weak verb-noun combinations. Whenever possible, replace such combinations with their strong verb counterparts. Change "made an estimate" to "estimated," "gave approval" to "approved." Notice how revision tightens these sentences, making them livelier and less pretentious:

Original They *were* of the *belief* that the report was due next week.
Revised   They *believed* the report was due next week.

Original The technical adviser *effected* a *replacement* of the system.
Revised   The technical advisor *replaced* the system.

Delete Unnecessary Adverbs

Strong verbs can further tighten your writing by ridding it of unnecessary adverbs. "She *strolled* down the path" conveys the same message as "She *walked slowly* and *leisurely* down the path"—but more economically. Similarly, why write "The crime *was extremely difficult* for the police to solve" when you can simply write "The crime *mystified* the police"?

Adverbs such as *extremely, really,* and *very* usually weaken writing. Although they are called "intensifiers," they make writing less, not more, intense. Notice that the following sentence reads more emphatically *without* the intensifier:

Original Although the professor's lectures are controversial, no one denies that they are *really* brilliant.
Revised   Although the professor's lectures are controversial, no one denies that they are brilliant.

"Qualifiers" such as *quite, rather,* and *somewhat* also tend to weaken writing. When you spot one, try to delete it:

Original When planning a summer trip to the mountains, remember to pack warm clothes; it turns *quite* cool at night.
Revised   When planning a summer trip to the mountains, remember to pack warm clothes; it turns cool at night.

Use Original Figures of Speech

Another strategy for adding vitality to your writing is to create imaginative, nonliteral comparisons, called **figures of speech.** For example, you might describe midsummer humidity this way: "Going from an air-conditioned building to the street is like being hit in the face with peanut butter." Or you might describe someone's raw, sunburned face by saying it is "as red as a skinned tomato." Notice that in both cases the comparisons yoke essentially dissimilar things (humidity and peanut butter, a face and a tomato). Such unexpected connections surprise readers and help keep their interest.

Figures of speech also tighten writing. Since they create sharp images in the reader's mind, you don't need many words to convey as much information. If someone writes "My teenage years were like perpetual root canal," the reader immediately knows how painful and never-ending the author found adolescence.

Similes, Metaphors, Personification

Figures of speech come in several varieties. A **simile** is a direct comparison of two unlike things using the word *like* or *as:* "The moon brightened the yard *like* a floodlight." In a **metaphor,** the comparison is implied rather than directly stated: "The girl's *barbed-wire hair* set off *electric shocks* in her parents." In **personification,** an inanimate object is given human characteristics: "The couple robbed the store without noticing a silent, hidden eyewitness who later would tell all—a video camera." (For more on figures of speech, see pages 159–60.)

Avoid Clichés

Trite and overused, some figures of speech signal a lack of imagination: *a tough nut to crack, cool as a cucumber, green with envy.* Such expressions, called **clichés,** are so predictable that you can hear the first few words (*Life is a bowl of . . .*) and fill in the rest (*cherries*). Clichés lull writer and reader alike into passivity since they encourage rote, habitual thinking.

When revising, either eliminate tired figures of speech or give them an unexpected twist. For example, seeking a humorous effect, you might write "Beneath his rough exterior beat a heart of lead" (instead of "gold"); rather than "Last but not least," you might write "Last but also least."

Two Other Cautions

First, if you include figures of speech, *don't pile one on top of the other,* as in the following sentence:

> Whenever the dorm residents prepared for the first party of the season, hairdryers howled like a windstorm, hairspray rained down in torrents, stereos vibrated like an earthquake, and shouts of excitement shook the walls like an avalanche.

Second, guard against *illogical* or *mixed* figures of speech. In the following example, note the ludicrous and contradictory comparisons:

> They rode the roller coaster of high finance, dodging bullets and avoiding ambushes from those trying to lasso their streak of good luck.

To detect outlandish comparisons, visualize each figure of speech. If it calls up some unintentionally humorous or impossible image, revise or eliminate it.

Avoid Sexist Language

Sexist language gives the impression that one sex is more important, powerful, or valuable than the other. You may have noticed such language in certain reading selections in this book—for example, selections that refer to the average person as *he*. Some of these essays were written before people became alert to sexist overtones; others reveal the tenacity of long-standing habits and attitudes. Fortunately, a growing number of writers—female and male—are replacing sexist language with **gender-neutral** or **nonsexist** terms that convey no sexual prejudice. You, too, can avoid sexist language. But to do so, you need to be aware of the situations in which it is apt to occur.

Sexist Vocabulary

Using nonsexist vocabulary means staying away from terms that demean or exclude one of the sexes. Such slang words as *stud, jock, chick,* and *fox* portray people as one-dimensional. Just as adult males should be called *men,* adult females should be referred to as *women,* not *girls.* Similarly, men shouldn't be empowered with professional and honorary titles while professional women are assigned only personal titles. Why, for example, should Ronald Reagan have been referred to as *President* Reagan while the Prime Minister of England, Margaret Thatcher, was called *Mrs.* Thatcher? In addition, consider replacing *Mrs.* and *Miss* with *Ms.*; like *Mr., Ms.* doesn't indicate marital status.

Be alert as well to the fact that words not inherently sexist can become so in certain contexts. Asking "What does the *man* in the street think of the teachers' strike?" excludes the possibility of asking women for their reactions.

Because language in our culture tends to exclude women rather than men, we list here a number of common words that exclude women. When you write (or speak), make an effort to use the more inclusive alternatives given.

Sexist	Nonsexist
the average guy	the average person
chairman	chairperson, chair
congressman	congressional representative
fireman	fire fighter
foreman	supervisor
layman	layperson
mailman	mail carrier, letter carrier
mankind, man	people, humans, human beings
policeman	police officer
salesman	salesperson
statesman	diplomat
spokesman	spokesperson
workmen	workers

Also, be on the lookout for phrases that suggest a given profession or talent is unusual for someone of a particular sex: *woman judge, woman doctor, male secretary, male nurse.*

Sexist Pronoun Use

Indefinite singular nouns—those representing a general group of people consisting of both genders—can lead to **sexist pronoun use:** "On *his* first day of school, a young child often experiences separation anxiety," or "Each professor should be responsible for monitoring *his* own students' progress." These sentences exclude female children and female professors from consideration, although the situations being described apply equally to them. But writing "On *her* first day of school, a young child often experiences separation anxiety" or "Each professor should be responsible for monitoring *her* own students' progress" is similarly sexist because the language excludes males.

Indefinite *pronouns* such as *anyone, each,* and *everybody* may also pave the way to sexist language. Although such pronouns often refer to a number of individuals, they are considered singular. So, wanting to be grammatically correct, you may write a sentence like the following: "Everybody wants *his* favorite candidate to win." The sentence, however, is sexist because *everybody* is certainly not restricted to men. But writing "Everybody wants *her* candidate to win" is equally sexist because now males aren't included.

Here's one way to avoid these kinds of sexist constructions: Use *both* male and female pronouns, instead of just one or the other. For example, you could write "On *his or her* first day of school, a young child often experiences separation anxiety" or "Everybody wants *his or her* favorite candidate to win." If you use both pronouns, you might try to vary their order; that is, alternate *he/she* with *she/he, his or her* with *her or his,* and so on. Another approach is to use *s/he* in place of *he* or *she* alone. A third possibility is to use the gender-neutral pronouns *they, their,* or *themselves:* "Everybody wants *their* favorite candidate to win." Be warned, though. Some people object to using these plural pronouns with singular indefinite pronouns, even though the practice is common in everyday speech. To be on the safe side, ask your instructors if they object to any of the approaches described here. If not, feel free to choose whichever nonsexist construction seems most graceful and least obtrusive.

If you're still unhappy with the result, two alternative strategies enable you to eliminate the need for *any* gender-marked singular pronouns. First, you can change singular general nouns or indefinite pronouns to their plural equivalents and then use nonsexist plural pronouns:

Original   A *workaholic* feels anxious when *he* isn't involved in a task-related project.
Revised   *Workaholics* feel anxious when *they*'re not involved in task-related projects.

Original   *Everyone* in the room expressed *his* opinion freely.
Revised   *Those* in the room expressed *their* opinions freely.

Revising Sentences and Words

Second, you can recast the sentence to omit the singular pronoun:

Original A *manager* usually spends part of each day settling squabbles among *his* staff.
Revised A manager usually spends part of each day settling *staff squabbles*.

Original No *one* wants *his* taxes raised.
Revised No one wants *to pay more taxes*.

The following checklist is designed to help you and your readers evaluate the words in a draft. (Activities at the end of the chapter will refer you to this checklist when you revise several essays.) To see how one student, Harriet Davids, used the checklist when revising, turn to page 128.

> ✓ REVISE WORDS: A CHECKLIST
>
> ▫ Which words seem inconsistent with the essay's tone? What words would be more appropriate?
>
> ▫ Where is language overly formal? Which words are unnecessarily long or specialized? Where is language too informal (colloquial or slangy)? Where do unintended shifts in diction level create a jarring effect?
>
> ▫ Which words overstate? Which understate? What alternatives would be less misleading?
>
> ▫ Which words carry connotations unsuited to the essay's purpose and tone? What synonyms would be more appropriate?
>
> ▫ Where would more specific and concrete words add vitality and clarify meaning?
>
> ▫ Where could weak verbs be replaced by vigorous ones? Which *to be* and linking verb forms should be changed to action verbs? Which passive verbs could be replaced by active ones? Where could a noun-verb combination be replaced by a strong verb?
>
> ▫ Which adverbs, especially intensifiers (*very*) and qualifiers (*quite*), could be eliminated?
>
> ▫ Where would original similes, metaphors, and personifications add power? Which figures of speech are hackneyed, illogical, or mixed? How could these problems be fixed?
>
> ▫ Where does sexist language appear? What gender-neutral terms could replace sexist ones? How could sexist pronouns be eliminated?

SAMPLE STUDENT REVISION OF SENTENCES AND WORDS

Reprinted here is the introduction to Harriet Davids's first draft—as it looked after she entered on a word processor the changes she made in overall meaning, structure, and paragraph development (see page 97). To help identify problems with words and sentences, Harriet asked someone in her editing group to read the revised version aloud. Then she welcomed comments from the group. The marginal notes indicate her ranking of those comments in order of importance. The above-line changes show how Harriet revised in response to these suggestions for improving the paragraph's sentences and words.

① *Combine into one sentence idea of 50s/60s parents and TV shows*

② *Make each family's problems a separate sentence*

③ *Use stronger verbs (not "telling")*

④ *Make "dangerous situations" more specific*

~~In the 50s and 60s, parents had it easy,~~ *Reruns of* TV comedies ~~of that period~~ *from the 50s and 60s dramatize the kinds of problems that parents used to have.* ~~show~~ The Cleavers scold~~ing~~ Beaver about his dirty hands, the Andersons *ground for not* ~~telling~~ Bud, to do his homework, ~~and~~ the Nelsons *dock* ~~telling~~ Ricky, *'s allowance because he forgets* to clean his room. Being a parent today is much more difficult, *then it was a generation ago.* Nowadays parents must protect their children from many things--from a growing number of distractions, from sexually explicit material, and from *life-threatening* ~~dangerous~~ situations.

(If you'd like to see Harriet's final draft, turn to page 137.)

Once you, like Harriet, have carefully revised sentences and words, your essay needs only to be edited (for errors in grammar, punctuation, and spelling) and proofread. In the next chapter, you'll read about these final steps. You'll also see a student essay that has gone through all phases of the writing process.

ACTIVITIES: REVISING SENTENCES AND WORDS

1. Revise the following wordy, muddy sentences, making them economical and clear.

    a. What a person should do before subletting a rental apartment is make sure to have the sublet agreement written up in a formal contract.
    b. In high school, it often happens that young people deny liking poetry because of the fact that they fear running the risk of having people mock or make fun of them because they actually enjoy poetry.
    c. In light of the fact that college students are rare in my home neighborhood, being a college student gives me immediate and instant status.
    d. There were a number of people who have made the observation that the new wing of the library looks similar in appearance to several nearby buildings with considerable historical significance.
    e. It was, in my opinion, an apt comment when the professor noted that most of the students who complain about how demanding the requirements of a course are tend to work at part-time or even full-time jobs.

2. Using only simple or simple and compound sentences, write a paragraph based on one of the following topic sentences. Then rewrite the paragraph, making some of the sentences complex and others compound-complex. Examine your two versions of the paragraph. What differences do you see in meaning and emphasis?

    a. The campus parking lot is dangerous at night.
    b. Some students have trouble getting along with their roommates.
    c. Silent body language speaks loudly.
    d. Getting on a teacher's good side is an easily mastered skill.

3. Write four new versions of each of the following sentence sets. Each version, consisting of one sentence, should illustrate a different pattern: subject-verb-modifier, modifiers first, embedded modifiers, distributed modifiers. (See pages 111–12 for a model of this activity.)

    a. The student slumps at her desk. She awaits her final exam. Her hair is an uncombed tangle. Her eyes are glazed from lack of sleep. Her desk is strewn with five sharpened pencils.

b. Some men experiment with their appearance. They grow beards and mustaches. They wear unusual jewelry. Some even get tattooed.
c. Both former long-distance runners are only in their thirties. They are dying of heart disease. They started taking muscle-building steroids in their teens.

4. The following sentences could be more emphatic. Examine each one to determine its focus; then revise the sentence, using one of the following strategies: placing the most important item first or last, parallelism, inverted word order, a fragment. Try to use a different strategy in each sentence.

   a. The old stallion's mane was tangled, and he had chipped hooves, and his coat was scraggly.
   b. Most of us find rude salespeople difficult to deal with.
   c. The politician promises, "I'll solve all your problems."
   d. We meet female stereotypes such as the gold digger, the dangerous vixen, and the "girl next door" in the movies.
   e. It's a wise teacher who encourages discussion of controversial issues in the classroom.

5. The following paragraph is pretentious and murky. Revise to make it crisp and clear.

   Since its founding, the student senate on this campus has maintained essentially one goal: to upgrade the quality of its student-related services. Two years ago, the senate, supported by the opinions of three consultants provided by the National Council of Student Governing Boards, was confident it was operating from a base of quality but felt that, if given additional monetary support from the administration, a significant improvement in student services would be facilitated. This was a valid prediction, for that is exactly what transpired in the past fifteen months once additional monetary resources were, in fact, allocated by the administration to the senate and its activities.

6. Write a sentence for each word in the series that follows, making sure your details reinforce each word's connotations:

   a. chubby, voluptuous, portly
   b. stroll, trudge, loiter
   c. turmoil, anarchy, hubbub

7. Write three versions of a brief letter voicing a complaint to a store, a person, or an organization. One version should be charged with negative connotations; the other should "soft pedal" the problem. The final version should present your complaint using neutral, objective words. Which letter do you prefer? Why?

Revising Sentences and Words

8. Describe each of the following in one or two sentences, using a creative figure of speech to convey each item's distinctive quality:

   a. a baby's hand
   b. a pile of dead leaves
   c. a sophisticated personal computer
   d. an empty room
   e. an old car

9. Enliven the following dull, vague sentences. Use your knowledge of sentence structure to dramatize key elements. Also, replace weak verbs with vigorous ones and make language more specific and concrete.

   a. I got sick on the holiday.
   b. He stopped the car at the crowded intersection.
   c. A bird appeared in the corner of the yard.
   d. The class grew restless.
   e. The TV broadcaster put on a concerned air as she announced the tragedy.

10. The following paragraph contains too many linking verbs, passives, adverbs, and prepositions. In addition, noun forms are sometimes used where their verb counterparts would be more effective. Revise the paragraph by eliminating unnecessary prepositions and providing more vigorous verbs. Then add specific, concrete words that dramatize what is being described.

    The farmers in the area conducted a meeting during which they formulated a discussion of the vandalism problem in the county in which they live. They made the estimate that, on the average, each of them had at least an acre of crops destroyed the past few weekends by gangs of motorcylists who have been driving maliciously over their land. The increase in such vandalism has been caused by the encroachment of the suburbs on rural areas.

11. Revise the following sentences to eliminate sexist language.

   a. The manager of a convenience store has to guard his cash register carefully.
   b. When I broke my arm in a car accident, a male nurse, aided by a physician's assistant, treated my injury.
   c. All of us should contact our congressman if we're not satisfied with his performance.
   d. The chemistry professors agree that nobody should have to buy her own Bunsen burner.

An important note: When revising essay drafts in activities 12 and 13, don't worry too much about grammar, punctuation, and spelling. However, do save your revisions, so you can focus on these matters after reading the next chapter.

12. In response to activity 1 in Chapter 7 (page 98), you revised the overall meaning, structure, and paragraph development of Harriet Davids's first draft. Find that revision so that you can now focus on its sentences and words. Get together with at least one other person and ask yourselves questions like these: "Where should sentence type, length, or pattern be more varied?" and "Where would more specific and concrete words add vitality and clarify meaning?" For further guidance, refer to the checklists on pages 116 and 127. Summarize and rank any perceived problems in marginal annotations or a feedback chart. Then type your changes into a word processor or enter them between the lines of the draft. (Save your revision so you can edit and proofread it after reading the next chapter.)

13. Return to the draft you prepared in response to activity 2, activity 3, activity 4, or activity 5 in Chapter 7 (pages 98–100). Get together with several people and request that one of them read the draft aloud. Then, using the checklists on pages 116 and 127, ask the group members focused questions about any sentences and words that you feel need sharpening. After evaluating the feedback, revise the draft. Either key your changes into a word processor or do your revising by hand. (Save your revision so you can edit and proofread it after reading the next chapter.)

9
EDITING AND PROOFREADING

It happens all too often. A student works hard to revise an essay, reading it over, making changes (some of them extensive), refining sentences and words, all to arrive at the best version possible. Then the student types the paper and hands it in without even a glance.

Wanting to get a piece of writing off your desk is a human response to so much work. But, if you don't edit and proofread—that is, closely check your writing for grammar, spelling, and typographical errors—you run the risk of sabotaging your previous efforts. Readers may assume that a piece of writing isn't worth their time if they're jolted by surface flaws that make it difficult to read. So, to make sure that your good ideas get a fair hearing, you should do the following:

- Edit,
- Use the appropriate manuscript format, and
- Proofread.

(For hints about editing and proofreading on a word processor, see page 148 in Chapter 10.)

EDIT CAREFULLY

When revising the paper, you probably spotted some errors in grammar, punctuation, or spelling, perhaps flagging them for later correction. Now—after you're satisfied with the essay's organization, development, and style—it's time to fix these errors. It's also time to search for and correct errors that have slipped by you so far.

If you're working with pen and paper or on a typewritten or word-processed draft with handwritten annotations, use a different color ink, so your new corrections will stand out. Because most writers find it easier to locate errors on a clean copy of their text, consider retyping your draft before editing it. If you use a word processor, search for errors both on the screen and on a printout. If your software includes a spelling check, your search for misspellings will be greatly simplified. Be aware, however, that such programs may not find errors in the spelling of proper nouns, and that they won't flag errors that constitute legitimate words (for example, *he* when you meant *the* or *their* when you meant *there*).

To be a successful editor of your own work, you need two standard tools: a grammar handbook and a good dictionary. One way to keep track of the errors you're prone to make is to record them on a simple chart. Divide the chart into three columns: (1) *Error,* (2) *Rules for Correcting Error,* and (3) *Error Corrected.* When your instructor returns an essay, copy representative mistakes you've made into the first column. Look up in a handbook the rules that apply and enter them in the second column. Then, in the last column, rewrite the phrase or sentence from your paper with the error corrected. As the semester goes on, you'll develop a *personalized inventory* of writing errors to use in checking your own work.

If you're weak in spelling, make a similar inventory of spelling errors and corrections. Use four columns for this list: (1) *Word Misspelled,* (2) *Part of Word Misspelled,* (3) *Spelling Rule,* and (4) *Word Corrected.*

USE THE APPROPRIATE MANUSCRIPT FORMAT

After correcting all grammar and spelling problems, you're ready to produce the final copy. In doing so, you should follow accepted academic practice, adapted to your instructor's requirements. Most instructors will require that you type your papers. Even if this isn't the case, typed or computer-printed papers look neater, are easier to grade, and show that you have made the transition to college-level format.

The following checklist on manuscript format describes the basic rules for college essays as well as special rules for typed, computer-generated, and handwritten papers.

☑ **APPROPRIATE MANUSCRIPT FORMAT: A CHECKLIST**

Typed Papers
- Use standard-size (8-½ by 11 inches), good-quality white typing paper. Don't use "erasable" paper or onion skin. The result is often a smudged look, and the instructor may have a difficult time getting the paper to accept inked-in comments.

- Use a typewriter with a standard type style. Avoid script or other hard-to-read typefaces.
- Make sure the typewriter prints in dark black ink. Keep the type clean and change the ribbon as needed.
- Double-space throughout the paper, and type on only one side of the page.

Computer-Generated Papers
- Use good-quality white paper.
- Never hand in a written piece on spread-sheet paper. Tear off sheet edges at the perforations, separate the pages, and arrange them in correct order. Don't rip the paper from the printer, rush to class, and hand in the accordion-folded sheets!
- Double-space throughout the paper, and make sure your printer uses legible, easy-to-read characters. An ink-jet, daisy wheel, or laser printer is best, but a dot-matrix printer that approximates "letter quality" is also acceptable.

Handwritten Papers
- Use white, lined paper with a margin rule on the left side. The paper may have holes for insertion in a notebook, but don't rip pages out of a spiral notebook unless there are perforations that permit you to do so neatly.
- Use only standard-size paper: 8-½ by 10 or 11 inches.
- Write on only one side of the page, using dark blue or black ink, never pencil.
- Don't skip lines, except between paragraphs.
- Write legibly and carefully, in a moderate size. Eliminate exaggerated mannerisms from your handwriting, such as curlicues and extreme slants.

All Papers
- Leave adequate margins: one inch at the top and bottom and right and left of each page should be sufficient.
- If you include a title page, place the title about one-third of the way down the page. Enter the title, and double-space between lines of the title and your name. Course and section, instructor's name, and date, on separate lines, are double-spaced and centered.
- If you don't include a title page, use a standard heading, as specified by your instructor, at the top of the first page. One standard format for the heading consists of your name, the instructor's name, the course title and number, and the date on double-spaced lines in the upper-left corner, an inch from the top.

> - Center the title of your paper one double space below the heading. Capitalize only the first letters of all main words. Don't use all caps, underlining, or quotation marks. Double-space a title having more than one line.
> - Double-space between the title and the first paragraph of your essay.
> - With the exception of the title page, number each page, including the first, by putting an arabic numeral in the upper-right corner one-half inch below the top of the page. Avoid putting *p.* or *page* with the page number. Include your last name before each page number, in case pages become separated.
> - Indent the first line of each paragraph five spaces.
> - Paper clip or staple your essay's pages, placing the outline wherever your instructor requests. Don't use the corner "rip and fold" method; it doesn't hold, and it spoils the look of a carefully typed paper.
> - Don't use a report cover unless your instructor requests it.
>
> (For examples of correct manuscript format, see pages 137 and 516.)

PROOFREAD CLOSELY

Proofreading means checking your final copy carefully for "typos" or other mistakes. One trick is to read your material backwards: If you read from the end of each paragraph to the beginning, you can focus on each word individually to make sure no letters have been left out or transposed. This technique prevents you from getting caught up in the flow of ideas and missing small defects, which is easy to do when you've read your own words many times.

What should you do when you find a typo? Simply use a pen with dark ink to make an above-line correction. The following standard proofreader's marks will help you indicate some common types of corrections:

Proofreader's Mark	Meaning	Example
∧	insert missing letter or word	televsion
ℓ	delete	reports the the findings
∾	reverse order	the gang's here all
¶	start new paragraph	to dry. Next, put
#	add space	the girls
⌢	close up space	boy cott

If you make so many corrections on a page that it begins to look like a draft, retype the page. If you're using a computer, make the corrections on the disk and reprint the page.

Editing and Proofreading 137

STUDENT ESSAY: FROM PREWRITING THROUGH PROOFREADING

In the last several chapters, we've taken you through the various stages in the writing process—from prewriting to proofreading. You've seen how Harriet Davids used prewriting (pages 26–28 and 32–33) and outlining (pages 33–34) to arrive at her first draft (pages 80–81). You also saw how Harriet revised, first, her draft's overall meaning and paragraph development (page 97) and, second, its sentences and words (page 128). In this chapter, you'll look at Harriet's final draft—the paper she submitted to her instructor after completing all the stages of the writing process.

Harriet, a thirty-eight-year-old college student and mother of two teenagers, wanted to write an informative paper with a straightforward, serious tone. While preparing her essay, she kept in mind that her audience would include her course instructor as well as her classmates, most of them considerably younger than she. This is the assignment that prompted Harriet's essay:

> Because the world these days is a difficult, even dangerous place, parents understandably worry about their children. Write an essay supporting the idea that today's world is, in many ways, hostile—particularly to children.

Harriet's essay is annotated so you can see how it illustrates the essay format described in Chapter 6 (page 79). As you read the essay, try to determine how well it reflects the principles of effective writing. The commentary following the paper will help you look at the essay more closely and give you some sense of the way Harriet went about revising her first draft.

Harriet Davids
Professor Kinne
College Composition, Section 203
October 4, 19 ___

Challenges for Today's Parents

1   Reruns of situation comedies from the 1950s and early 1960s dramatize the kinds of problems that parents used to have with their children. The Cleavers scold Beaver for not washing his hands before dinner; the Andersons ground Bud for not doing his homework; the Nelsons dock little Ricky's allowance because he keeps forgetting to clean his room. But times have changed dramatically. Being a parent today is much more difficult than it was a generation ago. Parents nowadays must protect their children from a growing number of distractions, from sexually explicit material, and from life-threatening situations.

Introduction

Thesis

Plan of development

First supporting paragraph

Topic sentence

Today's parents must try, first of all, to control all the new distractions that tempt children away from schoolwork. At home, a child may have a room furnished with a stereo and television. Not many young people can resist the urge to listen to a CD or watch MTV--especially if it is time to do schoolwork. Outside the home, the distractions are even more alluring. Children no longer "hang out" on a neighborhood corner within earshot of Mom or Dad's reminder to come in and do homework. Instead, they congregate in vast shopping malls, buzzing video arcades, and gleaming fast-food restaurants. Parents and school assignments have obvious difficulty competing with such enticing alternatives.

Second supporting paragraph

Topic sentence with link to previous paragraph

Besides dealing with these distractions, parents have to shield their children from a flood of sexually explicit materials. Today, children can find sex magazines and pornographic paperbacks in the same corner store that once offered only comics and candy. Children will not see the fuzzily photographed nudes that a previous generation did but will encounter the hard-core raunchiness of <u>Hustler</u> or <u>Penthouse</u>. Moreover, the movies young people attend often focus on highly sexual situations. It is difficult to teach children traditional values when films show teachers seducing students and young people treating sex as a casual sport. An even more difficult matter for parents is the heavily sexual content of programs on television. With just a flick of the dial, children can see soap-opera stars cavorting in bed or watch cable programs where nudity is common.

Third supporting paragraph

Topic sentence with emphasis signal

Most disturbing to parents today, however, is the increase in life-threatening dangers that face young people. When children are small, parents fear that their youngsters may be victims of violence. Every news program seems to carry a report about a mass murderer who preys on young girls, a deviant who has buried six boys in his backyard, or an organized child pornography ring that molests preschoolers. When children are older, parents begin to worry about their kids' use of drugs. Peer pressure to experiment with drugs is often stronger than parents' warnings. This pressure to experiment can be fatal. Finally, even if young people escape the hazards associated with drugs, they must still resist the pressure to drink. Although alcohol has always held an attraction for teenagers, reports indicate that they are drinking more than ever before. As many parents know, the consequences of this attraction can be deadly --especially when drinking is combined with driving.

Editing and Proofreading   139

5   Within one generation, the world as a place to raise children has changed dramatically. One wonders how yesterday's parents would have dealt with today's problems. Could the Andersons have kept Bud away from MTV? Could the Nelsons have shielded little Ricky from sexually explicit material? Could the Cleavers have protected Beaver from drugs and alcohol? Parents must be aware of all these distractions and dangers yet be willing to give their children the freedom they need to become responsible adults. It is not an easy task.

Conclusion

References to TV shows recall introduction

Commentary

Introduction and Thesis

The opening paragraph attracts readers' interest by recalling several vintage television shows that have almost become part of our cultural heritage. Harriet begins with these examples from the past because they offer such a sharp contrast to the present, thus underscoring the idea expressed in her *thesis*: "Being a parent today is much more difficult than it was a generation ago." Opening in this way, with material that serves as a striking contrast to what follows, is a common and effective strategy. Note, too, that Harriet's thesis states the paper's subject (being a parent) as well as her attitude toward the subject (the job is more demanding that it was years ago).

Plan of Development

Harriet follows her thesis with a *plan of development* that anticipates the three major points to be covered in the essay's supporting paragraphs. Unfortunately, this particular plan of development is somewhat mechanical, with the major points being trotted past the reader in one long, awkward sentence. To deal with the problem, Harriet could have rewritten the sentence or eliminated the plan of development altogether, ending the introduction with her thesis.

Patterns of Development

Although Harriet develops her thesis primarily through *examples*, she also draws on two other patterns of development. The whole paper implies a *contrast* between the way life and parenting are now and the way they used to be. The essay also contains an element of *causal analysis* since all the factors that Harriet cites affect children and the way they are raised.

Purpose, Audience, Tone, and Point of View

Give the essay's *purpose* and *audience*, Harriet adopts a serious *tone*, providing no-nonsense evidence to support her thesis. Note, too, that she uses the *third-person point of view*. Although she writes from the perspective of a mother of two teenage daughters, she doesn't write in the first person or refer specifically to her own experiences and those of her daughters. She adopts this objective stance because she wants to keep the focus on the issue rather than on her family.

What if Harriet had been asked by her daughters' school newspaper to write a humorous column about the trials and tribulations that parents face raising children? Aiming for a different tone, purpose, and audience, Harriet probably would have taken another approach. Drawing upon her personal experience, she might have confessed how she survives MTV's flash and dazzle, as well as the din of stereos blasting rock music at all hours: she stuffs her ears with cotton, hides her daughters' tapes, and cuts off the electricity. This material—with its first-person perspective, exaggeration, and light tone—would be appropriate.

Organization

Structuring the essay around a series of *relevant* and *specific examples,* Harriet uses *emphatic order* to sequence the paper's three main points: that a growing number of distractions, sexually explicit materials, and life-threatening situations make parenting difficult nowadays. The third supporting paragraph begins with the words "Most disturbing to parents today . . . ," signaling that Harriet feels particular concern about the physical dangers children face. Moreover, she uses basic organizational strategies to sequence the supporting examples within each paragraph. The details in the first supporting paragraph are organized *spatially,* starting with distractions at home and moving to those outside the home. The second supporting paragraph arranges examples *emphatically.* Harriet starts with sexually explicit publications and ends with the "even more difficult matter" of sexuality on television. The third and final supporting paragraph is organized *chronologically;* it begins by discussing dangers to small children and concludes by talking about teenagers.

The essay also displays Harriet's familiarity with other kinds of organizational strategies. Each supporting paragraph opens with a *topic sentence.* Further, *signal devices* are used throughout the paper to show the relationship among ideas: *transitions* ("*Instead,* they congregate in vast shopping malls"; "*Moreover,* the movies young people attend often focus on highly sexual situations"); *repetition* ("*sexual* situations" and "*sexual* content"); *synonyms* ("distractions . . . enticing alternatives" and "life-threatening . . . fatal"); *pronouns* ("young people . . . *they*"); and *bridging sentences* ("Besides dealing with these distractions, parents have to shield their children from a flood of sexually explicit materials").

A Minor Problem

Harriet's efforts to write a well-organized essay result in a somewhat predictable structure. It might have been better had she rewritten one of the paragraphs, perhaps embedding the topic sentence in the middle of the paragraph or saving it for the end. Similarly, Harriet's signal devices are a little heavy-handed. Even so, an essay with a sharp focus and clear signals is preferable to one with a confusing or inaccessible structure. As she gains more experience, Harriet can work on making the structure of her essays more subtle.

Conclusion

Harriet brings the essay to a satisfying *close* by reminding readers of the paper's central idea and three main points. The final paragraph also extends the essay's scope by introducing a new but related issue: that parents have to strike a balance between their need to provide limitations and their children's need for freedom.

Revising the First Draft

As you saw on pages 97 and 128, Harriet reworked her essay a number of times. For a clearer sense of her revision process, compare the final version of her conclusion (on page 139) with the original version reprinted here. Harriet wisely waited to rework her conclusion until after she had finetuned the rest of the essay. The marginal annotations, ranked in order of importance, indicate the problems that Harriet and her editing group detected in the conclusion:

1) Paragraph seems tacked on

Original Conclusion

Most adults love their children and want to be good parents. But it's difficult because the world seems stacked against young people. Even Holden Caulfield had trouble dealing with society's pressures. Parents must give their children some freedom but not so much that kids lose sight of what's important.

3) Boring sentence—too vague

2) Inappropriate reference to Holden

As soon as Harriet heard her paper read aloud during a group session, she realized her conclusion didn't work at all. Rather than bringing the essay to a pleasing finish, the final paragraph seemed like a tired afterthought. A classmate also pointed out that her allusion to *The Catcher in the Rye* misrepresented the essay's focus since Harriet discusses children of all ages, not just teens.

Keeping these points in mind, Harriet decided to scrap her original conclusion. Working at a word processor, she prepared a new, much stronger concluding paragraph. Besides eliminating the distracting reference to Holden Caulfield, she replaced the shopworn opening sentence ("Most adults love their children....") with three interesting and rhythmical questions ("Could the Andersons ... Could the Nelsons ... Could the Cleavers ... ?"). Because these questions recall the essay's main points and echo the introduction's reference to vintage television shows, they help unify Harriet's paper and bring it to a satisfying close.

These are just a few of the changes Harriet made when reworking her essay. Realizing that writing is a process, she left herself enough time to revise. She was gratified by her classmates' responses to what she had written and pleased by the lively discussion her essay provoked. Early in her composition course, Harriet learned that attention to the various stages in the writing process yields satisfying results, for writer and reader alike.

ACTIVITIES: EDITING AND PROOFREADING

1. Applying for a job, a student wrote the following letter. Edit and proofread it carefully, as if it were your own. If you have trouble spotting many grammar, spelling, and typing errors, that's a sign you need to review your grammar handbook.

Dear Mr. Eno:

    I am a sophmore at Harper College who will be returning home to Brooktown this June, hopefully, to fine a job for the the summer. One that would give me further experience in the retail field. I have heard from my freind, Sarah Snyder, that your hiring college studnets as assistant mangers, I would be greatly intrested in such a postion.

    I have quite a bit of experience in retail sales. Having worked after school in a "Dress Place" shop at Mason Mall, Pennsylvania. I started their as a sales clerk, by my second year I was serving as assistant manger.

    I am reliable and responsible, and truely enjoy sales work. Mary Carver, the owner of the "Dress Place," can verify my qualifications, she was my supervisor for two years.

    I will be visiting Brooktown from April 25 to 30. I hope to have an oppurtunity to speak to you about possible summer jobs at that time, and will be available for interview at your convience. Thank-you for you're consideration.

                                                    Sincerley,

                                                    Joan Ackerman

                                                    Joan Ackerman

2. Retrieve the revised essay you prepared in response to either activity 12 or activity 13 in Chapter 8 (page 132). Following the guidelines described on the preceding pages, edit and proofread your revision. After making whatever changes are needed, prepare your final draft of the essay, using the appropriate manuscript format. Before submitting your paper to your instructor, ask someone else to check it for grammar, spelling, and typographical errors that may have slipped by you undetected.

10
WRITING ON A WORD PROCESSOR

EVEN if you've never gone within ten feet of a computer, you'll probably have the chance to use one in college for **word processing**—that is, for writing, editing, and printing texts (or *documents* in computer talk). These days, most computers are easy to use. Text can be rearranged with only a few keystrokes; commands tend to be easy to remember; and instruction manuals are usually accurate and readable.

At your college, there's probably at least one room of computers for student use, if not several computer centers. Often, students can arrange for free computer instruction or get on-the-spot assistance as they work.

Many colleges have arrangements with computer manufacturers allowing students to buy computers at a discount. If you decide to purchase one, don't be shy about asking any computer-savvy folks you know for advice. Most computer buffs like to share their enthusiasm and their knowledge. They can recommend the kind of computer (*hardware*) and programs (*software*) best suited to your needs. Basic word-processing software (available on *floppy disks*) allows you to insert, delete, and move words, phrases, sentences, even entire sections of text. It also formats your text for margins, spacing, page numbering, and the like. In addition, many word-processing programs include spelling checks, ready-to-fill-in outline forms, and automatic footnoting options.

SOME OBSERVATIONS AND HINTS ABOUT USING A WORD PROCESSOR

There's no single way to use a word processor. Some people use one in all phases of the writing process; others save the computer for revising and editing. As you become increasingly comfortable with a word processor, you'll probably use it more and more in all stages.

Word processing is wonderfully fluid. The ease with which you can move ideas around helps you capture the often helter-skelter nature of the thinking process. After a while, writing in longhand or on a typewriter may seem slow and confining.

Here are some general tips for using a word processor to write a college essay:

- Be sure to use the computer's "save" function at frequent intervals. Otherwise, you risk losing a hefty chunk of text through a keystroke error, power failure, or system glitch.
- Always keep a backup disk of work in progress—a spare disk with a copy of your work to date.
- If you use a computer in your college's computer center, don't go to the center an hour before a paper is due expecting to produce a final draft. You may wind up with nothing to hand in but an excuse like "The computers were all taken" or "I accidentally deleted two pages." To avoid these problems, you need to plan your time wisely.
- To focus your work in each stage of the writing process, print out any material from the previous phase and move to the end of the file any material you plan to work on in the next phase.
- Before making significant on-screen changes, print out a copy of the original material. Once you have an intact version, you're free to make whatever on-screen modifications you wish; if the changes don't work out, you can still retrieve whatever you need from the original.
- Use a *single-space format* when typing so you get the maximum amount on screen. Similarly, prepare a single-spaced printout of your work (especially an outline or draft) to get a general impression of your material's overall effectiveness.
- Before asking friends or classmates to respond to your work, do a "spell check" and a "grammar check" so readers won't be distracted by mechanical errors.
- When asking readers to respond to what you've prepared, provide them with a *double-spaced* printout with wide margins. The extra space gives readers plenty of room to record their comments.

The following sections discuss ways to use a word processor in successive stages of the writing process.

Writing on a Word Processor

PREWRITE

In the prewriting stage, a computer's speed can help you capture even the most fleeting thoughts generated by, say, brainstorming, freewriting, or journal writing. For example, you might want to record your journal entries on a computer disk. Simply get down all your thoughts as fast as you can, filing the entries by date. If you work in a computer lab, save your entries on your own disk and, then, for privacy's sake, delete the entries from the lab's start-up disk or hard drive.

Generating material about a subject also moves along quickly when you use a word processor. Here's how you can proceed. Take a moment to type and then print out your purpose, audience, tone, and point of view. Having that material in front of you will keep you focused as you freewrite, brainstorm, use the mapping technique, and so on. To encourage a free and uncensored flow of ideas, try not to look at your words as you type your rough, preliminary thoughts. Instead, stare into space or turn down the screen's brightness.

Once you're ready to pull together a scratch outline of your raw material, you may find that adding, grouping, and deleting points proceed most smoothly when you work directly on screen. Indeed, you might want to experiment with any split-screen function that your software provides. Put your raw material in one window and your scratch outline in the other. With the two documents in view, you can jump from one to the other, editing either or both.

Rather than working directly on screen, you may decide to shape your prewriting by working on a printed version of your raw material. Such an approach allows you to see everything all at once, not just a screen's worth at a time. If you work from a printout, reread your rough ideas, marking points that seem workable, crossing out those that don't, and so on. Then, with your marked-up printout beside you, type your scratch outline into the computer. You can then delete your raw material from the disk since you have a copy to consult if you decide to retrieve points later on.

IDENTIFY A THESIS

The ease of computing means that you can play out all your hunches about a possible thesis. Simply type in as many versions of the thesis as you can generate. Then, if your software has a split-screen function, you can view your scratch outline in one window and the alternative thesis statements in the other. This simultaneous view of the scratch outline and alternative thesis statements helps clarify which thesis best fits the material in the scratch outline. Be sure, though, to save the alternative thesis statements; later on, you may decide that a previously rejected thesis is the most effective after all.

SUPPORT THE THESIS WITH EVIDENCE

When you're ready to generate evidence for your thesis, call up all your working material so far: your purpose, audience, tone, and point of view; your scratch outline; and your thesis. Start by moving all these items to one location at the top of the screen. Then add space between the points in your scratch outline. As you move among points, locate spots where additional evidence is needed. At such places, return to a prewriting technique to collect more facts, examples, reasons, and details. If you're using material from outside sources, key in that information as well as the names of the sources. Finally, evaluate all the evidence by printing out the material or by scrolling through it on screen. Make whatever modifications are needed.

ORGANIZE THE EVIDENCE

When moving evidence into an outline format, you'll find that the computer's flexibility helps you identify which sequence of ideas is most effective. To start, move your purpose, audience, tone, point of view, and thesis to the top of an empty screen. Underneath, place the latest version of your scratch outline, including any newly generated evidence. Next, review all the material, and decide which organizational approach (spatial, chronological, emphatic, or simple-to-complex) and which pattern of development (cause-effect, comparison-contrast, and so on) you'll use to structure the evidence. Then start moving the material around to reflect your concept of how different parts of the evidence should fit together. Finally, use tab stops or your software's outlining mode to create indentations for different levels of support. (Some software programs have a function that provides a ready-to-fill-in skeleton outline.)

WRITE THE FIRST DRAFT

Although some people write the first draft in longhand and then type it into the computer for revising, others write the first draft directly on screen. If you feel comfortable with the latter approach, you might begin by typing your purpose, audience, tone, point of view, and thesis at the top of the screen. With these considerations firmly in mind, review your outline; either print out the outline or place it in a split-screen window so you can look at it while you type your first draft in the other window.

As you draft the body paragraphs, don't waste time retyping supporting facts, statistics, anecdotes, and so forth from your outline; instead, use the computer's "cut and paste" functions to move such material into your draft. At this point, there's no need to blend in the transferred material seamlessly; you can smooth out any rough edges later. When writing the body paragraphs, you may find yourself "zapping" out several versions of the paragraph. That's fine. If you're typing, say, the third paragraph and decide the first part of the paragraph belongs at the end of the previous paragraph, just select the material to be moved, tap the appropriate keys, and relocate the sentences in question.

When you're ready to write the introductory and concluding paragraphs, scroll back through your prewriting and rough supporting evidence to see if there are any striking examples or facts that you didn't include in the body paragraphs. Some of these "leftovers" might provide an effective opening or closing. Remember, though, that the material you use to open and close the essay must fit the paper's purpose, audience, tone, point of view, and thesis. So, before typing in the introduction and conclusion, scroll through the body paragraphs to reinforce your sense of the whole essay. Then key in the essay's opening and closing paragraphs.

REVISE OVERALL MEANING, STRUCTURE, AND PARAGRAPH DEVELOPMENT

It is during revision that word processors reveal their full glory. With only a few keystrokes, for example, you can add, move, or delete words, sentences, or whole sections of text. You can recast a paragraph with ease and—if you dislike the result—make it disappear.

When reworking meaning, structure, and paragraph development, you may feel most comfortable combining longhand revision with on-screen modification. In such a case, it's a good idea to print out your draft for another look. Ask some classmates or friends to react to the draft; then synthesize their comments in a feedback chart or in marginal annotations. That done, enter by hand any changes in your draft. Finally, key in your changes and make a printout of the revised version, leaving extra space for you and others to continue revising.

Instead of working in longhand, you may feel most comfortable revising almost exclusively at the computer. If that's your preference, scroll through your entire first draft, making notes about overall meaning, structure, and paragraph development. (On another piece of paper, note any word or sentence problems you want to tackle later on.) Then, moving from paragraph to paragraph, type in your changes.

REVISE SENTENCES AND WORDS

Now you're ready to have readers respond to the essay's sentences and words. Show them the latest version of your essay and record their observations and suggestions. Also dig out any notes you made earlier about areas needing work and scroll through the essay once again, this time identifying other spots where sentences and words aren't as effective as they could be. If you're unsure which word or which version of a sentence works best in a paragraph, print out just the paragraph, including alternative options, and ask someone to help you decide. Having taken these steps, you're ready to type in your changes.

EDIT AND PROOFREAD

It's difficult to detect problems in grammar and spelling by looking at a computer screen. So, for best results, work from a printout when editing and proofreading. There is, though, some risk in seeing your draft neatly printed out; you might feel so pleased with your material's professional look that you fail to read it closely. Be sure not to shortchange this vital final stage in the writing process.

Work from a double-spaced printout that uses correct manuscript form. Be sure to take advantage of any "spelling check" and "grammar check" functions your computer might have. But remember: A spell check can't tell you that you should have used *affect* instead of *effect* or *whose* instead of *who's*. It can only flag a spelling that doesn't match *any* word in its dictionary. You may find that you can detect previously hidden mechanical errors if you "de-familiarize" your essay by adjusting its margins so that the text appears as if it were a newspaper column. Type in any needed changes; read through the on-screen text one more time to catch any remaining problems; then restore the appropriate format and print out your final version.

The time you spend learning how to use a word processor will be well worth it. Once you have the knack of thinking at the keyboard, you may never go back to writing in longhand or using a typewriter. However, if you find that writing in longhand or on a typewriter provides better results, then you should do what works for you. As we emphasize throughout this book, professional and student writers alike must find their own best ways for approaching the writing process.

PART III

THE PATTERNS OF DEVELOPMENT

11
AN OVERVIEW OF THE PATTERNS OF DEVELOPMENT

THROUGHOUT Part II, you saw how the patterns of development—narration, process analysis, definition, and so on—are used as strategies for generating, developing, and organizing ideas for essays. You also learned that, in practice, most types of writing combine two or more patterns. This chapter, the first in Part III, provides additional information about these important points. Once you have a clear understanding of the patterns in general, you'll be ready to move on to the remaining chapters in Part III. There you'll learn more about the unique characteristics of each pattern.

THE PATTERNS IN ACTION: DURING THE WRITING PROCESS

As you know, the patterns of development come into play throughout the composing process. In the prewriting stage, awareness of the patterns encourages you to think about your subject in fresh, new ways. Assume, for example, that you've been asked to write an essay about the way children are disciplined in school. However, you draw a blank as soon as you try to limit this general subject. To break the logjam, you could apply one or more patterns of development to your subject. *Comparison-contrast* might prompt you to write an essay investigating the differences between your parents' and your own feelings about school discipline. *Division-classification* might lead you to another paper—one that categorizes the kinds of discipline used in school. And *cause-effect* might point to still another essay—one that explores the way students react to being suspended.

Further along in the writing process—after you've identified your limited subject and your thesis—the patterns of development can help you generate your paper's evidence. Imagine that your thesis is "Teachers shouldn't discipline students publicly just to make an example of them." You're not sure, though, how to develop this thesis. Calling upon the patterns might spark some promising possibilities. *Narration* might encourage you to recount the disastrous time you were singled out and punished for the misdeeds of an entire class. Using *definition*, you might explain what is meant by an *autocratic* disciplinary style. *Argumentation-persuasion* might prompt you to advocate a new plan for disciplining students fairly and effectively.

The patterns of development also help you organize your ideas by pointing the way to an appropriate framework for a paper. Suppose you plan to write an essay for the campus newspaper about the disturbingly high incidence of shoplifting among college students; your purpose is to warn young people away from this tempting, supposedly victimless crime. You believe that many readers will be deterred from shoplifting if you tell them about the harrowing *process* set in motion once a shoplifter is detected. With this step-by-step explanation in mind, you can now map out the essay's content: what happens when a shoplifter is detained by a salesperson, questioned by store security personnel, led to a police car, booked at the police station, and tried in a courtroom.

THE PATTERNS IN ACTION: IN AN ESSAY

Although Part III devotes a separate chapter to each of the nine patterns of development, all chapters emphasize the same important point: Most writing consists of several patterns, with the dominant pattern providing the piece's organizational framework. To reinforce this point, each chapter contains a section, "How [the Pattern] Fits Your Purpose and Audience," that shows how a writer's purpose often leads to a blending of patterns. You'll also notice that one of the "Questions About the Writer's Craft" following each professional selection often asks you to analyze the piece's combination of patterns. Further, the "Writing Assignments Using Other Patterns of Development" encourage you to discover for yourself which mix of patterns would work best in a given piece of writing. In short, all through *The Macmillan Writer*, we emphasize that the patterns of development are far from being mechanical formulas. On the contrary: They are practical strategies that open up options in every stage of the composing process.

Before studying how the writers in Part III combine patterns of development, you'll probably find it helpful to glance back at pages 30–31 so you can review

An Overview of the Patterns of Development

the broad purpose of each pattern. That done, you'll be ready to analyze the selections in this part of the book. The following checklist will help you look more closely at the selections.

> ✔ ANALYZING HOW A WRITER COMBINES PATTERNS:
> A CHECKLIST
>
> ☐ What are the writer's purpose and thesis?
> ☐ Which pattern of development dominates the essay?
> ☐ How does this pattern help the writer support the essay's thesis and fulfill the essay's purpose?
> ☐ What other patterns appear in the essay?
> ☐ How do these patterns help the writer support the essay's thesis and fulfill the essay's purpose?

Your responses to these checklist questions will reward you with a richer understanding of the way skilled prose stylists use the patterns of development in their work.

12 DESCRIPTION

WHAT IS DESCRIPTION?

ALL of us respond in a strong way to sensory stimulation. The sweet perfume of a candy shop takes us back to childhood; the blank white walls of the campus infirmary remind us of long vigils at a hospital where a grandmother lay dying; the screech of a subway car sets our nerves on edge.

Without any sensory stimulation, we sink into a less-than-human state. Neglected babies, left alone with no human touch, no colors, no lullabies, become withdrawn and unresponsive. And prisoners dread solitary confinement, knowing that the sensory deprivation can be unbearable, even to the point of madness.

Because sensory impressions are so potent, descriptive writing has a unique power and appeal. **Description** can be defined as the expression, in vivid language, of what the five senses experience. A richly rendered description freezes a subject in time, evoking sights, smells, sounds, textures, and tastes in such a way that readers become one with the writer's world.

HOW DESCRIPTION FITS YOUR PURPOSE AND AUDIENCE

Description can be a supportive technique that develops part of an essay, or it can be the dominant technique used throughout an essay. Here are some examples of the way description can help you meet the objective of an essay developed chiefly through another pattern of development:

- In a *causal analysis* showing the *consequences* of pet overpopulation, you might describe the desperate appearance of a pack of starving stray dogs.

- In an *argumentation-persuasion* essay urging more rigorous handgun control, you might start with a description of a violent family confrontation that ended in murder.
- In a *process analysis* explaining the pleasure of making ice cream at home, you might describe the beauty of an old-fashioned, hand-cranked ice cream maker.
- In a *narrative essay* recounting a day in the life of a street musician, you might describe the musician's energy and the joyous appreciation of passersby.

In each case, the essay's overall purpose would affect the amount of description needed.

Your readers also influence how much description to include. As you write, ask yourself, "What do my particular readers need to know to understand and experience keenly what I'm describing? What descriptive details will they enjoy most?" Your answers to these and similar questions will help you tailor your description to specific readers. Consider an article intended for professional horticulturists; its purpose is to explain a new technique for controlling spider mites. Because of readers' expertise, there would be little need for a lengthy description of the insects. Written for a college newspaper, however, the article would probably provide a detailed description of the mites so student gardeners could spot them with ease.

While your purpose and audience define *how much* to describe, you have great freedom deciding *what* to describe. Description is especially suited to objects (your car or desk, for example), but you can also describe a person, an animal, a place, a time, and a phenomenon or concept. You might write an effective description about a friend who runs marathons (person), a pair of ducks that returns each year to a neighbor's pond (animals), the kitchen of a fast-food restaurant (place), a period when you were unemployed (time), the "fight or flight" response to danger (phenomenon or concept).

Description can be divided into two types: objective and subjective. In an **objective description,** you describe the subject in a straightforward and literal way, without revealing your attitude or feelings. Reporters, as well as technical and scientific writers, specialize in objective description; their jobs depend on their ability to detail experiences without emotional bias. For example, a reporter may write an unemotional account of a township meeting that ended in a fistfight. Or a marine biologist may write a factual report describing the way sea mammals are killed by the plastic refuse (sandwich wrappings, straws, fishing lines) that humans throw into the ocean.

In contrast, when writing a **subjective description,** you convey a highly personal view of your subject and seek to elicit a strong emotional response from your readers. Such subjective descriptions often take the form of reflective pieces or character studies. For example, in an essay describing the rich plant life in an inner-city garden, you might reflect on people's longing to connect with the soil and express admiration for the gardeners' hard work—an admiration you'd like readers to share. Or, in a character study of your grandfather, you might describe his stern appearance and gentle behavior, hoping that the contradiction will move readers as much as it moves you.

The *tone* of a subjective description is determined by your purpose, your attitude toward the subject, and the reader response you wish to evoke. Consider an essay about a dynamic woman who runs a center for disturbed children. If your goal is to make readers admire the woman, your tone will be serious and appreciative. But if you want to criticize the woman's high-pressure tactics and create distaste for her management style, your tone will be disapproving and severe.

The language of a descriptive piece also depends, to a great extent, on whether your purpose is primarily objective or subjective. If the description is objective, the language is straightforward, precise, and factual. Such *denotative* language consists of neutral dictionary meanings. If you want to describe as dispassionately as possible fans' violent behavior at a football game, you might write about the "large crowd" and its "mass movement onto the field." But if you are shocked by the fans' behavior and want to write a subjective piece that inspires similar outrage in readers, then you might write about the "swelling mob" and its "rowdy stampede onto the field." In the latter case, the language used would be *connotative* and emotionally charged so that readers would share your feelings. (For more on denotation and connotation, see page 22 and pages 119–20.)

Subjective and objective descriptions often overlap. Sometimes a single sentence contains both objective and subjective elements: "Although his hands were large and misshapen by arthritis, they were gentle to the touch, inspiring confidence and trust." Other times, part of an essay may provide a factual description (the physical appearance of a summer cabin your family rented), while another part of the essay may be highly subjective (how you felt in the cabin, sitting in front of a fire on a rainy day).

PREWRITING STRATEGIES

The following checklist shows how you can apply to description some of the prewriting strategies discussed in Chapter 2.

> ✔ **DESCRIPTION: A PREWRITING CHECKLIST**
>
> *Choose a Subject to Describe*
> ☐ Might a photograph, postcard, prized possession, or journal entry suggest a subject worth describing?
> ☐ Will you describe a person, animal, object, place, time period, or phenomenon? Is the subject readily observable, or will you have to reconstruct it from memory?
>
> *Determine Your Purpose, Audience, Tone, and Point of View*
> ☐ Is your purpose to inform or to evoke an emotional response? If you want to do both, which is your predominant purpose?
> ☐ What audience are you writing for? How much does the audience already know about the subject you plan to describe?

Description   157

> - What tone and point of view will best serve your purpose and make readers receptive to your description?
>
> *Use Prewriting to Generate Details About the Subject*
> - How could freewriting, journal entries, or brainstorming help you gather sensory specifics about your subject?
> - What relevant details about your subject come to mind when you apply the questioning technique to each of the five senses? What sounds (pitch, volume, and quality) predominate? What can you touch and how does it feel (temperature, weight, texture)? What do you see (color, pattern, shape, size)? What smells (pleasant, unpleasant) can't you forget? What tastes (agreeable, disagreeable) remain memorable?

STRATEGIES FOR USING DESCRIPTION IN AN ESSAY

After prewriting, you're ready to draft your essay. The following suggestions will be helpful whether you use description as a dominant or supportive pattern of development.

1. Focus a descriptive essay around a dominant impression. Like other kinds of writing, a descriptive essay must have a thesis, or main point. In a descriptive essay with a subjective slant, the thesis usually centers on the **dominant impression** you have about your subject. Suppose you decide to write an essay on your ninth-grade history teacher, Ms. Hazzard. You want the paper to convey how unconventional and flamboyant she was. The essay could, of course, focus on a different dominant impression—how insensitive she could be to students, for example. What's important is that you establish—early in the paper—the dominant impression you intend to convey. Although descriptive essays often imply, rather than explicitly state, the dominant impression, that impression should be unmistakable.

2. Select the details to include. The prewriting techniques discussed on pages 25–31 can help you develop heightened powers of observation and recall. Practice in noting significant details can lead you to become—in the words of novelist Henry James—"one of those people on whom nothing is lost." The power of description hinges on your ability to select from all possible details *only those that support the dominant impression*. All others—no matter how vivid or interesting—must be left out. If you were describing how flamboyant Ms. Hazzard could be, the details in the following paragraph would be appropriate:

A large-boned woman, Ms. Hazzard wore her bright red hair piled on top of her head, where it perched precariously. By the end of class, wayward strands of hair tumbled down and fell into eyes fringed by spiky false eyelashes. Ms. Hazzard's nails, filed into crisp points, were painted either bloody burgundy or neon pink. Plastic bangle bracelets, also either burgundy or pink, clattered up and down her ample arms as she scrawled on the board the historical dates that had, she claimed, "changed the world."

Such details—the heavy eye makeup, stiletto nails, gaudy bracelets—contribute to the impression of a flamboyant, unusual person. Even if you remembered times that Ms. Hazzard seemed perfectly conventional and understated, most likely you wouldn't describe those times because they would contradict the dominant impression.

You must also be selective in the *number of details* you include. Having a dominant impression helps you eliminate many details gathered during prewriting, but there still will be choices to make. For example, it would be inappropriate to describe in exhaustive detail everything in a messy room:

> The brown desk, made of a grained plastic laminate, is directly under a small window covered by a torn yellow-and-gold plaid curtain. In the left corner of the desk are four crumbled balls of blue-lined yellow paper, three red markers (all without caps), two fine-point blue pens, a crumbling pink eraser, and four letters, two bearing special wildlife stamps. A green down-filled vest and an out-of-shape red cable-knit sweater are thrown over the back of the bright blue metal bridge chair pushed under the desk. Under the chair is an oval braided rug, its once brilliant blues and greens spotted by soda and coffee stains.

Readers will be reluctant to wade through such undifferentiated specifics. Even more importantly, such excessive detailing dilutes the essay's focus. You end up with a seemingly endless list of specifics, rather than with a carefully crafted word picture. In this regard, sculptors and writers are similar—what they take away is as important as what they leave in.

3. Organize the descriptive details. It's important to select the organizational pattern (or combination of patterns) that best supports your dominant impression. The paragraphs in a descriptive essay are usually sequenced *spatially* (from top to bottom, interior to exterior, near to far) or *chronologically* (as the subject is experienced in time). But the paragraphs can also be ordered *emphatically* (ending with your subject's most striking elements) or by *sensory impression* (first smell, then taste, then touch, and so on).

You might, for instance, use a *spatial* pattern to organize a description of a large city as you viewed it from the air, a taxi, or a subway car. A description of your first day on a new job might move *chronologically,* starting with how you felt when you woke up that morning and proceeding through the day's events. In a paper describing a bout with the flu, you might arrange details *emphatically,* beginning with a description of your low-level aches and pains and concluding with

Description

an account of your raging fever. An essay about a neighborhood garbage dump could be organized by *sensory impressions:* the sights of the dump, its smells, its sounds. Regardless of the organizational pattern you use, provide enough *signal devices (about, next, worst of all)* so that readers can follow the description easily.

Finally, although descriptive essays don't always have conventional topic sentences, each descriptive paragraph should have a clear focus. Often this focus is indicated by a sentence early in the paragraph that names the scene, object, or individual to be described. Such a sentence functions as a kind of *informal topic sentence;* the paragraph's descriptive details then develop that topic sentence.

4. Use vivid sensory language and varied sentence structure. The connotative language typical of subjective description should be richly evocative. The words you select must etch in readers' minds the same picture that you have in yours. For this reason, rather than relying on vague generalities, you must use language that involves readers' senses. Consider the difference between the following paired descriptions:

Vague	**Vivid**
The food was unappetizing.	The stew congealed into an oval pool of milky-brown fat.
The toothpaste was refreshing.	The toothpaste, minty sweet, tingled against my bare teeth, finally free from braces.
Filled with passengers and baggage, the car moved slowly down the road.	Burdened with its load of clamoring children and well-worn suitcases, the car labored down the interstate on bald tires and worn shocks, emitting puffs of blue exhaust and an occasional backfire.

Unlike the *concrete, sensory-packed* sentences on the right, the sentences on the left fail to create vivid word pictures that engage readers. While all good writing blends abstract and concrete language, descriptive writing demands an abundance of specific sensory language. (For more on concrete and specific language, see pages 120–21 in Chapter 8.)

Although you should aim for rich, sensory images, avoid overloading your sentences with *too many adjectives:* "A stark, smooth, blinding glass cylinder, the fifty-story skyscraper dominated the crowded city street." Delete unnecessary words, retaining only the most powerful: "A blinding glass cylinder, the skyscraper dominated the street."

Remember too, that *verbs pack more of a wallop* than adverbs. The following sentence has to rely on adverbs (italicized) because its verbs are so weak: "She walked *casually* into the room and *deliberately* tried not to pay attention to their stares." Rewritten, so that verbs (italicized), not adverbs, do the bulk of the work, the sentence becomes more powerful: "She *strolled* into the room and *ignored* their stares." *Onomatopoetic* verbs, like *buzz, sizzle,* and *zoom,* can be especially effective because their sounds convey their meaning. (For more on vigorous verbs, see pages 121–22 in Chapter 8).

Figures of speech—nonliteral, imaginative comparisons between two basically dissimilar things—are another way to enliven descriptive writing. *Similes* use the word *like* or *as* when comparing; *metaphors* state or imply that the two things being compared are alike; and *personification* attributes human characteristics to inanimate things. (For further discussion of figures of speech, refer to pages 123–24 in Chapter 8.)

The examples that follow show how effective figurative language can be in descriptive writing:

Simile

> Moving as jerkily as a marionette on strings, the old man picked himself up off the sidewalk and staggered down the street.

Metaphor

> Stalking their prey, the hall monitors remained hidden in the corridors, motionless and ready to spring on any unsuspecting student who tried to sneak into class late.

Personification

> The scoop of vanilla ice cream, plain and unadorned, cried out for hot fudge sauce and a sprinkling of sliced pecans.

(For suggestions on avoiding clichéd figures of speech, see page 124 in Chapter 8.)

Finally, when writing descriptive passages, you need to *vary sentence structure.* Don't use the same subject-verb pattern in all sentences. The second example above, for instance, could have been written as follows: "The hall monitors stalked their prey. They hid in the corridors. They remained motionless and ready to spring on any unsuspecting student who tried to sneak into class late." But the sentence is richer and more interesting when the descriptive elements are embedded, eliminating what would otherwise have been a clipped and predictable subject-verb pattern. (For more on sentence variety, see pages 105–112 in Chapter 8.)

REVISION STRATEGIES

Once you have a draft of the essay, you're ready to revise. The following checklist will help you and those giving you feedback apply to description some of the revision techniques discussed in Chapters 7 and 8.

☑ **DESCRIPTION: A REVISION CHECKLIST**

Revise Overall Meaning and Structure

- What dominant impression does the essay convey? Is the dominant impression stated or implied? Where? Should it be made more obvious or more subtle? Why?

- Is the essay primarily objective or subjective? Should the essay be more personal and emotionally charged or less so?
- Which descriptive details don't support the dominant impression? Should they be deleted, or should the dominant impression be adjusted to encompass the details?

Revise Paragraph Development

- How are the essay's descriptive paragraphs (or passages) organized—spatially, chronologically, emphatically, or by sensory impressions? Would another organizational pattern be more effective? Which one(s)? Why?
- Which paragraphs lack a distinctive focus?
- Which descriptive paragraphs (or passages) deteriorate into a mere list of sensory impressions?
- Which descriptive paragraphs (or passages) are too abstract or general? Which fail to engage the reader's senses? How could they be made more concrete and specific?

Revise Sentences and Words

- What signal devices (*such as above, next, worst of all*) guide readers through the description? Are there enough signals? Too many?
- Where should sentence structure be varied so that it is less predictable and monotonous?
- Which sentences lack sensory images? How could they be made more evocative?
- Where should flat verbs and adverbs be replaced with vigorous verbs? Where would onomatopoeia enliven a sentence?
- Where are there too many adjectives? Which could be deleted?
- What figures of speech appear in the essay? Which seem contrived or trite?

STUDENT ESSAY: FROM PREWRITING THROUGH REVISION

The student essay that follows was written by Marie Martinez in response to this assignment:

> The essay "Once More to the Lake" is an evocative piece about a spot that had special meaning in E. B. White's life. Write an essay about a place that holds rich significance for you, centering the description on a dominant impression.

After deciding to write on the salt marsh near her grandparents' home, Marie used the prewriting technique of *questioning* to gather sensory details about this special place. To enhance her power of recall, she focused, one at a time, on each of the five senses. Then, typing as quickly as she could, she listed the sensory specifics that came to mind.

When Marie later reviewed the details listed under each sensory heading, she concluded that her essay's dominant impression should be the marsh's peaceful beauty. With that dominant impression in mind, she added some details to her prewriting and deleted others. Here is Marie's original prewriting; the handwritten insertions indicate her later efforts to develop the material:

Questioning Technique

<u>See</u>: <u>What do I see at the marsh?</u>
- line of tall, waving reeds *bordering the creek*
- path--flattened grass
- spring--bright green *(brilliant green)*
- autumn--gold *(tawny)*
- winter--gray
- soil--spongy
- dark soil
- blue crabs
- creek--narrow, sinuous can't see beginning or end *less than 15' wide*
- birds--little, brown
- low tide--steep bank of creek
- ~~an occasional beer can or potato chip bag~~
- grass under the water--green waves, shimmers
- fish--tiny, with silvery *(minnows)* sides, dart through water and vegetation *and underwater tangles*
- center of creek--everything water and sky

<u>Hear</u>: <u>How does it sound there?</u>
- chirping of birds *("tweep tweep")*
- splash of turtle or otter
- mainly silent

<u>Feel</u>: <u>How does it feel?</u>
- soil--spongy
- water--warmer than ocean; rub my face and neck; mucky *and oily*
- mud--slimy *(through toes)*
- crabs brush my legs
- feel buoyant, weightless

<u>Smell</u>: <u>Why can't I forget its smell?</u>
- salt
- soil

When Marie reviewed her annotated prewriting, she decided that, in the essay, she would order her brainstormed impressions by location rather than by sensory type. Using a spatial method of organization, she would present details as she moved from place to place—from her grandparents' home to the creek. The arrangement of details was now so clear to Marie that she felt comfortable moving to a first draft without further shaping her prewriting or preparing an outline. As she wrote, though, she frequently referred to her prewriting to retrieve sensory details about each location.

Now read Marie's paper, "Salt Marsh," noting the similarities and differences between her prewriting and final essay. You'll see that the essay's introduction and conclusion weren't drawn from the prewriting material, whereas most of the sensory details were. Notice, too, that when she wrote the essay, Marie expanded these details by adding more specifics and providing several powerful similes. Finally, consider how well the essay applies the principles of description discussed in this chapter. (The commentary that follows the paper will help you look at the essay more closely and will give you some sense of how Marie went about revising her first draft.)

Salt Marsh
by Marie Martinez

1   In one of his journals, Thoreau told of the difficulty he had escaping the obligations and cares of society: "It sometimes happens that I cannot easily shake off the village. The thought of some work will run in my head and I am not where my body is--I am out of my senses. In my walks I . . . return to my senses." All of us feel out of our senses at times. Overwhelmed by problems or everyday annoyances, we lose touch with sensory pleasures as we spend our days in noisy cities and stuffy classrooms. Just as Thoreau walked in the woods to return to his senses, I have a special place where I return to mine: the salt marsh behind my grandparents' house. *— Introduction / Dominant impression (thesis)*

2   My grandparents live on the East Coast, a mile or so inland from the sea. Between the ocean and the mainland is a wide fringe of salt marsh. A salt marsh is not a swamp, but an expanse of dark, spongy soil threaded with saltwater creeks and clothed in a kind of grass called salt meadow hay. All the water in the marsh rises and falls daily with the ocean tides, an endless cycle that changes the look of the marsh--partly flooded or mostly dry--as the day progresses. *— Informal topic sentence: Definition paragraph*

3   Heading out to the marsh from my grandparents' house, I follow a short path through the woods. As I walk along, a sharp smell of salt mixed *— Informal topic sentence: First paragraph in a four-part spatial sequence*

with the rich aroma of peaty soil fills my nostrils. I am always amazed by the way the path changes with the seasons. Sometimes I walk in the brilliant green of spring, sometimes in the tawny gold of autumn, sometimes in the grayish-tan of winter. No matter the season, the grass flanking the trail is often flattened into swirls, like thick Van Gogh brush strokes that curve and recurve in circular patterns. No people come here. The peacefulness heals me like a soothing drug.

After a few minutes, the trail suddenly opens up to a view that calms me no matter how upset or discouraged I might be: a line of tall waving reeds bordering and nearly hiding the salt marsh creek. To get to the creek, I part the reeds.

The creek is a narrow body of water no more than fifteen feet wide, and it ebbs and flows as the ocean currents sweep toward the land or rush back toward the sea. The creek winds in a sinuous pattern so that I cannot see its beginning or end, the places where it trickles into the marsh or spills into the open ocean. Little brown birds dip in and out of the reeds on the far shore of the creek, making a special "tweep-tweep" sound peculiar to the marsh. When I stand at low tide on the shore of the creek, I am on a miniature cliff, for the bank of the creek falls abruptly and steeply into the water. Below me, green grasses wave and shimmer under the water while tiny minnows flash their silvery sides as they dart through the underwater tangles.

The creek water is often much warmer than the ocean, so I can swim there in three seasons. Sitting on the edge of the creek, I scoop some water into my hand, rub my face and neck, then ease into the water. Where the creek is shallow, my feet sink into a foot of muck that feels like mashed potatoes mixed with motor oil. But once I become accustomed to it, I enjoy squishing the slimy mud through my toes. Sometimes I feel brushing past my legs the blue crabs that live in the creek. Other times, I hear the splash of a turtle or otter as it slips from the shore into the water. Otherwise, it is silent. The salty water is buoyant and lifts my spirits as I stroke through it to reach the middle of the creek. There in the center, I float weightlessly, surrounded by tall reeds that reduce the world to water and sky. I am at peace.

The salt marsh is not the kind of dramatic landscape found on picture postcards. There are no soaring mountains, sandy beaches, or lush valleys. The marsh is a flat world that some consider dull and uninviting. I am glad most people do not respond to the marsh's subtle beauty because that means I can be alone there. Just as the rising tide sweeps over the marsh, floating debris out to the ocean, the marsh washes away my concerns and restores me to my senses.

— Echo of idea in introduction

Commentary

The Dominant Impression

Marie responded to the assignment by writing a moving tribute to a place having special meaning for her—the salt marsh near her grandparents' home. Like most descriptive pieces, Marie's essay is organized around a *dominant impression:* the marsh's peaceful solitude and gentle, natural beauty. The essay's introduction provides a context for the dominant impression by comparing the pleasure Marie experiences in the marsh to the happiness Thoreau felt in his walks around Walden Pond.

Other Patterns of Development

Before developing the essay's dominant impression, Marie uses the second paragraph to *define* a salt marsh. An *objective description,* the definition clarifies that a salt marsh—with its spongy soil, haylike grass, and ebbing tides—is not to be confused with a swamp. Because Marie offers such a factual definition, readers have the background needed to enjoy the personalized view that follows.

Besides the definition paragraph and the comparison in the opening paragraph, the essay contains a strong element of *causal analysis:* Throughout, Marie describes the marsh's effect on her.

Sensory Language

At times, Marie develops the essay's dominant impression explicitly, as when she writes "No people come here" (paragraph 3) and "I am at peace" (6). But Marie generally uses the more subtle techniques characteristic of *subjective description* to convey the dominant impression. First of all, she fills the essay with strong *connotative language,* rich with *sensory images.* The third paragraph describes what she smells (the "sharp smell of salt mixed with the rich aroma of peaty soil") and what she sees ("brilliant green," "tawny gold," and "grayish-tan"). In the fifth paragraph, she uses *onomatopoeia* ("tweep tweep") to convey the birds' chirping sound. And the sixth paragraph includes vigorous descriptions of how the marsh feels to Marie's touch. She splashes water on her face and neck; she digs her toes into the mud at the bottom of the creek; she delights in the delicate brushing of crabs against her legs.

Figurative Language, Vigorous Verbs, and Varied Sentence Structure

You might also have noted that *figurative language, energetic verbs,* and *varied sentence patterns* contribute to the essay's descriptive power. Marie develops a *simile* in the third paragraph when she compares the flattened swirls of swamp grass to the brush strokes in a painting by Van Gogh. Later she uses another simile when she writes that the creek's thick mud feels "like mashed potatoes mixed with motor oil." Moreover, throughout the essay, she uses lively verbs ("shimmer," "flash") to capture the marsh's magical quality. Similarly, Marie enhances descriptive passages by varying the length of her sentences. Long, fairly elaborate sentences are interspersed with short, dramatic statements. In the third paragraph, for example, the long sentence describing the circular swirls of swamp grass is followed by the brief statement "No people come here." And the sixth paragraph uses two short sentences ("Otherwise, it is silent" and "I am at peace") to punctuate the paragraph's longer sentences.

Organization

We can follow Marie's journey through the marsh because she uses an easy-to-follow combination of *spatial, chronological,* and *emphatic* patterns to sequence her experience. The essay relies primarily on a spatial arrangement since the four body paragraphs focus on the different spots that Marie reaches: first, the path behind her grandparents' house (paragraph 3); then the area bordering the creek (4); next, her view of the creek (5); last, the creek itself (6). Each stage of her walk is signaled by an *informal topic sentence* near the start of each paragraph. Furthermore, *signal devices* (marked by italics here) indicate not only her location but also the chronological passage of time: "*As* I walk along, a sharp smell . . . fills my nostrils" (3); "*After* a few minutes, the trail suddenly opens up . . ." (4); "*Below* me, green grasses wave . . ." (5). And to call attention to the creek's serene beauty, Marie saves for last the description of the peace she feels while floating in the creek.

An Inappropriate Figure of Speech

Although the four body paragraphs focus on the distinctive qualities of each location, Marie runs into a minor problem in the third paragraph. Take a moment to reread that paragraph's last sentence. Comparing the peace of the marsh to the effect of a "soothing drug" is jarring. The effectiveness of Marie's essay hinges on her ability to create a picture of a pure, natural world. A reference to drugs is inappropriate. Now, reread the paragraph aloud, stopping after "No people come here." Note how much more in keeping with the essay's dominant impression the paragraph is when the reference to drugs is omitted.

Conclusion

The concluding paragraph brings the essay to a graceful close. The powerful *simile* found in the last sentence contains an implied reference to Thoreau and to Marie's earlier statement about the joy to be found in special places having restorative powers. Such an allusion echoes, with good effect, the paper's opening comments.

Description

Revising the First Draft

When Marie met with some classmates during a group feedback session, the students agreed that Marie's first draft was strong and moving. But they also said that they had difficulty following her route through the marsh; they found her third paragraph especially confusing. Marie kept track of her classmates' comments on a separate piece of paper and then entered them, numbered in order of importance, in the margin of her first draft. Reprinted here is the original version of Marie's third paragraph, along with her annotations:

Original Version of Third Paragraph

As I head out to the marsh from the house, I follow a short trail through the woods. A smell of salt and soil fills my nostrils. The end of the trail suddenly opens up to a view that calms me no matter how upset or discouraged I might be: a line of tall, waving reeds bordering the salt marsh creek. Civilization seems far away as I walk the path of flattened grass and finally reach my goal, the salt marsh creek hidden behind the tall, waving reeds. The path changes with the seasons; sometimes I walk in the brilliant green of spring, sometimes in the tawny gold of autumn, sometimes in the gray of winter. In some areas, the grass is flattened into swirls that make the marsh resemble one of those paintings by Van Gogh. No people come here. The peacefulness heals me like a soothing drug. The path stops at the line of tall, waving reeds standing upright at the border of the creek. I part the reeds to get to the creek.

① *Chronology is confusing*

③ *Make more specific*

② *Develop more fully—maybe use a simile*

When Marie looked more carefully at the paragraph, she agreed it was confusing. For one thing, the paragraph's third and fourth sentences indicated that she had come to the path's end and had reached the reeds bordering the creek. In the following sentences, however, she was on the path again. Then, at the end, she was back at the creek, as if she had just arrived there. Marie resolved this confusion by breaking the single paragraph into two separate ones—the first describing the walk along the path, the second describing her arrival at the creek. This restructuring, especially when combined with clearer transitions, eliminated the confusion.

While revising her essay, Marie also intensified the sensory images in her original paragraph. She changed the "smell of salt and soil" to the "sharp smell of salt mixed with the rich aroma of peaty soil." And when she added the phrase "thick Van Gogh brush strokes that curve and recurve in circular patterns," she made the comparison between the marsh grass and a Van Gogh painting more vivid.

These are just some of the changes Marie made while rewriting the paper. Her skillful revisions provided the polish needed to make an already strong essay even more evocative.

ACTIVITIES: DESCRIPTION

Prewriting Activities

1. Imagine you're writing two essays: One explains how students get "burned out"; the other contends that being a spendthrift is better (or worse) than being frugal. Jot down ways you might use description in each essay.

2. Go to a place on campus where students congregate. In preparation for an *objective* description of this place, make notes of various sights, sounds, smells, and textures, as well as the overall "feel" of the place. Then, in preparation for a *subjective* description, observe and take notes on another sheet of paper. Compare the two sets of material. What differences do you see in word choice and selection of details?

3. Prepare to interview an interesting person by outlining several questions ahead of time. When you visit that person's home or workplace, bring a notebook in which to record his or her responses. During the interview, observe the person's surroundings, voice, body language, dress, and so on. As soon as the interview is over, make notes on these matters. Then review your notes and identify your dominant impression of the person. With that impression in mind, which details would you omit if you were writing an essay? Which would you elaborate? Which organizational pattern (spatial, emphatic, chronological, or sensory) would you select to organize your description? Why?

Revising Activities

4. Revise each of the following sentence sets twice. The first time, create an unmistakable mood; the second time, create a sharply contrasting mood. To convey atmosphere, vary sentence structure, use vigorous verbs, provide rich sensory details, and pay special attention to words' connotations.

  a. The card players sat around the table. The table was old. The players were, too.
  b. A long line formed outside the movie theater. People didn't want to miss the show. The movie had received a lot of attention recently.

Description

   c. A girl walked down the street in her first pair of high heels. This was a new experience for her.

5. The following sentences contain clichés. Rewrite each sentence, supplying a fresh and imaginative figure of speech. Add whatever descriptive details are needed to provide a context for the figure of speech.

   a. They were as quiet as mice.
   b. My brother used to get green with envy if I had a date and he didn't.
   c. The little girl is proud as a peacock of her Girl Scout uniform.
   d. The professor is as dull as dishwater.

6. The following descriptive paragraph is from the first draft of an essay showing that personal growth may result when romanticized notions and reality collide. How effective is the paragraph in illustrating the essay's thesis? Which details are powerful? Which could be more concrete? Which should be deleted? Where should sentence structure be more varied? How could the description be made more coherent? Revise the paragraph, correcting any problems you discover and adding whatever sensory details are needed to enliven the description. Feel free to break the paragraph into one or more separate ones.

   As a child, I was intrigued by stories about the farm in Harrison County, Maine, where my father spent his teens. Being raised on a farm seemed more interesting than growing up in the suburbs. So about a year ago, I decided to see for myself what the farm was like. I got there by driving on Route 334, a surprisingly easy-to-drive, four-lane highway that had recently been built with matching state and federal funds. I turned into the dirt road leading to the farm and got out of my car. It had been washed and waxed for the occasion. Then I headed for a dirt-colored barn. Its roof was full of huge, rotted holes. As I rounded the bushes, I saw the house. It too was dirt-colored. Its paint must have worn off decades ago. A couple of dead-looking old cars were sprawled in front of the barn. They were dented and windowless. Also by the barn was an ancient refrigerator, crushed like a discarded accordion. The porch steps to the house were slanted and wobbly. Through the open windows came a stale smell and the sound of television. Looking in the front door screen, I could see two chickens jumping around inside. Everything looked dirty both inside and out. Secretly grateful that no one answered my knock, I bolted down the stairs, got into my clean, shiny car, and drove away.

PROFESSIONAL SELECTIONS: DESCRIPTION

E. B. WHITE

Recipient of the Presidential Medal of Freedom and the National Medal for Literature, Elwyn Brooks White (1899–1985) is considered one of America's foremost essayists. Known for his graceful prose, White wrote the *New Yorker's* "Talk of the Town" column for many years. He also authored, with William Strunk, Jr., the renowned guide for writers *The Elements of Style*. White's books for children include the beloved classic *Charlotte's Web* (1952). This selection is taken from *The Essays of E. B. White* (1977).

ONCE MORE TO THE LAKE

One summer, along about 1904, my father rented a camp on a lake in Maine and took us all there for the month of August. We all got ringworm from some kittens and had to rub Pond's Extract on our arms and legs night and morning, and my father rolled over in a canoe with all his clothes on; but outside of that the vacation was a success and from then on none of us ever thought there was any place in the world like that lake in Maine. We returned summer after summer—always on August 1 for one month. I have since become a salt-water man, but sometimes in summer there are days when the restlessness of the tides and the fearful cold of the sea water and the incessant wind that blows across the afternoon and into the evening make me wish for the placidity of a lake in the woods. A few weeks ago this feeling got so strong I bought myself a couple of bass hooks and a spinner and returned to the lake where we used to go, for a week's fishing and to revisit old haunts.

I took along my son, who had never had any fresh water up his nose and who had seen lily pads only from train windows. On the journey over to the lake I began to wonder what it would be like. I wondered how time would have marred this unique, this holy spot—the coves and streams, the hills that the sun set behind, the camps and the paths behind the camps. I was sure that the tarred road would have found it out, and I wondered in what other ways it would be desolated. It is strange how much you can remember about places like that once you allow your mind to return into the grooves that lead back. You remember one thing, and that suddenly reminds you of another thing. I guess I remembered clearest of all the early mornings, when the lake was cool and motionless, remembered how the bedroom smelled of the lumber it was made of and of the wet woods whose scent entered through the screen. The partitions in the camp were thin and did not extend clear to the top of the rooms, and as I was always the first up I would dress softly so as not to wake the others, and sneak out into the sweet outdoors and start out in the canoe, keeping close along the shore in the long shadows of the pines. I remembered being very careful never to rub my paddle against the gunwale for fear of disturbing the stillness of the cathedral.

Description

3   The lake had never been what you would call a wild lake. There were cottages sprinkled around the shores, and it was in farming country although the shores of the lake were quite heavily wooded. Some of the cottages were owned by nearby farmers, and you would live at the shore and eat your meals at the farmhouse. That's what our family did. But although it wasn't wild, it was a fairly large and undisturbed lake and there were places in it that, to a child at least, seemed infinitely remote and primeval.

4   I was right about the tar: it led to within half a mile of the shore. But when I got back there, with my boy, and we settled into a camp near a farmhouse and into the kind of summertime I had known, I could tell that it was going to be pretty much the same as it had been before—I knew it, lying in bed the first morning, smelling the bedroom and hearing the boy sneak quietly out and go off along the shore in a boat. I began to sustain the illusion that he was I, and therefore, by simple transposition, that I was my father. This sensation persisted, kept cropping up all the time we were there. It was not an entirely new feeling, but in this setting it grew much stronger. I seemed to be living a dual existence. I would be in the middle of some simple act, I would be picking up a bait box or laying down a table fork, or I would be saying something, and suddenly it would be not I but my father who was saying the words or making the gesture. It gave me a creepy sensation.

5   We went fishing the first morning. I felt the same damp moss covering the worms in the bait can, and saw the dragonfly alight on the tip of my rod as it hovered a few inches from the surface of the water. It was the arrival of this fly that convinced me beyond any doubt that everything was as it always had been, that the years were a mirage and that there had been no years. The small waves were the same, chucking the rowboat under the chin as we fished at anchor, and the boat was the same boat, the same color green and the ribs broken in the same places, and under the floorboards the same fresh-water leavings and débris—the dead helgramite, the wisps of moss, the rusty discarded fishhook, the dried blood from yesterday's catch. We stared silently at the tips of our rods, at the dragonflies that came and went. I lowered the tip of mine into the water, tentatively, pensively dislodging the fly, which darted two feet away, poised, darted two feet back, and came to rest again a little farther up the rod. There had been no years between the ducking of this dragonfly and the other one—the one that was part of memory. I looked at the boy, who was silently watching his fly, and it was my hands that held his rod, my eyes watching. I felt dizzy and didn't know which rod I was at the end of.

6   We caught two bass, hauling them in briskly as though they were mackerel, pulling them over the side of the boat in a businesslike manner without any landing net, and stunning them with a blow on the back of the head. When we got back for a swim before lunch, the lake was exactly where we had left it, the same number of inches from the dock, and there was only the merest suggestion of a breeze. This seemed an utterly enchanted sea, this lake you could leave to its own devices for a few hours and come back to, and find that it had not stirred, this constant and trustworthy body of water. In the shallows, the dark, water-soaked sticks and twigs, smooth and old, were undulating in clusters on the bottom against the clean ribbed sand, and the track of the mussel was plain. A school of minnows swam by, each minnow with its small individual shadow, doubling the attendance, so clear and sharp in the sunlight. Some of the other campers were in swimming, along the shore, one of them with a cake of soap, and the water felt thin and clear and unsubstantial. Over the years there had been this person with the cake of soap, this cultist, and here he was. There had been no years.

Up to the farmhouse to dinner through the teeming, dusty field, the road under our sneakers was only a two-track road. The middle track was missing, the one with the marks of the hooves and the splotches of dried, flaky manure. There had always been three tracks to choose from in choosing which track to walk in; now the choice was narrowed down to two. For a moment I missed terribly the middle alternative. But the way led past the tennis court, and something about the way it lay there in the sun reassured me; the tape had loosened along the backline, the alleys were green with plantains and other weeds, and the net (installed in June and removed in September) sagged in the dry noon, and the whole place steamed with midday heat and hunger and emptiness. There was a choice of pie for dessert, and one was blueberry and one was apple, and the waitresses were the same country girls, there having been no passage of time, only the illusion of it as in a dropped curtain—the waitresses were still fifteen; their hair had been washed, that was the only difference—they had been to the movies and seen the pretty girls with the clean hair. 7

Summertime, oh, summertime, pattern of life indelible, the fade-proof lake, the woods unshatterable, the pasture with the sweetfern and the juniper forever and ever, summer without end; this was the background, and the life along the shore was the design, the cottagers with their innocent and tranquil design, their tiny docks with the flagpole and the American flag floating against the white clouds in the blue sky, the little paths over the roots of the trees leading from camp to camp and the paths leading back to the outhouses and the can of lime for sprinkling, and at the souvenir counters at the store the miniature birch-bark canoes and the postcards that showed things looking a little better than they looked. This was the American family at play, escaping the city heat, wondering whether the newcomers in the camp at the head of the cove were "common" or "nice," wondering whether it was true that the people who drove up for Sunday dinner at the farmhouse were turned away because there wasn't enough chicken. 8

It seemed to me, as I kept remembering all this, that those times and those summers had been infinitely precious and worth saving. There had been jollity and peace and goodness. The arriving (at the beginning of August) had been so big a business in itself, at the railway station the farm wagon drawn up, the first smell of the pine-laden air, the first glimpse of the smiling farmer, and the great importance of the trunks and your father's enormous authority in such matters, and the feel of the wagon under you for the long ten-mile haul, and at the top of the last long hill catching the first view of the lake after eleven months of not seeing this cherished body of water. The shouts and cries of the other campers when they saw you, and the trunks to be unpacked, to give up their rich burden. (Arriving was less exciting nowadays, when you sneaked up in your car and parked it under a tree near the camp and took out the bags and in five minutes it was all over, no fuss, no loud wonderful fuss about trunks.) 9

Peace and goodness and jollity. The only thing that was wrong now, really, was the sound of the place, an unfamiliar nervous sound of the outboard motors. This was the note that jarred, the one thing that would sometimes break the illusion and set the years moving. In those other summertimes all motors were inboard; and when they were at a little distance, the noise they made was a sedative, an ingredient of summer sleep. They were one-cylinder and two-cylinder engines, and some were make-and-break and some were jump-spark, but they all made a sleepy sound across the lake. The one-lungers throbbed and fluttered, and the twin-cylinder ones purred and purred, and that was a quiet sound, too. But now the campers all had outboards. In the daytime, in the hot mornings, these motors made a petulant, irritable sound; at night, in the still evening when the afterglow lit the water, they whined about one's ears like mosquitoes. My boy loved our rented outboard, and his great desire was to 10

Description

achieve single-handed mastery over it, and authority, and he soon learned the trick of choking it a little (but not too much), and the adjustment of the needle valve. Watching him I would remember the things you could do with the old one-cylinder engine with the heavy flywheel, how you could have it eating out of your hand if you got really close to it spiritually. Motorboats in those days didn't have clutches, and you would make a landing by shutting off the motor at the proper time and coasting in with a dead rudder. But there was a way of reversing them, if you learned the trick, by cutting the switch and putting it on again exactly on the final dying revolution of the flywheel, so that it would kick back against compression and begin reversing. Approaching a dock in a strong following breeze, it was difficult to slow up sufficiently by the ordinary coasting method, and if a boy felt he had complete mastery over his motor, he was tempted to keep it running beyond its time and then reverse it a few feet from the dock. It took a cool nerve, because if you threw the switch a twentieth of a second too soon you would catch the flywheel when it still had speed enough to go up past center, and the boat would leap ahead, charging bullfashion at the dock.

11   We had a good week at the camp. The bass were biting well and the sun shone endlessly, day after day. We would be tired at night and lie down in the accumulated heat of the little bedrooms after the long hot day and the breeze would stir almost imperceptibly outside and the smell of the swamp drift in through the rusty screens. Sleep would come easily and in the morning the red squirrel would be on the roof, tapping out his gay routine. I kept remembering everything, lying in bed in the mornings—the small steamboat that had a long rounded stern like the lip of a Ubangi, and how quietly she ran on the moonlight sails, when the older boys played their mandolins and the girls sang and we ate doughnuts dipped in sugar, and how sweet the music was on the water in the shining night, and what it had felt like to think about girls then. After breakfast we would go up to the store and the things were in the same place—the minnows in a bottle, the plugs and spinners disarranged and pawed over by the youngsters from the boys' camp, the Fig Newtons and the Beeman's gum. Outside, the road was tarred and cars stood in front of the store. Inside, all was just as it had always been, except there was more Coca-Cola and not so much Moxie and root beer and birch beer and sarsaparilla. We would walk out with the bottle of pop apiece and sometimes the pop would backfire up our noses and hurt. We explored the streams, quietly, where the turtles slid off the sunny logs and dug their way into the soft bottom; and we lay on the town wharf and fed worms to the tame bass. Everywhere we went I had trouble making out which was I, the one walking at my side, the one walking in my pants.

12   One afternoon while we were there at the lake a thunderstorm came up. It was like the revival of an old melodrama that I had seen long ago with childish awe. The second-act climax of the drama of the electrical disturbance over a lake in America had not changed in any important respect. This was the big scene, still the big scene. The whole thing was so familiar, the first feeling of oppression and heat and a general air around camp of not wanting to go very far away. In midafternoon (it was all the same) a curious darkening of the sky, and a lull in everything that had made life tick; and then the way the boats suddenly swung the other way at their moorings with the coming of a breeze out of the new quarter, and the premonitory rumble. Then the kettle drum, then the snare, then the bass drum and cymbals, then crackling light against the dark, and the gods grinning and licking their chops in the hills. Afterward the calm, the rain steadily rustling in the calm lake, the return of light and hope and spirits, and the campers running out in joy and relief to go swimming in the rain, their bright cries perpetuating the deathless joke about how they were getting simply drenched, and the children screaming with delight at the new sensation of bathing in

the rain, and the joke about getting drenched linking the generations in a strong indestructible chain. And the comedian who waded in carrying an umbrella.

When the others went swimming, my son said he was going in, too. He pulled his dripping trunks from the line where they had hung all through the shower and wrung them out. Languidly, and with no thought of going in, I watched him, his hard little body, skinny and bare, saw him wince slightly as he pulled up around his vitals the small, soggy, icy garment. As he buckled the swollen belt, suddenly my groin felt the chill of death. 13

Questions for Close Reading

1. What is the selection's thesis (or dominant impression)? Locate the sentence(s) in which White states his main idea. If he doesn't state the thesis explicitly, express it in your own words.

2. Why does White return to the lake in Maine he had visited as a child? Why do you think he has waited to revisit it until he has a young son to bring along?

3. Several times in the essay, White notes that he felt as if he were his own father—and that his son became his childhood self. What event first prompts this sensation? What actions and thoughts cause it to recur?

4. How is the latest visit to the lake similar to White's childhood summers? What differences does White notice? What effects do the differences have on him?

5. Refer to your dictionary as needed to define the following words used in the selection: *incessant* (paragraph 1), *placidity* (1), *primeval* (3), *transposition* (4), *undulating* (6), *indelible* (8), *petulant* (10), and *languidly* (13).

Questions About the Writer's Craft

1. The pattern. Through vivid language, descriptive writing evokes sensory experiences. In "Once More to the Lake," White overlays two sets of sensory details: those of the present-day lake and those of the lake as it was in his boyhood. Which set of details is more objective? Which seems sharper and more powerful? Why?

2. To describe the lake, White chooses many words and phrases with religious connotations. Give some examples. What might have been his purpose in using such language?

3. Other patterns. In paragraph 12, White uses a metaphor to describe a thunderstorm. To what does he compare a thunderstorm? Why does he make this comparison?

4. White refers to "the chill of death" in the final paragraph. What brings on this feeling? Why does he feel it "in his groin"? Where has this idea been hinted at previously in the essay?

Writing Assignments Using Description as a Pattern of Development

1. Write a descriptive essay about a special place in your life. The place need not be a natural setting like White's lake; it could be a city or building that has meant a great deal to you. Use sensory details and figurative language, as White does, to enliven your description and convey the place's significance for you.

2. White was fortunate that his lake had remained virtually unchanged. But many other special spots have been destroyed or are threatened with destruction. Write a descriptive essay about a place (a park, a school, an old-fashioned ice cream parlor) that is "infinitely precious and worth saving." For your dominant theme, show which aspects of your subject make it worthy of being preserved for future generations. Joseph H. Suina's "And Then I Went to School" (page 339) may spark some helpful ideas since it details the special qualities of a place threatened with extinction.

Writing Assignments Using Other Patterns of Development

3. Sometimes, we, like White, are suddenly reminded of the nearness of death: a crushed animal lies in the road, a politician is assassinated, a classmate is killed in a car crash. Write an essay about a time you were forced to think about mortality. Explain what happened and describe your thoughts and feelings afterwards.

4. Have your older relatives attempted to share with you some special experiences of their younger years? Have you done the same thing with your own children, nephews, or nieces? You may have taken loved ones to a special place, as White did, or listened to stories or looked at photographs. Write an essay recounting such an experience. Explain the motivations of the older generation and the effects on the younger one. Before planning your paper, you may want to read the following essay by Maxine Hong Kingston, "Photographs of My Parents"; it depicts two generations' sharing of the past.

MAXINE HONG KINGSTON

An instructor of creative writing at the University of Hawaii, Maxine Hong Kingston (1940–) is the author of the highly praised *The Woman Warrior: Memoirs from a Girlhood Among Ghosts* (1975), *China Men* (1980), and *Tripmaster Monkey* (1989). This selection is taken from *The Woman Warrior*.

PHOTOGRAPHS OF MY PARENTS

1   Once in a long while, four times so far for me, my mother brings out the metal tube that holds her medical diploma. On the tube are gold circles crossed with seven red

lines each—"joy" ideographs* in abstract. There are also little flowers that look like gears for a gold machine. According to the scraps of labels with Chinese and American addresses, stamps, and postmarks, the family airmailed the can from Hong Kong in 1950. It got crushed in the middle, and whoever tried to peel the labels off stopped because the red and gold paint came off too, leaving silver scratches that rust. Somebody tried to pry the end off before discovering that the tube pulls apart. When I open it, the smell of China flies out, a thousand-year-old bat flying heavy-headed out of the Chinese caverns where bats are as white as dust, a smell that comes from long ago, far back in the brain. Crates from Canton, Hong Kong, Singapore, and Taiwan have that smell too, only stronger because they are more recently come from the Chinese.

Inside the can are three scrolls, one inside another. The largest says that in the twenty-third year of the National Republic, the To Keung School of Midwifery, where she has had two years of instruction and Hospital Practice, awards its Diploma to my mother, who has shown through oral and written examination her Proficiency in Midwifery, Pediatrics, Gynecology, "Medecine," "Surgary," Therapeutics, Ophthalmology, Bacteriology, Dermatology, Nursing and Bandage. This document has eight stamps on it: one, the school's English and Chinese names embossed together in a circle; one, as the Chinese enumerate, a stork and a big baby in lavender ink; one, the school's Chinese seal; one, an orangish paper stamp pasted in the border design; one, the red seal of Dr. Wu Pak-liang, M.D., Lyon, Berlin, president and "Ex-assistant étranger à la clinique chirugicale et d'accouchement de l'université de Lyon";** one, the red seal of Dean Woo Yin-kam, M.D.; one, my mother's seal, her chop mark[†] larger than the president's and the dean's; and one, the number 1279 on the back. Dean Woo's signature is followed by "(Hackett)." I read in a history book that Hackett Medical College for Women at Canton was founded in the nineteenth century by European women doctors.

The school seal has been pressed over a photograph of my mother at the age of thirty-seven. The diploma gives her age as twenty-seven. She looks younger than I do, her eyebrows are thicker, her lips fuller. Her naturally curly hair is parted on the left, one wavy wisp tendrilling off to the right. She wears a scholar's white gown, and she is not thinking about her appearance. She stares straight ahead as if she could see me and past me to her grandchildren and grandchildren's grandchildren. She has spacy eyes, as all people recently from Asia have. Her eyes do not focus on the camera. My mother is not smiling; Chinese do not smile for photographs. Their faces command relatives in foreign lands—"Send money"—and posterity forever—"Put food in front of this picture." My mother does not understand Chinese-American snapshots. "What are you laughing at?" she asks.

The second scroll is a long narrow photograph of the graduating class with the school officials seated in front. I picked out my mother immediately. Her face is exactly her own, though forty years younger. She is so familiar, I can only tell whether or not she is pretty or happy or smart by comparing her to the other women. For this formal group picture she straightened her hair with oil to make a chinlength bob like the others'. On the other women, strangers, I can recognize a curled lip, a sidelong glance, pinched shoulders. My mother is not soft; the girl with the small nose and dimpled underlip is soft. My mother is not humorous, not like the girl at the end who

---

*Chinese letters symbolizing the word *joy* (editors' note).
**Foreign ex-assistant instructor at the surgical and maternity clinic of Lyons in France (editors' note).
[†]Chinese seal.

Description

lifts her mocking chin to pose like Girl Graduate. My mother does not have smiling eyes; the old woman teacher (Dean Woo?) in front crinkles happily, and the one faculty member in the western suit smiles westernly. Most of the graduates are girls whose faces have not yet formed; my mother's face will not change anymore, except to age. She is intelligent, alert, pretty. I can't tell if she's happy.

5   The graduates seem to have been looking elsewhere when they pinned the rose, zinnia, or chrysanthemum on their precise black dresses. One thin girl wears hers in the middle of her chest. A few have a flower over a left or right nipple. My mother put hers, a chrysanthemum, below her left breast. Chinese dresses at that time were dartless, cut as if women did not have breasts; these young doctors, unaccustomed to decorations, may have seen their chests as black expanses with no reference points for flowers. Perhaps they couldn't shorten that far gaze that lasts only a few years after a Chinese emigrates. In this picture too my mother's eyes are big with what they held—reaches of oceans beyond China, land beyond oceans. Most emigrants learn the barbarians' directness—how to gather themselves and stare rudely into talking faces as if trying to catch lies. In America my mother has eyes as strong as boulders, never once skittering off a face, but she has not learned to place decorations and phonograph needles, nor has she stopped seeing land on the other side of the oceans. Now her eyes include the relatives in China, as they once included my father smiling and smiling in his many western outfits, a different one for each photograph that he sent from America.

6   He and his friends took pictures of one another in bathing suits at Coney Island beach, the salt wind from the Atlantic blowing their hair. He's the one in the middle with his arms about the necks of his buddies. They pose in the cockpit of a biplane, on a motorcycle, and on a lawn beside the "Keep Off the Grass" sign. They are always laughing. My father, white shirt sleeves rolled up, smiles in front of a wall of clean laundry. In the spring he wears a new straw hat, cocked at a Fred Astaire angle. He steps out, dancing down the stairs, one foot forward, one back, a hand in his pocket. He wrote to her about the American custom of stomping on straw hats come fall. "If you want to save your hat for next year," he said, "you have to put it away early, or else when you're riding the subway or walking along Fifth Avenue, any stranger can snatch it off your head and put his foot through it. That's the way they celebrate the change of seasons here." In the winter he wears a gray felt hat with his gray overcoat. He is sitting on a rock in Central Park. In one snapshot he is not smiling; someone took it when he was studying, blurred in the glare of the desk lamp.

7   There are no snapshots of my mother. In two small portraits, however, there is a black thumbprint on her forehead, as if someone had inked in bangs, as if someone had marked her.

8   "Mother, did bangs come into fashion after you had the picture taken?" One time she said yes. Another time when I asked, "Why do you have fingerprints on your forehead?" she said, "Your First Uncle did that." I disliked the unsureness in her voice.

9   The last scroll has columns of Chinese words. The only English is "Department of Health, Canton," imprinted on my mother's face, the same photograph as on the diploma. I keep looking to see whether she was afraid. Year after year my father did not come home or send for her. Their two children had been dead for ten years. If he did not return soon, there would be no more children. ("They were three and two years old, a boy and a girl. They could talk already.") My father did send money regularly, though, and she had nobody to spend it on but herself. She bought good clothes and shoes. Then she decided to use the money for becoming a doctor. She did not leave for Canton immediately after the children died. In China there was time to complete feelings. As my father had done, my mother left the village by ship. There was a sea bird painted on the ship to protect it against shipwreck and winds. She was in luck.

The following ship was boarded by river pirates, who kidnapped every passenger, even old ladies. "Sixty dollars for an old lady" was what the bandits used to say. "I sailed alone," she says, "to the capital of the entire province." She took a brown leather suitcase and a seabag stuffed with two quilts.

Questions for Close Reading

1. What is the selection's thesis (or dominant impression)? Locate the sentence(s) in which Kingston states her main idea. If she doesn't state the thesis explicitly, express it in your own words.

2. What do the photographs of Kingston's mother reveal about her appearance? What personality traits do they suggest?

3. How are the pictures of Kingston's father different from those of her mother?

4. Kingston writes that she continues to look at her mother's photographs "to see whether she was afraid." What might her mother have feared? Which of her mother's actions indicate a *lack* of fear?

5. Refer to your dictionary as needed to define the following words used in the selection: *midwifery* (paragraph 2) and *barbarian* (5).

Questions About the Writer's Craft

1. The pattern. The essay's first paragraph provides rich sensory details that allow us to see, feel, and smell the tube holding the diplomas. Why do you think Kingston took the time to paint such a careful word picture of this tube before describing its contents?

2. Other patterns. Why do you suppose Kingston compares the "smell of China" to a "thousand-year-old bat"? What is the metaphor's effect?

3. Where does Kingston shift from writing about her mother to writing about her father? Why do you think she makes the transition in this way?

4. What seems to have been Kingston's purpose in this selection?

Writing Assignments Using Description as a Pattern of Development

1. Write a descriptive essay based on what a particular photograph reveals about a family member. Try to look at the person as if he or she were new to you. Organize your description around a dominant impression.

2. Like Kingston's mother, many people have a special possession. Describe such a possession. (It may belong to you or someone else.) Include a variety of sensory impressions that suggest how significant this possession is to its owner.

Description

Writing Assignments Using Other Patterns of Development

3. Talk with an older family member or friend about an important event of his or her younger days. Then write a narrative essay about that incident, making sure that your details help readers understand the event's significance.

4. Although born in the United States, Kingston obviously takes pride in her Chinese heritage. Write an essay illustrating what aspects of your own racial, religious, or family heritage mean the most to you. To get some ideas about the importance of ethnic pride, you might want to read Malcolm X's "My First Conk" (page 307).

JOHN CIARDI

John Ciardi (1916–86) was born in Boston and is known primarily for his richly textured yet accessible poetry. He taught at Rutgers University in the 1950s and for almost twenty years served as the poetry editor of the magazine *Saturday Review*. In addition to translating the medieval epic poem *The Divine Comedy*, Ciardi wrote several children's books and a college-level text on poetry, *How Does a Poem Mean?* (1959). His own poetry is available in the collections *As If: New and Selected Poems* (1955) and *For Instance* (1979). The following essay is from *Manner of Speaking* (1982).

DAWN WATCH

1 Unless a man is up for the dawn and for the half hour or so of first light, he has missed the best of the day.

2 The traffic has just started, not yet a roar and a stink. One car at a time goes by, the tires humming almost like the sound of a brook a half mile down in the crease of a mountain I know—a sound that carries not because it is loud but because everything else is still.

3 It isn't exactly a mist that hangs in the thickets but more nearly the ghost of a mist—a phenomenon like side vision. Look hard and it isn't there, but glance without focusing and something registers, an exhalation that will be gone three minutes after the sun comes over the treetops.

4 The lawns shine with a dew not exactly dew. There is a rabbit bobbing about on the lawn and then freezing. If it were truly a dew, his tracks would shine black on the grass, and he leaves no visible track. Yet, there is something on the grass that makes it glow a depth of green it will not show again all day. Or is that something in the dawn air?

5 Our cardinals know what time it is. They drop pure tones from the hemlock tops. The black gang of grackles that makes a slum of the pin oak also knows the time but can only grate at it. They sound like a convention of broken universal joints grating uphill. The grackles creak and squeak, and the cardinals form tones that only occasionally sound through the noise. I scatter sunflower seeds by the birdbath for the cardinals and hope the grackles won't find them.

6 My neighbor's tomcat comes across the lawn, probably on his way home from passion, or only acting as if he had had a big night. I suspect him of being one of

those poolroom braggarts who can't get next to a girl but who likes to let on that he is a hot stud. This one is too can-fed and too lazy to hunt for anything. Here he comes now, ignoring the rabbit. And there he goes.

As soon as he has hopped the fence, I let my dog out. The dog charges the rabbit, watches it jump the fence, shakes himself in a self-satisfied way, then trots dutifully into the thicket for his morning service, stopping to sniff everything on the way back.

There is an old mountain laurel on the island of the driveway turnaround. From somewhere on the wind a white morning-glory rooted next to it and has climbed it. Now the laurel is woven full of white bells tinged pink by the first rays through the not quite mist. Only in earliest morning can they be seen. Come out two hours from now and there will be no morning-glories.

Dawn, too, is the hour of a weed I know only as day flower—a bright blue button that closes in full sunlight. I have weeded bales of it out of my flower beds, its one daytime virtue being the shallowness of its root system that allows it to be pulled out effortlessly in great handfuls. Yet, now it shines. Had it a few more hours of such shining in its cycle, I would cultivate it as a ground cover, but dawn is its one hour, and a garden is for whole days.

There is another blue morning weed whose name I do not know. This one grows from a bulb to pulpy stems and a bedraggled daytime sprawl. Only a shovel will dig it out. Try weeding it by hand and the stems will break off to be replaced by new ones and to sprawl over the chosen plants in the flower bed. Yet, now and for another hour it outshines its betters, its flowers about the size of a quarter and paler than those of the day flower but somehow more brilliant, perhaps because of the contrast of its paler foliage.

And now the sun is slanting in full. It is bright enough to make the leaves of the Japanese red maple seem a transparent red bronze when the tree is between me and the light. There must be others, but this is the only tree I know whose leaves let the sun through in this way—except, that is, when the fall colors start. Aspen leaves, when they first yellow and before they dry, are transparent in this way. I tell myself it must have something to do with the red-yellow range of the spectrum. Green takes sunlight and holds it, but red and yellow let it through.

The damned crabgrass is wrestling with the zinnias, and I stop to weed it out. The stuff weaves too close to the zinnias to make the iron claw usable. And it won't do to pull at the stalks. Crabgrass (at least in a mulched bed) can be weeded only with dirty fingers. Thumb and forefinger have to pincer into the dirt and grab the root-center. Weeding, of course, is an illusion of hope. Pulling out the root only stirs the soil and brings new crabgrass seeds into germinating position. Take a walk around the block and a new clump will have sprouted by the time you get back. But I am not ready to walk around the block. I fill a small basket with the plucked clumps, and for the instant I look at them, the zinnias are weedless.

Don't look back. I dump the weeds in the thicket where they will be smothered by the grass clippings I will pile on at the next cutting. On the way back I see the cardinals come down for the sunflower seeds, and the jays join them, and then the grackles start ganging in, gatecrashing the buffet and clattering all over it. The dog stops chewing his rawhide and makes a dash into the puddle of birds, which splashes away from him.

I hear a brake-squeak I have been waiting for and know the paper has arrived. As usual, the news turns out to be another disaster count. The function of the wire services is to bring us tragedies faster than we can pity. In the end we shall all be inured, numb, and ready for emotionless programming. I sit on the patio and read until the sun grows too bright on the page. The cardinals have stopped singing, and the grackles have flown off. It's the end of birdsong again.

15   Then suddenly—better than song for its instant—a hummingbird the color of green crushed velvet hovers in the throat of my favorite lily, a lovely high-bloomer I got the bulbs for but not the name. The lily is a crest of white horns with red dots and red velvet tongues along the insides of the petals and with an odor that drowns the patio. The hummingbird darts in and out of each horn in turn, then hovers an instant, and disappears.

16   Even without the sun, I have had enough of the paper. I'll take that hummingbird as my news for this dawn. It is over now. I smoke one more cigarette too many and decide that, if I go to bed now, no one in the family need know I have stayed up for it again. Why do they insist on shaking their heads when they find me still up for breakfast, after having scribbled through the dark hours? They always do. They seem compelled to express pity for an old loony who can't find his own way to bed. Why won't they understand that this is the one hour of any day that must not be missed, as it is the one hour I couldn't imagine getting up for, though I can still get to it by staying up? It makes sense to me. There comes a time when the windows lighten and the twittering starts. I look up and know it's time to leave the papers in their mess. I could slip quietly into bed and avoid the family's headshakes, but this stroll-around first hour is too good to miss. Even my dog, still sniffing and circling, knows what hour this is.

17   Come on, boy. It's time to go in. The rabbit won't come back till tomorrow, and the birds have work to do. The dawn's over. It's time to call it a day.

Questions for Close Reading

1. What is the selection's thesis (or dominant impression)? Locate the sentence(s) in which Ciardi states his main idea. If he doesn't state the thesis explicitly, express it in your own words.

2. What might Ciardi mean by saying that dawn is the "best" part of the day?

3. What details indicate that the scene Ciardi observes is one with which he is thoroughly familiar and one in which he himself plays a role?

4. What do you think Ciardi means by saying he has had "enough of the paper" and will "take that hummingbird as my news for this dawn" (paragraph 16)? What can you infer from these statements about Ciardi's view of the everyday world?

5. Refer to your dictionary as needed to define the following words used in the selection: *exhalation* (paragraph 3), *grackles* (5 and 13), *aspen* (11), *spectrum* (11), *germinating* (12), and *inured* (14).

Questions About the Writer's Craft

1. The pattern. What sensory impressions does Ciardi draw upon when describing the dawn? What method of organization does he use to structure these impressions?

2. Ciardi uses several striking metaphors to convey the dawn's sensory richness. Locate some of these metaphors. How do they reinforce the essay's dominant impression?

3. Other patterns. In detailing the scenes and events of the dawn, Ciardi describes several processes. Locate some of these in his essay and explain what they reveal about Ciardi's attitude toward the dawn.

4. Examine Ciardi's concluding paragraph. To whom is Ciardi talking? What is the effect of this sudden shift away from speaking to the reader? Why does the sentence "It's time to call it a day" make an especially apt closing line?

Writing Assignments Using Description as a Pattern of Development

1. Like Ciardi, most people have fond feelings about a specific place at a specific time of day. Brainstorm the sensory details that make a particular place and time especially attractive to you. Then write a description of your subject. Include both conventionally beautiful and nonpoetic elements so that your description, like Ciardi's, is down-to-earth rather than romanticized or sentimentalized.

2. Solitude is a major component of Ciardi's dawn watch. Write an essay about a place whose essential nature emerges in the absence of people. Possible subjects include a vacant city lot, a neighborhood garden, a section of ocean boardwalk. Rather than stating your thesis explicitly, choose sensory details that convey what it is about your subject that makes it worth describing. To see how two skilled prose stylists write about places having a magic of their own, you might want to read E. B. White's "Once More to the Lake" (page 170) and Anne Morrow Lindbergh's "Channelled Whelk" (page 237).

Writing Assignments Using Other Patterns of Development

3. Choose a block of time that you feel too few people appreciate. Then write an essay that refutes the reasons people might have for overlooking the value of this span of time. You might, for example, argue the importance of time spent commuting in a car, waiting for class to begin, or standing in line at the supermarket. Your essay may be serious or light in tone.

4. In his essay, Ciardi defines the "best" of the day. In an essay of your own, define the "best" of some important aspect of your life. For instance, you could define your "best" learning experience, your "best" decision, your "best" accomplishment. Use evocative sensory images and strong narrative details to support your definition of the "best."

ADDITIONAL WRITING TOPICS: DESCRIPTION

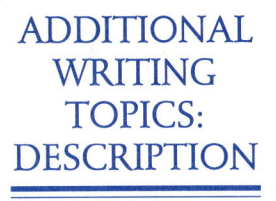

General Assignments

Write an essay using description to develop one of the following topics.

1. A favorite item of clothing
2. A school as a young child sees it
3. A hospital room you have visited or stayed in
4. An individualist's appearance
5. A coffee shop, bus shelter, newsstand, or some other small place
6. A parade or victory celebration
7. A banana, squash, or other fruit or vegetable
8. A particular drawer
9. A houseplant
10. A "media event"
11. A dorm room
12. An elderly person
13. An attractive man or woman
14. A prosthetic device or wheelchair
15. A TV, film, or music celebrity
16. A student lounge
17. A once-in-a-lifetime event
18. The inside of something, such as a cave, boat, car, shed, or machine
19. A friend, roommate, or other person you know well
20. An essential gadget or a useless gadget

Assignments with a Specific Purpose, Audience, and Point of View

1. For an audience of incoming first-year students, prepare a speech describing registration day at your college. Use specific details to help prepare students for

the actual event. Choose an adjective that represents your dominant impression of the experience, and keep that word in mind as you write.

2. As a subscriber to a dating service, you've been asked to submit a description of the kind of person you'd like to meet. Describe your ideal date. Focus on specifics about physical appearance, personal habits, character traits, and interests.

3. Your college has decided to replace an old campus structure (for example, a dorm or dining hall) with a new version. Write a letter of protest to the administration, describing the place so vividly and appealingly that its value and need for preservation are unquestionable.

4. As a staff member of the campus newspaper, you have been asked to write a weekly column of social news and gossip. For your first column, you plan to describe a recent campus event—a dance, party, concert, or other social activity. With a straightforward or tongue-in-cheek tone, describe where the event was held, the appearance of the people who attended, and so on.

5. You are part of a student–faculty group responsible for revising the college catalog at your school. Write a full and accurate description of a course with which you're familiar. Tell exactly what the course is about, who teaches it, and how it is run.

6. As a resident of a particular town, you're angered by the appearance of a certain spot and by the activities that take place there. Write a letter to the town council, describing in detail the undesirable nature of this place (a video arcade, an adult bookstore, a bar, a bus station, a neglected park or beach). End with some suggestions about ways to improve the situation.

13
NARRATION

WHAT IS NARRATION?

HUMAN beings are instinctively storytellers. In prehistoric times, our ancestors huddled around campfires to hear tales of hunting and magic. In ancient times, warriors gathered in halls to listen to bards praise in song the exploits of epic heroes. Things are no different today. Boisterous children invariably settle down to listen when their parents read to them; millions of people tune in day after day to the ongoing drama of their favorite soap operas; vacationers sit motionless on the beach, caught up in the latest best-sellers; and all of us enjoy saying, "Just listen to what happened to me today." Our hunger for storytelling is basic.

Narration means telling a single story or several related stories. The story can be a means to an end, a way to support a main idea or thesis. To demonstrate that television has become the constant companion of many children, you might narrate a typical child's day in front of the television—starting with cartoons in the morning and ending with situation comedies at night. Or to support the point that the college registration process should be reformed, you could tell the tale of a chaotic morning spent trying to enroll in classes.

Narration is powerful. Every public speaker, from politician to classroom teacher, knows that stories capture the attention of listeners as nothing else can. We want to know what happened to others, not simply because we're curious, but also because their experiences shed light on our own lives. Narration lends force to opinion, triggers the flow of memory, and evokes places, times, and people in ways that are compelling and affecting.

HOW NARRATION FITS YOUR PURPOSE AND AUDIENCE

Since narratives tell a story, you may think they're found only in novels or short stories. But narration can also appear in essays, sometimes as a supplemental pattern of development. For example, if your purpose in a paper is to *persuade* apathetic readers that airport security regulations must be followed strictly, you might lead off with a brief account of an armed terrorist who easily boarded a plane. In a paper *defining* good teaching, you might keep readers engaged by including satirical anecdotes about one hapless instructor, the antithesis of an effective teacher. An essay on the *effects* of an overburdened judicial system might provide—in an attempt to involve readers—a dramatic account of the way one clearly guilty murderer plea-bargained his way to freedom.

In addition to providing effective support in one section of your paper, narration can also serve as an essay's dominant pattern of development. In fact, most of this chapter shows you how to use a single narrative to convey a central point and share with readers your view of what happened. You might choose to narrate the events of an afternoon spent with your three-year-old nephew as a way of revealing how you rediscovered the importance of family life. Or you might relate the story of your roommate's mugging, evoking the powerlessness and terror of being a victim.

Although some narratives relate unusual experiences, most tread familiar ground, telling tales of joy, love, loss, frustration, fear—all common emotions experienced during life. Narratives can take the ordinary and transmute it into something significant, even extraordinary. As Willa Cather, the American novelist, wrote: "There are only two or three human stories and they go on repeating themselves as fiercely as if they had never happened before." The challenge lies in applying your own vision to a tale, thereby making it unique.

PREWRITING STRATEGIES

The following checklist shows how you can apply to narration some of the prewriting strategies discussed in Chapter 2.

> ☑ **NARRATION: A PREWRITING CHECKLIST**
>
> *Select Your Narrative Event(s)*
> ☐ What event evokes strong emotion in you and is likely to have a powerful effect on your readers?
> ☐ Does your journal suggest any promising subjects—for example, an entry about a bully's surprisingly respectful behavior toward a handicapped student or a painful encounter with racial prejudice?

- Does a scrapbook souvenir, snapshot, old letter, or prized object (an athletic trophy, a political button) point to an event worth writing about?
- Will you focus on a personal experience (your high school graduation ceremony), an incident in someone else's life (a friend's battle with chronic illness), or a public event (a community effort to save a beached whale)?
- Can you recount your story effectively, given the length of a typical college essay? If not, will relating one key incident from the fuller, more complete event enable you to convey the point and feeling of the entire experience?
- If you write about an event in someone else's life, will you have time to interview the person: "Why did you cross the picket line?" "What did you do when your boss told you to lie?"

Focus on the Conflict in the Event
- What is the source of tension in the event: one person's internal dilemma, a conflict between characters, or a struggle between a character and a social institution or natural phenomenon?
- Will the conflict create enough tension to "hook" readers and keep them interested?
- What point does the conflict and its resolution convey to readers?
- What tone is appropriate for recounting the conflict?

Use Prewriting to Generate Specifics About the Conflict
- Would the questioning technique ("Why did the argument occur?"), brainstorming, freewriting, mapping, or interviewing help you generate details about the conflict? Does your journal suggest ways to explore aspects of the conflict? ("When my friends participated in the violence at the rock concert, why didn't I try to stop them?")

STRATEGIES FOR USING NARRATION IN AN ESSAY

After prewriting, you're ready to draft your essay. The following suggestions will be helpful whether you use narration as a dominant or supportive pattern of development.

1. Identify the point of the narrative conflict. As you know, most narratives center around a conflict (see the preceding checklist). When you relate a story, it's up to you to convey the *significance* or *meaning* of the event's conflict. In *The*

Adventures of Huckleberry Finn, Mark Twain warned: "Persons attempting to find a motive in this narrative will be prosecuted; persons attempting to find a moral in it will be banished...." Twain was, of course, being ironic; his novel's richness lies in its "motives" and "morals." Similarly, when recounting your narrative, be sure to begin with a clear sense of your *narrative point*, or *thesis*. Then either state that point directly or select details and a tone that imply the point you want readers to take away from your story.

For example, suppose you decide to write about the time you got locked in a mall late at night. Your narrative might focus on the way the mall looked after hours and the way you struggled with mounting terror. But you would also use the narrative to make a point. Perhaps you want to emphasize that fear can be instructive. Or your point might be that malls have a disturbing, surreal underside. You could state this thesis explicitly. ("After hours, the mall shed its cheerful daytime demeanor for a more sinister quality.") Or you could refrain from stating the thesis directly, relying on your details and language to convey the point of the narrative: "The mannequins stared at me with glazed eyes and frozen smiles" and "The steel grates pulled over each store glinted in the cold light, making each shop look like a prison cell."

2. Develop only those details that advance the narrative point. Nothing is more boring than a storyteller who gets sidetracked and drags out a story with nonessential details. When telling a story, you maintain an effective narrative pace by focusing on your point and eliminating any details that don't support it. A good narrative depends not only on what is included, but also on what has been left out.

How do you determine which specifics to omit, which to treat briefly, and which to emphasize? Having a clear sense of your narrative point and knowing your audience are crucial. Assume you're writing a narrative about a disastrous get-acquainted dance sponsored by your college the first week of the academic year. In addition to telling what happened, you also want to make a point; perhaps you want to emphasize that, despite the college's good intentions, such "official" events actually make it difficult to meet people. With this purpose in mind, you might write about how stiff and unnatural students seemed, all dressed up in their best clothes; you might narrate snatches of strained conversation you overheard; you might describe the way males gathered on one side of the room, females on the other—reverting to behaviors supposedly abandoned in fifth grade. All these details would support your narrative point.

Because you don't want to lead away from that point, you would leave out details about the top-notch band and the appetizing refreshments at the dance. The music and food may have been surprisingly good, but since these details don't advance the point you want to make, they should not be included in your narrative.

You also need to keep your audience in mind when selecting narrative details. If the audience consists of your instructor and other students—all of them familiar with the new student center where the dance was held—specific details about the center probably wouldn't have to be provided. But imagine that the essay is going to appear in the quarterly magazine published by the college's community relations office. Many of the magazine's readers are former graduates who haven't been on campus for several years. They may need additional specifics about the student center: its location, how many people it holds, how it is furnished.

As you write, keep asking yourself, "Is this detail or character or snippet of conversation essential? Does my audience need this detail to understand the conflict in the situation? Does this detail advance or intensify the narrative action?" Summarize details that have some importance but do not deserve lengthy treatment ("Two hours went by ..."). And try to limit *narrative commentary*—statements that tell rather than show what happened—since such remarks interrupt the narrative flow. Focus instead on the specifics that propel action forward in a vigorous way.

Sometimes, especially if the narrative re-creates an event from the past, you won't be able to remember what happened detail for detail. In such a case, you should take advantage of what is called **dramatic license.** Using your current perspective as a guide, feel free to add or reshape details to suit your narrative point.

3. Organize the narrative sequence. All of us know the traditional beginning of fairy tales: "Once upon a time...." Every narrative begins somewhere, presents a span of time, and ends at a certain point. Frequently, you will want to use a straightforward time order, following the event *chronologically* from beginning to end: first this happened, next this happened, finally this happened.

But sometimes a strict chronological recounting may not be effective—especially if the high point of the narrative gets lost somewhere in the middle of the time sequence. To avoid that possibility, you may want to disrupt chronology, plunge the reader into the middle of the story, and then return in a **flashback** to the tale's beginning. You are probably familiar with the way flashback is used on television and in film. You see someone appealing to the main characters for financial help, then return in a flashback to an earlier time when both were students in the same class. Narratives can also use **flashforward**—you give readers a glimpse of the future (the main character being jailed) before the story continues in the present (the events leading to the arrest). These techniques shift the story onto several planes and keep it from becoming a step-by-step, predictable account. Reserve flashforwards and flashbacks, however, for crucial incidents only, since breaking out of chronological order acts as emphasis. Here are examples of how flashback and flashforward can be used in narrative writing:

Flashback

Standing behind the wooden counter, Greg wielded his knife expertly as he shucked clams--one every ten seconds--with practiced ease. The scene contrasted sharply with his first day on the job, when his hands broke out in blisters and when splitting each shell was like prying open a safe.

Flashforward

Rushing to move my car from the no-parking zone, I waved a quick goodbye to Karen as she climbed the steps to the bus. I didn't know then that by the time I picked her up at the bus station later that day, she had made a decision that would affect both our lives.

Whether or not you choose to include flashbacks or flashforwards in an essay, remember to limit the time span covered by the narrative. Otherwise, you'll have trouble generating the details needed to give the story depth and meaning. Also regardless of the time sequence you select, organize the tale so it drives toward a strong finish. Be careful that your story doesn't trail off into minor, anticlimactic details.

4. Make the narrative easy to follow. Describing each distinct action in a separate paragraph helps readers grasp the flow of events. Although narrative essays don't always have conventional topic sentences, each narrative paragraph should have a clear focus. Often this focus is indicated by a sentence early in the paragraph that directs attention to the action taking place. Such a sentence functions as a kind of *informal topic sentence;* the rest of the paragraph then develops that topic sentence. You should also be sure to use time signals when narrating a story. Words like *now, then, next, after,* and *later* ensure that your reader won't get lost as the story progresses.

5. Make the narrative vigorous and immediate. A compelling narrative provides an abundance of specific details, making readers feel as if they're experiencing the story being told. Readers must be able to see, hear, touch, smell, and taste the event you're narrating. *Vivid sensory description* is, therefore, an essential part of an effective narrative. (See page 68 in Chapter 6 and pages 120—21 in Chapter 8 for more on concrete, sensory language.) Not only do specific sensory details make writing a pleasure to read—we all enjoy learning the particulars about people, places, and things—but they also give the narrative the stamp of reality. The specifics convince the reader that the event being described actually did, or could, occur.

Compare the following excerpts from a narrative essay. The first version is lifeless and dull; the revised version, packed with sensory images, grabs readers with its sense of foreboding:

Original Version

That eventful day started out like every other summer day. My sister Tricia and I made several elaborate mud pies which we decorated with care. A little later on, as we were spraying each other with the garden hose, we heard my father walk up the path.

Revised

That sad summer day started out uneventfully enough. My sister Tricia and I spent a few hours mixing and decorating mud pies. Our hands caked with dry mud, we sprinkled each lopsided pie with alternating rows of dandelion and clover petals. Later, when the sun got hotter, we tossed our white T-shirts over the red picket fence--forgetting my grandmother's frequent warnings to be more ladylike. Our sweaty backs bared to the sun, we doused each other with icy sprays from the garden hose. Caught up in the primitive pleasure of it all, we barely heard my father as he walked up the garden path, the gravel crunching under his heavy work boots.

A caution: Sensory language enlivens narration, but it also slows the pace. Be sure that the slower pace suits your purpose. For example, a lengthy description fits an account of a leisurely summer vacation but is inappropriate in a tale about a frantic search for a misplaced wallet.

Another way to create an aura of narrative immediacy is to use **dialog** while telling a story. Our sense of other people comes, in part, from what they say and the way they sound. Conversational exchanges allow the reader to experience characters directly. Compare the following fragments of a narrative, one with dialog and one without, noting how much more energetic the second version is.

Original

As soon as I found my way back to the campsite, the trail guide commented on my disheveled appearance. I explained that I had heard some gunshots and had run back to camp as soon as I could.

Revised

As soon as I found my way back to the campsite, the trail guide took one look at me and drawled, "What on earth happened to you, Daniel Boone? You look as though you've been dragged through a haystack backwards."

"I'd look a lot worse if I hadn't run back here. When a bullet whizzes by me, I don't stick around to see who's doing the shooting."

Note that, when using dialog, you generally begin a new paragraph to indicate a shift from one person's speech to another's (as in the second example above). Dialog can also be used to convey a person's inner thoughts. Like conversation between people, such interior dialog is enclosed in quotation marks.

The challenge in writing dialog, both exterior and interior, is to make each character's speech distinctive and convincing. Reading the dialog aloud—even asking friends or family members to speak the lines—will help you develop an ear for authentic speech. What sounds most natural is often a compressed and reshaped version of what was actually said. As with other narrative details, include only those portions of dialog that serve your purpose, fit the mood you want to create, and reveal character.

Another way to enliven narratives is to use *varied sentence structure.* Sentences that plod along with the same predictable pattern put readers to sleep. Experiment with your sentences by varying their length and type; mix long and short sentences, simple and complex. (For more on sentence structure, see pages 105–112 in Chapter 8.) Compare the following original and revised versions to get an idea of how effective varied sentence structure can be in narrative writing:

Original

The store manager went to the walk-in refrigerator every day. The heavy metal door clanged shut behind her. I had visions of her freezing to death among the hanging carcasses. The shiny door finally swung open. She waddled out.

Revised

Each time the store manager went to the walk-in refrigerator, the heavy metal door clanged shut behind her. Visions of her freezing to death among the hanging carcasses crept into my mind until, finally, the shiny door swung open and out she waddled.

Original

The yellow-and-blue striped fish struggled on the line. Its scales shimmered in the sunlight. Its tail waved frantically. I saw its desire to live. I decided to let it go.

Revised

Scales shimmering in the sunlight, tail waving frantically, the yellow-and-blue striped fish struggled on the line. Seeing its desire to live, I let it go.

Finally, *vigorous verbs* lend energy to narratives. Use active verb forms ("The boss *yelled at* him") rather than passive ones ("He *was yelled at* by the boss"), and try to replace anemic *to be* verbs ("She *was* a good basketball player") with more dynamic constructions ("She *played* basketball well"). (For more on strong verbs, see pages 121–23 in Chapter 8.)

6. Keep your point of view and verb tense consistent. All stories have a *narrator*, the person who tells the story. If you, as narrator, tell a story as you experienced it, the story is written in the *first-person point of view* ("I saw the dog pull loose"). But if you observed the event (or heard about it from others) and want to tell how someone else experienced the incident, you would use the *third-person point of view* ("Anne saw the dog pull loose"). Each point of view has advantages and limitations. First person allows you to express ordinarily private thoughts and to re-create an event as you actually experienced it. This point of view is limited, though, in its ability to depict the inner thoughts of other people involved in the event. By way of contrast, third person makes it easier to provide insight into the thoughts of all the participants. However, its objective, broad perspective may undercut some of the subjective immediacy typical of the "I was there" point of view. No matter which point of view you select, stay with that vantage point throughout the entire narrative. (For more on point of view, see pages 23–24 in Chapter 2.)

Knowing whether to use the *past* or *present tense* ("I *strolled* into the room" as opposed to "I *stroll* into the room") is important. In most narrations, the past tense

Narration

predominates, enabling the writer to span a considerable period of time. Although more rarely used, the present tense can be powerful for events of short duration—a wrestling match or a medical emergency, for instance. A narrative in the present tense prolongs each moment, intensifying the reader's sense of participation. Be careful, though; unless the event is intense and fast-paced, the present tense can seem contrived. Whichever tense you choose, avoid shifting midstream—starting, let's say, in the past tense ("she skated") and switching to the present tense ("she runs").

REVISION STRATEGIES

Once you have a draft of the essay, you're ready to revise. The following checklist will help you and those giving you feedback apply to narration some of the revision techniques discussed in Chapters 7 and 8.

✔ NARRATION: A REVISION CHECKLIST

Revise Overall Meaning and Structure
- What is the essay's narrative point? Is it stated explicitly? If so, where? If not, where is it implied? Could the point be conveyed more clearly? How?
- What is the narrative's conflict? Is it stated explicitly? If so, where? If not, where is it implied? Could the conflict be made more dramatic? How?
- From what point of view is the narrative told? Is that the most effective point of view for this essay? Why or why not?

Revise Paragraph Development
- Which paragraphs (or passages) fail to advance the action, reveal character, or contribute to the story's mood? Should these sections be condensed or eliminated?
- Where do commentary and description slow the narrative pace? Is such an effect intended? If not, should the sections be tightened or eliminated?
- Where is it difficult to follow the chronology of events? Where should paragraph order be changed? Why? Where would chronology be clearer if there were separate paragraphs for distinct time periods? Where would additional time signals help?
- How could flashback or flashforward paragraphs (or passages) be used to highlight key events?
- What can be done to make the essay's opening paragraph more compelling? Would a dramatic bit of dialog or a mood-setting descriptive passage help?

- What could be done to make the essay's closing paragraph more effective? If the final paragraph seems anticlimactic, would it help to end earlier? If the ending doesn't round off the essay in a satisfying way, what could be added that would echo an idea or image in the opening?

Revise Sentences and Words
- Where is sentence structure monotonous? How would combining sentences, mixing sentence type, and alternating sentence length help?
- Where should the narrative pace be slowed down with long sentences or quickened with short ones?
- Where could dialog effectively convey character and propel the story forward? Where could dialog replace commentary?
- Which sentences and words are inconsistent with the essay's tone?
- Which sentences would benefit from sensory details that heighten the narrative mood?
- Where do vigorous verbs convey action? Where could active verbs ("Many of us *made* the same error") replace passive ones ("The same error *was made* by many of us")? Where could dull *to be* verbs ("The room *was* dark") be converted to more dynamic forms ("The room *darkened*")?
- Where are there inappropriate shifts in point of view or verb tense?

STUDENT ESSAY: FROM PREWRITING THROUGH REVISION

The student essay that follows was written by Paul Monahan in response to this assignment:

> In "Shooting an Elephant," George Orwell tells about an incident that forced him to act in a manner contrary to his better instincts. Write a narrative about a time you faced a disturbing conflict and ended up doing something you later regretted.

After deciding to write about an encounter he had with an elderly woman in the store where he worked, Paul did some *freewriting* on a word processor to gather material on his subject. When he later reviewed this freewriting, he crossed out unnecessary commentary, wrote notes signaling where dialog and descriptive details were needed, and indicated where paragraph breaks might occur. After annotating his freewriting in this manner, Paul felt comfortable launching into his first draft, without further shaping his freewriting or preparing an outline. As he wrote, though, he frequently referred to his warm-up material to organize his narrative and retrieve details. Paul's original freewriting

Narration

is shown here; the handwritten marks indicate Paul's later efforts to shape and develop this material:

Freewriting

An (old woman) entered the (store). She pushed the door, hobbled in, coughed, and seemed to be in pain. She wore a faded dress and a sweater that was much too small for her. The night was cold, but she didn't wear any stockings. You could see her veins. She strolled around the store, sneezing and hacking. She picked up a can of corn and stared at it. ~~She made me nervous.~~ I walked over to see what was going on. Asked if she needed help.

Set up contrast
Give details about her appearance
Add dialog

I was the one to do this because I was on duty. Had worked at 7-11 for two years. Felt confident. Always tried to be friendly and polite. Hadn't had any trouble. ~~But the old woman worried me.~~

Background information— move to first paragraph

"I need food," she said. I told her how much the corn cost and also that the bologna was on sale (what a stupid, insensitive thing to do!). She said she couldn't pay. I almost told her to take the can of corn, but all the rules stopped me. Be polite, stay in control. I told her I couldn't give anything away. Her face looked even more saggy. She kind of shook and put the can back. <u>She left. I rushed out</u> after her. Too late. Felt ashamed about acting like a robot. Mad at myself. (If only I'd acted differently.)

Add dialog
More specifics
Good title?

Now read Paul's paper, "If Only," noting the similarities and differences between his prewriting and final essay. You'll notice, for example, that Paul decided to move background information to the essay's opening, and that he ended up using as his title a shortened version of the final sentence in his prewriting. Finally, consider how well the essay applies the principles of narration discussed in this chapter. (The commentary that follows the paper will help you look at Paul's essay more closely and will give you some sense of how he went about revising his first draft.)

If Only

by Paul Monahan

1   Having worked at a 7-Eleven store for two years, I thought I had become successful at what our manager calls "customer relations." I firmly believed that a friendly smile and an automatic "sir," "ma'am," and "thank you" would see me through any situation that might arise, from soothing impatient or unpleasant people to apologizing for giving out the

Introduction

Narrative point (thesis) — wrong change. But the other night an old woman shattered my belief that a glib response could smooth over the rough spots of dealing with other human beings.

Informal topic sentence — The moment she entered, the woman presented a sharp contrast to our shiny store with its bright lighting and neatly arranged shelves. Walking as if each step were painful, she slowly pushed open the glass door and hobbled down the nearest aisle. *Sensory details* — She coughed dryly, wheezing with each breath. On a forty-degree night, she was wearing only a faded print dress, a thin, light-beige sweater too small to button, and black vinyl slippers with the backs cut out to expose calloused heels. There were no stockings or socks on her splotchy, blue-veined legs.

After strolling around the store for several minutes, the old woman stopped in front of the rows of canned vegetables. She picked up some corn niblets and stared with a strange intensity at the label. *Informal topic sentence* — At that point, I decided to be a good, courteous employee and asked her if she needed help. As I stood close to her, my smile became harder to maintain; *Sensory details* — her red-rimmed eyes were partially closed by yellowish crusts; her hands were covered with layer upon layer of grime, and the stale smell of sweat rose in a thick vaporous cloud from her clothes.

Start of dialog — "I need some food," she muttered in reply to my bright "Can I help you?"

"Are you looking for corn, ma'am?"

"I need some food," she repeated. "Any kind."

"Well, the corn is ninety-five cents," I said in my most helpful voice. "Or, if you like, we have a special on bologna today."

"I can't pay," she said.

Conflict established — For a second, I was tempted to say, "Take the corn." But the employee rules flooded into my mind: Remain polite, but do not let customers get the best of you. Let them know that you are in control. For a moment, I even entertained the idea that this was some sort of test, and that this woman was someone from the head office, testing my loyalty. I responded dutifully, "I'm sorry, ma'am, but I can't give away anything for free."

Informal topic sentence — The old woman's face collapsed a bit more, if that were possible, and her hands trembled as she put the can back on the shelf. She shuffled past me toward the door, her torn and dirty clothing barely covering her bent back.

11   Moments after she left, I rushed out the door with the can of corn, but she was nowhere in sight. For the rest of my shift, the image of the woman haunted me. I had been young, healthy, and smug. She had been old, sick, and desperate. Wishing with all my heart that I had acted like a human being rather than a robot, I was saddened to realize how fragile a hold we have on our better instincts.

Conclusion

Echoing of narrative point in the introduction

Commentary

Point of View, Tense, and Conflict

Paul chose to write "If Only" from the *first-person point of view*, a logical choice because he appears as a main character in his own story. Using the *past tense*, Paul recounts an incident filled with *conflict*—between him and the woman and between his fear of breaking the rules and his human instinct to help someone in need.

Narrative Point

It isn't always necessary to state the *narrative point* of an essay; it can be implied. But Paul decided to express the controlling idea of his narrative in two places—in the introduction ("But the other night an old woman shattered my belief that a glib response could smooth over the rough spots of dealing with other human beings") and again in the conclusion, where he expands his idea about rote responses overriding impulses of independent judgment and compassion. All of the essay's *narrative details* contribute to the point of the piece; Paul does not include any extraneous information that would detract from the central idea he wants to convey.

Organization and Other Patterns of Development

The narrative is *organized chronologically,* from the moment the woman enters the store to Paul's reaction after she leaves. Paul limits the narrative's time span. The entire incident probably occurs in under ten minutes, yet the introduction serves as a kind of *flashback* by providing some necessary background about Paul's past experiences. To help the reader follow the course of the narrative, Paul uses *time signals:* "The moment she entered, the woman presented a sharp contrast" (paragraph 2); "At that point, I decided to be a good, courteous employee" (3); "For the rest of my shift, the image of the woman haunted me" (11).

The paragraphs (except for those consisting solely of dialog) also contain *informal topic sentences* that direct attention to the specific stage of action being narrated. Indeed, each paragraph focuses on a distinct event: the elderly woman's actions when she first enters the store, the encounter between Paul and the woman, Paul's resulting inner conflict, the woman's subsequent response, and Paul's delayed reaction.

This chain of events, with one action leading to another, illustrates that the *cause-effect* pattern underlies the essay's basic structure. And another pattern—*description*—gives dramatic immediacy to the events being recounted. Throughout, rich sensory details engage the reader's interest. For instance, the sentence "her red-rimmed eyes were partially closed by yellowish crusts" (3) vividly re-creates the woman's appearance while also suggesting Paul's inner reaction to the woman.

Dialog and Sentence Structure

Paul uses other techniques to add energy and interest to his narrative. For one thing, he dramatizes his conflict with the woman through *dialog* that crackles with tension. And he achieves a vigorous narrative pace by *varying the length and structure of his sentences.* In the second paragraph, a short sentence ("There were no stockings or socks on her splotchy, blue-veined legs") alternates with a longer one ("On a forty-degree night, she was wearing only a faded print dress, a thin, light-beige sweater too small to button, and black vinyl slippers with the backs cut out to expose calloused heels." Some sentences in the essay open with a subject and verb ("She coughed dryly"), while others start with dependent clauses or participial phrases ("As I stood close to her, my smile became harder to maintain"; "Walking as if each step were painful, she slowly pushed open the glass door") or with a prepositional phrase ("For a second, I was tempted").

Revising the First Draft

To get a sense of how Paul went about revising his essay, take a moment to look at the original version of his third paragraph shown here. The handwritten annotations, numbered in order of importance, represent Paul's ideas for revision. Compare this preliminary version with the final version in the full essay:

Original Version of Third Paragraph

③ Inappropriate words—sound humorous
① Boring—not enough details
② Choppy sentences

After (sneezing) and (hacking) her way around the store, the old woman stopped in front of the vegetable shelves. (She) picked up a can of corn and stared at the label. (She) stayed like this for several minutes. Then I walked over to her and asked if I could be of help.

As you can see, Paul realized the paragraph lacked power, so he decided to add compelling descriptive details about the woman ("the stale smell of sweat," for example). When revising, he also worked to reduce the paragraph's choppiness. By expanding and combining sentences, he gave the paragraph an easier, more graceful rhythm. Much of the time, revision involves paring down excess material. In this case, though, Paul made the right decision to elaborate his sentences. Furthermore, he added the following comment to the third paragraph: "I decided to be a good, courteous employee." These few words introduce an appropriate note of irony and serve to echo the essay's controlling idea.

Finally, Paul decided to omit the words "sneezing and hacking" because he realized they were too comic or light for his subject. Still, the first sentence in the revised paragraph is somewhat jarring. The word *strolling* isn't quite appropriate since it implies a leisurely grace inconsistent with the impression he wants to convey. Replacing *strolling* with, say, *shuffling* would bring the image more into line with the essay's overall mood.

Despite this slight problem, Paul's revisions are right on the mark. The changes he made strengthened his essay, turning it into a more evocative, more polished piece of narrative writing.

ACTIVITIES: NARRATION

Prewriting Activities

1. Imagine you're writing two essays: One analyzes the effect of insensitive teachers on young children; the other argues the importance of family traditions. With the help of your journal or freewriting, identify different narratives you could use to open each essay.

2. Use brainstorming or any other prewriting technique to generate narrative details about *one* of the following events. After examining your raw material, identify two or three narrative points (thesis statements) that might focus an essay. Then edit the prewriting material for each narrative point, noting which items would be appropriate, which would be inappropriate, which would have to be developed more fully.

    a. An injury you received
    b. The loss of an important object
    c. An event that made you wish you had a certain skill

3. For each of the following situations, identify two different conflicts that would make a story worth relating:

    a. Going to the supermarket with a friend
    b. Telling your parents which college you've decided to attend

c. Participating in a demonstration
   d. Preparing for an exam in a difficult course

4. Prepare six to ten lines of vivid and natural-sounding dialog to convey the conflict in *two* of the following situations:

   a. One member of a couple trying to break up with the other
   b. A ten-year-old brother and a teenage sister shopping for a parent's birthday present
   c. A teacher talking to a student who plagiarized a paper
   d. A young person talking to his or her parents about dropping out of college for a semester

Revising Activities

5. Revise each of the following narrative sentence groups twice: once with words that carry negative connotations, and again with words that carry positive connotations. Use varied sentence structure, sensory details, and vigorous verbs to convey mood.

   a. The bell rang. It rang loudly. Students knew the last day of class was over.
   b. Last weekend, our neighbors burned leaves in their yard. We went over to speak with them.
   c. The sun shone in through my bedroom window. It made me sit up in bed. Daylight was finally here, I told myself.

6. The following paragraph is the introduction from the first draft of an essay proposing harsher penalties for drunk drivers. Revise this narrative paragraph to make it more effective. How can you make sentence structure less predictable? Which details should you delete? As you revise, provide language that conveys the event's sights, smells, and sounds. Also, clarify the chronological sequence.

   As I drove down the street in my bright-blue sports car, I saw a car coming rapidly around the curve. The car didn't slow down as it headed toward the traffic light. The light turned yellow and then red. A young couple, dressed like models, started crossing the street. When the woman saw the car, she called out to her husband. He jumped onto the shoulder. The man wasn't hurt but, seconds later, it was clear the woman was. I ran to a nearby emergency phone and called the police. The ambulance arrived, but the woman was already dead. The driver, who looked terrible, failed the sobriety test, and the police found out that he had two previous offenses. It's apparent that better ways have to be found for getting drunk drivers off the road.

PROFESSIONAL SELECTIONS: NARRATION

GEORGE ORWELL

Born Eric Blair in the British colony of India, George Orwell (1903–50) is best known for his two novels *Animal Farm* (1946) and *1984* (1949)—both searing depictions of totalitarian societies. A fierce critic of political and economic injustice, Orwell also wrote a number of essays about the desperate lives of English factory workers and miners. Orwell's position with the Indian Imperial Police provided the basis for the following essay, which is taken from the collection *"Shooting an Elephant" and Other Essays* (1950).

SHOOTING AN ELEPHANT

1   In Moulmein, in Lower Burma, I was hated by large numbers of people—the only time in my life that I have been important enough for this to happen to me. I was subdivisional police officer of the town, and in an aimless, petty kind of way anti-European feeling was very bitter. No one had the guts to raise a riot, but if a European woman went through the bazaars alone somebody would probably spit betel juice over her dress. As a police officer I was an obvious target and was baited whenever it seemed safe to do so. When a nimble Burman tripped me up on the football field and the referee (another Burman) looked the other way, the crowd yelled with hideous laughter. This happened more than once. In the end the sneering yellow faces of young men that met me everywhere, the insults hooted after me when I was at a safe distance, got badly on my nerves. The young Buddhist priests were the worst of all. There were several thousand of them in the town and none of them seemed to have anything to do except stand on street corners and jeer at Europeans.

2   All this was perplexing and upsetting. For at that time I had already made up my mind that imperialism was an evil thing and the sooner I chucked up my job and got out of it the better. Theoretically—and secretly, of course—I was all for the Burmese and all against their oppressors, the British. As for the job I was doing, I hated it more bitterly than I can perhaps make clear. In a job like that you see the dirty work of Empire at close quarters. The wretched prisoners huddling in the stinking cages of the lock-ups, the grey, cowed faces of the long-term convicts, the scarred buttocks of the men who had been flogged with bamboos—all these oppressed me with an intolerable sense of guilt. But I could get nothing into perspective. I was young and ill-educated and I had to think out my problems in the utter silence that is imposed on every Englishman in the East. I did not even know that the British Empire is dying, still less did I know that it is a great deal better than the younger empires that are going to supplant it. All I knew was that I was stuck between my hatred of the empire I served

and my rage against the evil-spirited little beasts who tried to make my job impossible. With one part of my mind I thought of the British Raj as an unbreakable tyranny, as something clamped down, *in saecula saeculorum,** upon the will of prostrate peoples; with another part I thought that the greatest joy in the world would be to drive a bayonet into a Buddhist priest's guts. Feelings like these are the normal by-products of imperialism; ask any Anglo-Indian official, if you can catch him off duty.

One day something happened which in a roundabout way was enlightening. It was a tiny incident in itself, but it gave me a better glimpse than I had had before of the real nature of imperialism—the real motives for which despotic governments act. Early one morning the sub-inspector at a police station the other end of the town rang me up on the 'phone and said that an elephant was ravaging the bazaar. Would I please come and do something about it? I did not know what I could do, but I wanted to see what was happening and I got onto a pony and started out. I took my rifle, an old .44 Winchester and much too small to kill an elephant, but I thought the noise might be useful *in terrorem.*** Various Burmans stopped me on the way and told me about the elephant's doings. It was not, of course, a wild elephant, but a tame one which had gone "must." It had been chained up, as tame elephants always are when their attack of "must" is due, but on the previous night it had broken its chain and escaped. Its mahout, the only person who could manage it when it was in that state, had set out in pursuit, but had taken the wrong direction and was now twelve hours' journey away, and in the morning the elephant had suddenly reappeared in the town. The Burmese population had no weapons and were quite helpless against it. It had already destroyed somebody's bamboo hut, killed a cow and raided some fruit-stalls and devoured the stock; also it had met the municipal rubbish van and, when the driver jumped out and took to his heels, had turned the van over and inflicted violences upon it.

The Burmese sub-inspector and some Indian constables were waiting for me in the quarter where the elephant had been seen. It was a very poor quarter, a labyrinth of squalid bamboo huts, thatched with palm-leaf, winding all over a steep hillside. I remember that it was a cloudy, stuffy morning at the beginning of the rains. We began questioning the people as to where the elephant had gone and, as usual, failed to get any definite information. That is invariably the case in the East; a story always sounds clear enough at a distance, but the nearer you get to the scene of events the vaguer it becomes. Some of the people said that the elephant had gone in one direction, some said that he had gone in another, some professed not even to have heard of any elephant. I had almost made up my mind that the whole story was a pack of lies, when we heard yells a little distance away. There was a loud, scandalized cry of "Go away, child! Go away this instant!" and an old woman with a switch in her hand came round the corner of a hut, violently shooing away a crowd of naked children. Some more women followed, clicking their tongues and exclaiming; evidently there was something that the children ought not to have seen. I rounded the hut and saw a man's dead body sprawling in the mud. He was an Indian, a black Dravidian coolie, almost naked, and he could not have been dead many minutes. The people said that the elephant had come suddenly upon him round the corner of the hut, caught him with its trunk, put its foot on his back and ground him into the earth. This was the rainy season and the ground was soft, and his face had scored a trench

---

*For ever and ever (editors' note).
**As a warning (editors' note).

Narration

a foot deep and a couple of yards long. He was lying on his belly with arms crucified and head sharply twisted to one side. His face was coated with mud, the eyes wide open, the teeth bared and grinning with an expression of unendurable agony. (Never tell me, by the way, that the dead look peaceful. Most of the corpses I have seen looked devilish.) The friction of the great beast's foot had stripped the skin from his back as neatly as one skins a rabbit. As soon as I saw the dead man I sent an orderly to a friend's house nearby to borrow an elephant rifle. I had already sent back the pony, not wanting it to go mad with fright and throw me if it smelt the elephant.

5   The orderly came back in a few minutes with a rifle and five cartridges, and meanwhile some Burmans had arrived and told us that the elephant was in the paddy fields below, only a few hundred yards away. As I started forward practically the whole population of the quarter flocked out of the houses and followed me. They had seen the rifle and were all shouting excitedly that I was going to shoot the elephant. They had not shown much interest in the elephant when he was merely ravaging their homes, but it was different now that he was going to be shot. It was a bit of fun to them, as it would be to an English crowd; besides they wanted the meat. It made me vaguely uneasy. I had no intention of shooting the elephant—I had merely sent for the rifle to defend myself if necessary—and it is always unnerving to have a crowd following you. I marched down the hill looking and feeling a fool, with the rifle over my shoulder and an ever-growing army of people jostling at my heels. At the bottom, when you got away from the huts, there was a metalled road and beyond that a miry waste of paddy fields a thousand yards across, not yet ploughed but soggy from the first rains and dotted with coarse grass. The elephant was standing eight yards from the road, his left side towards us. He took not the slightest notice of the crowd's approach. He was tearing up bunches of grass, beating them against his knees to clean them and stuffing them into his mouth.

6   I had halted on the road. As soon as I saw the elephant I knew with perfect certainty that I ought not to shoot him. It is a serious matter to shoot a working elephant—it is comparable to destroying a huge and costly piece of machinery—and obviously one ought not to do it if it can possibly be avoided. And at that distance, peacefully eating, the elephant looked no more dangerous than a cow. I thought then and I think now that his attack of "must" was already passing off; in which case he would merely wander harmlessly about until the mahout came back and caught him. Moreover, I did not in the least want to shoot him. I decided that I would watch him for a little while to make sure that he did not turn savage again, and then go home.

7   But at that moment I glanced round at the crowd that had followed me. It was an immense crowd, two thousand at the least and growing every minute. It blocked the road for a long distance on either side. I looked at the sea of yellow faces above the garish clothes—faces all happy and excited over this bit of fun, all certain that the elephant was going to be shot. They were watching me as they would watch a conjurer about to perform a trick. They did not like me, but with the magical rifle in my hands I was momentarily worth watching. And suddenly I realized that I should have to shoot the elephant after all. The people expected it of me and I had got to do it; I could feel their two thousand wills pressing me forward, irresistibly. And it was at this moment, as I stood there with the rifle in my hands, that I first grasped the hollowness, the futility of the white man's dominion in the East. Here was I, the white man with his gun, standing in front of the unarmed native crowd—seemingly the leading actor of the piece; but in reality I was only an absurd puppet pushed to and fro by the will of those yellow faces behind. I perceived in this moment that when the white man turns tyrant it is his own freedom that he destroys. He becomes a sort of

hollow, posing dummy, the conventionalized figure of a sahib. For it is the condition of his rule that he shall spend his life in trying to impress the "natives," and so in every crisis he has got to do what the "natives" expect of him. He wears a mask, and his face grows to fit it. I had got to shoot the elephant. I had committed myself to doing it when I sent for the rifle. A sahib has got to act like a sahib; he has got to appear resolute, to know his own mind and do definite things. To come all that way, rifle in hand, with two thousand people marching at my heels, and then to trail feebly away, having done nothing—no, that was impossible. The crowd would laugh at me. And my whole life, every white man's life in the East, was one long struggle not to be laughed at.

But I did not want to shoot the elephant. I watched him beating his bunch of grass against his knees, with that preoccupied grandmotherly air that elephants have. It seemed to me that it would be murder to shoot him. At that age I was not squeamish about killing animals, but I had never shot an elephant and never wanted to. (Somehow it always seems worse to kill a *large* animal.) Besides, there was the beast's owner to be considered. Alive, the elephant was worth at least a hundred pounds; dead, he would only be worth the value of his tusks, five pounds, possibly. But I had got to act quickly. I turned to some experienced-looking Burmans who had been there when we arrived, and asked them how the elephant had been behaving. They all said the same thing: he took no notice of you if you left him alone, but he might charge if you went too close to him. 8

It was perfectly clear to me what I ought to do. I ought to walk up to within, say, twenty-five yards of the elephant and test his behavior. If he charged, I could shoot; if he took notice of me, it would be safe to leave him until the mahout came back. But also I knew that I was going to do no such thing. I was a poor shot with a rifle and the ground was soft mud into which one would sink at every step. If the elephant charged and I missed him, I should have about as much chance as a toad under a steam-roller. But even then I was not thinking particularly of my own skin, only of the watchful yellow faces behind. For at that moment, with the crowd watching me, I was not afraid in the ordinary sense, as I would have been if I had been alone. A white man mustn't be frightened in front of "natives"; and so, in general he isn't frightened. The sole thought in my mind was that if anything went wrong those two thousand Burmans would see me pursued, caught, trampled on and reduced to a grinning corpse like that Indian up the hill. And if that happened it was quite probable that some of them would laugh. That would never do. There was only one alternative. I shoved the cartridges into the magazine and lay down on the road to get a better aim. 9

The crowd grew very still, and a deep, low, happy sigh, as of people who see the theatre curtain go up at last, breathed from innumerable throats. They were going to have their bit of fun after all. The rifle was a beautiful German thing with cross-hair sights. I did not then know that in shooting an elephant one would shoot to cut an imaginary bar running from ear-hole to ear-hole. I ought, therefore, as the elephant was sideway on, to have aimed straight at his ear-hole; actually I aimed several inches in front of this, thinking the brain would be further forward. 10

When I pulled the trigger I did not hear the bang or feel the kick—one never does when a shot goes home—but I heard the devilish roar of glee that went up from the crowd. In that instant, in too short a time, one would have thought, even for the bullet to get there, a mysterious, terrible change had come over the elephant. He neither stirred nor fell, but every line of his body had altered. He looked suddenly stricken, shrunken, immensely old, as though the frightful impact of the bullet had paralyzed him without knocking him down. At last, after what seemed a long time—it might have been five seconds, I dare say—he sagged flabbily to his knees. His mouth 11 slobbered. An enormous senility seemed to have settled upon him. One could have imagined him thousands of years old. I fired again into the same spot. At the second shot he did not collapse but climbed with desperate slowness to his feet and stood weakly upright, with legs sagging and head drooping. I fired a third time. That was the shot that did for him. You could see the agony of it jolt his whole body and knock the last remnant of strength from his legs. But in falling he seemed for a moment to rise, for as his hind legs collapsed beneath him he seemed to tower upward like a huge rock toppling, his trunk reaching skywards like a tree. He trumpeted, for the first and only time. And then down he came, his belly towards me, with a crash that seemed to shake the ground even where I lay.

12   I got up. The Burmans were already racing past me across the mud. It was obvious that the elephant would never rise again, but he was not dead. He was breathing very rhythmically with long rattling gasps, his great mound of a side painfully rising and falling. His mouth was wide open—I could see far down into caverns of pale pink throat. I waited a long time for him to die, but his breathing did not weaken. Finally I fired my two remaining shots into the spot where I thought his heart must be. The thick blood welled out of him like red velvet, but still he did not die. His body did not even jerk when the shots hit him, the tortured breathing continued without a pause. He was dying, very slowly and in great agony, but in some world remote from me where not even a bullet could damage him further. I felt that I had got to put an end to that dreadful noise. It seemed dreadful to see the great beast lying there, powerless to move and yet powerless to die, and not even to be able to finish him. I sent back for my small rifle and poured shot after shot into his heart and down his throat. They seemed to make no impression. The tortured gasps continued as steadily as the ticking of a clock.

13   In the end I could not stand it any longer and went away. I heard later that it took him half an hour to die. Burmans were bringing dahs and baskets even before I left, and I was told they had stripped the body almost to the bones by the afternoon.

14   Afterwards, of course, there were endless discussions about the shooting of the elephant. The owner was furious, but he was only an Indian and could do nothing. Besides, legally I had done the right thing, for a mad elephant has to be killed, like a mad dog, if its owner fails to control it. Among the Europeans opinion was divided. The older men said I was right, the younger men said it was a damn shame to shoot an elephant for killing a coolie, because an elephant was worth more than any damn Coringhee coolie. And afterwards I was very glad that the coolie had been killed; it put me legally in the right and it gave me a sufficient pretext for shooting the elephant. I often wondered whether any of the others grasped that I had done it solely to avoid looking a fool.

Questions for Close Reading

1. What is the selection's thesis (or narrative point)? Locate the sentence(s) in which Orwell states his main idea. If he doesn't state the thesis explicitly, express it in your own words.

2. How does Orwell feel about the Burmans? What words does he use to describe them?

3. What reasons does Orwell give for shooting the elephant?

4. In paragraph 3, Orwell says that the elephant incident gave him a better understanding of "the real motives for which despotic governments act." What do you think he means? Before you answer, reread paragraph 7 carefully.

5. Refer to your dictionary as needed to define the following words used in the selection: *imperialism* (paragraph 2), *prostrate* (2), *despotic* (3), *mahout* (3), *miry* (5), *conjurer* (7), *futility* (7), and *sahib* (7).

Questions About the Writer's Craft

1. The Pattern. Most effective narratives encompass a restricted time span. How much time elapses from the moment Orwell gets his gun to the death of the elephant? What time signals does Orwell provide to help the reader follow the sequence of events in this limited time span?

2. Orwell doesn't actually begin his narrative until the third paragraph. What purposes do the first two paragraphs serve?

3. In paragraph 6, Orwell says that shooting a working elephant "is comparable to destroying a huge and costly piece of machinery." This kind of comparison is called an *analogy*—describing something unfamiliar, often abstract, in terms of something more familiar and concrete. Find at least three additional analogies in Orwell's essay. What effect do they have?

4. Other Patterns. Much of the power of Orwell's narrative comes from his ability to convey sensory impressions—what he saw, heard, smelled. Orwell's description becomes most vivid when he writes about the elephant's death in paragraphs 11 and 12. Find some evocative words and phrases that give the description its power.

Writing Assignments Using Narration as a Pattern of Development

1. Orwell recounts a time he acted under great pressure. Write a narrative about an action you once took simply because you felt pressured. Perhaps you were attempting to avoid ridicule or to fulfill someone else's expectations. Like Orwell, use vivid details to bring the incident to life and to convey its effect on you. Reading Malcolm X's "My First Conk" (page 307) will help you appreciate the power of the need to conform.

2. Write a narrative essay about an experience that gave you, like Orwell, a deeper insight into your own nature. You may have discovered, for instance, that you can be surprisingly naive, compassionate, petty, brave, rebellious, or good at something.

Writing Assignments Using Other Patterns of Development

3. Was Orwell justified in shooting the elephant? Write an essay arguing either that Orwell was justified *or* that he was not. To develop your thesis, cite several specific reasons, each supported by details drawn from the essay. Here are some

Narration

points you might consider: the legality of Orwell's act, the elephant's temperament, the crowd's presence, the aftermath of the elephant's death, the death itself.

4. Orwell's essay concerns, in part, the tendency to conceal indecision and confusion with a facade of authority. Focusing on one or two groups of people (parents, teachers, doctors, politicians, and so on), write an essay about the way people in authority sometimes *pretend* to know what they are doing so that subordinates won't suspect their insecurity or incompetence. Part of your essay should focus on the consequences of such behaviors.

MAYA ANGELOU

Born Marguerite Johnson in 1928, Maya Angelou rose from a difficult childhood in Stamps, Arkansas, to become a multitalented performer and writer. A professor at Wake Forest University since 1991, she has danced professionally; starred in an off-Broadway play; acted on television; and become a prolific, highly regarded writer. At the 1993 inauguration of President Clinton and Vice President Gore, Angelou delivered a stirring poem written for the occasion. Her work includes poetry, *Oh Pray My Wings Are Gonna Fit Me Well* (1975) and *Now Sheba Sings the Song* (1988), as well as a five-part autobiography, with *I Know Why the Caged Bird Sings* being the most well-known book in the series. The following selection is taken from another book in the series, *Singin' and Swingin' and Gettin' Merry Like Christmas* (1976).

LOUISE COX

1 Music was my refuge. I could crawl into the spaces between the notes and curl my back to loneliness.

2 In my rented room (cooking privileges down the hall), I would play a record, then put my arms around the shoulders of the song. As we danced, glued together, I would nuzzle into its neck, kissing the skin, and rubbing its cheek with my own.

3 The Melrose Record Shop on Fillmore was a center for music, musicians, music lovers and record collectors. Blasts from its loudspeaker poured out into the street with all the insistence of a false mourner at a graveside. Along one wall of its dark interior, stalls were arranged like open telephone booths. Customers stood playing their selections on turntables and listening through earphones. I had two hours between jobs. Occasionally I went to the library or, if the hours coincided, to a free dance class at the YWCA. But most often I directed myself to the melodious Melrose Record Store, where I could wallow, rutting in music.

4 Louise Cox, a short blonde who was part owner of the store, flitted between customers like a fickle butterfly in a rose garden. She was white, wore perfume and smiled openly with the Negro customers, so I knew she was sophisticated. Other people's sophistication tended to make me nervous and I stayed shy of Louise. My music tastes seesawed between the blues of John Lee Hooker and the bubbling silver sounds of Charlie Parker. For a year I had been collecting their records.

5 On one visit to the store, Louise came over to the booth where I was listening to a record.

"Hi, I'm Louise. What's your name?"

I thought of "Puddin' in tame. Ask me again, I'll tell you the same." That was a cruel childhood rhyme meant to insult.

The last white woman who had asked me anything other than "May I help you?" had been my high school teacher. I looked at the little woman, at her cashmere sweater and pearls, at her slick hair and pink lips, and decided she couldn't hurt me, so I'd give her the name I had given to all white people.

"Marguerite Annie Johnson." I had been named for two grandmothers.

"Marguerite? That's a pretty name."

I was surprised. She pronounced it like my grandmother. Not Margarite, but Marg-you-reet.

"A new Charlie Parker came in last week. I saved it for you."

That showed her good business sense.

"I know you like John Lee Hooker, but I've got somebody I want you to hear." She stopped the turntable and removed my record and put on another in its place.

"Lord I wonder, do she ever think of me,
Lord I wonder, do she ever think of me,
I wonder, I wonder, will my baby come back to me?"

The singer's voice groaned a longing I seemed to have known my life long. But I couldn't say that to Louise. She watched my face and I forced it still.

"Well, I ain't got no special reason here,
No, I ain't got no special reason here,
I'm gonna leave 'cause I don't feel welcome here."

The music fitted me like tailor-made clothes.

She said, "That's Arthur Crudup. Isn't he great?"; excitement lighted her face.

"It's nice. Thank you for letting me hear it."

It wasn't wise to reveal one's real feelings to strangers. And nothing on earth was stranger to me than a friendly white woman.

"Shall I wrap it for you? Along with the Bird?"*

My salary from the little real estate office and the dress shop downtown barely paid rent and my son's baby-sitter.

"I'll pick them both up next week. Thank you for thinking of me." Courtesy cost nothing as long as one had dignity. My grandmother, Annie Henderson, had taught me that.

She turned and walked back to the counter, taking the record with her. I counseled myself not to feel badly. I hadn't rejected an offer of friendship, I had simply fielded a commercial come-on.

I walked to the counter.

"Thank you, Louise. See you next week." When I laid the record on the counter, she pushed a wrapped package toward me.

"Take these, Marg-you-reet. I've started an account for you." She turned to another customer. I couldn't refuse because I didn't know how to do so gracefully.

Outside on the evening street, I examined the woman's intention. What did I have that she wanted? Why did she allow me to walk away with her property? She didn't know me. Even my name might have been constructed on the spot. She couldn't have been seeking friendship; after all she was white, and as far as I knew, white women

---

*"Bird" was Charlie Parker's nickname (editors' note).

Narration

were never lonely, except in books. White men adored them, Black men desired them and Black women worked for them. There was no ready explanation for her gesture of trust.

34 At home I squeezed enough from the emergency money I kept in a drawer to repay her. Back at the store, she accepted the money and said, "Thanks, Marg-you-reet. But you didn't have to make a special trip. I trust you."

35 "Why?" That ought to get her. "You don't know me."

36 "Because I like you."

37 "But you don't know me. How can you like someone you don't know?"

38 "Because my heart tells me and I trust my heart."

39 For weeks I pondered over Louise Cox. What could I possibly have that she could possibly want? My mind, it was certain, was a well-oiled mechanism which worked swiftly and seminoiselessly. I often competed with radio contestants on quiz programs and usually won hands down in my living room. Oh, my mental machine could have excited anyone. I meant anyone interested in a person who had memorized the Presidents of the United States in chronological order, the capitals of the world, the minerals of the earth and the generic names of various species. There weren't too many callers for those qualifications and I had to admit that I was greatly lacking in the popular attractions of physical beauty and womanly wiles.

40 All my life, my body had been in successful rebellion against my finer nature. I was too tall and raw-skinny. My large extroverted teeth protruded in an excitement to be seen, and I, attempting to thwart their success, rarely smiled. Although I lathered Dixie Peach in my hair, the thick black mass crinkled and kinked and resisted the smothering pomade to burst free around my head like a cloud of angry bees. No, in support of truth, I had to admit Louise Cox was not friendly to me because of my beauty.

41 Maybe she offered friendship because she pitied me. The idea was a string winding at first frayed and loose, then tightening, binding into my consciousness. My spirit started at the intrusion. A white woman? Feeling sorry for me? She wouldn't dare. I would go to the store and show her. I would roll her distasteful pity into a ball and throw it in her face. I would smash her nose deep into the unasked-for sympathy until her eyes dribbled tears and she learned that I was a queen, not to be approached by peasants like her, even on bended knees, and wailing.

42 Louise was bent over the counter talking to a small Black boy. She didn't interrupt her conversation to acknowledge my entrance.

43 "Exactly how many boxes have you folded, J.C.?" Her intonation was sober.

44 "Eighteen." The boy's answer matched her seriousness. His head barely reached the counter top. She took a small box from a shelf behind her.

45 "Then here's eighteen cents." She pushed the coins around counting them, then poured them into his cupped palms.

46 "O.K." He turned on unsure young legs and collided with me. He mumbled "Thank you."

47 Louise rounded the counter, following the little voice. She ran past me and caught the door a second after he slammed it.

48 "J.C." She stood, arms akimbo on the sidewalk, and raised her voice. "J.C., I'll see you next Saturday." She came back into the store and looked at me.

49 "Hi, Marg-you-reet. Boy, am I glad to see you. Excuse that scene. I had to pay off one of my workers."

50 I waited for her to continue. Waited for her to tell me how precious he was and how poor and wasn't it all a shame. She went behind the counter and began slipping records into paper jackets.

"When I first opened the shop, all the neighborhood kids came in. They either demanded that I 'gi' them a penny' "—I hated whites' imitation of the Black accent—"or play records for them. I explained that the only way I'd give them anything was if they worked for it and that I'd play records for their parents, but not for them until they were tall enough to reach the turntables."

"So I let them fold empty record boxes for a penny apiece." She went on, "I'm glad to see you because I want to offer you a job."

I had done many things to make a living, but I drew the line at cleaning white folks' houses. I had tried that and lasted only one day. The waxed tables, cut flowers, closets of other people's clothes totally disoriented me. I hated the figured carpets, tiled kitchens and refrigerators filled with someone else's dinner leftovers.

"Really?" The ice in my voice turned my accent to upper-class Vivien Leigh (before *Gone with the Wind*).

"My sister has been helping me in the shop, but she's going back to school. I thought you'd be perfect to take her place."

My resolve began to knuckle under me like weak knees.

"I don't know if you know it, but I have a large clientele and try to keep in stock a supply, however small, of every record by Negro artists. And if I don't have something, there's a comprehensive catalog and I can order it. What do you think?"

Her face was open and her smile simple. I pried into her eyes for hidden meaning and found nothing. Even so, I had to show my own strength.

"I don't like to hear white folks imitate Negroes. Did the children really ask you to 'gi' them a penny'? Oh, come now."

She said, "You are right—they didn't ask. They demanded that I 'gi' them a penny.' " The smile left her face. "You say it."

"Give me a penny." My teeth pressed my bottom lip, stressing the *v*.

She reached for the box and handed me a coin. "Don't forget that you've been to school and let neither of us forget that we're both grown-up. I'd be pleased if you'd take the job." She told me the salary, the hours and what my duties would be.

"Thank you very much for the offer. I'll think about it." I left the shop, head up, back straight. I tried to exude indifference, like octopus ink, to camouflage my excitement.

I had to talk to Ivonne Broadnax, the Realist. She was my closest friend. Ivonne had escaped the hindrance of romantic blindness, which was my lifelong affliction. She had the clear, clean eyes of a born survivor. I went to her Ellis Street house, where she, at twenty-five, was bringing up an eight-year-old daughter and a fifteen-year-old sister.

"Vonne, you know that woman that runs the record store?"

"That short white woman with the crooked smile?" Her voice was small and keen and the sound had to force itself past white, even teeth.

"Yes."

"Why?"

"She offered me a job."

"Doing what?" I knew I could count on her cynicism.

"Salesgirl."

"Why?"

"That's what I've been trying to figure out. Why? And why me?"

Ivonne sat very still, thinking. She possessed a great beauty which she carried nonchalantly. Her cupid's-bow lips pursed, and when she raised her head her face was flushed pink and cream from the racing blood.

"Is she funny that way?"

We both knew that was the only logical explanation.

Narration

77 "No. I'm sure that she's not."
78 Ivonne bent her head again. She raised it and looked at me.
79 "Did you ask her?"
80 "No."
81 "I mean did you ask her for the job?"
82 "No. She offered it." I added just a little indignation to my answer.
83 Ivonne said, "You know white people are strange. I don't even know if they know why they do things." Ivonne had grown up in a small Mississippi town, and I, in a smaller town in Arkansas. Whites were as constant in our history as the seasons and as unfamiliar as affluence.
84 "Maybe she's trying to prove something." She waited. "What kind of pay she offering?"
85 "Enough so I can quit both jobs and bring the baby home."
86 "Well, take it."
87 "I'll have to order records and take inventories and all that." The odor of an improvement in my life had barely touched my nostrils and it made me jittery.
88 "Come on, Maya" (she called me by the family name). "If you could run a hook shop, you can run a record shop."
89 Once when I was eighteen in San Diego I had managed a house of prostitution, where two qualified workers entertained and I, as financial backer, took a percentage. I had since layered that experience over and over in my mind with forgiveness and a conscious affectation of innocence. But it was true, I did have a certain talent for administration.
90 "Tell her you'll take the job and then watch her like a hawk. You know white women. They pull off their drawers, lay down first, then scream rape. If you're not careful, she'll get weak and faint on you, then before you know it you'll be washing windows, and scrubbing the floor." We cackled like two old crones, remembering a secret past. The laughter was sour and not really directed at white women. It was a traditional ruse that was used to shield the Black vulnerability; we laughed to keep from crying.
91 I took the job, but kept Louise under constant surveillance. None of her actions went unheeded, no conversation unrecorded. The question was not if she would divulge her racism but when and how the revelation would occur. For a few months I was a character in a living thriller plot. I listened to her intonations and trailed her glances.
92 On Sundays, when the older people came in after church services to listen to the Reverend Joe May's sermons on 78 rpm records, I trembled with the chase's excitement. Large, corseted women gathered around the record players, their bosoms bloated with religious fervor, while their dark-suited husbands leaned into the music, faces blank in surrender to the spirit, their black and brown fingers restive on clutched Bibles.
93 Louise offered folding chairs to the ladies and moved back behind the counter to her books. I waited for one smirk, one roll of her eyes to the besieged heavens and I would have my evidence that she thought her whiteness was a superior quality which she and God had contrived for their own convenience.
94 After two months, vigilance had exhausted me and I had found no thread of prejudice. I began to relax and enjoy the wealth of a world of music. Early mornings were given over to Bartok and Schoenberg.* Midmorning I treated myself to the vocals of Billy Eckstine, Billie Holiday, Nat Cole, Louis Jordan and Bull Moose Jackson.

---

*Bartok was a Hungarian pianist and composer (1881–1945); Schoenberg was an Austrian-born composer and conductor (1874–1951). Both are important figures in the world of classical music. The other musicians mentioned are American blues and/or jazz artists (editors' note).

A piroshki from the Russian delicatessen next door was lunch and then the giants of bebop flipped through the air. Charlie Parker and Max Roach, Dizzy Gillespie, Sarah Vaughan and Al Haig and Howard McGhee. Blues belonged to late afternoons and the singers' lyrics of lost love spoke to my solitude.

I ordered stock and played records on request, emptied ashtrays and dusted the windows' cardboard displays. Louise and her partner, David Rosenbaum, showed their pleasure by giving me a raise, and although I was grateful to them for the job and my first introduction to an amiable black-white relationship, I could exhibit my feelings only by being punctual in coming to the shop and being efficient at work and coolly, grayly respectful.

95

Questions for Close Reading

1. What is the selection's thesis (or narrative point)? Locate the sentence(s) in which Angelou states her main idea. If she doesn't state the thesis explicitly, express it in your own words.

2. Angelou begins her essay with the statement, "Music was my refuge." Based on other statements she makes in the selection, what does she need refuge from? What is her life like at the time she meets Louise Cox?

3. What previous experiences has Angelou had with white people? What preconceptions about them has she developed? How do these notions affect her initial reactions to Louise Cox?

4. Why can't Angelou repay Cox's friendliness in kind? Why, even after working for Cox for two months, does she remain "coolly, grayly respectful" (paragraph 95)?

5. Refer to your dictionary as needed to define the following words used in the selection: *rutting* (paragraph 3), *extroverted* (40), *pomade* (40), *intrusion* (41), *akimbo* (48), *exude* (63), *nonchalantly* (74), *vulnerability* (90), *restive* (92), and *piroshki* (94).

Questions About the Writer's Craft

1. The pattern. Narrative essays center around a conflict. What conflicts do you detect in this selection? Are the conflicts resolved? How do the conflicts help convey the narrative point?

2. Locate some of Angelou's unusual and striking metaphors. What do the metaphors reveal about the author? How do they help readers understand the situation that she faces?

3. Other patterns. In paragraphs 15–17 and 19–21, Angelou quotes some lyrics from the music that Cox played for her. What effect do you think Angelou hoped the song lyrics would have on readers?

4. The essay devotes most of its time to portraying Louise Cox and describing Angelou's interpretations of Cox's behavior. But in paragraphs 64–90, Angelou describes a conversation she had with her best friend at the time. Why do you suppose Angelou includes this conversation? How does the dialog reinforce her narrative point?

Writing Assignments Using Narration as a Pattern of Development

1. In a narrative essay, tell about a time that you—like Angelou—had trouble recognizing another person's authentic nature because you accepted the validity of a commonly held stereotype. Conversely, you may write about a time when someone was unable to see the real you. In either case, explain what you learned from the event, and include only those conversational exchanges and details that dramatize your narrative point. Brent Staples's "Black Men and Public Space" (page 374) will provide insight into the corrosive effect of stereotyped assumptions.

2. "The odor of an improvement in my life . . . made me jittery," Angelou writes. In a narrative essay, write about a time in your life when a new opportunity—promising but also frightening—presented itself. You may have been offered a chance to travel, work as a volunteer, or take a course. Using vigorous narrative details, show what your reaction was to this attractive but frightening opportunity, whether you passed it up or seized it, and what happened as a result.

Writing Assignments Using Other Patterns of Development

3. With characteristic vigor, Angelou recounts her intense involvement with music. Write an essay in which you show how one of your passions—perhaps music, reading, dancing, cooking, or traveling—affects you. Like Angelou, use vivid language to convey the compelling nature of the activity and its powerful effect on you.

4. As Angelou shows, a new experience often brings about unexpected change. Select a major event in your life (the birth of a baby, a divorce, going away to school) or in the life of someone you know well. Then write an essay comparing and contrasting what life was like before and after the change. Joseph H. Suina's "And Then I Went to School" (page 339) dramatizes the way a new experience can alter a life forever.

ALICE WALKER

Alice Walker (1944–) is a noted proponent of the rights of blacks, women, and non-human animals. In addition to two collections of essays, she has written several books, including *The Color Purple* (1982), which won a Pulitzer Prize, *The Temple of My Familiar* (1989), and *Possessing the Secret of Joy* (1992). The essay reprinted here, first published in *Ms.* magazine (1986), is from Walker's 1988 collection of essays, *Living by the Word*.

AM I BLUE?

For about three years my companion and I rented a small house in the country that stood on the edge of a large meadow that appeared to run from the end of our deck straight into the mountains. The mountains, however, were quite far away, and between us and them there was, in fact, a town. It was one of the many pleasant aspects of the house that you never really were aware of this.

It was a house of many windows, low, wide, nearly floor to ceiling in the living room, which faced the meadow, and it was from one of these that I first saw our closest neighbor, a large white horse, cropping grass, flipping its mane, and ambling about—not over the entire meadow, which stretched well out of sight of the house, but over the five or so fenced-in acres that were next to the 20-odd that we had rented. I soon learned that the horse, whose name was Blue, belonged to a man who lived in another town, but was boarded by our neighbors next door. Occasionally, one of the children, usually a stocky teenager, but sometimes a much younger girl or boy, could be seen riding Blue. They would appear in the meadow, climb up on his back, ride furiously for 10 or 15 minutes, then get off, slap Blue on the flanks, and not be seen again for a month or more.

There were many apple trees in our yard, and one by the fence that Blue could almost reach. We were soon in the habit of feeding him apples, which he relished, especially because by the middle of summer the meadow grasses—so green and succulent since January—had dried out from lack of rain, and Blue stumbled about munching the dried stalks half-heartedly. Sometimes he would stand very still just by the apple tree, and when one of us came out he would whinny, snort loudly, or stamp the ground. This meant, of course: I want an apple.

It was quite wonderful to pick a few apples, or collect those that had fallen to the ground overnight, and patiently hold them, one by one, up to his large, toothy mouth. I remained as thrilled as a child by his flexible dark lips, huge, cubelike teeth that crunched the apples, core and all, with such finality, and his high, broad-breasted *enormity*; beside which I felt small indeed. When I was a child, I used to ride horses, and was especially friendly with one named Nan until one day I was riding and my brother deliberately spooked her and I was thrown, head first, against the trunk of a tree. When I came to, I was in bed and my mother was bending worriedly over me; we silently agreed that perhaps horseback riding was not the safest sport for me. Since then I have walked, and prefer walking to horseback riding—but I had forgotten the depth of feeling one could see in horses' eyes.

I was therefore unprepared for the expression in Blue's. Blue was lonely. Blue was horribly lonely and bored. I was not shocked that this should be the case; five acres to tramp by yourself, endlessly, even in the most beautiful of meadows, cannot provide many interesting events. No, I was shocked that I had forgotten that human animals and non-human animals can communicate quite well; if we are brought up around animals as children we take this for granted. By the time we are adults we no longer remember. However, the animals have not changed. It is their nature to express themselves. And they do. And, generally speaking, they are ignored.

After giving Blue the apples, I would wander back to the house, aware that he was observing me. Were more apples not forthcoming then? Was that to be his sole entertainment for the day? My partner's small son had decided he wanted to learn how to piece a quilt; we worked in silence on our respective squares as I thought. . . .

Well, about slavery: about white children, who were raised by black people, who knew their first all-accepting love from black women, and then, when they were 12 or so, were told they must "forget" the deep levels of communication between themselves and the "mammy" that they knew. Later they would be able to relate quite calmly: "My old mammy was sold to another good family." "My old mammy was —— ——." Fill in the blank. Many more years later the same person would say: "I can't understand these Negroes, these blacks. What do they want? They're so different from us."

8   And about the Indians, considered to be "like animals" by the "settlers" (a very benign euphemism for what the settlers actually were), who did not understand their description as a compliment.

9   And about the thousands of American men who marry Japanese, Korean, Filipina, and other non-English-speaking women and of how happy they report they are; "blissfully," until their brides learn to speak English, at which point the marriages tend to fall apart. What then did the men see, when they looked into the eyes of the women they married, before they could speak English? Apparently only their own reflections.

10 I thought of society's impatience with the young. "Why are they playing the music so loud?" Perhaps the children have listened to much of the music of oppressed people their parents danced to before they were born, with its passionate but soft cries for acceptance and love, and they have wondered why their parents failed to hear.

11 I do not know how long Blue had inhabited his five beautiful, boring acres before we moved into our house; a year after we had arrived he was still there.

12 But then, in our second year at the house, something happened in Blue's life. One morning, looking out the window at the fog that lay like a ribbon over the meadow, I saw another horse, a brown one, at the other end of Blue's field. Blue appeared to be afraid of it, and for several days made no attempt to go near. We went away for a week. When we returned, Blue had decided to make friends and the two horses ambled or galloped along together, and Blue did not come nearly as often to the fence underneath the apple tree.

13 When he did, bringing his new friend with him, there was a different look in his eyes. A look of independence, of self-possession, of inalienable *horse*ness. His friend eventually became pregnant. For months and months there was, it seemed to me, a mutual feeling between me and the horses—of justice, of peace. I fed apples to them both. The look in Blue's eyes was one of unabashed "this is *it*ness."

14 It did not, however, last forever. One day, after a visit to the city, I went out to give Blue some apples. He stood waiting, or so I thought, though not beneath the tree. When I shook the tree and jumped back from the shower of apples, he made no move. I carried some over to him. He managed to half-crunch one. The rest he let fall to the ground. I dreaded looking into his eyes—because I had of course noticed that Brown, his partner, had gone—but I did look. If I had been born into slavery, and my partner had been sold or killed, my eyes would have looked like that. The children next door explained that Blue's partner had been "put with him" (the same expression that old people in the South used when speaking of an ancestor during slavery who had been impregnated by her owner) so that they could mate and she conceive. Since that was accomplished, she had been taken back by her owner, who lived somewhere else.

15 Will she be back? I asked.

16 They didn't know.

17 Blue was like a crazed person. Blue *was*, to me, a crazed person. He galloped furiously, as if he were being ridden, around and around his five beautiful acres. He whinnied until he couldn't. He tore at the ground with his hooves. He butted himself

against his single shade tree. He looked always and always toward the road down which his partner had gone. And then, occasionally, when he came up for apples, or I took apples to him, he looked at me. It was a look so piercing, so full of grief, a look so *human,* I almost laughed (I felt too sad to cry) to think there are people who do not know that animals suffer. People like me who have forgotten, and daily forget, all that animals try to tell us. "Everything you do to us will happen to you; we are your teachers, as you are ours." There are those who never once have even considered animals' rights: those who have been taught that animals actually want to be used and abused by us, just as small children "love" to be frightened, or women "love" to be mutilated and raped. . . . They are the great-grandchildren of those people who honestly thought, because someone taught them this: "Women can't think," and "niggers can't faint." But most disturbing of all, in Blue's large brown eyes was a new look, more painful than the look of despair: the look of disgust with human beings, with life; the look of hatred. And it was odd what the look of hatred did. It gave him, for the first time, the look of a beast. And what that meant was that he had put up a barrier within to protect himself from further violence; all the apples in the world wouldn't change that fact.

And so Blue remained, a beautiful part of our landscape, very peaceful to look at from the window, white against the grass. Once a friend came to visit and said, looking out on the soothing view: "And it *would* have to be a *white* horse; the very image of freedom." And I thought, yes, the animals are forced to become for us merely "images" of what they once so beautifully expressed. And we are used to drinking milk from containers showing "contented" cows, whose real lives we want to hear nothing about, eating eggs and drumsticks from "happy" hens, and munching hamburgers advertised by bulls of integrity who seem to command their fate. 18

As we talked of freedom and justice one day for all, we sat down to steaks. I am eating misery, I thought, as I took the first bite. And spit it out. 19

Questions for Close Reading

1. What is the selection's thesis (or narrative point)? Locate the sentence(s) in which Walker states her main idea. If she doesn't state the thesis explicitly, express it in your own words.

2. How did Walker come to know Blue? Which words or phrases indicate her initial attitude toward him?

3. What feelings does Walker recognize in the horse? What is Walker implying about Blue—and other animals?

4. What false images of animals does Walker feel we gain from the culture around us?

5. Refer to your dictionary as needed to define the following words used in the selection: *benign* (paragraph 8) and *euphemism* (8).

Questions About the Writer's Craft

1. The Pattern. Walker interrupts her narrative with a long meditation on the human condition (paragraphs 7–10). What is the effect of this interruption?

2. Why might Walker have titled her narrative "Am I Blue?" What levels of meaning do you find in the title?

3. **Other Patterns.** Locate places in the essay where Walker attributes to Blue qualities and emotions typically associated with human beings. What effect do you think Walker intends to achieve with this strategy?

4. In paragraph 18, Walker refers to "contented" cows and "happy" hens. Why does she place these words in quotation marks? How does this technique reinforce Walker's thesis?

Writing Assignments Using Narration as a Pattern of Development

1. Write, as Walker does, a narrative revealing the hardships of a group all too often ignored, misunderstood, or mistreated (for example, the homeless, the disabled, the overweight). Focus on one representative of this group, and use narrative details to make a strong case for treating the group more fairly.

∞ 2. In "Am I Blue?" Walker narrates a series of events that helped change her mind about eating meat. Write a narrative essay about an episode that changed your behavior or attitude in some way. Save the announcement of your change in attitude for the essay's final paragraph, letting the narrative details do the explaining for you. To see how a skilled prose stylist recounts such a change of heart, read Maya Angelou's "Louise Cox" (page 207).

Writing Assignments Using Other Patterns of Development

∞ 3. At the end of her essay, Walker suggests that advertising misrepresents the reality of food-animals' lives. Identify some television commercials or magazine advertisements that you feel portray false images of one aspect of life (parent-child relationships, dating, old age). Then write an essay describing these commercials so vividly that your readers can easily see how distorted they are. To sharpen your understanding of advertising strategies, you might want to read Ann McClintock's "Propaganda Techniques in Today's Advertising" (page 271).

∞ 4. The animal-rights issue has received much attention in recent years. Focus on one aspect of this controversy (for example, wearing fur, eating veal, using animals in medical experiments), and research both sides of the issue. Then write an essay in which you support your point of view by refuting as many of the opposing arguments as you can. Beth Johnson Ruth's "Our Drug Problem" (page 449) illustrates a strategy for refuting opposing opinions.

ADDITIONAL WRITING TOPICS: NARRATION

General Assignments

Write an essay using description to develop one of the following topics.

1. An emergency that brought out the best or worst in you
2. The hazards of taking children out to eat
3. An incident that made you believe in fate
4. Your best or worst day at school or work
5. A major decision
6. An encounter with a machine
7. An important learning experience
8. A narrow escape
9. Your first date, first day on the job, or first anything
10. A memorable childhood experience
11. A fairy tale the way you would like to hear it told
12. A painful moment
13. An incredible but true story
14. A significant family event
15. An experience in which a certain emotion (pride, anger, regret, or some other) was dominant

Assignments with a Specific Purpose, Audience, and Point of View

1. As fund-raiser for a particular organization (for example, Red Cross, SPCA, Big Brothers/Big Sisters), you're sending a newsletter to contributors. Support your cause by telling the story of a time when your organization made all the difference—the blood donation that saved a life, the animal that was rescued from abuse, and so on.

2. A friend of yours has seen someone cheat on a test, shoplift, or violate an employer's trust. In a letter, convince this friend to inform the instructor, store

owner, or employer, by narrating an incident in which a witness did (or did not) speak up in such a situation. Tell what happened as a result.

3. You have had a disturbing encounter with one of the people who seems to have "fallen through the cracks" of society—a street person, an unwanted child, or anyone else who is alone and abandoned. Write a letter to the local newspaper describing this encounter. Your purpose is to arouse people's indignation and compassion and to get help for such unfortunates.

4. Write an article for your old high school newspaper. The article will be read primarily by seniors who are planning to go away to college next year. In the article, narrate a story that points to some truth about the "breaking away" stage of life.

5. A close friend has written a letter to you telling about a bad experience that he or she had with a teacher, employer, doctor, repairperson, or some other professional. Based on that single experience, your friend now negatively stereotypes the entire profession. Write a letter to your friend balancing his or her cynical picture by narrating a story that shows the "flip side" of this profession—someone who made every effort to help.

6. Your younger brother, sister, relative, or neighborhood friend can't wait to be your age. By narrating an appropriate story, show the young person that your age isn't as wonderful as he or she thinks. Be sure to select a story that the person can understand and appreciate.

14
ILLUSTRATION

WHAT IS ILLUSTRATION?

IF someone asked you, "Have you been to any good restaurants lately?" you probably wouldn't answer "Yes" and then immediately change the subject. Most likely, you would go on to **illustrate** with examples. Perhaps you'd give the names of restaurants you've enjoyed and talk briefly about the specific things you liked: the attractive prices, the tasty main courses, the pleasant service, the tempting desserts. Such examples and details are needed to convince others that your opinion—in this or any matter—is valid. Similarly, when you talk about larger and more important issues, people won't pay much attention to your opinion if all you do is string together vague generalizations: "We have to do something about acid rain. It's had disastrous consequences for the environment. Its negative effects increase every year. Action must be taken to control the problem." To be taken seriously and convince others that your point is well-founded, you must provide specific supporting examples: "The forests in the Adirondacks are dying"; "yesterday's rainfall was fifty times more acidic than normal"; "Pine Lake, in the northern part of the state, was once a great fishing spot but now has no fish population."

Examples are equally important when you write an essay. It's not vague generalities and highfaluting abstractions that make writing impressive. Just the opposite is true. Facts, details, anecdotes, statistics, expert opinion, and personal observations are at the heart of effective writing, giving your work substance and solidity.

HOW ILLUSTRATION FITS YOUR PURPOSE AND AUDIENCE

The wording of assignments and essay exam questions may signal the need for illustration:

> Soap operas, whether shown during the day or in the evening, are among the most popular television programs. Why do you think this is so? Provide specific examples to support your position.

> Some observers claim that college students are less interested in learning than in getting ahead in their careers. Cite evidence to support or refute this claim.

> A growing number of people feel that parents should not allow young children to participate in highly competitive team sports. Basing your conclusion on your own experiences and observations, indicate whether you think this point of view is reasonable.

Such phrases as "Provide specific examples," "Cite evidence," and "Basing your conclusion on your own experiences and observations" signal that each essay would be developed through illustration.

Usually, though, you won't be told so explicitly to provide examples. Instead, as you think about the best way to achieve your essay's purpose, you'll see the need for illustrative details—no matter which patterns of development you use. For instance, to *persuade* skeptical readers that the country needs a national health system, you might mention specific cases to dramatize the inadequacy of our current health-care system: a family bankrupted by medical bills; an uninsured accident victim turned away by a hospital; a chronically ill person rapidly deteriorating because he didn't have enough money to visit a doctor. Or imagine a lightly satiric piece that pokes fun at cat lovers. Insisting that "cat people" are pretty strange creatures, you might make your point—and make readers chuckle—with a series of examples *contrasting* cat lovers and dog lovers: the qualities admired by each group (loyalty in dogs versus independence in cats) and the different expectations each group has for its pets (dog lovers want Fido to be obedient and lovable, whereas cat lovers are satisfied with Felix's occasional spurts of docility and affection). Similarly, you would supply examples in a *causal analysis* speculating on the likely impact of a proposed tuition hike at your college. To convince the college administration of the probable negative effects of such a hike, you might cite the following examples: articles reporting a nationwide upswing in student transfers to less expensive schools; statistics indicating a significant drop in grades among already employed students forced to work more hours to pay increased tuition costs; interviews with students too financially strapped to continue their college education.

Whether you use illustration as a primary or supplemental method of development, it serves a number of important purposes. For one thing, illustrations make writing *interesting*. Assume you're writing an essay about the bias against women in television commercials. Your essay would be lifeless and boring if all it did was repeat, in a general way, that commercials present stereotyped views of men and women:

Original

An anti-female bias is rampant in television commercials. It is very much alive, yet most viewers seem to take it all in stride. Few people protest the obviously sexist characters and statements on such commercials. Surely, these commercials misrepresent the way most of us live.

Without interesting particulars, readers may respond, "Who cares?" But if you provide specific examples, you'll attract your readers' attention:

Revised

An anti-female bias is rampant in television commercials. Although millions of women hold responsible jobs outside the home, commercials continue to portray women as simple creatures who spend much of their time thinking about wax buildup, cottony-soft bathroom tissue, and static-free clothes. Men, apparently, have better things to do than fret over such mundane household matters. How many commercials can you recall that depict men proclaiming the virtues of squeaky-clean dishes or sparkling bathrooms? Not many.

Illustrations also make writing *persuasive*. Most writing conveys a point, but many readers are reluctant to accept someone else's point of view unless evidence demonstrates its validity. Imagine you're writing an essay showing that latchkey children are more self-sufficient and emotionally secure than children who return from school to a home where a parent awaits them. Your thesis is obviously controversial. Without specific examples—from your own experience, personal observations, or research studies—your readers would undoubtedly question your position's validity.

Further, illustrations help *explain* difficult, abstract, or unusual ideas. Suppose you're assigned an essay on a complex subject such as inflation, zero population growth, or radiation exposure. As a writer, you have a responsibility to your readers to make these difficult concepts concrete and understandable. If writing an essay on radiation exposure in everyday life, you might start by providing specific examples of home appliances that emit radiation—color televisions, computers, and microwave ovens—and tell exactly how much radiation we absorb in a typical day from such equipment. To illustrate further the extent of our radiation exposure, you could also provide specifics about unavoidable sources of natural radiation (the sun, for instance) and details about the widespread use of radiation in medicine (X-rays, radiation therapy). These examples would ground your discussion, making it immediate and concrete, preventing it from flying off into the vague and theoretical.

Finally, examples help *prevent unintended ambiguity.* All of us have experienced the frustration of having someone misinterpret what we say. In face-to-face communication, we can provide on-the-spot clarification. In writing, however, instantaneous feedback isn't available, so it's crucial that meaning be as unambiguous as possible. Illustrations will help. Assume you're writing an essay asserting that ineffective teaching is on the rise in today's high schools. To clarify what you mean by "ineffective," you provide illustrations: the instructor who spends so much time disciplining unruly students that he never gets around to teaching; the moonlighting teacher who is so tired in class that she regularly takes naps during tests; the teacher who accepts obviously plagiarized reports because he's grateful that students hand in something. Without such concrete examples, your readers will supply their own ideas—and these may not be what you had in mind. Readers might imagine "ineffective" to mean harsh and punitive, whereas concrete examples would show that you intend it to mean out of control and irresponsible.

PREWRITING STRATEGIES

The following checklist shows how you can apply to illustration some of the prewriting techniques discussed in Chapter 2.

✔ ILLUSTRATION: A PREWRITING CHECKLIST

Choose a Subject to Illustrate
- What general situation or phenomenon (for example, campus apathy, organic farming) can you depict through illustration?
- What difficult or misunderstood concept (nuclear winter, passive aggression) would examples help to explain and make concrete?

Determine Your Purpose, Audience, Tone, and Point of View
- What is your purpose in writing?
- What audience do you have in mind?
- What tone and point of view will best serve your purpose and lead readers to adopt the desired attitude toward the subject being illustrated?

Use Prewriting to Generate Examples
- How can brainstorming, freewriting, journal entries, or mapping help you generate relevant examples (events, facts, anecdotes, quotations) from your own or others' experiences?
- How could library research help you gather pertinent examples (expert opinion, case studies, statistics)?

STRATEGIES FOR USING ILLUSTRATION IN AN ESSAY

After prewriting, you're ready to draft your essay. The following suggestions will be helpful whether you use illustration as a dominant or supportive pattern of development.

1. Select the examples to include. Examples can take several forms, including specific names (of people, places, products, and so on), anecdotes, personal observations, expert opinion, as well as facts, statistics, and case studies gathered through research. Once you've used prewriting to generate as many examples as possible, you're ready to limit your examples to the strongest. Keeping your thesis, audience, tone, and point of view in mind, ask yourself several key questions: "Which examples support my thesis? Which do not? Which are most convincing? Which are most likely to interest readers and clarify meaning?"

Usually, you'll need to provide *several examples* to achieve your purpose. An essay with the thesis "Rock videos are dangerously violent" wouldn't be convincing if you gave only one example of a violent rock video. Several strong examples would be needed for readers to feel you had illustrated your point sufficiently.

As a general rule, you should strive for variety in the kinds of examples you include. For instance, you might choose a *personal-experience example* drawn from your own life or from the life of someone you know. Such examples pack the wallop of personal authority and lend drama to writing. Or you might include a *typical-case example,* an actual event or situation that did occur—but not to you or to anyone you know. (Perhaps you learned about the event through a magazine article, newspaper account, or television report.) The objective nature of such cases makes them especially convincing. You might also include a speculative or *hypothetical example* ("Imagine how difficult it must be for an elderly person to carry bags of groceries from the market to a bus stop several blocks away"). You'll find that hypothetical cases are effective for clarifying and dramatizing key points, but be sure to acknowledge that the example is indeed invented ("*Suppose* that . . ." or "Let's for a moment *assume* that . . ."). Make certain, too, that the invented situation is easily imagined and could conceivably happen. Finally, you might create a *generalized example*—one that is a composite of the typical or usual. Such generalized examples are often signaled by words that involve the reader ("*All of us*, at one time or another, have been driven to distraction by a trivial annoyance like the buzzing of a fly or the sting of a papercut"), or they may refer to humanity in general ("When *most people* get a compliment, they perk up, preen, and think the praise-giver is blessed with astute powers of observation").

Occasionally, *one extended example,* fully developed with many details, can support an essay. It might be possible, for instance, to support the thesis "Federal legislation should raise the legal drinking age to twenty-one" with a single compelling, highly detailed example of the effects of one teenager's drunken-driving spree.

The examples you choose must also be *relevant*; that is, they must have direct bearing on the point you want to make. You would have a hard time convincing readers that Americans have callous attitudes toward the elderly if you described the wide range of new programs, all staffed by volunteers, at a well-financed center for senior citizens. Because these examples *contradict*, rather than support, your thesis, readers are apt to dismiss what you have to say.

In addition, try to select *dramatic* examples. Say you're writing an essay to show that society needs to take more steps to protect children from abuse. Simply stating that many parents hit their children isn't likely to form a strong impression in the reader's mind. However, graphic examples (children with stab wounds, welts, and burn marks) are apt to create a sense of urgency in the reader.

Make certain, too, that your examples are *accurate*. Exercise special caution when using statistics. An old saying warns that there are lies, damned lies, and statistics—meaning that statistics can be misleading. A commercial may claim, "In a taste test, eighty percent of those questioned indicated that they preferred Fizzy Cola." Impressed? Don't be—at least, not until you find out how the test was conducted. Perhaps the participants had to choose between Fizzy Cola and battery acid, or perhaps there were only five participants, all Fizzy Cola vice presidents.

Finally, select *representative* examples. Picking the oddball, one-in-a-million example to support a point—and passing it off as typical—is dishonest. Consider an essay with the thesis "Part-time jobs contribute to academic success." Citing only one example of a student who works at a job twenty-five hours a week while earning straight *A*'s isn't playing fair. Why not? You've made a *sweeping generalization* based on only one case. To be convincing, you need to show how holding down a job affects *most* students' academic performance. (For more on sweeping generalizations, see pages 419–21.)

2. Develop your examples sufficiently. To ensure that you get your ideas across, your examples must be *specific*. An essay on the types of heroes in American movies wouldn't succeed if you simply strung together a series of undeveloped examples in paragraphs like this one:

Original

Heroes in American movies usually fall into types. One kind of hero is the tight-lipped loner, men like Clint Eastwood and Humphrey Bogart. Another movie hero is the quiet, shy, or fumbling type who has appeared in movies since the beginning. The main characteristic of this hero is lovableness, as seen in actors like Jimmy Stewart. Perhaps the most one-dimensional and predictable hero is the superman who battles tough odds. This kind of hero is best illustrated by Sylvester Stallone as Rocky and Rambo.

If you developed the essay in this way—moving from one undeveloped example to another—you would be doing little more than making a list. To be effective, key examples must be expanded in sufficient detail. The examples in the preceding paragraph could be developed in paragraphs of their own. You could, for instance, develop the first example this way:

Revised

    Heroes can be tight-lipped loners who appear out of nowhere, form no permanent attachments, and walk, drive, or ride off into the sunset. In most of his Westerns, from the low-budget "spaghetti Westerns" of the 1960s to <u>Pale Rider</u> in 1985, Clint Eastwood personifies this kind of hero. He is remote, mysterious, and untalkative. Yet he guns down an evil sheriff, runs other villains out of town, and helps a handicapped girl--acts that cement his heroic status. The loner might also be Sam Spade as played by Humphrey Bogart. Spade solves the crime and sends the guilty off to jail, yet he holds his emotions in check and has no permanent ties beyond his faithful secretary and shabby office. One gets the feeling that he could walk away from these, too, if necessary. Even in <u>The Right Stuff</u>, an account of America's early astronauts, the scriptwriters mold Chuck Yeager, the man who broke the sound barrier, into a classic loner. Yeager, portrayed by the aloof Sam Shepherd, has a wife, but he is nevertheless insular. Taking mute pride in his ability to distance himself from politicians, bureaucrats, even colleagues, he soars into space, dignified and detached.

(For hints on making evidence specific, see pages 66–68 in Chapter 6.)

3. Organize the examples. If, as is usually the case, several examples support your point, be sure to present the examples in an *organized* manner. Often you'll find that other *patterns of development* (cause-effect, comparison-contrast, definition, and so on) suggest ways to sequence examples. Let's say you're writing an essay showing that stay-at-home vacations offer numerous opportunities to relax. You might begin the essay with examples that *contrast* stay-at-home and get-away vacations. Then you might move to a *process analysis* that illustrates different techniques for unwinding at home. The essay might end with examples showing the *effect* of such leisurely at-home breaks.

    Finally, you need to select an *organizational approach consistent* with your *purpose* and *thesis*. Imagine you're writing an essay about students' adjustment during the first months of college. The supporting examples could be arranged *chronologically*. You might start by illustrating the ambivalence many students feel the first day of college when their parents leave for home; you might then offer an anecdote or two about students' frequent calls to Mom and Dad during the opening weeks of the semester; the essay might close with an account of students' reluctance to leave campus at the midyear break.

    Similarly, an essay demonstrating that a room often reflects the character of its occupant might be organized *spatially:* from the empty soda cans on the floor to the spitballs on the ceiling. In an essay illustrating the kinds of skills taught in a composition course, you might move from *simple* to *complex* examples: starting with relatively matter-of-fact skills like spelling and punctuation and ending with more conceptually difficult skills like formulating a thesis and organizing an essay. Last, the *emphatic sequence*—in which you lead from your first example to your final, most significant one—is another effective way to organize an essay with many examples. A paper about Americans' characteristic impatience might progress from minor examples (dependence on fast food, obsession with ever-faster mail delivery) to more disturbing manifestations of impatience (using drugs as quick solutions to problems, advocating simple answers to complex international problems: "Bomb them!").

4. Choose a point of view. Many essays developed by illustration place the subject in the foreground and the writer in the background. Such an approach calls for the *third-person point of view*. For example, even if you draw examples from your own personal experience, you can present them without using the *first-person* "I." You might convert such personal material into generalized examples (see page 224), or you might describe the personal experience as if it happened to someone else. Of course, you may use the first person if the use of "I" will make the example more believable and dramatic. But remember: Just because an event happened to you personally doesn't mean you have to use the first-person point of view.

REVISION STRATEGIES

Once you have a draft of the essay, you're ready to revise. The following checklist will help you and those giving you feedback apply to illustration some of the revision techniques discussed in Chapters 7 and 8.

✔ ILLUSTRATION: A REVISION CHECKLIST

Revise Overall Meaning and Structure

- What thesis is being advanced? Which examples don't support the thesis? Should these examples be deleted, or should the thesis be reshaped to fit the examples? Why?
- Which patterns of development and methods of organization (chronological, spatial, simple-to-complex, emphatic) provide the essay's framework? Would other ordering principles be more effective? If so, which ones?

Revise Paragraph Development

- Which paragraphs contain too many or too few examples? Which contain examples that are too brief or too extended? Which include insufficiently or overly detailed examples?

- Which paragraphs rely on predictable examples? How could the examples be made more compelling?
- Which paragraphs include examples that are atypical or inaccurate?

Revise Sentences and Words

- What signal devices (*for example, for instance, in particular, such as*) introduce examples and clarify the line of thought? Where are there too many or too few of these devices?
- Where would more varied sentence structure heighten the effect of the essay's illustrations?
- Where would more concrete and specific words make the examples more effective?

STUDENT ESSAY: FROM PREWRITING THROUGH REVISION

The student essay that follows was written by Michael Pagano in response to this assignment:

> Anne Morrow Lindbergh states in "Channelled Whelk" that Americans impose unnecessary complications on their lives. Observe closely the way you and others conduct your daily lives. Use your observations to generate evidence for an essay that supports or refutes Lindbergh's point of view.

After deciding to write an essay on the way possessions complicate life, Michael sat down at his word processor and did some *freewriting* to generate material on the topic. His original freewriting is shown here; the handwritten comments indicate Michael's later efforts to develop and shape this material. Note that Michael deleted some points, added others, and made several items more specific; he also labeled and sequenced key ideas. These annotations paved the way for a sentence outline, which is presented after the freewriting.

Freewriting

(1) Buying

I shop too much. So do my parents--practically every weekend and ~~nearly every holiday except Christmas and Easter. All those Washington's Birthday sales.~~ Then they yell at us kids for watching so much TV, although they're not around to do much with us. In fact, Mom and Dad were the ones who thought our old *19-inch* black-and-white TV wasn't good

(4) Discarding items

enough anymore so they replaced it with a huge *25-inch* color set. I remember all
classified section
those annoying phone calls when they put the ad in the paper to sell the black and white. People coming and going. Then Mom and Dad only got

Illustration

$25 for it anyway. ~~It wasn't worth paying for the ad.~~ They never seem to come out ahead. No wonder Mom works part-time at the library and Dad stays so late at the office. I'm getting into the same situation. Already up to my ears in debt, paying off the car. I spend hours washing it and waxing it, and it doesn't even fit into the garage, which is loaded with discarded junk. The whole house is cluttered. Maybe that's why people move so much--to escape the clutter. There was hardly room for my new word processor in my room. I also have to shove my new clothes into the closets and drawers. My snazzy new jeans get all wrinkled. They shrank when I washed them. Now they're too tight. I should have sent them to the dry cleaners. But I'd already paid enough for them. ~~Well, everything's shoddy nowadays.~~ Possessions don't hold up. So what lasts? Basic values --love, family, friends.

Annotations (right margin, in script):
- (5) *Running into debt*
- *2nd job* (above "part-time")
- *overtime* (above "stays so late")
- *time payments* (above "paying off")
- (3) *vacuuming car-maintenance*
- (2) *Running out of room*
- (3) *Having maintenance problems*
- *My computer's giving me trouble.*
- *conclusion?*

Outline

Thesis: We clutter our lives with material goods.

I. We waste a lot of time deciding what to buy.
    A. We window-shop for good-looking footwear.
    B. We look through magazines for stereos and exercise equipment.
    C. Family life suffers when everyone is out shopping.

II. Once we take our new purchases home, we find we don't have enough room for them.
    A. We stack things in crowded closets, garages, and basements.
    B. When things get too cluttered, we simply move.

III. Our possessions require continual maintenance.
    A. Cars have to be washed and waxed.
    B. New jeans have to go to the cleaners.
    C. Word processors and other items break down and have to be replaced.

IV. Before we replace broken items, we try to get rid of them by placing ads in the classified section.
    A. We have to deal with annoying phone calls.
    B. We have to deal with people coming to the house to see the items.

V. Our mania for possessions puts us in debt.
    A. We accumulate enormous credit-card balances.
    B. We take second jobs or work overtime to make time payments.

Now read Michael's paper, "Pursuit of Possessions," noting the similarities and differences among his freewriting, outline, and final essay. You'll see, for example, that Michael changed the "I" of his freewriting to the more general "We" in the outline and essay. He made this change because he wanted readers to see themselves in the situations being illustrated. In addition, Michael's outline, while more detailed than his freewriting, doesn't include highly concrete examples, but the essay does. In the outline, for instance, he simply states, "Word processors and other items break down...." In the essay, though, he spins out this point with vivid details: "The home computer starts to lose data, the microwave has to have its temperature controls adjusted, and the videocassette recorder has to be serviced when a cassette becomes jammed."

As you read Michael's essay, also consider how well it applies the principles of illustration. (The commentary that follows the paper will help you look at the essay more closely and will give you some sense of how Michael went about revising his first draft.)

Pursuit of Possessions
by Michael Pagano

Introduction — In the essay "Channelled Whelk," Anne Morrow Lindbergh states that Americans "who could choose simplicity, choose complication." Lindbergh herself is a prime example of the phenomenon she discusses. A wife and a mother, as well as a writer, Lindbergh has many obligations that make for a complicated life. Even so, Lindbergh attempts to simplify her life by escaping to a beach cottage that is bare except for driftwood and shells for decoration; there she is happy. But very few of us would be willing to simplify our lives as Lindbergh does. *Thesis* — Instead, we choose to clutter our lives with a stream of material possessions. And what is the result of this mania for possessions? *Plan of development* — Much of our time goes into buying new things, dealing with the complications they create, and working madly to buy more things or pay for the things we already have.

Topic sentence — We devote a great deal of our lives to acquiring the material goods we imagine are essential to our well-being. Hours are spent planning and thinking about our future purchases. We window-shop for designer jogging shoes; we leaf through magazines looking at ads for elaborate stereo equipment; we research back issues of Consumer Reports to find out about recent developments in exercise equipment. Moreover, once we find what we are looking for, more time is taken up when we decide to actually buy the items. How do we find this time? That's easy. We turn evenings, weekends, and holidays--times that used to be set aside for

The first of three paragraphs in a chronological sequence

1

2

Illustration   231

family and friends--into shopping expeditions. No wonder family life is
deteriorating and children spend so much time in front of television sets.
Their parents are seldom around.

3   As soon as we take our new purchases home, they begin to — Topic sentence
complicate our lives. A sleek new sports car has to be washed, waxed,
and vacuumed. A fashionable pair of skintight jeans can't be thrown in the   The second
washing machine but has to be taken to the dry cleaner. New stereo   paragraph in the
equipment has to be connected with a tangled network of cables to the   chronological
TV, radio, and cassette deck. Eventually, of course, the inevitable   sequence
happens. Our indispensable possessions break down and need to be
repaired. The home computer starts to lose data, the microwave has to   A paragraph with
have its temperature controls adjusted, and the videotape recorder has to   many specific
be serviced when a cassette becomes jammed in the machine.   examples

4   After more time has gone by, we sometimes discover that our — Topic sentence
purchases don't suit us anymore, and so we decide to replace them.
Before making our replacement purchases, though, we have to find ways   The third
to get rid of the old items. If we want to replace our black-and-white 19-   paragraph in the
inch television set with a 25-inch color set, we have to find time to put an chronological
ad in the classified section of the paper. Then we have to handle phone   sequence
calls and set up times people can come to look at the TV. We could store
the set in the basement--if we are lucky enough to find a spot that isn't
already filled with other discarded purchases.

5   Worst of all, this mania for possessions often influences our
approach to work. It is not unusual for people to take a second or even a   Topic sentence
third job to pay off the debt they fall into because they have overbought.   with emphasis
After paying for food, clothing, and shelter, many people see the rest of   signal
their paycheck go to Visa, MasterCard, department store charge accounts,
and time payments. Panic sets in when they realize there simply is not
enough money to cover all their expenses. Just to stay afloat, people may
have to work overtime or take on additional jobs.

6   It is clear that many of us have allowed the pursuit of possessions to   Conclusion
dominate our lives. We are so busy buying, maintaining, and paying for
our worldly goods that we do not have much time to think about what is
really important. We should try to step back from our compulsive need for
more of everything and get in touch with the basic values that are the real
point of our lives.

Commentary

Thesis, Other Patterns of Development, and Plan of Development

In "Pursuit of Possessions," Michael analyzes the American mania for acquiring material goods. He begins with a quotation from Anne Morrow Lindbergh's "Channelled Whelk" and briefly explains Lindbergh's strategy for simplifying her life. The reference to Lindbergh gives Michael a chance to *contrast* the way she tries to lead her life with the acquisitive and frenzied way many Americans lead theirs. This contrast leads logically to the essay's *thesis*: "We choose to clutter our lives with a stream of material possessions."

Besides introducing the basic contrast at the heart of the essay, Michael's opening paragraph helps readers see that the essay contains an element of *causal analysis*. Michael asks, "What is the result of this mania for possessions?" and then answers that question in the next sequence. This sentence also serves as the essay's *plan of development* and reveals that Michael feels the pursuit of possessions negatively affects our lives in three key ways.

Essays of this length often don't need a plan of development. But since Michael's paper is filled with many *examples*, the plan of development helps readers see how all the details relate to the essay's central point.

Evidence

Support for the thesis consists of numerous examples presented in the *first-person plural point of view* ("*We* choose to clutter our lives...," "*We* devote a great deal of our lives..." and so on). Many of these examples seem drawn from Michael's, his friends', or his family's experiences; however, to emphasize the events' universality, Michael converts these essentially personal examples into generalized ones that "we" all experience.

These examples, in turn, are organized around the three major points signaled by the plan of development. Michael uses one paragraph to develop his first and third points and two paragraphs to develop his second point. Each of the four supporting paragraphs is focused by a *topic sentence* that appears at the start of the paragraph. The transitional phrase "Worst of all" (paragraph 5) signals that Michael has sequenced his major points *emphatically*, saving for last the issue he considers most significant: how the "mania for possessions ... influences our approach to work."

Organizational Strategies

Emphatic order isn't Michael's only organizational technique. When reading the paper, you probably felt that there was an easy flow from one supporting paragraph to the next. How does Michael achieve such *coherence between paragraphs*? For one thing, he sequences paragraphs 2–4 *chronologically*: what happens before a purchase is made; what happens afterward. Secondly, topic sentences in paragraphs 3 and 4 include *signal devices* that indicate this passage of time. The topic sentences also strengthen coherence by *linking back* to the preceding paragraph: "As soon as we take our new purchases home, they ...

Illustration

complicate our lives" and *"After more time has gone by,* we ... discover that our purchases don't suit us anymore."

The same organizing strategies are used *within paragraphs* to make the essay coherent. Details in paragraphs 2–4 are sequenced *chronologically,* and to help readers follow the chronology, Michael uses *signal devices:* "*Moreover, once* we find what we are looking for, more time is taken up ..." (2); "*Eventually,* of course, the inevitable happens" (3); "*Then* we have to handle phone calls ..." (4).

Problems with Paragraph Development

You probably recall that an essay developed primarily through illustration must include examples that are *relevant, interesting, convincing, representative, accurate,* and *specific.* On the whole, Michael's examples meet these requirements. The third and fourth paragraphs, especially, include vigorous details that show how our mania for buying things can govern our lives. We may even laugh with self-recognition when reading about "skintight jeans that can't be thrown in the washing machine" or a basement "filled ... with discarded purchases."

The fifth paragraph, however, is underdeveloped. We know that this paragraph presents what Michael considers his most significant point, but the paragraph's examples are rather *flat* and *unconvincing.* To make this final section more compelling, Michael could mention specific people who overspend, revealing how much they are in debt and how much they have to work to become solvent again. Or he could cite a television documentary or magazine article dealing with the issue of consumer debt. Such specifics would give the paragraph the solidity it now lacks.

Shift in Tone

The fifth paragraph has a second, more subtle problem: a *shift in tone.* Although Michael has, up to this point, been critical of our possession-mad culture, he has poked fun at our obsession and kept his tone conversational and gently satiric. In this paragraph, though, he adopts a serious tone, and, in the next paragraph, his tone becomes even weightier, almost preachy. It is, of course, legitimate to have a serious message in a lightly satiric piece. In fact, most satiric writing has such an additional layer of meaning. But because Michael has trouble blending these two moods, there's a jarring shift in the essay.

Shift in Focus

The second paragraph shows another kind of shift—in *focus.* The paragraph's controlling idea is that too much time is spent acquiring possessions. However, starting with "No wonder family life is deteriorating," Michael includes two sentences that introduce a complex issue beyond the scope of the essay. Since the sentences disrupt the paragraph's unity, they should be deleted.

Revising the First Draft

Although the final version of the essay needs work in spots, it's much stronger than Michael's first draft. To see how Michael went about revising the draft, compare his paper's second and third supporting paragraphs with his draft version reprinted here. The annotations, numbered in order of importance, show the ideas Michael hit upon when he returned to his first draft and reworked this section.

Original Version of the Second Paragraph

② Awkward first sentence

① Paragraph goes in too many directions. Cut idea about moving since not enough space.

③ Make problem with jeans more specific

④ Develop more fully

Our lives are spent not only buying things but in dealing with the inevitable complications that are created by our newly acquired possessions. First, we have to find places to put all the objects we bring home. More clothes demand more closets; a second car demands more garage space; a home-entertainment center requires elaborate shelving. We shouldn't be surprised that the average American family moves once every three years. A good many families move simply because they need more space to store all the things they buy. In addition, our possessions demand maintenance time. A person who gets a new car will spend hours washing it, waxing it, and vacuuming it. A new pair of jeans has to go to the dry cleaners. New stereo systems have to be connected to already existing equipment. Eventually, of course, the inevitable happens. Our new items need to be repaired. Or we get sick of them and decide to replace them. Before making our replacement purchases, though, we have to get rid of the old items. That can be a real inconvenience.

Referring to the revision checklist on pages 227–28 helped Michael see that the paragraph rambled and lacked energy. He started to revise by tightening the first sentence, making it more focused and less awkward. Certainly, the revised sentence ("As soon as we take our new purchases home, they begin to complicate our lives") is crisper than the original. Next, he decided to omit the discussion about finding places to put new possessions; these sentences about inadequate closet, garage, and shelf space were so exaggerated that they undercut the valid point he wanted to make. He also chose to eliminate the sentences about the mobility of American families. This was, he felt, an interesting point, but it introduced an issue too complex to be included in the paragraph.

Michael strengthened the rest of the paragraph by making his examples more specific. A "new car" became a "sleek new sports car," and a "pair of jeans" became a "fashionable pair of skintight jeans." Michael also realized he had to do more than merely write, "Eventually, . . . our new items need to be repaired." This point had to be dramatized by sharp, convincing details. Therefore, Michael added lively examples to describe how high-tech possessions—microwaves, home computers, VCRs—break down. Similarly, Michael realized it wasn't enough simply to say, as he had in the original, that we run into problems when we try to replace out-of-favor purchases. Vigorous details were again needed to illustrate the point. Michael thus used a typical "replaceable" (an old black-and-white TV) as his key example and showed the annoyance involved in handling phone calls and setting up appointments so that people could see the TV.

After adding these specifics, Michael realized that he had enough material to devote a separate paragraph to the problems associated with replacing old purchases. By dividing his original paragraph, Michael ended up with two well-focused paragraphs, rather than a single rambling one.

In short, Michael strengthened his essay through substantial revision. Another round of rewriting would have made the essay stronger still. Even without this additional work, Michael's essay provides an interesting perspective on an American preoccupation.

ACTIVITIES: ILLUSTRATION

Prewriting Activities

1. Imagine you're writing two essays: One is a serious paper analyzing why large numbers of public school teachers leave the profession each year; the other is a light essay defining *preppie, head banger,* or some other slang term used to describe a kind of person. Jot down ways you might use examples in each essay.

2. Use mapping or another prewriting technique to gather examples illustrating the truth of *one* of the following familiar sayings. Then, using the same or a different prewriting technique, accumulate examples that counter the saying. Weigh both sets of examples to determine the saying's validity. After developing an appropriate thesis, decide which examples you would elaborate in an essay.

   a. Haste makes waste.
   b. There's no use crying over spilled milk.
   c. A bird in the hand is worth two in the bush.

3. Turn back to activity 4 and activity 5 in Chapter 4, and select *one* thesis statement for which you didn't develop supporting evidence earlier. Identify a purpose, audience, tone, and point of view for an essay with this thesis. Then meet with at least one other person to generate as many examples as possible to support the thesis. Next, evaluate the material to determine which examples should be eliminated. Finally, from the remaining examples, take the strongest one and develop it as fully as you can.

4. Freewrite or use your journal to generate examples illustrating how widespread a recent fad or trend has become. After reviewing your prewriting to determine a possible thesis, narrow the examples to those you would retain for an essay. How might the patterns of development or a chronological, emphatic, spatial, or simple-to-complex approach help you sequence the examples?

Revising Activities

5. The following paragraph is from the first draft of an essay about the decline of small-town shopping districts. The paragraph is meant to show what small towns can do to revitalize business. Revise the paragraph, strengthening it with specific and convincing examples.

> A small town can compete with a large new mall for shoppers. But merchants must work together, modernizing the stores and making the town's main street pleasant, even fun to walk. They should also copy the malls' example by including attention-getting events as often as possible.

6. The paragraph that follows is from the first draft of an essay showing how knowledge of psychology can help us understand behavior that might otherwise seem baffling. The paragraph is intended to illustrate the meaning of the psychological term *superego*. Revise the paragraph, replacing its vague, unconvincing examples with one extended example that conveys the meaning of *superego* clearly and dramatically.

> The superego is the part of us that makes us feel guilty when we do something that we know is wrong. When we act foolishly or wildly, we usually feel qualms about our actions later on. If we imagine ourselves getting revenge, we most likely discover that the thoughts make us feel bad. All of these are examples of the superego at work.

7. Reprinted here is a paragraph from the first draft of a light-spirited essay showing that Americans' pursuit of change for change's sake has drawbacks. The paragraph is meant to illustrate that infatuation with newness costs consumers money yet leads to no improvement in product quality. How effective is the paragraph? Which examples are specific and convincing? Which are not? Do any seem nonrepresentative, offensive, or sexist? How could the paragraph's organization be improved? Consider these questions as you rewrite the paragraph. Add specific examples where needed. Depending on the way you revise, you may want to break this one paragraph into several.

> We end up paying for our passion for the new and improved. Trendy clothing styles convince us that last year's outfits are outdated, even though our old clothes are fine. Women are especially vulnerable in this regard. What, though, about items that have to be replaced periodically, like shampoo? Even

slight changes lead to new formulations requiring retooling of the production process. That means increased manufacturing costs per item--all of which get passed on to us, the consumer. Then there are those items that tout new, trend-setting features that make earlier versions supposedly obsolete. Some manufacturers, for example, boast that their stereo or CD systems transmit an expanded-frequency range. The problem is that humans can't even hear such frequencies. But the high-tech feature dazzles men who are too naive to realize they're being hoodwinked.

PROFESSIONAL SELECTIONS: ILLUSTRATION

ANNE MORROW LINDBERGH

Anne Morrow Lindbergh (1906–) is a distinguished novelist, diarist, essayist, and poet. Her books include the novels *Dearly Beloved* (1962) and *Earth Shine* (1969), as well as the essay collection *Gift from the Sea* (1955), where the following selection first appeared.

CHANNELLED WHELK

1   The shell in my hand is deserted. It once housed a whelk, a snail-like creature, and then temporarily, after the death of the first occupant, a little hermit crab, who has run away, leaving his tracks behind him like a delicate vine on the sand. He ran away, and left me his shell. It was once a protection to him. I turn the shell in my hand, gazing into the wide open door from which he made his exit. Had it become an encumbrance? Why did he run away? Did he hope to find a better home, a better mode of living? I too have run away, I realize, I have shed the shell of my life, for these few weeks of vacation.

2   But his shell—it is simple; it is bare, it is beautiful. Small, only the size of my thumb, its architecture is perfect, down to the finest detail. Its shape, swelling like a pear in the center, winds in a gentle spiral to the pointed apex. Its color, dull gold, is whitened by a wash of salt from the sea. Each whorl, each faint knob, each criss-cross vein in its egg-shell texture, is as clearly defined as on the day of creation. My eye follows with delight the outer circumference of that diminutive winding staircase up which this tenant used to travel.

My shell is not like this, I think. How untidy it has become! Blurred with moss, knobby with barnacles, its shape is hardly recognizable any more. Surely, it had a shape once. It has a shape still in my mind. What is the shape of my life? 3

The shape of my life today starts with a family. I have a husband, five children and a home just beyond the suburbs of New York. I have also a craft, writing, and therefore work I want to pursue. The shape of my life is, of course, determined by many other things; my background and childhood, my mind and its education, my conscience and its pressures, my heart and its desires. I want to give and take from my children and husband, to share with friends and community, to carry out my obligations to man and to the world as a woman, as an artist, as a citizen. 4

But I want first of all—in fact, as an end to these other desires—to be at peace with myself. I want a singleness of eye, a purity of intention, a central core to my life that will enable me to carry out these obligations and activities as well as I can. I want, in fact—to borrow from the language of the saints—to live "in grace" as much of the time as possible. I am not using this term in a strictly theological sense. By grace I mean an inner harmony, essentially spiritual, which can be translated into outward harmony. I am seeking perhaps what Socrates asked for in the prayer from the *Phaedrus* when he said, "May the outward and inward man be at one." I would like to achieve a state of inner spiritual grace from which I could function and give as I was meant to in the eye of God. 5

Vague as this definition may be, I believe most people are aware of periods in their lives when they seem to be "in grace" and other periods when they feel "out of grace," even though they may use different words to describe these states. In the first happy condition, one seems to carry all one's tasks before one lightly, as if borne along on a great tide; and in the opposite state one can hardly tie a shoestring. It is true that a large part of life consists in learning a technique of tying the shoe-string, whether one is in grace or not. But there are techniques of living too; there are even techniques in the search for grace. And techniques can be cultivated. I have learned by some experience, by many examples, and by the writings of countless others before me, also occupied in the search, that certain environments, certain modes of life, certain rules of conduct are more conducive to inner and outer harmony than others. There are, in fact, certain roads that one may follow. Simplification of life is one of them. 6

I mean to lead a simple life, to choose a simple shell I can carry easily—like a hermit crab. But I do not. I find that my frame of life does not foster simplicity. My husband and five children must make their way in the world. The life I have chosen as wife and mother entrains a whole caravan of complications. It involves a house in the suburbs and either household drudgery or household help which wavers between scarcity and non-existence for most of us. It involves food and shelter; meals, planning, marketing, bills, and making the ends meet in a thousand ways. It involves not only the butcher, the baker, the candlestickmaker but countless other experts to keep my modern house with its modern "simplifications" (electricity, plumbing, refrigerator, gas-stove, oil-burner, dish-washer, radios, car, and numerous other labor-saving devices) functioning properly. It involves health; doctors, dentists, appointments, medicine, cod-liver oil, vitamins, trips to the drugstore. It involves education, spiritual, intellectual, physical; schools, school conferences, carpools, extra trips for basket-ball or orchestra practice; tutoring; camps, camp equipment and transportation. It involves clothes, shopping, laundry, cleaning, mending, letting skirts down and sewing buttons on, or finding someone else to do it. It involves friends, my husband's, my children's, my own, and endless arrangements to get together; letters, invitations, telephone calls and transportation hither and yon. 7

8   For life today in America is based on the premise of ever-widening circles of contact and communication. It involves not only family demands, but community demands, national demands, international demands on the good citizen, through social and cultural pressures, through newspapers, magazines, radio programs, political drives, charitable appeals, and so on. My mind reels with it. What a circus act we women perform every day of our lives. It puts the trapeze artist to shame. Look at us. We run a tightrope daily, balancing a pile of books on the head. Baby-carriage, parasol, kitchen chair, still under control. Steady now!

9   This is not the life of simplicity but the life of multiplicity that the wise men warn us of. It leads not to unification but to fragmentation. It does not bring grace; it destroys the soul. And this is not only true of my life, I am forced to conclude; it is the life of millions of women in America. I stress America, because today, the American woman more than any other has the privilege of choosing such a life. Woman in large parts of the civilized world has been forced back by war, by poverty, by collapse, by the sheer struggle to survive, into a smaller circle of immediate time and space, immediate family life, immediate problems of existence. The American woman is still relatively free to choose the wider life. How long she will hold this enviable and precarious position no one knows. But her particular situation has a significance far above its apparent economic, national or even sex limitations.

10   For the problem of the multiplicity of life not only confronts the American woman, but also the American man. And it is not merely the concern of the American as such, but of our whole modern civilization, since life in America today is held up as the ideal of a large part of the rest of the world. And finally, it is not limited to our present civilization, though we are faced with it now in an exaggerated form. It has always been one of the pitfalls of mankind. Plotinus was preaching the dangers of multiplicity of the world back in the third century. Yet, the problem is particularly and essentially woman's. Distraction is, always has been, and probably always will be, inherent in woman's life.

11   For to be a woman is to have interests and duties, raying out in all directions from the central mother-core, like spokes from the hub of a wheel. The pattern of our lives is essentially circular. We must be open to all points of the compass; husband, children, friends, home, community; stretched out, exposed, sensitive like a spider's web to each breeze that blows, to each call that comes. How difficult for us, then, to achieve a balance in the midst of these contradictory tensions, and yet how necessary for the proper functioning of our lives. How much we need, and how arduous of attainment is that steadiness preached in all rules for holy living. How desirable and distant is the ideal of the contemplative, artist, or saint—the inner inviolable core, the single eye.

12   With a new awareness, both painful and humorous, I begin to understand why the saints were rarely married women. I am convinced it has nothing inherently to do, as I once supposed, with chastity or children. It has to do primarily with distractions. The bearing, rearing, feeding and educating of children; the running of a house with its thousand details; human relationships with their myriad pulls—woman's normal occupations in general run counter to creative life, or contemplative life, or saintly life. The problem is not merely one of *Woman and Career, Woman and the Home, Woman and Independence.* It is more basically: how to remain whole in the midst of the distractions of life; how to remain balanced, no matter what centrifugal forces tend to pull one off center; how to remain strong, no matter what shocks come in at the periphery and tend to crack the hub of the wheel.

13   What is the answer? There is no easy answer, no complete answer. I have only clues, shells from the sea. The bare beauty of the channelled whelk tells me that one

answer, and perhaps a first step, is in simplification of life, in cutting out some of the distractions. But how? Total retirement is not possible. I cannot shed my responsibilities. I cannot permanently inhabit a desert island. I cannot be a nun in the midst of family life. I would not want to be. The solution for me, surely, is neither in total renunciation of the world, nor in total acceptance of it. I must find a balance somewhere, or an alternating rhythm between these two extremes; a swinging of the pendulum between solitude and communion, between retreat and return. In my periods of retreat, perhaps I can learn something to carry into my worldly life. I can at least practice for these two weeks the simplification of outward life, as a beginning. I can follow this superficial clue, and see where it leads. Here, in beach living, I can try.

14   One learns first of all in beach living the art of shedding; how little one can get along with, not how much. Physical shedding to begin with, which then mysteriously spreads into other fields. Clothes, first. Of course, one needs less in the sun. But one needs less anyway, one finds suddenly. One does not need a closet-full, only a small suitcase-full. And what a relief it is! Less taking up and down of hems, less mending, and—best of all—less worry about what to wear. One finds one is shedding not only clothes—but vanity.

15   Next, shelter. One does not need the airtight shelter one has in winter in the North. Here I live in a bare sea-shell of a cottage. No heat, no telephone, no plumbing to speak of, no hot water, a two-burner oil stove, no gadgets to go wrong. No rugs. There were some, but I rolled them up the first day; it is easier to sweep the sand off a bare floor. But I find I don't bustle about with unnecessary sweeping and cleaning here. I am no longer aware of the dust. I have shed my Puritan conscience about absolute tidiness and cleanliness. Is it possible that, too, is a material burden? No curtains. I do not need them for privacy; the pines around my house are enough protection. I want the windows open all the time, and I don't want to worry about rain. I begin to shed my Martha-like anxiety about many things. Washable slipcovers, faded and old—I hardly see them; I don't worry about the impression they make on other people. I am shedding pride. As little furniture as possible; I shall not need much. I shall ask into my shell only those friends with whom I can be completely honest. I find I am shedding hypocrisy in human relationships. What a rest that will be! The most exhausting thing in life, I have discovered, is being insincere. That is why so much of social life is exhausting; one is wearing a mask. I have shed my mask.

16   I find I live quite happily without those things I think necessary in winter in the North. And as I write these words, I remember, with some shock at the disparity in our lives, a similar statement made by a friend of mine in France who spent three years in a German prison camp. Of course, he said, qualifying his remark, they did not get enough to eat, they were sometimes atrociously treated, they had little physical freedom. And yet, prison life taught him how little one can get along with, and what extraordinary spiritual freedom and peace such simplification can bring. I remember again, ironically, that today more of us in America than anywhere else in the world have the luxury of choice between simplicity and complication of life. And for the most part, we, who could choose simplicity, choose complication. War, prison, survival periods, enforce a form of simplicity on man. The monk and the nun choose it of their own free will. But if one accidentally finds it, as I have for a few days, one finds also the serenity it brings.

17   Is it not rather ugly, one may ask? One collects material possessions not only for security, comfort or vanity, but for beauty as well. Is your sea-shell house not ugly and

bare? No, it is beautiful, my house. It is bare, of course, but the wind, the sun, the smell of the pines blow through its bareness. The unfinished beams in the roof are veiled by cobwebs. They are lovely, I think, gazing up at them with new eyes; they soften the hard lines of the rafters as grey hairs soften the lines on a middle-aged face. I no longer pull out grey hairs or sweep down cobwebs. As for the walls, it is true they looked forbidding at first. I felt cramped and enclosed by their blank faces. I wanted to knock holes in them, to give them another dimension with pictures or windows. So I dragged home from the beach grey arms of driftwood, worn satin-smooth by wind and sand. I gathered trailing green vines with floppy red-tipped leaves. I picked up the whitened skeletons of conchshells, their curious hollowed-out shapes faintly reminiscent of abstract sculpture. With these tacked to walls and propped up in corners, I am satisfied. I have a periscope out to the world. I have a window, a view, a point of flight from my sedentary base.

18   I am content. I sit down at my desk, a bare kitchen table with a blotter, a bottle of ink, a sand dollar to weight down one corner, a clam shell for a pen tray, the broken tip of a conch, pink-tinged, to finger, and a row of shells to set my thoughts spinning.

19   I love my sea-shell of a house. I wish I could live in it always. I wish I could transport it home. But I cannot. It will not hold a husband, five children and the necessities and trappings of daily life. I can only carry back my little channelled whelk. It will sit on my desk in Connecticut, to remind me of the ideal of a simplified life, to encourage me in the game I played on the beach. To ask how little, not how much, can I get along with. To say—is it necessary?—when I am tempted to add one more accumulation to my life, when I am pulled toward one more centrifugal activity.

20   Simplification of outward life is not enough. It is merely the outside. But I am starting with the outside. I am looking at the outside of a shell, the outside of my life—the shell. The complete answer is not to be found on the outside, in an outward mode of living. This is only a technique, a road to grace. The final answer, I know, is always inside. But the outside can give a clue, can help one to find the inside answer. One is free, like the hermit crab, to change one's shell.

21   Channelled whelk, I put you down again, but you have set my mind on a journey, up an inwardly winding spiral staircase of thought.

Questions for Close Reading

1. What is the selection's thesis? Locate the sentence(s) in which Lindbergh states her main idea. If she doesn't state the thesis explicitly, express it in your own words.

2. What does Lindbergh find appealing about the shell of the channelled whelk?

3. Why, according to Lindbergh, are distraction and "multiplicity" so much a problem for women? Why are they less of a problem for men?

4. Since Lindbergh prefers the life at the beach house, why doesn't she remain there? Why does she take the shell away with her?

5. Refer to your dictionary as needed to define the following words used in the selection: *apex* (paragraph 2), *conducive* (6), *myriad* (12), *periphery* (12), and *sedentary* (17).

Questions About the Writer's Craft

1. The pattern. Illustrative essays often develop key points through extended examples. In what paragraphs does Lindbergh use extended illustrations to clarify what she means by "simplification"? What's the effect of these extended illustrations?

2. Other patterns. Why do you suppose Lindbergh begins her essay with a few paragraphs describing a whelk shell? Where does she return to the shell? What does the shell come to represent?

3. In paragraph 6, the author uses the image of "tying a shoestring." To what aspects of life is she referring? At what point do you recognize that "tying a shoestring" serves as a metaphor for a larger part of life?

4. Why do you think Lindbergh ends the essay with a short "speech" or address to the whelk shell? How does this last paragraph extend an idea suggested in the preceding paragraph?

Writing Assignments Using Illustration as a Pattern of Development

1. Write an essay about the excess of possessions in people's lives today. Give examples of people you know or have heard about who are obsessed with possessions. Part of your essay should discuss the effect these possessions have on people's lives.

2. Lindbergh writes that she often feels fragmented into a series of selves because of the numerous demands—family, community, and political—made on her. Analyze your own life to identify the different roles you play. Write an essay detailing the "balancing act" you perform in your life. When describing each of your roles, be sure to provide specific examples of the demands claiming your attention. In the conclusion, point briefly to some things you could do to make your life less fragmented and more harmonious.

Writing Assignments Using Other Patterns of Development

3. Imagine simplifying your own life to achieve greater inner harmony. How would you go about it? Write an essay describing such a process. For each step, include specific examples of activities, objects, relationships, and the like that you would eliminate.

4. Taking a position opposed to Lindbergh's, contend that we benefit from the multiplicity of our lives. Argue that material possessions and numerous "circles of contact" are necessary and advantageous. Your tone can be either serious or humorous. In either case, be sure to acknowledge dissenting views.

Illustration

ALLEEN PACE NILSEN

A specialist in children's literature, Alleen Pace Nilsen (1936–) teaches at Arizona State University and edits a newsletter on adolescent literature. Nilsen's doctoral dissertation concerned linguistic sexism in books written for children. She coauthored the text *Literature for Today's Young Adults* (1982). The following selection is from *Sexism and Language* (1977), a collection of essays published by the National Council of Teachers of English.

SEXISM AND LANGUAGE

1   Over the last hundred years, American anthropologists have travelled to the corners of the earth to study primitive cultures. They either became linguists themselves or they took linguists with them to help in learning and analyzing languages. Even if the culture was one that no longer existed, they were interested in learning its language because besides being tools of communication, the vocabulary and structure of a language tell much about the values held by its speakers.

2   However, the culture need not be primitive, nor do the people making observations need to be anthropologists and linguists. Anyone living in the United States who listens with a keen ear or reads with a perceptive eye can come up with startling new insights about the way American English reflects our values.

Animal Terms for People—Mirrors of the Double Standard

3   If we look at just one semantic area of English, that of animal terms in relation to people, we can uncover some interesting insights into how our culture views males and females. References to identical animals can have negative connotations when related to a female, but positive or neutral connotations when related to a male. For example, a *shrew* has come to mean "a scolding, nagging, evil-tempered woman," while *shrewd* means "keen-witted, clever, or sharp in practical affairs; astute . . . businessman, etc." (*Webster's New World Dictionary of the American Language*, 1964).

4   A *lucky dog* or a *gay dog* may be a very interesting fellow, but when a woman is a *dog*, she is unattractive, and when she's a *bitch* she's the personification of whatever is undesirable in the mind of the speaker. When a man is self-confident, he may be described as *cocksure* or even *cocky*, but in a woman this same self-confidence is likely to result in her being called a *cocky bitch*, which is not only a mixed metaphor, but also probably the most insulting animal metaphor we have. *Bitch* has taken on such negative connotations—children are taught it is a swear word—that in everyday American English, speakers are hesitant to call a female dog a *bitch*. Most of us feel that we would be insulting the dog. When we want to insult a man by comparing him to a dog, we call him a *son of a bitch*, which quite literally is an insult to his mother rather than to him.

5   If the female is called a *vixen* (a female fox), the dictionary says this means she is "an ill-tempered, shrewish, or malicious woman." The female seems both to attract and to hold on longer to animal metaphors with negative connotations. A *vampire* was originally a corpse that came alive to suck the blood of living persons. The word acquired the general meaning of an unscrupulous person such as a blackmailer and then, the specialized meaning of "a beautiful but unscrupulous woman who seduces

men and leads them to their ruin." From this latter meaning we get the word *vamp*. The popularity of this term and of the name *vampire bat* may contribute to the idea that a female being is referred to in a phrase such as *the old bat*.

Other animal metaphors do not have definitely derogatory connotations for the female, but they do seem to indicate frivolity or unimportance, as in *social butterfly* and *flapper*. Look at the differences between the connotations of participating in a *hen party* and in a *bull session*. Male metaphors, even when they are negative in connotation, still relate to strength and conquest. Metaphors related to aggressive sex roles, for example, *buck, stag, wolf,* and *stud,* will undoubtedly remain attached to males. Perhaps one of the reasons that in the late sixties it was so shocking to hear policemen called *pigs* was that the connotations of *pig* are very different from the other animal metaphors we usually apply to males.

When I was living in Afghanistan, I was surprised at the cruelty and unfairness of a proverb that said, "When you see an old man, sit down and take a lesson; when you see an old woman, throw a stone." In looking at Afghan folk literature, I found that young girls were pictured as delightful and enticing, middle-aged women were sometimes interesting but more often just tolerable, while old women were always grotesque and villainous. Probably the reason for the negative connotation of old age in women is that women are valued for their bodies while men are valued for their accomplishments and their wisdom. Bodies deteriorate with age but wisdom and accomplishments grow greater.

When we returned home from Afghanistan, I was shocked to discover that we have remnants of this same attitude in America. We see it in our animal metaphors. If both the animal and the woman are young, the connotation is positive, but if the animal and the woman are old, the connotation is negative. Hugh Hefner might never have made it to the big time if he had called his girls *rabbits* instead of *bunnies*. He probably chose *bunny* because he wanted something close to, but not quite so obvious as *kitten* or *cat*—the all-time winners for connoting female sexuality. Also *bunny*, as in the skiers' *snow bunny*, already had some of the connotations Hefner wanted. Compare the connotations of *filly* to *old nag; bird* to *old crow* or *old bat;* and *lamb* to *crone* (apparently related to the early modern Dutch *kronje, old ewe* but now *withered old woman*).

Probably the most striking examples of the contrast between young and old women are animal metaphors relating to cats and chickens. A young girl is encouraged to be *kittenish,* but not *catty*. And though most of us wouldn't mind living next door to a *sex kitten,* we wouldn't want to live next door to a *cat house*. Parents might name their daughter *Kitty* but not *Puss* or *Pussy,* which used to be a fairly common nickname for girls. It has now developed such sexual connotations that it is used mostly for humor, as in the James Bond movie featuring Pussy Galore and her flying felines.

In the chicken metaphors, a young girl is a *chick*. When she gets old enough she marries and soon begins feeling *cooped up*. To relieve the boredom she goes to *hen parties* and *cackles* with her friends. Eventually she has her *brood,* begins to *henpeck* her husband, and finally turns into an *old biddy*.

How English Glorifies Maleness

Throughout the ages physical strength has been very important, and because men are physically stronger than women, they have been valued more. Only now in the machine age, when the difference in strength between males and females pales into insignificance in comparison to the strength of earth-moving machinery, airplanes, and guns, males no longer have such an inherent advantage. Today a man of intellect

Illustration

is more valued than a physical laborer, and since women can compete intellectually with men, their value is on the rise. But language lags far behind cultural changes, so the language still reflects this emphasis on the importance of being male. For example, when we want to compliment a male, all we need to do is stress the fact that he is male by saying he is a *he-man,* or he is *manly,* or he is *virile.* Both *virile* and *virtuous* come from the Latin *vir,* meaning *man.*

12   The command or encouragement that males receive in sentences like "Be a man!" implies that *to be a man* is to be honorable, strong, righteous, and whatever else the speaker thinks desirable. But in contrast to this, a girl is never told to be a *woman.* And when she is told to be a *lady,* she is simply being encouraged to "act feminine," which means sitting with her knees together, walking gracefully, and talking softly.

13   The armed forces, particularly the Marines, use the positive masculine connotation as part of their recruitment psychology. They promote the idea that to join the Marines (or the Army, Navy, or Air Force) guarantees that you will become a man. But this brings up a problem, because much of the work that is necessary to keep a large organization running is what is traditionally thought of as *women's work.* Now, how can the Marines ask someone who has signed up for a *man-sized job* to do *women's work*? Since they can't, they euphemize and give the jobs titles that either are more prestigious or, at least, don't make people think of females. Waitresses are called *orderlies,* secretaries are called *clerk-typists,* nurses are called *medics,* assistants are called *adjutants,* and cleaning up an area is called *policing* the area. The same kind of word glorification is used in civilian life to bolster a man's ego when he is doing such tasks as cooking and sewing. For example, a *chef* has higher prestige than a *cook* and a *tailor* has higher prestige than a *seamstress.*

14   Little girls learn early in life that the boy's role is one to be envied and emulated. Child psychologists have pointed out that experimenting with the role of the opposite sex is much more acceptable for little girls than it is for little boys. For example, girls are free to dress in boys' clothes, but certainly not the other way around. Most parents are amused if they have a daughter who is a *tomboy,* but they are genuinely distressed if they have a son who is a *sissy.* The names we give to young children reflect this same attitude. It is all right for girls to have boys' names, but pity the boy who has a girl's name! Because parents keep giving boys' names to girls, the number of acceptable boys' names keeps shrinking. Currently popular names for girls include *Jo, Kelly, Teri, Chris, Pat, Shawn, Toni,* and *Sam* (short for *Samantha*). *Evelyn, Carroll, Gayle, Hazel, Lynn, Beverley, Marion, Francis,* and *Shirley* once were acceptable names for males. But as they were given to females, they became less and less acceptable. Today, men who are stuck with them self-consciously go by their initials or by abbreviated forms such as *Haze, Shirl, Frank,* or *Ev.* And they seldom pass these names on to their sons.

15   Many common words have come into the language from people's names. These lexical items again show the importance of maleness compared to the triviality of the feminine activities being described. Words derived from the names of women include *Melba toast,* named for the Australian singer Dame Nellie Melba; *Sally Lunn cakes,* named after an eighteenth-century woman who first made them; *pompadour,* a hair style named after Madame Pompadour; and the word *maudlin,* as in *maudlin sentiment,* from Mary Magdalene, who was often portrayed by artists as displaying exaggerated sorrow.

16   There are trivial items named after men—*teddy bear* after Theodore Roosevelt and *sideburns* after General Burnside—but most words that come from men's names relate to significant inventions or developments. These include *pasteurization* after Louis Pasteur, *sousaphone* after John Philip Sousa, *mason jar* after John L. Mason, *boysenberry* after Rudolph Boysen, *pullman car* after George M. Pullman, *braille* after Louis Braille,

franklin stove after Benjamin Franklin, *diesel engine* after Rudolf Diesel, *ferris wheel* after George W. G. Ferris, and the verb *to lynch* after William Lynch, who was a vigilante captain in Virginia in 1780.

The latter is an example of a whole set of English words dealing with violence. These words have strongly negative connotations. From research using free association and semantic differentials, with university students as subjects, James Ney concluded that English reflects both an anti-male and an anti-female bias because these biases exist in the culture (*Etc.: A Review of General Semantics,* March 1976, pp. 67–76). The students consistently marked as masculine such words as *killer, murderer, robber, attacker, fighter, stabber, rapist, assassin, gang, hood, arsonist, criminal, hijacker, villain,* and *bully,* even though most of these words contain nothing to specify that they are masculine. An example of bias against males, Ney observed, is the absence in English of a pejorative term for women equivalent to *rapist.* Outcomes of his free association test indicated that if "English speakers want to call a man something bad, there seems to be a large vocabulary available to them but if they want to use a term which is good to describe a male, there is a small vocabulary available. The reverse is true for women."

Certainly we do not always think positively about males; witness such words as *jerk, creep, crumb, slob, fink,* and *jackass.* But much of what determines our positive and negative feelings relates to the roles people play. We have very negative feelings toward someone who is hurting us or threatening us or in some way making our lives miserable. To be able to do this, the person has to have power over us and this power usually belongs to males.

On the other hand, when someone helps us or makes our life more pleasant, we have positive feelings toward that person or that role. *Mother* is one of the positive female terms in English, and we see such extensions of it as *Mother Nature, Mother Earth, mother lode, mother superior,* etc. But even though a word like *mother* is positive it is still not a word of power. In the minds of English speakers being female and being powerless or passive are so closely related that we use the terms *feminine* and *lady* either to mean female or to describe a certain kind of quiet and unobtrusive behavior.

Words Labelling Women as Things

Because of our expectations of passivity, we like to compare females to items that people acquire for their pleasure. For example, in a . . . commercial for the television show "Happy Days," one of the characters announced that in the coming season they were going to have not only "cars, motorcycles, and girls," but also a band. Another example of this kind of thinking is the comparison of females to food since food is something we all enjoy, even though it is extremely passive. We describe females as such delectable morsels as a *dish, a cookie, a tart, cheesecake, sugar and spice, a cute tomato, honey, a sharp cookie,* and *sweetie pie.* We say a particular girl has a *peaches and cream complexion* or "she looks good enough to eat." And parents give their daughters such names as *Candy* and *Cherry.*

Other pleasurable items that we compare females to are toys. Young girls are called *little dolls* or *China dolls,* while older girls—if they are attractive—are simply called *dolls.* We might say about a woman, "She's pretty as a picture," or "She's a fashion plate." And we might compare a girl to a plant by saying she is a *clinging vine, a shrinking violet,* or a *wallflower.* And we might name our daughters after plants such as *Rose, Lily, Ivy, Daisy, Iris,* and *Petunia.* Compare these names to boys' names such as

Illustration

Martin which means warlike, *Ernest* which means resolute fighter, *Nicholas* which means victory, *Val* which means strong or valiant, and *Leo* which means lion. We would be very hesitant to give a boy the name of something as passive as a flower although we might say about a man that he is a *late-bloomer.* This is making a comparison between a man and the most active thing a plant can do, which is to bloom. The only other familiar plant metaphor used for a man is the insulting *pansy,* implying that he is like a woman.

Questions for Close Reading

1. What is the selection's thesis? Locate the sentence(s) in which Nilsen states her main idea. If she doesn't state the thesis explicitly, express it in your own words.

2. According to Nilsen, what do animal metaphors usually imply when used to describe women? What do male animal metaphors usually imply?

3. Why, according to Nilsen, do some professions have different names depending on whether the job is performed by a male or a female? What is suggested by the existence of two different terms for the same occupation?

4. When positive terms are used for women, what personality characteristics do such terms suggest? Why are words connoting violence most often applied to men?

5. Refer to your dictionary as needed to define the following words used in the selection: *unscrupulous* (paragraph 5), *enticing* (7), *connotation* (8), *virile* (11), *lexical* (15), *maudlin* (15), and *vigilante* (16).

Questions About the Writer's Craft

1. The pattern. Why does Nilsen use so many examples to illustrate each type of sexism in the English language? What point of view is she trying to anticipate and counteract?

2. What three main sexist motifs in English does Nilsen examine? How does she signal her movement from one motif to the next?

3. Other patterns. Why do you think Nilsen begins by discussing animal terms for humans? What effect does placing this section first have on the reader?

4. What is Nilsen's tone? What terms and expressions reveal her personal viewpoint on sexism in our language?

Writing Assignments Using Illustration as a Pattern of Development

1. Nilsen claims that our language glorifies maleness and denigrates femaleness. Are there other areas of our lives where the typical behavior and attitudes of one sex are valued more than the typical roles and characteristics of the other sex?

Consider such areas as dating, marriage, sports, clothing, and occupations. Focusing on a single area, write an essay showing that our culture glorifies one sex over the other. Nancy Gibbs's "When Is It Rape?" (page 379) and Caryl Rivers's "What Should Be Done About Rock Lyrics?" (page 443) should spark some ideas worth exploring.

2. The English language embodies many prejudices besides sexism. Many words and expressions, for example, reflect prejudice against skin color, old age, youth, left-handedness, shortness, fatness, and so on. Focusing on *one* such area, write an essay using specific examples of prejudicial language to show how the words we use reflect our stereotypes and biases.

Writing Assignments Using Other Patterns of Development

3. Would your life have been different if you had been born the opposite sex? Would you have been treated differently by your parents, teachers, and friends? Are there any specific experiences or events that would have turned out differently had you been a different sex? Write an essay persuading readers that your life would have been essentially the same *or* very different had you been born exactly as you were except for your sex.

4. Gender-based stereotyping exists in many areas of our culture besides language. Imagine you're a visitor to the United States and know nothing about the culture—perhaps you're a visitor from Mars. You observe people, watch TV for a week, and study several issues of a popular general interest magazine, like *People, Time,* or *Newsweek.* Then you write a report back to your home about the differences in the United States between males and females. Providing numerous examples to explain the dissimilarities, cover one or two of the following in your analysis: occupations, recreational activities, friendships, and so forth.

BOB GREENE

Journalist Bob Greene (1947–) has served as a contributing editor and columnist at *Esquire Magazine,* and his columns for the *Chicago Tribune* are syndicated in more than two hundred American newspapers. In his popular book *Good Morning Merry Sunshine* (1984), Greene expresses the delights of fatherhood. His observations on American life can be found in his books *American Beat* (1983); *Cheeseburgers* (1985); *He Was a Midwestern Boy on His Own* (1991); and *Hang Time* (1992), written with basketball superstar Michael Jordan. The following selection first appeared in the *Chicago Tribune* in 1984.

UNWRITTEN RULES CIRCUMSCRIBE OUR LIVES

The restaurant was almost full. A steady hum of conversation hung over the room; people spoke with each other and worked on their meals.

Suddenly, from a table near the center of the room, came a screaming voice:

"Damn it, Sylvia...."

4   The man was shouting at the top of his voice. His face was reddened, and he yelled at the woman sitting opposite him for about 15 seconds. In the crowded restaurant, it seemed like an hour. All other conversation in the room stopped, and everyone looked at the man. He must have realized this, because as abruptly as he had started, he stopped; he lowered his voice and finished whatever it was he had to say in a tone the rest of us could not hear.

5   It was startling precisely because it almost never happens; there are no laws against such an outburst, and with the pressures of our modern world you would almost expect to run into such a thing on a regular basis. But you don't; as a matter of fact, when I thought about it I realized that it was the first time in my life I had witnessed such a demonstration. In all the meals I have had in all the restaurants, I had never seen a person start screaming at the top of his lungs.

6   When you are eating among other people, you do not raise your voice; it is just an example of the unwritten rules we live by. When you consider it, you recognize that those rules probably govern our lives on a more absolute basis than the ones you could find if you looked in the lawbooks. The customs that govern us are what make a civilization; there would be chaos without them, and yet for some reason—even in the disintegrating society of the '80s—we obey them.

7   How many times have you been stopped at a red light late at night? You can see in all directions; there is no one else around—no headlights, no police cruiser idling behind you. You are tired and you are in a hurry. But you wait for the light to change. There is no one to catch you if you don't, but you do it anyway. Is it for safety's sake? No; you can see that there would be no accident if you drove on. Is it to avoid getting arrested? No; you are alone. But you sit and wait.

8   At major athletic events, it is not uncommon to find 80,000 or 90,000 or 100,000 people sitting in the stands. On the playing field are two dozen athletes; maybe fewer. There are nowhere near enough security guards on hand to keep the people from getting out of their seats and walking onto the field en masse. But it never happens. Regardless of the emotion of the contest, the spectators stay in their places, and the athletes are safe in their part of the arena. The invisible barrier always holds.

9   In restaurants and coffee shops, people pay their checks. A simple enough concept. Yet it would be remarkably easy to wander away from a meal without paying at the end. Especially in these difficult economic times, you might expect that to become a common form of cheating. It doesn't happen very often. For whatever the unwritten rules of human conduct are, people automatically make good for their meals. They would no sooner walk out on a check than start screaming.

10 Restrooms are marked "Men" and "Women." Often there are long lines at one or another of them, but males wait to enter their own washrooms, and women to enter theirs. In an era of sexual egalitarianism, you would expect impatient people to violate this rule on occasion; after all, there are private stalls inside, and it would be less inconvenient to use them than to wait. In Cleveland—why Cleveland I don't know—this custom has begun to change. At public events in Cleveland it is not unusual to find women getting out of line at the women's restroom and walking into the men's room. Elsewhere it just isn't done. People obey the signs.

11 Even criminals obey the signs. I once covered a murder which centered around that rule being broken. A man wanted to harm a woman—which woman apparently didn't matter. So he did the simplest thing possible. He went to a public park and walked into a restroom marked "Women"—the surest place to find what he wanted. He found it. He attacked with a knife the first woman to come in there. Her husband and young child waited outside, and the man killed her. Such a crime is not commonplace, even in a world grown accustomed to nastiness. Even the most evil

elements of our society generally obey the unspoken rule: If you are not a woman, you do not go past a door marked "Women."

I know a man who, when he pulls his car up to a parking meter, will put change in the meter even if there is time left on it. He regards it as the right thing to do; he says he is not doing it just to extend the time remaining—even if there is sufficient time on the meter to cover whatever task he has to perform at the location, he will pay his own way. He believes that you are supposed to purchase your own time; the fellow before you purchased only his. 12

I knew another man who stole tips at bars. It was easy enough; when the person sitting next to this man would depart for the evening and leave some silver or a couple dollars for the bartender, this guy would wait until he thought no one was looking and then sweep the money over in front of him. The thing that made it unusual is that I never knew anyone else who even tried this; the rules of civility stated that you left someone else's tip on the bar until it got to the bartender, and this man stood out because he refused to comply. 13

There are so many rules like these—rules we all obey—that we think about them only when that rare person violates them. In the restaurant, after the man had yelled "Damn it, Sylvia" and had then completed his short tirade, there was a tentative aura among the other diners for half an hour after it happened. They weren't sure what disturbed them about what they had witnessed; they knew, though, that it violated something very basic about the way we are supposed to behave. And it bothered them—which in itself is a hopeful sign that things, more often than not, are well. 14

Questions for Close Reading

1. What is the selection's thesis? Locate the sentence(s) in which Greene states his main idea. If he doesn't state the thesis explicitly, express it in your own words.

2. What does Greene mean by "the unwritten rules"? How do these rules differ from the written laws that govern us?

3. What makes people obey unwritten laws?

4. Why does Greene say that there would be chaos without unwritten rules?

5. Refer to your dictionary as needed to define the following words used in the selection: *circumscribe* (title), *absolute* (paragraph 6), *en masse* (8), *egalitarianism* (10), *civility* (13), *tirade* (14), and *aura* (14).

Questions About the Writer's Craft

1. The pattern. Locate examples in the essay that show people violating unwritten rules. Why might Greene have included such negative examples? How do these negative examples support the writer's thesis?

2. Other patterns. Where does Greene use comparison-contrast? How does his use of comparison-contrast clarify what he means by "the unwritten rules"?

3. Consider Greene's introduction and conclusion. Why might he have chosen to quote the shouting man's words in the introductory anecdote? What effect does he achieve by returning to this anecdote at the end of the essay?

4. What specific techniques does Greene use to give his essay an easy, informal style? Why do you think Greene chose to write in this style?

Writing Assignments Using Illustration as a Pattern of Development

1. Greene maintains that people generally comply with society's unwritten rules. Think of *one* area of life where you have seen people *not* comply with the rules. You might focus on people's behavior in a classroom, in a restaurant, at a party, and so on. Determine exactly which unwritten behavioral codes are being ignored. Then, using several convincing examples, write an essay illustrating that this violation of unwritten rules has significantly negative consequences. Martin Gottfried's "Rambos of the Road" (page 403) may spark some ideas for your paper.

2. College life has unspoken rules that govern behavior. Drawing on vivid examples, write an essay showing that several unwritten rules of campus life are meaningless and should be ignored. Your essay may be serious or playful in tone.

Writing Assignments Using Other Patterns of Development

3. Research the term *civil disobedience* by looking it up in a dictionary and in an encyclopedia. Then write an essay defining the term. Develop your definition by showing how civil disobedience could be an effective force for change in a specific situation that needs remedying. The situation could be on campus, in an organization, in a community, or on the national or international scene.

4. Interview people who are a generation older than you to find rules of behavior that have changed over time. Focus your discussion on behavioral codes in one or two settings (for example, in a family or at a social gathering). Then write an essay comparing and contrasting customs of the past with those of today. Your discussion should make clear which generation seems more "civilized."

ADDITIONAL WRITING TOPICS: ILLUSTRATION

General Assignments

Use illustration to develop one of the following topics into a well-organized essay.

1. Many of today's drivers have dangerous habits.

2. Drug and alcohol abuse is (or is not) a serious problem among many young people.
3. One rule of restaurant dining is, "Management often seems oblivious to problems that are perfectly obvious to customers."
4. Children today are not encouraged to use their imaginations.
5. The best things in life are definitely not free.
6. A part-time job is an important experience that every college student should have.
7. Television commercials stereotype the elderly (or another minority group).
8. Today, salespeople act as if they're doing you a favor by taking your money.
9. Most people behave decently in their daily interactions with each other.
10. You can tell a lot about people by observing what they eat.

Assignments with a Specific Purpose, Audience, and Point of View

1. A friend of yours has taken a job in a big city or moved to a small town. To prepare your friend for this new environment, write a letter giving examples of what life in a big city or small town is like. You might focus on those benefits or dangers with which your friend is unlikely to be familiar.

2. Shopping for a new car, you become annoyed at how many safety features are available only as expensive options. Write a letter of complaint to the auto manufacturer, citing at least three examples of such options. Avoid sounding hostile.

3. Lately, many people at your college or workplace have been experiencing stress. As a member of the campus (or company) Committee on Morale, you've been asked to prepare a pamphlet illustrating different strategies for reducing stress. Decide what strategies you'll discuss and explain them with helpful examples.

4. Assume that you're an elementary school principal planning to give a speech in which you'll try to convince parents that television distorts children's perceptions of reality. Write the speech, illustrating your point with vivid examples.

5. A pet food company is having an annual contest to choose a new animal to feature in its advertising. To win the contest, you must convince the company that your pet is personable, playful, unique. Write an essay giving examples of your pet's special qualities.

6. For your college humor magazine, write an article on what you consider to be the "three best consumer products of the past twenty-five years." Support your opinion with lively, engaging specifics that are consistent with the magazine's offbeat and slightly ironic tone.

15

DIVISION-CLASSIFICATION

WHAT IS DIVISION-CLASSIFICATION?

IMAGINE what life would be like if this were how an average day unfolded:

You plan to stop at the supermarket for only a few items, but your marketing takes over an hour because all the items in the store are jumbled together. Clerks put new shipments anywhere they please; milk is with vegetables on Monday but with laundry detergent on Thursday. Next, you go to the drugstore to pick up some photos you left to be developed. You don't have time, though, to wait while the cashier roots through the large carton into which all the pick-up envelopes have been thrown. You return to your car and decide to stop at the town hall to pay a parking ticket. But the town hall baffles you. The offices are unmarked, and there isn't even a directory to tell you on which floor the Violations Bureau can be found. Annoyed, you get back into your car and, minutes later, end up colliding with another car that was driving toward you in your lane. When you wake up in the hospital, you find there are three other patients in your room: a middle-aged man with a heart problem, a young boy ready to have his tonsils removed, and a woman about to go into labor.

Such a muddled world, lacking the most basic forms of organization, would make daily life chaotic. All of us instinctively look for ways to order our environment. Without systems, categories, or sorting mechanisms, we would be overwhelmed by life's complexity. An organization like a college or university, for example, is made manageable by being divided into various schools (Liberal Arts, Performing Arts, Engineering, and so on). The schools are then separated into departments (English, History, Political Science), and each department's offerings are grouped into distinct categories—English, for instance, into Literature and Composition—before being further divided into specific courses.

The kind of ordering system we've been discussing is called **division-classification,** a way of thinking that allows us to make sense of a complex world. Division and classification, though separate processes, often complement each other. **Division** involves taking a single unit or concept, breaking it down into parts, and then analyzing the connection among the parts and between the parts and the whole. For instance, if we wanted to organize the chaotic hospital described at the start of the chapter, we might think about how the single concept *hospital* could be broken down into its components. We might come up with the following breakdown: pediatric wing, cardiac wing, maternity wing, and so on.

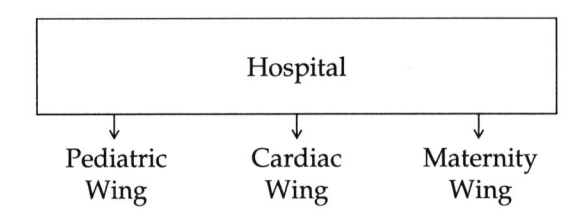

```
          ┌─────────────────────────┐
          │        Hospital         │
          └─────────────────────────┘
               ↓        ↓        ↓
           Pediatric  Cardiac  Maternity
             Wing      Wing      Wing
```

What we have just done involves division: We've taken a single entity (a hospital) and divided it into some of its component parts (wings), each with its own facilities and patients.

In contrast, **classification** brings two or more related items together and categorizes them according to type or kind. If the disorganized supermarket described earlier were to be restructured, the clerks would have to classify the separate items arriving at the store. Cartons of lettuce, tomatoes, cucumbers, butter, yogurt, milk, shampoo, conditioner, and setting lotion would be assigned to the appropriate categories:

```
   Lettuce            Butter           Shampoo
   Tomatoes           Yogurt           Conditioner
   Cucumbers          Milk             Setting lotion
      ↓                 ↓                  ↓
 ┌──────────┐     ┌──────────┐      ┌──────────────┐
 │ Produce  │     │  Dairy   │      │ Hair Products│
 └──────────┘     └──────────┘      └──────────────┘
```

HOW DIVISION-CLASSIFICATION FITS YOUR PURPOSE AND AUDIENCE

The reorganized hospital and supermarket show the way division and classification work in everyday life. But division and classification also come into

Division-Classification

play during the writing process. Because division involves breaking a subject into parts, it can be a helpful strategy during prewriting, especially if you're analyzing a broad, complex subject: the structure of a film; the motivation of a character in a novel; the problem your community has with vandalism; the controversy surrounding school prayer. An editorial examining a recent hostage crisis, for example, might divide the crisis into three areas: how the hostages were treated by (1) their captors, (2) the governments negotiating their release, and (3) the media. The purpose of the editorial might be to show readers that the governments' treatment of the hostages was particularly exploitative.

Classification can be useful for imposing order on the hodgepodge of ideas generated during prewriting. You examine that material to see which of your rough ideas are alike and which are dissimilar, so that you can cluster related items in the same category. Classification would, then, be a helpful strategy when analyzing topics like these: techniques for impressing teachers; comic styles of talk-show hosts; views on abortion; reasons for the current rise in volunteerism. You might, for instance, use classification in a paper showing that Americans are undermining their health through their obsessive pursuit of various diets. Perhaps you begin by brainstorming all the diets that have gained popularity in recent years (Weight Watchers, Slim-Fast, Jenny Craig, whatever). Then you categorize the diets according to type: high fiber, low protein, high carbohydrate, and so on. Once the diets are grouped, you can discuss the problems within each category, demonstrating to readers that none of the diets is safe or effective.

Division-classification can be crucial when responding to college assignments like the following:

> Based on your observations, what kinds of appeals do television advertisers use when selling automobiles? In your view, are any of these appeals morally irresponsible?

> Analyze the components that go into being an effective parent. Indicate those you consider most vital for raising confident, well-adjusted children.

> Describe the hierarchy of the typical high school clique, identifying the various parts of the hierarchy. Use your analysis to support or refute the view that adolescence is a period of rigid conformity.

> Many social commentators have observed that discourtesy is on the rise. Indicate whether you think this is a valid observation by characterizing the types of everyday encounters you have with people.

These assignments suggest division-classification through the use of such words as *kinds, components, parts,* and *types*. Generally, though, you won't receive such clear signals to use division-classification. Instead, the broad purpose of the essay—and the point you want to make—will lead you to the analytical thinking characteristic of division-classification.

Sometimes division-classification will be the dominant technique for structuring an essay; other times it will be used as a supplemental pattern in an essay organized primarily according to another pattern of development. Let's look at some examples. Say you want to write a paper *explaining a process* (surviving divorce; creating a hit recording; shepherding a bill through Congress; using the

Heimlich maneuver on people who are choking). You could *divide* the process into parts or stages, showing, for instance, that the Heimlich maneuver is an easily mastered skill that readers should acquire. Or imagine you plan to write a light-spirited essay analyzing the *effect* that increased awareness of sexual stereotypes has had on college students' social lives. In such a case, you might use *classification*. To show readers that shifting gender roles make young men and women comically self-conscious, you could categorize the places where students scout each other out: in class, at the library, at parties, in dorms. You could then show how students—not wishing to be macho or coyly feminine—approach each other with laughable tentativeness in these four environments.

Now imagine that you're writing an *argumentation-persuasion* essay urging that the federal government prohibit the use of growth-inducing antibiotics in livestock feed. The paper could begin by *dividing* the antibiotics cycle into stages: the effects of antibiotics on livestock; the short-term effects on humans who consume the animals; the possible long-term effects of consuming antibiotic-tainted meat. To increase readers' understanding of the problem, you might also discuss the antibiotics controversy in terms of an even larger issue: the dangerous ways food is treated before being consumed. In this case, you would consider the various procedures (use of additives, preservatives, artificial colors, and so on), *classifying* these treatments into several types—from least harmful (some additives or artificial colors, perhaps) to most harmful (you might slot the antibiotics here). Such an essay would be developed using both division *and* classification: first, the division of the antibiotics cycle and then the classification of the various food treatments. Frequently, this interdependence will be reversed, and classification will precede rather than follow division.

PREWRITING STRATEGIES

The following checklist shows how you can apply to division-classification some of the prewriting techniques discussed in Chapter 2.

✔ DIVISION-CLASSIFICATION: A PREWRITING CHECKLIST

Choose a Subject to Analyze
- What fairly complex subject (sibling rivalry, religious cults) can be made more understandable through division-classification?
- Will you divide a single entity or concept (domestic violence) into parts (toward spouse, parent, or child)? Will you classify a number of similar things (college courses) into categories (easy, of average difficulty, tough)? Or will you use both division and classification?

Determine Your Purpose, Audience, Tone, and Point of View
- What is the purpose of your analysis?

Division-Classification 257

> - Toward what audience will you direct your explanation?
> - What tone and point of view will make readers receptive to your explanation?
>
> *Use Prewriting to Generate Material on Parts or Types*
> - How can brainstorming, mapping, or any other prewriting technique help you divide your subject into parts? What differences or similarities among parts will you emphasize?
> - How can brainstorming, mapping, or any other prewriting technique help you categorize your subjects? What differences or similarities among categories will you emphasize?
> - How can the patterns of development help you generate material about your subjects' parts or categories? How can you describe the parts or categories? What can you narrate about them? What examples illustrate them? What process do they help explain? How can they be compared or contrasted? What causes them? What are their effects? How can they be defined? What argument do they support?

STRATEGIES FOR USING DIVISION-CLASSIFICATION IN AN ESSAY

After prewriting, you're ready to draft your essay. The following suggestions will be helpful whether you use division-classification as a dominant or supportive pattern of development.

1. Select a principle of division-classification consistent with your purpose. Most subjects can be divided or classified according to *several different principles.* For example, when writing about an ideal vacation, you could divide your subject according to any of these principles: location, cost, recreation available. Similarly, when analyzing students at your college, you could base your classification on a variety of principles: students' majors, their racial or ethnic background, whether they belong to a fraternity or sorority. In all cases, though, the principle of division-classification you select must meet one stringent requirement: It must help you meet your overall purpose and reinforce your central point.

Sometimes a principle of division-classification seems so attractive that you latch on to it without examining whether it's consistent with your purpose. Suppose you want to write a paper asserting that several episodes of a new television comedy are destined to become classics. Here's how you might go wrong. You begin by doing some brainstorming about the episodes. Then, as you start to organize the prewriting material, you hit upon a possible principle of classification: grouping the characters in the show according to the frequency with which they appear (main characters appearing in every show, supporting characters appearing in most shows, and guest characters appearing once or twice). You name the characters and explain which characters fit where. But is this principle of classification significant? Has it anything to do with why the shows will become classics? No, it hasn't. Such an essay would be little more than a meaningless exercise.

In contrast, a significant principle of classification might involve categorizing a number of shows according to the easily recognized human types portrayed: the Pompous Know-It-All, the Boss Who's Out of Control, the Lovable Grouch, the Surprisingly Savvy Innocent. You might illustrate the way certain episodes offer delightful twists on these stock figures, making such shows models of comic plotting and humor.

When you write an essay that uses division-classification as its primary method of development, a *single principle* of division-classification provides the foundation for each major section of the paper. Imagine you're writing an essay showing that the success of contemporary music groups has less to do with musical talent than with the group's ability to market themselves to a distinct segment of the listening audience. To develop your point, you might categorize several performers according to the age groups they appeal to (preteens, adolescents, people in their late twenties) and then analyze the marketing strategies the musicians use to gain their fans' support. The essay's logic would be undermined if you switched, in the middle of your analysis, to another principle of classification—say, the influence of earlier groups on today's music scene.

Don't, however, take this caution to mean that essays can never use more than one principle of division-classification as they unfold. They can—as long as the *shift from one principle to another* occurs in *different parts* of the paper. Imagine you want to write about widespread disillusionment with student government leaders at your college. You could develop this point by breaking down the dissatisfaction into the following: disappointment with the students' qualifications for office; disenchantment with their campaign tactics; frustration with their performance once elected. That section of the essay completed, you might move to a second principle of division—how students can get involved in campus government. Perhaps you break the proposed involvement into the following possibilities: serving on nominating committees; helping to run candidates' campaigns; attending open sessions of the student government.

2. Apply the principle of division-classification logically. In an essay using division-classification, you need to demonstrate to readers that your analysis is the result of careful thought. First of all, your division-classification should be as *complete* as possible. Your analysis should include—within reason—all the parts into which you can divide your subject, or all the types into which you can categorize your subjects. Let's say you're writing an essay showing that where college students live is an important factor in determining how satisfied they are with college life. Keeping your purpose in mind, you classify students according to where they live: with parents, in dorms, in fraternity and sorority houses. But what about all the students who live in rented apartments, houses, or rooms off campus? If these places of residence are ignored, your classification won't be complete; you will lose credibility with your readers because they'll probably realize that you have overlooked several important considerations.

Your division-classification should also be *consistent:* the parts into which you break your subject or the groups into which you place your subjects should be as mutually exclusive as possible. The parts or categories should not be mixed, nor should they overlap. Assume you're writing an essay describing the animals at the zoo in a nearby city. You decide to describe the zoo's mammals, reptiles, birds, and endangered species. But such a classification is inconsistent. You begin by categorizing the animals according to scientific class (mammals, birds, reptiles), then switch to another principle when you classify some animals according to whether they are endangered. Because you drift over to a different principle of classification, your categories are no longer mutually exclusive: endangered species could overlap with any of the other categories. In which section of the paper, for instance, would you describe an exotic parrot that is obviously a bird but is also nearly extinct? And how would you categorize the zoo's rare mountain gorilla? This impressive creature is a mammal, but it is also an endangered species. Such overlapping categories undercut the logic that gives an essay its integrity.

3. Prepare an effective thesis. If your essay uses division-classification as its dominant method of development, it might be helpful to prepare a thesis that does more than signal the paper's subject and suggest your attitude toward that subject. You might also want the thesis to state the principle of division-classification at the heart of the essay. Furthermore, you might want the thesis to reveal which part or category you regard as most important.

Consider the two thesis statements that follow:

Thesis 1

As the observant beachcomber moves from the tidal area to the upper beach to the sandy dunes, rich variations in marine life become apparent.

Thesis 2

Although most people focus on the dangers associated with the disposal of toxic waste in the land and ocean, the incineration of toxic matter may pose an even more serious threat to human life.

The first thesis statement makes clear that the writer will organize the paper by classifying forms of marine life according to location. Since the purpose of the essay is to inform as objectively as possible, the thesis doesn't suggest the writer's opinion about which category is most significant.

The second thesis signals that the essay will evolve by dividing the issue of toxic waste according to methods of disposal. Moreover, because the paper takes a stance on a controversial subject, the thesis is worded to reveal which aspect of the topic the writer considers most important. Such a clear statement of the writer's position is an effective strategy in an essay of this kind.

You may have noted that each thesis statement also signals the paper's plan of development. The first essay, for example, will use specific facts, examples, and details to describe the kinds of marine life found in the tidal area, upper beach, and dunes. However, thesis statements in papers developed primarily through division-classification don't have to be so structured. If a paper is well written, your principle of division-classification, your opinion about which part or category is most important, and the essay's plan of development will become apparent as the essay unfolds.

4. Organize the paper logically. Whether your paper is developed wholly or in part by division-classification, it should have a logical structure. As much as possible, you should try to discuss *comparable points* in each section of the paper. In the essay on seashore life, for example, you might describe life in the tidal area by discussing the mollusks, crustaceans, birds, and amphibians that live or feed there. You would then follow through, as much as possible, with this arrangement in the paper's other sections (upper beach and dunes). Forgetting to describe the birdlife thriving in the dunes, especially when you had discussed birdlife in the tidal and upper-beach areas, would compromise the paper's structure. Of course, perfect parallelism is not always possible—there are no mollusks in the dunes, for instance. You should also use *signal devices* to connect various parts of the paper: "*Another* characteristic of marine life battered by the tides"; "A *final* important trait of both tidal and upper-beach crustaceans"; "*Unlike* the creatures of the tidal area and the upper beach." Such signals clarify the connections among the essay's ideas.

5. State any conclusions or recommendations in the paper's final section. The analytic thinking that occurs during division-classification often leads to surprising insights. Such insights may be introduced early on, or they may be reserved for the end, where they are stated as conclusions or recommendations. A paper might categorize different kinds of coaches—from inspiring to incompetent—and make the point that athletes learn a great deal about human relations simply by having to get along with their coaches, regardless of the coaches' skills. Such a paper might conclude that participation in a team sport teaches more about human nature than several courses in psychology. Or the essay might end with a proposal: Rookies and seasoned team members should be paired, so that novice players can get advice on dealing with coaching eccentricities.

REVISION STRATEGIES

Once you have a draft of the essay, you're ready to revise. The following checklist will help you and those giving you feedback apply to division-classification some of the revision techniques discussed in Chapters 7 and 8.

✔ DIVISION-CLASSIFICATION: A REVISION CHECKLIST

Revise Overall Meaning and Structure
- What is the principle of division-classification at the heart of the essay? How does this principle contribute to the essay's overall purpose and thesis?

Division-Classification

> - Does the thesis state the essay's principle of division-classification? Should it? Does the thesis signal which part or category is most important? Should it? Does the thesis reveal the essay's plan of development? Should it?
> - Is the essay organized primarily through division, classification, or a blend of both?
> - If the essay is organized mainly through division, is the subject sufficiently broad and complex to be broken down into parts? What are the parts?
> - If the essay is organized mainly through classification, what are the categories? How does this categorizing reveal similarities and/or differences that would otherwise not be apparent?
>
> *Revise Paragraph Development*
> - Are comparable points discussed in each of the paper's sections? What are these points?
> - In which paragraphs does the division-classification seem illogical, incomplete, or inconsistent? In which paragraphs are parts or categories not clearly explained?
> - Are the subject's different parts or categories discussed in separate paragraphs? Should they be?
> - What conclusions or recommendations are stated or implied in the closing paragraph(s)?
>
> *Revise Sentences and Words*
> - What signal devices ("Another characteristic"; "A third type"; "The most important trait") help integrate the paper? Are there enough signals? Too many?
> - Where should sentences and words be made more concrete and specific in order to clarify the parts and categories being discussed?

STUDENT ESSAY: FROM PREWRITING THROUGH REVISION

The student essay that follows was written by Gail Oremland in response to this assignment:

> In "Propaganda Techniques in Today's Advertising," Ann McClintock describes the flaws in many of the persuasive strategies used by advertisers. Choose another group of people whose job is also to communicate—for example, parents, bosses, teachers. Then, in an essay of your own, divide the group into types according to the flaws they reveal when communicating.

Gail wanted to prepare a light-spirited paper about college professors' foibles. Right from the start, she decided to focus on three kinds of professors: the "Knowledgeable One," the "Leader of Intellectual Discussion," and the "Buddy." She used the *patterns of development* to generate prewriting material about each kind, typing whatever ideas came to mind as she focused on one pattern at a time. Reprinted here is Gail's prewriting for the Knowledgeable One. Note that not every pattern sparked ideas. When Gail later reviewed her prewriting, she added some details and deleted others. The handwritten marks on the prewriting indicate Gail's later efforts to refine her rough material.

After annotating her prewriting for all the categories, Gail prepared her first draft, without shaping her prewriting further or making an outline. As she wrote, though, she frequently referred to her warm-up material to retrieve specifics about each professorial type.

Prewriting Using the Patterns of Development

Knowledgeable One

Even in a blizzard or hurricane

Narration: Enters, walks to podium, puts notes on stand, begins lecture exactly on schedule. Talks on and on, stating facts. ~~Even when she had a cold, she kept on lecturing, although we could hardly hear her and her voice kept cracking.~~ Always ends lecture exactly on time. Packs her notes. Hurries away. *Shoots out the back door. Back to the privacy of her office, away from students.*

Description: Self-important air, yellowed notes, all weather, drones, students' glazed eyes, yawns

Doesn't stop, so students feel they can't interrupt

Cause-Effect: Thinks she's an expert and that students are ignorant, so students are intimidated. States one dry fact after another, so students get bored. Addresses students as "Mr." or "Miss," so she establishes distance.

Definition: A fact person

Illustration: History prof who knows death toll of every battle; biology prof who knows all the molecules; accounting prof who knows every clause of tax form

Comparison-Contrast: Interest in specialized academic area vs. no interest in students

Division-Classification

Now read Gail's paper, "The Truth About College Teachers," noting the similarities and differences between her prewriting and final essay. As you may imagine, the patterns of development that yielded the most details during prewriting became especially prominent in the final essay. Note, too, that Gail's prewriting consisted of unconnected details within each pattern, whereas the essay flows easily. To achieve such coherence, Gail used commentary and transitional phrases to connect the prewriting details. As you read the essay, also consider how well it applies the principles of division-classification discussed in this chapter. (The commentary that follows the paper will help you look at the essay more closely and will give you some sense of how Gail went about revising her first draft.)

The Truth About College Teachers
by Gail Oremland

1   A recent TV news story told about a group of college professors from a nearby university who were hired by a local school system to help upgrade the teaching in the community's public schools. The professors were to visit classrooms, analyze teachers' skills, and then conduct workshops to help the teachers become more effective at their jobs. But after the first round of workshops, the superintendent of schools decided to cancel the whole project. He fired the learned professors and sent them back to their ivory tower. Why did the project fall apart? There was a simple reason. The college professors, who were supposedly going to show the public school teachers how to be more effective, were themselves poor teachers. Many college students could have predicted such a disastrous outcome. They know, firsthand, that college teachers are strange. They know that professors often exhibit bizarre behaviors, relating to students in ways that make it difficult for students to stay awake, or--if awake--to learn. *— Introduction* *— Thesis*

2   One type of professor assumes, legitimately enough, that her function is to pass on to students the vast store of knowledge she has acquired. But because the "Knowledgeable One" regards herself as an expert and her students as the ignorant masses, she adopts an elitist approach that sabotages learning. The Knowledgeable One enters a lecture hall with a self-important air, walks to the podium, places her yellowed-with-age notes on the stand, and begins her lecture at the exact second the class is officially scheduled to begin. There can be a blizzard or *— Topic sentence* *The first of three paragraphs on the first category of teacher*

The first paragraph in a three-part chronological sequence: What happens before *class*

hurricane raging outside the lecture hall; students can be running through freezing sleet and howling winds to get to class on time. Will the Knowledgeable One wait for them to arrive before beginning her lecture? Probably not. The Knowledgeable One's time is precious. She's there, set to begin, and that's what matters.

Topic sentence ⟶ Once the monologue begins, the Knowledgeable One drones on and on. The Knowledgeable One is a fact person. She may be the history prof who knows the death toll of every Civil War battle, the biology prof who can diagram all the common biological molecules, the accounting prof who enumerates every clause of the federal tax form. Oblivious to students' glazed eyes and stifled yawns, the Knowledgeable One delivers her monologue, dispensing one dry fact after another. The only advantage to being on the receiving end of this boring monologue is that students do not have to worry about being called on to question a point or provide an opinion; the Knowledgeable One is not willing to relinquish one minute of her time by giving students a voice. Assume for one improbable moment that a student actually manages to stay awake during the monologue and is brave enough to ask a question. In such a case, the Knowledgeable One will address the questioning student as "Mr." or "Miss." This formality does not, as some students mistakenly suppose, indicate respect for the student as a fledgling member of the academic community. Not at all. This impersonality represents the Knowledgeable One's desire to keep as wide a distance as possible between her and her students.

The second paragraph on the first category of teacher

The second paragraph in the chronological sequence: What happens during *class*

Topic sentence ⟶ The Knowledgeable One's monologue always comes to a close at the precise second the class is scheduled to end. No sooner has she delivered her last forgettable word than the Knowledgeable One packs up her notes and shoots out the door, heading back to the privacy of her office, where she can pursue her specialized academic interests--free of any possible interruption from students. The Knowledgeable One's hasty departure from the lecture hall makes it clear she has no desire to talk with students. In her eyes, she has met her obligations; she has taken time away from her research to transmit to students what she knows. Any closer contact might mean she would risk contagion from students, that great unwashed mass. Such a danger is to be avoided at all costs.

The third paragraph on the first category of teacher

The final paragraph in the chronological sequence: What happens after *class*

Unlike the Knowledgeable One, the "Leader of Intellectual Discussion" seems to respect students. Emphasizing class discussion, the Leader encourages students to confront ideas ("What is Twain's view of

Division-Classification

morality?" "Was our intervention in Vietnam justified?" "Should big business be given tax breaks?" and discover their own truths. Then, about three weeks into the semester, it becomes clear that the Leader wants students to discover *his* version of the truth. Behind the Leader's democratic guise lurks a dictator. When a student voices an opinion that the Leader accepts, the student is rewarded by hearty nods of approval and "Good point, good point." But if a student is rash enough to advance a conflicting viewpoint, the Leader responds with killing politeness: "Well, yes, that's an interesting perspective. But don't you think that . . .?" Grade-conscious students soon learn not to chime in with their viewpoint. They know that when the Leader, with seeming honesty, says, "I'd be interested in hearing what you think. Let's open this up for discussion," they had better figure out what the Leader wants to hear before advancing their own theories. "Me-tooism" rather than independent thinking, they discover, guarantees good grades in the Leader's class.

— Topic sentence

Paragraph on the second category of teacher

6   Then there is the professor who comes across as the students' "Buddy." This kind of professor does not see himself as an imparter of knowledge or a leader of discussion but as a pal, just one in a community of equals. The Buddy may start his course this way. "All of us know that this college stuff--grades, degrees, exams, required reading--is a game. So let's not play it, okay?" Dressed in jeans, sweatshirt, and scuffed sneakers, the Buddy projects a relaxed, casual attitude. He arranges the class seats in a circle (he would never take a position in front of the room) and insists that students call him by his first name. He uses no syllabus and gives few tests, believing that such constraints keep students from directing their own learning. A free spirit, the Buddy often teaches courses like "The Psychology of Interpersonal Relations" or "The Social Dynamics of the Family." If students choose to use class time to discuss the course material, that's fine. If they want to discuss something else, that's fine, too. It's the self-expression, the honest dialog, that counts. In fact, the Buddy seems especially fond of digressions from academic subjects. By talking about his political views, his marital problems, his tendency to drink one too many beers, the Buddy lets students see that he is a regular guy--just like them. At first, students look forward to classes with the Buddy. They enjoy the informality, the chitchat, the lack of pressure. But after a while, they wonder why they are paying for a course

— Topic sentence

Paragraph on the third category of teacher

where they learn nothing. They might as well stay home and watch the soaps.

Conclusion

Obviously, some college professors are excellent. They are learned, hardworking, and imaginative; they enjoy their work and like being with students. On the whole, though, college professors are a strange lot. Despite their advanced degrees and their own exposure to many different kinds of teachers, they do not seem to understand how to relate to students. Rather than being hired as consultants to help others upgrade their teaching skills, college professors should themselves hire consultants to tell them what they are doing wrong and how they can improve. Who should these consultants be? That's easy: the people who know them best--their students.

Echoes opening anecdote

7

Commentary

Introduction and Thesis

After years of being graded by teachers, Gail took special pleasure in writing an essay that gave her a chance to evaluate her teachers—in this case, her college professors. Even the essay's title, "The Truth About College Teachers," implies that Gail is going to have fun knocking profs down from their ivory towers. To introduce her subject, she uses a timely news story. This brief anecdote leads directly to the essay's *thesis:* "Professors often exhibit bizarre behaviors, relating to students in ways that make it difficult for students to stay awake, or—if awake—to learn." Note that Gail's thesis isn't highly structured; it doesn't, for example, name the specific categories to be discussed. Still, her thesis suggests that the essay is going to *categorize* a range of teaching behaviors, using as a *principle of classification* the strange ways that college profs relate to students.

Purpose

As with all good papers developed through division-classification, Gail's essay doesn't use classification as an end in itself. Gail uses classification because it helps her achieve a broader *purpose*. She wants to *convince* readers—without moralizing or abandoning her humorous tone—that such teaching styles inhibit learning. In other words, there's a serious underside to her essay. This additional layer of meaning is characteristic of satiric writing.

Categories and Topic Sentences

The essay's body, consisting of five paragraphs, presents the three categories that make up Gail's analysis. According to Gail, college teachers can be categorized as the Knowledgeable One (paragraphs 2–4), the Leader of Intellectual Discussion (5), or the Buddy (6). Obviously, there are other ways professors might be classified. But given Gail's purpose, audience, tone, and point of view,

Division-Classification

her categories are appropriate; they are reasonably *complete, consistent,* and *mutually exclusive.* Note, too, that Gail uses *topic sentences* near the beginning of each category to help readers see which professorial type she's discussing.

Overall Organization and Paragraph Structure

Gail is able to shift smoothly and easily from one category to the next. How does she achieve such graceful transitions? Take a moment to reread the sentences that introduce her second and third categories (paragraphs 5 and 6). Look at the way each sentence's beginning (in italics here) links back to the preceding category or categories: "*Unlike the Knowledgeable One,* the 'Leader of Intellectual Discussion' seems to respect students"; and the "Buddy . . . *does not see himself as an imparter of knowledge or a leader of discussion* but as a pal. . . ."

Gail is equally careful about providing an easy-to-follow structure within each section. She uses a *chronological sequence* to organize her three-paragraph discussion of the Knowledgeable One. The first paragraph deals with the beginning of the Knowledgeable One's lecture; the second, with the lecture itself; the third, with the end of the lecture. And the paragraphs' *topic sentences* clearly indicate this passage of time. Similarly, *transitions* are used in the paragraphs on the Leader of Intellectual Discussion and the Buddy to ensure a logical progression of points: "*Then,* about three weeks into the semester, it becomes clear that the Leader wants students to discover *his* version of the truth" (5), and "*At first,* students look forward to classes with the Buddy. . . . But *after a while,* they wonder why they are paying for a course where they learn nothing" (6).

Tone

The essay's unity can also be traced to Gail's skill in sustaining her satiric tone. Throughout the essay, Gail selects details that fit her gently mocking attitude. She depicts the Knowledgeable One lecturing from "yellowed-with-age notes . . . , oblivious to students' glazed eyes and stifled yawns," unwilling to wait for students who "run . . . through freezing sleet and howling winds to get to class on time." Then she presents another tongue-in-cheek description, this one focusing on the way the Leader of Intellectual Discussion conducts class: "Good point, good point. . . . Well, yes, that's an interesting perspective. But don't you think that. . . ?" Finally, with similar killing accuracy, Gail portrays the Buddy, democratically garbed in "jeans, sweatshirt, and scuffed sneakers."

Other Patterns of Development

Gail's satiric depiction of her three professorial types employs a number of techniques associated with *narrative* and *descriptive writing:* vigorous images, highly connotative language, and dialog. *Definition, illustration, causal analysis,* and *comparison-contrast* also come into play. Gail defines the characteristics of each type of professor; she provides numerous examples to support her categories; she explains the effects of the different teaching styles on students; and, in her description of the Leader of Intellectual Discussion, she contrasts the appearance of democracy with the dictatorial reality.

Unequal Development of Categories

Although Gail's essay is unified, organized, and well developed, you may have felt that the first category outweighs the other two. There is, of course, no need to balance the categories exactly. But Gail's extended treatment of the first category sets up an expectation that the others will be treated as fully. One way to remedy this problem would be to delete some material from the discussion of the Knowledgeable One. Gail might, for instance, omit the first five sentences in the third paragraph (about the professor's habit of addressing students as Mr. or Miss). Such a change could be made without taking the bite out of her portrayal. Even better, Gail could simply switch the order of her sections, putting the portrait of the Knowledgeable One at the essay's end. Here, the extended discussion wouldn't seem out of proportion. Instead, the sections would appear in *emphatic order,* with the most detailed category saved for last.

Revising the First Draft

It's apparent that an essay as engaging as Gail's must have undergone a good deal of revising. Along the way, Gail made many changes in her draft, but it's particularly interesting to see how she changed her original introduction (reprinted here). The annotation represents her general impressions of the paragraph's problems.

Original Version of the Introduction

Too serious. Doesn't fit rest of essay.

Despite their high IQs, advanced degrees, and published papers, some college professors just don't know how to teach. Found almost in any department, in tenured and untenured positions, they prompt student apathy. They fail to convey ideas effectively and to challenge or inspire students. Students thus finish their courses having learned very little. Contrary to popular opinion, these professors' ineptitude is not simply a matter of delivering boring lectures or not caring about students. Many of them care a great deal. Their failure actually stems from their unrealistic perceptions of what a teacher should be. Specifically, they adopt teaching styles or roles that alienate students and undermine learning. Three of the most common ones are "The Knowledgeable One," "The Leader of Intellectual Discussion," and "The Buddy."

When Gail showed the first draft of the essay to her composition instructor, he laughed—and occasionally squirmed—as he read what she had prepared. He was enthusiastic about the paper but felt there was a problem with the introduction's tone; it was too serious when compared to the playful, lightly satiric mood of the rest of the essay. When Gail reread the paragraph, she agreed, but she was uncertain about the best way to remedy the problem. After revising other sections of the essay, she decided to let the paper sit for a while before going back to rewrite the introduction.

In the meantime, Gail switched on the TV. The timing couldn't have been better; she tuned into a news story about several supposedly learned professors who had been fired from a consulting job because they had turned out to know so little about teaching. This was exactly the kind of item Gail needed to start her essay. Now she was able to prepare a completely new introduction, making it consistent in spirit with the rest of the paper.

With this stronger introduction and the rest of the essay well in hand, Gail was ready to write a conclusion. Now, as she worked on the concluding paragraph, she deliberately shaped it to recall the story about the fired consultants. By echoing the opening anecdote in her conclusion, Gail was able to end the paper with another poke at professors—a perfect way to close her clever and insightful essay.

ACTIVITIES: DIVISION-CLASSIFICATION

Prewriting Activities

1. Imagine you're writing two essays: One is a humorous paper showing how to impress college instructors; the other is a serious essay explaining why volunteerism is on the rise. What about the topics might you divide and/or classify?

2. Use group brainstorming to identify at least three possible principles of division for *one* of the following topics. For each principle, determine what your thesis might be if you were writing an essay.

  a. Prejudice
  b. Rock music
  c. A shopping mall
  d. A good horror movie

3. Through group brainstorming, identify three different principles of classification that might provide the structure for an essay about the possible effects of a controversial decision to expand your college's enrollment. Focusing on one of the principles, decide what your thesis might be. How would you sequence the categories?

Revising Activities

4. Following is a scratch outline for an essay developed through division-classification. On what principle of division-classification is the essay based? What problem do you see in the way the principle is applied? How could the problem be remedied?

Thesis: The same experience often teaches opposite things to different people.

- What working as a fast-food cook teaches: Some learn responsibility; others learn to take a "quick and dirty" approach.
- What a negative experience teaches optimists: Some learn from their mistakes; others continue to maintain a positive outlook.
- What a difficult course teaches: Some learn to study hard; others learn to avoid demanding courses.
- What the breakup of a close relationship teaches: Some learn how to negotiate differences; others learn to avoid intimacy.

5. Following is a paragraph from the first draft of an essay urging that day-care centers adopt play programs tailored to children's developmental needs. What principle of division-classification focuses the paragraph? Is the principle applied consistently and logically? Are parts/categories developed sufficiently? Revise the paragraph, eliminating any problems you discover and adding specific details where needed.

Within a few years, preschool children move from self-absorbed to interactive play. Babies and toddlers engage in solitary play. Although they sometimes prefer being near other children, they focus primarily on their own actions. This is very different from the highly interactive play of the elementary school years. Sometime in children's second year, solitary play is replaced by parallel play, during which children engage in similar activities near one another. However, they interact only occasionally. By age three, most children show at least some cooperative play, a form that involves interaction and cooperative role-taking. Such role-taking can be found in the "pretend" games that children play to explore adult relationships (games of "Mommy and Daddy") and anatomy (games of "Doctor"). Additional signs of youngsters' growing awareness of peers can be seen at about age four. At this age, many children begin showing a special devotion to one other child and may want to play only with that child. During this time, children also begin to take special delight in physical activities such as running and jumping, often going off by themselves to expend their abundant physical energy.

PROFESSIONAL SELECTIONS: DIVISION-CLASSIFICATION

ANN McCLINTOCK

Currently Director of Occupational Therapy at Ancora State Hospital in New Jersey, Ann McClintock (1946–) has also worked as a free-lance writer and editor. She speaks frequently to community groups about the effects of advertising on American life. The following essay, revised for this collection, is part of a work-in-progress about the use of propaganda techniques in the marketing of products and candidates.

PROPAGANDA TECHNIQUES IN TODAY'S ADVERTISING

1   Americans, adults and children alike, are being seduced. They are being brainwashed. And few of us protest. Why? Because the seducers and the brainwashers are the advertisers we willingly invite into our homes. We are victims, content—even eager—to be victimized. We read advertisers' propaganda messages in newspapers and magazines; we watch their alluring images on television. We absorb their messages and images into our subconscious. We all do it—even those of us who claim to see through advertisers' tricks and therefore feel immune to advertising's charm. Advertisers lean heavily on propaganda to sell their products, whether the "products" are a brand of toothpaste, a candidate for office, or a particular political viewpoint.

2   *Propaganda* is a systematic effort to influence people's opinions, to win them over to a certain view or side. Propaganda is not necessarily concerned with what is true or false, good or bad. Propagandists simply want people to believe the messages being sent. Often, propagandists will use outright lies or more subtle deceptions to sway people's opinions. In a propaganda war, any tactic is considered fair.

3   When we hear the word "propaganda," we usually think of a foreign menace: anti-American radio programs broadcast by a totalitarian regime or brainwashing tactics practiced on hostages. Although propaganda may seem relevant only in the political arena, the concept can be applied fruitfully to the way products and ideas are sold in advertising. Indeed, the vast majority of us are targets in advertisers' propaganda war. Every day, we are bombarded with slogans, print ads, commercials, packaging claims, billboards, trademarks, logos, and designer brands—all forms of propaganda. One study reports that each of us, during an average day, is exposed to over *five hundred* advertising claims of various types. This saturation may even increase in the future since current trends include ads on movie screens, shopping carts, video cassettes, even public television.

4   What kind of propaganda techniques do advertisers use? There are seven basic types:

1. *Name Calling* Name calling is a propaganda tactic in which negatively charged names are hurled against the opposing side or competitor. By using such names, propagandists try to arouse feelings of mistrust, fear, and hate in their audiences. For example, a political advertisement may label an opposing candidate a "loser," "fence-sitter," or "warmonger." Depending on the advertiser's target market, labels such as "a friend of big business" or "a dues-paying member of the party in power" can be the epithets that damage an opponent. Ads for products may also use name calling. An American manufacturer may refer, for instance, to a "foreign car" in its commercial—not an "imported" one. The label of foreignness will have unpleasant connotations in many people's minds. A childhood rhyme claims that "names can never hurt me," but name calling is an effective way to damage the opposition, whether it is another car maker or a congressional candidate.

2. *Glittering Generalities* Using glittering generalities is the opposite of name calling. In this case, advertisers surround their products with attractive—and slippery—words and phrases. They use vague terms that are difficult to define and that may have different meanings to different people: *freedom, democratic, all-American, progressive, Christian,* and *justice.* Many such words have strong, affirmative overtones. This kind of language stirs positive feelings in people, feelings that may spill over to the product or idea being pitched. As with name calling, the emotional response may overwhelm logic. Target audiences accept the product without thinking very much about what the glittering generalities mean—or whether they even apply to the product. After all, how can anyone oppose "truth, justice, and the American way"?

The ads for politicians and political causes often use glittering generalities because such "buzz words" can influence votes. Election slogans include high-sounding but basically empty phrases like the following:

"He cares about people." (That's nice, but is he a better candidate than his opponent?)

"Vote for progress." (Progress by *whose* standards?)

"They'll make this country great again." (What does "great" mean? Does "great" mean the same thing to others as it does to me?)

"Vote for the future." (What kind of future?)

"If you love America, vote for Phyllis Smith." (If I don't vote for Smith, does that mean I don't love America?)

Ads for consumer goods are also sprinkled with glittering generalities. Product names, for instance, are supposed to evoke good feelings: *Luvs* diapers, *New Freedom* feminine hygiene products, *Joy* liquid detergent, *Loving Care* hair color, *Almost Home* cookies, *Yankee Doodle* pastries. Product slogans lean heavily on vague but comforting phrases: Kinney is "The Great American Shoe Store," General Electric "brings good things to life," and Dow Chemical "lets you do great things." Chevrolet, we are told, is the "heartbeat of America," and Chrysler boasts cars that are "built by Americans for Americans."

3. *Transfer* In transfer, advertisers try to improve the image of a product by associating it with a symbol most people respect, like the American flag or Uncle Sam. The advertisers hope that the prestige attached to the symbol will carry over to the product. Many companies use transfer devices to identify their products: Lincoln Insurance shows a profile of the President; Continental Insurance portrays a Revolutionary War minuteman; Amtrak's logo is red, white, and blue; Liberty Mutual's

Division-Classification

corporate symbol is the Statue of Liberty; Allstate's name is cradled by a pair of protective, fatherly hands.

10   Corporations also use the transfer technique when they sponsor prestigious shows on radio and television. These shows function as symbols of dignity and class. Kraft Corporation, for instance, sponsored a "Leonard Bernstein Conducts Beethoven" concert, while Gulf Oil is the sponsor of *National Geographic* specials and Mobil supports public television's *Masterpiece Theater*. In this way, corporations can reach an educated, influential audience and, perhaps, improve their public image by associating themselves with quality programming.

11   Political ads, of course, practically wrap themselves in the flag. Ads for a political candidate often show either the Washington Monument, a Fourth of July parade, the Stars and Stripes, a bald eagle soaring over the mountains, or a white-steepled church on the village green. The national anthem or "America the Beautiful" may play softly in the background. Such appeals to Americans' love of country can surround the candidate with an aura of patriotism and integrity.

12   *4. Testimonial* The testimonial is one of advertisers' most-loved and most-used propaganda techniques. Similar to the transfer device, the testimonial capitalizes on the admiration people have for a celebrity to make the product shine more brightly—even though the celebrity is not an expert on the product being sold.

13   Print and television ads offer a nonstop parade of testimonials: here's Cher for Holiday Spas; here's basketball star Michael Jordan eating Wheaties; Michael Jackson sings about Pepsi; American Express features a slew of well-known people who assure us that they never go anywhere without their American Express card. Testimonials can sell movies too; newspaper ads for films often feature favorable comments by well-known reviewers. And, in recent years, testimonials have played an important role in pitching books; the backs of paperbacks frequently list complimentary blurbs by celebrities.

14   Political candidates, as well as their ad agencies, know the value of testimonials. Barbara Streisand lent her star appeal to the presidential campaign of Bill Clinton, while Arnold Schwarzenegger endorsed George Bush. Even controversial social issues are debated by celebrities. The nuclear freeze, for instance, starred Paul Newman for the pro side and Charlton Heston for the con.

15   As illogical as testimonials sometimes are (Pepsi's Michael Jackson, for instance, is a health-food adherent who does not drink soft drinks), they are effective propaganda. We like the *person* so much that we like the *product* too.

16   *5. Plain Folks* The plain folks approach says, in effect, "Buy me or vote for me. I'm just like you." Regular folks will surely like Bob Evans' Down on the Farm Country Sausage or good old-fashioned Countrytime Lemonade. Some ads emphasize the idea that "we're all in the same boat." We see people making long-distance calls for just the reasons we do—to put the baby on the phone to Grandma or to tell Mom we love her. And how do these folksy, warmhearted (usually saccharine) scenes affect us? They're supposed to make us feel that AT&T—the multinational corporate giant—has the same values we do. Similarly, we are introduced to the little people at Ford, the ordinary folks who work on the assembly line, not to bigwigs in their executive offices. What's the purpose of such an approach? To encourage us to buy a car built by these honest, hardworking "everyday Joes" who care about quality as much as we do.

17   Political advertisements make almost as much use of the "plain folks" appeal as they do of transfer devices. Candidates wear hard hats, farmers' caps, and assemblyline coveralls. They jog around the block and carry their own luggage through the

airport. The idea is to convince voters that the candidates are average people, not the elite—not wealthy lawyers or executives but the common citizen.

6. *Card Stacking* When people say that "the cards were stacked against me," they mean that they were never given a fair chance. Applied to propaganda, card stacking means that one side may suppress or distort evidence, tell half-truths, oversimplify the facts, or set up a "straw man"—a false target—to divert attention from the issue at hand. Card stacking is a difficult form of propaganda both to detect and to combat. When a candidate claims that an opponent has "changed his mind five times on this important issue," we tend to accept the claim without investigating whether the candidate had good reasons for changing his mind. Many people are simply swayed by the distorted claim that the candidate is "waffling" on the issue.

Advertisers often stack the cards in favor of the products they are pushing. They may, for instance, use what are called "weasel words." These are small words that usually slip right past us, but that make the difference between reality and illusion. The weasel words are underlined in the following claims:

"Helps control dandruff symptoms." (The audience usually interprets this as *stops* dandruff.)

"Most dentists surveyed recommend sugarless gum for their patients who chew gum." (We hear the "most dentists" and "for their patients," but we don't think about how many were surveyed or whether or not the dentists first recommended that the patients not chew gum at all.)

"Sticker price $1000 lower than most comparable cars." (How many is "most"? What car does the advertiser consider "comparable"?)

Advertisers also use a card stacking trick when they make an unfinished claim. For example, they will say that their product has "twice as much pain reliever." We are left with a favorable impression. We don't usually ask, "Twice as much pain reliever as what?" Or advertisers may make extremely vague claims that sound alluring but have no substance: Toyota's "Oh, what a feeling!"; Vantage cigarettes' "the taste of success"; "The spirit of Marlboro"; Coke's "the real thing." Another way to stack the cards in favor of a certain product is to use scientific-sounding claims that are not supported by sound research. When Ford claimed that its LTD model was "400% quieter," many people assumed that the LTD must be quieter than all other cars. When taken to court, however, Ford admitted that the phrase referred to the difference between the noise level inside and outside the LTD. Other scientific-sounding claims use mysterious ingredients that are never explained as selling points: "Retsyn," "special whitening agents," "the ingredient doctors recommend."

7. *Bandwagon* In the bandwagon technique, advertisers pressure, "Everyone's doing it. Why don't you?" This kind of propaganda often succeeds because many people have a deep desire not to be different. Political ads tell us to vote for the "winning candidate." The advertisers know we tend to feel comfortable doing what others do; we want to be on the winning team. Or ads show a series of people proclaiming, "I'm voting for the Senator. I don't know why anyone wouldn't." Again, the audience feels under pressure to conform.

In the marketplace, the bandwagon approach lures buyers. Ads tell us that "nobody doesn't like Sara Lee" (the message is that you must be weird if you don't). They tell us that "most people prefer Brand X two to one over other leading brands" (to be like the majority, we should buy Brand X). If we don't drink Pepsi, we're left out of

Division-Classification

"the Pepsi generation." To take part in "America's favorite health kick," the National Dairy Council urges us to drink milk. And Honda motorcycle ads, praising the virtues of being a follower, tell us, "Follow the leader. He's on a Honda."

23   Why do these propaganda techniques work? Why do so many of us buy the products, viewpoints, and candidates urged on us by propaganda messages? They work because they appeal to our emotions, not to our minds. Often, in fact, they capitalize on our prejudices and biases. For example, if we are convinced that environmentalists are radicals who want to destroy America's record of industrial growth and progress, then we will applaud the candidate who refers to them as "treehuggers." Clear thinking requires hard work: analyzing a claim, researching the facts, examining both sides of an issue, using logic to see the flaws in an argument. Many of us would rather let the propagandists do our thinking for us.

24   Because propaganda is so effective, it is important to detect it and understand how it is used. We may conclude, after close examination, that some propaganda sends a truthful, worthwhile message. Some advertising, for instance, urges us not to drive drunk, to become volunteers, to contribute to charity. Even so, we must be aware that propaganda is being used. Otherwise, we will have consented to handing over to others our independence of thought and action.

Questions for Close Reading

1. What is the selection's thesis? Locate the sentence(s) in which McClintock states her main idea. If she doesn't state the thesis explicitly, express it in your own words.

2. What is *propaganda*? What mistaken associations do people often have with this term?

3. What are "weasel words"? How do they trick listeners?

4. Why does McClintock believe we should be better informed about propaganda techniques?

5. Refer to your dictionary as needed to define the following words used in the selection: *seduced* (paragraph 1), *warmonger* (5), and *elite* (17).

Questions About the Writer's Craft

1. The pattern and other patterns. Before explaining the categories into which propaganda techniques can be grouped, McClintock provides a definition of propaganda. Is the definition purely informative, or does it have a larger objective? If you think the latter, what is the definition's broader purpose?

2. In her introduction, McClintock uses loaded words like *seduced* and *brainwashed*. What effect do these words have on the reader?

3. Locate places where McClintock uses questions. Which are rhetorical and which are genuine queries?

4. What kind of conclusion does McClintock provide for the essay?

Writing Assignments Using Division-Classification as a Pattern of Development

1. McClintock cautions us to be sensitive to propaganda in advertising. Young children, however, aren't capable of this kind of awareness. With pen or pencil in hand, watch some commercials aimed at children, such as those for toys, cereals, and fast food. Then analyze the use of propaganda techniques in these commercials. Using division-classification, write an essay describing the main propaganda techniques you observed. Support your analysis with examples drawn from the commercials. Remember to provide a thesis that indicates your opinion of the advertising techniques.

2. Like advertising techniques, television shows can be classified. Avoiding the obvious system of classifying according to game shows, detective shows, and situation comedies, come up with your own original division-classification principle. Possibilities include how family life is depicted, the way work is presented, how male-female relationships are portrayed. Using one such principle, write an essay in which you categorize popular TV shows into three types. Refer to specific shows to support your classification system. Your attitude toward the shows being discussed should be clear.

Writing Assignments Using Other Patterns of Development

3. McClintock says that card stacking "distort[s] evidence, tell[s] half-truths, oversimplif[ies] the facts" (18). Focusing on an editorial, a political campaign, a print ad, or a television commercial, analyze the extent to which card stacking is used as a persuasive strategy.

4. To increase further your sensitivity to the moral dimensions of propaganda, write a proposal outlining an ad campaign for a real or imaginary product or elected official. The introduction to your proposal should identify who or what is to be promoted, and the thesis or plan of development should indicate the specific propaganda techniques you suggest. In the paper's supporting paragraphs, explain how these techniques would be used to promote your product or candidate.

RUSSELL BAKER

The winner of a Pulitzer Prize in journalism, Russell Baker (1925–) began his career as a writer for the *Baltimore Sun* and, in the 1950s, moved to the *New York Times,* where he still writes a regular column, "The Observer." Baker's works include two autobiographies, *Growing Up* (1982) and *The Good Times* (1989), as well as several collections of essays, among them *There's a Country in My Cellar* (1990). The selection that follows first appeared in the *New York Times* in 1968.

Division-Classification

THE PLOT AGAINST PEOPLE

1. Inanimate objects are classified scientifically into three major categories—those that break down, those that get lost, and those that don't work.

2. The goal of all inanimate objects is to resist man and ultimately to defeat him, and the three major classifications are based on the method each object uses to achieve its purpose. As a general rule, any object capable of breaking down at the moment when it is most needed will do so. The automobile is typical of the category.

3. With the cunning peculiar to its breed, the automobile never breaks down while entering a filling station which has a large staff of idle mechanics. It waits until it reaches a downtown intersection in the middle of the rush hour, or until it is fully loaded with family and luggage on the Ohio Turnpike. Thus it creates maximum inconvenience, frustration, and irritability, thereby reducing its owner's lifespan.

4. Washing machines, garbage disposals, lawn mowers, furnaces, TV sets, tape recorders, slide projectors—all are in league with the automobile to take their turn at breaking down whenever life threatens to flow smoothly for their enemies.

5. Many inanimate objects, of course, find it extremely difficult to break down. Pliers, for example, and gloves and keys are almost totally incapable of breaking down. Therefore, they have had to evolve a different technique for resisting man.

6. They get lost. Science has still not solved the mystery of how they do it, and no man has ever caught one of them in the act. The most plausible theory is that they have developed a secret method of locomotion which they are able to conceal from human eyes.

7. It is not uncommon for a pair of pliers to climb all the way from the cellar to the attic in its single-minded determination to raise its owner's blood pressure. Keys have been known to burrow three feet under mattresses. Women's purses, despite their great weight, frequently travel through six or seven rooms to find hiding space under a couch.

8. Scientists have been struck by the fact that things that break down virtually never get lost, while things that get lost hardly ever break down. A furnace, for example, will invariably break down at the depth of the first winter cold wave, but it will never get lost. A woman's purse hardly ever breaks down; it almost invariably chooses to get lost.

9. Some persons believe this constitutes evidence that inanimate objects are not entirely hostile to man. After all, they point out, a furnace could infuriate a man even more thoroughly by getting lost than by breaking down, just as a glove could upset him far more by breaking down than by getting lost.

10. Not everyone agrees, however, that this indicates a conciliatory attitude. Many say it merely proves that furnaces, gloves and pliers are incredibly stupid.

11. The third class of objects—those that don't work—is the most curious of all. These include such objects as barometers, car clocks, cigarette lighters, flashlights and toy-train locomotives. It is inaccurate, of course, to say that they *never* work. They work once, usually for the first few hours after being brought home, and then quit. Thereafter, they never work again.

12. In fact, it is widely assumed that they are built for the purpose of not working. Some people have reached advanced ages without ever seeing some of these objects—barometers, for example—in working order.

13. Science is utterly baffled by the entire category. There are many theories about it. The most interesting holds that the things that don't work have attained the highest state possible for an inanimate object, the state to which things that break down and things that get lost can still only aspire.

They have truly defeated man by conditioning him never to expect anything of them. When his cigarette lighter won't light or his flashlight fails to illuminate, it does not raise his blood pressure. Objects that don't work have given man the only peace he receives from inanimate society.

Questions for Close Reading

1. What is the selection's thesis? Locate the sentence(s) in which Baker states his main idea. If he doesn't state the thesis explicitly, express it in your own words.

2. According to Baker, what is the goal of inanimate objects? Why do these objects fall into three types?

3. What is especially infuriating about the way in which many objects break down?

4. Baker says that people disagree about the reasons that objects behave as they do. What diverse conclusions have people reached?

5. Refer to your dictionary as needed to define the following words used in the selection: *plausible* (paragraph 6), *locomotion* (6), and *conciliatory* (10).

Questions About the Writer's Craft

1. The pattern. What is Baker's principle of classification? Through what categories does he develop his essay? Why do you suppose Baker sequenced the categories as he did?

2. Where in the essay does Baker move from his first to his second category? How does he signal this shift?

3. What effect does Baker achieve by beginning his essay with a one-sentence paragraph?

4. To a large degree, the humor in this essay is derived from Baker's ironic depiction of inanimate objects as having a will of their own. What words and phrases does Baker use to make objects seem alive?

Writing Assignments Using Division-Classification as a Pattern of Development

1. Baker's classification of inanimate objects is, of course, tongue-in-cheek. Choose another topic and write your own humorous classification essay. For example, you could write about types of cafeteria food (bland, mysterious, and lethal), types of roommates, or types of study methods.

2. In a light-spirited division-classification essay, show three kinds of responses that you, or people in general, often have to the types of "uncooperative" objects that Baker describes.

Writing Assignments Using Other Patterns of Development

3. Like Baker, we all have stories of some inanimate object that failed us at a crucial moment. Write a narrative about your experience with an appliance, machine, or other possession that let you down. Whether you adopt a humorous or a serious tone, be sure to explain exactly what went wrong and what you tried to do about it.

4. Do all cars break down? Do all cameras jam just before you take a picture? Maybe not. Write an essay showing the superiority of a particular car, camera, VCR, TV, compact-disc player, computer, or other product. Illustrate the item's quality by contrasting it with inferior examples of the same product.

MEG GREENFIELD

A graduate of Smith College, Meg Greenfield (1930–) began her journalism career as a researcher for *Reporter* magazine and joined the *Washington Post* in 1968. She won a Pulitzer Prize in 1978 for editorial writing and, since 1979, has served as the editor of the *Post's* editorial page. The following essay first appeared in 1986 as one of her columns for *Newsweek*.

WHY NOTHING IS "WRONG" ANYMORE

1   There has been an awful lot of talk about sin, crime and plain old antisocial behavior this summer—drugs and pornography at home, terror and brutality abroad. Maybe it's just the heat; or maybe these categories of conduct (sin, crime, etc.) are really on the rise. What strikes me is our curiously deficient, not to say defective, way of talking about them. We don't seem to have a word anymore for "wrong" in the moral sense, as in, for example, "theft is wrong."

2   Let me quickly qualify. There is surely no shortage of people condemning other people on such grounds, especially their political opponents or characters they just don't care for. Name-calling is still very much in vogue. But where the concept of wrong is really important—as a guide to one's own behavior or that of one's own side in some dispute—it is missing; and this is as true of those on the religious right who are going around pronouncing great masses of us sinners as it is of their principal antagonists, those on the secular left who can forgive or "understand" just about anything so long as it has not been perpetrated by a right-winger.

3   There is a fairly awesome literature that attempts to explain how we have changed as a people with the advent of psychiatry, the weakening of religious institutions and so forth, but you don't need to address these matters to take note of a simple fact. As a guide and a standard to live by, you don't hear so much about "right and wrong" these days. The very notion is considered politically, not to say personally, embarrassing, since it has such a repressive, Neanderthal ring to it. So we have developed a broad range of alternatives to "right and wrong." I'll name a few.

4   **Right and stupid:** This is the one you use when your candidate gets caught stealing, or, for that matter, when anyone on your side does something reprehensible.

"It was really so dumb of him"—head must shake here—"I just can't understand it." Bad is dumb, breathtakingly dumb and therefore unfathomable; so, conveniently enough, the effort to fathom it might just as well be called off. This one had a big play during Watergate and has had mini-revivals ever since whenever congressmen and senators investigating administration crimes turn out to be guilty of something similar themselves.

Right and not necessarily unconstitutional: I don't know at quite what point along the way we came to this one, the avoidance of admitting that something is wrong by pointing out that it is not specifically or even inferentially prohibited by the Constitution or, for that matter, mentioned by name in the criminal code or the Ten Commandments. The various parties that prevail in civil-liberty and civil-rights disputes before the Supreme Court have gotten quite good at making this spurious connection: it is legally permissible, therefore it is morally acceptable, possibly even good. But both as individuals and as a society we do things every day that we know to be wrong even though they may not fall within the class of legally punishable acts or tickets to eternal damnation.

Right and sick: Crime or lesser wrongdoing defined as physical and/or psychological disorder—this one has been around for ages now and as long ago as 1957 was made the butt of a great joke in the "Gee Officer Krupke!" song in "West Side Story." Still, I think no one could have foreseen the degree to which an originally reasonable and humane assumption (that some of what once was regarded as wrongdoing is committed by people acting out of ailment rather than moral choice) would be seized upon and exploited to exonerate every kind of misfeasance. This route is a particular favorite of caught-out officeholders who, when there is at last no other recourse, hold a press conference, announce that they are "sick" in some wise and throw themselves and their generally stunned families on our mercy. At which point it becomes gross to pick on them; instead we are exhorted to admire them for their "courage."

Right and only to be expected: You could call this the tit-for-tat school; it is related to the argument that holds moral wrongdoing to be evidence of sickness, but it is much more pervasive and insidious these days. In fact it is probably the most popular dodge, being used to justify, or at least avoid owning up to, every kind of lapse: the other guy, or sometimes just plain circumstance, "asked for it." For instance, I think most of us could agree that setting fire to live people, no matter what their political offense, is—dare I say it?—wrong. Yet if it is done by those for whom we have sympathy in a conflict, there is a tendency to extenuate or disbelieve it, receiving it less as evidence of wrongdoing on our side than as evidence of the severity of the provocation or as enemy-supplied disinformation. Thus the hesitation of many in the antiapartheid movement to confront the brutality of so-called "necklacing," and thus the immediate leap of Sen. Jesse Helms to the defense of the Chilean government after the horrifying incineration of protesters there.

Right and complex: This one hardly takes a moment to describe; you know it well. "Complex" is the new "controversial," a word used as "controversial" was for so long to flag trouble of some unspecified, dismaying sort that the speaker doesn't want to have to step up to. "Well, you know, it's very complex. . . ." I still can't get this one out of my own vocabulary.

In addition to these various sophistries, we also have created a rash of "ethics committees" in our government, of course, whose function seems to be to dither around writing rules that allow people who have clearly done wrong—and should have known it and probably did—to get away because the rules don't cover their offense (see Right and not necessarily unconstitutional). But we don't need any more committees or artful dodges for that matter. As I listen to the moral arguments swirling about us this summer I become ever more persuaded that our real problem is this: the "still, small voice" of conscience has become far too small—and utterly still.

Questions for Close Reading

1. What is the selection's thesis? Locate the sentence(s) in which Greenfield states her main idea. If she doesn't state the thesis explicitly, express it in your own words.

2. What is the "simple fact" that Greenfield refers to in paragraph 3?

3. How many excuses does Greenfield cite to illustrate her belief that wrongdoing is widely condoned these days? What are the excuses?

4. In particular, whose ethics does Greenfield question? Locate places in the essay where she indicates who her actual target is.

5. Refer to your dictionary as needed to define the following words used in the selection: *antagonists* (paragraph 2), *perpetrated* (2), *repressive* (3), *Neanderthal* (3), *reprehensible* (4), *unfathomable* (4), *inferentially* (5), *spurious* (5), *misfeasance* (6), *insidious* (7), *extenuate* (7), *antiapartheid* (7), and *sophistries* (9).

Questions About the Writer's Craft

1. The pattern. Does Greenfield use division, classification, or both to organize her essay? Does she apply her principle of division-classification consistently?

2. Greenfield repeats the phrase "right and" before each of her alternatives to "wrong." Why do you suppose she uses this strategy? How is this repetition related to her thesis?

3. Locate places in the essay where Greenfield employs the first person. What effect does her use of "I" have on the essay's tone and persuasiveness?

4. How does Greenfield tie her opening and closing paragraphs together? What issue in her introductory paragraph does she resolve in her conclusion?

Writing Assignments Using Division-Classification as a Pattern of Development

1. Greenfield names various excuses that politicians and others use in uncomfortable situations. Choose a disquieting situation in which people sometimes find themselves, and write an essay categorizing the excuses they typically devise. For example, you could write about the types of excuses that students use when they hand in late papers or that drivers use to justify speeding. Like Greenfield, reveal your attitude toward these people.

2. Using a personal, authoritative tone like Greenfield's, write an essay classifying the kinds of mistakes that people make in a specific situation. You might, for example, write about people's bumbling attempts to improve their social lives or their errors of judgment in selecting a college. Your essay might be light or serious.

Writing Assignments Using Other Patterns of Development

3. What does the concept *wrong* mean to you? Write an essay defining this word and clarifying your standards for determining if an action is "wrong."

4. In an essay, draw on either several vivid illustrations or a single compelling example to show that people are capable of highly moral, even altruistic behavior. Bob Greene's "Unwritten Rules Circumscribe Our Lives" (page 248) and Fern Kupfer's "Institution Is Not a Dirty Word" (page 439) should spark some thoughts about the more generous side of human nature.

ADDITIONAL WRITING TOPICS: DIVISION-CLASSIFICATION

General Assignments

Choose one of the following subjects and write an essay developed wholly or in part through division-classification.

Division

1. A shopping mall
2. A video or stereo system
3. A particular kind of team
4. A school library
5. A playground, gym, or other recreational area
6. A significant event
7. A college campus
8. A television show or movie

Classification

1. People in a waiting room
2. Parents
3. Holidays
4. Students in a class
5. Summer movies
6. College courses
7. Television watchers
8. Commercials

Assignments with a Specific Purpose, Audience, and Point of View

1. You are a dorm counselor. During orientation week, you'll be talking to students on your floor about the different kinds of problems they may have with roommates. Write your talk, describing each kind of problem and explaining how to cope.

2. As a driving instructor, you decide to prepare a lecture on the types of drivers that your students are likely to encounter on the road. In your lecture, categorize drivers according to a specific principle and show the behaviors of each type.

3. You have been asked to write a pamphlet for "new recruits"—new workers on your job, new students in your college class, new members of your sports team, or the like. In the pamphlet, identify at least three general qualities needed for the recruits' success.

4. A seasoned camp counselor, you've been asked to prepare, for new counselors, an informational sheet on children's emotional needs. Categorizing those needs into types, explain what counselors can do to nurture youngsters emotionally.

5. As your college newspaper's TV critic, you plan to write a review of the fall shows, most of which—in your opinion—lack originality. To show how stereotypical the programs are, select one type (for example, situation comedies or crime dramas). Then use a specific division-classification principle to illustrate that the same stale formulas are trotted out from show to show.

6. Asked to write an editorial for the campus paper, you decide to do a half-serious piece on taking "mental health" days off from classes. Structure your essay around three kinds of occasions when "playing hooky" is essential for maintaining sanity.

16
PROCESS ANALYSIS

WHAT IS PROCESS ANALYSIS?

PERHAPS you've noticed the dogged determination of small children when they learn how to do something new. Whether trying to tie their shoelaces or tell time, little children struggle along, creating knotted tangles, confusing the hour with the minute hand. But they don't give up. Mastering such basic skills makes them feel less dependent on the adults of the world—all of whom seem to know how to do everything. Actually, none of us is born knowing how to do very much. We spend a good deal of our lives learning—everything from speaking our first word to balancing our first bank statement. Indeed, the milestones in our lives are often linked to the processes we have mastered: how to cross the street alone; how to drive a car; how to make a speech without being paralyzed by fear.

Process analysis, a technique that explains the steps or sequence involved in doing something, satisfies our need to learn as well as our curiosity about how the world works. All the self-help books flooding the market today (*Managing Stress, How to Make a Million in Real Estate, Ten Days to a Perfect Body*) are examples of process analysis. The instructions on the federal tax form and the recipes in a cookbook are also process analyses. Several television classics, now seen in reruns, capitalize on our desire to learn how things happen: *The Wild Kingdom* shows how animals survive in faraway lands, and *Mission: Impossible* has great fun detailing elaborate plans for preventing the triumph of evil. Process analysis can be more than merely interesting or entertaining, though; it can be of critical importance. Consider a waiter hurriedly skimming the "Choking Aid" instructions posted on a restaurant wall or an air-traffic controller following emergency procedures in an effort to prevent a midair collision. In these last examples, the consequences could be fatal if the process analyses are slipshod, inaccurate, or confusing.

Process Analysis 285

Undoubtedly, all of us have experienced less dramatic effects of poorly written process analyses. Perhaps you've tried to assemble a bicycle and spent hours sorting through a stack of parts, only to end up with one or two extra pieces never mentioned in the instructions. Or maybe you were baffled when putting up a set of wall shelves because the instructions used unfamiliar terms like *mitered cleat, wing nut,* and *dowel pin.* No wonder many people stay clear of anything that actually admits "assembly required."

HOW PROCESS ANALYSIS FITS YOUR PURPOSE AND AUDIENCE

You will use process analysis in two types of writing situations: (1) when you want to give step-by-step instructions to readers showing how they can do something, or (2) when you want readers to understand how something happens even though they won't actually follow the steps outlined. The first kind of process analysis is **directional**; the second is **informational.**

When you look at the cooking instructions on a package of frozen vegetables or follow guidelines for completing a job application, you're reading directional process analysis. A serious essay explaining how to select a college and a humorous essay telling readers how to get on the good side of a professor are also examples of directional process analysis. Using a variety of tones, informational process analyses can range over equally diverse subjects; they can describe mechanical, scientific, historical, sociological, artistic, or psychological processes: for example, how the core of a nuclear power plant melts down; how television became so important in political campaigns; how abstract painters use color; how to survive a blind date.

Process analysis, both directional and informational, is often appropriate in *problem-solving situations.* In such cases, you say, "Here's the problem and here's what should be done to solve the problem." Indeed, college assignments frequently take the form of problem-solving process analyses. Consider these examples:

> Because many colleges and universities have changed the eligibility requirements for financial aid, fewer students can depend on loans or scholarships. How can students cope with the increasing costs of obtaining a higher education?

> Over the years, there have been many reports citing the abuse of small children in day-care centers. What can parents do to guard against the mistreatment of their children?

> Community officials have been accused of mismanaging recent unrest over the public housing ordinance. Describe the steps the officials took, indicating why you think their strategy was unwise. Then explain how you think the situation should have been handled.

Note that the last assignment asks students to explain what's wrong with the current approach before they present their own step-by-step solution. Problem-solving process analyses are often organized in this way. You may also have noticed that none of the assignments explicitly requires an essay response using process analysis. However, the wording of the assignments—"*Describe* the *steps*," "*What* can parents *do*," "*How* can students *cope*"—indicates that process analysis would be an appropriate strategy for developing the responses.

Assignments don't always signal the use of process analysis so clearly. But during the prewriting stage, as you generate material to support your thesis, you'll often realize that you can best achieve your purpose by developing the essay—or part of it—using process analysis.

Sometimes process analysis will be the primary strategy for organizing an essay; other times it will be used to help make a point in an essay organized around another pattern of development. Let's take a look at process analysis as a supporting strategy.

Assume that you're writing a *causal analysis* examining the impact of television commercials on people's buying behavior. To help readers see that commercials create a need where none existed before, you might describe the various stages in an advertising campaign to pitch a new, completely frivolous product. In an essay *defining* a good boss, you could convey the point that effective managers must be skilled at settling disputes by explaining the steps your boss took to resolve a heated disagreement between two employees. If you write an *argumentation-persuasion* paper urging the funding of programs to ease the plight of the homeless, you would have to dramatize for readers the tragedy of these people's lives. To achieve your purpose, you could devote part of the paper to an explanation of how the typical street person goes about finding a place to sleep and getting food to eat.

PREWRITING STRATEGIES

The following checklist shows how you can apply to process analysis some of the prewriting strategies discussed in Chapter 2.

✔ PROCESS ANALYSIS: A PREWRITING CHECKLIST

Choose a Process to Analyze

- What processes do you know well and feel you can explain clearly (for example, how to jog without injury, how lobbyists influence legislators)?
- What processes have you wondered about (how to meditate; how the greenhouse effect works)?
- What process needs changing if a current problem is to be solved?

Determine Your Purpose, Audience, Tone, and Point of View
- What is the central purpose of your process analysis? Do you want to inform readers so that they will acquire a new skill (how to buy a used car)? Do you want readers to gain a better understanding of a complex process (how young children develop a conscience)? Do you want to persuade readers to accept your point of view about a process, perhaps even urge them to adopt a particular course of action ("If you disagree with the proposed plan for reorganizing academic advisement, you should take the following steps to register your protest with college officials").
- What audience are you writing for? What will they need to know to understand the process? What will they not need to know?
- What point of view will you adopt when addressing the audience?
- What tone do you want to project? Do you want to come across as serious, humorous, sarcastic, ironic, objective, impassioned?

Use Prewriting to Generate the Stages of the Process
- How could brainstorming or mapping help you identify primary and secondary steps in the process?
- How could brainstorming or mapping help you identify the ingredients or materials that the reader will need?

STRATEGIES FOR USING PROCESS ANALYSIS IN AN ESSAY

After prewriting, you're ready to draft your essay. The following suggestions will be helpful whether you use process analysis as a dominant or supportive pattern of development.

1. Formulate a thesis that clarifies your attitude toward the process. Like the thesis in any other paper, the thesis in a process analysis should do more than announce your subject ("Here's how the college's work-study program operates"). It should also state or imply your attitude toward the process: "Enrolling in the college's work-study program has become unnecessarily complicated. The procedure could be simplified if the college adopted the helpful guidelines prepared by the Student Senate."

2. Keep your audience in mind when deciding what to cover. Only after you gauge how much your readers already know (or don't know) about the process can you determine how much explanation to provide. Suppose you've been asked to write an article informing students of the best way to use the university computer center. The article will be published in a newsletter for computer science majors. You would seriously misjudge your audience—and probably put them to sleep—if you explained in detail how to transfer material from disk to disk or how to delete information from a file. However, an article on the same topic prepared for a general audience—your composition class, for instance—would probably require such detailed instructions. The audience's level of knowledge also determines whether you should define technical terms. The computer science majors wouldn't need terms such as "modem," "interface," and "byte" defined, whereas students in your composition class would likely require easy-to-understand explanations. Indeed, with any general audience, you should use as little specialized language as possible.

To determine how much explanation is needed, put yourself in your readers' shoes. Don't assume readers will know something just because you do. Ask questions like these about your audience: "Will my readers need some background about the process before I describe it in depth?" and "If my essay is directional, should I specify near the beginning the ingredients, materials, and equipment needed to perform the process?" (For more help in analyzing your audience, see the checklist on page 21.)

3. Focusing on your purpose, thesis, and audience, explain the process—one step at a time. After using prewriting techniques to identify primary and secondary steps and needed equipment, you're ready to organize your raw material into an easy-to-follow sequence. At times your purpose will be to explain a process with a *fairly fixed chronological sequence:* how to make pizza, how to pot a plant, how to change a tire. In such cases, you should include all necessary steps, in the correct chronological order. However, if a strict chronological ordering of steps means that a particularly important part of the sequence gets buried in the middle, the sequence probably should be juggled so that the crucial step receives the attention it deserves.

Other times your goal will be to describe a process having *no commonly accepted sequence.* For example, in an essay explaining how to discipline a child or how to pull yourself out of a blue mood, you will have to come up with your own definition of the key steps and then arrange those steps in some logical order. You may also use process analysis to *reject* or *reformulate* a traditional sequence. In this case, you would propose a more logical series of steps: "Our system for electing congressional representatives is inefficient and undemocratic; it should be reformed in the following ways."

Whether the essay describes a generally agreed-on process or one that is not commonly accepted, you must provide all the details needed to explain the process. Your readers should be able to understand, even visualize, the process. There should be no fuzzy patches or confusing cuts from one step to another. Don't, however, go into obsessive detail about minor stages or steps. If you dwell for several hundred words on how to butter the pan, your readers will never stay with you long enough to learn how to make the omelet.

It's not unusual, especially in less defined sequences, for some steps in a process to occur simultaneously and overlap. When this happens, you should present the steps in the most logical order, being sure to tell your readers that several steps are not perfectly distinct and may merge. For example, in an essay explaining how a species becomes extinct, you would have to indicate that overpopulation of hardy strains and destruction of endangered breeds are often simultaneous events. You would also need to clarify that the depletion of food sources both precedes and follows the demise of a species.

4. Sort out the directional and informational aspects of the process analysis. As you may have discovered when prewriting, directional and informational process analyses are not always distinct. In fact, they may be complementary: You may need to provide background information about a process before outlining its steps. For example, in a paper describing a step-by-step approach for losing weight, you might first need to explain how the body burns calories. Or, in a paper on gardening, you could provide some theory about the way organic fertilizers work before detailing a plan for growing vegetables. Although both approaches may be appropriate in a paper, one generally predominates.

The kind of process analysis chosen has implications for the way you will relate to your reader. When the process analysis is *directional*, the reader is addressed in the *second person:* "You should first rinse the residue from the radiator by . . . ," or "Wrap the injured person in a blanket and then. . . ." (In the second example, the pronoun *you* is implied.)

If the process analysis has an *informational* purpose, you won't address the reader directly but will choose from a number of other options. For example, you might use the *first person.* In a humorous essay explaining how not to prepare for finals, you could cite your own disastrous study habits: "Filled with good intentions, I sit on my bed, pick up a pencil, open my notebook, and promptly fall asleep." The *third-person singular or plural* can also be used in informational process essays: "The door-to-door salesperson walks up the front walk, heart pounding, more than a bit nervous, but also challenged by the prospect of striking a deal," or "The new recruits next underwent a series of important balance tests in what was called the 'horror chamber.' " Whether you use the first, second, or third person, avoid shifting point of view midstream.

You might have noticed that in the third-person examples, the present tense ("walks up") is used in one sentence, the past tense ("underwent") in the other. The past tense is appropriate for events already completed, whereas the present tense is used for habitual or ongoing actions. ("A dominant male goose usually flies at the head of the V-wedge during migration.") The present tense is also effective when you want to lend a sense of dramatic immediacy to a process, even if the steps were performed in the past. ("The surgeon gently separates the facial skin and muscle from the underlying bony skull.") As with point of view, be on guard against changing tenses in the middle of your explanation.

5. Provide readers with the help they need to follow the sequence. As you move through the steps of a process analysis, don't forget to *warn readers about difficulties* they might encounter. For example, in a paper on the artistry involved in butterflying a shrimp, you might write something like this:

> Next, make a shallow cut with your sharpened knife along the convex curve of the shrimp's intestinal tract. The tract, usually a faint black line along

the outside curve of the shrimp, is faintly visible beneath the translucent flesh. But some shrimp have a thick orange, blue, or gray line instead of a thin black one. In all cases, be careful not to slice too deeply, or you will end up with two shrimp halves instead of one butterflied shrimp.

You have told readers what to look for, citing the exceptions, and have warned them against making too deep a cut. Anticipating spots where communication might break down is a key part of writing an effective process analysis.

Transitional words and phrases are also critical in helping readers understand the order of the steps being described. Time signals like *first, next, now, while, after, before,* and *finally* provide readers with a clear sense of the sequence. Entire sentences can also be used to link parts of the process, reminding your audience of what has already been discussed and indicating what will now be explained: "Once the panel of experts finishes its evaluation of the exam questions, randomly selected items are field-tested in schools throughout the country."

6. Select and maintain an appropriate tone. When writing a process analysis essay, be sure your tone is consistent with your purpose, your attitude toward your subject, and the effect you want to have on readers. When explaining how fraternities and sororities recruit new members, do you want to use an objective, nonjudgmental tone, or do you want to project an angry, even accusatory tone? To decide, take into account readers' attitudes toward your subject. Does your audience have a financial or emotional investment in the process being described? Does your own interest in the process coincide or conflict with that of your audience? Awareness of your readers' stance can be crucial. Consider another example: Assume you're writing a letter to the director of the student health center proposing a new system to replace the currently chaotic one. You'd do well to be tactful in your criticisms. Offend your reader, and your cause is lost. If, however, the letter is slated for the college newspaper and directed primarily to other students, you could adopt a more pointed, even sarcastic tone. Readers, you would assume, will probably share your view and favor change.

Once you settle on the essay's tone, maintain it throughout. If you're writing a light piece on the way computers are taking over our lives, you wouldn't include a grim step-by-step analysis of the way confidential computerized medical records may become public.

7. Open and close the process analysis effectively. A paper developed primarily through process analysis should have a strong beginning. The introduction should state the process to be described and imply whether the essay has an informational or directional intent.

If you suspect readers are indifferent to your subject, use the introduction to motivate them, telling them how important the subject is:

Do you enjoy the salad bars found in many restaurants? If you do, you probably have noticed that the vegetables are always crisp and fresh—no matter how many hours they have been exposed to the air. What are the restaurants doing to make the vegetables look so inviting? There's a simple answer. Many restaurants dip and spray the vegetables with potent chemicals to make them look appetizing.

If you think your audience may be intimidated by your subject (perhaps because it's complex or relatively obscure), the introduction is the perfect spot to reassure them that the process being described is not beyond their grasp:

> Studies show that many people prefer to accept a defective product rather than deal with the uncomfortable process of making a complaint. But once a few easy-to-learn basics are mastered, anyone can register a complaint that gets results.

Most process analysis essays don't end as soon as the last step in the sequence is explained. Instead, they usually include some brief final comments that round out the piece and bring it to a satisfying close. This final section of the essay may summarize the main steps in the process—not by repeating the steps verbatim but by rephrasing and condensing them in several concise sentences. The conclusion can also be an effective spot to underscore the significance of the process, recalling what may have been said in the introduction about the subject's importance. Or the essay can end by echoing the note of reassurance that may have been included at the start.

REVISION STRATEGIES

Once you have a draft of the essay, you're ready to revise. The following checklist will help you and those giving you feedback apply to process analysis some of the revision techniques discussed in Chapters 7 and 8.

> ☑ PROCESS ANALYSIS: A REVISION CHECKLIST
>
> *Revise Overall Meaning and Structure*
> - What purpose does the process analysis serve? To inform, to persuade, or to do both?
> - Where does the process seem confusing? Where have steps been left out? Which steps need simplifying?
> - What tone does the essay project? Is the tone appropriate for the essay's purpose and readers? Where are there distracting shifts in tone?

> *Revise Paragraph Development*
> - Does the introduction specify the process to be described? Does it provide an overview? Should it? Does it mention ingredients or materials the reader needs to know about? Should it?
> - Which paragraphs are difficult to follow? Have any steps been explained in unnecessary detail? Have key steps been omitted? Which paragraphs should warn readers about potential trouble spots or overlapping steps?
> - Where do time signals (*after, before, next*) clarify the sequence within and between paragraphs? Where does overreliance on time signals make the sequence awkward and mechanical?
> - Which paragraph describes the most crucial step in the sequence? How has the step been highlighted?
> - What closing comments round out the piece? Would the conclusion be more effective if the main stages were summarized? Or would such a conclusion be too repetitive?
>
> *Revise Sentences and Words*
> - What technical or specialized terms appear in the essay? Have they been sufficiently defined or explained? Where could simpler, less technical language be used?
> - Are there any places where the essay awkwardly switches from, say, second person to third person? How could this problem be corrected?
> - Does the essay use correct verb tenses—the past tense for completed events, the present tense for habitual or ongoing actions?
> - Where does the essay use the passive voice ("The earth is hoed")? Would the active voice ("You hoe the earth") be more effective?

STUDENT ESSAY: FROM PREWRITING THROUGH REVISION

The student essay that follows was written by Robert Barry in response to this assignment:

> In "The Jeaning of America—and the World," Carin Quinn details the evolution of that unmistakable symbol of American culture—blue jeans. Think of another symbol of popular culture and show, step by step, how it has worked its way into Americans' everyday life. Your essay, either serious or light in tone, might focus on a form of entertainment, a pastime, an invention, or the like.

Process Analysis

Before writing his essay, Robert used the prewriting strategy of *mapping* to generate material for the subject he decided to write on: VCR addiction. Then, with his map as a foundation, he prepared a topic outline that organized and developed his thoughts more fully. Both the map and the outline are reprinted here.

Mapping

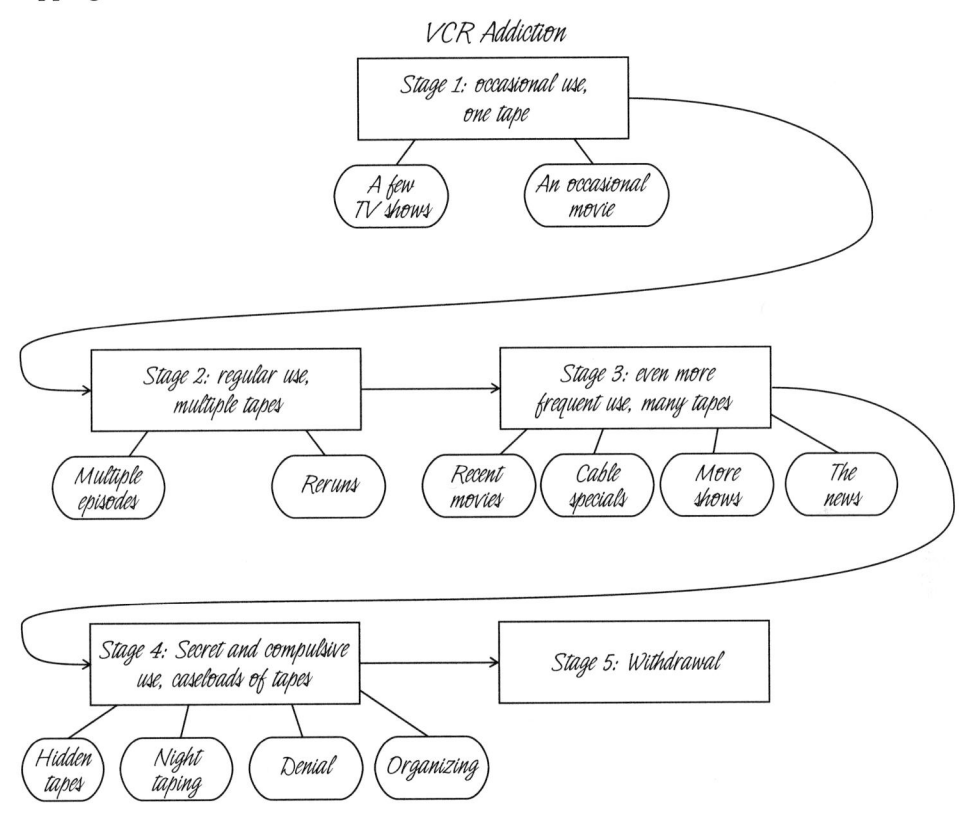

VCR Addiction

- Stage 1: occasional use, one tape
  - A few TV shows
  - An occasional movie
- Stage 2: regular use, multiple tapes
  - Multiple episodes
  - Reruns
- Stage 3: even more frequent use, many tapes
  - Recent movies
  - Cable specials
  - More shows
  - The news
- Stage 4: Secret and compulsive use, caseloads of tapes
  - Hidden tapes
  - Night taping
  - Denial
  - Organizing
- Stage 5: Withdrawal

Outline

Thesis: Without realizing it, a person can turn into a compulsive videotaper. This movement from innocent hobby to full-blown addiction occurs in several stages.

I. Stage One: Occasional use (only one tape)
    A. TV show reruns
        1. <u>Star Trek</u>
        2. <u>Miami Vice</u>
    B. An occasional movie

II. Stage Two: More frequent use (more tapes)
  A. Many episodes of Star Trek
  B. Reruns of The Honeymooners and Mission: Impossible
III. Stage Three: Much more frequent use (stockpile of tapes)
  A. Taping of news shows
  B. Taping of recent movies--add examples
  C. Not enough time to watch taped cable shows plus regularly taped shows
IV. Stage Four: Secret and compulsive use (caseloads of tapes)
  A. Reaction to family's concern
    1. Denial
    2. Hiding tapes in suitcase
    3. Nighttime taping
  B. Obsessive organization of tapes
V. Stage Five: Withdrawal
  A. Forced withdrawal at college
  B. Success at last

Now read Robert's paper, "Becoming a Videoholic," noting the similarities and differences among his map, outline, and final essay. You'll see that Robert dropped one idea (taping news shows), expanded other points (his obsessive organization of tapes into Westerns, comedies, and horror movies), and added some completely new details (his near backsliding during withdrawal). Note, too, that the analogy between VCR addiction and alcoholism doesn't appear in either the map or the outline. The analogy didn't occur to Robert until he began writing his first draft. Despite these differences, the map and outline depict essentially the same five stages in VCR addiction as the essay. Finally, as you read the essay, consider how well it applies the principles of process analysis discussed in this chapter. (The commentary that follows the paper will help you look at Robert's essay more closely and will give you some sense of how he went about revising.)

Becoming a Videoholic
by Robert Barry

Introduction — In the last several years, videocassette recorders (VCRs) have become popular additions in many American homes. A recent newspaper article notes that one in three households has a VCR, with sales continuing to climb every day. VCRs seem to be the most popular technological breakthrough since television itself. No consumer warning labels are attached to these rapidly multiplying VCRs, but they should be. *Start of two-sentence thesis* → VCRs can be dangerous. Barely aware of what is happening, a person can turn into a compulsive videotaper. The descent from innocent hobby to full-blown addiction takes place in several stages.

In the first innocent stage, the unsuspecting person buys a VCR for occasional use. I was at this stage when I asked my parents if they would buy me a VCR as a combined birthday and high school graduation gift. With the VCR, I could tape reruns of Star Trek and Miami Vice, shows I would otherwise miss on nights I was at work. The VCR was perfect. I hooked it up to the old TV in my bedroom, recorded the intergalactic adventures of Captain Kirk and the high-voltage escapades of Sonny Crockett, then watched the tapes the next day. Occasionally, I taped a movie that my friends and I watched over the weekend. I had just one cassette, but that was all I needed since I watched every show I recorded and simply taped over the preceding show when I recorded another. In these early days, my VCR was the equivalent of light social drinking.

In the second phase on the road to videoholism, an individual uses the VCR more frequently and begins to stockpile tapes rather than watch them. My troubles began in July when my family went to the shore for a week's vacation. I programmed the VCR to tape all five episodes of Star Trek while I was at the beach perfecting my tan. Since I used the VCR's long-play mode, I could get all five Star Treks on one cassette. But that ended up creating a problem. Even I, an avid Trekkie, didn't want to watch five shows in one sitting. I viewed two shows, but the three unwatched shows tied up my tape, making it impossible to record other shows. How did I resolve this dilemma? Very easily. I went out and bought several more cassettes. Once I had these additional tapes, I was free to record as many Star Treks as I wanted, plus I could tape reruns of classics like The Honeymooners and Mission: Impossible. Very quickly, I accumulated six Star Treks, four Honeymooners, and three Mission: Impossibles. Then a friend--who shall go nameless--told me that only eighty-two episodes of Star Trek were ever made. Excited by the thought that I could acquire as impressive a collection of tapes as a Hollywood executive, I continued recording Star Trek, even taping shows while I watched them. Clearly, my once innocent hobby was getting out of control. I was now using the VCR on a regular basis--the equivalent of several stiff drinks a day.

In the third stage of videoholism, the amount of taping increases significantly, leading to an even more irrational stockpiling of cassettes.

Third stage in process

Continuation of analogy

The catalyst that propelled me into this third stage was my parents' decision to get cable TV. Selfless guy that I am, I volunteered to move my VCR and hook it up to the TV in the living room, where the cable outlet was located. Now I could tape all the most recent movies and cable specials. With that delightful possibility in mind, I went out and bought two six-packs of blank tapes. Then, in addition to my regulars, I began to record a couple of other shows every day. I taped <u>Rocky III</u>, <u>Magnum Force</u>, a James Bond movie, an HBO comedy special with Eddie Murphy, and an MTV concert featuring Mick Jagger. Where did I get time to watch all these tapes? I didn't. Taping at this point was more satisfying than watching. Reason and common sense were abandoned. Getting things on tape had become an obsession, and I was taping all the time.

Topic sentence

Fourth stage in process

Continuation of analogy

In the fourth stage, videoholism creeps into other parts of the addict's life, influencing behavior in strange ways. Secrecy becomes commonplace. One day, my mother came into my room and saw my bookcase filled with tapes--rather than with the paperbacks that used to be there. "Robert," she exclaimed, "isn't this getting a bit out of hand?" I assured her it was just a hobby, but I started hiding my tapes, putting them in a suitcase stored in my closet. I also taped at night, slipping downstairs to turn on the VCR after my parents had gone to bed and getting down first thing in the morning to turn off the VCR and remove the cassette before my parents noticed. Also, denial is not unusual during this stage of VCR addiction. At the dinner table, when my younger sister commented, "Robert tapes all the time," I laughingly told everyone-- including myself--that the taping was no big deal. I was getting bored with it and was going to stop any day, I assured my family. Obsessive behavior also characterizes the fourth stage of videoholism. Each week, I pulled out the TV magazine from the Sunday paper and went through it carefully, circling in red all the shows I wanted to tape. Another sign of addiction was my compulsive organization of all the tapes I had stockpiled. Working more diligently than I ever had for any term paper, I typed up labels and attached them to each cassette. I also created an elaborate list that showed my tapes broken down into categories such as Westerns, horror movies, and comedies.

Topic sentence

Continuation of analogy

In the final stage of an addiction, the individual either succumbs completely to the addiction or is able to break away from the habit. I broke my addiction, and I broke it cold turkey. This total withdrawal occurred when I went off to college. There was no point in taking my VCR to school because TVs were not allowed in the freshman dorms. Even though there were many things to occupy my time during the school week, cold sweats overcame me whenever I though about everything on TV I was not taping. I even considered calling home and asking members of my family to tape things for me, but I knew they would think I was crazy. At the beginning of the semester, I also had to resist the overwhelming desire to travel the three hours home every weekend so I could get my fix. But after a while, the urgent need to tape subsided. Now, months later, as I write this, I feel detached and sober. *Final stage in process*

7   I have no illusions, though. I know that once a videoholic, always a videoholic. Soon I will return home for the holidays, which, as everyone knows, can be a time for excess eating--and taping. But I will cope with the pressure. I will take each day one at a time. I will ask my little sister to hide my blank tapes. And if I feel myself succumbing to the temptations of taping, I will pick up the telephone and dial the videoholics' hot line: (800) VCR-TAPE. I will win the battle. *Conclusion* *Final references to analogy*

Commentary

Purpose, Thesis, and Tone

Robert's essay is an example of *informational process analysis;* his purpose is to describe—rather than teach—the process of becoming a "videoholic." The title, with its coined term *videoholic,* tips us off that the essay is going to be entertaining. And the introductory paragraph clearly establishes the essay's playful, mock-serious tone. The tone established, Robert briefly defines the term *videoholic* as a "compulsive videotaper" and then moves to the essay's *thesis:* "Barely aware of what is happening, a person can turn into a compulsive videotaper. The descent from innocent hobby to full-blown addiction takes place in several stages."

Throughout the essay, Robert sustains the introduction's humor by mocking his own motivations and poking fun at his quirks: "Selfless guy that I am, I volunteered to move my VCR" (paragraph 4), and "Working more diligently than I ever had for any term paper, I typed up labels" (5). Robert probably uses a bit of *dramatic license* when reporting some of his obsessive behavior, and we, as readers, understand that he's exaggerating for comic effect. Most likely he didn't break out in a cold sweat at the thought of the TV shows he was unable to tape, and he probably didn't hide his tapes in a suitcase. Nevertheless, this tinkering with the truth is legitimate because it allows Robert to create material that fits the essay's lightly satiric tone.

Organization and Topic Sentences

To meet the requirements of the assignment, Robert needed to provide a *step-by-step* explanation of a process. And because he invented the term *videoholism*, Robert also needed to invent the stages in the progression of his addiction. During his prewriting, Robert discovered five stages in his videoholism. Presented *chronologically*, these stages provide the organizing focus for his paper. Specifically, each supporting paragraph is devoted to one stage, with the *topic sentence* for each paragraph indicating the stage's distinctive characteristics.

Transitions

Although Robert's essay is playful, it is nonetheless a process analysis and so must have an easy-to-follow structure. Keeping this in mind, Robert wisely includes *transitions* to signal what happened at each stage of his videoholism: "*Once* I had these additional tapes, I was free to record" (paragraph 3); "*Then*, in addition to my regulars, I began to record" (4); "*One day*, my mother came into my room" (5); and "*But after a while*, the urgent need to tape subsided" (6). In addition to such transitions, Robert uses crisp questions to move from idea to idea within a paragraph: "How did I resolve this dilemma? Very easily. I . . . bought several more cassettes" (3), and "Where did I get time to watch all these tapes? I didn't" (4).

Other Patterns of Development

Even though Robert's essay is a process analysis, it contains elements of other patterns of development. For example, his paper is unified by an *analogy*—a sustained *comparison* between Robert's video addiction and the obviously more serious addiction to alcohol. Handled incorrectly, the analogy could have been offensive, but Robert makes the comparison work to his advantage. The analogy is stated specifically in several spots: "In these early days, my VCR was the equivalent of light social drinking" (2); "I was now using the VCR on a regular basis—the equivalent of several stiff drinks a day" (3). Another place where Robert touches wittily on the analogy occurs in the middle of the fourth paragraph: "I went out and bought two six-packs of blank tapes." To illustrate his progression toward videoholism, Robert depicts the *effects* of his addiction. Finally, he generates numerous lively details or *examples* to illustrate the different stages in his addiction.

Two Unnecessary Sentences

Perhaps you noticed that Robert runs into a minor problem at the end of the fourth paragraph. Starting with the sentence "Reason and common sense were abandoned," he begins to ramble and repeat himself. The paragraph's last two sentences fail to add anything substantial. Take a moment to read paragraph 4 aloud, omitting the last two sentences. Note how much sharper the new conclusion is: "Where did I get time to watch all these tapes? I didn't. Taping at this point was more satisfying than watching." This new ending says all that needs to be said.

Revising the First Draft

When it was time to revise, Robert—in spite of his apprehension—showed his paper to his roommate and asked him to read it out loud. Robert knew this strategy would provide a more objective point of view on his work. His roommate, at first an unwilling recruit, nonetheless laughed as he read the essay aloud. That was just the response Robert wanted. But when his roommate got to the conclusion, Robert heard that the closing paragraph was flat and anticlimactic. His roommate agreed, so the two of them brainstormed ways to make the conclusion livelier and more in spirit with the rest of the essay.

Reprinted here is Robert's original conclusion. The handwritten notes, numbered in order of importance, represent both Robert's ideas for revision and those of his roommate.

Original Version of the Conclusion

I have no illusions, though, that I am over my videoholism. Soon I will be returning home for the holidays, which can be a time for excess taping. All I can do is ask my little sister to hide my blank tapes. After that, I will hope for the best.

③ Shorten first sentence
① Get back to analogy
② Boring. Add humor.

As you can see, Robert and his roommate decided that the best approach would be to reinforce the playful, mock-serious tone that characterized earlier parts of the essay. Robert thus made three major changes to his conclusion. First, he tightened the first sentence of the paragraph ("I have no illusions, though, that I am over my videoholism"), making it crisper and more dramatic: "I have no illusions, though." Second, he added a few sentences to sustain the light, self-deprecating tone he had used earlier: "I know that once a videoholic, always a videoholic"; "But I will cope with the pressure"; "I will win the battle." Third, and perhaps most important, he returned to the alcoholism analogy: "I will take each day one at a time. . . . And if I feel myself succumbing to the temptations of taping, I will pick up the telephone and dial the videoholics' hotline. . . ."

These weren't the only changes Robert made while reworking his paper, but they help illustrate how sensitive he was to the effect he wanted to achieve. Certainly, the recasting of the conclusion was critical to the overall success of this amusing essay.

ACTIVITIES: PROCESS ANALYSIS

Prewriting Activities

1. Imagine you're writing two essays: One defines the term *comparison shopping;* the other contrasts two different teaching styles. Jot down ways you might use process analysis in each essay.

2. Look at the essay topics that follow. Assuming that your readers will be students in your composition class, which topics would lend themselves to directional process analysis, informational process analysis, or a blend of both? Explain your responses.

   a. Going on a job interview
   b. Using a computer in the college library
   c. Cleaning up oil spills
   d. Negotiating personal conflicts
   e. Curing a cold
   f. Growing vegetables organically

3. For *one* of the following essay topics, decide—given the audience indicated in parentheses—what your purpose, tone, and point of view might be. Then use brainstorming, questioning, mapping, or another prewriting technique to identify the steps you'd include in a process analysis for that audience. After reviewing the material generated, delete, add, and combine points as needed. Then organize the material in the most logical sequence.

   a. How to write effective essays (*college students*)
   b. How to get along with parents (*high school students*)
   c. How the college administration handled a controversial campus issue (*alumni*)
   d. How to deal with a bully (*elementary school children*)
   e. How a specific ceremony is performed in your religion (*an adult unfamiliar with the practice*)
   f. How malls encourage spending sprees (*general public*)

4. Select *one* of the essay topics that follow and determine what your purpose, tone, and point of view would be for each audience indicated in parentheses. Then use prewriting to identify the points you'd cover for each audience. Finally, organize the raw material, noting the differences in emphasis and sequence for each group of readers.

   a. How to buy a car (*young people who have just gotten a driver's license; established professionals*)

Process Analysis

  b. How children acquire their values (*first-time parents; elementary school teachers*)
  c. How to manage money (*grade-school children; college students*)
  d. How loans or scholarships are awarded to incoming students on your campus (*high school graduates applying for financial aid; high school guidance counselors*)
  e. How arguments can strengthen relationships (*preteen children; young adults*)
  f. How to relax (*college students; parents with young children*).

5. For *one* of the following process topics, identify an appropriate audience, purpose, tone, and point of view. Then use prewriting to generate raw material showing that there's a problem with the way the process is performed. After organizing that material, use prewriting once again—this time to identify how the process *should* be performed. Sequence this new material in a logical order.

  a. How students select a college or a major
  b. How local television news covers national events
  c. How a specific group of people mismanage their finances
  d. How your campus or your community is handling a difficult situation

Revising Activities

6. The following paragraph is from an essay making the point that over-the-phone sales can be a challenging career. The paragraph, written as a process analysis, describes the steps involved in making a sales call. Revise the paragraph, deleting any material that undermines the paragraph's unity, organizing the steps in a logical sequence, and supplying transitions where needed. Also be sure to correct any inappropriate shifts in person. Finally, do some brainstorming—individually or in a group—to generate details to bolster underdeveloped steps in the sequence.

Establishing rapport with potential customers is the most challenging part of phone sales. The longer you can keep customers on the phone, the more you can get a sense of their needs. And the more you know about customers, the more successful the salesperson is bound to be. Your opening comments are critical. After setting the right tone, you gently introduce your product. There are a number of ways you can move gracefully from your opening remarks to the actual selling phase of the call. Remember: Don't try to sell the customer at the beginning. Instead, try in a friendly way to keep the prospective customer on the phone. Maintaining such a connection is easier than you think because many people have an almost desperate need to talk. Their lives are isolated and lonely--a sad fact of contemporary life. Once you shift to the distinctly selling phase of the call, you should present the advantages of the product, especially the advantages of price and convenience. Mentioning installment payments is often effective. If the customer says that he or she isn't interested, the salesperson should try to determine--in a genial way--why the person is reluctant to buy. Don't, however, push aggressively for reasons or try to steamroll the person into thinking his or her reservations are invalid. Once the person agrees to buy, try to encourage credit card payment, rather than check or money order. The salesperson can explain that credit card payment means the customer will receive the product sooner. End the call as you began--in an easy, personable way.

7. Reprinted here is a paragraph from the first draft of a humorous essay advising shy college students how to get through a typical day. Written as a process analysis, the paragraph outlines techniques for surviving class. Revise the paragraph, deleting digressions that disrupt the paragraph's unity, eliminating unnecessary repetition, and sequencing the steps in the proper order. Also correct inappropriate shifts in person and add transitions where needed. Feel free to add any telling details.

Simply attending class can be stressful for shy people. Several strategies, though, can lesson the trauma. Shy students should time their arrival to coincide with that of most other class members--about two minutes before the class is scheduled to begin. If you arrive too early, you may be seen sitting alone or, even worse, may actually be forced to talk with another early arrival. If you arrive late, all eyes will be upon you. Before heading to class, the shy student should dress in the least conspicuous manner possible--say, in the blue jeans, sweatshirt, and sneakers that 99.9 percent of your classmates wear. That way you won't stand out from everyone else. Take a seat near the back of the room. Don't, however, sit at the very back since professors often take sadistic pleasure in calling on students back there, assuming they chose those seats because they didn't want to be called on. A friend of mine who is far from shy uses just the opposite ploy. In an attempt to get in good with her professors, she sits in the front row and, incredibly enough, volunteers to participate. However, since shy people don't want to call attention to themselves, they should stifle any urge to sneeze or cough. You run the risk of having people look at you or offer you a tissue or cough drop. And of course, never, ever volunteer to answer. Such a display of intelligence is sure to focus all eyes on you. In other words, make yourself as inconspicuous as possible. How, you might wonder, can you be inconspicuous if you're blessed (or cursed) with great looks? Well, . . . have you ever considered earning your degree through the mail?

PROFESSIONAL SELECTIONS: PROCESS ANALYSIS

MORTIMER ADLER

A prolific writer, Mortimer Adler (1902–) is a strong advocate for the life of the mind. Although he refused to complete requirements for both a high school diploma and a bachelor's degree, Adler received his doctorate from Columbia University in 1928. He went on to achieve recognition as the editor of the fifteenth edition of the *Encyclopedia Britannica*. Adler's *How to Read a Book: The Art of Getting a Liberal Education* was a best-seller in 1940. His other books include two autobiographies and several works of popular philosophy, such as *The Great Ideas: One Hundred Two Essays* (1992). The following essay first appeared in the magazine *Saturday Review* in 1940.

HOW TO MARK A BOOK

1   You know you have to read "between the lines" to get the most out of anything. I want to persuade you to do something equally important in the course of your reading. I want to persuade you to "write between the lines." Unless you do, you are not likely to do the most efficient kind of reading.

2   I contend, quite bluntly, that marking up a book is not an act of mutilation but of love....

3   There are two ways in which one can own a book. The first is the property right you establish by paying for it, just as you pay for clothes and furniture. But this act of purchase is only the prelude to possession. Full ownership comes only when you have made it a part of yourself, and the best way to make yourself a part of it is by writing in it....

4   Is it false respect, you may ask, to preserve intact and unblemished a beautifully printed book, an elegantly bound edition? Of course not. I'd no more scribble all over a first edition of *Paradise Lost** than I'd give my baby a set of crayons and an original Rembrandt! I wouldn't mark up a painting or a statue. Its soul, so to speak, is inseparable from its body. And the beauty of a rare edition or of a richly manufactured volume is like that of a painting or a statue.

5   But the soul of a book *can* be separated from its body. A book is more like the score of a piece of music than it is like a painting. No great musician confuses a symphony with the printed sheets of music. Arturo Toscanini reveres Brahms,** but Toscanini's

---

*An epic poem written in 1667 by the English poet John Milton (editors' note).
**Arturo Toscanini (1867–1957) was a celebrated cellist and conductor; Brahms (1833–97) was a renowned pianist and composer (editors' note).

score of the C-minor Symphony is so thoroughly marked up that no one but the maestro himself can read it. The reason why a great conductor makes notations on his musical scores—marks them up again and again each time he returns to study them—is the reason why you should mark your books. If your respect for magnificent binding or typography gets in the way, buy yourself a cheap edition and pay your respects to the author.

Why is marking up a book indispensable to reading? First, it keeps you awake. (And I don't mean merely conscious; I mean wide awake.) In the second place, reading, if it is active, is thinking, and thinking tends to express itself in words, spoken or written. The marked book is usually the thought-through book. Finally, writing helps you remember the thoughts you had, or the thoughts the author expressed. . . .

[T]he physical act of writing, with your own hand, brings words and sentences more sharply before your mind and preserves them better in your memory. To set down your reaction to important words and sentences you have read, and the questions they have raised in your mind, is to preserve those reactions and sharpen those questions. . . .

And, best of all, your marks and notes become an integral part of the book and stay there forever. You can pick up the book the following week or year, and there are all your points of agreement, disagreement, doubt, and inquiry. It's like resuming an interrupted conversation with the advantage of being able to pick up where you left off.

And that is exactly what reading a book should be: a conversation between you and the author. Presumably he knows more about the subject than you do; naturally, you'll have the proper humility as you approach him. But don't let anybody tell you that a reader is supposed to be solely on the receiving end. Understanding is a two-way operation; learning doesn't consist in being an empty receptacle. The learner has to question himself and question the teacher. He even has to argue with the teacher, once he understands what the teacher is saying. And marking a book is literally an expression of your differences, or agreements of opinion, with the author.

There are all kinds of devices for marking a book intelligently and fruitfully. Here's the way I do it:

1. *Underlining:* of major points, of important or forceful statements.
2. *Vertical lines at the margin:* to emphasize a statement already underlined.
3. *Star, asterisk, or other doo-dad at the margin:* to be used sparingly, to emphasize the ten or twenty most important statements in the book. (You may want to fold the bottom corner of each page on which you use such marks. It won't hurt the sturdy paper on which most modern books are printed, and you will be able to take the book off the shelf at any time and, by opening it at the folded-corner page, refresh your recollection of the book.)
4. *Numbers in the margin:* to indicate the sequence of points the author makes in developing a single argument.
5. *Numbers of other pages in the margin:* to indicate where else in the book the author made points relevant to the point marked; to tie up the ideas in a book, which, though they may be separated by many pages, belong together.
6. *Circling of key words or phrases.*
7. *Writing in the margin, or at the top or bottom of the page, for the sake of:* recording questions (and perhaps answers) which a passage raised in your mind; reducing a complicated discussion to a simple statement; recording the sequence of major points right through the books. I use the end-papers at the back of the book to make a personal index of the author's points in the order of their appearance.

18   The front end-papers are, to me, the most important. Some people reserve them for a fancy bookplate. I reserve them for fancy thinking. After I have finished reading the book and making my personal index on the back end-papers, I turn to the front and try to outline the book, not page by page, or point by point (I've already done that at the back), but as an integrated structure, with a basic unity and an order of parts. This outline is, to me, the measure of my understanding of the work.

19   If you're a die-hard anti-book-marker, you may object that the margins, the space between the lines, and the end-papers don't give you room enough. All right. How about using a scratch pad slightly smaller than the page-size of the book—so that the edges of the sheets won't protrude? Make your index, outlines, and even your notes on the pad, and then insert these sheets permanently inside the front and back covers of the book.

20   Or, you may say that this business of marking books is going to slow up your reading. It probably will. That's one of the reasons for doing it. Most of us have been taken in by the notion that speed of reading is a measure of our intelligence. There is no such thing as the right speed for intelligent reading. Some things should be read quickly and effortlessly, and some should be read slowly and even laboriously. The sign of intelligence in reading is the ability to read different things differently according to their worth. In the case of good books, the point is not to see how many of them you can get through, but rather how many can get through you—how many you can make your own. A few friends are better than a thousand acquaintances. If this be your aim, as it should be, you will not be impatient if it takes more time and effort to read a great book than it does a newspaper.

21   You may have one final objection to marking books. You can't lend them to your friends because nobody else can read them without being distracted by your notes. Furthermore, you won't want to lend them because a marked copy is a kind of intellectual diary, and lending it is almost like giving your mind away.

22   If your friend wishes to read your *Plutarch's Lives,** Shakespeare*, or *The Federalist Papers*,** tell him gently but firmly to buy a copy. You will lend him your car or your coat—but your books are as much a part of you as your head or your heart.

Questions for Close Reading

1. What is the selection's thesis? Locate the sentence(s) in which Adler states his main idea. If he doesn't state the thesis explicitly, express it in your own words.

2. According to Adler, why is marking a book so crucial to the process of understanding its ideas?

3. What objections to marking books does Adler anticipate his readers might have? How does Adler deal with these objections?

4. What does Adler mean in paragraph 20 when he writes that "the point is not to see how many of them [good books] you can get through, but rather how many can get through you . . ."?

---

*A series of biographies of famous Greeks and Romans, written by Plutarch at some undetermined point during the first two decades of the second century AD (editors' note).
**Eighty-five essays—written by Alexander Hamilton, James Madison, and John Jay and published in 1787–88—analyzing the Constitution and advocating its adoption (editors' note).

5. Refer to your dictionary as needed to define the following words used in the selection: *prelude* (paragraph 3), *typography* (5), *indispensable* (6), *bookplate* (18), and *integrated* (18).

Questions About the Writer's Craft

1. The pattern. What indications are there that Adler has taken his audience into account when introducing his subject and when presenting his process analysis? Where does he show awareness of his audience's concerns?

2. Other patterns. Where in the essay does Adler use the comparison-contrast pattern of development? How does the pattern contribute to the persuasiveness of his point of view?

3. What signal devices does Adler use to help readers follow the progression of his ideas? What is the effect of these techniques?

4. Look closely at Adler's sentence structure and word choice. What effect do these two elements have on Adler's tone and credibility?

Writing Assignments Using Process Analysis as a Pattern of Development

1. Hoping to encourage readers to follow his advice, Adler describes his technique for marking a book. In an essay of your own, describe for readers your way of doing something. You might describe the steps you take to prepare for a job interview, to meet new people, to plant a vegetable garden, and so on. Like Adler, project enthusiasm for your subject and describe the process so clearly that readers will have no trouble following the steps outlined.

2. Unlike Adler, who takes great pleasure in reading, many people consider reading a chore—even though they felt considerable pleasure and pride when they learned to read as children. Write an essay detailing the steps that schools *or* families *or* communities can take to encourage a lifelong enthusiasm for books. To underscore the need for the steps you present, begin the essay with a vivid example showing that people do indeed avoid reading.

Writing Assignments Using Other Patterns of Development

3. Think of an activity that you take as seriously as Adler takes reading—perhaps serving on a campus committee, doing crafts, watching or participating in a sport. Write an essay persuading readers that despite their reservations or objections, this is a significant and worthwhile activity. Like Adler, use vivid examples and an easy, personal tone to show readers what is so compelling about the activity.

4. Adler writes in paragraph 9, "Understanding is a two-way operation; learning doesn't consist in being an empty receptacle." In an essay, narrate a time that you were actively engaged in learning because someone encouraged you, as Adler puts it, to "question" and "argue." The person might have been a friend, a teacher, a family member, a coach, or an employer. Include only those narrative details and conversational exchanges that convey the intensity of your learning experience.

MALCOLM X

Malcolm X (1925–65) was born Malcolm Little but took the name Malcolm X when he became a Black Muslim. An impassioned speaker and influential civil rights leader, Malcolm X was assassinated by a follower of a rival political and religious group. The following selection is from *The Autobiography of Malcolm X* (1964), which was originally dictated to Alex Haley, later known as the author of *Roots*.

MY FIRST CONK

1   Shorty soon decided that my hair was finally long enough to be conked. He had promised to school me in how to beat the barbershops' three- and four-dollar price by making up congolene, and then conking ourselves.

2   I took the little list of ingredients he had printed out for me, and went to a grocery store, where I got a can of Red Devil lye, two eggs, and two medium-sized white potatoes. Then at a drugstore near the poolroom, I asked for a large jar of Vaseline, a large bar of soap, a large-toothed comb and a fine-toothed comb, one of those rubber hoses with a metal spray-head, a rubber apron and a pair of gloves.

3   "Going to lay on that first conk?" the drugstore man asked me. I proudly told him, grinning, "Right!"

4   Shorty paid six dollars a week for a room in his cousin's shabby apartment. His cousin wasn't at home. "It's like the pad's mine, he spends so much time with his woman," Shorty said. "Now, you watch me—"

5   He peeled the potatoes and thin-sliced them into a quart-sized Mason fruit jar, then started stirring them with a wooden spoon as he gradually poured in a little over half the can of lye. "Never use a metal spoon; the lye will turn it black," he told me.

6   A jelly-like, starchy-looking glop resulted from the lye and potatoes, and Shorty broke in the two eggs, stirring real fast—his own conk and dark face bent down close. The congolene turned pale-yellowish. "Feel the jar," Shorty said. I cupped my hand against the outside, and snatched it away. "Damn right, it's hot, that's the lye," he said. "So you know it's going to burn when I comb it in—it burns bad. But the longer you can stand it, the straighter the hair."

7   He made me sit down, and he tied the string of the new rubber apron tightly around my neck, and combed up my bush of hair. Then, from the big Vaseline jar, he took a handful and massaged it hard all through my hair and into the scalp. He also thickly Vaselined my neck, ears and forehead. "When I get to washing out your head, be sure to tell me anywhere you feel any little stinging," Shorty warned me, washing his hands, then pulling on the rubber gloves, and tying on his own rubber apron. "You always got to remember that any congolene left in burns a sore into your head."

The congolene just felt warm when Shorty started combing it in. But then my head caught fire.

I gritted my teeth and tried to pull the sides of the kitchen table together. The comb felt as if it was raking my skin off.

My eyes watered, my nose was running. I couldn't stand it any longer; I bolted to the washbasin. I was cursing Shorty with every name I could think of when he got the spray going and started soap-lathering my head.

He lathered and spray-rinsed, lathered and spray-rinsed, maybe ten or twelve times, each time gradually closing the hot-water faucet, until the rinse was cold, and that helped some.

"You feel any stinging spots?"

"No," I managed to say. My knees were trembling.

"Sit back down, then. I think we got it all out okay."

The flame came back as Shorty, with a thick towel, started drying my head, rubbing hard. "*Easy, man, easy!*" I kept shouting.

"The first time's always worst. You get used to it better before long. You took it real good, homeboy. You got a good conk."

When Shorty let me stand up and see in the mirror, my hair hung down in limp, damp strings. My scalp still flamed, but not as badly; I could bear it. He draped the towel around my shoulders, over my rubber apron, and began again Vaselining my hair.

I could feel him combing, straight back, first the big comb, then the fine-tooth one.

Then, he was using a razor, very delicately, on the back of my neck. Then finally, shaping the sideburns.

My first view in the mirror blotted out the hurting. I'd seen some pretty conks, but when it's the first time, on your *own* head, the transformation, after the lifetime of kinks, is staggering.

The mirror reflected Shorty behind me. We both were grinning and sweating. And on top of my head was this thick, smooth sheen of shining red hair—real red—as straight as any white man's.

How ridiculous I was! Stupid enough to stand there simply lost in admiration of my hair now looking "white," reflected in the mirror in Shorty's room. I vowed that I'd never again be without a conk, and I never was for many years.

This was my first really big step toward self-degradation: when I endured all of that pain, literally burning my flesh to have it look like a white man's hair. I had joined that multitude of Negro men and women in America who are brainwashed into believing that the black people are "inferior"—and white people "superior"—that they will even violate and mutilate their God-created bodies to try to look "pretty" by white standards.

Look around today, in every small town and big city, from two-bit catfish and soda-pop joints into the "integrated" lobby of the Waldorf-Astoria, and you'll see conks on black men. And you'll see black women wearing these green and pink and purple and red and platinum-blonde wigs. They're all more ridiculous than a slapstick comedy. It makes you wonder if the Negro has completely lost his sense of identity, lost touch with himself.

You'll see the conk worn by many, many so-called "upper class" Negroes, and, as much as I hate to say it about them, on all too many Negro entertainers. One of the reasons that I've especially admired some of them, like Lionel Hampton and Sidney Poitier, among others, is that they have kept their natural hair and fought to the top. I admire any Negro man who has never had himself conked, or who has had the sense to get rid of it—as I finally did.

26   I don't know which kind of self-defacing conk is the greater shame—the one you'll see on the heads of the black so-called "middle class" and "upper class," who ought to know better, or the one you'll see on the heads of the poorest, most downtrodden, ignorant black men. I mean the legal-minimum-wage ghetto-dwelling kind of Negro, as I was when I got my first one. It's generally among these poor fools that you'll see a black kerchief over the man's head, like Aunt Jemima; he's trying to make his conk last longer, between trips to the barbershop. Only for special occasions is this kerchief-protected conk exposed—to show off how "sharp" and "hip" its owner is. The ironic thing is that I have never heard any woman, white or black, express any admiration for a conk. Of course, any white woman with a black man isn't thinking about his hair. But I don't see how on earth a black woman with any race pride could walk down the street with any black man wearing a conk—the emblem of his shame that he is black.

27   To my own shame, when I say all of this I'm talking first of all about myself—because you can't show me any Negro who ever conked more faithfully than I did. I'm speaking from personal experience when I say of any black man who conks today, or any white-wigged black woman, that if they gave the brains in their heads just half as much attention as they do their hair, they would be a thousand times better off.

Questions for Close Reading

1. What is the selection's thesis? Locate the sentence(s) in which Malcolm X states his main idea. If he doesn't state the thesis explicitly, express it in your own words.

2. What are the ingredients of "congolene"? What is their effect? Why are the Vaseline, soap, spray hose, apron, and gloves needed?

3. Why does Malcolm X permit his friend Shorty to give him a "conk"? Why does he refer to it as "My first really big step toward self-degradation"?

4. What kind of black man does Malcolm X say he admires? What does he imply is more important than trying to change one's appearance?

5. Refer to your dictionary as needed to define the following words used in the selection: *self-degradation* (paragraph 23) and *self-defacing* (26).

Questions About the Writer's Craft

1. The pattern. After detailing the steps in the process of conking, Malcolm X places conking in the context of another, larger process. What is that process? How is it related to Malcolm X's purpose in writing this essay?

2. Other patterns. Why do you think Malcolm X chose to narrate his own experience rather than someone else's?

3. In paragraphs 22–26, Malcolm X places quotation marks around a number of words. How do these quotation marks reinforce the essay's thesis?

4. Do you think Malcolm X is writing primarily for a black audience or for a white one? How can you tell?

Writing Assignments Using Process Analysis as a Pattern of Development

1. Malcolm X writes of the pressure to conform to majority opinions and practices. Relate the steps you took to resist pressures exerted by a specific group (your family, an employer, the educational system). Explain whether your resistance was or was not in your own best interests. George Orwell's "Shooting an Elephant" (page 201) and Joseph H. Suina's "And Then I Went to School" (page 339) offer insights into the possible effects of the need to conform.

2. Malcolm X describes an arduous process that had a demoralizing effect. In an essay, show how your mastery of a difficult process increased your self-esteem. Guide readers through the process step by step, revealing how your achievement enhanced your self-image.

Writing Assignments Using Other Patterns of Development

3. In his youth, Malcolm X valued the straight hair of many whites. As he matured, however, he took pride in his natural appearance. Select some quality you possess or a custom you follow that you presently value more or less than you used to. Contrast your current attitude with your earlier one. Reveal what brought about the change.

4. Narrate a time you initially misjudged someone because of his or her appearance. Convey the individual's genuine character, as well as your progressive discovery of the real person behind the appearance. To get a better idea of how prejudice can distort our perception of others, you might want to read Maya Angelou's "Louise Cox" (page 207) and Brent Staples's "Black Men and Public Space" (page 373).

CARIN QUINN

A graduate of California State University at Los Angeles, Carin Quinn holds a Master of Arts in American Studies. The essay that follows was first published in *American Heritage* magazine in 1978.

THE JEANING OF AMERICA—AND THE WORLD

This is the story of a sturdy American symbol which has now spread throughout most of the world. The symbol is not the dollar. It is not even Coca-Cola. It is a simple pair of pants called blue jeans, and what the pants symbolize is what Alexis de Tocqueville called "a manly and legitimate passion for equality...." Blue jeans are favored equally by bureaucrats and cowboys; bankers and deadbeats; fashion designers and beer drinkers. They draw no distinctions and recognize no classes; they are merely American. Yet they are sought after almost everywhere in the world—

including Russia, where authorities recently broke up a teen-aged gang that was selling them on the black market for two hundred dollars a pair. They have been around for a long time, and it seems likely that they will outlive even the necktie.

2   This ubiquitous American symbol was the invention of a Bavarian-born Jew. His name was Levi Strauss.

3   He was born in Bad Ocheim, Germany, in 1829, and during the European political turmoil of 1848 decided to take his chances in New York, to which his two brothers already had emigrated. Upon arrival, Levi soon found out that his two brothers had exaggerated their tales of an easy life in the land of the main chance. They were landowners, they had told him; instead, he found them pushing needles, thread, pots, pans, ribbons, yarn, scissors, and buttons to housewives. For two years he was a lowly peddler, hauling some 180 pounds of sundries door-to-door to eke out a marginal living. When a married sister in San Francisco offered to pay his way West in 1850, he jumped at the opportunity, taking with him bolts of canvas he hoped to sell for a living.

4   It was the wrong kind of canvas for that purpose, but while talking with a miner down from the mother lode, he learned that pants—sturdy pants that would stand up to the rigors of the diggings—were almost impossible to find. Opportunity beckoned. On the spot, Strauss measured the man's girth and inseam with a piece of string and for six dollars in gold dust, had them tailored into a pair of stiff but rugged pants. The miner was delighted with the result, word got around about "those pants of Levi's," and Strauss was in business. The company has been in business ever since.

5   When Strauss ran out of canvas, he wrote his two brothers to send more. He received instead a tough, brown cotton cloth made in Nimes, France—called *serge de Nimes* and swiftly shortened to "denim" (the word "jeans" derives from *Gênes*, the French word for Genoa, where a similar cloth was produced). Almost from the first, Strauss had his cloth dyed the distinctive indigo that gave blue jeans their name, but it was not until the 1870s that he added the copper rivets which have long since become a company trademark. The rivets were the idea of a Virginia City, Nevada, tailor, Jacob W. Davis, who added them to pacify a mean-tempered miner called Alkali Ike. Alkali, the story goes, complained that the pockets of his jeans always tore when he stuffed them with ore samples and demanded that Davis do something about it. As a kind of joke, Davis took the pants to a blacksmith and had the pockets riveted; once again, the idea worked so well that word got around; in 1873 Strauss appropriated and patented the gimmick—and hired Davis as a regional manager.

6   By this time, Strauss had taken both his brothers and two brothers-in-law into the company and was ready for his third San Francisco store. Over the ensuing years the company prospered locally, and by the time of his death in 1902, Strauss had become a man of prominence in California. For three decades thereafter the business remained profitable though small, with sales largely confined to the working people of the West—cowboys, lumberjacks, railroad workers, and the like. Levi's jeans were first introduced to the East, apparently, during the dude-ranch craze of the 1930s, when vacationing Easterners returned and spread the word about the wonderful pants with rivets. Another boost came in World War II, when blue jeans were declared an essential commodity and were sold only to people engaged in defense work. From a company with fifteen salespeople, two plants, and almost no business east of the Mississippi in 1946, the organization grew in thirty years to include a sales force of more than twenty-two thousand, with fifty plants and offices in thirty-five countries. Each year, more than 250,000,000 items of Levi's

clothing are sold—including more than 83,000,000 pairs of riveted blue jeans. They have become, through marketing, word of mouth, and demonstrable reliability, the common pants of America. They can be purchased pre-washed, pre-faded, and pre-shrunk for the suitably proletarian look. They adapt themselves to any sort of idiosyncratic use; women slit them at the inseams and convert them into long skirts, men chop them off above the knees and turn them into something to be worn while challenging the surf. Decorations and ornamentations abound.

The pants have become a tradition, and along the way have acquired a history of their own—so much so that the company has opened a museum in San Francisco. There was, for example, the turn-of-the-century trainman who replaced a faulty coupling with a pair of jeans; the Wyoming man who used his jeans as a towrope to haul his car out of a ditch; the Californian who found several pairs in an abandoned mine, wore them, then discovered they were sixty-three years old and still as good as new and turned them over to the Smithsonian as a tribute to their toughness. And then there is the particularly terrifying story of the careless construction worker who dangled fifty-two stories above the street until rescued, his sole support the Levi's belt loop through which his rope was hooked. 7

Questions for Close Reading

1. What is the selection's thesis? Locate the sentence(s) in which Quinn states her main idea. If she doesn't state the thesis explicitly, express it in your own words.

2. How did the immigrant Levi Strauss decide to manufacture pants? For what reasons were his pants such an immediate success?

3. What is the story behind the trademark rivets on the pockets of Levi's jeans?

4. What factors made jeans, a Western working-man's uniform, popular among Easterners? Why does Quinn refer to today's blue jeans as an "American symbol"?

5. Refer to your dictionary as needed to define the following words used in the selection: *ubiquitous* (paragraph 2), *sundries* (3), *girth* (4), *indigo* (5), and *proletarian* (6).

Questions About the Writer's Craft

1. The pattern. Quinn recounts a process she calls "jeaning." What steps in the development of the classic blue jean does she identify? What other process does she discuss in paragraph 6?

2. How does Quinn help readers keep track of the sequence of events?

3. What strategy does Quinn use in the first paragraph to introduce her subject? (To review introductory strategies, see pages 74–76.) How does this strategy help establish the essay's tone?

4. Paragraph 2 consists of two brief sentences. What effect does Quinn achieve by making the paragraph so short?

Writing Assignments Using Process Analysis as a Pattern of Development

1. According to Quinn, Strauss invented blue jeans to solve a problem in work clothes. Explain a process you used to solve a specific problem. It might be a problem you had in studying efficiently or arguing fairly. Present the process in such a way that readers can follow the steps easily.

2. Quinn's essay is partly biography; it shows the process by which an immigrant achieved success in America. Write an essay about a person whose biography demonstrates a process. You could, for example, use this person's experience to explain the process of selecting a career, becoming committed to a cause, or being Americanized.

Writing Assignments Using Other Patterns of Development

3. The dollar, Coca-Cola, and blue jeans are just a few symbols of the American way of life. If you had to pick a symbol for our country—not the flag or the eagle, but a new one that represents contemporary American society—what would it be? The symbol can be either positive or negative. Write an essay defending your choice with abundant examples.

4. In an essay, define what the word *success* means to you. Does it necessarily entail financial or business achievement, like Levi Strauss's, or does it mean something else to you? Provide concrete examples to develop your definition.

ADDITIONAL WRITING TOPICS: PROCESS ANALYSIS

General Assignments

Using process analysis, write an essay on one of the following topics.

Directional: How to Do Something

1. How to improve a course you have taken
2. How to drive defensively
3. How to get away with _____
4. How to improve the place where you work or study

5. How to relax
6. How to show appreciation to others
7. How to get through school despite personal problems
8. How to complain effectively

Informational: How Something Happens

1. How a student becomes burned out
2. How a library's card catalog or computerized catalog organizes books
3. How a dead thing decays (or some other natural process)
4. How the college registration process works
5. How *homo sapiens* choose a mate
6. How a VCR (or some other machine) works
7. How a bad habit develops
8. How people fall into debt

Assignments with a Specific Purpose, Audience, and Point of View

1. An author of books for elementary school children, you want to show children how to do something—take care of a pet, get along with siblings, keep a room clean. Explain the process in terms a child would understand yet not find condescending.

2. To help a sixteen-year-old friend learn how to drive, explain a specific driving maneuver one step at a time. You might, for example, describe how to make a three-point turn, parallel park, or handle a skid. Remember, your friend lacks self-confidence and experience.

3. Write an article for *Consumer Reports* on how to shop for a certain product. Give specific steps explaining how to save money, buy a quality product, and the like.

4. Write a process analysis showing how to save a life by CPR, rescue breathing, the Heimlich maneuver, or some other method. Your audience will be people from your neighborhood who are taking a first-aid class.

5. Your best friend plans to move into his or her own apartment but doesn't know the first thing about how to choose one. Explain the process of selecting an apartment—where to look, what to investigate, what questions to ask before signing a lease.

6. You write an "advice to the lovelorn" column for the campus newspaper. A correspondent writes saying that he or she wants to break up with a steady boyfriend/girlfriend but doesn't know how to do it without hurting the person. Give the writer guidance on how to end a meaningful relationship with a minimal amount of pain.

17
COMPARISON-CONTRAST

WHAT IS COMPARISON-CONTRAST?

WE frequently try to make sense of the world by finding similarities and differences in our experiences. Seeing how things are alike (**comparing**) and seeing how they are different (**contrasting**) helps us impose meaning on experiences that otherwise might remain fragmented and disconnected. Barely aware of the fact that we're comparing and contrasting, we may think to ourselves, "I woke up in a great mood this morning, but now I feel uneasy and anxious. I wonder why I feel so different." This inner questioning, which often occurs in a flash, is just one example of the way we use comparison and contrast to understand ourselves and our world.

Comparing and contrasting also helps us make choices. We compare and contrast everything—from two brands of soap we might buy to two colleges we might attend. We listen to a favorite radio station, watch a preferred nightly news show, select a particular dessert from a menu—all because we have done some degree of comparing and contrasting. We often weigh these alternatives in an unstudied, casual manner, as when we flip from one radio station to another. But when we have to make important decisions, we tend to think rigorously about how things are alike or different: Should I live in a dorm or rent an apartment? Should I accept the higher-paying job or the lower-paying one that offers more challenges? Such a deliberate approach to comparison-contrast may also provide us with needed insight into complex contemporary issues: Is television's coverage of political candidates more or less objective than it used to be? What are the merits of the various positions on abortion?

HOW COMPARISON-CONTRAST FITS YOUR PURPOSE AND AUDIENCE

When is it appropriate in writing to use the comparison-contrast pattern of development? Often an assignment's wording signals clearly that comparison-contrast is called for:

Compare the way male and female relationships are depicted in *Cosmopolitan, Ms., Playboy,* and *Esquire*. Which publication has the most limited view of men and women? Which has the broadest perspective?

Many social commentators have observed that both college students and their parents feel that colleges should equip young people with immediately marketable skills. Indicate whether you think this is an accurate assessment by comparing your own beliefs about the purpose of a college degree with those of your parents.

Football, basketball, and baseball differ in the ways they appeal to fans. Contrast the unique drawing power of each sport and arrive at some conclusions about the nature of each sport's following.

The issue of prayer in public school continues to receive attention. Take a position on the controversy by contrasting the views of those who believe prayer should be allowed in public schools with those who believe it should be prohibited.

Other assignments will, in less obvious ways, lend themselves to comparison-contrast. For instance, although the words *compare* and *contrast* don't appear in the following assignments, essay responses to the assignments could be organized around the comparison-contrast format:

The emergence of the two-career family is one of the major phenomena of our culture. Discuss the advantages and disadvantages of having both parents work, showing how you feel about such two-career households.

Some people believe that the 1950s, often called the golden age of television, produced several never-to-be equaled comedy classics. Do you agree that such shows as *I Love Lucy* and *The Honeymooners* are superior to the situation comedies aired on television today?

There has been considerable criticism recently of the news coverage by the city's two leading newspapers, the *Herald* and the *Beacon*. Indicate whether you think the criticism is valid by discussing the similarities and differences in the two papers' news coverage.

Note: The last assignment shows that a comparison-contrast essay may cover similarities *and* differences, not just one or the other.

As you have seen, comparison-contrast can be the key strategy for achieving an essay's purpose. But comparison-contrast can also be a supplemental method used to help make a point in an essay organized chiefly around another pattern of development. A serious, informative essay intended for laypeople might *define* clinical depression by contrasting that state of mind with ordinary run-of-the-mill blues. Writing humorously about the exhausting *effects* of trying to get in

Comparison-Contrast

shape, you might dramatize your plight for readers by contrasting the leisurely way you used to spend your day with your current rigidly compulsive exercise regimen. Or, in an urgent *argumentation-persuasion* essay on the need for stricter controls over drug abuse in the workplace, you might provide readers with background by comparing several companies' approaches to the problem.

PREWRITING STRATEGIES

The following checklist shows how you can apply to comparison-contrast some of the prewriting strategies discussed in Chapter 2.

✔ COMPARISON-CONTRAST: A PREWRITING CHECKLIST

Choose Subjects to Compare and Contrast

- What have you recently needed to compare and contrast (subjects to major in, events to attend, ways to resolve a disagreement) in order to make a choice? What would a comparison-contrast analysis disclose about the alternatives, your priorities, and the criteria by which you judge?
- Can you show a need for change by contrasting one way of doing something (say, the way your college awards athletic scholarships) with a better way (either imagined or actual)?
- Do any people you know show some striking similarities and differences? What would a comparison-contrast analysis reveal about their characters and the personal qualities you prize?
- How does your view on an issue (the legal drinking age, birth control, a new policy at your college) differ from that of other people (your parents, a friend, most students at your college)? What would a comparison-contrast analysis of these views indicate about your values?

Determine Your Purpose, Audience, Tone, and Point of View

- Is your purpose primarily to inform readers of similarities and differences? To evaluate your subjects' relative merits? To persuade readers to choose between alternative courses of action?
- What audience are you writing for? To what tone and point of view will they be most receptive?

Use Prewriting to Generate Points of Comparison-Contrast

- How could brainstorming, freewriting, mapping, or journal entries help you gather information about your subjects' most significant similarities and differences?

STRATEGIES FOR USING COMPARISON-CONTRAST IN AN ESSAY

After prewriting, you're ready to draft your essay. The following suggestions will be helpful whether you use comparison-contrast as a dominant or supportive pattern of development.

1. Be sure your subjects are at least somewhat alike. Unless you plan to develop an *analogy* (see the following numbered suggestion), the subjects you choose to compare or contrast should share some obvious characteristics or qualities. It makes sense to compare different parts of the country, two comedians, or several college teachers. But a reasonable paper wouldn't result from, let's say, a comparison of a television game show with a soap opera. Your subjects must belong to the same general group so that your comparison-contrast stays within logical bounds and doesn't veer off into pointlessness.

2. Stay focused on your purpose. When writing, remember that comparison-contrast isn't an end in itself. That is, your objective isn't to turn an essay into a mechanical list of "how *A* differs from *B*" or "how *A* is like *B*." As with the other patterns of development discussed in this book, comparison-contrast is a strategy for making a point or meeting a larger purpose.

Consider the assignment on page 316 about the two newspapers. Your purpose here might be simply to *inform*, to present information as objectively as possible: "This is what the *Herald's* news coverage is like. This is what the *Beacon's* news coverage is like."

More frequently, though, you'll use comparison-contrast to *evaluate* your subjects' pros and cons, your goal being to reach a conclusion or make a judgment: "Both the *Herald* and the *Beacon* spend too much time reporting local news," or "The *Herald's* analysis of the recent hostage crisis was more insightful than the *Beacon's*." Comparison-contrast can also be used to *persuade* readers to take action: "People interested in thorough coverage of international events should read the *Herald* rather than the *Beacon*." Persuasive essays may also propose a change, contrasting what now exists with a more ideal situation: "For the *Beacon* to compete with the *Herald*, it must assign more reporters to international stories."

Yet another purpose you might have in writing a comparison-contrast essay is to *clear up misconceptions* by revealing previously hidden similarities or differences. For example, perhaps your town's two newspapers are thought to be sharply different. However, a comparison-contrast analysis might reveal that—although one paper specializes in sensationalized stories while the other adopts a more muted approach—both resort to biased, emotionally charged analyses of local politics. Or the essay might illustrate that the tabloid's treatment of the local arts scene is surprisingly more comprehensive than that of its competitor.

Comparing and contrasting also make it possible to *draw an analogy* between two seemingly unrelated subjects. An analogy is an imaginative comparison that delves beneath the surface differences of subjects in order to expose their significant and often unsuspected similarities or differences. Your purpose may be to show that singles bars and zoos share a number of striking similarities. Or you may want to illustrate that wolves and humans raise their young in much the same way, but that wolves go about the process in a more civilized manner. The analogical approach can make a complex subject easier to understand—as, for example, when the national deficit is compared to a household budget gone awry. Analogies are often dramatic and instructive, challenging you and your audience to consider subjects in a new light. But analogies don't speak for themselves. You must make clear to the reader how the analogy demonstrates your purpose.

3. Formulate a strong thesis. An essay that is developed primarily through comparison-contrast should be focused by a solid thesis. Besides revealing your attitude, the thesis will often do the following:

- Name the subjects being compared and contrasted.
- Indicate whether the essay focuses on the subjects' similarities, differences, or both.
- State the essay's main point of comparison or contrast.

Not all comparison-contrast essays need thesis statements as structured as those that follow. Even so, these examples can serve as models of clarity. Note that the first thesis statement signals similarities, the second differences, and the last both similarities and differences:

Middle-aged parents are often in a good position to empathize with adolescent children because the emotional upheavals experienced by the two age groups are much the same.

The priorities of most retired people are more conducive to health and happiness than the priorities of most young professionals.

College students in their thirties and forties face many of the same pressures as younger students, but they are better equipped to withstand these pressures.

4. Select the points to be discussed. Once you have identified the essay's subject, purpose, and thesis, you need to decide which of the many points generated during prewriting you will discuss: You have to identify which aspects of the subjects to compare or contrast. College professors, for instance, could be compared and contrasted on the basis of their testing methods, ability to motivate students, confidence in front of a classroom, personalities, level of enthusiasm, and so forth.

When selecting points to cover, be sure to consider your audience. Ask yourself: "Will my readers be familiar with this item? Will I need it to get my message across? Will my audience find this item interesting or convincing?" What your readers know, what they don't know, and what you can project about their reactions should influence your choices. And, of course, you need to select points that support your thesis. If your essay explains the differences between healthy, sensible diets and dangerous crash diets, it wouldn't be appropriate to talk about aerobic exercise. Similarly, imagine you want to write an essay making the point that, despite their differences, hard rock of the 1960s and punk rock of the 1970s both reflected young people's disillusionment with society. It wouldn't make much sense to contrast the long uncombed hairstyles of the 1960s with the short spikey cuts of the 1970s. But contrasting song lyrics (protest versus nihilistic messages) would help support your thesis and lead to interesting insights.

5. Organize the points to be discussed. After deciding which points to include, you should use a systematic, logical plan for presenting those ideas. If the points aren't organized, your essay will be little more than a confusing jumble of ideas. There are two common ways to organize an essay developed wholly or in part by comparison-contrast: the one-side-at-a-time method and the point-by-point method. Although both strategies may be used in a paper, one method usually predominates.

In the **one-side-at-a-time method** of organization, you discuss everything relevant about one subject before moving to another subject. For example, responding to the earlier assignment that asked you to analyze the news coverage in two local papers, you might first talk about the *Herald*'s coverage of international, national, and local news; then you would discuss the *Beacon*'s coverage of the same categories. Note that the areas discussed should be the same for both newspapers. It wouldn't be logical to review the *Herald*'s coverage of international, national, and local news and then to detail the *Beacon*'s magazine supplements, modern living section, and comics page. Moreover, the areas compared and contrasted should be presented in the same order.

This is how you would organize the essay using the one-side-at-a-time method:

Everything about subject A   *Herald*'s news coverage:
- International
- National
- Local

Everything about subject B   *Beacon*'s news coverage:
- International
- National
- Local

In the **point-by-point method** of organization, you alternate from one aspect of the first subject to the same aspect of your other subject(s). For example, to use this method when comparing or contrasting the *Herald* and the *Beacon,* you would first discuss the *Herald*'s international coverage, then the *Beacon*'s international coverage; next, the *Herald*'s national coverage, then the *Beacon*'s; and finally, the *Herald*'s local coverage, then the *Beacon*'s.

An essay using the point-by-point method would be organized like this:

First aspect of subjects A and B	*Beacon:* International coverage
	Herald: International coverage
Second aspect of subjects A and B	*Beacon:* National coverage
	Herald: National coverage
Third aspect of subjects A and B	*Beacon:* Local coverage
	Herald: Local coverage

Deciding which of these two methods of organization to use is largely a personal choice, though there are several factors to consider. The one-side-at-a-time method tends to convey a more unified feeling because it highlights broad similarities and differences. It is, therefore, an effective approach for subjects that are fairly uncomplicated. This strategy also works well when essays are brief; the reader won't find it difficult to remember what has been said about subject *A* when reading about subject *B*.

Because the point-by-point method permits more extensive coverage of similarities and differences, it is often a wise choice when subjects are complex. This pattern is also useful for lengthy essays since readers would probably find it difficult to remember, let's say, ten pages of information about subject *A* while reading the next ten pages about subject *B*. The point-by-point approach, however, may cause readers to lose sight of the broader picture, so remember to keep them focused on your central point.

6. Supply the reader with clear transitions. Although a well-organized comparison-contrast format is important, it doesn't guarantee that readers will be able to follow your line of thought easily. *Transitions*—especially those signaling similarities or differences—are needed to show readers where they have been and where they are going. Such cues are essential in all writing, but they're especially crucial in a paper using comparison-contrast. By indicating clearly when subjects are being compared or contrasted, the transitions help weave the discussion into a coherent whole.

The transitions (in boldface) in the following examples could be used to *signal similarities* in an essay discussing the news coverage in the *Herald* and the *Beacon*:

- The *Beacon* **also** allots only a small portion of the front page to global news.
- **In the same way,** the *Herald* tries to include at least three local stories on the first page.
- **Likewise,** the *Beacon* emphasizes the importance of up-to-date reporting of town meetings.
- The *Herald* is **similarly** committed to extensive coverage of high school and college sports.

The transitions (in boldface) in these examples could be used to *signal differences:*

- **By way of contrast,** the *Herald*'s editorial page deals with national matters on the average of three times a week.
- **On the other hand,** the *Beacon* does not share the *Herald*'s enthusiasm for interviews with national figures.
- The *Beacon,* **however,** does not encourage its reporters to tackle national stories the way the *Herald* does.
- **But** the *Herald*'s coverage of the Washington scene is much more comprehensive than its competitor's.

REVISION STRATEGIES

Once you have a draft of the essay, you're ready to revise. The following checklist will help you and those giving you feedback apply to comparison-contrast some of the revision techniques discussed in Chapters 7 and 8.

✔ COMPARISON-CONTRAST: A REVISION CHECKLIST

Revise Overall Meaning and Structure

- Are the subjects sufficiently alike for the comparison-contrast to be logical and meaningful?
- What purpose does the essay serve? Does it inform? Evaluate? Persuade readers to accept a viewpoint and perhaps take action? Eliminate misconceptions or draw a surprising analogy?
- What is the essay's thesis? How could the thesis be stated more effectively?
- Is the overall essay organized primarily by the one-side-at-a-time method or by the point-by-point method? What is the advantage of that strategy for this essay?
- Regardless of the method used to organize the essay, are the same features discussed for each subject? What are the features? Are they discussed in the same order?
- Which points of comparison and/or contrast might be unfamiliar to readers? Do these need further development? Which points should be deleted because they're unconvincing or irrelevant? Where do significant points seem to be missing? How has the most important point of similarity or difference been emphasized?

Comparison-Contrast

Revise Paragraph Development
- If the essay uses the one-side-at-a-time method, which paragraph marks the switch from one subject to another?
- If the essay uses the point-by-point method, do paragraphs consistently alternate between subjects (one aspect of one subject, then the same aspect for another subject, and so on)? If this alternation becomes too elaborate or predictable, what could be done to eliminate the problem?
- If the essay uses both the one-side-at-a-time and the point-by-point methods, which paragraph marks the switch from one method to the other? If the switch is confusing, how could it be made less so?
- Where would transitions signaling similarities (*also, likewise, in the same way*) and differences (*on the other hand, however, in contrast*) make it easier to follow the line of thought within and between paragraphs?

Revise Sentences and Words
- Where do too many transitions make sentences awkward and mechanical?
- Which sentences and words fail to convey the intended tone?

STUDENT ESSAY: FROM PREWRITING THROUGH REVISION

The student essay that follows was written by Carol Siskin in response to this assignment:

> In "Neat People vs. Sloppy People," Suzanne Britt contrasts two personality types, extolling the one normally considered less praiseworthy. In an essay of your own, contrast two personality types, life-styles, or stages of life, showing that the one most people consider inferior is actually superior.

Having recently turned forty, Carol decided to write an essay taking issue with the idea that being young is better than being old. From time to time, Carol had used her *journal* to explore what it means to grow older. Rather than writing a new journal entry on the subject, she decided to look at earlier entries to see if they contained any helpful material for the assignment. One rather free-ranging entry, typewritten the evening of her birthday, proved especially valuable. The original entry is shown on the next page. The handwritten marks indicate Carol's later efforts to shape and develop this raw material. Note the way Carol added details, circled main ideas, and indicated a possible sequence.

These annotations paved the way for her outline, which is presented after the journal entry.

Journal Entry

Forty years old today. At 20 I thought 40 would mean the end of everything, but that's not the case at all. I'm much happier now.

Possible conclusion

Mom and Dad made a dinner for the occasion. Talking of happy, they look great. Mom said this is the best part of their lives. They love retirement--and obviously each other. I hope Mitch and I will be that happy when we're in our sixties. And Dave and Elaine seem as good as ever. They look right together. What a pleasure it is to be a couple. I remember how lonely I was before Mitch and how lonely Dave was after his divorce. I sure don't envy young singles.

I (Appearance)

My diets. Hated big waist and legs.

Dave seems content now. He looks handsome and robust, partly because he feels good about his life, partly because he tries to run pretty regularly. I remember how desperately he used to work out with weights because he worried about his appearance. I'm glad I don't have to be obsessed with my appearance the way I used to be. Mitch loves me the way I am. And I'm not obsessed anymore with being super stylish. Or thin. In fact, tonight, with no qualms whatever, I ate two healthy slices of birthday cake.

blazers vs. leather jackets

II (Decisions)

Dave says that Nancy (I can't believe she's 22) is thinking of going to graduate school, but she's not sure what to study. I can remember all the confusion I felt about schools and majors. I don't miss those days at all. Dave thinks Nancy is just plain confused about who she is and what she wants. Her goals change from day to day, especially because she's trying to please everyone. One day she feels confident; the next she's frightened. And she blames her parents' unhappy marriage for her confusion. No wonder she can't decide whether to marry and have kids. What chaos!

III (Sense of self)

II

Tonight, though, was anything but chaos and confusion. It was an evening of quiet contentment. All of us enjoyed each other and got along. Quite different from the way it used to be. How I used to fight with Mom and Dad. I remember slamming the door and yelling, "It's your fault I was born." What unhappy times those were.

Comparison-Contrast

Outline

Thesis: Being young is good, but being older is better.

I. Appearance
   A. Dave and I when young
      1. Dave's weight lifting to build himself up
      2. My constant dieting to change my body
      3. Both begging for "right" clothes
   B. Attitudes now
      1. My contentment with my rounded shape
      2. Dave's satisfaction with his thinness
      3. Our clothes fashionable but comfortable

II. Decisions
   A. My major decisions mostly in the past
      1. About education
      2. About marriage and children
   B. Nancy's major decisions mostly in the future
      1. About education
      2. About marriage and children

III. Sense of self
   A. Nancy's uncertainty
      1. Unclear values and goals
      2. Strong need to be liked
      3. Unresolved feelings about parents
   B. Older person's surer self-identity
      1. Have clearer values and goals
      2. Can stand being unliked
      3. Don't blame parents

Now read Carol's paper, "The Virtues of Growing Older," noting the similarities and differences among her journal entry, outline, and final essay. You'll see that the essay is more developed than either the journal entry or outline. In the essay, Carol added numerous specific details—like those about Dave gobbling vitamins and milk shakes when he was a teen. In contrast, she omitted from the essay some journal material because it would have required burdensome explanations. For instance, if she hadn't eliminated the reference to Nancy, it would have been necessary to explain that Nancy is the daughter of Dave's wife by her first marriage. Despite these differences, you'll note that the essay's basic plan is derived largely from the journal entry and outline. As you read the essay, also consider how well it applies the principles of comparison-contrast discussed in this chapter. (The commentary that follows the paper will help you look at Carol's essay more closely and will give you some sense of how she went about revising her first draft.)

The Virtues of Growing Older
by Carol Siskin

The first of a two-paragraph introduction

Our society worships youth. Advertisements convince us to buy Grecian Formula and Oil of Olay so we can hide the gray in our hair and smooth the lines on our face. Television shows feature attractive young stars with firm bodies, perfect complexions, and thick manes of hair. Middle-aged folks work out in gyms and jog down the street, trying to delay the effects of age.

The second introductory paragraph

Thesis

Wouldn't any person over thirty gladly sign with the devil just to be young again? Isn't aging an experience to be dreaded? Perhaps it is un-American to say so, but I believe the answer is "No." Being young is often pleasant, but being older has distinct advantages.

First half of topic sentence for point 1: Appearance

Start of what it's like being young

When young, you are apt to be obsessed with your appearance. When my brother Dave and I were teens, we worked feverishly to perfect the bodies we had. Dave lifted weights, took megadoses of vitamins, and drank a half-dozen milk shakes a day in order to turn his wiry adolescent frame into some muscular ideal. And as a teenager, I dieted constantly. No matter what I weighed, though, I was never satisfied with the way I looked. My legs were too heavy, my shoulders too broad, my waist too big. When Dave and I were young, we begged and pleaded for the "right" clothes. If our parents didn't get them for us, we felt our world would fall apart. How could we go to school wearing loose-fitting blazers when everyone else would be wearing smartly tailored leather jackets? We could be considered freaks. I often wonder how my parents, and parents in general, manage to tolerate their children during the adolescent years.

Second half of topic sentence for point 1

Start of what it's like being older

Now, however, Dave and I are beyond such adolescent agonies. My rounded figure seems fine, and I don't deny myself a slice of pecan pie if I feel in the mood. Dave still works out, but he has actually become fond of his tall, lanky frame. The two of us enjoy wearing fashionable clothes, but we are no longer slaves to style. And women, I'm embarrassed to admit, even more than men, have always seemed to be at the mercy of fashion. Now my clothes--and my brother's--are attractive yet easy to wear. We no longer feel anxious about what others will think. As long as we feel good about how we look, we are happy.

Being older is preferable to being younger in another way. Obviously, I still have important choices to make about my life, but I have already made many of the critical decisions that confront those just starting out. I chose the man I wanted to marry. I decided to have children. I elected to return to college to complete my education. But when you are young, major decisions await you at every turn. "What college should I attend? What career should I pursue? Should I get married? Should I have children?" There are just a few of the issues facing young people. It's no wonder that, despite their carefree facade, they are often confused, uncertain, and troubled by all the unknowns in their future.

But the greatest benefit of being forty is knowing who I am. The most unsettling aspect of youth is the uncertainty you feel about your values, goals, and dreams. Being young means wondering what is worth working for. Being young means feeling happy with yourself one day and wishing you were never born the next. It means trying on new selves by taking up with different crowds. It means resenting your parents and their way of life one minute and then feeling you will never be as good or as accomplished as they are. By way of contrast, forty is sanity. I have a surer self-identity now. I don't laugh at jokes I don't think are funny. I can make a speech in front of a town meeting or complain in a store because I am no longer terrified that people will laugh at me; I am no longer anxious that everyone must like me. I no longer blame my parents for my every personality quirk or keep a running score of everything they did wrong raising me. Life has taught me that I, not they, am responsible for who I am. We are all human beings--neither saints nor devils.

Most Americans blindly accept the idea that newer is automatically better. But a human life contradicts this premise. There is a great deal of happiness to be found as we grow older. My own parents, now in their sixties, recently told me that they are happier now than they have ever been. They would not want to be my age. Did this surprise me? At first, yes. Then it gladdened me. Their contentment holds out great promise for me as I move into the next--perhaps even better--phase of my life.

Commentary

Purpose and Thesis

In her essay, Carol disproves the widespread belief that being young is preferable to being old. The *comparison-contrast* pattern allows her to analyze the drawbacks of one and the merits of the other, thus providing the essay with an *evaluative purpose*. Using the title to indicate her point of view, Carol places the *thesis* at the end of her two-paragraph introduction: "Being young is often pleasant, but being older has distinct advantages." Note that the thesis accomplishes several things. It names the two subjects to be discussed and clarifies Carol's point of view about her subjects. The thesis also implies that the essay will focus on the contrasts between these two periods of life.

Points of Support and Overall Organization

To support her assertion that older is better, Carol supplies examples from her own life and organizes the examples around three main points: attitudes about appearance, decisions about life choices, and questions of self-concept. Using the *point-by-point method* to organize the overall essay, she explores each of these key ideas in a separate paragraph. Each paragraph is further focused by one or two sentences that serve as a topic sentence.

Sequence of Points, Organizational Cues, and Paragraph Development

Let's look more closely at the way Carol presents her three central points in the essay. She obviously considers appearance the least important of a person's worries, life choices more important, and self-concept the most critical. So she uses *emphatic order* to sequence the supporting paragraphs, with the phrase "But the greatest benefit" signaling the special significance of the last issue. Carol is also careful to use *transitions* to help readers follow her line of thinking: "*Now, however,* Dave and I are beyond such adolescent agonies" (3); "*But* when you are young, major decisions await you at every turn" (4); and "*By way of contrast,* forty is sanity" (5).

Although Carol has worked hard to write a well-organized paper—and has on the whole been successful—she doesn't feel compelled to make the paper fit a rigid format. As you've seen, the essay as a whole uses the point-by-point method, but each supporting paragraph uses the *one-side-at-a-time method*—that is, everything about one age group is discussed before there is a shift to the other age group. Notice too that the third and fifth paragraphs start with young people and then move to adults, whereas the fourth paragraph reverses the sequence by starting with older people.

Other Patterns of Development

Carol obviously uses the comparison-contrast format to organize her ideas, but other patterns of development also come into play. To illustrate her points, she makes extensive use of *illustration,* and her discussion also contains elements typical of *causal analysis.* Throughout the essay, for instance, she traces the effect of being a certain age on her brother, herself, and her parents.

Comparison-Contrast

A Problem with Unity

As you read the third paragraph, you might have noted that Carol's essay runs into a problem. Two sentences in the paragraph disrupt the *unity* of Carol's discussion: "I often wonder how my parents, and parents in general, manage to tolerate their children during the adolescent years," and "women, I'm embarrassed to admit . . . have always seemed to be at the mercy of fashion." These sentences should be deleted because they don't develop the idea that adolescents are overly concerned with appearance.

Conclusion

Carol's final paragraph brings the essay to a pleasing and interesting close. The conclusion recalls the point made in the introduction: Americans overvalue youth. Carol also uses the conclusion to broaden the scope of her discussion. Rather than continuing to focus on herself, she briefly mentions her parents and the pleasure they take in life. By bringing her parents into the essay, Carol is able to make a gently philosophical observation about the promise that awaits her as she grows older. The implication is that a similarly positive future awaits us, too.

Revising the First Draft

To help guide her revision, Carol asked her husband to read her first draft aloud. As he did, Carol took notes on what she sensed were the paper's strengths and weaknesses. She then jotted down her observations, as well as her husband's, onto the draft. Because Carol wasn't certain which observations were most valid, she didn't rank them. Carol made a number of changes when revising the essay. You'll get a good sense of how she proceeded if you compare the annotated original introduction reprinted here with the final version in the full essay.

Original Version of the Introduction

America is a land filled with people who worship youth. We admire dynamic young achievers; our middle-aged citizens work out in gyms; all of us wear tight tops and colorful sneakers--clothes that look fine on the young but ridiculous on aging bodies. Television shows revolve around perfect-looking young stars, while commercials entice us with products that will keep us young.

Wouldn't every older person want to be young again? Isn't aging to be avoided? It may be slightly unpatriotic to say so, but I believe the answer is "No." Being young may be pleasant at times, but I would rather be my forty-year-old self. I no longer have to agonize about my physical appearance, I have already made many of my crucial life decisions, and I am much less confused about who I am.

Boring paragraph
First sentence dull
Cut?

Make point about TV more specific

Make questions more vigorous

Maybe cut plan of development

After hearing her original two-paragraph introduction read aloud, Carol was dissatisfied with what she had written. Although she wasn't quite sure how to proceed, she knew that the paragraphs were flat and that they failed to open the essay on a strong note. She decided to start by whittling down the opening sentence, making it crisper and more powerful: "Our society worships youth." That done, she eliminated two bland statements ("We admire dynamic young achievers," and "all of us wear tight tops and colorful sneakers") and made several vague references more concrete and interesting. For example, "Commercials entice us with products that will keep us young" became "Grecian Formula and Oil of Olay . . . hide the gray in our hair and smooth the lines on our face"; "perfect-looking young stars" became "attractive young stars with firm bodies, perfect complexions, and thick manes of hair." With the addition of these specifics, the first paragraph became more vigorous and interesting.

Carol next made some subtle changes in the two questions that opened the second paragraph of the original introduction. She replaced "Wouldn't every older person want to be young again?" and "Isn't aging to be avoided?" with two more emphatic questions: "Wouldn't any person over thirty gladly sign with the devil just to be young again?" and "Isn't aging an experience to be dreaded?" Carol also made some changes at the end of the original second paragraph. Because the paper is relatively short and the subject matter easy to understand, she decided to omit her somewhat awkward *plan of development* ("I no longer have to agonize about my physical appearance, I have already made many of my crucial life decisions, and I am much less confused about who I am"). This deletion made it possible to end the introduction with a clear statement of the essay's thesis.

Once these revisions were made, Carol was confident that her essay got off to a stronger start. Feeling reassured, she moved ahead and made changes in other sections of her paper. Such work enabled her to prepare a solid piece of writing that offers food for thought.

ACTIVITIES: COMPARISON-CONTRAST

Prewriting Activities

1. Imagine you're writing two essays: One explores the effects of holding a job while in college; the other explains how to budget money wisely. Jot down ways you might use comparison-contrast in each essay.

2. Suppose you plan to write a series of articles for your college newspaper. What purpose might you have for comparing and/or contrasting each of the following subject pairs?

   a. Audio tapes and compact discs
   b. Paper or plastic bags at the supermarket
   c. Two courses—one taught by an inexperienced newcomer, the other by an old pro
   d. Cutting class and not showing up at work

3. Use the patterns of development or another prewriting technique to compare and/or contrast a current situation with the way you would like it to be. After reviewing your prewriting material, decide what your purpose, audience, tone, and point of view might be if you were to write an essay. Finally, write out your thesis and main supporting points.

4. Using your journal or freewriting, jot down the advantages and disadvantages of two ways of doing something (for example, watching movies in the theater versus watching them on a VCR at home; following trends versus ignoring them; dating one person versus playing the field; and so on). Reread your prewriting and determine what your thesis, purpose, audience, tone, and point of view might be if you were to write an essay. Make a scratch list of the main ideas you would cover. Would a point-by-point or a one-side-at-a-time method of organization work more effectively?

Revising Activities

5. Of the statements that follow, which would *not* make effective thesis statements for comparison-contrast essays? Identify the problem(s) in the faulty statements and revise them accordingly.

   a. Although their classroom duties often overlap, teacher aides are not as equipped as teachers to handle disciplinary problems.
   b. This college provides more assistance to its students than most schools.
   c. During the state's last congressional election, both candidates relied heavily on television to communicate their messages.
   d. There are many differences between American and foreign cars.

6. The following paragraph is from the draft of an essay detailing the qualities of a skillful manager. How effective is this comparison-contrast paragraph? What revisions would help focus the paragraph on the point made in the topic sentence? Where should details be added or deleted? Rewrite the paragraph, providing necessary transitions and details.

A manager encourages creativity and treats employees courteously, while a boss discourages staff resourcefulness and views it as a threat. At the hardware store where I work, I got my boss's approval to develop a system for organizing excess stock in the storeroom. I shelved items in roughly the same order as they were displayed in the store. The system was helpful to all the salespeople, not just to me, since everyone was stymied by the boss's helter-skelter system. What he did was store overstocked items according to each wholesaler, even though most of us weren't there long enough to know which items came from which wholesaler. His supposed system created chaos. When he saw what I had done, he was furious and insisted that we continue to follow the old slap-dash system. I had assumed he would welcome my ideas the way my manager did last summer when I worked in a drugstore. But he didn't and I had to scrap my work and go back to his eccentric system. He certainly could learn something about employee relations from the drugstore manager.

PROFESSIONAL SELECTIONS: COMPARISON-CONTRAST

SUZANNE BRITT

Suzanne Britt has written for such diverse publications as *Books and Religion,* the *New York Times,* the *Baltimore Sun,* and *Newsday.* Her books include *Skinny People Are Dull and Crunchy Like Carrots* (1982); *Show and Tell* (1983), from which the following essay is taken; and *A Writer's Rhetoric* (1988).

NEAT PEOPLE VS. SLOPPY PEOPLE

1   I've finally figured out the difference between neat people and sloppy people. The distinction is, as always, moral. Neat people are lazier and meaner than sloppy people.

2   Sloppy people, you see, are not really sloppy. Their sloppiness is merely the unfortunate consequence of their extreme moral rectitude. Sloppy people carry in their mind's eye a heavenly vision, a precise plan, that is so stupendous, so perfect, it can't be achieved in this world or the next.

3   Sloppy people live in Never-Never Land. Someday is their métier. Someday they are planning to alphabetize all their books and set up home catalogues. Someday they will go through their wardrobes and mark certain items for tentative mending and certain items for passing on to relatives of similar shape and size. Someday sloppy people will make family scrapbooks into which they will put newspaper clippings, postcards, locks of hair, and the dried corsage from their senior prom. Someday they will file everything on the surface of their desks, including the cash receipts from coffee

purchases at the snack shop. Someday they will sit down and read all the back issues of *The New Yorker.*

4   For all these noble reasons and more, sloppy people never get neat. They aim too high and wide. They save everything, planning someday to file, order, and straighten out the world. But while these ambitious plans take clearer and clearer shape in their heads, the books spill from the shelves onto the floor, the clothes pile up in the hamper and closet, the family mementos accumulate in every drawer, the surface of the desk is buried under mounds of paper and the unread magazines threaten to reach the ceiling.

5   Sloppy people can't bear to part with anything. They give loving attention to every detail. When sloppy people say they're going to tackle the surface of the desk, they really mean it. Not a paper will go unturned; not a rubber band will go unboxed. Four hours or two weeks into the excavation, the desk looks exactly the same, primarily because the sloppy person is meticulously creating new piles of papers with new headings and scrupulously stopping to read all the old book catalogs before he throws them away. A neat person would just bulldoze the desk.

6   Neat people are bums and clods at heart. They have cavalier attitudes toward possessions, including family heirlooms. Everything is just another dust-catcher to them. If anything collects dust, it's got to go and that's that. Neat people will toy with the idea of throwing the children out of the house just to cut down on the clutter.

7   Neat people don't care about process. They like results. What they want to do is get the whole thing over with so they can sit down and watch the rasslin' on TV. Neat people operate on two unvarying principles: Never handle any item twice, and throw everything away.

8   The only thing messy in a neat person's house is the trash can. The minute something comes to a neat person's hand, he will look at it, try to decide if it has immediate use and, finding none, throw it in the trash.

9   Neat people are especially vicious with mail. They never go through their mail unless they are standing directly over a trash can. If the trash can is beside the mailbox, even better. All ads, catalogs, pleas for charitable contributions, church bulletins and money-saving coupons go straight into the trash can without being opened. All letters from home, postcards from Europe, bills and paychecks are opened, immediately responded to, then dropped in the trash can. Neat people keep their receipts only for tax purposes. That's it. No sentimental salvaging of birthday cards or the last letter a dying relative ever wrote. Into the trash it goes.

10 Neat people place neatness above everything, even economics. They are incredibly wasteful. Neat people throw away several toys every time they walk through the den. I knew a neat person once who threw away a perfectly good dish drainer because it had mold on it. The drainer was too much trouble to wash. And neat people sell their furniture when they move. They will sell a La-Z-Boy recliner while you are reclining in it.

11 Neat people are no good to borrow from. Neat people buy everything in expensive little single portions. They get their flour and sugar in two-pound bags. They wouldn't consider clipping a coupon, saving a leftover, reusing plastic non-dairy whipped cream containers or rinsing off tin foil and draping it over the unmoldy dish drainer. You can never borrow a neat person's newspaper to see what's playing at the movies. Neat people have the paper all wadded up and in the trash by 7:05 a.m.

12 Neat people cut a clean swath through the organic as well as the inorganic world. People, animals, and things are all one to them. They are so insensitive. After they've finished with the pantry, the medicine cabinet, and the attic, they will throw out the red geranium (too many leaves), sell the dog (too many fleas), and send the children off to boarding school (too many scuffmarks on the hardwood floors).

Questions for Close Reading

1. What is the selection's thesis? Locate the sentence(s) in which Britt states her main idea. If she doesn't state the thesis explicitly, express it in your own words.

2. According to Britt, the sloppy person has "noble reasons" (paragraph 4) for being sloppy. What are they?

3. What does Britt criticize about neat people's attitude toward things?

4. What type would you guess that Britt is—neat or sloppy? Why do you feel this way?

5. Refer to your dictionary as needed to define the following words used in the selection: *rectitude* (paragraph 2), *métier* (3), *cavalier* (6), and *swath* (12).

Questions About the Writer's Craft

1. The pattern. Which comparison-contrast format does Britt use to organize her essay? Why do you suppose she selected this approach?

2. Why do you think Britt discusses sloppy and neat people in the order she does?

3. Britt makes extensive use of short sentences in the paragraphs on neat people. What is the effect? What sentence length predominates in the discussion of sloppy people? What is the effect?

4. How does Britt achieve her humorous tone? What kinds of words and images does she use to make readers chuckle?

Writing Assignments Using Comparison-Contrast as a Pattern of Development

1. Britt contrasts two types of people and finds superior the type we usually criticize. Write your own tongue-in-cheek contrast essay showing that a personality type we generally consider inferior is actually superior to its opposite. For example, you might show that being shy is better than being extroverted or that being a class cut-up is preferable to being a conscientious student.

2. Write a serious or playful essay contrasting the characteristics of two kinds of people belonging to the same general category (for example, two teachers, coaches, rock musicians). You might, for instance, contrast "old-fashioned grandmas" with "trend-setting grandmothers." Either imply or state your attitude toward the two types.

Writing Assignments Using Other Patterns of Development

3. What kind of person are you—organized or disorganized, carefree or careworn, casual or formal? Write a straightforward or tongue-in-cheek essay describing yourself. Be sure to provide abundant details to develop your self-portrait.

4. Sloppy people aren't the only ones who follow the "someday" approach to life. Focusing either on personal experience (your own or someone else's) or on a campus or community situation, write an essay that examines the effects of procrastination. Your essay may be humorous or serious.

JACK NEWFIELD

Journalist Jack Newfield (1939–) served as editor and columnist for the *Village Voice* until 1988, when he joined the editorial staff of the *New York Daily News*. His numerous books include *Robert Kennedy: A Memoir* (1969) and *City for Sale* (1989), which describes the reign of New York City Mayor Ed Koch. The following essay first appeared in *Playboy* magazine in 1986.

STALLONE VS. SPRINGSTEEN

1   Bruce Springsteen and Sylvester Stallone are the two great working-class heroes of American mass culture. Springsteen had the best-selling album of 1985 and Stallone had the second most successful movie. On the surface, they share stunning similarities of biceps, bandannas, American flags, Vietnam themes, praise from President Reagan and uplifting feelings of national pride. Bumper stickers proclaim, BRUCE—THE RAMBO OF ROCK.

2   But beneath the surface—and between the lines—these two American heroes of the eighties are sending opposite messages. They are subtly pulling the 18-to-35-year-old generation toward two competing visions of the American future.

3   Stallone's *Rocky* and *Rambo* films—especially the latter—are about violence and revenge in a context of fantasy. Rambo never pays a price in body bags or pain or blood or doubt or remorse or fear. The enemy is stereotyped and therefore dehumanized. The emotions Stallone liberates are hostility and aggression: Audiences come out of the theater wanting to kick some Commie ass in Nicaragua.

4   By contrast, the essential human feeling Springsteen liberates is empathy—compassion for the common man trapped in the dead-end world of the hourly wage. The realistic words of Springsteen's best songs are about the hurt of unemployed workers; about reconciliation with estranged parents through understanding *their* lives; about staying hopeful even though experience falls short of the American dream.

5   In *Rambo* Stallone depicts the Vietnam veteran as a killing machine, a deranged, rampaging executioner. In "Born in the U.S.A.," Springsteen depicts the Vietnam veteran as neglected—wanting to be reintegrated into society as a normal person but getting the brush-off from a bureaucrat at the Veterans Administration. Recall the misunderstood and misheard words of the Springsteen anthem:

> Got in a little hometown jam,
> So they put a rifle in my hand.
> Sent me off to a foreign land
> To go and kill the yellow man. . . .
> Come back home to the refinery.
> Hiring man says, "Son, if it was up to me. . . ."

Went down to see my VA man;
He said, "Son, don't you understand now?"
I had a brother at Khé Sanh
Fighting off the Viet Cong.
They're still there; he's all gone.
He had a woman he loved in Saigon—
I got a picture of him in her arms now. . . .

The difference between Stallone and Springsteen is perhaps best illuminated by reading an essay George Orwell wrote in 1945, before either Stallone or Springsteen was born. In the essay, "Notes on Nationalism," Orwell makes a distinction between nationalism and patriotism and then suggests that they are, in fact, opposites.

> By "nationalism" I mean first of all the habit of assuming that human beings can be classified like insects and that whole blocks of millions or tens of millions of people can confidently be labeled "good" or "bad." But secondly—and this is much more important—I mean the habit of identifying oneself with a single nation or other unit, placing it beyond good and evil and recognizing no other duty than that of advancing its interests. Nationalism is not to be confused with patriotism . . . since two different and even opposing ideas are involved. By "patriotism" I mean a devotion to a particular place and a particular way of life, which one believes to be the best in the world but has no wish to force upon other people. Patriotism is of its nature defensive, both militarily and culturally. Nationalism, on the other hand, is inseparable from the desire for power. . . .
>
> It can plausibly be argued, for instance—it is even probably true—that patriotism is an inoculation against nationalism.

Stallone as Rambo snarls, "Damn Russian bastards" and kills a few more. Springsteen introduces "This Land is Your Land," the first encore at all his concerts, as "the greatest song ever written about America," and then reminds his fans, "Remember, *nobody wins unless everybody wins.*" That's one difference between nationalism and patriotism.

Stallone manipulates Americans' feelings of frustration over the lost Vietnam war and helps create a jingoistic climate of emotion in which a future war might be welcomed. Springsteen asks us to honor the neglected and rejected Vietnam veterans, so that we won't glide gleefully into the next war without remembering the real cost of the last one. That's a second difference between nationalism and patriotism.

"It's a right-wing fantasy," said Stallone, talking to *Time* about last summer's big hit. "What Rambo is saying is that if they could fight again, it would be different." He added that he was looking for another "open wound" as a site for a sequel, possibly Iran or Afghanistan.

Ron Kovic is a paraplegic author and Vietnam veteran. As an honored guest at Springsteen's opening-night concert last August at the Giants' stadium in New Jersey, Kovic told reporters, "I've been sitting in this wheelchair for the past 18 years. And I can only thank Bruce Springsteen for all he has done for Vietnam veterans. 'Born in the U.S.A.' is a beautiful song that helped me personally to heal." The difference between looking for another open wound as a movie backdrop and creating music that is healing—that's a third distinction between nationalism and patriotism. . . .

Nationalism, as defined by Orwell, is an intoxicating but essentially negative emotion, because it is, by its very nature, intolerant. It does not respect the rights of minorities or the dignity of neighbors. It is a will to power that negates complexity. Its most extreme avatars are monstrous lunatics such as Khomeini, Qaddafi, Botha, Farrakhan and Kahane.

Comparison-Contrast

14   The milder form of nationalism, as represented by Stallone, is less harmful. Stallone doesn't have Governmental power, and he doesn't push the issue; he usually retreats behind his movie character and tells most interviewers he is nonpolitical.

15   But the messages his images communicate to masses of impressionable young people sometimes do have damaging consequences. For example, the week *Rambo*, with its negative stereotypes of Asians, opened in Boston last spring, there were two incidents in which Southeast Asian refugees were badly beaten up by gangs of white youths.

16   In the more recent *Rocky IV*—which Stallone wrote, directed and starred in—the villainous foe is a Russian who fights dirty, takes illegal steroid injections and wears a black mouthpiece. Cleverly named Ivan Drago, he is depicted as a robotlike extension of the Evil Empire. Critics have written that it is the most simplistic and one-dimensional of all the *Rocky* movies. It lacks the interesting subplots and realistic blue-collar atmosphere of the original *Rocky*, with its loan shark and neighborhood gym; this time, Stallone literally and figuratively wraps himself in the American flag—proving that sequels are the last refuge of nationalists.

17   The worst features of Stallone's nationalism are the values it enshrines and reinforces: racism, violence, militarism and—possibly most subversive of all—simplicity. The convergence of these emotions can make war and foreign intervention seem like a sporting event. Or a movie.

18   Bruce Springsteen's patriotism is rooted in a different set of values, apparent in his songs: the old-fashioned virtues of work, family, community, loyalty, dignity, perseverance, love of country. His fundamental theme is the gap between America's promise and performance and his resilient faith in the eventual redemption of that promise. He sees America as it is, with all its jobless veterans, homeless people and urban ghettos. And he retains his idealism *in spite of everything,* because his patriotism has room for paradox. At a Springsteen concert, one song makes you want to cheer for America; the next makes you want to cry for America—and then change it.

19   Springsteen conveys compassion for the casualty, for the ordinary person who may not be articulate. His empathy is for men with "debts no honest man can pay." From his immense pride in his home town comes a homage to closed textile mills and "Main Street's white-washed windows and vacant stores." Out of his populist patriotism comes his affection for people who feel "like a dog that's been beat too much" and his reconciling respect for his working-class father:

> Daddy worked his whole life for nothing but the pain.
> Now he walks up these empty rooms, looking for something to blame.

These songs are social, not political. They don't offer platforms, slogans or rhetoric. They don't imply easy remedies and they don't endorse politicians. Springsteen himself says he has not voted since 1972, and he is enrolled in no political party....

20   Springsteen and Stallone, two messiahs of American mass culture, two muscular men—tugging this country's flag in different directions.

21   Sylvester Stallone, at bottom, is a faker, feeding us fantasies as therapy for our national neuroses. He is appealing to the dark side that exists in all of us, the part of us that wants to get even with everyone who has ever gotten the better of us, the part that finds it easier to understand a stereotype than an individual, the part that dreams of vengeance that never fails and never leaves an aftertaste of guilt.

22   Bruce Springsteen appeals to the best in all of us. His songs ask us to forgive the sinner but to remember the sin; to respect one another but to question authority; to

refuse to compromise our ideals ("no retreat, no surrender"); to keep growing but to continue to love our parents and our home towns; to feel a responsibility for sharing with our countrymen who have less property and less power.

"I think what's happening now," Springsteen told one interviewer, "is people want to forget. There was Vietnam, there was Watergate, there was Iran—we were beaten, we were hustled and then we were humiliated. And I think people got a need to feel good about the country they live in. But what's happening, I think, is that need—which is a good thing—is gettin' manipulated and exploited...." 23

"One of the things that was always on my mind was to maintain connections with the people I'd grown up with and the sense of community where I came from. That's why I stayed in New Jersey. The danger of fame is in *forgetting*." 24

Questions for Close Reading

1. What is the selection's thesis? Locate the sentence(s) in which Newfield states his main idea. If he doesn't state the thesis explicitly, express it in your own words.

2. In what ways are Springsteen and Stallone alike?

3. According to the Orwell essay that Newfield cites (paragraph 7), what is the difference between nationalism and patriotism? What evidence does Newfield offer to show that Stallone's movies express nationalism rather than patriotism?

4. In what ways, according to Newfield, does Springsteen appeal to the best in us?

5. Refer to your dictionary as needed to define the following words used in the selection: *empathy* (paragraph 4), *estranged* (4), *jingoistic* (10), *avatars* (13), *simplistic* (16), *convergence* (17), *resilient* (18), *rhetoric* (19), and *messiahs* (20).

Questions About the Writer's Craft

1. **The pattern.** Which method for organizing comparison-contrast essays does Newfield use? Why might he have selected this method?

2. Comparison-contrast is never an end in itself; it always serves another purpose. Where in his essay does Newfield announce his purpose? What is it?

3. Why do you suppose Newfield reproduces Springsteen's lyrics as well as Stallone's remarks in a *Time* interview? What is the effect of including this quoted material?

4. How would you describe Newfield's tone? Select several paragraphs, and explain what they reveal about Newfield's attitude toward his subjects.

Writing Assignments Using Comparison-Contrast as a Pattern of Development

1. Build the case that either Springsteen's or Stallone's vision of America is prevalent among popular musicians and actors. Develop your view by pointing out other performers' similarities to either Springsteen or Stallone.

Comparison-Contrast

2. In "Stallone vs. Springsteen," Newfield describes two distinct personalities, as well as two opposing philosophies. Write an essay contrasting your own personality, values, and goals with those of a sibling or longtime friend. Show how different two people who have grown up together can be.

Writing Assignments Using Other Patterns of Development

3. Newfield states that part of Stallone's appeal is that he "liberates ... hostility and aggression." Focus on a specific area of life (the library, store, workplace) and narrate one or two instances of hostile behavior, your response to the behavior, and what happened as a result. End by describing steps that people can take to deal with belligerence. Before writing your paper, you may want to read Bob Greene's "Unwritten Rules Circumscribe Our Lives" (page 248) and Martin Gottfried's "Rambos of the Road" (page 403)—two essays that take opposing views on the issue of aggression in everyday life.

4. Newfield uses Orwell's definitions of nationalism and patriotism to clarify the difference between these two concepts and the behaviors that each exemplifies. Write an essay defining two other concepts that might appear similar but that are really quite different: assertiveness and rudeness; authoritative and authoritarian behavior; love and infatuation.

JOSEPH H. SUINA

Still living on the Cochiti Pueblo Reservation in New Mexico where he grew up, Joseph H. Suina (1944–) teaches in the Multicultural Teacher Education Program at the University of New Mexico. Suina's work as an educator led to his coauthoring a book for teachers, *The Learning Environment: An Instructional Strategy* (1982). The following selection first appeared in *Linguistic and Cultural Influences on Learning Mathematics*, edited by Rodney Cocking and Jose Mestre (1988).

AND THEN I WENT TO SCHOOL

1   I lived with my grandmother from the ages of 5 through 9. It was the early 1950s when electricity had not yet invaded the homes of the Cochiti Indians. The village day school and health clinic were first to have it and to the unsuspecting Cochitis this was the approach of a new era in their uncomplicated lives.

2   Transportation was simple then. Two good horses and a sturdy wagon met most needs of a villager. Only five or six individuals possessed an automobile in the Pueblo of 300. A flatbed truck fixed with wooden rails and a canvas top made a regular Saturday trip to Santa Fe. It was always loaded beyond capacity with Cochitis taking their wares to town for a few staples. With an escort of a dozen barking dogs, the straining truck made a noisy exit, northbound from the village.

3   During those years, Grandmother and I lived beside the plaza in a one-room house. It consisted of a traditional fireplace, a makeshift cabinet for our few tin cups and dishes, and a wooden crate that held our two buckets of all-purpose water. At the far

end of the room were two rolls of bedding we used as comfortable sitting "couches." Consisting of thick quilts, sheepskin, and assorted blankets, these bed rolls were undone each night. A wooden pole the length of one side of the room was suspended about 10 inches from the ceiling beams. A modest collection of colorful shawls, blankets, and sashes was draped over the pole making this part of the room most interesting. In one corner was a bulky metal trunk for our ceremonial wear and a few valuables. A dresser, which was traded for some of my grandmother's well-known pottery, held the few articles of clothing we owned and the "goody bag." Grandmother always had a flour sack filled with candy, store bought cookies, and Fig Newtons. These were saturated with a sharp odor of moth balls. Nevertheless, they made a fine snack with coffee before we turned in for the night. Tucked securely in my blankets, I listened to one of her stories or accounts of how it was when she was a little girl. These accounts seemed so old fashioned compared to the way we lived. Sometimes she softly sang a song from a ceremony. In this way I fell asleep each night.

4   Earlier in the evening we would make our way to a relative's house if someone had not already come to visit us. I would play with the children while the adults caught up on all the latest. Ten-cent comic books were finding their way into the Pueblo homes. For us children, these were the first link to the world beyond the Pueblo. We enjoyed looking at them and role playing as one of the heroes rounding up the villains. Everyone preferred being a cowboy rather than an Indian because cowboys were always victorious. Sometimes, stories were related to both children and adults. These get-togethers were highlighted by refreshments of coffee and sweet bread or fruit pies baked in the outdoor oven. Winter months would most likely include roasted pinon nuts or dried deer meat for all to share. These evening gatherings and sense of closeness diminished as the radios and televisions increased over the following years. It was never to be the same again.

5   The winter months are among my fondest recollections. A warm fire crackled and danced brightly in the fireplace and the aroma of delicious stew filled our one-room house. To me the house was just right. The thick adobe walls wrapped around the two of us protectingly during the long freezing nights. Grandmother's affection completed the warmth and security I will always remember.

6   Being the only child at Grandmother's, I had lots of attention and plenty of reasons to feel good about myself. As a pre-schooler, I already had the chores of chopping firewood and hauling in fresh water each day. After "heavy work," I would run to her and flex what I was certain were my gigantic biceps. Grandmother would state that at the rate I was going I would soon attain the status of a man like the adult males in the village. Her shower of praises made me feel like the Indian Superman of all times. At age 5, I suppose I was as close to that concept of myself as anyone.

7   In spite of her many years, Grandmother was still active in the village ceremonial setting. She was a member of an important women's society and attended all the functions, taking me along to many of them. I would wear one of my colorful shirts she handmade for just such occasions. Grandmother taught me the appropriate behavior at these events. Through modeling she taught me to pray properly. Barefooted, I would greet the sun each morning with a handful of cornmeal. At night I would look to the stars in wonderment and let a prayer slip through my lips. I learned to appreciate cooperation in nature and my fellowmen early in life. About food and material things, Grandmother would say, "There is enough for everyone to share and it all comes from above, my child." I felt very much a part of the world and our way of life. I knew I had a place in it and I felt good about me.

Comparison-Contrast

8   At age 6, like the rest of the Cochiti 6-year-olds that year, I had to begin my schooling. It was a new and bewildering experience. One I will not forget. The strange surroundings, new concepts about time and expectations, and a foreign tongue were overwhelming to us beginners. It took some effort to return the second day and many times thereafter.

9   To begin with, unlike my grandmother, the teacher did not have pretty brown skin and a colorful dress. She was not plump and friendly. Her clothes were one color and drab. Her pale and skinny form made me worry that she was very ill. I thought that explained why she did not have time just for me and the disappointed looks and orders she seemed to always direct my way. I didn't think she was so smart because she couldn't understand my language. "Surely that was why we had to leave our 'Indian' at home." But then I did not feel so bright either. All I could say in her language was "yes teacher," "my name is Joseph Henry," and "when is lunch time." The teacher's odor took some getting used to also. In fact, many times it make me sick right before lunch. Later, I learned from the girls that this odor was something she wore called perfume.

10 The classroom too had its odd characteristics. It was terribly huge and smelled of medicine like the village clinic I feared so much. The walls and ceiling were artificial and uncaring. They were too far from me and I felt naked. The fluorescent light tubes were eerie and blinked suspiciously above me. This was quite a contrast to the fire and sunlight that my eyes were accustomed to. I thought maybe the lighting did not seem right because it was man-made, and it was not natural. Our confinement to rows of desks was another unnatural demand from our active little bodies. We had to sit at these hard things for what seemed like forever before relief (recess) came midway through the morning and afternoon. Running carefree in the village and fields was but a sweet memory of days gone by. We all went home for lunch because we lived within walking distance of the school. It took coaxing and sometimes bribing to get me to return and complete the remainder of the school day.

11 School was a painful experience during those early years. The English language and the new set of values caused me much anxiety and embarrassment. I could not comprehend everything that was happening but yet I could understand very well when I messed up or was not doing so well. The negative aspect was communicated too effectively and I became unsure of myself more and more. How I wished I could understand other things just as well in school.

12 The value conflict was not only in school performance but in other areas of my life as well. For example, many of us students had a problem with head lice due to "the lack of sanitary conditions in our homes." Consequently, we received a severe shampooing that was rough on both the scalp and the ego. Cleanliness was crucial and a washing of this type indicated to the class how filthy a home setting we came from. I recall that after one such treatment I was humiliated before my peers with a statement that I had "She'na" (lice) so tough that I must have been born with them. Needless to say, my Super Indian self-image was no longer intact.

13 My language, too, was questionable from the beginning of my school career. "Leave your Indian (language) at home" was like a trademark of school. Speaking it accidentally or otherwise was a sure reprimand in the form of a dirty look or a whack with a ruler. This punishment was for speaking the language of my people which meant so much to me. It was the language of my grandmother and I spoke it well. With it, I sang beautiful songs and prayed from my heart. At that young and tender age, comprehending why I had to part with it was most difficult for me. And yet at home I was encouraged to attend school so that I might have a better life in the future.

I knew I had a good village life already but this was communicated less and less each day I was in school. . . .

I had to leave my beloved village of Cochiti for my education beyond Grade 6. I left to attend a Bureau of Indian Affairs boarding school 30 miles from home. Shined shoes and pressed shirt and pants were the order of the day. I managed to adjust to this just as I had to most of the things the school shoved at me or took away from me. Adjusting to leaving home and the village was tough indeed. It seemed the older I got, the further away I became from the ways I was so much a part of. Because my parents did not own an automobile, I saw them only once a month when they came up in the community truck. They never failed to come supplied with "eats" for me. I enjoyed the outdoor oven bread, dried meat, and tamales they usually brought. It took a while to get accustomed to the diet of the school. I longed for my grandmother and my younger brothers and sisters. I longed for my house. I longed to take part in a Buffalo Dance. I longed to be free.

I came home for the 4-day Thanksgiving break. At first, home did not feel right anymore. It was much too small and stuffy. The lack of running water and bathroom facilities were too inconvenient. Everything got dusty so quickly and hardly anyone spoke English. I did not realize I was beginning to take on the white man's ways, the ways that belittled my own. However, it did not take long to "get back with it." Once I established my relationships with family, relatives, and friends I knew I was where I came from and where I belonged.

Leaving for the boarding school the following Sunday evening was one of the saddest events in my entire life. Although I enjoyed myself immensely the last few days, I realized then that life would never be the same again. I could not turn back the time just as I could not do away with school and the ways of the white man. They were here to stay and would creep more and more into my life. The effort to make sense of both worlds together was painful and I had no choice but to do so. The schools, television, automobiles, and other white man's ways and values had chipped away at the simple cooperative life I grew up in. The people of Cochiti were changing. The winter evening gatherings, exchanging of stories, and even the performing of certain ceremonies were already only a memory that someone commented about now and then. Still the demands of both worlds were there. The white man's was flashy, less personal, but comfortable. The Indian was both attracted and pushed toward these new ways that he had little to say about. There was no choice left but to compete with the white man on his terms for survival. For that I knew I had to give up a part of my life.

Determined not to cry, I left for school that dreadfully lonely night. My right hand clutched tightly the mound of cornmeal Grandmother placed there and my left hand brushed away a tear as I made my way back to school.

Questions for Close Reading

1. What is the selection's thesis? Locate the sentence(s) in which Suina states his main idea. If he doesn't state the thesis explicitly, express it in your own words.

2. How did the Cochiti instill their values and native culture in their children? How was the Cochiti approach different from the teaching methods used in the white school Suina attended?

Comparison-Contrast

3. What non-native influences appear in Suina's town and life before he starts attending school?

4. Why is Suina forced to attend a white school and learn about the whites' life-style and language? What does he find confusing about school? How does school change him?

5. Refer to your dictionary as needed to define the following words used in the selection: *adobe* (paragraph 5), *ego* (12), and *belittled* (15).

Questions About the Writer's Craft

1. The pattern. Comparison-contrast essays organize material according to the point-by-point or one-side-at-a-time method. Which method predominates in this essay? Why do you think Suina uses this method? Locate places where Suina uses the other method of organization.

2. Other patterns. Suina uses description to evoke the simple, emotional warmth of the Native American life-style as well as the sterile, stark coldness of the white school. Locate places in the essay where Suina provides sensory details to help readers understand the differences between the two cultures.

3. Consider Suina's word choice in the opening paragraph. How do the words "invade" and "unsuspecting" help establish the essay's overall tone? What do these terms reveal about Suina's attitude toward the transformation of Native American culture?

4. Where in paragraph 14 does Suina use repetition? What is the effect of the repetition?

Writing Assignments Using Comparison-Contrast as a Pattern of Development

1. As a Native American, Suina is made to feel like an outsider in the white school. But cultural differences aren't the only factors that cause children to feel uncomfortable in school. For example, they may have trouble fitting in because they have a learning disability, are shy, are extroverted, or need more (or less) structure than the school provides. Focusing on *one* such problem, write an essay comparing and contrasting present-day education with the way it should be.

2. After attending boarding school for a few months, Suina reappraises his home and earlier life-style. In a similar way, separation can cause the rest of us to view our home, our school, another institution, or an individual in a more positive or a more negative light. Write an essay comparing and contrasting the feelings you had for a person, place, or institution with your attitude after being separated for a while. Provide vigorous details to show why your attitude changed.

Writing Assignments Using Other Patterns of Development

3. Suina reports that his grandmother showered him with praise and made him feel like a "Superman." However, once he entered school, the constant scoldings, dirty looks, and ruler slaps eroded his self-esteem. Write an essay illustrating how a person affected your view of yourself, either by praising or by criticizing your efforts. Provide several dramatic examples or a single, richly detailed example to illustrate how this person affected you.

4. In school, Suina is pressured to abandon the language of his home and to speak only English. Conduct some library research on the subject of bilingualism in education. Then write an essay arguing that schools either should or should not teach non-English-speaking students in their native language until they become sufficiently proficient in English to join regular classes. At some point, you should acknowledge and perhaps refute opposing views.

ADDITIONAL WRITING TOPICS: COMPARISON-CONTRAST

General Assignments

Using comparison-contrast, write an essay on one of the following topics.

1. Two-career family versus one-career family
2. Two approaches for dealing with problems
3. Children's pastimes today and yesterday
4. Two attitudes toward money
5. Watching a movie on television versus viewing it in a theater
6. Two approaches to parenting
7. Two approaches to studying
8. Marriage versus living together
9. Two views on a controversial issue
10. The coverage of an event on television versus its coverage in a newspaper

Assignments with a Specific Purpose, Audience, and Point of View

1. You would like to change your campus living arrangements. Perhaps you want to move from a dormitory to an off-campus apartment or from home to a dorm. Before you do, though, you'll have to convince your parents (who are paying most of your college costs) that the move will be beneficial. Write out what you would say to your parents. Contrast your current situation with your proposed one, explaining why the new arrangement would be better.

2. As a store manager, you decide to write a memo to all sales personnel explaining how to keep customers happy. Compare and/or contrast the needs and shopping habits of several different consumer groups (by age, spending ability, or sex), and show how to make each group comfortable in your store.

3. Write a guide on "Passing Exams" for first-year college students, contrasting the right and wrong ways to prepare for and take exams. Although your purpose is basically serious, leaven the section on how *not* to approach exams with some humor.

4. You work as a volunteer for a mental health hot line. Many people call simply because they feel "stressed out." Prepare a brochure for these people, recommending a "Type B" approach to stressful situations. Focus the brochure on the contrast between "Type A" and "Type B" personalities: the former is nervous, hard-driving, competitive; the latter is relaxed and noncompetitive. Give specific examples of how each "type" tends to act in stressful situations.

5. As president of your student senate, you're concerned about the way your school is dealing with a particular situation (for example, advisement, parking, financial assistance). Write a letter to your college president contrasting the way your school handles the situation with another school's approach. In your conclusion, point out the advantages of adopting the other college's strategy.

6. Your old high school has invited you back to make a speech before an audience of seniors. The topic will be "how to choose the college that is right for you." Write your speech in the form of a comparison-contrast analysis. Focus on the choices available (two-year versus four-year schools, large versus small, local versus faraway, and so on), showing the advantages and/or disadvantages of each.

18
CAUSE-EFFECT

WHAT IS CAUSE-EFFECT?

SUPERSTITION has it that curiosity killed the cat. Maybe so. Yet our science, technology, storytelling, and fascination with the past and future all spring from our determination to know "Why" and "What if." Seeking explanations, young children barrage adults with endless questions: "Why do trees grow tall?" "What would happen if the sun didn't shine?" But children aren't the only ones who wonder in this way. All of us think in terms of cause and effect, sometimes consciously, sometimes unconsciously: "Why did they give me such an odd look?" we wonder, or "How would I do at another college?" we speculate. This exploration of reasons and results is also at the heart of most professions: "What led to our involvement in Vietnam?" historians question; "What will happen if we administer this experimental drug?" scientists ask.

Cause-effect writing, often called **causal analysis**, is rooted in this elemental need to make connections. Because the drive to understand reasons and results is so fundamental, causal analysis is a common kind of writing. An article analyzing the unexpected outcome of an election, a report linking poor nutrition to low academic achievement, an editorial analyzing the impact of a proposed tax cut—all are examples of cause-effect writing.

Done well, cause-effect pieces uncover the subtle and often surprising connections between events or phenomena. By rooting out causes and projecting effects, causal analysis enables us to make sense of our experiences, revealing a world that is somewhat less arbitrary and chaotic.

Cause-Effect 347

HOW CAUSE-EFFECT FITS YOUR PURPOSE AND AUDIENCE

Many assignments and exam questions in college involve writing essays that analyze causes, effects, or both. Sometimes, as in the following examples, you'll be asked to write an essay developed primarily through the cause-effect pattern:

> Although divorces have leveled off in the last few years, the number of marriages ending in divorce is still greater than it was a generation ago. What do you think are the causes of this phenomenon?

> Political commentators were surprised that so few people voted in the last election. Discuss the probable causes of this weak voter turnout.

> Americans never seem to tire of gossip about the rich and famous. What effect has this fascination with celebrities had on American culture?

> The federal government is expected to pass legislation that will significantly reduce the funding of student loans. Analyze the possible effects of such a cutback.

Other assignments and exam questions may not explicitly ask you to address causes and effects, but they may use words that suggest causal analysis would be appropriate. Consider these examples, paying special attention to the italicized words:

Cause

> In contrast to the socially involved youth of the 1960s, many young people today tend to remove themselves from political issues. What do you think are the *sources* of the political apathy found among 18- to 25-year-olds?

Effect

> A number of experts forecast that drug abuse will be the most significant factor affecting American productivity in the coming decade. Evaluate the validity of this observation by discussing the *impact* of drugs on the workplace.

Cause and Effect

> According to school officials, a predictable percentage of entering students drop out of college at some point during their first year. What *motivates* students to drop out? What *happens* to them once they leave?

In addition to serving as the primary strategy for achieving an essay's purpose, causal analysis can also be a supplemental method used to help make a point in an essay developed chiefly through another pattern of development. Assume, for example, that you want to write an essay *defining* the term *the homeless*. To help readers see that unfavorable circumstances can result in nearly anyone becoming homeless, you might discuss some of the unavoidable, everyday factors causing people to live on streets and in subway stations. Similarly, in a *persuasive* proposal urging your college administration to institute an honors program, you would probably spend some time analyzing the positive effect of such a program on students and faculty.

PREWRITING STRATEGIES

The following checklist shows how you can apply to cause-effect some of the prewriting techniques discussed in Chapter 2.

> ✔ **CAUSE-EFFECT: A PREWRITING CHECKLIST**
>
> *Choose a Topic*
> - Do your journal entries reflect an ongoing interest in the causes for and/or effects of something? (What causes friends to drop out of school? What will be the effect of recent legislation regarding abortion?)
> - Will you analyze a personal phenomenon (for example, your decision to stop smoking), a change at your college (new requirements for graduation), a nationwide trend (the growing popularity of "tabloid television"), or a historical event (the defeat of the Equal Rights Amendment)?
> - Does your subject intrigue, anger, puzzle you? Is it likely to interest your readers as well?
>
> *Make Sure the Topic is Manageable*
> - Can you tackle your subject—especially if it's a social trend or historical event—in the number of pages allotted?
> - Can you gather enough information for your analysis? Does the topic require library research? Do you have time for such research?
> - Will you examine causes (why your parents got divorced), effects (how their separation changed you), or both? Will your topic still be manageable if you discuss both causes and effects?
>
> *Identify Your Purpose, Audience, Tone, and Point of View*
> - Is the purpose of your causal analysis to inform (the reasons for a rock star's climb to fame)? To persuade (why the rock star merits his or her success)? To speculate about possibilities (whether the rock star will continue to grow as an artist)? Do you want to combine purposes?
> - Given your purpose and audience, what tone and point of view should you adopt?
>
> *Use Individual and Group Brainstorming, Mapping, and/or Freewriting to Explore Causes and Effects*
> - *Causes:* What happened? What are the possible reasons? Which are most likely? Who was involved? Why?
> - *Effects:* What happened? Who was involved? What were the observable results? What are some possible future consequences? Which consequences are negative? Which are positive?

STRATEGIES FOR USING CAUSE-EFFECT IN AN ESSAY

After prewriting, you're ready to draft your essay. The following suggestions will be helpful whether you use causal analysis as a dominant or supportive pattern of development.

1. Stay focused on the purpose of your analysis. When writing a causal analysis, don't lose sight of your overall purpose. Consider, for example, an essay on the causes of widespread child abuse. If you're concerned primarily with explaining the problem of child abuse to your readers, you might take a purely *informative* approach:

> Although parental stress is the immediate cause of child abuse, the more compelling reason for such behavior lies in the way parents were themselves mistreated as children.

Or you might want to *persuade* your audience about some point or idea concerning child abuse:

> The tragic consequences of child abuse provide strong support for more aggressive handling of such cases by social workers and judges.

Then again, you could choose a *speculative* approach, your main purpose being to suggest possibilities:

> Psychologists disagree about the potential effect on youngsters of all the media attention given to child abuse. Will children exposed to this media coverage grow up assertive, self-confident, and able to protect themselves? Or will they become fearful and distrustful?

These examples illustrate that an essay's causal analysis may have more than one purpose. For instance, although the last example points to a paper with a primarily speculative purpose, the essay would probably start by informing readers of experts' conflicting views. The paper would also have a persuasive slant if it ended by urging readers to complain to the media about their sensationalized treatment of the child-abuse issue.

2. Adapt content and tone to your purpose and readers. Your purpose and audience determine what supporting material and what tone will be most effective in a cause-effect essay. Assume you want to direct your essay on child abuse to general readers who know little about the subject. To *inform* readers, you might use facts, statistics, and expert opinion to provide an objective discussion of the causes of child abuse. Your analysis might show the following: (1) adults who were themselves mistreated as children tend to abuse their own offspring; (2) marital stress contributes to the mistreatment of children; and (3) certain personality disorders increase the likelihood of child abuse. Sensitive to what your readers would and wouldn't understand, you would stay away from a formal tone. Rather than writing "Pathological pre-abuse symptomatology predicts adult transference of high aggressivity," you would say "Psychologists can often predict, on the basis of family histories, who will abuse children."

Now imagine that your purpose is to *convince* future social workers that the failure of social service agencies to act authoritatively in child-abuse cases often has tragic consequences. Hoping to encourage more responsible behavior in the prospective social workers, you would adopt a more emotional tone in the essay, perhaps citing wrenching case histories that dramatize what happens when child abuse isn't taken seriously.

3. Think rigorously about causes and effects. Cause-effect relationships are usually complex. To write a meaningful analysis, you should do some careful thinking about your subject. (The two sets of questions at the end of this chapter's Prewriting Checklist [page 348] will help you think creatively about causes and effects.)

If you look beyond the obvious, you'll discover that a cause may have many effects. Imagine you're writing a paper on the effects of cigarette smoking. A number of consequences might be discussed, some less obvious but perhaps more interesting than others: increased risk of lung cancer and heart disease, evidence of harm done by secondhand smoke, legal battles regarding the rights of smokers and nonsmokers, lower birth weights in babies of mothers who smoke, and developmental problems experienced by such underweight infants.

In the same way, an effect may have multiple causes. An essay analyzing the reasons for world hunger could discuss many causes, again some less evident but perhaps more thought-provoking than others: overpopulation, climatic changes, inefficient use of land, and poor management of international relief funds.

Your analysis may also uncover a **causal chain** in which one cause (or effect) brings about another, which, in turn, brings about another, and so on. Here's an example of a causal chain: Prohibition went into effect; bootleggers and organized crime stepped in to supply public demand for alcoholic beverages; ordinary citizens began breaking the law by buying illegal alcohol and patronizing speakeasies; disrespect for legal authority became widespread and acceptable. As you can see, a causal chain often leads to interesting points. In this case, the subject of Prohibition leads not just to the obvious (illegal consumption of alcohol) but also to the more complex issue of society's decreasing respect for legal authority.

Don't grapple with so complex a chain, however, that you become hopelessly entangled. If your subject involves multiple causes and effects, limit what you'll discuss. Identify which causes and effects are *primary* and which are *secondary*. How extensively you cover secondary factors will depend on your purpose and audience. In an essay intended to inform a general audience about the harmful effects of pesticides, you would most likely focus on everyday dangers—polluted drinking water, residues in food, and the like. You probably wouldn't include a discussion of more long-range consequences (evolution of resistant insects, disruption of the soil's acid-alkaline balance).

Similarly, decide whether to focus on *immediate*, more obvious causes and effects, or on less obvious, more *remote* ones. Or perhaps you need to focus on both. In an essay about a faculty strike at your college, should you attribute the strike simply to the faculty's failure to receive a salary increase? Or should you also examine other factors: the union's failure to accept a salary package that satisfied most professors; the administration's inability to coordinate its negotiating efforts? It may be more difficult to explore more remote causes and effects, but it can also lead to more original and revealing essays. Thoughtful analyses take these less obvious considerations into account.

When developing a causal analysis, be careful to avoid the ***post hoc* fallacy.** Named after the Latin phrase *post hoc, ergo propter hoc,* meaning "after this, therefore because of this," this kind of faulty thinking occurs when you assume that simply because one event *followed* another, the first event *caused* the second. For example, if the Republicans win a majority of seats in Congress and, several months later, the economy collapses, can you conclude that the Republicans caused the collapse? A quick assumption of "Yes" fails the test of logic, for the timing of events could be coincidental and not indicative of any cause-effect relationship. The collapse may have been triggered by uncontrolled inflation that began well before the congressional elections. (For more on *post hoc* thinking, see page 424 in Chapter 20.)

Also, be careful not to mistake *correlation* for *causation*. Two events correlate when they occur at about the same time. Such co-occurrence, however, doesn't guarantee a cause-effect relationship. For instance, while the number of ice cream cones eaten and the instances of heat prostration both increase during the summer months, this doesn't mean that eating ice cream causes heat prostration! A third factor—in this case, summer heat—is the actual cause. When writing causal analyses, then, use with caution words that imply a causal link (such as *therefore* and *because*). Words that express simply time of occurrence (*following* and *previously*) are safer and more objective.

Finally, keep in mind that a rigorous causal analysis involves more than loose generalizations about causes and effects. Creating plausible connections may require library research, interviewing, or both. Often you'll need to provide facts, statistics, details, personal observations, or other corroborative material if readers are going to accept the reasoning behind your analysis.

4. Write a thesis that focuses the paper on causes, effects, or both. The thesis in an essay developed through causal analysis often indicates whether the essay will deal mostly with causes, effects, or both. Here, for example, are three thesis statements for causal analyses dealing with the public school system. You'll see that each thesis signals that essay's particular emphasis:

Causes

Our school system has been weakened by an overemphasis on trendy electives.

Effects

An ineffectual school system has led to crippling teachers' strikes and widespread disrespect for the teaching profession.

Causes and Effects

Bureaucratic inefficiency has created a school system unresponsive to children's emotional, physical, and intellectual needs.

Note that the thesis statement—in addition to signaling whether the paper will discuss causes or effects or both—may also point to the essay's plan of development. Consider the last thesis statement; it makes clear that the paper will discuss children's emotional needs first, their physical needs second, and their intellectual needs last.

The thesis statement in a causal analysis doesn't have to specify whether the essay will discuss causes, effects, or both. Nor does the thesis have to be worded in such a way that the essay's plan of development is apparent. But when first writing cause-effect essays, you may find that a highly focused thesis will help keep your analysis on track.

5. Choose an organizational pattern. There are two basic ways to organize the points in a cause-effect essay: you may use a chronological or an emphatic sequence. If you select *chronological order,* you discuss causes and effects in the order in which they occur or will occur. Suppose you're writing an essay on the causes for the popularity of imported cars. These causes might be discussed in chronological sequence: American plant workers became frustrated and dissatisfied on the job; some workers got careless while others deliberately sabotaged the production of sound cars; a growing number of defective cars hit the market; consumers grew dissatisfied with American cars and switched to imports.

Chronology might also be used to organize a discussion about effects. Imagine you want to write an essay about the need to guard against disrupting delicate balances in the country's wildlife. You might start the essay by discussing what happened when the starling, a non-native bird, was introduced into the American environment. Because the starling had few natural predators, the starling population soared out of control; the starlings took over food sources and habitats of native species; the bluebird, a native species, declined and is now threatened with extinction.

Although a chronological pattern can be an effective way to organize material, a strict time sequence can present a problem if your primary cause or effect ends up buried in the middle of the sequence. In such a case, you might use *emphatic order,* reserving the most significant cause or effect for the end. For example, time order could be used to present the reasons behind a candidate's unexpected victory: Less than a month after the candidate's earlier defeat, a full-scale fund-raising campaign for the next election was started; the candidate spoke to many crucial power groups early in the campaign; the candidate did exceptionally well in the pre-election debates; good weather and large voter turnout on election day favored the candidate. However, if you believe that the candidate's appearance before influential groups was the key factor in the victory, it would

Cause-Effect

be more effective to emphasize that point by saving it for the end. This is what is meant by emphatic order—saving the most important point for last.

Emphatic order is an especially effective way to sequence cause-effect points when readers hold what, in your opinion, are mistaken or narrow views about a subject. To encourage readers to look more closely at the issues, you present what you consider the erroneous or obvious views first, show why they are unsound or limited, then present what you feel to be the actual causes and effects. Such a sequence nudges the audience into giving further thought to the causes and effects you have discovered. Here are informal outlines for two causal analyses using this approach:

Subject: The causes of the riot at a rock concert
1. Some commentators blame the excessively hot weather.
2. Others cite drug use among the concertgoers.
3. Still others blame the liquor sold at the concessions.
4. But the real cause of the disaster was poor planning by the concert promoters.

Subject: The effects of campus crime
1. Immediate problems
    a. Students feel insecure and fearful.
    b. Many night-time campus activities have been curtailed.
2. More significant long-term problems
    a. Unfavorable publicity about campus crime will affect future student enrollment.
    b. Unfavorable publicity about campus crime will make it difficult to recruit top-notch faculty.

When using emphatic order, you might want to word the thesis in such a way that it signals which point your essay will stress. Look at the following thesis statements:

Although many immigrants arrive in this country without marketable skills, their most pressing problem is learning how to make their way in a society whose language they don't know.

The space program has led to dramatic advances in computer technology and medical science. Even more importantly, though, the program has helped change many people's attitudes toward the planet we live on.

These thesis statements reflect an awareness of the complex nature of cause-effect relationships. While not dismissing secondary issues, the statements establish which points the writer considers most noteworthy. The second thesis, for instance, indicates that the paper will touch on the technological and medical advances made possible by the space program but will emphasize the way the program has changed people's attitudes toward the earth.

Whether you use a chronological or emphatic pattern to organize your essay, you'll need to provide clear *signals* to identify when you're discussing causes and when you're discussing effects. Expressions such as "Another reason" and "A final outcome" help readers follow your line of thought.

6. Use language that hints at the complexity of cause-effect relationships. Because it's difficult—if not impossible—to identify causes and effects with certainty, you should avoid such absolutes as "It must be obvious" and "There is no doubt." Instead, try phrases like "Most likely" or "It is probable." Such language isn't indecisive; it's reasonable and reflects your understanding of the often tangled nature of causes and effects. Don't, however, go to the other extreme and be reluctant to take a stand on the issues. If you have thought carefully about causes and effects, you have a right to state your analysis with conviction.

REVISION STRATEGIES

Once you have a draft of the essay, you're ready to revise. The following checklist will help you and those giving you feedback apply to cause-effect writing some of the revision techniques discussed in Chapters 7 and 8.

✔ CAUSE-EFFECT: A REVISION CHECKLIST

Revise Overall Meaning and Structure
- Is the essay's purpose informative, persuasive, speculative, or a combination of these?
- What is the essay's thesis? Is it stated specifically or implied? Where? Could it be made any clearer? How?
- Does the essay focus on causes, effects, or both? How do you know?
- Where has correlation been mistaken for causation? Where is the essay weakened by *post hoc* thinking?
- Where does the essay distinguish between primary and secondary causes and effects? How do the most critical causes and effects receive special attention?
- Where does the essay dwell on the obvious?

Revise Paragraph Development
- Which paragraphs fail to support the essay's thesis?
- Are the essay's paragraphs sequenced chronologically or emphatically? Was the decision to use that order a good one? Why, or why not?

Cause-Effect   355

> - Where would signal devices (such as *afterward*, *before*, *then*, and *next*) make it easier to follow the progression of thought within and between paragraphs?
> - Which paragraphs would be strengthened by vivid examples, such as statistics, fact, anecdotes, or personal observations, that support the causal analysis?
>
> *Revise Sentences and Words*
> - Where do expressions like *as a result*, *because*, and *therefore* mislead the reader by implying a cause-effect relationship? Would words such as *following* and *previously* eliminate the problem?
> - Do any words or phrases convey an arrogant or dogmatic tone (*There is no question*, *undoubtedly*, *always*, *never*)? What other expressions (*most likely*, *probably*) would improve credibility?

STUDENT ESSAY: FROM PREWRITING THROUGH REVISION

The student essay that follows was written by Carl Novack in response to this assignment:

> In "Black Men and Public Space," Brent Staples reminds us that, sadly, racist attitudes have not changed much over the years. There are, though, some areas in which people's attitudes *have* changed dramatically. Identify a significant shift in an activity, practice, or institution. Then write an essay in which you discuss the factors that you believe are responsible for the attitudinal change.

After deciding to write about Americans' changing food habits, Carl used the *mapping technique* to generate material on his subject. His map is shown on page 356. The marks in color indicate Carl's later efforts to organize and elaborate the original map. Note that he added some branches, eliminated others, drew arrows indicating that some topics should be moved, and changed the wording of some key ideas. These annotations paved the way for Carl's topic outline, which is presented after the map.

Mapping

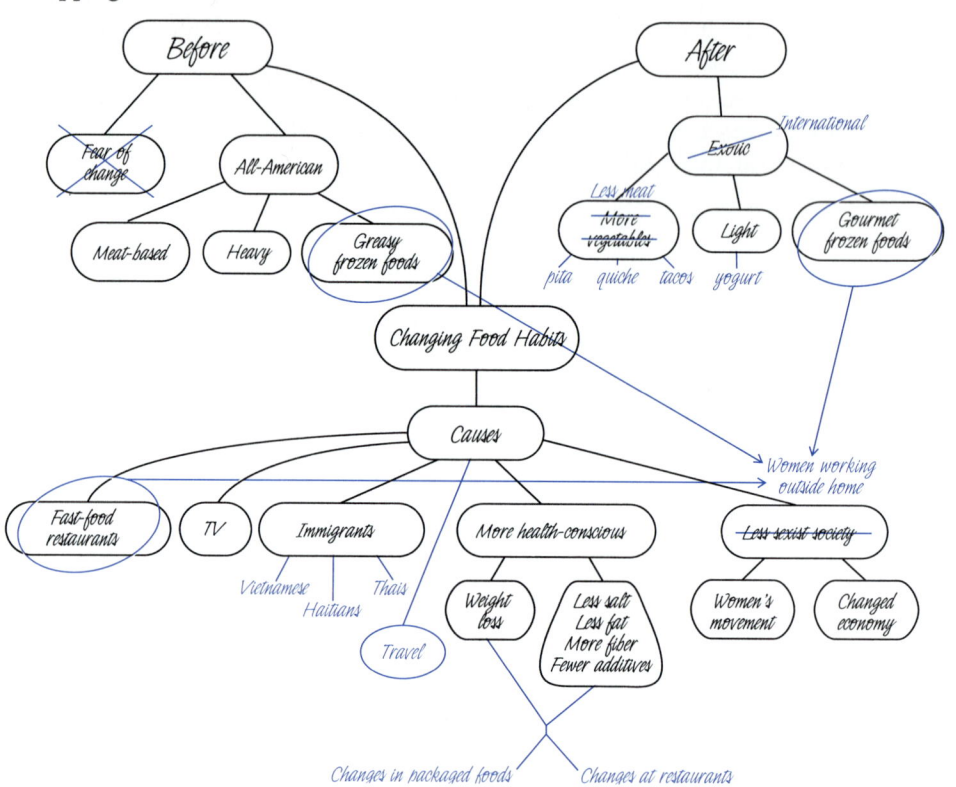

[Mapping diagram:

Before branches to:
- ~~Fear of change~~
- All-American
  - Meat-based
  - Heavy
  - (Greasy frozen foods) [circled]

After branches to:
- *International*
- ~~Exotic~~
  - *Less meat* / ~~More vegetables~~ — *pita, quiche, tacos, yogurt*
  - Light
  - Gourmet frozen foods [circled] → *Women working outside home*

Both connect to **Changing Food Habits** → **Causes**:
- Fast-food restaurants [circled]
- TV
- Immigrants — *Vietnamese, Haitians, Thais*; *Travel* [circled]
- More health-conscious
  - Weight loss
  - Less salt, Less fat, More fiber, Fewer additives
- ~~Less sexist society~~
  - Women's movement
  - Changed economy

Changes in packaged foods   Changes at restaurants]

Outline

Thesis: America has changed and so has what we Americans eat and how we eat.

   I. We used to eat "All-American" meals.
      A. Heavy
      B. Meat-based
  II. Now our tastes are more international.
      A. Lighter--yogurt
      B. Less meat--pita, quiche, tacos
 III. There are several reasons for our tastes becoming more international.
      A. Television
      B. Travel abroad
      C. Immigrants in this country

Cause-Effect 357

IV. Two social trends have also changed how and what we eat.
   A. Health consciousness
      1. Concern about weight
      2. Concern about salt, fat, fiber, additives
         a. Changes in packaged foods (lunch meat, canned vegetables, soups)
         b. Changes in restaurants (salad bars)
   B. More women working outside the home because of the economy and the women's movement
      1. Increase in fast-food restaurants
      2. More frozen foods, some even gourmet

Now read Carl's paper, "Americans and Food," noting the similarities and differences among his map, outline, and final essay. See, for example, how the diagram suggests a "before" and "after" contrast—a contrast the essay develops. Also note Carl's decision to move "frozen foods" and "fast-food restaurants" to the "women working outside home" section of the diagram. This decision is reflected in the outline and in the final essay, where frozen foods and fast-food restaurants are discussed in the same paragraph. As you read the essay, also consider how well it applies the principles of causal analysis discussed in this chapter. (The commentary that follows the paper will help you look at Carl's essay more closely and will give you some sense of how he went about revising his first draft.)

Americans and Food
by Carl Novack

1   An offbeat but timely cartoon recently appeared in the local newspaper. The single panel showed a gravel-pit operation with piles of raw earth and large cranes. Next to one of the cranes stood the owner of the gravel pit--a grizzled, tough-looking character, hammer in hand, pointing proudly to the new sign he had just tacked up. The sign read, "Fred's Fill Dirt and Croissants." The cartoon illustrates an interesting phenomenon: the changing food habits of Americans. Our meals used to consist of something like home-cooked pot roast, mashed potatoes laced with butter and salt, a thick slice of apple pie topped with a healthy scoop of vanilla ice cream--plain, heavy meals, cooked from scratch, and eaten leisurely at home. But America has changed, and as it has, so have what we Americans eat and how we eat it. —Introduction / Thesis

2   We used to have simple, unsophisticated tastes and looked with suspicion at anything more exotic than hamburger. Admittedly, we did

adopt some foods from the various immigrant groups who flocked to our shores. We learned to eat Chinese food, pizza, and bagels. But in the last few years, the international character of our diet has grown tremendously. We can walk into any mall in Middle America and buy pita bread, quiche, and tacos. Such foods are often changed on their journey from exotic imports to ordinary "American" meals (no Pakistani, for example, eats frozen-on-a-stick boysenberry-flavored yogurt), but the imports are still a long way from hamburger on a bun.

Why have we become more worldly in our tastes? For one thing, television blankets the country with information about new food products and trends. Viewers in rural Montana know that the latest craving in Washington, D.C., is Cajun cooking or that something called tofu is now available in the local supermarket. Another reason for the growing international flavor of our food is that many young Americans have traveled abroad and gotten hooked on new tastes and flavors. Backpacking students and young professionals vacationing in Europe come home with cravings for authentic French bread or German beer. Finally, continuing waves of immigrants settle in the cities where many of us live, causing significant changes in what we eat. Vietnamese, Haitians, and Thais, for instance, bring their native foods and cooking styles with them and eventually open small markets or restaurants. In time, the new food will become Americanized enough to take its place in our national diet.

Our growing concern with health has also affected the way we eat. For the last few years, the media have warned us about the dangers of our traditional diet, high in salt and fat, low in fiber. The media also began to educate us about the dangers of processed foods pumped full of chemical additives. As a result, consumers began to demand healthier foods, and manufacturers started to change some of their products. Many foods, such as lunch meat, canned vegetables, and soups, were made available in low-fat, low-sodium versions. Whole-grain cereals and high-fiber breads also began to appear on the grocery shelves. Moreover, the food industry started to produce all-natural products--everything from potato chips to ice cream--without additives and preservatives. Not surprisingly, the restaurant industry responded to this switch to healthier foods, luring customers with salad bars, broiled fish, and steamed vegetables.

Cause-Effect 359

5   Our food habits are being affected, too, by the rapid increase in the number of women working outside the home. Sociologists and other experts believe that two important factors triggered this phenomenon: the women's movement and a changing economic climate. Women were assured that it was acceptable, even rewarding, to work outside the home; many women also discovered that they had to work just to keep up with the cost of living. As the traditional role of homemaker changed, so did the way families ate. With Mom working, there wasn't time for her to prepare the traditional three square meals a day. Instead, families began looking for alternatives to provide quick meals. What was the result? For one thing, there was a boom in fast-food restaurants. The suburban or downtown strip that once contained a lone McDonald's now features Wendy's, Roy Rogers, Taco Bell, Burger King, and Pizza Hut. Families also began to depend on frozen foods as another time-saving alternative. Once again, though, demand changed the kind of frozen food available. Frozen foods no longer consist of foil trays divided into greasy fried chicken, watery corn niblets, and lumpy mashed potatoes. Supermarkets now stock a range of supposedly gourmet frozen dinners--from fettucini in cream sauce to braised beef en brochette. *Topic sentence: Another cause* *Start of a causal chain*

6   It may not be possible to pick up a ton of fill dirt and a half-dozen croissants at the same place, but America's food habits are definitely changing. If it is true that "you are what you eat," then America's identity is evolving along with its diet. *Conclusion*

Commentary

Title and Introduction

  Asked to prepare a paper analyzing the reasons behind a change in our lives, Carl decided to write about a shift he had noticed in Americans' eating habits. The title of the essay, "Americans and Food," identifies Carl's subject but could be livelier and more interesting.
  Despite his rather uninspired title, Carl starts his *causal analysis* in an engaging way—with the vivid description of a cartoon. He then connects the cartoon to his subject with the following sentence: "The cartoon illustrates an interesting phenomenon: the changing food habits of Americans." To back up his belief that there has been a revolution in our eating habits, Carl uses the first paragraph to summarize the kind of meal that people used to eat. He then moves to his *thesis:* "But America has changed, and as it has, so have what Americans eat and how we eat it." The thesis implies that Carl's paper will focus on both causes and effects.

Purpose

Carl's purpose was to write an *informative* causal analysis. But before he could present the causes of the change in eating habits, he needed to show that such a change had, in fact, taken place. He therefore uses the second paragraph to document one aspect of this change—the internationalization of our eating habits.

Topic Sentences

At the start of the third paragraph, Carl uses a question—"Why have we become more worldly in our tastes?"—to signal that his discussion of causes is about to begin. This question also serves as the paragraph's *topic sentence*, indicating that the paragraph will focus on reasons for the increasingly international flavor of our food. The next two paragraphs, also focused by topic sentences, identify two other major reasons for the change in eating habits: "Our growing concern with health has also affected the way we eat" (paragraph 4), and "Our food habits are being affected, too, by the rapid increase in the number of women working outside the home" (5).

Other Patterns of Development

Carl draws on two patterns of development—*comparison-contrast* and *illustration*—to develop his causal analysis. At the heart of the essay is a basic *contrast* between the way we used to eat and the way we eat now. And throughout his essay, Carl provides convincing *examples* to demonstrate the validity of his points. Consider for a moment the third paragraph. Here Carl asserts that one reason for our new eating habits is our growing exposure to international foods. He then presents concrete evidence to show that we have indeed become more familiar with international cuisine: Television exposes rural Montana to Cajun cooking; students traveling abroad take a liking to French bread; urban dwellers enjoy the exotic fare served by numerous immigrant groups. The fourth and fifth paragraphs use similarly specific evidence (for example, "low-fat, low-sodium versions" of "lunchmeat, canned vegetables, and soups") to illustrate the soundness of key ideas.

Causal Chains

Let's look more closely at the evidence in the essay. Not satisfied with obvious explanations, Carl thought through his ideas carefully and even brainstormed with friends to arrive at as comprehensive an analysis as possible. Not surprisingly, much of the evidence Carl uncovered took the form of *causal chains*. In the fourth paragraph, Carl writes, "The media also began to educate us about the dangers of processed foods pumped full of chemical additives. As a result, consumers began to demand healthier foods, and manufacturers started to change some of their products." And the next paragraph shows how the changing role of American women caused families to look for alternative ways of eating. This shift, in turn, caused the restaurant and food industries to respond with a wide range of food alternatives.

Making the Paper Easy to Follow

Although Carl's analysis digs beneath the surface and reveals complex cause-effect relationships, he wisely limits his pursuit of causal chains to *primary* causes and effects. He doesn't let the complexities distract him from his main purpose: to show why and how the American diet is changing. Carl is also careful to provide his essay with abundant *connecting devices*, making it easy for readers to see the links between points. Consider the use of *transitions* (signaled by italics) in the following sentences: "*Another* reason for the growing international flavor of our food is that many young Americans have traveled abroad" (paragraph 3); "*As a result*, consumers began to demand healthier foods" (4); and "*As* the traditional role of homemaker changed, so did the way families ate" (5).

A Problem with the Essay's Close

As you read the essay, you probably noticed that Carl's conclusion is a bit weak. Although his reference to the cartoon works well, the rest of the paragraph limps to a tired close. Ending an otherwise vigorous essay with such a slight conclusion undercuts the effectiveness of the whole paper. Carl spent so much energy developing the body of his essay that he ran out of the stamina needed to conclude the piece more forcefully. Careful budgeting of his time would have allowed him to prepare a stronger concluding paragraph.

Revising the First Draft

When Carl was ready to revise, he showed the first draft of his essay to several classmates who used the revision checklist on pages 354–55 to focus their feedback. Listening carefully, Carl jotted down their most helpful comments and eventually transferred them, numbered in order of importance, to his draft. Comparing Carl's original version of his fourth paragraph (shown here) with his final version in the essay will show you how he went about revising.

Original Version of the Fourth Paragraph

(A growing concern with health has also affected the way we eat, especially because the media has sent us warnings the last few years about the dangers of salt, sugar, food additives, and high-fat and low-fiber diets. We have started to worry that our traditional meals may have been shortening our lives. As a result, consumers demanded healthier foods and manufacturers started taking some of the salt and sugar out of canned foods. "All-natural" became an effective selling point, leading to many preservative-free products. Restaurants, too, adapted their menus, luring customers with light meals. Because we now know about the link between overweight and a variety of health problems, including heart attacks, we are counting calories. In turn, food companies made fortunes on diet beer and diet cola. Sometimes, though, we seem a bit confused about the health issue; we drink soda that is sugar-free but loaded with chemical sweeteners. Still, we believe we are lengthening our lives through changing our diets.

② *First sentence cluttered, too long*

③ *Add specifics*

① *Doesn't fit point being made*

On the advice of his classmates, Carl decided to omit all references to the way our concern with weight has affected our eating habits. It's true, of course, that calorie-counting has changed how we eat. But as soon as Carl started to discuss this point, he got involved in a causal chain that undercut the paragraph's unity. He ended up describing the paradoxical situation in which we find ourselves: In an attempt to eat healthy, we stay away from sugar and turn to possibly harmful artificial sweeteners. This is an interesting issue, but it detracts from Carl's main point—that our concern with health has affected our eating habits in a *positive* way.

Carl's editing team also pointed out that the fourth paragraph's first sentence contained too much material to be an effective topic sentence. Carl corrected the problem by breaking the overlong sentence into two short ones: "Our growing concern with health has also affected the way we eat. For the last few years, the media have warned us about the dangers of our traditional diet, high in salt and fat, low in fiber." The first of these sentences serves as a crisp topic sentence that focuses the rest of the paragraph.

Finally, when Carl heard the essay read aloud, he realized the fourth paragraph lacked convincing specifics. When revising, he changed "manufacturers started taking some of the salt and sugar out of canned foods" to the more specific "Many foods, such as lunch meats, canned vegetables, and soups, were made available in low-fat, low-sodium versions." Similarly, generalizations about "light meals" and "all-natural products" gained life through the addition of concrete examples: restaurants lured "customers with salad bars, broiled fish, and steamed vegetables," and the food industry produced "everything from potato chips to ice cream—without additives and preservatives."

Carl did an equally good job revising other sections of his paper. With the exception of the weak spots already discussed, he made the changes needed to craft a well-reasoned essay, one that demonstrates his ability to analyze a complex phenomenon.

ACTIVITIES: CAUSE-EFFECT

Prewriting Activities

1. Imagine you're writing two essays: One proposes the need for high school courses in personal finance (how to budget money, balance a checkbook, and the like); the other explains how to show appreciation. Jot down ways you might use cause-effect in each essay.

2. Use mapping, collaborative brainstorming, or another prewriting technique to generate possible causes and/or effects for *one* of the following topics. Then organize your raw material into a brief outline, with related causes and effects grouped in the same section.

   a. Pressure on students to do well
   b. Children's access to soft-core pornography on cable television
   c. Being physically fit
   d. Spiraling costs of a college education

3. For the topic you selected in activity 2, note the two potential audiences indicated below in parentheses. For each audience, devise a thesis and decide whether your essay's purpose would be informative, persuasive, speculative, or some combination of these. Then, with your thesis statements and purposes in mind, review the outline you prepared for the preceding activity. How would you change it to fit each audience? What points should be added? What points would be primary causes and effects for one audience but secondary for the other? Which organizational pattern—chronological, spatial, or emphatic—would be most effective for each audience?

   a. Pressure on students to do well (*college students, parents of elementary school children*)
   b. Children's access to soft-core pornography on cable television (*cable executives, parents of young children*)
   c. Being physically fit (*those who show a reasonable degree of concern, those who are obsessed with being fit*)
   d. Spiraling costs of a college education (*college officials, high school students planning to attend college*)

Revising Activities

4. Explain how the following statements demonstrate *post hoc* thinking and confuse correlation and cause-effect.

   a. Our city now has many immigrants from Latin American countries. The crime rate in our city has increased. Latin American immigrants are the cause of the crime wave.
   b. The divorce rate has skyrocketed. More women are working outside the home than ever before. Working outside the home destroys marriages.
   c. A high percentage of people in Dixville have developed cancer. The landfill, used by XYZ Industries, has been located in Dixville for twenty years. The XYZ landfill has caused cancer in Dixville residents.

5. The following paragraph is from the first draft of an essay arguing that technological advances can diminish the quality of life. How solid is the paragraph's causal analysis? Which causes and/or effects should be eliminated? Where is the analysis simplistic? Where does the writer make absolute claims even though cause-effect relationships are no more than a possibility? Keeping these questions in mind, revise the paragraph.

How did the banking industry respond to inflation? It simply introduced a new technology--the automated teller machine (ATM). By making money more available to the average person, the ATM gives people the cash to buy inflated goods--whether or not they can afford them. Not surprisingly, automatic teller machines have had a number of negative consequences for the average individual. Since people know they can get cash at any time, they use their lunch hours for something other than going to the bank. How do they spend this new-found time? They go shopping, and machine-vended money means more impulse buying, even more than with a credit card. Also, because people don't need their checkbooks to withdraw money, they can't keep track of their accounts and therefore develop a casual attitude toward financial matters. It's no wonder children don't appreciate the value of money. Another problem is that people who would never dream of robbing a bank try to trick the machine into dispensing money "for free." There's no doubt that this kind of fraud contributes to the immoral climate in the country.

PROFESSIONAL SELECTIONS: CAUSE-EFFECT

GEORGE GALLUP, JR.

The author of numerous articles on contemporary social issues, George Gallup, Jr. (1930–) is president of the Gallup Poll, the well-known research firm that measures public opinion. His books include *America's Search for Faith* (1980), with David Poling; *Forecast 2000* (1985), with William Proctor; and *One Hundred Questions and Answers: Religion in America* (1989), with Sara Jones. The following essay is taken from *Forecast 2000*.

THE FALTERING FAMILY

In a recent Sunday school class in a United Methodist Church in the Northeast, a group of eight- to ten-year-olds were in a deep discussion with their two teachers. When asked to choose which of ten stated possibilities they most feared happening, their response was unanimous. All the children most dreaded a divorce between their parents. 1

Later, as the teachers, a man and a woman in their late thirties, reflected on the lesson, they both agreed they'd been shocked at the response. When they were the same age as their students, they said, the possibility of their parents' being divorced never entered their heads. Yet in just one generation, children seemed to feel much less security in their family ties. 2

3   Nor is the experience of these two Sunday school teachers an isolated one. Psychiatrists revealed in one recent newspaper investigation that the fears of children definitely do change in different periods; and in recent times, divorce has become one of the most frequently mentioned anxieties. In one case, for example, a four-year-old insisted that his father rather than his mother walk him to nursery school each day. The reason? He said many of his friends had "no daddy living at home, and I'm scared that will happen to me" (*The New York Times,* May 2, 1983).

4   In line with such reports, our opinion leaders expressed great concern about the present and future status of the American family. In the poll 33 percent of the responses listed decline in family structure, divorce, and other family-oriented concerns as one of the five major problems facing the nation today. And 26 percent of the responses included such family difficulties as one of the five major problems for the United States in the year 2000.

5   Historical and sociological trends add strong support to these expressions of concern. For example, today about one marriage in every two ends in divorce. Moreover, the situation seems to be getting worse, rather than better. In 1962, the number of divorces was 2.2 per 1,000 people, according to the National Center for Health Statistics. By 1982, the figure had jumped to 5.1 divorces per 1,000 people—a rate that had more than doubled in two decades.

6   One common concern expressed about the rise in divorces and decline in stability of the family is that the family unit has traditionally been a key factor in transmitting stable cultural and moral values from generation to generation. Various studies have shown that educational and religious institutions often can have only a limited impact on children without strong family support.

7   Even grandparents are contributing to the divorce statistics. One recent study revealed that about 100,000 people over the age of fifty-five get divorced in the United States each year. These divorces are usually initiated by men who face retirement, and the relationships being ended are those that have endured for thirty years or more (*The New York Times Magazine,* December 19, 1982).

8   What are the pressures that have emerged in the past twenty years that cause long-standing family bonds to be broken?

9   Many now agree that the sexual revolution of the 1960s worked a profound change on our society's family values and personal relationships. Certainly, the seeds of upheaval were present before that critical decade. But a major change that occurred in the mid-sixties was an explicit widespread rejection of the common values about sexual and family relationships that most Americans in the past had held up as an ideal.

10 We're just beginning to sort through all the changes in social standards that have occurred. Here are some of the major pressures that have contributed to those changes.

Pressure One: Alternative Lifestyles

11 Twenty years ago, the typical American family was depicted as a man and woman who were married to each other and who produced children (usually two) and lived happily ever after. This was the pattern that young people expected to follow in order to become "full" or "normal" members of society. Of course, some people have always chosen a different route—remaining single, taking many partners, or living with a member of their own sex. But they were always considered somewhat odd, and outside the social order of the traditional family.

In the last two decades, this picture has changed dramatically. In addition to the proliferation of single people through divorce, we also have these developments:

- Gay men and women have petitioned the courts for the right to marry each other and to adopt children. These demands are being given serious consideration, and there may be a trend of sorts in this direction. For example, the National Association of Social Workers is increasingly supporting full adoption rights for gay people (*The New York Times*, January 10, 1983).

- Many heterosexual single adults have been permitted to adopt children and set up single-parent families. So being unattached no longer excludes people from the joys of parenthood.

- Some women have deliberately chosen to bear children out of wedlock and raise them alone. In the past, many of these children would have been given up for adoption, but no longer.

- A most unusual case involved an unmarried psychologist, Dr. Afton Blake, who recently gave birth after being artificially inseminated with sperm from a sperm bank to which Nobel Prize winners had contributed (*The New York Times*, September 6, 1983).

- In a recent Gallup Youth Poll, 64 percent of the teenagers questioned said that they hoped their lives would be different from those of their parents. This included having more money, pursuing a different kind of profession, living in a different area, having more free time—and staying single longer.

    Most surveys show increasing numbers of unmarried couples living together. Also, there are periodic reports of experiments in communal living, "open marriages," and other such arrangements. Although the more radical approaches to relationships tend to come and go and never seem to attract large numbers of people, the practice of living together without getting married seems to be something that's here to stay. The law is beginning to respond to these arrangements with awards for "palimony"—compensation for long-term unmarried partners in a relationship. But the legal and social status of unmarried people who live together is still quite uncertain—especially as far as any children of the union are concerned.

- Increasing numbers of married couples are choosing to remain childless. Planned Parenthood has even established workshops for couples to assist them in making this decision (*Los Angeles Herald-Examiner*, November 27, 1979).

So clearly, a situation has arisen during the last twenty years in which traditional values are no longer as important. Also, a wide variety of alternatives to the traditional family has arisen. Individuals may feel that old-fashioned marriage is just one of many options.

Pressure Two: Sexual Morality

Attitudes toward sexual morality have changed as dramatically in the last two decades as have the alternatives to traditional marriage. Hear what a widely used college textbook, published in 1953, said about premarital sex:

> The arguments against premarital coitus outweigh those in its favor. Except for the matter of temporary physical pleasure, all arguments about gains tend to be highly theoretical, while the risks and unpleasant consequences tend to be in equal degree highly practical. . . .

23 The promiscuity of young men is certainly poor preparation for marital fidelity and successful family life. For girls it is certainly no better and sometimes leads still further to the physical and psychological shock of abortion or the more prolonged suffering of bearing an illegitimate child and giving it up to others. From the viewpoint of ethical and religious leaders, the spread of disease through unrestrained sex activities is far more than a health problem. They see it as undermining the dependable standards of character and the spiritual values that raise life to the level of the "good society."

(This comes from *Marriage and the Family* by Professor Ray E. Baber of Pomona College, California, which was part of the McGraw-Hill Series in Sociology and Anthropology and required reading for some college courses.)

24 Clearly, attitudes have changed a great deal in just three decades. Teenagers have accepted the idea of premarital sex as the norm. In one recent national poll, 52 percent of girls and 66 percent of boys favored having sexual relations in their teens. Ironically, however, 46 percent of the teenagers thought that virginity in their future marital partner was fairly important. Youngsters, in other words, display some confusion about what they want to do sexually, and what they expect from a future mate.

25 But of course, only part of the problem of defining sexual standards lies with young people and premarital sex. The strong emphasis on achieving an active and rewarding sex life has probably played some role in encouraging many husbands and wives into rejecting monogamy. Here's some of the evidence that's been accumulating:

26 • Half of the men in a recent nationwide study admitted cheating on their wives (*Pensacola Journal,* May 30, 1978).

27 • Psychiatrists today say they see more patients who are thinking about having an extramarital affair and who wonder if it would harm their marriage (*New York Post*, November 18, 1976).

28 • A psychiatrist at the Albert Einstein College of Medicine says, "In my practice I have been particularly struck by how many women have been able to use an affair to raise their consciousness and their confidence."

29 So the desire for unrestrained sex now tends to take a place among other more traditional priorities, and this can be expected to continue to exert strong pressure on marriage relationships.

Pressure Three: The Economy

30 The number of married women working outside the home has been increasing steadily, and most of these women are working out of economic necessity. As a result, neither spouse may have time to concentrate on the nurturing of the children or of the marriage relationship.

31 One mother we interviewed in New Jersey told us about her feelings when she was forced to work full time in a library after her husband lost his job.

32 "It's the idea that I have no choice that really bothers me," she said. "I have to work, or we won't eat or have a roof over our heads. I didn't mind working part-time just to have extra money. I suppose that it's selfish, but I hate having to work every day and then to come home, fix dinner, and have to start doing housework. Both my husband and I were raised in traditional families, where the father went to work and the mother stayed home and took care of the house and children. [My husband] would never think of cooking or doing housework. I've raised my boys the same way, and now I'm paying for it. Sometimes, I almost hate my husband, even though I know it's not his fault."

Unfortunately, such pressures probably won't ease in the future. Even if the economy improves and the number of unemployed workers decreases, few women are likely to give up their jobs. Economists agree that working-class women who have become breadwinners during a recession can be expected to remain in the workforce. One reason is that many unemployed men aren't going to get their old jobs back, even when the economy improves.

"To the extent that [the men] may have to take lower-paying service jobs, their families will need a second income," says Michelle Brandman, associate economist at Chase Econometrics. "The trend to two-paycheck families as a means of maintaining family income is going to continue" (*The Wall Street Journal,* December 8, 1982).

In addition to the pressures of unemployment, the cost of having, rearing, and educating children is steadily going up. Researchers have found that middle-class families with two children *think* they're spending only about 15 percent of their income on their children. Usually, though, they *actually* spend about 40 percent of their money on them. To put the cost in dollars and cents, if you had a baby in 1977, the estimated cost of raising that child to the age of eighteen will be $85,000, and that figure has of course been on the rise for babies born since then (*New York Daily News,* July 24, 1977).

Another important factor that promises to keep both spouses working full time in the future is the attitude of today's teenagers toward these issues. They're not so much concerned about global issues like overpopulation as they are about the high cost of living. Both boys and girls place a lot of emphasis on having enough money so that they can go out and do things. Consequently, most teenage girls surveyed say they expect to pursue careers, even after they get married.

So it would seem that by the year 2000 we can expect to see more working mothers in the United States. The woman who doesn't hold down any sort of outside job but stays at home to care for her children represents a small percentage of wives today. By the end of the century, with a few exceptions here and there, she may well have become a part of America's quaint past.

As women have joined the workforce in response to economic needs, one result has been increased emotional strains on the marriage and family relationships. But there's another set of pressures that has encouraged women to pursue careers. That's the power of feminist philosophy to permeate attitudes in grassroots America during the past couple of decades.

Pressure Four: Grassroots Feminist Philosophy

Many women may not agree with the most radical expressions of feminist philosophy that have arisen in the past decade or so. But most younger women—and indeed, a majority of women in the United States—tend to agree with most of the objectives that even the radical feminist groups have been trying to achieve. The basic feminist philosophy has filtered down to the grass roots, and young boys and girls are growing up with feminist assumptions that may have been foreign to their parents and grandparents.

For example, child care and housework are no longer regarded strictly as "women's work" by the younger people we've polled. Also, according to the Gallup Youth Poll, most teenage girls want to go to college and pursue a career. Moreover, they expect to marry later in life and to continue working after they're married. Another poll, conducted by *The New York Times* and *CBS News,* revealed that only 2 percent of the youngest age group interviewed—that is, those eighteen to twenty-nine years old—

preferred "traditional marriage." By this, they meant a marriage in which the husband is exclusively a provider and the wife is exclusively a homemaker and mother.

41 If these young people continue to hold views similar to these into later life, it's likely that the changes that are occurring today in the traditional family structure will continue. For one thing, more day-care centers for children will have to be established. Consequently, the rearing of children will no longer be regarded as solely the responsibility of the family, but will become a community or institutional responsibility.

42 But while such developments may lessen the strain on mothers and fathers, they may also weaken the bonds that hold families together. Among other things, it may become psychologically easier to get a divorce if a person is not getting along with a spouse, because the divorcing spouses will believe it's less likely that the lives of the children will be disrupted.

43 So the concept of broadening the rights of women vis-à-vis their husbands and families has certainly encouraged women to enter the working world in greater numbers. They're also more inclined to seek a personal identity that isn't tied up so much in their homelife.

44 These grassroots feminist forces have brought greater benefits to many, but at the same time they've often worked against traditional family ties, and we remain uncertain about what is going to replace them. Feminists may argue that the traditional family caused its own demise—or else why would supposedly content wives and daughters have worked so hard to transform it? Whatever its theories, though, feminism is still a factor that, in its present form, appears to exert a destabilizing influence on many traditional familial relationships among husbands, wives, and children.

45 As things stand now, our family lives are in a state of flux and will probably continue to be out of balance until the year 2000. The pressures we've discussed will continue to have an impact on our family lives in future years. But at the same time, counterforces, which tend to drive families back together again, are also at work.

46 One of these factors is a traditionalist strain in the large majority of American women. The vast majority of women in this country—74 percent—continue to view marriage with children as the most interesting and satisfying life for them personally, according to a Gallup Poll for the White House Conference on Families released in June, 1980.

47 Another force supporting family life is the attitude of American teenagers toward divorce. According to a recent Gallup Youth Poll, 55 percent feel that divorces are too easy to get today. Also, they're concerned about the high rate of divorce, and they want to have enduring marriages themselves. But at the same time—in a response that reflects the confusion of many adult Americans on this subject—67 percent of the teens in this same poll say it's right to get a divorce if a couple doesn't get along together. In other words, they place little importance on trying to improve or salvage a relationship that has run into serious trouble.

48 There's a similar ambivalence in the experts we polled. As we've seen, 33 percent of them consider family problems as a top concern today, and 26 percent think these problems will be a big difficulty in the year 2000. But ironically, less than 3 percent suggest that strengthening family relationships is an important consideration in planning for the future! It's obvious, then, that we're confused and ambivalent in our feelings about marriage and the family. Most people know instinctively, without having to read a poll or a book, that happiness and satisfaction in life are rooted largely in the quality of our personal relationships. Furthermore, the most important of those relationships usually begin at home. So one of the greatest challenges we

face before the year 2000, both as a nation and as individuals, is how to make our all-important family ties strong and healthy. It's only upon such a firm personal foundation that we can hope to venture forth and grapple effectively with more public problems.

Questions for Close Reading

1. What is the selection's thesis? Locate the sentence(s) in which Gallup states his main idea. If he doesn't state the thesis explicitly, express it in your own words.

2. According to Gallup, what are the major pressures that have caused the change in American attitudes toward marriage and family?

3. What new styles of pairing up and parenting have entered the American mainstream and now compete with traditional marriage?

4. Why are more and more women choosing to work outside the home? Why does the author believe that this is a permanent life-style change for American women?

5. Refer to your dictionary as needed to define the following words used in the selection: *explicit* (paragraph 9), *proliferation* (12), *inseminated* (16), *salvage* (47), and *ambivalence* (48).

Questions About the Writer's Craft

1. The pattern. In this selection, Gallup tries to account for changes in the American ideals of marriage and family. Why do you think he uses the term *pressures* rather than *causes*?

2. What techniques does Gallup use to introduce the selection? What feeling toward marriage and family does this introduction create in you? How is the introduction related to the data presented in the selection?

3. Other patterns. Examine the supporting evidence that Gallup provides to illustrate each "pressure." For which ones does he provide facts or statistics? What kinds of evidence does he provide to illustrate the other pressures?

4. How does Gallup create a sense of his objectivity? Which word choices suggest his personal opinions about the transformation in American family values?

Writing Assignments Using Cause-Effect as a Pattern of Development

1. Writing in 1985, Gallup places much of the blame for the family's decline on women. He ignores a number of other factors (both personal and societal) that add stress to family life. Substance abuse, mental illness, homelessness, and industry's failure to provide day-care services to employees with young children are just some of the factors that come to mind. Select *one* of these factors, or

Cause-Effect 371

another that seems important to you, and write an essay analyzing its effect on the family.

2. Write an essay explaining how people are affected when those close to them choose an alternative life-style. For example, think of someone you know who has chosen divorce, single parenthood, a gay life-style, cohabitation, or some other nontraditional way of life. Decide what positive and/or negative effects resulted from this choice, and discuss these effects in your essay. You may wish to evaluate the choice on the basis of how it turned out, but avoid generalizing from one case to universal rules of behavior.

Writing Assignments Using Other Patterns of Development

3. When a family breaks apart, many lives are disrupted. Parents, children, grandparents, other relatives, friends, even neighbors must cope with disorder and confusion. Choose one of these groups and write an essay illustrating the kinds of turmoil that the group may face. Develop the paper by drawing on your own and/or other people's experience. Include some brief recommendations about how the group might cope with the situation.

4. To what extent, and in what light, do alternative life-styles (extramarital affairs, divorce, single parenthood, and so on) appear in the plots of television sitcoms and dramas? To get some idea, watch TV for a week and take notes. Write up your findings in the form of a letter to *TV Guide*, either criticizing or praising the TV networks for the way they present one or two such life-styles. Support your argument with specific references to the shows you viewed.

JACQUES COUSTEAU

An oceanographer, author, and film producer, Jacques Cousteau (1910–) helped invent the Aqualung and, during his long career, developed numerous techniques for exploring the ocean. Three of Cousteau's films about sea life have won Academy Awards. His books include *The Silent World* (1953), *World Without Sun* (1964), and *The Bounty of the Sea* (1965), from which the following selection is taken.

THE BOUNTY OF THE SEA

1   During the past thirty years, I have observed and studied the oceans closely, and with my own two eyes I have seen them sicken. Certain reefs that teemed with fish only ten years ago are now almost lifeless. The ocean bottom has been raped by trawlers. Priceless wetlands have been destroyed by landfill. And everywhere are sticky globs of oil, plastic refuse, and unseen clouds of poisonous effluents. Often, when I describe the symptoms of the oceans' sickness, I hear remarks like "they're only fish" or "they're only whales" or "they're only birds." But I assure you that our destinies are linked with theirs in the most profound and fundamental manner. For if the oceans should die—by which I mean

that all life in the sea would finally cease—this would signal the end not only for marine life but for all other animals and plants of this earth, including man.

With life departed, the ocean would become, in effect, one enormous cesspool. Billions of decaying bodies, large and small, would create such an insupportable stench that man would be forced to leave all the coastal regions. But far worse would follow.

The ocean acts as the earth's buffer. It maintains a fine balance between the many salts and gases which make life possible. But dead seas would have no buffering effect. The carbon dioxide content of the atmosphere would start on a steady and remorseless climb, and when it reached a certain level a "greenhouse effect" would be created. The heat that normally radiates outward from the earth to space would be blocked by the CO_2, and sea level temperatures would dramatically increase.

One catastrophic effect of this heat would be melting of the icecaps at both the North and South Poles. As a result, the ocean would rise by 100 feet or more, enough to flood almost all the world's major cities. These rising waters would drive one-third of the earth's billions inland, creating famine, fighting, chaos, and disease on a scale almost impossible to imagine.

Meanwhile, the surface of the ocean would have scummed over with a thick film of decayed matter, and would no longer be able to give water freely to the skies through evaporation. Rain would become a rarity, creating global drought and even more famine.

But the final act is yet to come. The wretched remnant of the human race would now be packed cheek by jowl on the remaining highlands, bewildered, starving, struggling to survive from hour to hour. Then would be visited upon them the final plague, anoxia (lack of oxygen). This would be caused by the extinction of plankton algae and the reduction of land vegetation, the two sources that supply the oxygen you are now breathing.

And so man would finally die, slowly gasping out his life on some barren hill. He would have survived the oceans by perhaps thirty years. And his heirs would be bacteria and a few scavenger insects.

Questions for Close Reading

1. What is the selection's thesis? Locate the sentence(s) in which Cousteau states his main idea. If he doesn't state the thesis explicitly, express it in your own words.

2. According to Cousteau, what evidence is there that the oceans may be dying? How convincing is his evidence?

3. What is the "greenhouse effect"? How is it related to the death of the ocean?

4. What are the factors that would cause the migration of humans toward interior highlands? According to Cousteau, what would inevitably happen to humans after this migration occurred?

5. Refer to your dictionary as needed to define the following words used in the selection: *trawlers* (paragraph 1), *effluents* (1), *buffer* (3), and *plankton* (6).

Questions About the Writer's Craft

1. The pattern. How many chains of effects resulting from the ocean's death does Cousteau describe? Why do you suppose he sequences the effects the way he does?

Cause-Effect

2. What transitions does Cousteau use to move from one chain of effects to another? Which of these transitions indicate Cousteau's attitude toward his subject?

3. Why do you think Cousteau decided to start his essay in the first person? What might have been his reason for shifting to the third person in the rest of the essay?

4. Other patterns. Cousteau uses descriptive, highly connotative words like "cesspool" and "scummed over." Locate additional examples of emotionally charged, often strongly visual language. Why might Cousteau have chosen to use this kind of emotive language?

Writing Assignments Using Cause-Effect as a Pattern of Development

1. Cousteau graphically shows the effect of the death of our oceans. Focus on some other less global environmental problem in a community: graffiti on a public building; beer cans thrown in a neighborhood park; the loss of farmland to commercial development. Discuss the effects of this situation on the community and its people. Conclude with suggestions about possible ways to remedy the problem.

2. Think of a place or social institution that, like our oceans, is changing for the worse. In an essay, explain the reasons for this change. Collect information for your causal analysis by brainstorming with others and/or conducting library research.

Writing Assignments Using Other Patterns of Development

3. Identify an environmental or social problem that would be at least partly alleviated if people's attitudes and behavior changed. You might, for example, focus on the use of non-biodegradable packaging by fast-food restaurants or on the growing incidence of date rape. Brainstorm with others and/or conduct research to gather appropriate material; then write an essay outlining the steps that could be taken to reduce the problem. Before writing your paper, you may want to read Nancy Gibbs's "When Is It Rape?" (page 397)—an essay that shows how unexamined assumptions can lead to a serious social problem.

4. Cousteau projects a chain of events that, once started, could not be stopped by human intervention. Drawing on one example or several, write a narrative essay showing that a single person *can* make the difference in remedying a seemingly overwhelming problem.

BRENT STAPLES

After earning a Ph.D. in psychology from the University of Chicago, Brent Staples (1951–) soon became a nationally recognized essayist. He has worked on numerous newspapers and is now assistant metropolitan editor of the *New York Times*. This selection first appeared in slightly different form in *Ms.* magazine (1986) and then in *Harper's* (1987).

BLACK MEN AND PUBLIC SPACE

My first victim was a woman—white, well dressed, probably in her early twenties. I came upon her late one evening on a deserted street in Hyde Park, a relatively affluent neighborhood in an otherwise mean, impoverished section of Chicago. As I swung onto the avenue behind her, there seemed to be a discreet, uninflammatory distance between us. Not so. She cast back a worried glance. To her, the youngish black man—a broad six feet two inches with a beard and billowing hair, both hands shoved into the pockets of a bulky military jacket—seemed menacingly close. After a few more quick glimpses, she picked up her pace and was soon running in earnest. Within seconds she disappeared into a cross street.

That was more than a decade ago. I was twenty-two years old, a graduate student newly arrived at the University of Chicago. It was in the echo of that terrified woman's footfalls that I first began to know the unwieldy inheritance I'd come into—the ability to alter public space in ugly ways. It was clear that she thought herself the quarry of a mugger, a rapist, or worse. Suffering a bout of insomnia, however, I was stalking sleep, not defenseless wayfarers. As a softy who is scarcely able to take a knife to a raw chicken—let alone hold one to a person's throat—I was surprised, embarrassed, and dismayed all at once. Her flight made me feel like an accomplice in tyranny. It also made it clear that I was indistinguishable from the muggers who occasionally seeped into the area from the surrounding ghetto. That first encounter, and those that followed, signified that a vast, unnerving gulf lay between nighttime pedestrians—particularly women—and me. And I soon gathered that being perceived as dangerous is a hazard in itself. I only needed to turn a corner into a dicey situation, or crowd some frightened, armed person in a foyer somewhere, or make an errant move after being pulled over by a policeman. Where fear and weapons meet—and they often do in urban America—there is always the possibility of death.

In that first year, my first away from my hometown, I was to become thoroughly familiar with the language of fear. At dark, shadowy intersections, I could cross in front of a car stopped at a traffic light and elicit the *thunk, thunk, thunk, thunk* of the driver—black, white, male, or female—hammering down the door locks. On less traveled streets after dark, I grew accustomed to but never comfortable with people crossing to the other side of the street rather than pass me. Then there were the standard unpleasantries with policemen, doormen, bouncers, cabdrivers, and others whose business it is to screen out troublesome individuals *before* there is any nastiness.

I moved to New York nearly two years ago and I have remained an avid night walker. In central Manhattan, the near-constant crowd cover minimizes tense one-on-one street encounters. Elsewhere—in SoHo, for example, where sidewalks are narrow and tightly spaced buildings shut out the sky—things can get very taut indeed.

After dark, on the warrenlike streets of Brooklyn where I live, I often see women who fear the worst from me. They seem to have set their faces on neutral, and with their purse straps strung across their chests bandolier-style, they forge ahead as though bracing themselves against being tackled. I understand, of course, that the danger they perceive is not a hallucination. Women are particularly vulnerable to street violence, and young black males are drastically overrepresented among the perpetrators of that violence. Yet these truths are no solace against the kind of alienation that comes of being ever the suspect, a fearsome entity with whom pedestrians avoid making eye contact.

6 It is not altogether clear to me how I reached the ripe old age of twenty-two without being conscious of the lethality nighttime pedestrians attributed to me. Perhaps it was because in Chester, Pennsylvania, the small, angry industrial town where I came of age in the 1960s, I was scarcely noticeable against a backdrop of gang warfare, street knifings, and murders. I grew up one of the good boys, had perhaps a half-dozen fistfights. In retrospect, my shyness of combat has clear sources.

7 As a boy, I saw countless tough guys locked away; I have since buried several, too. They were babies, really—a teenage cousin, a brother of twenty-two, a childhood friend in his mid-twenties—all gone down in episodes of bravado played out in the streets. I came to doubt the virtues of intimidation early on. I chose, perhaps unconsciously, to remain a shadow—timid, but a survivor.

8 The fearsomeness mistakenly attributed to me in public places often has a perilous flavor. The most frightening of these confusions occurred in the late 1970s and early 1980s, when I worked as a journalist in Chicago. One day, rushing into the office of a magazine I was writing for with a deadline story in hand, I was mistaken for a burglar. The office manager called security and, with an ad hoc posse, pursued me through the labyrinthine halls, nearly to my editor's door. I had no way of proving who I was. I could only move briskly toward the company of someone who knew me.

9 Another time I was on assignment for a local paper and killing time before an interview. I entered a jewelry store on the city's affluent Near North Side. The proprietor excused herself and returned with an enormous red Doberman pinscher straining at the end of a leash. She stood, the dog extended toward me, silent to my questions, her eyes bulging nearly out of her head. I took a cursory look around, nodded, and bade her good night.

10 Relatively speaking, however, I never fared as badly as another black male journalist. He went to nearby Waukegan, Illinois, a couple of summers ago to work on a story about a murderer who was born there. Mistaking the reporter for the killer, police officers hauled him from his car at gunpoint and but for his press credentials would probably have tried to book him. Such episodes are not uncommon. Black men trade tales like this all the time.

11 Over the years, I learned to smother the rage I felt at so often being taken for a criminal. Not to do so would surely have led to madness. I now take precautions to make myself less threatening. I move about with care, particularly late in the evening. I give a wide berth to nervous people on subway platforms during the wee hours, particularly when I have exchanged business clothes for jeans. If I happen to be entering a building behind some people who appear skittish, I may walk by, letting them clear the lobby before I return, so as not to seem to be following them. I have been calm and extremely congenial on those rare occasions when I've been pulled over by the police.

12 And on late-evening constitutionals I employ what has proved to be an excellent tension-reducing measure: I whistle melodies from Beethoven and Vivaldi and the more popular classical composers. Even steely New Yorkers hunching toward nighttime destinations seem to relax, and occasionally they even join in the tune. Virtually everybody seems to sense that a mugger wouldn't be warbling bright, sunny selections from Vivaldi's *Four Seasons*. It is my equivalent of the cowbell that hikers wear when they know they are in bear country.

Questions for Close Reading

1. What is the selection's thesis? Locate the sentence(s) in which Staples states his main idea. If he doesn't state the thesis explicitly, express it in your own words.

2. How did Staples first learn that he was considered a threat by many people? How did this discovery make him feel?

3. What are some of the dangers that Staples has encountered because of his color? How has he handled each dangerous situation?

4. What "precautions" does Staples take to appear nonthreatening to others? Why do these precautions work?

5. Refer to your dictionary as needed to define the following words used in the selection: *uninflammatory* (paragraph 1), *dicey* (2), *bandolier* (5), *lethality* (6), *bravado* (7), *berth* (11), and *constitutionals* (12).

Questions About the Writer's Craft

1. The pattern. Brent Staples reveals both causes and effects of people's reacting with fear to a black male. Does the essay end with a discussion of causes or of effects? Why do you suppose Staples concludes the essay as he does?

2. Other patterns. Why do you think Staples opens the piece with such a dramatic, yet intentionally misleading narrative? What effect does he achieve?

3. Is Staples writing primarily for whites, blacks, or both? How do you know?

4. What is Staples's tone? Why do you think he chose this tone?

Writing Assignments Using Cause-Effect as a Pattern of Development

1. Write an essay showing how your or someone else's entry into a specific public space (for example, a bus, party, elevator, or table at the library) influenced other people's behavior. Identify the possible reasons that others reacted as they did, and explain how their reactions, in turn, affected the newcomer. Use your analysis to reach some conclusions about human nature.

2. Staples describes circumstances that often result in fear. Focusing on a more positive emotion, like admiration or contentment, illustrate the situations that tend to elicit that emotion in you. Discuss why these circumstances have the effect they do.

Writing Assignments Using Other Patterns of Development

∞ **3.** Staples describes how others' expectations oblige him to alter his behavior. Narrate an event during which you felt forced to conform to what others expected. What did you learn from the experience? George Orwell's "Shooting an Elephant" (page 201), Malcolm X's "My First Conk" (page 307), and Joseph Suina's "And Then I Went to School" (page 339) may prompt some interesting thoughts on the issue of conformity.

4. When he encounters a startled pedestrian, Staples feels some fear but manages to control it. Write an essay showing the steps you took one time when you felt afraid but, like Staples, remained in control and got through safely. Convey your initial fear, your later relief, and any self-discovery that resulted from the experience.

ADDITIONAL WRITING TOPICS: CAUSE-EFFECT

General Assignments

Write an essay that analyzes the causes and/or effects of one of the following topics.

1. Sleep deprivation
2. Having the parents you have
3. Lack of communication in a relationship
4. Overexercising or not exercising
5. A particular TV or rock star's popularity
6. Skill or ineptitude in sports
7. A major life decision
8. Changing attitudes toward the environment
9. Voter apathy
10. An act of violence or cruelty

Assignments with a Specific Purpose, Audience, and Point of View

1. A debate about the prominence of athletics at colleges and universities is going to be broadcast on the local cable station. For this debate, prepare a speech pointing out either the harmful or beneficial effects of "big-time" college athletic programs.

2. Why do students "flunk out" of college? Write an article for the campus newspaper outlining the main causes of failure. Your goal is to steer students away from dangerous habits and situations that lead to poor grades or dropping out.

3. Write a letter to the editor of your favorite newspaper, analyzing the causes of the country's current "trash crisis." Be sure to mention the nationwide love affair with disposable items and the general disregard of the idea of thrift.

4. As part of a pamphlet for first-year college students, write an advice piece on the effects—both negative and positive—of combining a part-time job with college studies.

5. Why do you think teenage suicide is on the rise? Write a fact sheet for parents of teenagers and for high school guidance counselors, describing the factors that could make a young person desperate enough to attempt suicide. At the end, suggest what parents and counselors can do to help confused, unhappy young people.

6. Write a letter to the mayor of your town or city suggesting a "Turn Off the TV" public relations effort, convincing residents to stop watching television for a month. Cite the positive effects that "no TV" would have on parents, children, and the community in general.

19 DEFINITION

WHAT IS DEFINITION?

IN Lewis Carroll's wise and whimsical tale *Through the Looking Glass*, Humpty Dumpty proclaims, "When I use a word . . . it means just what I choose it to mean—neither more nor less." If the world were filled with characters like Humpty Dumpty, all of them bending the meanings of words to their own purposes and accepting no challenges to their personal definitions, communication would creak to a halt.

For language to communicate, words must have accepted definitions. Dictionaries, the sourcebooks for definitions, are compilations of current word meanings, enabling speakers of a language to understand one another. But as you might suspect, things are not as simple as they first appear. We all know that a word like *discipline* has a standard dictionary definition. We also know that parents argue every day over the meaning of *discipline*, as do teachers and school administrators. Moreover, many of the wrenching moral debates of our time are attempts to resolve questions of definition. Much of the controversy over abortion, for instance, centers on what is meant by "life" and when it "begins."

Words can, in short, be slippery. Each of us has unique experiences, attitudes, and values that influence the way we use words and the way we interpret the words of others. Lewis Carroll may have been exaggerating, but to some degree Humpty Dumpty's attitude exists in all of us.

In addition to the idiosyncratic interpretations we may attach to words, some words shift in meaning over time. The word *pedagogue*, for instance, originally meant "a teacher or leader of children." However, with the passage of time, *pedagogue* has come to mean "a dogmatic, pedantic teacher." And, of course, we invent new words as the need arises. For example, *modem* and *byte* are just two of many new words created in response to recent breakthroughs in computer technology.

Writing a **definition**, then, is no simple task. Primarily, the writer tries to answer basic questions: "What does _____ mean?" and "What is the special or true nature of _____?" The word to be defined may be an object, a concept, a type of person, a place, or a phenomenon. Potential subjects might be the "user-friendly" computer, animal rights, a model teacher, cabin fever. As you will see, there are various strategies for expanding definitions far beyond the single-word synonyms or brief phrases that dictionaries provide.

HOW DEFINITION FITS YOUR PURPOSE AND AUDIENCE

Many times, short-answer exam questions call for definitions. Consider the following examples:

Define the term *mob psychology*.
What is the difference between a metaphor and a simile?
How would you explain what a religious cult is?

In such cases, a good response might involve a definition of several sentences or several paragraphs.

Other times, definition may be used in an essay organized mainly around another pattern of development. In this situation, all that's needed is a brief formal definition or a short definition given in your own words. For instance, a *process analysis* showing readers how computers have revolutionized the typical business office might start with a textbook definition of the term *artificial intelligence*. In an *argumentation-persuasion* paper urging students to support recent efforts to abolish fraternities and sororities, you could refer to the definitions of *blackballing* and *hazing* found in the university handbook. Or your personal definition of *hero* could be the starting point for a *causal analysis* that explains to readers why there are few real heroes in today's world.

But the most complex use of definition, and the one we focus on in this chapter, involves exploring a subject through an **extended definition**. Extended definition allows you to apply a personal interpretation to a word, to propose a revisionist view of a commonly accepted meaning, to analyze words representing complex or controversial issues. *Pornography, gun control, secular humanism,* and *right to privacy* would be good subjects for extended definition; each is multifaceted, often misunderstood, and fraught with emotion. *Junk food, anger, leadership,* and *anxiety* could also make interesting subjects, especially if the extended definition helped readers develop a new understanding of the word. You might, for example, define *anxiety* not as a negative state but as a positive force that propels us to take action.

An extended definition may run several paragraphs or a few pages. Keep in mind, however, that some definitions require a chapter or even an entire book to

Definition

develop. Theologians, philosophers, and pop psychologists have devoted entire texts to concepts like *evil* and *love*.

PREWRITING STRATEGIES

The following checklist shows how you can apply to definition some of the prewriting techniques discussed in Chapter 2.

☑ DEFINITION: A PREWRITING CHECKLIST

Choose Something to Define
- Is there something you're especially qualified to define? What about that thing do you hope to convey?
- Do any of your journal entries reflect an attempt to pinpoint something's essence: courage, pornography, a well-rounded education?
- Will you define a concept (energy), an object (the microchip), a type of person (the bigot), a place (the desert), a phenomenon (the rise in volunteerism), a complex or controversial issue (euthanasia)?
- Can your topic be meaningfully defined within the space and time allotted?

Identify Your Purpose, Audience, Tone, and Point of View
- Do you want simply to inform and explain—that is, to make meaning clear? Or do you want to persuade readers to accept your understanding of a term? Do you want to do both?
- Will you offer a personal interpretation? Propose a revised meaning? Explain an obscure or technical term? Discuss shifts in meaning over time? Distinguish one term from another, closely related term? Show conflicts in definition?
- Are your readers apt to be open to your interpretation of a term? What information will they need to understand your definition and to feel that it is correct and insightful?
- What tone and point of view will make your readers receptive to your definition?

Use Prewriting to Develop the Definition
- How might mapping, brainstorming, freewriting, and speaking with others generate material that develops your definition?
- Which of the following prewriting questions would generate the most details and, therefore, suggest patterns for developing your definition?

Question	Pattern
How does X look, taste, smell, feel, and sound?	Description
What does X do? When? Where?	Narration
What are some typical instances of X?	Illustration
What are X's component parts? What different forms can X take?	Division-classification
How does X work?	Process analysis
What is X like or unlike?	Comparison-contrast
What leads to X? What are X's consequences?	Cause-effect

STRATEGIES FOR USING DEFINITION IN AN ESSAY

After prewriting, you're ready to draft your essay. The following suggestions will be helpful whether you use definition as a dominant or supportive pattern of development.

1. Stay focused on the essay's purpose, audience, and tone. Since your purpose for writing an extended definition shapes the entire paper, you need to keep that objective in mind when developing your definition. Suppose you decide to write an essay defining *jazz*. The essay could be purely *informative* and discuss the origins of jazz, its characteristic tonal patterns, and some of the great jazz musicians of the past. Or the essay could move beyond pure information and take on a *persuasive* edge. It might, for example, argue that jazz is the only contemporary form of music worth considering seriously.

Just as your purpose in writing will vary, so will your tone. A strictly informative definition will generally assume a detached, objective tone ("Apathy is an emotional state characterized by listlessness and indifference"). By way of contrast, a definition essay with a persuasive slant might be urgent in tone ("To combat student apathy, we must design programs that engage students in campus life"), or it might take a satiric approach ("An apathetic stance is a wise choice for any thinking student").

As you write, keep thinking about your audience as well. Not only do your readers determine what terms need to be defined (and in how much detail), but they also keep you focused on the essay's purpose and tone. For instance, you probably wouldn't write a serious, informative piece for the college newspaper about the "mystery meat" served in the campus cafeteria. Instead, you would adopt a light tone as you defined the culinary horror and might even make a persuasive pitch about improving the food prepared on campus.

2. Formulate an effective definition. A definition essay sometimes begins with a brief **formal definition**—the dictionary's, a textbook's, or the writer's—and

Definition

then expands that initial definition with supporting details. Formal definitions are traditionally worded as three-part statements, including (1) the **term**, (2) the **class** to which the term belongs, and (3) the **characteristics** that distinguish the term from other members of its class. Consider these examples of formal definition:

Term	Class	Characteristics
The peregrine falcon,	an endangered bird,	is the world's fastest flyer.
A bodice-ripper	is a paperback book,	usually read by women, that deals with highly charged romance in exotic places and faraway times.
Back to basics	is a trend in education	that emphasizes skill mastery through rote learning.

A definition that meets these three guidelines—term, class, and characteristics—will clarify what your subject *is* and what it *is not*. These guidelines also establish the boundaries or scope of your definition. For example, defining *back to basics* as a "trend that emphasizes rote learning" signals a certain boundary; it lets readers know that other educational trends (such as those that emphasize children's social or emotional development) won't be part of the essay's definition.

Because they are formulaic, formal definitions tend to be dull. For this reason, it's best to reserve them for clarifying potentially confusing words—perhaps words with multiple meanings. For example, the term *the West* can refer to the western section of the United States, to the United States and its non-Communist allies (as in the "Western world"), or to the entire Western Hemisphere. Before discussing the West, then, you would need to provide a formal definition that clarifies your use of the term. Highly specialized or technical terms may also require clarification. Few readers are likely to feel confident about their understanding of the term *cognitive dissonance* unless you supply them with a formal definition: "a conflict of thoughts arising when two or more ideas do not go together."

If you decide to include a formal definition in your essay, avoid tired openings like "the dictionary says" or "according to *Webster's*." Such weak starts lack imagination. You should also keep in mind that a strict dictionary definition may actually confuse readers. Suppose you're writing a paper on the way people tend to absorb their ideas and values from the media. Likening this automatic response to the process of osmosis, you decide to open the paper with a dictionary definition. If you write, "Osmosis is the tendency of a solvent to disperse through a semipermeable membrane into a more concentrated medium," readers are apt to be baffled. *Remember:* The purpose of a definition is to clarify meaning, not obscure it.

You should also stay clear of ungrammatical "is when" definitions: "Blind ambition is when you want to get ahead, no matter how much other people are hurt." Instead, write "Blind ambition is wanting to get ahead, no matter how much other people are hurt." A final pitfall to avoid in writing formal definitions is **circularity**, saying the same thing twice and therefore defining nothing: "A campus tribunal is a tribunal composed of various members of the university community." Circular definitions like this often repeat the term being defined (*tribunal*) or use words having the same meaning (*campus; university community*). In this case, we learn nothing about what a campus tribunal is; the writer says only that "X is X."

3. Develop the extended definition. You can use the patterns of development when formulating an extended definition. Description, narration, process analysis, comparison-contrast, or any of the other patterns discussed in this book may be drawn upon—alone or in combination. Imagine you're planning to write an extended definition of *robotics*. You might develop the term by providing *examples* of the way robots are currently being used in scientific research; by *comparing* and *contrasting* human and robot capabilities; or by *classifying* robots, starting with the most basic and moving to the most advanced or futuristic models. (To deepen your understanding of which patterns to use when developing a particular extended definition, take a moment to review the last item in this chapter's Prewriting Checklist.)

4. Organize the material that develops the definition. If you use a single pattern to develop the extended definition, apply the principles of organization suited to that pattern, as described in the appropriate chapter of this book. Assume that you're defining *fad* by means of *process analysis*. You might organize your paragraphs according to the steps in the process: a fad's slow start as something avant-garde or eccentric; its wildfire acceptance by the general public; the fad's demise as it becomes familiar or tiresome. If you want to define *character* by means of a single *narration*, you would probably organize paragraphs chronologically.

In a definition essay using several methods of development, you should devote separate paragraphs to each pattern. A definition of *relaxation*, for instance, might start with a paragraph that *narrates* a particularly relaxing day; then it might move to a paragraph that presents several *examples* of people who find it difficult to unwind; finally, it might end with a paragraph that explains a *process* for relaxing the mind and body.

5. Write an effective introduction. It can be helpful to provide—near the start of a definition essay—a brief formal definition of the term you're going to develop in the rest of the paper. Beyond this basic element, the introduction might include a number of other features. You may explain the *origin* of the term being defined: "*Acid rock* is a term first coined in the 1960s to describe music that was written or listened to under the influence of the drug LSD." Similarly, you may explain the *etymology*, or linguistic origin, of the key word that focuses the paper: "The term *vigilantism* is derived from a Latin word meaning 'to watch and be awake.'"

You may also use the introduction to clarify what your subject is *not*. Such **definition by negation** can be an effective strategy at a paper's beginning, especially if readers don't share your view of the subject. In such a case, you might write something like this: "The gorilla, far from being the vicious killer of jungle movies and popular imagination, is a sedentary, gentle creature living in a closely knit family group." Such a statement provides the special focus for your essay and signals some of the misconceptions or fallacies soon to be discussed.

Definition

In addition, you may include in the introduction a **stipulative definition**, one that puts special restrictions on a term: "Strictly defined, a mall refers to a one- or two-story enclosed building containing a variety of retail shops and at least two large anchor stores. Highway-strip shopping centers or downtown centers cannot be considered true malls." When a term has multiple meanings, or when its meaning has become fuzzy through misuse, a stipulative definition sets the record straight right at the start, so that readers know exactly what is, and is not, being defined.

Finally, the introduction may end with a *plan of development* that indicates how the essay will unfold. A student who returned to school after having raised a family decided to write a paper defining the mid-life crisis that had led to her enrollment in college. After providing a brief formal definition of *mid-life crisis*, the student rounded off her introduction with this sentence: "Such a mid-life crisis often starts with vague misgivings, turns into depression, and ends with a significant change in life-style."

REVISION STRATEGIES

Once you have a draft of the essay, you're ready to revise. The following checklist will help you and those giving you feedback apply to definition some of the revision techniques discussed in Chapters 7 and 8.

✓ DEFINITION: A REVISION CHECKLIST

Revise Overall Meaning and Structure

- Is your essay's purpose informative, persuasive, or both?
- Is the term being defined clearly distinguished from similar terms?
- Where does a circular definition cloud meaning?
- Where would a word's historical or linguistic origin clarify meaning? Where would a formal definition, stipulative definition, or definition by negation help?
- Where are technical, nonstandard, or ambiguous terms a source of confusion?
- Which patterns of development are used to develop the definition? How do these help the essay achieve its purpose?
- If the essay uses only one pattern, is the essay's method of organization characteristic of that pattern (step-by-step for process analysis, chronological for narration, and so on)?
- Where could a dry formal definition be deleted without sacrificing overall clarity?

> *Revise Paragraph Development*
> - If the essay uses several patterns of development, where would separate paragraphs for different patterns be appropriate?
> - Which paragraphs (or passages) are flat or unconvincing? How could they be made more compelling?
>
> *Revise Sentences and Words*
> - Which sentences and words are inconsistent with the essay's tone?
> - Where should overused phrases like "the dictionary says" and "according to *Webster's*" be replaced by more original wording?
> - Have "is when" definitions been avoided?

STUDENT ESSAY: FROM PREWRITING THROUGH REVISION

The student essay that follows was written by Laura Chen in response to this assignment:

> In "Entropy," K. C. Cole takes a scientific term from physics and gives it a broader definition and a wider application. Choose another specialized term and define it in such a way that you reveal something significant about contemporary life.

Before writing her essay, Laura sat down at a computer and *brainstormed* material on the subject she decided to write about: inertia in everyday life. Later on, when she started shaping this material, she jotted down notes in the margin, starred important ideas, crossed out an item, added other ideas, drew connecting arrows, and used numbers and letters to sequence points. In the process, the essay's underlying structure began to emerge so clearly that an outline seemed unnecessary; Laura felt she could move directly from her brainstormed material to a first draft. Laura's original brainstormed list is reprinted on page 387. The handwritten marks indicate her later efforts to organize the preliminary material.

Now read Laura's paper, "Physics in Everyday Life," noting the similarities and differences between her prewriting and final essay. You'll see, for example, that Laura's decision to discuss national inertia *after* individual inertia makes the essay's sequence of points more emphatic. Similarly, by moving the mention of gravity to the essay's end, Laura creates a satisfying symmetry: The paper now opens and closes with principles of physics. As you read the essay, also consider how well it applies the principles of definition discussed in this chapter. (The commentary that follows the paper will help you look at Laura's essay more closely and will give you some sense of how she went about revising her first draft.)

Definition

Brainstorming

Entropy--an imp. term in physics. *(Put in conclusion?)* Just like gravity.

Formal definition
Boulder sitting or rolling

*③ National inertia *(save broadest for last)*

3b We accept pollution

3a Accept shoddy products

~~Accept growing homelessness~~
3c Go ahead with genetic engineering even though uncomfortable

3d Keep producing nuclear arms

3e Watch too much TV, despite all the reports

1c Racial discrimination remains a problem *Move to section on the individual*

② Individual inertia, too

We resist change

1a Vote the same way all the time

Add example here
1b Need jolts to change (a perfect teenage daughter becomes pregnant)

② But on TV--no inertia

2a Soap operas, commercials--everyone changes easily *give specifics*

2b In real life--wear same hairstyle, use same products, wars and national problems drag on

Physics in Everyday Life
by Laura Chen

1   A boulder sits on a mountainside for a thousand years. The boulder   *Introduction*
will remain there forever unless an outside force intervenes. Suppose a
force does affect the boulder--an earthquake, for instance. Once the
boulder begins to thunder down the mountain, it will remain in motion
and head in one direction only--downhill--until another force interrupts its

progress. If the boulder tumbles into a gorge, it will finally come to rest as gravity anchors it to the earth once more. In both cases, the boulder is exhibiting the physical principle of inertia: the tendency of matter to remain at rest or, if moving, to keep moving in one direction unless affected by an outside force. Inertia, an important factor in the world of physics, also plays a crucial role in the human world. Inertia affects our individual lives as well as the direction taken by society as a whole.

Inertia often influences our value systems and personal growth. Inertia is at work, for example, when people cling to certain behaviors and views. Like the boulder firmly fixed to the mountain, most people are set in their ways. Without thinking, they vote Republican or Democratic because they have always voted that way. They regard with suspicion a couple having no children, simply because everyone else in the neighborhood has a large family. It is only when an outside force--a jolt of some sort--occurs that people change their views. A white American couple may think little about racial discrimination, for instance, until they adopt an Asian child and must comfort her when classmates tease her because she looks different. Parents may consider promiscuous any unmarried girl who has a baby until their 17-year-old honors student confesses that she is pregnant. Personal jolts like these force people to think, perhaps for the first time, about issues that now affect them directly.

To illustrate how inertia governs our lives, it is helpful to compare the world of television with real life. On TV, inertia does not exist. Television shows and commercials show people making all kinds of drastic changes. They switch brands of coffee or try a new hair color with no hesitation. In one car commercial, an ambitious young accountant abandons her career with a flourish and is seen driving off into the sunset as she heads for a small cabin by the sea to write poetry. In a soap opera, a character may progress from homemaker to hooker to nun in a single year. But in real life, inertia rules. People tend to stay where they are, to keep their jobs, to be loyal to products. A second major difference between television and real life is that, on television, everyone takes prompt and dramatic action to solve problems. The construction worker with a thudding headache is pain-free at the end of the sixty-second commercial; the police catch the murderer within an hour; the family learns to cope with their son's life-threatening drug addiction by the time the made-for-TV movie ends at eleven. But in the real world, inertia

Definition   389

persists, so that few problems are solved neatly or quickly. Illnesses drag on, few crimes are solved, and family conflicts last for years.

4   Inertia is, most importantly, a force at work in the life of our nation. —— Topic sentence
Again, inertia is two-sided. It keeps us from moving and, once we move, it keeps us pointed in one direction. We find ourselves mired in a certain path, accepting the inferior, even the dangerous. We settle for toys that —— Start of a series of examples
break, winter coats with no warmth, and rivers clogged with pollution. Inertia also compels our nation to keep moving in one direction--despite the uncomfortable suspicion that it is the wrong direction. We are not sure if manipulating genes is a good idea, yet we continue to fund scientific projects in genetic engineering. Nearly fifty years ago, we were shaken when we saw the devastation caused by an atomic bomb. But we went on to develop weapons hundreds of times more destructive. Although warned that excessive television viewing may be harmful, we continue to watch hours of television each day.

5   We have learned to defy gravity, one of the basic laws of physics; —— Conclusion
we fly high above the earth, even float in outer space. But most of us have not learned to defy inertia. Those special individuals who are able to act when everyone else seems paralyzed are rare. But the fact that such people do exist means that inertia is not all-powerful. If we use our reasoning ability and our creativity, we can conquer inertia, just as we have conquered gravity.

Commentary

Introduction

As the title of her essay suggests, Laura has taken a scientific term (*inertia*) from a specialized field and drawn on the term to help explain some everyday phenomena. Using the *simple-to-complex* approach to structure the introduction, she opens with a vivid *descriptive* example of inertia. This description is then followed by a *formal definition* of inertia: "the tendency of matter to remain at rest or, if moving, to keep moving in one direction unless affected by an outside force." Laura wisely begins the paper with the easy-to-understand description rather than with the more-difficult-to-grasp scientific definition. Had the order been reversed, the essay would not have gotten off to nearly as effective a start. She then ends her introductory paragraph with a *thesis*, "Inertia, an important factor in the world of physics, also plays a crucial role in the human world," and with a *plan of development*, "Inertia affects our individual lives as well as the direction taken by society as a whole."

Organization

To support her definition of inertia and her belief that it can rule our lives, Laura generates a number of compelling examples. She organizes these examples by grouping them into three major points, each point signaled by a *topic sentence* that opens each of the essay's three supporting paragraphs (2–4).

A definite organizational strategy determines the sequence of Laura's three central points. The essay moves from the way inertia affects the individual to the way it affects the nation. The phrase "most importantly" at the start of the fourth paragraph indicates that Laura has arranged her points emphatically, believing that inertia's impact on society is most critical.

A Weak Example

When reading the fourth paragraph, you might have noticed that Laura's examples aren't sequenced as effectively as they could be. To show that we, as a nation, tend to keep moving in the same direction, Laura discusses our ongoing uneasiness about genetic engineering, nuclear arms, and excessive television viewing. The point about nuclear weapons is most significant, yet it gets lost in the middle. The paragraph would be stronger if it ended with the point about nuclear arms. Moreover, the example about excessive television viewing doesn't belong in this paragraph since, at best, it has limited bearing on the issue being discussed.

Other Patterns of Development

In addition to using numerous *examples* to illustrate her points, Laura draws on several other patterns of development to show that inertia can be a powerful force. In the second and fourth paragraphs, she uses *causal analysis* to explain how inertia can paralyze people and nations. The second paragraph indicates that only "an outside force—a jolt of some sort—" can motivate inert people to change. To support this view, Laura provides two examples of parents who experience such jolts. Similarly, in the fourth paragraph, she contends that inertia causes the persistence of specific national problems: shoddy consumer goods and environmental pollution.

Another pattern, *comparison-contrast*, is used in the third paragraph to highlight the differences between television and real life: on television, people zoom into action, but in everyday life, people tend to stay put and muddle through. The essay also contains a distinct element of *argumentation-persuasion* since Laura clearly wants readers to accept her definition of inertia and her view that it often governs human behavior.

Conclusion

Laura's *conclusion* rounds off the essay nicely and brings it to a satisfying close. Laura refers to another law of physics, one with which we are all familiar—gravity. By creating an *analogy* between gravity and inertia, she suggests that our ability to defy gravity should encourage us to defy inertia. The analogy enlarges the scope of the essay; it allows Laura to reach out to her readers by challenging them to action. Such a challenge is, of course, appropriate in a definition essay having a persuasive bent.

Definition

Revising the First Draft

When it was time to rework her essay, Laura began by reading her paper out loud. Then, referring to the revision checklist on pages 385–86, she noted in the margin of her draft the problems she detected, numbering them in order of importance. After reviewing her notes, she started to revise in earnest, paying special attention to her third paragraph. The first draft of that paragraph, together with her annotations, is reprinted here:

Original Version of the Third Paragraph

The ordinary actions of daily life are, in part, determined by inertia. To understand this, it is helpful to compare the world of television with real life, for, in the TV-land of ads and entertainment, inertia does not exist. For example, on television, people are often shown making all kinds of drastic changes. They switch brands of coffee or try a new hair color with no hesitation. In one car commercial, a young accountant leaves her career and sets off for a cabin by the sea to write poetry. In a soap opera, a character may progress from homemaker to hooker to nun in a single year. In contrast, inertia rules in real life. People tend to stay where they are, to keep their jobs, to be loyal to products (wives get annoyed if a husband brings home the wrong brand or color of bathroom tissue from the market). Middle-aged people wear the hairstyles or makeup that suited them in high school. A second major difference between television and real life is that, on TV, everyone takes prompt and dramatic action to solve problems. A woman finds the solution to dull clothes at the end of a commercial; the police catch the murderer within an hour; the family learns to cope with a son's disturbing life-style by the time the movie is over. In contrast, the law of real-life inertia means that few problems are solved neatly or quickly. Things, once started, tend to stay as they are. Few crimes are actually solved. Medical problems are not easily diagnosed. Messy wars in foreign countries seem endless. National problems are identified, but Congress does not pass legislation to solve them.

Annotations:
1. *Paragraph rambles*
4. *First two sentences awkward*
7. *Make more specific*
3. *Delete part about annoyed wives and hairstyles*
5. *Trite—replace*
6. *Point about life-style not clear*
2. *Last two sentences don't belong*

After rereading her draft, Laura realized that her third paragraph rambled. To give it more focus, she removed the last two sentences ("Messy wars in foreign countries seem endless" and "National problems are identified, but Congress does not pass legislation. . . .") because they referred to national affairs but were located in a section focusing on the individual. Further, she eliminated two flat, unconvincing examples: wives who get annoyed when their husbands bring home the wrong brand of bathroom tissue and middle-aged people whose hairstyles and makeup are outdated. Condensing the two disjointed sentences that originally opened the paragraph also helped tighten this section of the essay. Note how much crisper the revised sentences are: "To illustrate how inertia rules our lives, it is helpful to compare the world of television with real life. On TV, inertia does not exist."

Laura also worked to make the details and the language in the paragraph more specific and vigorous. The vague sentence "A woman finds the solution to dull clothes at the end of the commercial" is replaced by the more dramatic "The construction worker with a thudding headache is pain-free at the end of the sixty-second commercial." Similarly, Laura changed a "son's disturbing lifestyle" to a "son's life-threatening drug addiction"; "by the time the movie is over" became "by the time the made-for-TV movie ends at eleven"; and "a young accountant leaves her career and sets off for a cabin by the sea to write poetry" was changed to "an ambitious young accountant abandons her career with a flourish and is seen driving off into the sunset as she heads for a small cabin by the sea to write poetry."

Once these changes were made, Laura decided to round off the paragraph with a powerful summary statement highlighting how real life differs from television: "Illnesses drag on, few crimes are solved, and family conflicts last for years."

These third-paragraph revisions are similar to those that Laura made elsewhere in her first draft. Her astute changes enabled her to turn an already effective paper into an especially thoughtful analysis of human behavior.

ACTIVITIES: DEFINITION

Prewriting Activities

1. Imagine you're writing two essays: One explains an effective strategy for registering a complaint; the other contrasts the styles of two stand-up comics. Jot down ways you might use definition in each essay.

2. Use the prewriting questions for the patterns of development on page 382 to generate material for an extended definition of *one* of the terms on the next page. Then answer these questions about your prewriting material: What thesis does the prewriting suggest? Which pattern(s) yielded the most supporting material? In what order would you present this support when writing an essay?

Definition

   a. popularity
   b. cruelty
   c. a "dweeb"
   d. self-esteem
   e. a "wimp"
   f. loneliness

3. Select a term whose meaning varies from person to person or one for which you have a personal definition. Some possibilities include:

success	femininity	a liberal
patriotism	affirmative action	a housewife
individuality	pornography	intelligence

Brainstorm with others to identify variations in the term's meaning. Then examine your prewriting material. What thesis comes to mind? If you were writing an essay, would your purpose be informative, persuasive, or both? Finally, prepare a scratch list of the points you might cover.

Revising Activities

4. Explain why each of the following is an effective or ineffective definition. Rewrite those you consider ineffective.

   a. *Passive aggression* is when people show their aggression passively.
   b. A *terrorist* tries to terrorize people.
   c. *Being assertive* means knowing how to express your wishes and goals in a positive, noncombative way.
   d. *Pop music* refers to music that is popular.
   e. *Loyalty* is when someone stays by another person during difficult times.

5. The following introductory paragraph is from the first draft of an essay contrasting walking and running as techniques for reducing tension. Although intended to be a definition paragraph, it actually doesn't tell us anything we don't already know. It also relies on the old-hat "*Webster's* says." Rewrite the paragraph so it is more imaginative. You might use a series of anecdotes or one extended example to define tension and introduce the essay's thesis more gracefully.

According to Webster's, tension is "mental or nervous strain, often accompanied by muscular tightness or tautness." Everyone feels tense at one time or another. It may occur when there's a deadline to meet. Or it could be caused by the stress of trying to fulfill academic, athletic, or social goals. Sometimes it comes from criticism by family, bosses, or teachers. Such tension puts wear and tear on our bodies and on our emotional well-being. Although some people run to relieve tension, research has found that walking is a more effective tension reducer.

PROFESSIONAL SELECTIONS: DEFINITION

K. C. COLE

K. C. Cole (1946–) has contributed articles on science to numerous national publications and has written a regular column for *Discovery* magazine. Her essays are collected in *Sympathetic Vibrations: Reflections on Physics as a Way of Life* (1985). She has written two books, *Facets of Light: Color Images and Things That Glow in the Dark* (1980) and *Order in the Universe: The Shape of Relative Motion* (1986). The selection that follows first appeared as a "Hers" column in the *New York Times* (1982).

ENTROPY

It was about two months ago when I realized that entropy was getting the better of me. On the same day my car broke down (again), my refrigerator conked out and I learned that I needed root-canal work in my right rear tooth. The windows in the bedroom were still leaking every time it rained and my son's baby sitter was still failing to show up every time I really needed her. My hair was turning gray and my typewriter was wearing out. The house needed paint and I needed glasses. My son's sneakers were developing holes and I was developing a deep sense of futility.

After all, what was the point of spending half of Saturday at the Laundromat if the clothes were dirty all over again the following Friday?

Disorder, alas, is the natural order of things in the universe. There is even a precise measure of the amount of disorder, called entropy. Unlike almost every other physical property (motion, gravity, energy), entropy does not work both ways. It can only increase. Once it's created it can never be destroyed. The road to disorder is a one-way street.

Because of its unnerving irreversibility, entropy has been called the arrow of time. We all understand this instinctively. Children's rooms, left on their own, tend to get messy, not neat. Wood rots, metal rusts, people wrinkle and flowers wither. Even mountains wear down; even the nuclei of atoms decay. In the city we see entropy in the rundown subways and worn-out sidewalks and torn-down buildings, in the increasing disorder of our lives. We know, without asking, what is old. If we were suddenly to see the paint jump back on an old building, we would know that something was wrong. If we saw an egg unscramble itself and jump back into its shell, we would laugh in the same way we laugh at a movie run backward.

Entropy is no laughing matter, however, because with every increase in entropy energy is wasted and opportunity is lost. Water flowing down a mountainside can be made to do some useful work on its way. But once all the water is at the same level it can work no more. That is entropy. When my refrigerator was working, it kept all the cold air ordered in one part of the kitchen and warmer air in another. Once it broke down the warm and cold mixed into a lukewarm mess that allowed my butter to melt, my milk to rot and my frozen vegetables to decay.

6. Of course the energy is not really lost, but it has defused and dissipated into a chaotic caldron of randomness that can do us no possible good. Entropy is chaos. It is loss of purpose.

7. People are often upset by the entropy they seem to see in the haphazardness of their own lives. Buffeted about like so many molecules in my tepid kitchen, they feel that they have lost their sense of direction, that they are wasting youth and opportunity at every turn. It is easy to see entropy in marriages, when the partners are too preoccupied to patch small things up, almost guaranteeing that they will fall apart. There is much entropy in the state of our country, in the relationships between nations—lost opportunities to stop the avalanche of disorders that seems ready to swallow us all.

8. Entropy is not inevitable everywhere, however. Crystals and snowflakes and galaxies are islands of incredibly ordered beauty in the midst of random events. If it was not for exceptions to entropy, the sky would be black and we would be able to see where the stars spend their days; it is only because air molecules in the atmosphere cluster in ordered groups that the sky is blue.

9. The most profound exception to entropy is the creation of life. A seed soaks up some soil and some carbon and some sunshine and some water and arranges it into a rose. A seed in the womb takes some oxygen and pizza and milk and transforms it into a baby.

10. The catch is that it takes a lot of energy to produce a baby. It also takes energy to make a tree. The road to disorder is all downhill but the road to creation takes work. Though combating entropy is possible, it also has its price. That's why it seems so hard to get ourselves together, so easy to let ourselves fall apart.

11. Worse, creating order in one corner of the universe always creates more disorder somewhere else. We create ordered energy from oil and coal at the price of the entropy of smog.

12. I recently took up playing the flute again after an absence of several months. As the uneven vibrations screeched through the house, my son covered his ears and said, "Mom, what's wrong with your flute?" Nothing was wrong with my flute, of course. It was my ability to play it that had atrophied, or entropied, as the case may be. The only way to stop that process was to practice every day, and sure enough my tone improved, though only at the price of constant work. Like anything else, abilities deteriorate when we stop applying our energies to them.

13. That's why entropy is depressing. It seems as if just breaking even is an uphill fight. There's a good reason that this should be so. The mechanics of entropy are a matter of chance. Take any ice-cold air molecule milling around my kitchen. The chances that it will wander in the direction of my refrigerator at any point are exactly 50-50. The chances that it will wander away from my refrigerator are also 50-50. But take billions of warm and cold molecules mixed together, and the chances that all the cold ones will wander toward the refrigerator and all the warm ones will wander away from it are virtually nil.

14. Entropy wins not because order is impossible but because there are always so many more paths toward disorder than toward order. There are so many more different ways to do a sloppy job than a good one, so many more ways to make a mess than to clean it up. The obstacles and accidents in our lives almost guarantee that constant collisions will bounce us on to random paths, get us off the track. Disorder is the path of least resistance, the easy but not the inevitable road.

Like so many others, I am distressed by the entropy I see around me today. I am afraid of the randomness of international events, of the lack of common purpose in the world; I am terrified that it will lead into the ultimate entropy of nuclear war. I am upset that I could not in the city where I live send my child to a public school; that people are unemployed and inflation is out of control; that tensions between sexes and races seem to be increasing again; that relationships everywhere seem to be falling apart.

Social institutions—like atoms and stars—decay if energy is not added to keep them ordered. Friendships and families and economies all fall apart unless we constantly make an effort to keep them working and well oiled. And far too few people, it seems to me, are willing to contribute consistently to those efforts.

Of course, the more complex things are, the harder it is. If there were only a dozen or so air molecules in my kitchen, it would be likely—if I waited a year or so—that at some point the six coldest ones would congregate inside the freezer. But the more factors in the equation—the more players in the game—the less likely it is that their paths will coincide in an orderly way. The more pieces in the puzzle, the harder it is to put back together once order is disturbed. "Irreversibility," said a physicist, "is the price we pay for complexity."

Questions for Close Reading

1. What is the selection's thesis? Locate the sentence(s) in which Cole states her main idea. If she doesn't state the thesis explicitly, express it in your own words.

2. How does entropy differ from the other properties of the physical world? Is the image "the arrow of time" helpful in establishing this difference?

3. Why is the creation of life an exception to entropy? What is the relationship between entropy and energy?

4. Why does Cole say that entropy "is no laughing matter"? What is so depressing about the entropy she describes?

5. Refer to your dictionary as needed to define the following words used in the selection: *futility* (paragraph 1), *dissipated* (6), *buffeted* (7), *tepid* (7), and *atrophied* (12).

Questions About the Writer's Craft

1. The pattern. What is Cole's underlying purpose in defining the scientific term *entropy*? What gives the essay its persuasive edge?

2. What tone does Cole adopt to make reading about a scientific concept more interesting? Identify places in the essay where her tone is especially prominent.

3. Cole uses such words as *futility, loss,* and *depressing*. How do these words affect you? Why do you suppose she chose such terms? Find similar words in the essay.

4. Other patterns. Many of Cole's sentences follow a two-part pattern involving a contrast: "The road to disorder is all downhill but the road to creation takes

Definition

work" (paragraph 10). Find other examples of this pattern in the essay. Why do you think Cole uses it so often?

Writing Assignments Using Definition as a Pattern of Development

1. Define *order* or *disorder* by applying the term to a system that you know well—for example, your school, dorm, family, or workplace. Develop your definition through any combination of writing patterns: by supplying examples, by showing contrasts, by analyzing the process underlying the system, and so on.

2. Choose, as Cole does, a technical term that you think will be unfamiliar to most readers. In a humorous or serious paper, define the term as it is used technically; then show how the term can shed light on some aspect of your life. For example, the concept in astronomy of a *supernova* could be used to explain your sudden emergence as a new star on the athletic field, in your schoolwork, or on the social scene. Here are a few suggested terms:

symbiosis	volatility	resonance
velocity	erosion	catalyst
neutralization	equilibrium	malleability

Writing Assignments Using Other Patterns of Development

3. Can one person make much difference in the amount of entropy—disorder and chaos—in the world? Share your view in an essay. Use examples of people who have tried to overcome the tendency of things to "fall apart." Make clear whether you think these people succeeded or failed in their attempts.

4. Cole claims that our lives contain a distressing amount of "haphazardness" (paragraph 7). Write an essay arguing that people either do or do not control their own fates. Support your point with a series of specific examples.

NANCY GIBBS

Employed by *Time* since 1985, Nancy Gibbs was named a senior editor in 1991. She has worked in a number of the magazine's departments, writing articles on a wide range of issues, including health care, child labor laws, and racism on campus. Gibbs's book, *Children of Light* (1985), is a history of Quaker education in New York City. The selection reprinted here first appeared in *Time* (1991).

WHEN IS IT RAPE?

1   Be careful of strangers and hurry home, says a mother to her daughter, knowing that the world is a frightful place but not wishing to swaddle a child in fear. Girls grow

up scarred by caution and enter adulthood eager to shake free of their parents' worst nightmares. They still know to be wary of strangers. What they don't know is whether they have more to fear from their friends.

Most women who get raped are raped by people they already know—like the boy in biology class, or the guy in the office down the hall, or their friend's brother. The familiarity is enough to make them let down their guard, sometimes even enough to make them wonder afterward whether they were "really raped." What people think of as "real rape"—the assault by a monstrous stranger lurking in the shadows—accounts for only one out of five attacks.

So the phrase "acquaintance rape" was coined to describe the rest, all the cases of forced sex between people who already knew each other, however casually. But that was too clinical for headline writers, and so the popular term is the narrower "date rape," which suggests an ugly ending to a raucous night on the town.

These are not idle distinctions. Behind the search for labels is the central mythology about rape: that rapists are always strangers, and victims are women who ask for it. The mythology is hard to dispel because the crime is so rarely exposed. The experts guess—that's all they can do under the circumstances—that while one in four women will be raped in her lifetime, less than 10 percent will report the assault, and less than 5 percent of the rapists will go to jail.

When a story of the crime lodges in the headlines, the myths have a way of cluttering the search for the truth. The tale of Good Friday in Palm Beach landed in the news because it involved a Kennedy,* but it may end up as a watershed case, because all the mysteries and passions surrounding date rape are here to be dissected. William Kennedy Smith met a woman at a bar, invited her back home late at night and apparently had sex with her on the lawn. She says it was rape, and the police believed her story enough to charge him with the crime. Perhaps it was the bruises on her leg; or the instincts of the investigators who found her, panicked and shaking, curled up in the fetal position on a couch; or the lie-detector tests she passed.

On the other side, Smith has adamantly protested that he is a man falsely accused. His friends and family testify to his gentle nature and moral fiber and insist that he could not possibly have committed such a crime. Maybe the truth will come out in court—but regardless of its finale, the case has shoved the debate over date rape into the minds of average men and women. Plant the topic in a conversation, and chances are it will ripen into a bitter argument or a jittery sequence of pale jokes.

Women charge that date rape is the hidden crime; men complain it is hard to prevent a crime they can't define. Women say it isn't taken seriously; men say it is a concept invented by women who like to tease but not take the consequences. Women say the date-rape debate is the first time the nation has talked frankly about sex; men say it is women's unconscious reaction to the excesses of the sexual revolution. Meanwhile, men and women argue among themselves about the "gray area" that surrounds the whole murky arena of sexual relations, and there is no consensus in sight.

In court, on campus, in conversation, the issue turns on the elasticity of the word *rape*, one of the few words in the language with the power to summon a shared image of a horrible crime.

At one extreme are those who argue that for the word to retain its impact, it must be strictly defined as forced sexual intercourse: a gang of thugs jumping a jogger in

---

*William Kennedy Smith, the nephew of John, Robert, and Edward Kennedy, was accused of raping a woman on Good Friday (1991) in Palm Beach, Florida. Kennedy was acquitted, but his trial, broadcast on television, generated heated debate on the issue of date rape.

Central Park, a psychopath preying on old women in a housing complex, a man with an ice pick in a side street. To stretch the definition of the word risks stripping away its power. In this view, if it happened on a date, it wasn't rape. A romantic encounter is a context in which sex *could* occur, and so what omniscient judge will decide whether there was genuine mutual consent?

10   Others are willing to concede that date rape sometimes occurs, that sometimes a man goes too far on a date without a woman's consent. But this infraction, they say, is not as ghastly a crime as street rape, and it should not be taken as seriously. The *New York Post*, alarmed by the Willy Smith case, wrote in a recent editorial, "If the sexual encounter, *forced or not,* has been preceded by a series of consensual activities—drinking, a trip to the man's home, a walk on a deserted beach at three in the morning—the charge that's leveled against the alleged offender should, it seems to us, be different than the one filed against, say, the youths who raped and beat the jogger."

11   This attitude sparks rage among women who carry scars received at the hands of men they knew. It makes no difference if the victim shared a drink or a moonlit walk or even a passionate kiss, they protest, if the encounter ended with her being thrown to the ground and forcibly violated. Date rape is not about a misunderstanding, they say. It is not a communications problem. It is not about a woman's having regrets in the morning for a decision she made the night before. It is not about a "decision" at all. Rape is rape, and any form of forced sex—even between neighbors, co-workers, classmates and casual friends—is a crime.

12   A more extreme form of that view comes from activists who see rape as a metaphor, its definition swelling to cover any kind of oppression of women. Rape, seen in this light, can occur not only on a date but also in a marriage, not only by violent assault but also by psychological pressure. A Swarthmore College training pamphlet once explained that acquaintance rape "spans a spectrum of incidents and behaviors, ranging from crimes legally defined as rape to verbal harassment and inappropriate innuendo."

13   No wonder, then, that the battles become so heated. When innuendo qualifies as rape, the definitions have become so slippery that the entire subject sinks into a political swamp. The only way to capture the hard reality is to tell the story.

14   A thirty-two-year-old woman was on business in Tampa last year for the Florida supreme court. Stranded at the courthouse, she accepted a lift from a lawyer involved in her project. As they chatted on the ride home, she recalls, "he was saying all the right things, so I started to trust him." She agreed to have dinner, and afterward, at her hotel door, he convinced her to let him come in to talk. "I went through the whole thing about being old-fashioned," she says. "I was a virgin until I was twenty-one. So I told him talk was all we were going to do."

15   But as they sat on the couch, she found herself falling asleep. "By now, I'm comfortable with him, and I put my head on his shoulder. He's not tried anything all evening, after all." Which is when the rape came. "I woke up to find him on top of me, forcing himself on me. I didn't scream or run. All I could think about was my business contacts and what if they saw me run out of my room screaming rape.

16   "I thought it was my fault. I felt so filthy, I washed myself over and over in hot water. Did he rape me?, I kept asking myself. I didn't consent. But who's gonna believe me? I had a man in my hotel room after midnight." More than a year later, she still can't tell the story without a visible struggle to maintain her composure. Police referred the case to the state attorney's office in Tampa, but without more evidence it decided not to prosecute. Although her attacker has admitted that he heard her say no, maintains the woman, "he says he didn't know that I meant no. He didn't feel he'd raped me, and he even wanted to see me again."

Her story is typical in many ways. The victim herself may not be sure right away that she has been raped, that she had said no and been physically forced into having sex anyway. And the rapist commonly hears but does not heed the protest. "A date rapist will follow through no matter what the woman wants because his agenda is to get laid," says Claire Walsh, a Florida-based consultant on sexual assaults. "First comes the dinner, then a dance, then a drink, then the coercion begins." Gentle persuasion gives way to physical intimidation, with alcohol as the ubiquitous lubricant. "When that fails, force is used," she says. "Real men don't take no for an answer." . . .

So here, of course, is the heart of the debate. If rape is sex without consent, how exactly should consent be defined and communicated, when and by whom? Those who view rape through a political lens tend to place all responsibility on men to make sure that their partners are consenting at every point of a sexual encounter. At the extreme, sexual relations come to resemble major surgery, requiring a signed consent form. Clinical psychologist Mary P. Koss of the University of Arizona in Tucson, who is a leading scholar on the issue, puts it rather bluntly: "It's the man's penis that is doing the raping, and ultimately he's responsible for where he puts it."

Historically, of course, this has never been the case, and there are some who argue that it shouldn't be—that women too must take responsibility for their behavior, and that the whole realm of intimate encounters defies regulation from on high. Anthropologist Lionel Tiger has little patience for trendy sexual politics that make no reference to biology. Since the dawn of time, he argues, men and women have always gone to bed with different goals. In the effort to keep one's genes in the gene pool, "it is to the male advantage to fertilize as many females as possible, as quickly as possible and as efficiently as possible." For the female, however, who looks at the large investment she will have to make in the offspring, the opposite is true. Her concern is to "select" who "will provide the best set up for their offspring." So, in general, "the pressure is on the male to be aggressive and on the female to be coy." . . .

What is lost in the ideological debate over date rape is the fact that men and women, especially when they are young, and drunk, and aroused, are not very good at communicating. "In many cases," says [Susan] Estrich,* "the man thought it was sex, and the woman thought it was rape, and they are both telling the truth." The man may envision a celluloid seduction, in which he is being commanding, she is being coy. A woman may experience the same event as a degrading violation of her will. That some men do not believe a woman's protests is scarcely surprising in a society so drenched with messages that women have rape fantasies and a desire to be overpowered.

By the time they reach college, men and women are loaded with cultural baggage, drawn from movies, television, music videos and "bodice ripper" romance novels. Over the years they have watched Rhett sweep Scarlett up the stairs in *Gone with the Wind*; or Errol Flynn, who was charged twice with statutory rape, overpower a protesting heroine who then melts in his arms; or Stanley rape his sister-in-law Blanche du Bois while his wife is in the hospital giving birth to a child in *A Streetcar Named Desire*. Higher up the cultural food chain, young people can read of date rape in Homer or Jane Austen, watch it in *Don Giovanni* or *Rigoletto*.**

---

*The victim of a rape in the 1970s, law professor Susan Estrich has written a book, *Real Rape*, about her ordeal (editors' note).
**Traditionally, the Greek poet Homer is conjectured to be the author of the epics *The Iliad* and *The Odyssey*, both dated around 850 BC. Jane Austen was an English novelist (1775–1817). *Don Giovanni*, an opera by Wolfgang Amadeus Mozart (1756–1791), tells the tale of a notorious

Definition

22   The messages come early and often, and nothing in the feminist revolution has been able to counter them. A recent survey of sixth- to ninth-graders in Rhode Island found that a fourth of the boys and a sixth of the girls said it was acceptable for a man to force a woman to kiss him or have sex if he has spent money on her. A third of the children said it would not be wrong for a man to rape a woman who had had previous sexual experiences.

23   Certainly cases like Palm Beach, movies like *The Accused* and novels like Avery Corman's *Prized Possessions** may force young people to re-examine assumptions they have inherited. The use of new terms, like acquaintance rape and date rape, while controversial, has given men and women the vocabulary they need to express their experiences with both force and precision. This dialogue would be useful if it helps strip away some of the dogmas, old and new, surrounding the issue. Those who hope to raise society's sensitivity to the problem of date rape would do well to concede that it is not precisely the same sort of crime as street rape, that there may be very murky issues of intent and degree involved.

24   On the other hand, those who downplay the problem should come to realize that date rape is a crime of uniquely intimate cruelty. While the body is violated, the spirit is maimed. How long will it take, once the wounds have healed, before it is possible to share a walk on a beach, a drive home from work or an evening's conversation without always listening for a quiet alarm to start ringing deep in the back of the memory of a terrible crime?

Questions for Close Reading

1. What is the selection's thesis? Locate the sentence(s) in which Gibbs states her main idea. If she doesn't state the thesis explicitly, express it in your own words.

2. What does Gibbs mean by the "elasticity of the word *rape*" (paragraph 8)? How does this "elasticity" lead to problems in definition?

3. What, in Gibbs's opinion, is the "typical" scenario in a case of date rape? According to the consultant that Gibbs quotes, what is it about men that causes them to enact this scenario?

4. An author cited by Gibbs states that in a case of rape both the man and the woman "are telling the truth" (20). What anthropological and cultural factors might contribute to this conflict in perception?

5. Refer to your dictionary as needed to define the following words used in the selection: *watershed* (paragraph 5), *fetal* (5), *psychopath* (9), *omniscient* (9), *infraction* (10), *innuendo* (12, 13), *coercion* (17), *intimidation* (17), *ubiquitous* (17), *ideological* (20), *celluloid* (20), *statutory* (21), and *dogmas* (23).

---

libertine and womanizer. *Rigoletto*, an opera by Giuseppe Verdi (1813–1901), recounts a story of abduction and seduction.
The Accused is a 1988 film about a woman who pursues retribution for a gang-rape she endured. *Prized Possessions* is a 1990 novel about the rape of a first-year college student.

Questions About the Writer's Craft

1. The pattern. Writers often use definition by negation in the beginning of a definition essay (see page 384). Where in the essay does Gibbs employ this strategy? How does it help her reinforce her thesis?

2. Other patterns. Definition essays frequently draw upon other patterns of development to explain the meaning of a term. Locate places in the selection where Gibbs uses comparison-contrast and narration. How do these patterns help clarify her definition of date rape?

3. What emotionally charged language does Gibbs use in her introduction and conclusion? What effect do you think she hoped these words would have on readers? How do these words help create an effective beginning and end for the piece?

4. Gibbs uses statistics (paragraphs 2 and 4), refers to several dramatic cases of rape (5–6, 9–10), often cites experts or writers in the field of sexual assault (17–20), and summarizes the results of recent opinion surveys (22). Why do you think she includes such factual material? What type of audience does she seem to assume will read her essay?

Writing Assignments Using Definition as a Pattern of Development

1. Interview some people, both male and female, to get their definitions of date rape. Then in an essay, point out any differences between the two sexes' perspectives. That done, present your own definition of date rape, explaining both what it is and what it isn't.

∞ 2. One of Gibbs's authorities on date rape comments sarcastically, "Real men don't take no for an answer" (paragraph 17). Brainstorm with several people to see how they define a "real man." After evaluating that material, write an essay constructing your own definition of a "real man." Alleen Pace Nilsen's "Sexism and Language" (page 243), Jack Newfield's "Stallone vs. Springsteen" (page 335), Martin Gottfried's "Rambos of the Road" (page 403), and Caryl Rivers's "What Should Be Done About Rock Lyrics?" (page 443) will prompt some ideas worth exploring.

Writing Assignments Using Other Patterns of Development

∞ 3. Date rape seems to be on the rise. Brainstorm with others to identify what may be causing its increased incidence. Focusing on several related factors, write an essay showing how these factors contribute to the problem. Some possible factors include the following: the way males and females are depicted in the media (advertisements, movies, television, rock videos); young people's use of

Definition

alcohol; the emergence of co-ed college dorms. At the end of the essay, offer some recommendations about what can be done to create a safer climate for dating. Alleen Pace Nilsen's "Sexism and Language" (page 243), Jack Newfield's "Stallone vs. Springfield" (page 335), Martin Gottfried's "Rambos of the Road" (page 403), and Caryl Rivers's "What Should Be Done About Rock Lyrics?" (page 443) may provide insights to draw upon in your paper.

4. Determine what your college is doing about date rape. Does it have a formal policy defining date rape, a hearing process, ongoing workshops, discussions for incoming students? Write a paper explaining how your college deals with date rape. Then argue either that more attention should be devoted to this issue or that your college has adopted measures sufficient to deal with the problem. If you feel the college should do more, indicate what steps should be taken.

MARTIN GOTTFRIED

A recipient of the George Jean Nathan Award for Dramatic Criticism, Martin Gottfried (1939–) has written for such publications as the *New York Post* and *Saturday Review*. His books include *Broadway Musicals* (1979), *The Curse of Genius* (1984), *All His Jazz: The Life and Death of Bob Fosse* (1990), and *More Broadway Musicals* (1991). The following essay first appeared in *Newsweek* in 1986.

RAMBOS OF THE ROAD

1   The car pulled up and its driver glared at us with such sullen intensity, such hatred, that I was truly afraid for our lives. Except for the Mohawk haircut he didn't have, he looked like Robert DeNiro in *Taxi Driver*, the sort of young man who, delirious for notoriety, might kill a president.

2   He was glaring because we had passed him and for that affront he pursued us to the next stoplight so as to express his indignation and affirm his masculinity. I was with two women and, believe it, was afraid for all three of us. It was nearly midnight and we were in a small, sleeping town with no other cars on the road.

3   When the light turned green, I raced ahead, knowing it was foolish and that I was not in a movie. He didn't merely follow, he chased, and with his headlights turned off. No matter what sudden turn I took, he followed. My passengers were silent. I knew they were alarmed, and I prayed that I wouldn't be called upon to protect them. In that cheerful frame of mind, I turned off my own lights so I couldn't be followed. It was lunacy. I was responding to a crazy *as a* crazy.

4   "I'll just drive to the police station," I finally said, and as if those were the magic words, he disappeared.

5   **Elbowing fenders:** It seems to me that there has recently been an epidemic of auto macho—a competition perceived and expressed in driving. People fight it out over parking spaces. They bully into line at the gas pump. A toll booth becomes a signal for elbowing fenders. And beetle-eyed drivers hunch over their steering wheels, squeezing the rims, glowering, preparing the excuse of not having seen you as they muscle you off the road. Approaching a highway on an entrance ramp recently, I was strong-armed by a trailer truck so immense that its driver all but blew me away by

blasting his horn. The behemoth was just inches from my hopelessly mismatched coupe when I fled for the safety of the shoulder.

And this is happening on city streets, too. A New York taxi driver told me that "intimidation is the name of the game. Drive as if you're deaf and blind. You don't hear the other guy's horn and you sure as hell don't see him."

The odd thing is that long before I was even able to drive, it seemed to me that people were at their finest and most civilized when in their cars. They seemed so orderly and considerate, so reasonable, staying in the right-hand lane unless passing, signaling all intentions. In those days you really eased into highway traffic, and the long, neat rows of cars seemed mobile testimony to the sanity of most people. Perhaps memory fails, perhaps there were always testy drivers, perhaps—but everyone didn't give you the finger.

A most amazing example of driver rage occurred recently at the Manhattan end of the Lincoln Tunnel. We were four cars abreast, stopped at a traffic light. And there was no moving even when the light had changed. A bus had stopped in the cross traffic, blocking our paths: it was a normal-for-New-York-City gridlock. Perhaps impatient, perhaps late for important appointments, three of us nonetheless accepted what, after all, we could not alter. One, however, would not. He would not be helpless. He would go where he was going even if he couldn't get there. A Wall Street type in suit and tie, he got out of his car and strode toward the bus, rapping smartly on its doors. When they opened, he exchanged words with the driver. The doors folded shut. He then stepped in front of the bus, took hold of one of its large windshield wipers and broke it.

The bus doors reopened and the driver appeared, apparently giving the fellow a good piece of his mind. If so, the lecture was wasted, for the man started his car and proceeded to drive directly *into the bus*. He rammed it. Even though the point at which he struck the bus, the folding doors, was its most vulnerable point, ramming the side of a bus with your car has to rank very high on a futility index. My first thought was that it had to be a rented car.

Lane merger: To tell the truth, I could not believe my eyes. The bus driver opened his doors as much as they could be opened and he stepped directly onto the hood of the attacking car, jumping up and down with both his feet. He then retreated into the bus, closing the doors behind him. Obviously a man of action, the car driver backed up and rammed the bus again. How this exercise in absurdity would have been resolved none of us will ever know for at that point the traffic unclogged and the bus moved on. And the rest of us, we passives of the world, proceeded, our cars crossing a field of battle as if nothing untoward had happened.

It is tempting to blame such belligerent, uncivil and even neurotic behavior on the nuts of the world, but in our cars we all become a little crazy. How many of us speed up when a driver signals his intention of pulling in front of us? Are we resentful and anxious to pass him? How many of us try to squeeze in, or race along the shoulder at a lane merger? We may not jump on hoods, but driving the gantlet, we seethe, cursing not so silently in the safety of our steel bodies on wheels—fortresses for cowards.

What is it within us that gives birth to such antisocial behavior and why, all of a sudden, have so many drivers gone around the bend? My friend Joel Katz, a Manhattan psychiatrist, calls it "a Rambo pattern. People are running around thinking the American way is to take the law into your own hands when anyone does anything wrong. And what constitutes 'wrong'? Anything that cramps your style."

It seems to me that it is a new America we see on the road now. It has the mentality of a hoodlum and the backbone of a coward. The car is its weapon and hiding place, and it is still a symbol even in this. Road Rambos no longer bespeak a self-reliant, civil people tooling around in family cruisers. In fact, there aren't families in these machines that charge headlong with their brights on in broad daylight, demanding we get out of their way. Bullies are loners, and they have perverted our liberty of the open road into drivers' license. They represent an America that derides the values of decency and good manners, then roam the highways riding shotgun and shrieking freedom. By allowing this to happen, the rest of us approve.

Questions for Close Reading

1. What is the selection's thesis? Locate the sentence(s) in which Gottfried states his main idea. If he doesn't state the thesis explicitly, express it in your own words.

2. What does Gottfried mean by "auto macho" (paragraph 5)? When has he experienced this phenomenon firsthand?

3. What evidence does Gottfried give that driving used to be a "testimony to the sanity of most people" (paragraph 7)?

4. What, according to Gottfried's psychiatrist friend, is the "Rambo pattern" that affects drivers? Does Gottfried feel this pattern is the exception these days—or the rule?

5. Refer to your dictionary as needed to define the following words used in the selection: *notoriety* (paragraph 1), *affront* (2), and *gantlet* (11).

Questions About the Writer's Craft

1. **The pattern.** Writers can use several patterns of development in an extended definition. Which does Gottfried use to define "Rambos of the Road"? Why might he have chosen these particular patterns?

2. **Other patterns.** What is the effect of Gottfried's three-paragraph narrative opening?

3. In paragraph 5, Gottfried says that aggressive driving behavior has become an "epidemic." Why do you think he selected this word? What details does he provide to support this analogy?

4. Although this selection is a good example of an extended definition, Gottfried does more than explain a contemporary phenomenon. What other purpose does he have in mind? How does he convey this purpose to his audience?

Writing Assignments Using Definition as a Pattern of Development

1. The "Rambo" mentality can manifest itself in settings other than the nation's roads. Write a definition essay showing how this kind of behavior is evident in some other context. You might, for example, call your essay "Campus Rambos"

or "The Husband as Rambo." Nancy Gibbs's "When Is It Rape?" (page 397) may provide insight into the prevalence of the "Rambo" syndrome.

2. Following Gottfried's lead, try your hand at extended definition by explaining a contemporary phenomenon familiar to you through either direct experience or media coverage. Possible topics include date rape, computeritis, male bonding, workaholism, and mall fever.

Writing Assignments Using Other Patterns of Development

3. Gottfried describes a problem but doesn't offer suggestions about how it might be solved. Write an essay proposing steps that parents, schools, or communities might take to promote more civilized driving habits.

4. Write an essay explaining what, in your opinion, accounts for the success of films (like the *Rambo* series or any Clint Eastwood movie) that depict a lone male on a violent mission of revenge. Might there be more to the films than simply vicarious adventure? To gain some insight into the popularity of such films, you may find it helpful to read Jack Newfield's "Stallone vs. Springsteen" (page 335) before writing your essay.

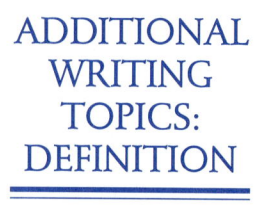

ADDITIONAL WRITING TOPICS: DEFINITION

General Assignments

Using definition, write an essay on one of the following topics.

1. Fads
2. Helplessness
3. An epiphany
4. Empowerment
5. A Yiddish term such as *mensch, klutz, chutzpah,* or *dreck,* or a term from some other ethnic group
6. Idiomatic expressions
7. Hypocrisy

8. Inner peace
9. Exploitation
10. A double bind

Assignments with a Specific Purpose, Audience, and Point of View

1. *Newsweek* magazine runs a popular column called "My Turn," consisting of readers' opinions on subjects of general interest. Write a piece for this column defining *today's college students*. Use the piece to dispel some negative stereotypes (for example, that college students are apathetic, ill-informed, self-centered, and materialistic).

2. You're an attorney arguing a case of sexual harassment—a charge your client has leveled against an employer. To win the case, you must present to the jury a clear definition of exactly what *sexual harassment* is and isn't. Write such a definition for your opening remarks in court.

3. You have been asked to write part of a pamphlet for students who come to the college health clinic. For this pamphlet, define *one* of the following conditions and its symptoms: *depression, stress, burnout, test anxiety, addiction* (to alcohol, drugs, or TV), *workaholism*. Part of the pamphlet should describe ways to cope with the condition described.

4. A new position has opened in your company. Write a job description to be sent to employment agencies that will screen candidates. Your description should define the job's purpose, state the duties involved, and outline essential qualifications.

5. Part of your job as a peer counselor in the student counseling center involves helping students communicate more effectively. To assist students, write a definition of some term that you think represents an essential component of a strong interpersonal relationship. You might, for example, define *respect, sharing, equality,* or *trust*. Part of the definition should employ definition by negation, a discussion of what the term is *not*.

6. Having waited on tables for several years at a resort hotel, you've been asked by the hotel manager to give some pointers to this year's new dining hall staff. Prepare a talk in which you define *courtesy*, the quality you consider most essential to the job. Use specific examples to illustrate your definition.

20
ARGUMENTATION-PERSUASION

WHAT IS ARGUMENTATION-PERSUASION?

"You can't possibly believe what you're saying."

"Look, I know what I'm talking about, and that's that."

Does this heated exchange sound familiar? Probably. When we hear the word *argument*, most of us think of a verbal battle propelled by stubbornness and irrational thought, with one person pitted against the other.

Argumentation in writing, though, is a different matter. Using clear thinking and logic, the writer tries to convince readers of the soundness of a particular opinion on a controversial issue. If, while trying to convince, the writer uses emotional language and dramatic appeals to readers' concerns, beliefs, and values, then the piece is called **persuasion.** Besides encouraging acceptance of an opinion, persuasion often urges readers (or another group) to commit themselves to a course of action. Assume you're writing an essay protesting the federal government's policy of offering aid to those suffering from hunger in other countries while many Americans go hungry. If your purpose is to document, coolly and objectively, the presence of hunger in the United States, you would prepare an argumentation essay. Such an essay would be filled with statistics, report findings, and expert opinion to demonstrate how widespread hunger is nationwide. If, however, your purpose is to shake up readers, even motivate them to write letters to their Congressional representatives and push for a change in policy, you would write a persuasive essay. In this case, your essay might contain emotional accounts of undernourished children, ill-fed pregnant women, and nearly starving elderly people.

Argumentation-Persuasion

Because people respond rationally *and* emotionally to situations, argumentation and persuasion are usually *combined*. Suppose you decide to write an article for the campus newspaper advocating a pre-Labor Day start for the school year. Your audience includes the college administration, students, and faculty. The article might begin by *arguing* that several schools starting the academic year earlier were able to close for the month of January and thus reduce heating and other maintenance expenses. Such an argument, supported by documented facts and figures, would help convince the administration. Realizing that you also have to gain student and faculty support for your idea, you might argue further that the proposed change would mean that students and faculty could leave for winter break with the semester behind them—papers written, exams taken, grades calculated and recorded. To make this part of your argument especially compelling, you could adopt a *persuasive* strategy by using emotional appeals and positively charged language: "Think how pleasant it would be to sleep late, spend time with family and friends, toast the New Year—without having to worry about work awaiting you back on campus."

When argumentation and persuasion blend in this way, emotion *supports* rather than *replaces* logic and sound reasoning. Although some writers resort to emotional appeals to the exclusion of rational thought, when you prepare argumentation-persuasion essays, you should advance your position through a balanced appeal to reason and emotion.

HOW ARGUMENTATION-PERSUASION FITS YOUR PURPOSE AND AUDIENCE

You probably realize that argumentation, persuasion, or a combination of the two is everywhere: an editorial urging the overhaul of an ill-managed literacy program; a commercial for a new shampoo; a scientific report advocating increased funding for AIDS research. Your own writing involves argumentation-persuasion as well. When you prepare a *causal analysis, descriptive piece, narrative,* or *definition essay,* you advance a specific point of view: MTV has a negative influence on teens' view of sex; Cape Cod in winter is imbued with a special kind of magic; a disillusioning experience can teach people much about themselves; *character* can be defined as the willingness to take unpopular positions on difficult issues. Indeed, an essay organized around any of the patterns of development described in this book may have a persuasive intent. You might, for example, encourage readers to try out a *process* you've explained, or to see one of the two movies you've *compared*.

Argumentation-persuasion, however, involves more than presenting a point of view and providing evidence. Unlike other forms of writing, it assumes controversy and addresses opposing viewpoints. Consider the following assignments, all of which require the writer to take a position on a controversial issue:

In parts of the country, communities established for older citizens or childless couples have refused to rent to families with children. How do you feel about this situation? What do you think are the rights of the parties involved?

Citing the fact that the highest percentage of automobile accidents involve young men, insurance companies consistently charge their highest rates to young males. Is this practice fair? Why or why not?

Some colleges and universities have instituted a "no pass, no play" policy for athletes. Explain why this policy is or is not appropriate.

It's impossible to predict with absolute certainty what will make readers accept the view you advance or take the action you propose. But the ancient Greeks, who formulated our basic concepts of logic, isolated three factors crucial to the effectiveness of argumentation-persuasion: *logos, pathos,* and *ethos.*

Your main concern in an argumentation-persuasion essay should be with the ***logos,*** or **soundness,** of your argument: the facts, statistics, examples, and authoritative statements you gather to support your viewpoint. This supporting evidence must be unified, specific, sufficient, accurate, and representative (see pages 46–49 and 66–69). Imagine, for instance, you want to convince people that a popular charity misappropriates the money it receives from the public. Your readers, inclined to believe in the good works of the charity, will probably dismiss your argument unless you can substantiate your claim with valid, well-documented evidence that enhances the *logos* of your position.

Sensitivity to the ***pathos,*** or the **emotional power of language,** is another key consideration for writers of argumentation-persuasion essays. *Pathos* appeals to readers' needs, values, and attitudes, encouraging them to commit themselves to a viewpoint or course of action. The *pathos* of a piece derives partly from the writer's language. *Connotative* language—words with strong emotional overtones—can move readers to accept a point of view and may even spur them to act.

Advertising and propaganda generally rely on *pathos* to the exclusion of logic, using emotion to influence and manipulate. Consider the following pitches for a man's cologne and a woman's perfume. The language—and the attitudes to which it appeals—is different in each case:

Brawn: Experience the power. Bold. Yet subtle. Clean. Masculine. The scent for the man who's in charge.

Black Lace is for you—the woman who dresses for success but who dares to be provocative, slightly naughty. Black Lace. Perfect with pearls by day and with diamonds by night.

The appeal to men plays on the impact that the words *Brawn, bold, power,* and *in charge* may have for some males. Similarly, the charged words *Black Lace, provocative, naughty,* and *diamonds* are intended to appeal to business women who—in the advertiser's mind, at least—may be looking for ways to reconcile sensuality and professionalism. (For more on slanted language, read Ann McClintock's "Propaganda Techniques in Today's Advertising," page 271).

Like an advertising copywriter, you must select language that reinforces your message. In a paper supporting an expanded immigration policy, you might use evocative phrases like "land of liberty," "a nation of immigrants," and "America's open-door policy." However, if you were arguing for strict immigration quotas, you might use language like "save jobs for unemployed Americans," "flood of unskilled labor," and "illegal aliens." Remember, though: Such language should *support, not supplant,* clear thinking.

Finally, whenever you write an argumentation-persuasion essay, you should establish your *ethos,* or **credibility** and **reliability.** You cannot expect readers to accept or act on your viewpoint unless you convince them that you know what you're talking about and that you're worth listening to. You will come across as knowledgeable and trustworthy if you present a logical, reasoned argument that takes opposing views into account. Make sure, too, that your appeals to emotion aren't excessive. Overwrought emotionalism undercuts credibility.

Writing an effective argumentation-persuasion essay involves an interplay of *logos, pathos,* and *ethos.* The exact balance among these factors is determined by your audience and purpose (that is, whether you want the audience simply to agree with your view or whether you also want them to take action). More than any other kind of writing, argumentation-persuasion requires that you *analyze your readers* and tailor your approach to them. You need to determine how much they know about the issue, how they feel about you and your position, what their values and attitudes are, what motivates them. (The checklists on pages 21 and 412–13 provide additional guidelines for analyzing your audience.)

In general, most readers will fall into one of three broad categories: supportive, wavering, or hostile. Each type of audience requires a different blend of *logos, pathos,* and *ethos* in an argumentation-persuasion essay.

1. A supportive audience. If your audience agrees with your position and trusts your credibility, you don't need a highly reasoned argument dense with facts, examples, and statistics. Although you may want to solidify support by providing additional information (*logos*), you can rely primarily on *pathos*—a strong emotional appeal—to reinforce readers' commitment to your shared viewpoint. Assume that you belong to a local fishing club and have volunteered to write an article encouraging members to support threatened fishing rights in state parks. You might begin by stating that fishing strengthens the fish population by thinning out overcrowded streams. Since your audience would certainly be familiar with this idea, you wouldn't need to devote much discussion to it. Instead, you would attempt to move them emotionally. You might evoke the camaraderie in the sport, the pleasure of a perfect cast, the beauty of the outdoors, and perhaps conclude with "If you want these enjoyments to continue, please make a generous contribution to our fund."

2. A wavering audience. At times, readers may be interested in what you have to say but may not be committed fully to your viewpoint. Or perhaps they're not as informed about the subject as they should be. In either case, because your readers need to be encouraged to give their complete support, you don't want to risk alienating them with a heavy-handed emotional appeal. Concentrate instead on *ethos* and *logos*, bolstering your image as a reliable source and providing the evidence needed to advance your position. If you want to convince an audience of high school seniors to take a year off to work between high school and college, you might establish your credibility by recounting the year you spent working and by showing the positive effects it had on your life (*ethos*). In addition, you could cite studies indicating that delayed entry into college is related to higher grade point averages. A year's savings, you would explain, allow students to study when they might otherwise need to hold down a job to earn money for tuition (*logos*).

3. A hostile audience. An apathetic, skeptical, or hostile audience is obviously most difficult to convince. With such an audience you should avoid emotional appeals because they might seem irrational, sentimental, or even comical. Instead, weigh the essay heavily in favor of logical reasoning and hard-to-dispute facts (*logos*). Assume your college administration is working to ban liquor from the student pub. You plan to submit to the campus newspaper an open letter supporting this generally unpopular effort. To sway other students, you cite the positive experiences of schools that have gone dry. Many colleges, you explain, have found their tavern revenues actually increase because all students—not just those of drinking age—can now support the pub. With the greater revenues, some schools have upgraded the food served in the pubs and have hired disc jockeys or musical groups to provide entertainment. Many schools have also seen a sharp reduction in alcohol-related vandalism. Readers may not be won over to your side, but your sound, logical argument may encourage them to be more tolerant of your viewpoint. Indeed, such increased receptivity may be all you can reasonably expect from a hostile audience.

PREWRITING STRATEGIES

The following checklist shows how you can apply to argumentation-persuasion some of the prewriting techniques discussed in Chapter 2.

> ✔ **ARGUMENTATION-PERSUASION: A PREWRITING CHECKLIST**
>
> *Choose a Controversial Issue*
> - What issue (academic, social, political, moral, economic) do you feel strongly about? With what issues are your journal entries concerned? What issues discussed in recent newspaper, television, or magazine reports have piqued your interest?
> - What is your view on the issue?

Argumentation-Persuasion

Determine Your Purpose, Audience, Tone, and Point of View
- Is your purpose limited to convincing readers to adopt your viewpoint, or do you also hope to spur them to action?
- Who is your audience? How much do your readers already know about the issue? How do you expect them to react to you, the issue, your viewpoint? Are they best characterized as supportive, wavering, or hostile? What values and needs may motivate readers to be responsive to your position?
- What tone is most likely to increase readers' commitment to your point of view? Should you convey strong emotion or cool objectivity?
- What point of view is most likely to enhance your credibility?

Use Prewriting to Generate Supporting Evidence
- How might brainstorming, journal entries, freewriting, or mapping help you identify personal experiences, observations, and examples to support your viewpoint?
- How might the various patterns of development help you generate supporting material? What about the issue can you describe? Narrate? Illustrate? Compare and contrast? Analyze in terms of process or cause-effect? Define or categorize in some especially revealing way?
- How might interviews or library research help you uncover relevant examples, facts, statistics, expert opinions?

STRATEGIES FOR USING ARGUMENTATION-PERSUASION IN AN ESSAY

After prewriting, you're ready to draft your essay. The following suggestions will help you prepare a convincing and logical argument.

1. At the beginning of the paper, identify the controversy surrounding the issue and state your position. Your introduction should clarify the controversy about the issue. In addition, it should provide as much background information as your readers are likely to need.

The thesis of an argumentation-persuasion paper is often called the **assertion** or **proposition**. Occasionally, the proposition appears at the paper's end, but it is usually stated at the beginning. If you state the thesis right away, your audience knows where you stand and is better able to evaluate the evidence presented.

Remember: Argumentation-persuasion assumes conflicting viewpoints. Be sure your proposition focuses on a controversial issue and indicates your view. Avoid a proposition that is merely factual; what is demonstrably true allows little room for debate. To see the difference between a factual statement and an effective thesis, examine the two statements that follow.

Fact

In the last few years, the nation's small farmers have suffered financial hardships.

Thesis

Inefficient management, rather than competition from agricultural conglomerates, is responsible for the financial plight of the nation's small farmers.

The first statement is certainly true. It would be difficult to find anyone who believes that these are easy times for small farmers. Because the statement invites little opposition, it can't serve as the focus of an argumentation-persuasion essay. The second statement, though, takes a controversial stance on a complex issue. Such a proposition is a valid starting point for a paper intended to argue and persuade. However, don't take this advice to mean that you should take a highly opinionated position in your thesis. A dogmatic, overstated proposition ("Campus security is staffed by overpaid, badge-flashing incompetents") is bound to alienate some readers.

Remember also to keep the proposition narrow and specific, so you can focus your thoughts in a purposeful way. Consider the following statements:

Broad Thesis

The welfare system has been abused over the years.

Narrowed Thesis

No one except the disabled and mothers of preschool-age children should be eligible for welfare.

If you tried to write a paper based on the first statement, you would face an unmanageable task—showing all the ways that welfare has been abused. Your readers would also be confused about what to expect in the paper: Will it discuss unscrupulous bureaucrats, fraudulent bookkeeping, dishonest recipients? In contrast, the revised thesis is limited and specific. It signals that the paper will propose restricting welfare payments to two groups. Such a proposal will surely have opponents and is thus appropriate for argumentation-persuasion.

The thesis in an argumentation-persuasion essay can simply state your opinion about an issue, or it can go a step further and call for some action:

Opinion

The lack of affordable day-care centers discriminates against low-income families.

Call for Action

The federal government should support the creation of more day-care centers in low-income neighborhoods.

In either case, your stand on the issue must be clear to your readers.

2. Offer readers strong support for your thesis. Finding evidence that relates to your readers' needs, values, and experience (see pages 21 and 413) is a crucial part of writing an argumentation-persuasion essay. Readers will be responsive to evidence that is *unified, adequate, specific, accurate, dramatic,* and *representative* (see pages 46–49 and 66–69). The evidence might consist of personal experiences or observations. Or it could be gathered from outside sources—statistics; facts; examples; or expert opinion taken from books, articles, reports, interviews, and documentaries. A paper arguing that elderly Americans are better off than they used to be might incorporate the following kinds of evidence:

- *Personal observation or experience:* A description of the writer's grandparents who are living comfortably on Social Security and pensions.
- *Statistics from a report:* A statement that the per-capita after-tax income of older Americans is $335 greater than the national average.
- *Fact from a newspaper article:* The point that the majority of elderly Americans do not live in nursing homes or on the streets; rather, they have their own houses or apartments.
- *Examples from interviews:* Accounts of several elderly couples living comfortably in well-managed retirement villages in Florida.
- *Expert opinion cited in a documentary:* A statement by Dr. Marie Sanchez, a specialist in geriatrics: "An over-sixty-five American today is likely to be healthier, and have a longer life expectancy, than a fifty-year-old living only a decade ago."

You may wonder whether to use the *first-person* ("I") or *third-person* ("he," "she," "they") point of view when presenting evidence based on personal observation, experience, or interviews. The subjective immediacy typical of the first person often delivers a jolt of persuasive power; however, many writers arguing a point prefer to present personal evidence in an objective way, using the third person to keep the focus on the issue rather than on themselves. When you write an argumentation-persuasion essay, your purpose, audience, and tone will help you decide which point of view will be most effective. If you're not sure which point of view to use, check with your instructor. Some encourage a first-person approach; others expect a more objective stance.

As you seek outside evidence, you may—perhaps to your dismay—come across information that undercuts your argument. Resist the temptation to ignore such material; instead, use the evidence to arrive at a more balanced, perhaps somewhat qualified viewpoint. Conversely, don't blindly accept or disregard flaws in the arguments made by sources agreeing with you. Retain a healthy skepticism, analyzing the material as rigorously as if it were advanced by the opposing side.

Also, keep in mind that outside sources aren't infallible. They may have biases that cause them to skew evidence. So be sure to evaluate your sources. If you're writing an essay supporting a woman's right to abortion, the National Abortion Rights Action League (NARAL) can supply abundant statistics, case studies, and reports. But realize that NARAL won't give you the complete picture; it will probably present evidence that supports its "pro-choice" position only. To counteract such bias, you should review what those with differing opinions have to say. You should, for example, examine material published by such "pro-life" organizations as the National Right-to-Life Committee—keeping in mind, of course, that this material is also bound to present support for its viewpoint only. Remember, too, that there are more than two sides to a complex issue. To get as broad a perspective as possible, you should track down sources that have no axe to grind—that is, sources that make a deliberate effort to examine all sides of the issue. For example, published proceedings from a debate on abortion or an in-depth article that aims to synthesize various views on abortion would broaden your understanding of this controversial subject.

Whatever sources you use, be sure to *document* (give credit to) that material. Otherwise, readers may dismiss your evidence as nothing more than your subjective opinion, or they may conclude that you have *plagiarized*—tried to pass off someone else's ideas as your own. (Documentation isn't necessary when material is commonly known or is a matter of historical or scientific record.) In brief informal papers, documentation may consist of simple citations like "Psychologist Aaron Beck believes depression is the result of distorted thoughts" or "*Newsweek* (May 1, 1989) reports that most college-admissions procedures are chaotic." (For information about documenting sources in longer, more formal papers, see Chapters 21 and 22.)

3. Seek to create goodwill. To avoid alienating readers who may not agree with you, stay away from condescending expressions like "Anyone can see that . . ." or "It's obvious that . . ." Also, guard against personalizing the debate and being confrontational: "*My opponents* find the law ineffective" sounds adversarial, whereas "*Those opposed* to the law find it ineffective" or "*Opponents* of the law find it ineffective" is more evenhanded. The last two statements also focus—as they should—on the issue, not on the people involved in the debate.

Goodwill can also be established by finding a *common ground*—some points on which all sides can agree, despite their differences. Assume a township council has voted to raise property taxes. The additional revenues will be used to preserve, as parkland, a wooded area that would otherwise be sold to developers. Before introducing its tax-hike proposal, the council would do well to remind homeowners of everyone's shared goals: maintaining the town's beauty and preventing the community's overdevelopment. This reminder of the common values shared by the town council and homeowners will probably make residents more receptive to the tax hike.

4. Organize the supporting evidence. The support for an argumentation-persuasion paper can be organized in a variety of ways. Any of the patterns of development described in this book (description, narration, definition, cause-effect, and so on) may be used—singly or in combination—to develop the essay's proposition. Imagine you're writing a paper arguing that car racing should be banned from television. Your essay might contain a *description* of a horrifying accident that was televised in graphic detail; you might devote part of the paper to a *causal analysis* showing that the broadcast of such races encourages teens to drive carelessly; you could include a *process analysis* to explain how young

Argumentation-Persuasion 417

drivers "soup up" their cars in a dangerous attempt to imitate the racers seen on television. If your essay includes several patterns, you may need a separate paragraph for each.

When presenting evidence, arrange it so you create the strongest possible effect. In general, you should end with your most compelling point, leaving readers with dramatic evidence that underscores your proposition's validity.

5. Acknowledge and perhaps refute differing viewpoints. If your essay has a clear thesis and strong logical support, you've taken important steps toward winning readers over. However, because argumentation-persuasion focuses on controversial issues, you should also take opposing views into account. As you think about and perhaps research your subject, seek out conflicting viewpoints. As journalist Walter Lippman argued more than sixty years ago in an essay aptly titled "The Indispensable Opposition," it is through the "confrontation of opinion in debate" that we test our views. A good argument seeks out contrary viewpoints, acknowledges them, perhaps even admits they have some merit. Such a strategy strengthens your argument in several ways. It helps you anticipate objections, alerts you to flaws in your own position, and makes you more aware of the other sides' weaknesses. Further, by acknowledging the dissenting views, you come across as reasonable and thorough—qualities that may disarm readers and leave them more receptive to your argument.

You can use a number of techniques to deal with dissenting positions. Here are three particularly effective strategies.

First, you can use a *two-part proposition* consisting of a subordinate clause followed by a main clause. The first part of the proposition (the subordinate clause) *acknowledges opposing opinions;* the second part (the main clause) *states your opinion* and implies that your view stands on more solid ground. With such an approach you may (but you don't have to) discuss opposing opinions. The following thesis statement illustrates this strategy (the opposing viewpoint is underlined once; the writer's position is underlined twice):

Although some instructors think that standardized finals restrict academic freedom, such exams are preferable to those prepared by individual professors.

Second, you can take one or two paragraphs to *summarize* arguments raised by *opposing viewpoints* and grant, when appropriate, the validity of some of those points ("It may be true that ..."). Then you go on to present evidence for your position ("Even so, ...").

Third, you can *refute* all or part of the *dissenting views* by pointing out their flaws. Refutation means pointing out problems with dissenting views and thereby highlighting your position's superiority. You may focus on the opposing sides' inaccurate or inadequate evidence, or you may point to their faulty logic. (Some common types of illogical thinking are discussed on pages 419–22 and 424–26.)

Let's consider how you could refute a competing position in an essay that supports sex education in public schools. You might start by acknowledging the opposing viewpoint's key argument: "Sex education should be the prerogative of parents." After granting the validity of this view in an ideal world, you might show that many parents don't provide such education. You could present statistics on the number of parents who avoid discussing sex with their children because the subject makes them uncomfortable; you could cite studies revealing that children in single-parent homes are likely to receive even less parental guidance about sex; and you could give examples of young people whose parents provided sketchy, even misleading information.

There are various ways to develop a paper's refutation section. The best method to use depends on the paper's length and the complexity of the issue. Two possible sequences are outlined here:

First Strategy	**Second Strategy**
State your proposition.	State your proposition.
Cite opposing viewpoints and the evidence for those views.	Cite opposing viewpoints and the evidence for those views.
Refute opposing viewpoints by presenting counterarguments.	Refute opposing viewpoints by presenting counterarguments.
	Present additional evidence for your proposition.

In the first strategy, you simply refute all or part of the opposing positions' arguments. The second strategy takes the first one a step further by presenting *additional evidence* to support your proposition. In such a case, the additional evidence *must be different* from the points made in the refutation. The additional evidence may appear at the essay's end (as in the preceding outline), or it may be given near the beginning (after the proposition); it may also be divided between the beginning and end.

No matter which strategy you select, you may refute opposing views *one side at a time* or *one point at a time*. (For more on comparing and contrasting the sides of an issue, see pages 320–21 in Chapter 17.) Throughout the essay, be sure to provide clear signals so that readers can distinguish your arguments from the other sides': "Despite the claims of those opposed to the plan, many think that . . ." and "Those not in agreement think that. . . ."

6. Use induction or deduction to think logically about your argument. The line of reasoning used to develop an argument is the surest indicator of how rigorously you have thought through your position. There are two basic ways to think about a subject: inductively and deductively. Though the following discussion treats induction and deduction as separate processes, the two often overlap and complement each other.

Inductive reasoning involves examination of specific cases, facts, or examples. Based on these specifics, you then draw a conclusion or make a generalization. This is the kind of thinking scientists use when they examine evidence (the results of experiments, for example) and then draw a *conclusion:* "Smoking increases the risk of cancer." All of us use inductive reasoning in everyday life. We might think the following: "My head is aching" (evidence); "My nose is stuffy" (evidence); "I'm coming down with a cold" (conclusion). Based on the conclusion, we might go a step further and take some action: "I'll take an aspirin."

Argumentation-Persuasion

With inductive reasoning, the conclusion reached can serve as the proposition for an argumentation-persuasion essay. If the paper advances a course of action, the proposition often mentions the action, signaling an essay with a distinctly persuasive purpose.

Let's suppose that you're writing a paper about a crime wave in the small town where you live. You might use inductive thinking to structure the essay's argument:

> Several people were mugged last month while shopping in the center of town. (*evidence*)
>
> Several homes and apartments were burglarized in the past few weeks. (*evidence*)
>
> Several cars were stolen from people's driveways over the weekend. (*evidence*)
>
> The police force hasn't adequately protected town residents. (*conclusion, or proposition, for an argumentation essay with probable elements of persuasion*)
>
> The police force should take steps to upgrade its protection of town residents. (*conclusion, or proposition, for an argumentation essay with a clearly persuasive intent*)

This inductive sequence highlights a possible structure for the essay. After providing a clear statement of your proposition, you might detail recent muggings, burglaries, and car thefts. Then you could move to the opposing viewpoint: a description of the steps the police say they have taken to protect town residents. At that point, you would refute the police's claim, citing additional evidence that shows the measures taken have not been sufficient. Finally, if you wanted your essay to have a decidedly persuasive purpose, you could end by recommending specific action the police should take to improve its protection of the community.

As in all essays, your evidence should be *unified, specific, accurate, dramatic, sufficient,* and *representative* (see pages 46–49 and 66–69). These last two characteristics are critical when you think inductively; they guarantee that your conclusion would be equally valid even if other evidence were presented. Insufficient or atypical evidence often leads to **hasty generalizations** that mar the essay's logic. For example, you might think the following: "Some elderly people are very wealthy and do not need Social Security checks" (evidence), and "Some Social Security recipients illegally collect several checks" (evidence). If you then conclude, "Social Security is a waste of taxpayers' money," your conclusion is invalid and hasty because it's based on only a few atypical examples. Millions of Social Security recipients aren't wealthy and don't abuse the system. If you've failed to consider the full range of evidence, any action you propose ("The Social Security system should be disbanded") will probably be considered suspect by thoughtful readers. It's possible, of course, that Social Security should be disbanded, but the evidence leading to such a conclusion must be sufficient and representative.

When reasoning inductively, you should also be careful that the evidence you collect is *recent* and *accurate*. No valid conclusion can result from dated or erroneous evidence. To ensure that your evidence is sound, you also need to evaluate the reliability of your sources. When a person who is legally drunk claims to have seen a flying saucer, the evidence is shaky, to say the least. But if two respected scientists, both with 20-20 vision, saw the saucer, their evidence is worth considering.

Finally, it's important to realize that there's always an element of uncertainty in inductive reasoning. The conclusion can never be more than an *inference,* involving what logicians call an **inductive leap.** There could be other explanations for the evidence cited and thus other positions to take and actions to advocate. For example, given a small town's crime wave, you might conclude not that the police force has been remiss but that residents are careless about protecting themselves and their property. In turn, you might call for a different kind of action—perhaps that the police conduct public workshops in self-defense and home security. In an inductive argument, your task is to weigh the evidence, consider alternative explanations, then choose the conclusion and course of action that seem most valid.

Unlike inductive reasoning, which starts with a specific case and moves toward a generalization or conclusion, **deductive reasoning** begins with a generalization that is then applied to a specific case. This movement from general to specific involves a three-step form of reasoning called a **syllogism.** The first part of a syllogism is called the **major premise,** a general statement about an entire group. The second part is the **minor premise,** a statement about an individual within that group. The syllogism ends with a **conclusion** about that individual.

Just as you use inductive thinking in everyday life, you use deductive thinking—often without being aware of it—to sort out your experiences. When trying to decide which car to buy, you might think as follows:

Major Premise   In an accident, large cars are safer than small cars.
Minor Premise   The Turbo Titan is a large car.
Conclusion   In an accident, the Turbo Titan will be safer than a small car.

Based on your conclusion, you might decide to take a specific action, buying the Turbo Titan rather than the smaller car you had first considered.

To create a valid syllogism and thus arrive at a sound conclusion, you need to avoid two major pitfalls of deductive reasoning. First, be sure not to start with a *sweeping* or *hasty generalization* (see page 225 in Chapter 14) as your *major premise*. Second, don't accept as truth a *faulty conclusion*. Let's look at each problem.

Sweeping major premise.   Perhaps you're concerned about a trash-to-steam incinerator scheduled to open near your home. Your thinking about the situation might follow these lines:

Major Premise   Trash-to-steam incinerators have had serious problems and pose significant threats to the well-being of people living near the plants.
Minor Premise   The proposed incinerator in my neighborhood will be a trash-to-steam plant.
Conclusion   The proposed trash-to-steam incinerator in my neighborhood will have serious problems and pose significant threats to the well-being of people living near the plant.

Argumentation-Persuasion

Having arrived at this conclusion, you might decide to join organized protests against the opening of the incinerator. But your thinking is somewhat illogical. Your *major premise* is a *sweeping* one because it indiscriminately groups all trash-to-steam plants into a single category. It's unlikely that you're familiar with all the trash-to-steam incinerators in this country and abroad; it's probably not true that *all* such plants have had serious difficulties that endangered the public. For your argument to reach a valid conclusion, the major premise must be based on repeated observations or verifiable facts. You would have a better argument, and thus reach a more valid conclusion, if you restricted or qualified the major premise, applying it to some, not all, of the group:

Major Premise A *number* of trash-to-steam incinerators have had serious problems and posed significant threats to the well-being of people living near the plants.
Minor Premise The proposed incinerator in my neighborhood will be a trash-to-steam plant.
Conclusion *It's possible* that the proposed trash-to-steam incinerator in my neighborhood will run into serious problems and pose significant threats to the well-being of people living near the plant.

This new conclusion, the result of more careful reasoning, would probably encourage you to learn more about trash-to-steam incinerators in general and about the proposed plant in particular. If further research still left you feeling uncomfortable about the plant, you would probably decide to join the protest. On the other hand, your research might convince you that the plant has incorporated into its design a number of safeguards that have been successful at other plants. This added information could reassure you that your original fears were unfounded. In either case, the revised deductive process would lead to a more informed conclusion and course of action.

Faulty conclusion. Your syllogism—and thus your reasoning—would also be invalid if your *conclusion reverses the "if . . . then" relationship implied in the major premise.* Assume you plan to write a letter to the college newspaper urging the resignation of the student government president. Perhaps you pursue a line of reasoning that goes like this:

Major Premise Students who plagiarize papers must appear before the Faculty Committee on Academic Policies and Procedures.
Minor Premise Yesterday Jennifer Kramer, president of the student government, appeared before the Faculty Committee on Academic Policies and Procedures.
Conclusion Jennifer must have plagiarized a paper.
Action Jennifer should resign her position as student government president.

Such a chain of reasoning is illogical and unfair. Here's why. *If* students plagiarize their term papers and are caught, *then* they must appear before the committee. However, the converse isn't necessarily true—that *if* students appear before the committee, *then* they must have plagiarized. In other words, not *all* students appearing before the Faculty Committee have been called up on plagiarism charges. For instance, Jennifer could have been speaking on behalf of another student; she could have been protesting some action taken by the committee; she could have been seeking the committee's help on an article she plans to write about academic honesty. The conclusion doesn't allow for these other possible explanations.

Now that you're aware of the problems associated with deductive reasoning, let's look at the way you can use a syllogism to structure an argumentation-persuasion essay. Suppose you decide to write a paper advocating support for a projected space mission. You know that controversy surrounds the space program, especially since seven astronauts died in a 1986 launch. Confident that the tragedy has led to more rigorous controls, you want to argue that the benefits of an upcoming mission outweigh its risks. A deductive pattern could be used to develop your argument. In fact, outlining your thinking as a syllogism might help you formulate a proposition, organize your evidence, deal with the opposing viewpoint, and—if appropriate—propose a course of action:

Major Premise	Space programs in the past have led to important developments in technology, especially in medical science.
Minor Premise	The *Cosmos* Mission is the newest space program.
Proposition (*essay might be persuasive*)	The *Cosmos* Mission will most likely lead to important developments in technology, especially in medical science.
Proposition (*essay is clearly persuasive*)	Congress should continue its funding of the *Cosmos* Mission.

Having outlined the deductive pattern of your thinking, you might begin by stating your proposition and then discuss some new procedures developed to protect the astronauts and the rocket system's structural integrity. With that background established, you could detail the opposing claim that little of value has been produced by the space program so far. You could then move to your refutation, citing significant medical advances derived from former space missions. Finally, the paper might conclude on a persuasive note, with a plea to Congress to continue funding the latest space mission.

7. Use Toulmin logic to establish a strong connection between your evidence and thesis. Whether you use an essentially inductive or deductive approach, your argument depends on strong evidence. In *The Uses of Argument*, Stephen Toulmin describes a useful approach for strengthening the connection between evidence and thesis. Toulmin divides a typical argument into three parts:

- **Claim**—the thesis, proposition, or conclusion
- **Data**—the evidence (facts, statistics, examples, observations, expert opinion) used to convince readers of the claim's validity
- **Warrant**—the underlying assumption that justifies moving from evidence to claim.

Argumentation-Persuasion

Here's a sample argument using Toulmin's terminology:

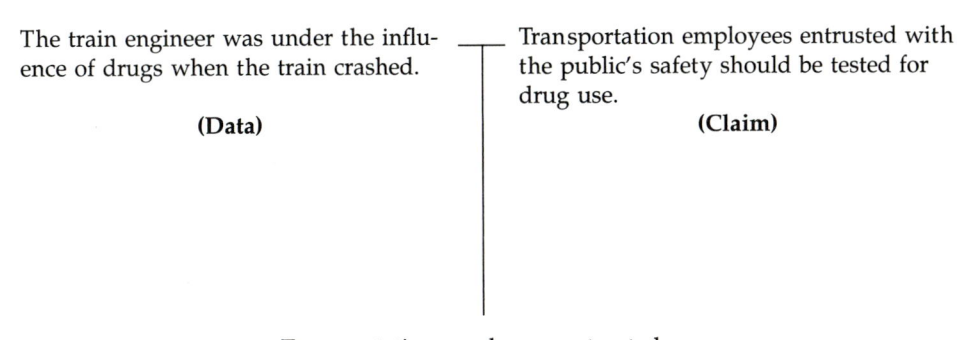

The train engineer was under the influence of drugs when the train crashed.	Transportation employees entrusted with the public's safety should be tested for drug use.
(Data)	**(Claim)**

Transportation employees entrusted with the public's safety should not be allowed on the job if they use drugs.
(Warrant)

As Toulmin explains in his book, readers are more apt to consider your argument valid if they know what your warrant is. Sometimes your warrant will be so obvious that you won't need to state it explicitly; an *implicit warrant* will be sufficient. Assume you want to argue that the use of live animals to test product toxicity should be outlawed. To support your claim, you cite the following evidence: first, current animal tests are painful and usually result in the animal's death; second, human cell cultures frequently offer more reliable information on how harmful a product may be to human tissue; and third, computer simulations often can more accurately rate a substance's toxicity. Your warrant, although not explicit, is nonetheless clear: "It is wrong to continue product testing on animals when more humane and valid test methods are available."

Other times, you'll do best to make your *warrant explicit.* Suppose you plan to argue that students should be involved in deciding which faculty members are granted tenure. To develop your claim, you present some evidence. You begin by noting that, currently, only faculty members and administrators review candidates for tenure. Next, you call attention to the controversy surrounding two professors, widely known by students to be poor teachers, who were nonetheless granted tenure. Finally, you cite a decision, made several years ago, to discontinue using student evaluations as part of the tenure process; you emphasize that since that time complaints about teachers' incompetence have risen dramatically. Some readers, though, still might wonder how you got from your evidence to your claim. In this case, your argument could be made stronger by stating your warrant explicitly: "Since students are as knowledgeable as the faculty and administrators about which professors are competent, they should be involved in the tenure process."

The more widely accepted your warrant, Toulmin explains, the more likely it is that readers will accept your argument. If there's no consensus about the warrant, you'll probably need to *back it up.* For the preceding example, you might mention several reports that found students evaluate faculty fairly (most students don't, for example, use the ratings to get back at professors against whom they have a personal grudge); further, students' ratings correlate strongly with those given by administrators and other faculty.

Toulmin describes another way to increase receptivity to an argument: *qualify the claim*—that is, explain under what circumstances it might be invalid or restricted. For instance, you might grant that most students know little about their instructors' research activities, scholarly publications, or participation in professional committees. You could, then, qualify your claim this way: "Because students don't have a comprehensive view of their instructors' professional activities, they should be involved in the tenure process but play a less prominent role than faculty and administrators."

As you can see, Toulmin's approach provides strategies for strengthening an argument. So, when prewriting or revising, take a few minutes to ask yourself the following questions:

- What data (*evidence*) should I provide to support my claim (*thesis*)?
- Is my warrant clear? Should I state it explicitly? What back-up can I provide to justify my warrant?
- Would qualifying my claim make my argument more convincing?

Your responses to these questions will help you structure a convincing and logical argument.

8. Recognize logical fallacies. When writing an argumentation-persuasion essay, you need to recognize **logical fallacies** both in your own argument and in points raised by the opposing side. Work to eliminate such gaps in logic from your own writing and, when they appear in the opposing argument, try to expose them in your refutation. Logicians have identified many logical fallacies—including the sweeping or hasty generalization and the faulty conclusion discussed earlier in this chapter. Other logical fallacies are described in Ann McClintock's "Propaganda Techniques in Today's Advertising" (page 271) and in the paragraphs that follow.

The *post hoc* **fallacy** (short for a Latin phrase meaning "after this, therefore because of this") occurs when you conclude that a cause-effect relationship exists simply because one event preceded another. Let's say you note the growing number of immigrants settling in a nearby city, observe the city's economic decline, and conclude that the immigrants' arrival caused the decline. Such a chain of thinking is faulty because it assumes a cause-effect relationship based purely on co-occurrence. Perhaps the immigrants' arrival was a factor in the economic slump, but there could also be other reasons: the lack of financial incentives to attract business to the city, restrictions on the size of the city's manufacturing facilities, citywide labor disputes that make companies leery of settling in the area. Your argument should also consider these possibilities. (For more on the *post hoc* fallacy, see page 351 in Chapter 18.)

The *non sequitur* **fallacy** (Latin for "it does not follow") is an even more blatant muddying of cause-effect relationships. In this case, a conclusion is drawn that has no logical connection to the evidence cited: "Millions of

Americans own cars, so there is no need to fund public transportation." The faulty conclusion disregards the millions of Americans who don't own cars; it also ignores pollution and road congestion, both of which could be reduced if people had access to safe, reliable public transportation.

An *ad hominem* **argument** (from the Latin meaning "to the man") occurs when someone attacks a person rather than a point of view. Suppose your college plans to sponsor a physicians' symposium on the abortion controversy. You decide to write a letter to the school paper opposing the symposium. Taking swipes at two of the invited doctors who disapprove of abortion, you mention that one was recently involved in a messy divorce and that the other is alleged to have a drinking problem. By hurling personal invective, you avoid discussing the issue. Mudslinging is a poor substitute for reasoned argument. And as politician Adlai Stevenson once said, "He who slings mud generally loses ground."

Appeals to questionable or faulty authority also weaken an argument. Most of us have developed a healthy suspicion of phrases like *sources close to, an unidentified spokesperson states, experts claim,* and *studies show*. If these people and reports are so reliable, they should be clearly identified.

Begging the question involves failure to establish proof for a debatable point. The writer expects readers to accept as given a premise that's actually controversial. For instance, you would have trouble convincing readers that prayer should be banned from public schools if you based your argument on the premise that school prayer violates the U.S. Constitution. If the Constitution does, either explicitly or implicitly, prohibit prayer in public education, your essay must demonstrate that fact. You can't build a strong argument if you pretend there's no controversy surrounding your premise.

A **false analogy** disregards significant dissimilarities and wrongly implies that because two things share *some* characteristics, they are therefore *alike in all respects*. You might, for example, compare nicotine and marijuana. Both, you could mention, involve health risks and have addictive properties. If, however, you go on to conclude, "Driving while smoking a cigarette isn't illegal, so driving while smoking marijuana shouldn't be illegal either," you're employing a false analogy. You've overlooked a major difference between tobacco and marijuana: Marijuana impairs perception and coordination—important aspects of driving—while there's no evidence that tobacco does the same.

The *either/or* **fallacy** occurs when you assume that a particular viewpoint or course of action can have only one of two diametrically opposed outcomes—either totally this or totally that. Say you argue as follows: "Unless colleges continue to offer scholarships based solely on financial need, no one who is underprivileged will be able to attend college." Such a statement ignores the fact that bright, underprivileged students could receive scholarships based on their potential or their demonstrated academic excellence.

Finally, a **red herring** argument is an intentional digression from the issue—a ploy to deflect attention from the matter being discussed. Imagine you're arguing that condoms shouldn't be dispensed to high school students. You would introduce a red herring if you began to rail against parents who fail to provide their children with any information about sex. Most people would agree that parents *should* provide such information. However, the issue being discussed is not parents' irresponsibility but the pros and cons of schools' distributing condoms to students.

REVISION STRATEGIES

Once you have a draft of the essay, you're ready to revise. The following checklist will help you and those giving you feedback apply to argumentation-persuasion some of the revision techniques discussed in Chapters 7 and 8.

> ✔ **ARGUMENTATION-PERSUASION: A REVISION CHECKLIST**
>
> *Revise Overall Meaning and Structure*
> - What issue is being discussed? What is controversial about it?
> - What is the essay's thesis? How does it differ from a generalization or mere statement of fact?
> - What is the essay's purpose? To win readers over to a point of view? To spur readers to action? What action?
> - For what audience is the essay written? What strategies are used to make readers receptive to the essay's thesis?
> - What tone does the essay project? Is the tone likely to win readers over? Why or why not?
> - If the essay's argument is essentially deductive, is the major premise sufficiently restricted? What repeated observations or verifiable facts is the premise based on? Are the minor premise and conclusion valid? If not, how could these problems be corrected?
> - Where is the essay weakened by hasty generalizations, a failure to weigh evidence honestly, or a failure to draw the most valid conclusion?
> - Where does the essay commit any of the following *logical* fallacies: Concluding that a cause-effect relationship exists simply because one event preceded another? Attacking a person rather than an issue? Drawing a conclusion that isn't logically related to the evidence? Failing to establish proof for a debatable point? Relying on questionable or vaguely specified authority? Drawing a false analogy? Resorting to *either/or* thinking?
>
> *Revise Paragraph Development*
> - How apparent is the link between the evidence (data) and the thesis (claim)? How could an explicit warrant clarify the connection? How would supporting the warrant or qualifying the claim strengthen the argument?

> - Which paragraphs lack sufficient evidence (facts, examples, statistics, and expert opinion)?
> - Which paragraphs lack unity? How could they be made more focused? In which paragraph does the evidence seem bland, overly general, unrepresentative, or inaccurate?
> - Which paragraphs take opposing views into account? Are these views refuted? If so, are they refuted *in toto* or one point at a time? Which counterarguments are ineffective? Why?
> - Where do outside sources require documentation?
>
> *Revise Sentences and Words*
> - What words and phrases ("Contrary to what opponents claim...") or "Those opposed feel...") help readers distinguish the essay's arguments from those advanced by the opposing side?
> - Which words carry strong emotional overtones? Is this connotative language excessive? Where does emotional language replace rather than reinforce clear thinking?
> - Where might dogmatic language ("Anyone can see that..." and "Obviously,...") alienate readers?

STUDENT ESSAY: FROM PREWRITING THROUGH REVISION

The student essay that follows was written by Mark Simmons in response to this assignment:

> In "Institution Is Not a Dirty Word," Fern Kupfer invites controversy by disputing the notion that placing a severely mentally handicapped child in an institution is cruel and irresponsible. Select another controversial issue, one that you feel strongly about. Using logic and solid evidence, convince readers that your viewpoint is valid.

Before writing his essay, Mark used the prewriting strategy of *group brainstorming* to generate material on the subject he decided to write about: compulsory national service. In a lively give-and-take with friends, Mark jotted down, as they occurred, ideas that seemed especially promising. Later on, he typed up his jottings so he could review them more easily. At that point, he began to organize the material.

Mark's typed version of the brainstormed list is on page 428. The handwritten marks indicate his later efforts to organize the material. As you can see, he started organizing the list by crossing out one item (the possibility of low morale) and adding several others (for example, that compulsory national service would be a relatively inexpensive way to repair bridges and roads). Then he labeled points raised by the opposing side and his counterarguments. In the process, the essay's underlying structure began to emerge so clearly that he had no trouble preparing an outline, which is presented on page 429.

Brainstorming

Definition   Compulsory service--ages 17-25

           Two years--military or public service

Example.   *Serve after high school or college*
Where to use?   Israel has it, and it works well

           Nazi Germany had it, too

           Too authoritarian   *Opposing position: Point 3 (potentially fascist)*

           Start of a dictatorship

           Can choose what kind of service

           No uniforms   *Refutation of point 3 (not fascist)*

           U.S. not a fascist country

           Americans very lucky--economic opportunity, right to vote, etc.

Introduction   Take without giving

           Should have to give--program provides that chance

           Program too expensive

           Pay--at least minimum wage   *Opposing position: Point 1 (too expensive)*

Less costly way to   Have to provide housing, too
repair bridges and   *Can live at home*
roads and help   Payments from participating towns, cities, states   *Refutation of point 1 (not expensive)*
elderly and
disabled   Could be like Peace Corps' small budget

           ~~Low morale because forced? (Unlike Volunteer Peace Corps)~~

           Demoralizing   *Opposing position: Point 2 (demoralizing)*

           Interfere with careers

           Learn skills   *Refutation of point 2 (not demoralizing)*

           Time to think about goals

           Make real contribution to society
           Feel good and worthwhile

Outline

Thesis: Compulsory national service would be good for both young people and the country.

I. Definition of compulsory national service
II. Cost of compulsory national service
    A. Would be expensive
        1. Would have high administrative costs
        2. Would have high salary and housing costs
    B. Wouldn't be expensive
        1. Could follow Peace Corps model
        2. Would require the towns, cities, and states using the corps to pay salary and housing costs
        3. Would cut costs by having young people live at home
        4. Would provide a cost-efficient way to repair deteriorating bridges, roads, and neighborhoods
        5. Would provide a cost-efficient way to help the elderly and homeless
III. Effect of compulsory national service on young people
    A. Would be demoralizing
        1. Would interrupt career plans
        2. Would waste young people's time by making them do work that isn't personally meaningful
    B. Wouldn't be demoralizing
        1. Would give young people time to evaluate life and career goals
        2. Would equip young people with marketable skills
        3. Would make young people from different backgrounds feel good about coming together to contribute to society
IV. Effect of compulsory national service on American democracy
    A. Could encourage fascism, as it did in Germany
    B. Wouldn't encourage fascism
        1. Wouldn't undermine our present system of checks and balances
        2. Would offer young people choices about when they would serve and in which branch they would serve
        3. Wouldn't require uniforms or confinement in a barracks
        4. Wouldn't be that different from a regular nine-to-five job

    Now read Mark's paper, "Compulsory National Service," noting the similarities and differences between his prewriting, outline, and final essay. One difference is especially striking: During prewriting, Mark and his friends tended to identify an objection to compulsory service, brainstorm an appropriate counterargument, then move to the next objection and its counterargument. Mark used the same *point-by-point* format in his outline. When drafting his paper, though, Mark decided to use the *one-side-at-a-time* format. He summarized all reservations first, then devoted the rest of the essay to a detailed refutation. This change in organization strengthened Mark's argument because his rebuttals acquired greater force when gathered together, instead of remaining scattered throughout the paper. As you read the essay, also consider how well it applies the principles of argumentation-persuasion discussed in this chapter. (The commentary that follows the paper will help you look at Mark's essay more closely and will give you some sense of how he went about revising his first draft.)

Compulsory National Service
by Mark Simmons

Introduction

Our high school history class spent several weeks studying the events of the 1960s. The most intriguing thing about that decade was the spirit of service and social commitment among young people. In the 60s, young people thought about issues beyond themselves; they joined the Peace Corps and participated in freedom marches against segregation. They accepted President Kennedy's urging to "Ask not what your country can do for you; ask what you can do for your country." Most young people today, despite their obvious concern with careers and getting ahead, would also like an opportunity to make a worthwhile contribution to society. By instituting a program of compulsory national service, our country could tap this desire in young people. Such a system would yield significant benefits.

Start of two-sentence thesis

Definition paragraph

Compulsory national service means that everyone between the ages of 17 and 25 would serve their country for two years. Young people could choose between two major options: military service or a public-service corps. They could serve their time at any point within the eight-year span. The unemployed or the uncertain could join immediately after high school; college-bound students could complete their education before joining the national service.

Topic sentence
Beginning of summary of three points raised by opposing viewpoint

The idea of compulsory national service has been discussed for many years, and some nations such as Israel have embraced it wholeheartedly. The idea could also be workable in this country. Unfortunately, detractors have prevented the idea from taking hold. Opponents contend, first of all, that the program would cost too much; they argue that a great

Argumentation-Persuasion

deal of money would have to be spent administering the program. In addition, young people would have to receive at least a minimum wage for their work, and some of them would need housing--both costly items. Another argument against compulsory national service is that it would demoralize young people; the plan would prevent the young from getting on with their careers and would make them feel as though they were engaged in work that had no personal reward. A final argument is that compulsory service would lay the groundwork for a military state. The picture is painted of an army of young robots totally at the mercy of the government, like the Hitler Youth of the Second World War.

4 — Despite opponents' claims that compulsory national service would involve exorbitant costs, the program would not have to be that expensive to run. The program might use as a model the Peace Corps, which has achieved great benefits even while being administered on a fairly modest budget. Also, the sums required for wages and housing could be reduced considerably through payments made by the towns, cities, and states using the corps' services. And the economic benefits of the program could be significant. The public-service corps could repair deteriorating bridges, highways, public buildings, and inner-city neighborhoods. The corps could organize recycling projects; it could staff public health clinics, day-care centers, legal aid centers, and homeless shelters. The corps could also monitor pollution, clean up litter, and help care for the country's growing elderly population. All of these projects would help solve many of the problems that plague our nation, and they would probably cost much less than if they were handled by traditional government bureaucracies or the private sector.

Topic sentence: Refutation of first point

5 — Also, rather than undermining the spirit of young people, as opponents contend, the program would probably boost their morale. Many young people feel enormous pressure and uncertainty. They are not sure what they want to do, or they have trouble finding a way to begin their careers. Compulsory national service could give young people a much-needed breathing space and could even equip them with the skills needed to start a career. Moreover, participating in compulsory national service could provide an emotional boost for the young; all of them would experience the pride that comes from working hard, reaching goals, acquiring skills, and handling responsibilities. A positive mind-set would also result from the sense of community that would be created by serving in the national service. All young-people--rich or poor, educated or not, regardless of sex

Topic sentence: Refutation of second point

or social class--would come together during this time. Young people would grow to understand one another and learn that every person has an ability to aid the welfare of the whole group. Each young person would have the satisfaction of knowing that he or she has made a real contribution to the nation.

Topic sentence: Refutation of third point

Finally, contrary to what opponents claim, compulsory national service would not signal the start of a dictatorship. Although the service would be required, young people would have complete freedom to choose any two years between the ages of 17 and 25. They would also have complete freedom to choose the branch of the military or public-service corps that suits them best. And the corps would not need to be outfitted in military uniforms or to live in barrack-like camps. It could be set up like a regular job, with young people living at home as much as possible, following a nine-to-five schedule, enjoying all the personal freedoms that would ordinarily be theirs. Also, a dictatorship would no more likely emerge from a program of compulsory national service than it has from our present military system. We would still have a series of checks and balances to prohibit the taking of power by one group or individual. We should also keep in mind that our system is different from that of fascist regimes; our long tradition of personal liberty makes improbable the seizing of absolute power by one person or faction. A related but even more important point to remember is that freedom does not mean people are guaranteed the right to pursue only their individual needs. That is mistaking selfishness for freedom. And, as everyone knows, selfishness leads only to misery. It cannot lead to a happy life. The national service would not take away freedom. On the contrary, it would help young people grasp this larger concept of freedom, a concept that is badly needed to counteract the deadly "look out for number one" attitude that is spreading like a poison across the nation.

Conclusion: echoes material in introduction

Perhaps there will never be a time like the 1960s when so many young people were concerned with remaking the world. Still, a good many of today's young people want meaningful work. They want to feel that what they do makes a difference. A program of compulsory national service would tap this willingness in young people, helping them realize the best in themselves. Such a program would also allow us as a nation to make sub-stantial headway against the social problems that haunt the country. It is apparent that compulsory national service is an idea whose time has come.

Commentary

Blend of Argumentation and Persuasion

In his essay, Mark tackles a controversial issue: He takes the position that compulsory national service would benefit both the country as a whole and its young people in particular. Mark's essay is a good example of the way argumentation and persuasion often mix; although the paper presents Mark's position in a logical, well-reasoned manner (argumentation), it also appeals to readers' personal values and suggests a course of action (persuasion).

Audience Analysis

When planning the essay, Mark realized that his audience—his composition class—would consist largely of two kinds of readers. Some, not sure of their views, would be inclined to agree with him if he presented his case well. Others would probably be reluctant to accept his view. Because of this mixed audience, Mark knew he couldn't depend on *pathos* (an appeal to emotion) to convince readers. Rather, his argument had to rely mainly on *logos* (reason) and *ethos* (credibility). So Mark organized his essay around a series of logical arguments and evoked his own authority, drawing on his knowledge of history and his "inside" knowledge of young people.

Introduction and Thesis

Mark introduces his subject by discussing an earlier decade when large numbers of young people worked for social change. Mark's references to the Peace Corps, freedom marches, and President Kennedy reinforce his image as a knowledgeable source and establish a context for his position. These historical references also lead into the two-sentence *thesis* at the end of the introduction: "By instituting a system of compulsory national service, our country could tap this desire in young people. Such a system would yield significant benefits."

Background Paragraph

The next paragraph is developed around a *definition* of compulsory national service. The definition guarantees that Mark's readers will share his understanding of the essay's central concept.

Acknowledging the Opposing Viewpoint

Mark is now in a good position to move into the body of his essay. Even though the assignment didn't call for research, Mark wisely decided to get together with some friends to brainstorm some issues that might be raised by the dissenting view. Using the *one-side-at-a-time* format, he acknowledges this position in the *topic sentence* of the essay's third paragraph: "Unfortunately, opponents have prevented the idea from taking hold." Next he summarizes the main points the dissenting opinion might advance: compulsory national service would be expensive, demoralizing to young people, and dangerously authoritarian. Mark uses the rest of the essay to counter these criticisms.

Refutation

The next three paragraphs (4–6) *refute* the opposing stance and present Mark's evidence for his position. Adapting material he brainstormed with friends, Mark structures the essay so that readers can follow his *counterargument* with ease. Each paragraph argues against one opposing point and begins with a *topic sentence* that serves as Mark's response to the dissenting view. Note the way the italicized portion of each topic sentence recalls a dissenting point cited earlier: "Despite opponents' claims that *compulsory national service would involve exorbitant costs,* the program would not have to be that expensive to run" (paragraph 4); "Also, rather than *undermining the spirit of young people,* as opponents contend, the program would probably boost their morale" (5); "Finally, contrary to what opponents claim, *compulsory national service would not signal the start of a dictatorship*" (6). Mark also guides the reader through the various points in the refutation by using *transitions* within paragraphs: "*And* the economic benefits ... could be significant" (4); "*Moreover,* participating in compulsory national service could provide an emotional boost..." (5); "*Also,* a dictatorship would no more likely emerge..." (6).

Some Problems with the Refutation

Overall, Mark's three-paragraph refutation is strong, but it would have been even more effective if the paragraphs had been resequenced. As it now stands, the last paragraph (6) seems anticlimactic. The refutation would have been more persuasive if Mark had placed the final paragraph in the refutation in a less emphatic position. He could, for example, have put it first or second in the sequence, saving for last either of the other two more convincing paragraphs.

You may also have felt that there's another problem with the third paragraph in the refutation. Here, Mark seems to lose control of his counterargument. Beginning with "And, as everyone knows...," Mark falls into the *logical fallacy* called *begging the question.* He shouldn't assume that everyone agrees that a selfish life inevitably brings misery. He also indulges in charged emotionalism when he refers—somewhat melodramatically—to the "deadly 'look out for number one' attitude that is spreading like a poison across the nation."

Inductive Reasoning

Mark arrived at his position *inductively*—through an *inference* or *inductive leap*. He started with a number of specific observations about the nation and its young people. To support those observations, he added his friends' comments and insights. Combined, this material led him to the general *conclusion* that compulsory national service would be both workable and beneficial. In other words, Mark's evidence, as thoughtful and convincing as it may be, consists not of researched fact but of reasonable speculation.

Other Patterns of Development

To develop his argument, Mark draws on several patterns of development. The second paragraph relies on *definition* to clarify what is meant by compulsory national service. The introduction and conclusion *compare* and *contrast* young people of the 1960s with those of today. Finally, to support his position, Mark uses a kind

Argumentation-Persuasion

of *causal analysis* that speculates on the likely consequences of compulsory national service.

Conclusion

Despite some minor problems along the way, Mark closes the essay effectively. He echoes the point made in the introduction about the 1960s and restates his thesis. The essay then ends with a crisp assertion that suggests a course of action.

Revising the First Draft

Mark revised his first draft with the help of two classmates, who used the checklist on pages 426–27 to focus their comments. After jotting his classmates' suggestions on a separate sheet, Mark transferred those he found most helpful to the margin of his paper. He then numbered the comments in order of importance. As Mark reviewed these notes, he realized that his introduction needed special attention.

A comparison of the introduction's original and final versions reveals the way Mark proceeded when revising. The annotations on the original (reprinted here) signal the problems that Mark and his partners saw in the first version.

Original Introduction

"There's no free lunch." "You can't get something for nothing." "You have to earn your way." In America, these sayings are not really true. In America, we gladly take but give back little. In America, we receive economic opportunity, legal protection, the right to vote, and, most of all, a personal freedom unequaled throughout the world. How do we repay our country for such gifts? In most cases, we don't. This unfair relationship must be changed. The best way to make a start is to institute a system of national compulsory service for young people. This system would be of real benefit to the country and its citizens.

③ *Choppy*

① *Focus right from start on young people—maybe mention youth of the 1960s*

② *Need stronger link between early part of paragraph and thesis*

Following his classmates' suggestion, Mark deleted the introduction's references to Americans in general. He made this change because the paper focuses not on all Americans but on American youth. To reinforce this emphasis, he also added the point about the social commitment characteristic of young people in the 1960s. Besides providing a logical lead-in to the thesis, this reference to an earlier period gave the discussion an important historical perspective and lent a note of authority to Mark's argument. Mark was also pleased to see that adding this new material helped unify and smooth out the paragraph.

These are just a few of the many changes Mark made while reworking his essay. Because he budgeted his time carefully, he was able to revise thoroughly. With the exception of some weak spots in the sixth paragraph, Mark's essay is well reasoned and convincing.

ACTIVITIES: ARGUMENTATION-PERSUASION

Prewriting Activities

1. Imagine you're writing two essays: One defines hypocrisy; the other contrasts license and freedom. Identify an audience for each essay (college students, professors, teenagers, parents, employers, employees, or some other group). Then jot down how each essay might argue the merits of certain ways of behaving.

2. Following are several thesis statements for argumentation-persuasion essays. For each thesis, determine whether the three audiences indicated in parentheses are apt to be supportive, wavering, or hostile. Then select *one* thesis and use group brainstorming to identify, for each audience, general concerns on which you might successfully base your persuasive appeal (for example, the concern for approval, for financial well-being, for self-respect, for the welfare of others).

   a. The minimum wage should be raised every two years (*low-income employees, employers, congressional representatives*).
   b. Students should not graduate from college until they have passed a comprehensive exam in their majors (*college students, their parents, college officials*).
   c. Abandoned homes owned by the city should be sold to low-income residents for a nominal fee (*city officials, low-income residents, general citizens*).
   d. The town should pass a law prohibiting residents near the reservoir from using pesticides on their lawns (*environmentalists, homeowners, members of the town council*).
   e. Faculty advisors to college newspapers should have the authority to prohibit the publication of articles that reflect negatively on the school (*alumni, college officials, student journalists*).

3. Using the thesis you selected in activity 2, focus—for each group indicated in parentheses—on one or two of the general concerns you identified. Then brainstorm with others to determine the specific points you'd make to persuade each group. What technique (pages 417–18) would you use to acknowledge the viewpoint of the most hostile audience?

4. Clip an effective advertisement from a magazine or newspaper. Through brainstorming, determine to what extent the ad depends on *logos, ethos,* and *pathos.* Consider the persuasive approaches described in Ann McClintock's "Propaganda Techniques in Today's Advertising" (page 271) as well as the logical fallacies discussed in this chapter. After reviewing your brainstorming,

Argumentation-Persuasion

devise a thesis that expresses your feelings about the ad's persuasive strategies. Are they responsible? Why or why not?

5. In a campus, local, or major newspaper, find an editorial with which you disagree. Using the patterns of development, freewriting, or another prewriting technique, generate points that refute the editorial. You may, for example, identify any logical fallacies in the editorial. Then, following one of the refutation strategies discussed in this chapter, organize your rebuttal.

Revising Activities

6. Examine the following sets, each containing *data* (evidence) and a *claim* (thesis). For each set, identify the implied *warrant*. Which sets would benefit from an explicit warrant? Why? How might the warrant be expressed? In which sets would it be helpful to support the warrant or qualify the claim? Why? How might the warrant be supported or the claim qualified?

a. *Data:* An increasing number of Americans are buying Japanese cars. The reason, they report, is that Japanese cars tend to have superior fuel efficiency and longevity. Japanese cars are currently manufactured under stricter quality control than American models.
Claim: Implementing stricter quality controls is one way for the American auto industry to compete with Japanese imports.

b. *Data:* Although laws guarantee learning-impaired children an education suitable to their needs, no laws safeguard the special needs of intellectually gifted children. There are, proportionately, far more programs that assist the slow learner than there are those that challenge the fast learner.
Claim: Our educational system is unfair to gifted children.

c. *Data:* To date, no woman or nonwhite and only one non-Protestant (John F. Kennedy) has ever been elected president of the United States.
Claim: Until prejudicial attitudes change, American voters will not elect a president who is a female, a member of a racial minority, or a non-Protestant.

d. *Data:* Minors aren't permitted to vote, marry without parental consent, or sign contracts. Nevertheless, the Supreme Court has ruled that a minor can receive the full penalty of the law—in some cases, even be executed—for a crime.
Claim: Minors who engage in criminal acts should be treated with greater leniency than adults.

7. Examine the faulty chains of reasoning that follow. Which use essentially inductive logic? Which use essentially deductive logic? In each set, determine, in general terms, why the conclusion is invalid. (The next activity offers practice in identifying specific logical fallacies that render conclusions invalid.)

a. Whenever I work in the college's computer lab, something goes wrong. The program crashes, the cursor freezes, the margins unset themselves.
Conclusion: The college needs to allocate additional funds to repair and upgrade the computers in the lab.

b. Many cars in the student parking lot are dented and look as though they have been in accidents.
Conclusion: Students are careless drivers.

c. Many researchers believe that children in families where both parents work develop confidence and independence. In a nearby community, the number of two-career families increased 15 percent over a two-year period.
Conclusion: Children in the nearby community will develop confidence and independence.

d. The local Chamber of Commerce elected a woman as president. The all-male Metropolitan Business Club approved a woman for membership.
Conclusion: Traditionally conservative male groups are starting to accept women's role in business.

e. Anyone found guilty of sexual harassment will be fired by XYZ Corporation. Curt A. was fired by XYZ Corporation.
Conclusion: Curt A. is guilty of sexual harassment.

8. Each set of statements that follows contains at least one of the logical fallacies described earlier in the chapter and in Ann McClintock's essay "Propaganda Techniques in Today's Advertising" (page 271). Identify the fallacy or fallacies in each set and explain why the statements are invalid.

a. Grades are irrelevant to learning. Students are in college to get an education, not good grades. The university should eliminate grading altogether.
b. The best policy is to put juvenile offenders in jail so that they can get a taste of reality. Otherwise, they will repeat their crimes over and over.
c. Legal experts say that this bill will weaken consumers' rights. Based on their views, we should petition legislators not to sign the bill.
d. So-called sex education programs do nothing to decrease the rate of teenage pregnancy. Further expenditures on these programs should be curtailed.
e. This country should research environmentally sound ways to use coal as an energy source. If we don't, we will become enslaved to the oil-rich Middle East nations.
f. If we allow abortion, people will think it's acceptable to kill the homeless or pull the plug on sick people—two groups that are also weak and frail.
g. The curfews that some towns impose on teenagers are as repressive as the curfews in totalitarian countries.
h. Each day, Americans throw out ton after ton of edible food; it isn't true that some Americans suffer from hunger.
i. Two members of the state legislature have introduced gun-control legislation. Both have led sheltered, pampered lives that prevent them from seeing how ordinary people need guns to protect themselves.
j. Some say that auto insurance rates need to be more strictly regulated, but how strict are regulations on health insurance?
k. Last year, a few students managed to avoid paying for their parking decals. This year's increased student parking fees unfairly penalize everyone for the dishonesty of a few.

Argumentation-Persuasion

9. Following is the introduction from the first draft of an essay advocating the elimination of mandatory dress codes in public schools. Revise the paragraph, being sure to consider these questions: How effectively does the writer deal with the opposing viewpoint? Does the paragraph encourage those who might disagree with the writer to read on? Why or why not? Do you see any logical fallacies in the writer's thinking? Where? Does the writer introduce anything that veers away from the point being discussed? Where? Before revising, you may find it helpful to do some brainstorming—individually or in a group—to find ways to strengthen the paragraph.

After reworking the paragraph, take a few minutes to consider how the rest of the essay might unfold. What persuasive strategies could be used, what points could be made, what action could be urged in the effort to build a convincing argument?

In three nearby towns recently, high school administrators joined forces to take an outrageously strong stand against students' constitutional rights. Acting like Fascists, they issued an edict in the form of a preposterous dress code that prohibits students from wearing expensive jewelry, designer jeans, leather jackets--anything that the administrators, in their supposed wisdom, consider ostentatious. Perhaps the next thing they'll want to do is forbid students to play rock music at school dances. What prompted the administrators' dictatorial prohibition against certain kinds of clothing? Somehow or other, they got it into their heads that having no restrictions on the way students dress creates an unhealthy environment, where students vie with each other for the flashiest attire. Students and parents alike should protest this and any other dress code. If such codes go into effect, we might as well throw out the Constitution.

PROFESSIONAL SELECTIONS: ARGUMENTATION-PERSUASION

FERN KUPFER

A teacher of writing at Iowa State University, Fern Kupfer (1946–) lectures nationally as an advocate for families with handicapped children. Her works include two novels, *Surviving the Seasons* (1989) and *No Regrets* (1990), as well as *Before and After Zachariah*

(1982), a book about the institutionalization of her severely handicapped son. The following essay first appeared in *Newsweek* in 1982.

INSTITUTION IS NOT A DIRTY WORD

1   I watched Phil Donahue recently. He had on mothers of handicapped children who talked about the pain and blessing of having a "special" child. As the mother of a severely handicapped six-year-old boy who cannot sit, who cannot walk, who will be in diapers all of his days, I understand the pain. The blessing part continues to elude me—notwithstanding the kind and caring people we've met through this tragedy.

2   What really makes my jaws clench, though, is the use of the word "special." The idea that our damaged children are "special," and that we as parents were somehow picked for the role, is one of the myths that come with the territory. It's reinforced by the popular media, which present us with heartwarming images of retarded people who marry, of quadriplegics who fly airplanes, of those fortunate few who struggle out of comas to teach us about the meaning of courage and love. I like these stories myself. But, of course, inspirational tales are only one side of the story. The other side deals with the daily care of a family member who might need more than many normal families can give. Parents who endure with silent stoicism or chin-up good humor are greeted with kudos and applause. "I don't know how you do it," the well-wishers say, not realizing, of course, that no one has a choice in this matter. No one would consciously choose to have a child anything less than healthy and normal. The other truth is not spoken aloud: "Thank God, it's not me."

3   One mother on the Donahue show talked about how difficult it was to care for her severely brain-damaged daughter, but in the end, she said serenely, "She gives much more than she takes from our family." And no, she would never institutionalize her child. She would never "put her away." For "she is my child," the woman firmly concluded as the audience clapped in approval. "I would never give her up."

4   Everyone always says how awful the institutions are. Don't they have bars on the windows and children lying neglected in crowded wards? Aren't all the workers sadists, taking direction from the legendary Big Nurse? Indeed, isn't institutionalizing a child tantamount to locking him away? Signing him out of your life forever? Isn't it proof of your failure as a parent—one who couldn't quite measure up and love your child, no matter what?

5   No, to all of the above. And love is beside the point.

6   Our child Zachariah has not lived at home for almost four years. I knew when we placed him, sorry as I was, that this was the right decision, for his care precluded any semblance of normal family life for the rest of us. I do not think that we "gave him up," although he is cared for daily by nurses, caseworkers, teachers and therapists, rather than by his mother and father. When we come to visit him at his "residential facility," a place housing 50 severely physically and mentally handicapped youngsters, we usually see him being held and rocked by a foster grandma who has spent the better part of the afternoon singing him nursery rhymes. I do not feel that we have "put him away." Perhaps it is just a question of language. I told another mother who was going through the difficult decision regarding placement for her retarded child, "Think of it as going to boarding school rather than institutionalization." Maybe euphemisms help ease the pain a little bit. But I've also seen enough to know that institution need not be a dirty word.

7   The media still relish those institution horror stories: a page-one photo of a retarded girl who was repeatedly molested by the janitor on night duty. Oh, the newspapers have a field day with something like that. And that is how it should be, I suppose. To protect against institutional abuse we need critical reporters with sharpened pencils and a keen investigative eye. But there are other scenes from the institution as well. I've seen a young caseworker talk lovingly as she changed the diapers of a teen-age boy. I've watched as an aide put red ribbons into the ponytail of a cerebral-palsied woman, wipe away the drool and kiss her on the cheek. When we bring Zach back to his facility after a visit home, the workers welcome him with hugs and notice if we gave him a haircut or a new shirt.

8   The reporters don't make news out of that simple stuff. It doesn't mesh with the anti-institutional bias prevalent in the last few years, or the tendency to canonize the handicapped and their accomplishments. This anti-institutional trend has some very frightening ramifications. We force mental patients out into the real world of cheap welfare hotels and call it "community placement." We parole youthful offenders because "jails are such dangerous places to be," making our city streets dangerous places for the law-abiding. We heap enormous guilt on the families that need, for their own survival, to put their no-longer-competent elderly in that dreaded last stop: the nursing home.

9   Another danger is that in a time of economic distress for all of us, funds could be cut for human-service programs under the guise of anti-institutionalization. We must make sure, before we close the doors of those "awful" institutions, that we have alternative facilities to care for the clientele. The humanitarians who tell us how terrible institutions are should be wary lest they become unwilling bedfellows to conservative politicians who want to walk a tight fiscal line. It takes a lot of money to run institutions. No politician is going to say he's against the handicapped, but he can talk in sanctimonious terms about efforts to preserve the family unit, about families remaining independent and self-sufficient. Translated, this means, "You got your troubles, I got mine."

10 Most retarded people do not belong in institutions any more than most people over 65 belong in nursing homes. What we need are options and alternatives for a heterogeneous population. We need group homes and halfway houses and government subsidies to families who choose to care for dependent members at home. We need accessible housing for independent handicapped people; we need to pay enough to foster-care families to show that a good home is worth paying for. We need institutions. And it shouldn't have to be a dirty word.

Questions for Close Reading

1. What is the selection's thesis? Locate the sentence(s) in which Kupfer states her main idea. If she doesn't state the thesis explicitly, express it in your own words.

2. What myths about handicapped children does Kupfer identify?

3. According to Kupfer, what role do the media play in determining how we think about the handicapped? What aspects of the problem do the media tend to ignore?

4. What are some of the negative effects of the "anti-institutional bias" that Kupfer points out?

5. Refer to your dictionary as needed to define the following words used in the selection: *quadriplegics* (paragraph 2), *stoicism* (2), *kudos* (2), *tantamount* (4), *fiscal* (9), *sanctimonious* (9), and *heterogeneous* (10).

Questions About the Writer's Craft

1. The pattern. The author of an argumentation-persuasion essay needs to establish his or her credibility. How does Kupfer do this?

2. Where does Kupfer refer to the opposing viewpoint? What strategy does she use to counter this view?

3. Other patterns. Locate places in the essay where Kupfer uses highly connotative, descriptive language. How do these descriptive passages affect her portrayal of the opposing view and help her develop her own position?

4. How would you describe Kupfer's tone? What roles do word choice, sentence structure, and punctuation (especially quotation marks) play in establishing this tone?

Writing Assignments Using Argumentation-Persuasion as a Pattern of Development

1. In paragraph 8, Kupfer mentions other institutions she believes our society is biased against: mental hospitals, jails for juvenile offenders, nursing homes for the elderly. In an essay, argue for or against one of these institutions as a way to handle a social problem. Devote at least one paragraph to refuting the opposing viewpoint.

2. As a lead-in to her argument, Kupfer describes a talk-show discussion. Watch or listen to a talk show dealing with a controversial life-style or community problem. After evaluating the points of view expressed, write an argumentation-persuasion essay that advances your position on the issue. Part of the essay should acknowledge, perhaps rebut, the opposing viewpoint.

Writing Assignments Using Other Patterns of Development

3. Kupfer's essay tells the "other side" of an experience. In an essay of your own, do the same. Contrast the way the media have portrayed some situation or event with the way it really is. For example, you might contrast your college newspaper's account of an unruly student senate meeting with what really happened. Or you might contrast television's glamorous depiction of two-career families with the grinding everyday reality.

4. Kupfer objects to the use of the word *special* for severely handicapped children. In an essay, explain why you object to some other term (perhaps *senior* *citizen, yuppie,* or *tree hugger*) used to describe a particular group of people. Use examples to show why you feel the term is inaccurate or unfair.

CARYL RIVERS

A journalism professor at Boston University, Caryl Rivers (1937–) has authored numerous articles for newspapers and magazines. Her many books include two novels, *Virgins* (1984) and *Intimate Enemies* (1987), as well as a work on contemporary culture, *More Joy Than Rage: Crossing Generations With the New Feminism* (1991). The following essay first appeared in the *Boston Globe* in 1985.

WHAT SHOULD BE DONE ABOUT ROCK LYRICS?

1   After a grisly series of murders in California, possibly inspired by the lyrics of a rock song, we are hearing a familiar chorus: don't blame rock and roll. Kids will be kids. They love to rebel, and the more shocking the stuff, the better they like it.

2   There's some truth in this, of course. I loved to watch Elvis shake his torso when I was a teenager, and it was even more fun when Ed Sullivan wouldn't let the cameras show him below the waist. I snickered at the forbidden "Rock With Me, Annie" lyrics by a black rhythm and blues group, which were deliciously naughty. But I am sorry, rock fans, that is not the same thing as hearing lyrics about how a man is going to force a woman to perform oral sex on him at gunpoint in a little number called "Eat Me Alive." It is not in the same league with a song about the delights of slipping into a woman's room while she is sleeping and murdering her, the theme of an AC/DC ballad that allegedly inspired the California slayer.

3   Make no mistake, it is not sex we are talking about here, but violence. Violence against women. Most rock songs are not violent—they are funky, sexy, rebellious, and sometimes witty. Please do not mistake me for a Mrs. Grundy. If Prince wants to leap about wearing only a purple jock strap, fine. Let Mick Jagger unzip his fly as he gyrates, if he wants to. But when either one of them starts garroting, beating, or sodomizing a woman in their number, that is another story.

4   I always find myself annoyed when "intellectual" men dismiss violence against women with a yawn, as if it were beneath their dignity to notice. I wonder if the reaction would be the same if the violence were directed against someone other than women. How many people would yawn and say, "Oh, kids will be kids" if a rock group did a nifty little number called "Lynchin," in which stringing up and stomping on black people were set to music? Who would chuckle and say, "Oh, just a little adolescent rebellion" if a group of rockers went on MTV dressed as Nazis, desecrating synagogues and beating up Jews to the beat of twanging guitars?

5   I'll tell you what would happen. Prestigious dailies would thunder on editorial pages; senators would fall over each other to get denunciations into the *Congressional Record.* The president would appoint a commission to clean up the music business.

6   But violence against women is greeted by silence. It shouldn't be.

7   This does not mean censorship, or book (or record) burning. In a society that protects free expression, we understand a lot of stuff will float up out of the sewer. Usually, we recognize the ugly stuff that advocates violence against any group as the garbage it is, and we consider its purveyors as moral lepers. We hold our nose and tolerate it, but we speak out against the values it proffers.

But images of violence against women are not staying on the fringes of society. No longer are they found only in tattered, paper-covered books or in movie houses where winos snooze and the scent of urine fills the air. They are entering the mainstream at a rapid rate. This is happening at a time when the media, more and more, set the agenda for the public debate. It is a powerful legitimizing force—especially television. Many people regard what they see on TV as the truth; Walter Cronkite once topped a poll as the most trusted man in America.

Now, with the advent of rock videos and all-music channels, rock music has grabbed a big chunk of legitimacy. American teenagers have instant access, in their living rooms, to the messages of rock, on the same vehicle that brought them *Sesame Street*. Who can blame them if they believe that the images they see are accurate reflections of adult reality, approved by adults? After all, Big Bird used to give them lessons on the same little box. Adults, by their silence, sanction the images. Do we really want our kids to think that rape and violence are what sexuality is all about?

This is not a trivial issue. Violence against women is a major social problem, one that's more than a cerebral issue to me. I teach at Boston University, and one of my most promising young journalism students was raped and murdered. Two others told me of being raped. Recently, one female student was assaulted and beaten so badly she had $5,000 worth of medical bills and permanent damage to her back and eyes.

It's nearly impossible, of course, to make a cause-and-effect link between lyrics and images and acts of violence. But images have a tremendous power to create an atmosphere in which violence against certain people is sanctioned. Nazi propagandists knew that full well when they portrayed Jews as ugly, greedy, and powerful.

The outcry over violence against women, particularly in a sexual context, is being legitimized in two ways: by the increasing movement of these images into the mainstream of the media in TV, films, magazines, albums, videos, and by the silence about it.

Violence, of course, is rampant in the media. But it is usually set in some kind of moral context. It's usually only the bad guys who commit violent acts against the innocent. When the good guys get violent, it's against those who deserve it. Dirty Harry blows away the scum; he doesn't walk up to a toddler and say, "Make my day." The A team does not shoot up suburban shopping malls.

But in some rock songs, it's the "heroes" who commit the acts. The people we are programmed to identify with are the ones being violent, with women on the receiving end. In a society where rape and assaults on women are endemic, this is no small problem, with millions of young boys watching on their TV screens and listening on their Walkmans.

I think something needs to be done. I'd like to see people in the industry respond to the problem. I'd love to see some women rock stars speak out against violence against women. I would like to see disc jockeys refuse air play to records and videos that contain such violence. At the very least, I want to see the end of the silence. I want journalists and parents and critics and performing artists to keep this issue alive in the public forum. I don't want people who are concerned about this issue labeled as bluenoses and bookburners and ignored.

And I wish it wasn't always just women who were speaking out. Men have as large a stake in the quality of our civilization as women do in the long run. Violence is a contagion that infects at random. Let's hear something, please, from the men.

Questions for Close Reading

1. What is the selection's thesis? Locate the sentence(s) in which Rivers states her main idea. If she doesn't state the thesis explicitly, express it in your own words.

2. What about rock music does Rivers find acceptable—even enjoyable? What does Rivers mean when she says in paragraph 3 that she doesn't want to be mistaken for a "Mrs. Grundy"?

3. How, according to Rivers, does television contribute to the problem of rock music's violence against women?

4. Why does Rivers think that the "outcry against violence" is legitimate, even necessary? What form does Rivers believe this outcry should take?

5. Refer to your dictionary as needed to define the following words used in the selection: *grisly* (paragraph 1), *garroting* (3), *purveyors* (7), *sanction* (9 and 11), *cerebral* (10), *propagandists* (11), *endemic* (14), and *contagion* (16).

Questions About the Writer's Craft

1. The pattern. When presenting her argument, Rivers often refers to opposing views. Which opposing views does she refute? Which does she concede? Why do you think she proceeds in this manner?

2. Other patterns. Rivers uses comparison-contrast in several places in the essay. Locate some of these comparisons and/or contrasts. How does Rivers's use of comparison-contrast help support her thesis?

3. Throughout much of her essay, Rivers writes in the first person and, in paragraph 2, she addresses the reader directly. What effect does her use of the first and second person have on her credibility and on her essay's tone?

4. Rivers sprinkles highly connotative language throughout the essay. Locate some of this language in the selection. What effect do you think Rivers hoped such language would have on the reader?

Writing Assignments Using Argumentation-Persuasion as a Pattern of Development

1. Spend some time watching rock videos on television, taking notes on those that support and those that refute Rivers's criticism. Weigh your observations carefully and decide whether you agree with Rivers that rock music's images and lyrics promote violence against women. Remembering to acknowledge opposing views, write an essay agreeing or disagreeing with Rivers. Use your observations to support your thesis.

2. Asserting that we live in a time when "assaults on women are endemic," Rivers attributes this problem mainly to rock lyrics. But there are other factors in our society that contribute to the problem: substance abuse, advertising messages, cultural definitions of appropriate male and female behavior, and so on. Select *one* of these factors, or another that seems important, and write an essay arguing that this factor is *more* critical than rock music in inciting violence against women. Near the beginning of the essay, point out the limitations of Rivers's perspective. Alleen Pace Nilsen's "Sexism and Language" (page 243) and Jack Newfield's "Stallone vs. Springsteen" (page 335) may provide some helpful insight.

Writing Assignments Using Other Patterns of Development

3. Rivers is outraged by the silence surrounding rock music's violence against women. In an essay, present the steps that *one* of the following—families, schools, or religious institutions—should take to end the silence. Before explaining what should be done, present several vivid examples to dramatize that there is indeed a problem that needs to be addressed.

4. Critics accuse not only rock videos but also television in general of fostering harmful images of women, men, teenagers, ethnic and racial minorities, and the elderly. Write an essay illustrating television's distorted depiction of *one* of these groups. Brainstorm with others to gather compelling examples to support your thesis.

LOUIS NIZER

Through his numerous books and articles, Louis Nizer (1902–) has become one of the nation's best-known attorneys. His books include *My Life in Court* (1962), *The Jury Returns* (1966), *Reflections Without Mirrors* (1978), and *Catspaw: One Man's Ordeal by Trial* (1992). The following essay first appeared in the *New York Times* in 1986.

LOW-COST DRUGS FOR ADDICTS?

We are losing the war against drug addiction. Our strategy is wrong. I propose a different approach.

The Government should create clinics, manned by psychiatrists, that would provide drugs for nominal charges or even free to addicts under controlled regulations. It would cost the Government only 20 cents for a heroin shot, for which the addicts must now pay the mob more than $100, and there are similar price discrepancies in cocaine, crack and other such substances.

Such a service, which would also include the staff support of psychiatrists and doctors, would cost a fraction of what the nation now spends to maintain the land, sea and air apparatus necessary to interdict illegal imports of drugs. There would also be a savings of hundreds of millions of dollars from the elimination of the prosecutorial procedures that stifle our courts and overcrowd our prisons.

We see in our newspapers the triumphant announcements by Government agents that they have intercepted huge caches of cocaine, the street prices of which are in the

Argumentation-Persuasion

tens of millions of dollars. Should we be gratified? Will this achievement reduce the number of addicts by one? All it will do is increase the cost to the addict of his illegal supply.

5   Many addicts who are caught committing a crime admit that they have mugged or stolen as many as six or seven times a day to accumulate the $100 needed for a fix. Since many of them need two or three fixes a day, particularly for crack, one can understand the terror in our streets and homes. It is estimated that there are in New York City alone 200,000 addicts, and this is typical of cities across the nation. Even if we were to assume that only a modest percentage of a city's addicts engage in criminal conduct to obtain the money for the habit, requiring multiple muggings and thefts each day, we could nevertheless account for many of the tens of thousands of crimes each day in New York City alone.

6   Not long ago, a Justice Department division issued a report stating that more than half the perpetrators of murder and other serious crimes were under the influence of drugs. This symbolizes the new domestic terror in our nation. This is why our citizens are unsafe in broad daylight on the most traveled thoroughfares. This is why typewriters and television sets are stolen from offices and homes and sold for a pittance. This is why parks are closed to the public and why murders are committed. This is why homes need multiple locks, and burglary systems, and why store windows, even in the most fashionable areas, require iron gates.

7   The benefits of the new strategy to control this terrorism would be immediate and profound.

8   First, the mob would lose the main source of its income. It could not compete against a free supply for which previously it exacted tribute estimated to be hundreds of millions of dollars, perhaps billions, from hopeless victims.

9   Second, pushers would be put out of business. There would be no purpose in creating addicts who would be driven by desperate compulsion to steal and kill for the money necessary to maintain their habit. Children would not be enticed. The mob's macabre public-relations program is to tempt children with free drugs in order to create customers for the future. The wave of street crimes in broad daylight would diminish to a trickle. Homes and stores would not have to be fortresses. Our recreational areas could again be used. Neighborhoods would not be scandalized by sordid street centers where addicts gather to obtain their supply from slimy merchants.

10 Third, police and other law-enforcement authorities, domestic or foreign, would be freed to deal with traditional nondrug crimes.

11 There are several objections that might be raised against such a salutary solution.

12 First, it could be argued that by providing free drugs to the addict we would consign him to permanent addiction. The answer is that medical and psychiatric help at the source would be more effective in controlling the addict's descent than the extremely limited remedies available to the victim today. I am not arguing that the new strategy will cure everything. But I do not see many addicts being freed from their bonds under the present system.

13 In addition, as between the addict's predicament and the safety of our innocent citizens, which deserves our primary concern? Drug-induced crime has become so common that almost every citizen knows someone in his immediate family or among his friends who has been mugged. It is these citizens who should be our chief concern.

14 Another possible objection is that addicts will cheat the system by obtaining more than the allowable free shot. Without discounting the resourcefulness of the bedeviled addict, it should be possible to have Government cards issued that would be punched so as to limit the free supply in accord with medical authorization.

Yet all objections become trivial when matched against the crisis itself. What we are witnessing is the demoralization of a great society: the ruination of its school children, athletes and executives, the corrosion of the workforce in general. 15

Many thoughtful sociologists consider the rapidly spreading drug use the greatest problem that our nation faces—greater and more real and urgent than nuclear bombs or economic reversal. In China, a similar crisis drove the authorities to apply capital punishment to those who trafficked in opium—an extreme solution that arose from the deepest reaches of frustration. 16

Free drugs will win the war against the domestic terrorism caused by illicit drugs. As a strategy, it is at once resourceful, sensible and simple. We are getting nowhere in our efforts to hold back the ocean of supply. The answer is to dry up demand. 17

Questions for Close Reading

1. What is the selection's thesis? Locate the sentence(s) in which Nizer states his main idea. If he doesn't state the thesis explicitly, express it in your own words.

2. Nizer believes his plan would yield numerous benefits. What are they?

3. Nizer acknowledges some possible objections to his plan. What are they? How does he refute these arguments?

4. How much concern does Nizer have for those addicted to drugs? How do you know?

5. Refer to your dictionary as needed to define the following words used in the selection: *nominal* (paragraph 2), *interdict* (3), *cache* (4), *macabre* (9), *salutary* (11), *consign* (12), and *illicit* (17).

Questions About the Writer's Craft

1. The pattern. Which of the two possible strategies for organizing a refutation (see page 418) does Nizer use in this essay?

2. Nizer's essay starts with a brief introductory paragraph consisting of three crisp, almost clipped sentences. What is the effect of this unusually brief introduction?

3. What words with militaristic connotations does Nizer use in his essay? What might have been Nizer's reason for using such language?

4. To what audience does Nizer seem to be addressing his proposal? How do you know?

Writing Assignments Using Argumentation-Persuasion as a Pattern of Development

∞ **1.** Read Beth Johnson Ruth's "Our Drug Problem" (page 449), an essay that takes exception to Nizer's view. Decide whether Nizer or Ruth presents a more convincing case. Then write an essay arguing that the *other writer* has trouble making a strong case for his or her position. Consider the merits and flaws (including any logical fallacies) in the argument, plus such issues as the writer's credibility, strategies for dealing with the opposing view, and use of emotional appeals. Throughout, support your opinion with specific examples drawn from the selection. Keep in mind that you're critiquing the effectiveness of the writer's argument. It's not appropriate, then, simply to explain why you agree or disagree with the writer's position or merely to summarize what the writer says.

2. Propose measures that *one* of the following groups might take to educate people about the effects of drug addiction: parent groups; public schools; colleges or universities; local, state, or federal government. Put your proposal in the form of a letter to the appropriate person (a high school principal, college president, and so on). Try to anticipate and rebut possible objections to your proposal.

Writing Assignments Using Other Patterns of Development

3. According to psychologists, many individuals have an "addictive personality." Referring to people you know well, write an essay defining this term. However, instead of focusing on addiction to a substance, illustrate the "addictive personality" by writing about the excessive need for approval, danger, competition, and the like.

4. Assume that the Dean of Students has asked you to write an open letter to be published in next year's orientation brochure for first-year college students. Your assignment is to warn incoming students about the long-term effects of drug abuse, or too much partying, or excessive procrastination—anything that might affect their well-being and success in college. Develop your letter by drawing on your own and other people's experiences. You might, in addition, use a source such as the *Readers' Guide to Periodical Literature* to track down helpful articles, so that you can include relevant facts, statistics, or expert opinion in your letter.

BETH JOHNSON RUTH

An educator and journalist, Beth Johnson Ruth (1956–) has taught at Goshen College and New England College. She has also worked as a public relations writer for a health center. The following selection, revised for this book, is taken from a collection of Ruth's essays about drug use and society.

OUR DRUG PROBLEM

1   In the eyes of some, legalizing narcotics is a tantalizing cure-all for America's drug problem. It's time, they say, to stop pouring enormous resources into the war on

drugs. The war has been lost. Drug use, they argue, is here to stay. Ignoring evidence that drug legalization can produce a permanent underclass of hopelessly addicted people, as has happened in Holland, they advocate removal of all legal restrictions on drug use.

Supporters of legalization include respected public figures like conservative columnist William F. Buckley, Jr., Nobel Prize-winning economist Milton Friedman, and Mayor Kurt Schmoke of Baltimore. Two U.S. Representatives, Fortney Stark of California and Steny Howyer of Maryland, have also recommended legalization. The idea, once espoused only by the radical fringe, has gained respectability. What, however, are its merits? Let's examine, one by one, the arguments put forth by proponents.

"Legalizing drugs would mean the end of drug-related crime." Presumably it's true that if narcotics were legalized, druglords, pushers, and drug gangs would no longer reap enormous profits. It does not follow, however, that the addicted would be any less driven to desperate measures to obtain a fix. To feed their habit, many would obtain money by resorting to robbery and prostitution. Indeed, as the number of addicts continued to grow, so would the number of drug-related crimes.

"The government could tax drug sales and regulate the purity of narcotics if they were sold legally." The advocates of legalization point out that two other addictive substances—alcohol and tobacco—are legal and subject to government regulation. True. But with what results? Alcohol and tobacco combined are responsible for about 500,000 deaths each year. In 1988, the reported death toll related to illegal drugs was 6,756. Would we consider it progress to have more people dying from injecting, inhaling, and consuming purer forms of poison?

"The war on drugs is simply too expensive and too ineffective. The country can't afford to continue spending money at this rate." No doubt about it, the price tag attached to fighting drug abuse is phenomenal. It's estimated that federal, state, and local governments spend about $8 billion a year on drug enforcement. Add to that the uncounted billions spent on feeding and housing those imprisoned for drug-related crimes (more than a third of all federal prisoners fall into this category), and you end up with some breathtaking sums.

True, the war on drugs is not being won. The courts are overflowing with cases waiting to be tried. Huge seizures of narcotics stop only a small fraction of the drugs coming into the country. Countless dragnets snare only the small-time pusher, not the drug kingpin. Clearly, as it is being waged now, the national fight against drug abuse is futile.

The only thing more costly than continuing the current war on drugs would be the legalization of narcotics; such a measure would claim innumerable human lives. "People say only 10 percent of those who drink are problem drinkers, so they assume that only 10 percent of the people who take drugs will become addicts," observes Mitchell Rosenthal, president of Phoenix House, a New York City-based drug rehabilitation program. "But there is no reason to believe that if we made [drugs such as] crack available ... that only 10 percent would be addicted; the number would probably be more like 75 percent."

Currently, drug abuse costs American industry over $70 billion per year through lost productivity. Imagine how that figure would soar if legal restraints were removed. If people didn't have to drive into a seedy neighborhood, didn't risk arrest and disgrace, how many more would try addictive drugs? Moreover, what would be the fate of addicts if narcotics were available legally? In the words of one cocaine addict,

"I'd be dead.... I'd just sit down with a big pile of the stuff and snort it until I dropped."

9   And there's one more number to consider: The health costs of treating drug abuse are estimated at $60 billion per year. Imagine what that figure might become if drugs were made legal.

10 Why, then, would anyone recommend legalizing narcotics? The answer has to do with racism, elitism, and sheer indifference to the suffering of others. "These people are going to kill themselves anyway," many middle-class Americans reason. "I'm not going to have my tax dollars used to try to save them. Besides, what does it matter if drugs wipe out a generation—as long as it's a generation of black and Hispanic kids?"

11 If you doubt that this kind of thinking is pervasive, consider the public indifference to the last decade's gutting of education and job-training programs. Such programs address the major causes of drug abuse: poverty and despair. When the number of families living beneath the poverty level increased more than six-fold between 1979 and 1988, did more fortunate Americans protest? Who objected when federal funds for low-income housing dropped from $32 to $9 billion between 1981 and 1988? There was little public protest when federal aid for public education decreased by nearly $6 billion in the 1980s. Nor did the average American complain when funding of job-training programs dropped by $40 billion from 1981 to 1988. And the minimum wage, despite a recent increase, has fallen to its lowest level in terms of buying power since 1955. Is it any wonder that poor teenagers choose the lucrative jobs offered by druglords over the chance to flip hamburgers at a fast-food restaurant? Given the harshness of their lives, it's not surprising that the underprivileged have turned to drugs in such massive numbers.

12 Legalizing narcotics, then, as the Dutch have learned, is not the solution; it's simply another way of ignoring the problem. Making drugs legal won't make them go away. What is needed is an all-out attack on the conditions that lead to drug abuse. Improved education, more affordable housing, new employment opportunities—these are the only effective weapons in the war against drugs.

Questions for Close Reading

1. What is the selection's thesis? Locate the sentence(s) in which Ruth states her main idea. If she doesn't state the thesis explicitly, express it in your own words.

2. According to Ruth, for what reasons do "respected public figures" advocate the legalization of narcotics?

3. How does the number of deaths from illegal drug abuse compare with the number of deaths from the abuse of alcohol and tobacco? In what ways does this information strengthen Ruth's argument?

4. Ruth admits that, as it is currently being fought, the war on drugs is ineffectual and costly. Why, then, is she against legalizing narcotics? What does she advocate instead?

5. Refer to your dictionary as needed to define the following words used in the selection: *espoused* (paragraph 2), *kingpin* (6), *elitism* (10), and *pervasive* (11).

Questions About the Writer's Craft

1. The pattern. Although Ruth works to refute opposing arguments, she also concedes points to the dissenting view. In paragraph 5, for example, she admits, "No doubt about it, the price tag attached to fighting drug abuse is phenomenal." Why do you think she makes such concessions?

2. Locate places in the essay where Ruth uses connotative language. What effect does such language have on her portrayal of the opposing position?

3. Other patterns. To support her argument, Ruth draws on facts, statistics, examples, and expert testimony. Find instances in the essay of each kind of illustration. What is the effect of this evidence?

4. Locate places in the essay where Ruth uses rhetorical questions. How do these questions reinforce the persuasiveness of her argument?

Writing Assignments Using Argumentation-Persuasion as a Pattern of Development

1. Ruth contends that "race, elitism, and sheer indifference to the suffering of others" are behind the proposal to legalize drugs. Write an essay in which you defend or challenge Ruth's charge. Remember to mention and, when possible, refute opposing arguments. Louis Nizer's "Low-Cost Drugs for Addicts?" (page 446) will familiarize you with a viewpoint sharply different from Ruth's.

2. Assume that your college's Office of Student Life has just hired you as a peer counselor whose job it is to reach out to students in distress. Your first task is to write a letter to students with drug and/or alcohol problems, persuading them to seek help through the college's professional and peer counseling services. The letter will be posted on campus bulletin boards and will appear in the student newspaper. As you write the letter, keep in mind that people in difficulty often resist offers of help. What persuasive strategies can you use to overcome this resistance?

Writing Assignments Using Other Patterns of Development

3. In an essay, examine the possible effects of mandatory drug testing on a specific group of people (for example, public school students, college athletes, airline employees). Be sure your paper expresses a clear attitude toward such a program. Brainstorm with others and conduct library research to gather material for your essay.

4. Assume that you're a student member of your college's Disciplinary Action Committee. On this week's agenda is the case of a student who has been caught selling drugs on campus. Write a brief report detailing the step-by-step procedure you think your college should follow with this and similar cases.

Argumentation-Persuasion

ADDITIONAL WRITING TOPICS: ARGUMENTATION-PERSUASION

General Assignments

Using argumentation-persuasion, develop one of the following topics in an essay.

1. Hiring quotas
2. Giving birth-control devices to teenagers
3. Prayer in the schools
4. Living off campus
5. Spouses sharing housework equally
6. Big-time sports in college
7. Music videos
8. Drugs and alcohol on campus
9. Requiring college students to pass a comprehensive exam in their majors before graduating
10. Putting elderly parents in nursing homes
11. Financial aid to college students

Assignments with a Specific Purpose, Audience, and Point of View

1. A college has rejected your or your child's application on the basis of low SAT scores. Write to the college admissions director, arguing that SAT scores are not a fair indicator of your or your child's abilities and potential.

2. As a staff writer for the college opinion magazine, you've been asked to nominate the "Outstanding Man or Woman on Campus," to be featured on the magazine's cover. Write a letter to your supervising editor in support of your nominee.

3. You and your parents don't agree on some aspect of your romantic life (you want to live with your boyfriend/girlfriend and they don't approve; you want to get married and they want you to wait; they simply don't like your partner). Write your parents a letter explaining why your preference is reasonable. Try hard to win them over to your side.

4. As a high school teacher, you support some additional restriction on students. The restriction might be "no radios in school," "no T-shirts," "no food in class," "no smoking on school grounds." Write an article for the school newspaper, justifying this new rule to the student body.

5. Someone you know is convinced that the music you listen to is trashy or boring. Write a letter to the person arguing that your music has value. Support your contention with specific references to lyrics, musical structure, and performers' talent.

6. Assume you're a member of a racial, ethnic, or social minority. You might, for example, be a Native American, an elderly person, a female executive. On a recent television show or in a TV commercial, you saw something that depicts your group in an offensive way. Write a letter (to the network or the advertiser) expressing your feelings and explaining why you feel the material should be taken off the air.

PART IV

THE RESEARCH PAPER

21
SELECTING A SUBJECT, USING THE LIBRARY, AND TAKING NOTES

SOME GENERAL COMMENTS ABOUT THE RESEARCH PAPER

IF you're like many of the students we know, **research papers** probably make you nervous. Why, you may wonder, do instructors assign them? Such projects take time, and the payoff, you may feel, doesn't seem worth the effort. If this *is* how you feel, we hope to show you that conducting research and writing up your findings can be rewarding, even fun.

Think of library research as a treasure hunt. The deeper you dig, the more you unearth material that's new to you. Besides experiencing the pleasure of such discovery, you become an expert of sorts in your subject and grow more comfortable with research methods. Most importantly, writing a research paper enlarges your perspective. As you test your own views against existing evidence, evaluate conflicting opinions, and learn how to detect other people's biases, you acquire analytic skills that will benefit you throughout life. These skills enable you to move beyond casual, off-the-top-of-the-head opinions to those that are well reasoned and thoughtful. In everyday conversation, most of us feel free to voice all kinds of opinions, even if they're based on nothing more than emotion and secondhand information. Researched opinions, though, are sounder and more logical. They're based on authoritative evidence rather than on limited personal experience, on fact rather than on hearsay. Instead of being rooted in unexamined personal belief, researched opinions emerge from a careful consideration of the evidence.

All of this may sound intimidating, but keep in mind that writing a research paper expands what you already know about writing essays; many of the steps are the same. The two major differences are the greater length of the research paper—usually five or more pages—and the kind of support you offer for your thesis. Rather than relying on your own experience or that of friends or family, you use published information and expert opinion to support your thesis. Even so, writing a research paper *can* be a challenge. One way to make the project more manageable is to view it as a process consisting of two major phases: (1) the **research stage,** when you find out all you can about your subject and identify a working thesis, and (2) the **writing stage,** when you present in an accepted format what you've discovered. This chapter focuses on the first stage; the next, Chapter 22, examines the second stage. Although we discuss the research process as a series of steps, we encourage you to modify the sequence to suit your subject, your personal approach to writing, and the requirements of a particular assignment.

During the first stage of the research process, you do the following:

- Plan the research.
- Find sources in the library.
- Prepare a working bibliography.
- Take notes to support the thesis with evidence.

PLAN THE RESEARCH

Understand the Paper's Boundaries

Your first step in planning the research is to *clarify the project's requirements.* How long is the paper supposed to be? How extensively should you deal with opposing viewpoints? Are there any restrictions about the number and type of sources? Are popular magazines and books acceptable, or should you use only scholarly sources? Has the instructor limited your subject choices?

Also, be sure you understand the paper's overall purpose. Unless you've been assigned a purely informative report ("explain several psychologists' theories of hostility"), your research paper shouldn't simply display all the information you have gathered. Instead of merely patching together ideas from a variety of sources, you should develop your own position, using outside sources to arrive at a balanced but definitive conclusion.

One more point: You should be aware that most instructors expect students to use the third-person point of view in research papers. If you plan to include any personal experiences, observations, or interviews (see below and pages 503–04) along with your outside research, ask your instructor whether the use of the first-person point of view would be appropriate.

Understand Primary Versus Secondary Research

You should determine whether your instructor expects you to conduct any **primary research**—information gathered from firsthand observations, personal interviews, and the like. Most college research papers involve **library** or **secondary research**—information gathered secondhand from published accounts, including statistics, facts, case studies, expert opinion, critical interpretations, and experimental results. Occasionally, though, you may want or be asked to conduct primary research. You may, for example, run an experiment, visit an organization, observe a situation, schedule an interview, or conduct a survey. In such cases of primary research, you'll need to prepare carefully and establish a strict deadline schedule for yourself. (See pages 503–04 for hints on incorporating primary research into a paper.)

Some Comments About Conducting Interviews

If you plan to go on an information-gathering interview, put some careful thought into how you will proceed. If you use a letter rather than a telephone call to request an interview, get feedback on the letter's overall effectiveness before mailing it. When you set up your appointment, request enough time (30–60 minutes) to discuss your topic in depth; keep in mind, however, that the person may not be able to set aside as much time as you'd like. If you hope to tape-record the interview, you must obtain permission to do so beforehand. (Some organizations don't permit employees to be recorded during interviews.) Also, when making the appointment, ask if you may quote the person directly; he or she is entitled to know that all comments will be "on record."

Most importantly, plan the interview carefully. First, determine what you want to accomplish: Do you want to gather general background material or do you want to clear up confusion about a specific point? Then, well in advance of the interview, prepare a list of questions geared toward that goal. During the interview, though, remain flexible—follow up on interesting remarks even if they diverge somewhat from your original plan. (If you discover that your interviewee isn't as informed as you had hoped, graciously request the names of other people who might help you further.) Throughout the interview, take accurate and complete notes (unless of course, you're taping). If certain remarks seem especially quotable, make sure you get the statements down correctly. Finally, soon after the interview ends, be sure to fill in any gaps in your notes.

Some Comments About Conducting Surveys

A survey helps you gather a good deal of information from many people (called "respondents")—and in a much shorter period of time than would be needed to interview each person individually. If you believe that citing the opinions of a group of people will strengthen your paper, you might want to conduct a survey. Bear in mind, though, that designing, administering, and interpreting a survey questionnaire are time-consuming tasks that demand considerable skill. Be sure, then, to have someone knowledgeable about surveys evaluate both your questionnaire and the responses it evokes.

When you write your survey questions, make them as clear and precise as possible. For example, if your goal is to determine the frequency with which something occurs, do not ask for vague responses such as "seldom," "often," and "occasionally." Instead, ask the respondents to identify more specific time periods: "weekly," "1–3 times a week," "4–6 times a week," and "daily." Also, steer away from questions that favor one side of an issue or that restrict the range of responses. Consider the following survey questions:

Should already overburdened college students be required to participate in a community-service activity before they can graduate?

Yes _____   No _____   Maybe _____

In your opinion, how knowledgeable are college students about jobs in their majors?

Knowledgeable _____   Not Knowledgeable _____

Both of the preceding questions need to be revised but for different reasons. The first, by assuming that students are "already overburdened," biases respondents to reply negatively. To make the question more neutral, you would have to eliminate the prejudicial words. The second question asks respondents to answer in terms of a simple contrast: "Knowledgeable" or "Not Knowledgeable." It ignores the likelihood that some respondents may wish to reply "Very Knowledgeable," "Somewhat Knowledgeable," and so on.

You should include in your survey only those items that will yield useful information. For example, if administering a survey to students on your campus, you would ask respondents some questions about their age, college year, major, and so forth—as long as you planned to break responses into subgroups. But these questions would be unnecessary if you didn't intend to analyze responses in such a manner. In any case, be sure to limit the number of questions you ask. If you don't, you'll regret it later on when you sort out the responses.

When you conduct a survey, it's unlikely that you'll be able to poll every member of the group whose opinions you seek. Instead, you must poll a *representative subgroup* of the whole. By *representative*, we mean "having characteristics similar to the group as a whole." Imagine you're writing a research paper on unfair employment practices. As part of your data collection, you decide to poll students on campus about their job experiences. If you, a first-year student, give the questionnaire only to students in your introductory courses, your sample won't be representative of the student body as a whole. Upper-level students might have significantly different work experiences and thus quite different opinions about employer fairness. So, to gauge students' attitudes at your college with accuracy, you'll have to hand out your survey in numerous places and on varied occasions on the campus. That way, your responses will be drawn from the whole spectrum of undergraduate backgrounds, majors, ages, and so forth.

This method of collecting student responses still wouldn't amount to what is called a *random sample*. To achieve a random sample, you must choose respondents by a scientific method—one that would, theoretically, give each person in the group to be studied the chance to respond. For example, to survey undergraduates on your campus, you would have to obtain a comprehensive list of all enrolled students. From this list, you would pick names at a regular interval, perhaps every tenth; to each tenth person, you would deliver (or mail) a survey, or you would telephone to ask the questions orally. With this method, every enrolled student has the potential of being chosen as a respondent.

Since there's so much cost and time involved in doing a random sample, you'll most likely use an informal method of collecting responses. Using the "street corner" approach, you might hand your survey to passersby or to people seated in classes, in student lounges, and so on. Or, if you're collecting information about the service provided at a particular facility, you might (with permission) place a short questionnaire where respondents can pick it up, quickly fill it out, and return it. Because of your informal methods, your results would be an *approximate* portrait of the group polled; however, the more people you survey, the more accurate your profile of the larger population is likely to be. (See pages 503–04 for hints on incorporating survey results into a research paper.)

Once you're sure of the paper's boundaries and understand your instructor's expectations regarding primary and secondary research, it's time for you to move on. At this point, you'll need to (1) choose a general subject, (2) limit that subject, (3) conduct preliminary research, (4) identify a working thesis, and (5) make a schedule.

Choose a General Subject

Your instructor may provide a list of acceptable topics for a research paper, or you may be free to select a topic on your own. In the latter case, your second step in planning the research is to *choose a general subject*. If you have an area of interest—say, Native American culture or animal rights—the subject might be suitable for a research paper. If you don't immediately know what you'd like to research, consider current events, journal entries, the courses you're taking, the reading you've done on your own, or some of the selections in this book. A sociology course may have piqued your interest in child abuse or the elderly. Current events might suggest research on water pollution or business ethics. Several of your journal entries may focus on an issue that concerns you—maybe, for example, use of drugs in college athletics. Perhaps you've come across a provocative article on nuclear power or the nation's health-care crisis. Maybe you find yourself disagreeing with what George Gallup says about divorce in "The Faltering Family," on pages 364–70 of this book. (In the activities at the end of this chapter, you'll find a list of suggested research topics derived from the readings in this text.)

If you're still not sure of what subject to research, use one or more prewriting techniques to identify areas that interest or puzzle you. Brainstorming, questioning, freewriting, and mapping (see pages 25–30) should help you generate ideas worth exploring. As soon as you have a list of possible topics, use the following checklist to help you determine which of these subjects would or would not be appropriate for a research paper.

> ☑ SELECTING AN APPROPRIATE SUBJECT TO RESEARCH: A CHECKLIST
>
> ☐ Will you enjoy learning about the subject for the substantial period of time you'll be working on the research paper? If you think you might get bored, select another subject.
>
> ☐ Can you obtain enough information on the subject? Recent developments (an ongoing government scandal or a controversial new program to help the homeless) can be investigated only through mass-circulation newspapers and magazines. Books as well as specialized or scholarly journal articles on recent events may not be available for some time.
>
> ☐ Has the topic been researched so often (the legalization of marijuana, violence in sports) that there's nothing new or interesting left to say about it?
>
> ☐ Is the topic surrounded by unreliable testimony (ESP, UFOs, the Bermuda Triangle), making it unsuitable for a research paper?
>
> ☐ Is the topic (a rock star's conflict with the recording industry, for example) too trivial for an academic project?
>
> ☐ Does the subject lend itself to or call for research? If it doesn't, think about selecting another topic. For example, the dangers of smoking are now almost universally acknowledged and so probably wouldn't make an appropriate topic for a research paper.
>
> ☐ Has the topic been written about by only one major source? If so, your research will be one-sided.
>
> ☐ Can you be objective about your topic? Researching both sides of an issue about which you feel strongly usually deepens your understanding of the issue's complexity. But if you feel so committed to a point of view that you'll have trouble considering opposing opinions, it's best to avoid that subject altogether.

Once you have a general topic in mind, you may want to clear it with your instructor. Or you can wait until the next stage to do so—after you've narrowed the topic further.

Prewrite to Limit the General Subject

The next step in planning your research is to *limit* or *narrow your topic*. "Pollution" is too broad a topic, but "The Effect of Acid Rain on Urban Structures" poses a realistic challenge. Similarly, "Cable Television" is way too general, but "Trends in Cable Comedy" is manageable. Remember, you aren't writing a book but a paper of probably five to fifteen pages.

Sometimes you'll know the particular aspect of a subject you want to explore. Usually, though, you'll have to do some work to restrict your subject. In such cases, try using the prewriting techniques of questioning, mapping, freewriting, and brainstorming described in Chapter 2. Discussing the topic with other people can also help you focus your thinking. (For more on limiting general subjects, see pages 24–27.)

Conduct Preliminary Research

Frequently, you won't be able to narrow your topic until you learn more about it. When that's the case, background reading, often called **preliminary research,** is necessary. Just as prewriting precedes a first draft, preliminary research precedes the in-depth research you conduct further along in the process.

At this point, you don't have to track down highly specialized material. Instead, you simply skim books and mass-market or newspaper articles on your topic to get an overview and to identify possible slants on your subject. If your broad subject is inspired by a class, you can check out the topic in your textbook. And, of course, you can consult library sources—the *computerized* or *card catalog*, the *reference section*, and *periodical indexes* such as the *Readers' Guide to Periodical Literature*. All of these sources break broad subjects into subtopics, thus helping you focus your research. These and other library resources, discussed in greater detail later in the chapter, are among the most valuable tools available to researchers.

After you locate several promising books or articles on your general subject, glance through the material rapidly to get a sense of issues and themes. Do the sources suggest a particular angle of inquiry? If you don't find much material on your subject, think about selecting another topic, one about which more has been written.

While conducting preliminary research, there's no need to take notes, unless you want to jot down possible limited topics. However, you should keep an informal record of the books and articles you skim. Using a sheet of paper or preferably an index card for each source, note the following information: For each book, record the author, title, and call number; for each article, record the date and the page numbers. Such basic information will help you relocate material later on, when you'll need to look at your sources more closely. Also, it's a good idea to jot down the authors and titles of other works mentioned in the sources you skim. You may decide to consult them at another point.

Once you arrive at your limited topic—or several possibilities—ask your instructor for feedback, listening carefully to any reservations he or she may have about your idea. Moreover, even though you've identified a limited subject, don't be surprised if it continues to shift and narrow further as you go along. Such reshaping is part of the research process.

Identify a Working Thesis

As long as you're confident there's sufficient material available on your limited topic, your next step is to form a **working thesis,** an idea of your own that is in some way original.

Having a tentative thesis guides your research and helps you determine which sources will be appropriate. However, general statements like "Congress should not make further cuts in social programs," "Prayer in public schools should not be allowed," and "Higher education is male-dominated" are so broad that they fail to restrict the scope of research. Whole books have been written on welfare, just one of many social programs. Be sure, then, that your working thesis focuses on a *limited subject*. The thesis should also take a stand by *expressing your point of view, or attitude, about the subject.* Note the difference between the broad statements above and the effective limited thesis statements that follow (the limited subjects are underlined once, the attitudes twice):

> The Congressional decision to reduce funding of school lunch programs has had unfortunate consequences for disadvantaged children.
>
> A moment of silence in public schools does not violate the constitutional separation of church and state.
>
> The funding of college athletics discriminates against women.

You should view your working thesis as tentative; you probably won't have a final thesis until your research is almost complete and all the facts are in. Indeed, if your thesis *doesn't* shift as you investigate your topic, you may not be tapping a wide enough range of sources, or you may be resisting challenges to your original point of view. *Remember:* Gathering information with a closed mind undermines the purpose of a research project.

In its final form, your thesis should accomplish at least one of three things. First, it may offer your personal synthesis of multiple findings, your own interpretation of "what it all means." Second, it may refine or extend other people's theories or interpretations. Third, it may offer a perspective that differs from or opposes the one you find expressed in most of your sources. (For more on thesis statements, see pages 37–41.)

Make a Schedule

Having identified your working thesis, you're nearly ready to begin the research stage of your project. Before you begin, though, *make a schedule.* First, list what you need to do. Then, working back from your paper's due date, set rough time limits for the different phases of the project: locating and reading relevant

Selecting a Subject, Using the Library, and Taking Notes

periodicals and books; taking notes; interviewing an expert or sending away for information; drafting, revising, and editing the paper.

FIND SOURCES IN THE LIBRARY

Now is the time to start your research in earnest. Always keep in mind that you're looking for material to support your working thesis. What should you do if you come across material that contradicts your thesis? Resist the temptation to disregard such material. Instead, evaluate it as objectively as you can, and use it to arrive at a more valid statement of your thesis.

Even if your paper contains some primary research, most of your information-gathering will take place in your college library or its equivalent. If the college library is new to you, look for informative handouts near the main desk, and sign up for a library tour if one is offered. Most college libraries contain several floors of bookshelves (often called *stacks*), with fiction and nonfiction arranged according to the Dewey Decimal or Library of Congress system of classification (see pages 467–68). You'll also find sections for periodicals, microfilm and microfiche files, reference works, reserved books, government documents, rare books, and the like. Special collections may be housed in the main library or elsewhere; for example, an extensive music library may be located in the music department. In any case, the main library catalog lists all the material contained in such special collections.

The pages ahead provide detailed information about using library resources—the computerized or card catalog, the reference section, and periodicals.

The Computerized Catalog

Many college libraries now have **computerized catalogs** of their book holdings. If computer technology makes you nervous, you'll be pleased to learn that most computerized systems are equipped with on-screen prompts that make it easy to search for sources.

In a typical on-line search you'll be asked by the computer whether you want to search by *author, title,* or *subject*. If you're searching by author or title, you type into the terminal the author's first and last names or the title, respectively. If you're searching by subject, you type in a key term that summarizes your topic. The screen will then list the books in the library for the author, title, or subject you typed in. To get complete bibliographic information about a specific book, follow the computer's instructions. The book's publisher, publication date, call number, and so on will appear on the screen. Most computerized catalogs also indicate the status of a book—whether it is out on loan, overdue, lost, or available on loan.

When searching books by subject, you may have to try several key terms to discover under what term the computer lists sources on that topic. If you can't locate any books on your subject, determine the right term to key in by consulting the *Library of Congress Subject Headings* (see below) or a bound or an on-screen thesaurus of headings used in your library's data base.

Once the computer identifies books on your subject, you can copy down the authors, titles, and call numbers of promising books, or, in many libraries, you can direct the computer to print out a list. By mastering your library's computerized catalog, you'll find that it will take only minutes to identify sources that in the past might have taken you several hours to track down. One caution, however, about computerized catalogs: Few libraries have their entire collections on-line. Special collections and older books may not be included. If the data base isn't posted near the terminals, check with the librarian. You'll have to use the traditional card catalog to track down those sources not covered by the computerized catalog.

The Card Catalog

If your library isn't computerized, you'll need to use the traditional **card catalog,** a file of cards listing all the books in the library. The catalog is arranged alphabetically by word rather than letter by letter: *music* would come before *musicians; social reformers* before *socialism.* If you're not sure with what word or term to start your search, consult a reference book that lists (alphabetically) the card catalog's subject headings. For libraries using the Dewey Decimal system, this book is the *Sears List of Subject Headings;* for libraries using the more common Library of Congress system, it is the *Library of Congress Subject Headings.*

Subject, Title, and Author Cards

To locate books on your topic, look under the appropriate subject headings; that is, use the catalog's **subject cards.** You'll find a card for each book the library owns on that subject. Suppose you want to research the kinds of classroom environments that encourage student initiative and independence. You could start by looking under the subject heading *Education,* jotting down the titles and call numbers of promising books. One might be Carl Rogers's *The Freedom to Learn.*

If you don't find any appropriate books cataloged under the first subject heading, try alternative headings. They are often listed on a separate card at the front of each catalog section devoted to a major subject heading. The *Education* card, for example, might list *Learning, styles of* and *Teaching strategies.* If you don't find such a cross-reference card, consult the *Library of Congress Subject Headings* or think of words related to your topic. You could, for instance, look under *Instruction* or *Schools.*

The catalog also indexes books by *title* and by *author.* Imagine you already know about Rogers's ground-breaking work and want to start your research by reading his book. To see if your library has the book, you would look under the title (*Freedom to Learn*) or under the author (Rogers). **Title cards** are arranged alphabetically according to the first word in the title, or according to the second

Selecting a Subject, Using the Library, and Taking Notes

word if the first is *A, An,* or *The*. **Author cards** are arranged alphabetically according to the author's last name. If a book has more than one author, there's a card for each.

Some libraries file author, title, and subject cards in a single catalog; others maintain one catalog for subject cards and a second for author and title cards.

Subject, title, and author cards contain the same information. The only difference is that subject cards have subject headings at the top, while title and author cards have, respectively, titles and authors' names at the top. Look carefully at the accompanying example of a subject card, paying special attention to the following:

1. The *call number,* in the left margin of the card, indicates the book's location in the library.
2. The book's *edition* and *year of publication* are given. If the catalog has cards for, say, the original and revised editions of a book, you should refer to the most recent one to obtain updated information.
3. At the bottom of the card, *other subject headings* under which the book is filed are identified. You should look under these headings for additional books on your topic.

Subject heading	EDUCATION
Call number	LB 1051 R636 1983
Author	Rogers, Carl R. (Carl Ransom), 1902-
Book title	Freedom to learn for the 80's / Carl R. Rogers; with special contributions by Julie Ann Allender . . . [et al.].—
Place of publication, publisher, year of publication	Columbus, Ohio: C. E. Merrill Pub. Co., © 1983. viii, 312 p.: ill.; 25 cm.
Revised edition	Rev. ed. of: Freedom to learn, 1969. Includes bibliographies and index. ISBN 0-675-20012-1
Other subject headings	1. Learning 2. Psychotherapy

How to Find a Book

To locate a book on the shelves, use its **call number.** Besides appearing in the upper-left corner of the catalog card, the call number is printed on the spine of the book. There are two systems of call numbers in use in the United States—the **Dewey Decimal** and the **Library of Congress.** Most college libraries use the latter system, though some still reference older books by the Dewey Decimal system and more recent acquisitions by the Library of Congress. Check with the librarian to see which system(s) your library uses. Listed here are both systems' call numbers and the subjects they represent:

Dewey Decimal System

000–099 General Works
100–199 Philosophy and Psychology
200–299 Religion
300–399 Social Science
400–499 Language

500–599 Pure Science
600–699 Technology (Applied Sciences)
700–799 The Arts
800–899 Literature
900–999 History

Library of Congress System

A	General works—Polygraphy
B	Philosophy—Religion
C	History—Auxiliary Sciences
D	History and Topography (except America)
E–F	America
G	Geography—Anthropology
H	Social Sciences
J	Political Science
K	Law
L	Education
M	Music
N	Fine Arts
P	Language and Literature
Q	Science
R	Medicine
S	Agriculture—Plant and Animal Industry
T	Technology
U	Military Science
V	Naval Science
Z	Bibliography and Library Science

Once you have a book's call number, consult a map or list posted near the card catalog to determine the book's location in the stacks. If you don't see a list, ask the librarian. In libraries with closed stacks, make out a call slip so that a member of the staff can get the book for you.

If you can't find a book in the stacks, don't assume that it's been checked out. Perhaps it's tossed on a table close by, or it may have been replaced carelessly; take a look at books tucked at the ends of the shelves and placed sideways. If you still can't locate the book, consult the person at the circulation desk. If the book has been checked out, you can usually fill out a form to have the current borrower notified that you're waiting for the book, which will be held for you as soon as it is returned. You might also check with a librarian to see if the book has been put on reserve or moved to a special collection, or if it is available through an inter-library loan system. In libraries with computerized circulation systems, all

Selecting a Subject, Using the Library, and Taking Notes

you need to do is type in the book's call number and the computer screen will tell you whether the book has been checked out, moved to a special location, or lost.

The Reference Section

As you already know, **reference works** can help you conduct preliminary research on a topic. Though they have limitations, reference volumes can also be useful at this point. Some reference works (*Encyclopaedia Britannica* and the *World Almanac and Book of Facts*) cover a wide range of subjects. Others (*Mathematics Dictionary* and *Dance Encyclopedia*) are more specialized and provide information about specific fields. Despite these differences, all reference volumes present significantly condensed information. They provide basic facts but not much interpretation. Explanations are brief. Most reference works are, then, unsuitable as sources for in-depth research. In fact, they're usually omitted from the list of Works Cited at the end of a paper.

How do you track down reference works that might be helpful? Start by looking up your subject in the main catalog or, if your library has one, in the separate card catalog for reference books. Record the call numbers and titles of those books marked "Ref" (Reference). The Library of Congress call number for reference is "Z," but a library may keep only some of its "Z" books in the reference section and the rest in the stacks. Most libraries arrange reference shelves alphabetically by subject ("Art," "Economics," "History"), making it easy to browse for other useful references once you've identified one on a subject. Keep in mind that reference materials don't circulate; that is, they cannot be checked out, so you must consult them while in the library.

Listed here are some of the common reference books found in most college libraries:

Biography

International Who's Who
Who's Who in America

Business/Economics

Dictionary of Banking and Finance
Encyclopedia of Economics

Ethnic/Feminist Studies

Encyclopedia of Feminism
Harvard Encyclopedia of American Ethnic Groups

Fine Arts

New Grove Dictionary of American Music
The New Harvard Dictionary of Music
The Oxford Companion to Art
The Thames and Hudson Dictionary of Art Terms

Literature/Film

The Oxford Companion to American Literature
The Oxford Companion to English Literature
World Encyclopedia of the Film

History/Political Science

Editorials on File
Encyclopedia of American Political History
Facts on File
A Political Handbook of the World

Philosophy/Religion

A Dictionary of Non-Christian Religions
The Encyclopedia of American Religions
An Encyclopedia of Philosophy

Science/Technology/Mathematics

A Dictionary of Mathematics
Encyclopedia of Medical History
McGraw-Hill Encyclopedia of Science and Technology
The Merck Index of Chemicals and Drugs

Psychology/Education

Encyclopedia of Education
Encyclopedia of Psychology
Encyclopedia of Special Education

Social Sciences

Dictionary of Anthropology
Encyclopedia of Crime and Justice
International Encyclopedia of the Social Sciences

Periodicals

Periodicals are publications issued at periodic (regular or intermittent) intervals throughout the year. There are three broad types of periodicals: general, scholarly, and serious.

General periodicals (daily newspapers and magazines such as *Time, Newsweek,* and *Psychology Today*) are designed for the average person. Such publications often adopt a personal or anecdotal writing style and offer easy-to-read overviews of subjects. Usually written by generalists rather than experts, the articles in such mass-market publications provide background information, but their lack of comprehensive coverage limits their usefulness for in-depth research. Moreover, since general circulation periodicals usually give only the briefest credit to the writers whose ideas they mention, readers have difficulty tracking down sources and being assured that information is reliable.

Intended for readers with specialized knowledge, **scholarly periodicals** (*Journal of Experimental Child Psychology, Renaissance Drama,* and *Veterinary Medicine*) provide objective, in-depth analyses written by authorities in the field. Such publications develop ideas with facts, studies, and well-reasoned commentary; they document fully the ideas they borrow.

Serious periodicals (*National Geographic, Scientific American,* and *Smithsonian*) are designed for well-educated laypeople rather than experts. These publications develop subjects with less depth than scholarly periodicals but provide a broader perspective. Like scholarly publications, they use a generally objective tone and back up their ideas with information and logic. Documentation is provided but often isn't as complete as it is in scholarly publications.

Periodical Indexes, Abstracts, and Bibliographies

Periodical indexes, issued anywhere from every two weeks to once a year, are cumulative directories that list articles published in certain journals, newspapers, and magazines. In addition, major newspapers, including the *New York Times,* publish annual subject directories. Most periodical indexes arrange listed articles under subject headings. Beneath the headings, individual articles are organized alphabetically by authors' last names.

To locate periodical indexes, you must learn how your library is organized. If there's a periodicals room, you'll probably find the periodical indexes located there, arranged alphabetically by title. In such a case, simply scan the shelves to find the index you want. Sometimes, periodical indexes are located in a separate alphabetically arranged section in the reference room, or, less helpfully, are shelved with reference volumes according to call number. Occasionally, you may find the periodical index to a highly specialized field shelved in the stacks near books in the same field of study. If you can't find the index you want in any of these locations, check with the librarian. You may have to use the computerized card catalog to find the index you want.

You're probably familiar with one index—the *Readers' Guide to Periodical Literature.* It lists general-interest articles published by popular newsstand magazines, such as *U.S. News & World Report* and *Sports Illustrated.* The *Readers' Guide* is issued twice a month in softcover volumes, which are compiled into quarterly, semiannual, and annual issues; once a year is ended, a library retains only the annual hardbound volume. When you were in high school, you probably used the *Readers' Guide* because it indexes accessible, nontechnical publications. To locate articles appropriate for college-level research, you'll need to consult indexes that list articles from more academic, professional, and specialized publications. The college equivalents of the *Readers' Guide* are the *Humanities Index* and the *Social Sciences Index* (see below). You should become familiar with these indexes as well as with the major indexes for the field in which you plan to major (see below).

Some specialized indexes provide brief descriptions of the articles they list. These indexes are usually called **abstracts.** Examples are *Abstracts of Folklore Studies, Criminal Justice Abstracts,* and *Psychological Abstracts.* Abstracts usually contain fewer listings than other types of indexes and are restricted to a limited field. In contrast to indexes that list only articles, **bibliographies** like the *Modern Language Association International Bibliography* list books as well as articles.

Listed here are representative indexes, abstracts, and bibliographies found in most college libraries. Check with the librarian to see which sources can be accessed through the library's computerized catalog or through CD-ROM. (For information on CD-ROM, see pages 473–74.)

General

Biography Index
Humanities Index
New York Times Index
Readers' Guide to Periodical Literature
Social Sciences Index
Speech Index

Arts/Literature

Art Index
Book Review Index
Film Literature Index
Modern Language Association International Bibliography
Music Index
New York Times Book Review Index
Play Index

Business/Economics

Business Periodicals Index
International Bibliography of Economics
Wall Street Journal Index

Education

Education Abstracts
Education Index
ERIC Research in Education

Selecting a Subject, Using the Library, and Taking Notes

History, Political Science, Government

Historical Abstracts
Monthly Index to United States Government Publications
Political Science Bibliographies
Vertical File Index

Philosophy/Religion

Philosopher's Index
Religion Index

Psychology/Sociology

Psychological Abstracts
Sociological Abstracts

Sciences

Applied Science and Technology Index
Biological Abstracts
Botanical Bibliographies
Chemical Abstracts
Engineering Index Annual
Environment Index
International Computer Bibliography

Women's and Ethnic Studies

Bibliography on Women
Index to Periodical Articles by and About Blacks

Computerized Indexes, Abstracts, and Bibliographies

A growing number of college libraries now offer computerized searches of many major indexes, abstracts, and bibliographies. In some libraries, a data base that groups directories alphabetically by subject is maintained in the same system as the computerized catalog for books (see pages 465–66). In other libraries, there may be a separate bank of terminals for searching periodical directories. These terminals are usually hooked up to a **CD-ROM** (compact disc, read-only memory) player containing compact discs on which are stored periodical indexes. The CDs are usually updated monthly so that the information is more current than that found in the bound versions of the directories.

Your college library may subscribe to a number of CD-ROM indexes, including the following: *Humanities Index, Social Sciences Index, Readers' Guide to Periodical Literature, Business Periodicals Index, Education Index, Modern Language Association International Bibliography, Art Index, Government Publications Index,*

Legal Trac, Health Index, and *National Newspaper Index* (covering the *New York Times* and other important newspapers).

Many libraries subscribe to the Info Trac *General Periodicals Index*, which includes over one thousand periodicals ranging from general interest to business, current events, the humanities, and the social sciences. Info Trac's *Academic Index* includes four hundred additional serious and scholarly periodicals, plus the previous six months of the *New York Times.*

Some libraries also offer telephone access to a data base located off campus or even out of state. Because access occurs through the telephone, there's usually a charge and possibly a time delay for retrieval of information. These telephone-access data bases not only list the titles of specific journal articles but also print out the articles themselves—a feature that certainly justifies the fee involved. Some major on-line data bases are Dialog, Wilsonline, and Nexis.

As you have no doubt concluded, library technology is changing rapidly. Many colleges foresee the day when book catalogs, periodical indexes, abstracts, bibliographies, as well as the texts of major reference works will be available not just on the library's computer terminals but campus-wide through a complex network of connecting terminals. Soon college students will be able to do in-depth research in their dorms at any time of the day or night.

Using Computerized and Printed Indexes. Many libraries offer indexes, abstracts, and bibliographies in both computerized and print form. Besides saving time, computerized directories have the advantage of being current; most are updated monthly rather than quarterly or annually, as is the case with print volumes. However, computerized data bases contain only the last three or so years of listings. If you're researching a topic that predates that time period, computerized indexes won't be helpful. For example, to discover how the J. D. Salinger novel *The Catcher in the Rye* was received by contemporaries when it was first published in 1951, you would need to identify articles and reviews written during that period. Bound volumes of the *Modern Language Association International Bibliography, Book Review Index,* and *New York Times Book Review Index* would provide you with the needed information.

Periodical directories, whether computerized or published in print form, use a similar format for listing articles. In both cases, articles are listed alphabetically by subject and by author. Under each subject, articles are arranged alphabetically by title. By looking under appropriate subject headings, you find the titles of articles, books, and studies on your subject. If you don't find your subject listed, try variations on it. Suppose, for example, you're researching the topic "Business ethics." You might look under "Bribery" or "Fraud," in addition to "Business ethics." Bibliographies also refer you to other headings under which related articles are listed. For example, under "Business ethics," you might find cross references to "Advertising ethics," "Banking, ethical aspects," and "Commercial crime."

If you know how to use one index, you can usually transfer these skills to other directories because the formats are similar. If you learned to use the *Readers' Guide* in high school, you should have no trouble using more specialized and scholarly directories. Take a look at the sample annotated *Readers' Guide* entry shown here. You would find that entry listed under the subject heading "Handicapped." Note

Selecting a Subject, Using the Library, and Taking Notes 475

that it provides all the information needed to find an article. Any abbreviations in an entry (of magazine titles, months, and so on) can be decoded by referring to the front of the directory where the abbreviations are explained.

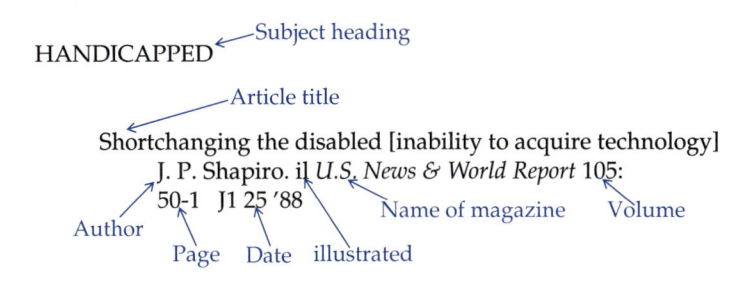

HANDICAPPED ←—Subject heading

←—Article title
Shortchanging the disabled [inability to acquire technology]
J. P. Shapiro. il *U.S. News & World Report* 105:
50-1 Jl 25 '88
Author   Name of magazine   Volume
Page   Date   illustrated

Be sure not to end your search for appropriate material until you've consulted the most pertinent indexes and bibliographies. For a paper on the psychology of child abuse, you might start with the *New York Times Index* and then move to more specialized volumes: *Child Development Abstracts* and *Mental Health Book Review Index*. To ensure that you don't miss important developments on your topic, always start with the most recent years and work your way back.

Locating Specific Issues of Periodicals

Once you have a list of article titles on your subject, you need to see whether the library carries the specific periodicals and issues you want. You also need to determine where the issues are located. Consult the *periodicals catalog*, usually located in the periodicals room or sometimes in the reference room. If your library doesn't have a separate periodicals catalog, look in the main catalog, by periodical title. A periodical card will often tell you the issues owned by the library, their call number, and their location(s). Issue numbers and dates given at the top of the card usually refer to the first issues published, not to the first issues owned by the library. Information about issues owned by the library generally appears at the bottom of the card.

If your library doesn't maintain periodical cards or if information in the periodical cards is incomplete, check with your librarian. He or she will direct you to a computer printout, a typed list, a special bound volume, microfilm, or a separate card file for the necessary information.

Recent issues of magazines, newspapers, and journals are kept in the library's current periodicals section, where they are arranged alphabetically by title. Less current issues can probably be found in bound volumes located in the periodicals room or in the stacks. These bound volumes don't circulate. Back issues of major newspapers are often stored on microfilm and kept in a separate location.

PREPARE A WORKING BIBLIOGRAPHY

As you gather promising books, reference volumes, and articles on your subject, prepare a **working bibliography**—a master list of potential sources. Having such a list means you won't have to waste time later tracking down a source whose title you remember only vaguely. It also means you'll have all the information needed to document your paper without having to return to the original sources.

Since you want to read as much as you can about your subject, the working bibliography will contain more sources than your instructor requires for the final paper. In the long run, you probably won't use all the sources in your working bibliography. Some will turn out to be less helpful than you thought they would be; others may focus on an aspect of your topic you decide not to cover after all.

The working bibliography may be compiled on standard notebook paper or, preferably, on index cards, one card for each source. We recommend 4 × 6-inch cards rather than 3 × 5-inch ones or sheets of paper. Unlike sheets of paper, index cards can be arranged in alphabetical order quickly, making it easy to prepare your Works Cited list (see page 497). And the larger index cards give you room to comment on a source's value ("Good discussion of landfill regulations") or availability ("See if book is on reserve").

Whether you use notebook paper or index cards to prepare your working bibliography, take time to record the following information (to see sample bibliography cards, turn to pages 479–80):

- If the source is a book, write down its title, author, and call number.
- If the source is an article in a reference volume, note the titles of both the article and the reference work, the article's author, and the reference work's call number.
- If the source is an article in a periodical, note the titles of both the article and periodical, the article's author, and the article's date and pages.

Recording this basic information helps you locate these potentially useful sources later on. In the next stage, as you start taking notes, you'll refine the information in your working bibliography.

TAKE NOTES TO SUPPORT THE THESIS WITH EVIDENCE

Why Take Notes?

Now that you've identified promising sources and compiled a working bibliography, it's almost time to take notes on your research material. At this point you may be wondering why you should take notes at all. Why not simply read the sources and then draft the research paper, referring to the sources when you need to check a fact or quote something?

Such an approach is bound to create problems. For one thing, you may have to return a source to the library before you're ready to start writing. Taking the time to go back to the library to retrieve the source later on can slow you down considerably—and, in fact, someone else could have checked out the only copy of the source. With notecards, though, you'll have all the necessary information at hand without having to return to the original source.

Moreover, if you have your sources in front of you as you write, you'll be tempted to move large chunks of material directly from your sources to your paper, without first evaluating and distilling the material. Writing directly from your sources also aggravates any tendency you may have to string together one quotation after another, without providing many ideas of your own. Worst of all, such an approach often leads to *plagiarism:* passing off someone else's work as your own. (For more on plagiarism, see pages 488–89 and 504–10.)

Note-taking can eliminate such problems. When done well, it encourages you to assess, synthesize, and react to your sources. Keeping your working thesis firmly in mind, you examine what others have to say about your subject. Some authors will support your working thesis; others will serve as "devil's advocates," prodding you to consider opposing viewpoints. In either case, note-taking helps you refine your position and develop a sound basis for your conclusions.

Before Note-taking: Evaluate Sources

You shouldn't take notes on a source until after you've evaluated its *relevance, timeliness, seriousness of approach,* and *objectivity.* Titles can be misleading. If a source turns out to be irrelevant, skip note-taking; just indicate on your working bibliography that you consulted the source and found it didn't relate to your topic. Next, consider the source's age. To some extent, the topic and kind of research you're doing determine whether a work is outdated. If you're researching a historical topic such as the internment of Japanese-Americans during World War II, you would most likely consult sources published in the 1940s and 1950s, as well as more up-to-date sources. In contrast, if you're investigating a recent scientific development—*in vitro* fertilization, for example—it would make sense to restrict your search to current material. For most college research, a source older than ten years is considered outdated unless it was the first to present key concepts in a field.

You should also ask yourself if each source is serious and scholarly enough for your purpose and your instructor's requirements. Finally, examine your sources for possible bias, keeping in mind that a strong conclusion or opinion is *not in itself* a sign of bias. As long as a writer doesn't ignore opposing positions or distort evidence, a source can't be considered biased. A biased source presents only those facts that fit the writer's predetermined conclusions. Such a source is often marked by emotionally charged language (see page 22). Publications sponsored by special interest groups—a particular industry, religious association, or political party—are usually biased. Reading such materials *does* familiarize you with a specific point of view, but remember that contrary evidence has probably been ignored or skewed.

A special problem occurs when you find a source that takes a position contrary to the one that you had previously considered credible. When you come across such conflicting material, you can be sure you've identified a pivotal issue within your topic. To decide which position is more valid, you need to take good notes from both sources (see pages 481–89) or carefully annotate your photocopies (see pages 483–84). Then evaluate each source for bias. On this basis alone, you might discover serious flaws in one or both sources. Also compare the key points and supporting evidence in the two sources. Where do they agree? Where do they disagree? Does one source argue against the other's position, perhaps even discrediting some of the opposing view's evidence? The answers to these questions may very well cause you to question the quality, completeness, or fairness of one or both sources. To resolve such a conflict of sources, you can also research your subject more fully. For example, if your conflicting sources are at the general or serious level (see page 471), you should probably turn to more scholarly sources. By referring to more authoritative material, you may be able to determine which of the conflicting sources is more valid.

When you try to resolve discrepancies between sources, be sure not to let your own bias come into play. Try not to favor one position over the other simply because it reflects your own views. Remember, your goal is to arrive at the most well-founded position you can. In fact, researching a topic may lead you to change your original viewpoint. In this case, you shouldn't hesitate to revise your working thesis to accord with the evidence you gather.

Before Note-taking: Refine Your Working Bibliography

After determining which sources are worth taking notes on, spend some time refining the relevant entries in your working bibliography. With the sources in front of you, use the following guidelines to check that you've recorded all necessary information:

- Take down the *authors' names* exactly as they appear on the title pages of the original works and in the order shown there. The author listed first is considered the primary author, so don't rearrange the names alphabetically. Occasionally, a work will be attributed to an organization, university, or institute rather than to a person. If so, consider that organization the author.
- For a *book,* record from the title page the full title (including any subtitle) and the publisher's name, noting only key words (Macmillan, *not* Macmillan Publishing Company). Also, record the publisher's location. If the publisher is international, use the publishing location in your country, if there is one. If several locations within your country are listed, use as the city of publication the one that's most prominent on the title page or the one nearest to you. Also record the copyright year, the most recent year in which the text was registered, as well as the volume number for multivolume books. If you have doubts whether your edition is the most recent, check the computerized on-line or the card catalog to see if the library has a later one. Remember, the

number of editions in which a book has appeared is not the same as the number of printings the book has gone through. A book may say "ninth printing," yet be only the second edition. Finally, don't forget to note the book's call number.
- For a *mass-publication magazine,* note the author's name (if any), the article title, the magazine title, the date (usually month and year), and the pages on which the article appears.
- For a *newspaper article,* take down the author's name (if any), the article title, the newspaper title, the date (month, day, and year), the edition, and the section and pages where the article appears.
- For an *article in a book-length collection,* record the authors of the article, the article title, the book title, the book's editor, the publisher and its location, the copyright date, and the specific book pages on which the article appears.
- For a *scholarly or serious journal,* note the authors' names, the article title, the journal title, the date (including volume and issue numbers, month, and year), and the pages on which the article appears. Take down publishing location only if two periodicals have the same name. In such a case, indicate the city of publication by placing it in parentheses after the periodical's name.
- For all periodicals, note the library location of relevant issues.

We suggest you display bibliographic information much as it appears in the sample cards on the next two pages. The arrangement there follows the MLA format. No matter which format you use on your cards, follow a consistent sequence. It will make your job much easier later when you prepare the paper's Works Cited or References page. If your working bibliography is well organized, accurate, and complete, you won't have to refer to your sources later on for the information you'll need to document your research paper.

E876
.E34
1990

Ehrenreich, Barbara. The Worst Years of Our Lives: Irreverent Notes from a Decade of Greed. New York: Pantheon, 1990.

Bibliography Card: Book

> *Microfiche*
>
> Linden, Eugene. "Last
> Stand for Africa's Elephants."
> <u>Time</u> 20 Feb. 1989: 76-77.

Bibliography Card: Article in a General-interest Magazine

> *Microfiche*
>
> Etzioni, Amitai. "Good
> Ethics Is Good Business — Really."
> <u>New York Times</u> 12 Feb. 1989,
> natl ed., sec. 3:2

Bibliography Card: Newspaper Article

> *periodical*
> *room*
>
> Grigg, Darryl N., & John D. Friesen. "Family
> Patterns Associated with
> Anorexia Nervosa." <u>Journal</u>
> <u>of Marital & Family Therapy</u>
> 15.1 (1989): 29-42

Bibliography Card: Article in a Scholarly Journal

Before Note-taking: Read Your Sources

At this point, you should spend some time analyzing each source for its *central ideas, main supporting points,* and *key details.* As you read, keep asking yourself how the source's content meshes with your working thesis and with what you know about your subject. Does the source repeat what you already know? If so, you may not need any notes. But if a source provides detailed support for important ideas, plan to take full notes.

When Note-taking: What to Select

What, specifically, should you take notes on? Your notes might include any of the following: facts, statistics, anecdotal accounts, expert opinion, case studies, surveys, reports, results of experiments. If a source suggests a new angle on your subject, thoughtful and extensive notes are in order. As you begin taking notes, you may not be able to judge how helpful a source will be. In that case, you probably should take fairly detailed notes. After a while, you'll become more selective.

As you go along, you may come across material that challenges your working thesis and forces you to think differently about your subject. Indeed, the more you learn, the more difficult it may be to state anything conclusively. This is a sign that you're synthesizing and weighing all the evidence. In time, the confusion will lessen, and you'll emerge with a clearer understanding of your subject.

When Note-taking: How to Record Statistics

As you read your sources, you'll probably come across statistics that reinforce points you want to make. Follow these guidelines when taking notes on statistics:

- Check that you record the figures accurately. Also note how and by whom the statistics were gathered as well as where and when they were first reported.
- Take down your source's interpretation of the statistics, but be sure to scrutinize the interpretation. Although the source's figures may be correct, they could have been given a "spin" that distorts them. For example, if 80 percent of Americans think violent crime is our number one national problem, that doesn't mean that violent crime *is* our main problem; it simply means that 80 percent of the people polled *think* it is. And if a "majority" of people think that homelessness should be among our top national priorities, it may be that a mere 51 percent—a bare majority—feels that way. In short, make sure the statistics mean what your sources say they mean.
- Examine each source for possible bias. If a source takes a highly impassioned stance, you should regard its statistics with healthy skepticism. Indeed, it's a good idea to corroborate such figures elsewhere; tracking down the original

source of a statistic is the best way to ensure that numbers are being reported fairly.
- Be suspicious of statistics that fail to indicate the number of respondents or that are based on a small nonrepresentative sample (see page 460–61). For instance, assume the claim is made that 90 percent of the people sampled wouldn't vote for a candidate who had an extramarital affair. However, if only ten people were polled one Sunday as they left church, then the 90 percent statistic is meaningless.

When Note-taking: Use Index Cards

With your sources and bibliography cards close at hand, you're ready to begin taking notes on a second set of index cards. Your instructor will probably ask you to take notes on 4 × 6-inch (or larger) cards. On each card, record notes from only *one source* and on only *one subtopic* of your subject.

Note cards have several advantages over sheets of paper. First, cards help you break information into small, easy-to-manage chunks. Second, they allow you to rearrange information since they can be piled and sorted, unlike information on pages, which must be cut and taped. You can also delete information easily by simply removing a card. Last, note cards save time once you begin writing; you can, for example, staple a quotation on a card right onto your first draft.

For every note card, do the following:

- *Key* each card *to the appropriate source* in your working bibliography by writing the author's last name on each note card. If you have more than one source by the same author, also record the source's title.
- Record the *page* or *pages* in the source that the note refers to. If the note card material is drawn from several pages, indicate clearly where the page breaks occur in the source. That way, if you use only a portion of the material later, you will know its exact page number.
- Write a key word or phrase at the top of each note card, indicating the gist of the note and the aspect of your topic the card focuses on. Often your key terms will themselves develop subtopics. For example, a paper on erosion may have two major stacks of cards: "Beach erosion" and "Mountain erosion," with beach erosion being divided into "Dune" and "Shoreline" erosion.
- Finally, write down the actual note. Pages 484–89 describe specific kinds of notes to take. In the meantime, here's some general advice. Some cards will have only a line or two; others will be quite full. If you run out of space on a card, don't use the other side; this makes it hard to see at a glance what the note is about. Instead, use a second card, being sure to record the source, page, and so on. Also label successive cards carefully (1 of 2, 2 of 2) and clip them to the first card in the series.

It's up to you where on the note card you place identifying information. The sample card shown here illustrates one way. Whichever way you set up your note cards, be consistent. When you scan your cards before finishing with a source, you'll be more inclined to notice any missing information if you've prepared them in some consistent style. You'll also find it easier to retrieve information later on from well-organized note cards.

> Unethical behavior: causes   Etzioni, p.22
>   Economists often think people's desire for profit causes them to cheat—cheat to stay ahead.
>   <u>But recent studies by social scientists show otherwise</u>—"social ties" and other "non-economic factors" cause ethical or noneth. behav.
>   Leading factors—"local cultures" and "social webs"

Note cards may also include your comments about a source. Enclosing your observations in square brackets ["helpful summary," "controversial interpretation"] keeps these interpretive remarks separate from your notes on a source. If taking notes sparks new ways of looking at your subject, get down such thoughts, carefully separating them from your source material. Write "Me" or "My idea" on the card, or enclose your observations in a box. If your own comments become extensive, use separate note cards, clearly labeling them as your own ideas.

Two Other Note-taking Approaches

Although index cards are the most efficient way to take notes, there are other methods available. If you can't get the hang of the note-card system, try using **sheets of paper.** To minimize the problems you may encounter later when you start organizing the paper, head each sheet with a key to the source. Then enter all notes from that source, along with page numbers, on the same sheet. If you run out of space, don't take notes on the other side. Instead, start a new sheet, entering on each a key to the source, and continue to keep track of the pages in the source from which you're taking notes. Mark each sheet in the sequence clearly (1 of 3, 2 of 3, and so on). Using key phrases to signal subtopics will also make it easier to organize your notes later.

Duplicating material is another way to gather information. You have the right to copy published work as long as you use it for your own research and give credit for borrowed material. Photocopying *does* have advantages. It allows unhurried analysis and reconsideration of research material at home. It can also be a way of ensuring accuracy since sources can be checked so easily. Duplicating can be especially useful if you need to retrieve a detail that initially seemed unimportant.

However, photocopying is not without dangers, especially if you're an inexperienced researcher. You may get a false sense of security if you convince yourself that once you've photocopied material, you've done most of the work. *Remember:* You still have to evaluate and synthesize your source material, figuring out what evidence supports your working thesis. That means you should dig into the photocopied material, underlining or boxing sections you might use, jotting subtopics in the margins, recording your reaction to the material.

There's one more pitfall to consider: Working with duplicated material can encourage *plagiarism.* Instead of recasting material in your own words, you may be tempted to copy others' language and ideas. If that is the case, you'd be better off steering clear of duplicating altogether. (For more on plagiarism, see pages 488–89 and 504–10.)

If you do photocopy, don't forget to include the duplicated sources in your working bibliography and to write complete source information on the photocopy itself.

Kinds of Notes

There are four broad kinds of notes: direct quotations, summaries, paraphrases, and combined notes. Knowing how and when to use each type is an important part of the research process.

Direct Quotations

A **quotation note** reproduces, word for word, that which is stated in a source. Although quoting can demonstrate the thoroughness with which you reviewed relevant sources, don't take one direct quote note card after another; such a string of quotations means you haven't evaluated and synthesized your sources sufficiently. When should you quote? If a source's ideas are unusual or controversial, record a representative quotation in your notes so you can include it in your paper to show you have accurately conveyed the source's viewpoint. And, of course, record a quotation if a source's wording or ideas are particularly eloquent or convincing. When taking notes, you might aim for one to three quotations from each major source. More than that can create a problem when you write the paper (see pages 508–10).

A card containing a direct quotation from a source should be clearly indicated by quotation marks, perhaps even a handwritten note like "Direct Quotation" or "DQ." Whenever your source quotes someone else (a secondary source) and you want to take notes on what that other person said, put the statement in quotes and indicate its original source. (See page 510 for more on quoting secondary sources.)

When copying a quotation, you must record the author's statement *exactly* as it appears in the original work, right down to the punctuation. As long as you don't change the meaning of the original, you may delete a phrase or sentence from a quotation if it's not pertinent to the point you're making. In such cases, insert three spaced periods, called an **ellipsis** (. . .), in place of the deleted words:

Original Passage

    The plot, with one exciting event after another, was representative of the usual historical novel. But *Gone With the Wind* placed its emphasis as much on the private individual as on the panorama.

Ellipsis Used to Show Material Omitted

"The plot . . . was representative of the usual historical novel. But <u>Gone With the Wind</u> placed its emphasis as much on the private individual as on the panorama."

    If you drop material from the end of a sentence, the period that ends the sentence appears in its usual place, followed by the three spaced periods that signal the omission:

Ellipsis at the End

"The plot, with one exciting event after another, was representative of the usual historical novel. . . ."

    You don't need an ellipsis if you omit material at the start of a quotation. Simply place the quotation marks where you begin quoting directly. Also, don't capitalize the first word in the quotation unless it ordinarily requires capitalization:

No Ellipsis Needed

<u>Gone With the Wind</u>'s piling up of "one exciting event after another" was typical of the historical potboiler.

    This last example also illustrates that you can omit the ellipsis if all you quote is a key term or short phrase. In such cases, just enclose the borrowed material in quotation marks. (For more examples of the ellipsis, see pages 505–06 and 508.)

    If, for clarity's sake, you need to add a word or short phrase to a quotation (for example, by changing a verb tense or replacing a vague pronoun with a noun), enclose your insertion in **brackets:**

"Not only did it [<u>Gone With the Wind</u>] for a short time become America's speediest-selling novel, but over the long haul, it became the nation's largest-selling novel."

    When a source you're quoting quotes another source, place single quotation marks around the words of the secondary source:

"Despite its massive scope, <u>Gone With the Wind</u> sustained, according to one reviewer, 'remarkable continuity in its plot and character development.' "

Summaries

By **summaries,** we mean *condensing* someone else's ideas and restating them *in your own words.* Skim the source; then, using your own language, condense the material to its central idea, main supporting points, and key details. Summary note cards may be written as lists, brief paragraphs, or both. You may use abbreviations and phrases as well as complete sentences. *A caution:* When summarizing, don't use the ellipsis to signal that you have omitted some ideas. The ellipsis is used only when quoting.

The length of the summary depends on your topic and purpose. Read the first eight paragraphs of George Gallup's essay, "The Faltering Family," on pages 364–70. Then look at the summary cards below. The notes were taken by two students using Gallup's essay to research different topics. The first student, writing on the effects of divorce on children, labeled the card, "Divorce statistics: effects on children" and prepared an in-depth summary card. The second

---

Divorce statistics: effects on children   Gallup, p.365

Trends are alarming: 1 in 2 marriages ends in divorce
Situation getting bleaker.
   In 1962: 2.2 div. per 1,000 people
      1982: 5.1 per 1,000 (double '62 rate)
         Stats from Nat'l Center for Health Statistics
NY Times (Dec. 1982) reports that annually 100,000 older
   Ams. (55 or over) leave long-term marriages.
All this makes kids fearful and insecure.

First Student's Summary Card

Family decline   Gallup, p.365

   Between 1962 & 1982 divorce rate doubled. 26% of opinion leaders feel family problems will be one of the nation's top five problems in the year 2000.

Second Student's Summary Card

Selecting a Subject, Using the Library, and Taking Notes

student, writing on likely changes in America by the year 2000, took a much shorter note under the heading "Family decline."

Summarizing problems.   The sample note cards on page 486 were prepared by students who were careful about translating ideas into their own language. The note cards below, however, were prepared by students who had difficulty recasting ideas from the Gallup passage. In the first example, the student was so determined to put things her own way that she added her own ideas and ended up *distorting* Gallup's meaning. For instance, note the way she changed "opinion leaders" to "government officials" and the way family decline became the country's "top problem," rather than one of five top problems. In the second example, the student worked so hard to compress material that he prepared an *overly condensed* note card. The fragmented and vague quality of the summary renders it almost meaningless.

> Concern over family   Gallup, p. 365
>
> Government officials concerned about the family's future. 33% think family disruptions will be the country's top problem in the year 2000.

Summary: Distorting the Original

> Divorce rate growing   Gallup, p. 365
>
> Now 1 in 2.
>
> Over 20 years, increased substantially.

Summary: Overly Condensed

Paraphrases

You may have heard of another kind of note prepared in your own words: **paraphrase notes.** Unlike a summary, which condenses the original, a paraphrase recasts material by using roughly the same number of words, retaining the same level of detail, and adopting the same style as the original. Since the research process requires you to distill information, you'll probably find summary note cards much more helpful than paraphrases.

Plagiarism. Paraphrasing can also lead to *plagiarism*—when a writer borrows someone else's ideas, facts, or language but doesn't properly credit that source. Look, for example, at the note card below. When preparing his paraphrase, the student stayed too close to the source and borrowed much of Gallup's language *word for word.* Note, for example, the underlined words, which are taken directly from Gallup. If the student transferred this phrasing to his paper without supplying quotation marks, he'd be guilty of plagiarism. Indeed, even if this student acknowledged Gallup in the paper, he'd still be plagiarizing—the lack of quotation marks implies that the language is the student's when, in fact, it is Gallup's.

> Divorce statistics   Gallup, p. 365
>
> <u>Historical and sociological trends add strong support</u> to the theory that family life is breaking apart. About <u>one marriage in every two ends in divorce.</u> And <u>the situation is getting worse</u>; it isn't improving.

Plagiarized Paraphrase: Word-for-Word

In the sample card on page 489, the student believed, erroneously, that if she changed a word here and omitted a word there, she'd be preparing an effective paraphrase. Note that the language is all Gallup's except for the underlined words, which signal the student's slight rephrasings of Gallup. Notice, too, that the student occasionally deleted a word from Gallup, thinking that such changes would constitute a legitimate paraphrase. For instance, Gallup's "support to these expressions of concern" became "support these concerns." The student couldn't place quotation marks around these *near-quotes* because her wording wasn't identical to that of the source. Yet to place the near-quotes in a paper without quotation marks would be deceptive; the lack of quotation marks would suggest that the language was the student's when actually it's substantially (but not exactly) Gallup's. Such near-quotes are also considered plagiarism, even if, when writing the paper, the student supplied a note citing the source. (For hints on steering clear of plagiarism when you actually write a research paper, see the discussion of documentation on pages 504–10.)

> *Divorce statistics*   *Gallup, p. 365*
>
> Historical and sociological <u>studies strongly</u> support these concerns. For <u>instance, nowadays roughly</u> one marriage in two ends in divorce. <u>And</u> the situation <u>is</u> getting worse, <u>not</u> better.

Plagiarized Paraphrase: Near-Quotes

Combined Notes

When taking notes, you may summarize someone else's ideas in your own words but also include some of the source's exact wording. The result, a **combined note,** is legitimate as long as you put quotation marks around the source's language. The sample combined note card shown below is based on the same passage from Gallup's essay.

Combination note cards are effective. They allow you to retain key phrases as well as eloquent or controversial statements from your source; you don't have to spend time recasting material that resists translation into your own words. At the same time, combined notes indicate that you're actively involved with your research material, that you're continually asking yourself, "What should I state in my own words? What is so informative, so interesting, so provocative that I want to use it exactly as it is, word for word?" Such questions prompt discipline and careful thought, two qualities that will serve you well as you move ahead to the next phase of your research—organizing and writing the paper, our focus in Chapter 22.

> *Divorce statistics*   *Gallup, p. 365*
>
> The National Center for Health Statistics reports:
>   1962 - 2.2 divorces per 1,000
>   1982 - 5.1 divorces per 1,000
>
> No wonder there are such "expressions of concern." The divorce rate "more than doubled in two decades."

Sample Combined Note Card

ACTIVITIES: SELECTING A SUBJECT, USING THE LIBRARY, AND TAKING NOTES

1. Use the card or computer catalog to answer the following questions:

   a. What are three books dealing with the subject of adoption? Of television? Nuclear power? Genetic research?
   b. What is the title of a book by Betty Friedan? By John Kenneth Galbraith?
   c. Who is the author of *Invisible Man*? Of *A Country Year*?

2. Examine this catalog card closely and then use it to answer the questions that follow:

   > LB1139
   > .L3F43
   >
   > FERGUSON, Charles Albert, 1921–   comp.
   >
   > Studies of child language development. Edited by Charles A. Ferguson and Dan Isaac Slobin. New York. Holt, Rinehart and Winston, 1973.
   >
   > xv, 645 p. illus. (24) cm.
   > Bibliography: p. 628–645.
   >
   > 1. Children—Language. 2. Psycholinguistics
   > I. Slobin, Dan Isaac 1930—joint comp. II. Title

   a. Which catalog system does this library use?
   b. Is this a subject, author, or title card?
   c. What is the title of the book? Does it have an author or an editor?
   d. Under what subjects is this book listed in the catalog?
   e. When was the book published?
   f. Assume you're writing a paper about the way children learn to speak. Considering the information on the card, would you try to locate this book? Why or why not?

3. Using reference works available in your library, find the answers to the following questions:

   a. What was the price of a barrel of crude oil in 1990?
   b. Who invented Kodachrome film, and when?

Selecting a Subject, Using the Library, and Taking Notes   491

   c. What is the medical condition *rosacea*?
   d. What television show won the Emmy in 1973–74 for Outstanding Comedy Series?
   e. What was artist John Sartain known for?
   f. When was an African American first elected to Congress?
   g. In economics, what is Pareto's Law?
   h. In art, what is *écorché*?
   i. Give two other names for a *mbira*, a musical instrument.
   j. In the religion of the Hopi Native Americans, what are *kachinas*?

4. Select *one* of the following limited topics. Then, using the appropriate periodical indexes and bibliographies (see pages 471–74), locate three periodicals that would be helpful in researching the topic. Examine each periodical to determine whether it is aimed at a general, serious, or scholarly audience.

   a. Drug testing of public transportation employees
   b. Ethical considerations in organ-transplant surgery
   c. Women in prison
   d. Deforestation of the Amazon rain forest
   e. The difference between *The Accidental Tourist* as a novel and as a film

5. Prepare a bibliography card for each of the following books. Gather all the information necessary at the library so that you can write accurate and complete bibliography cards:

   a. Barbara Tuchman, *Practicing History*
   b. L. Jacobs, *The Documentary Tradition*
   c. Margaret Mead, *Coming of Age in Samoa*
   d. Stephen Bank, *The Sibling Bond*
   e. Ronald Gross, *The New Old*
   f. Matthew Arnold, *Culture and Anarchy*

6. Select *one* of the following limited topics. Then refer to the appropriate periodical index or bibliography (see pages 471–74) to locate at least three relevant articles on the topic: one from a general-interest magazine, one from a newspaper, one from a serious or scholarly journal. Make a bibliography card for each article.

   a. Ordaining women in American churches
   b. Attempts to regulate pornography
   c. The popularity of novelist and essayist Isak Dinesen
   d. The growing interest in painter David Hockney
   e. AIDS education programs
   f. The greenhouse effect

7. Listed here are some of this book's professional essays, along with broad research topics that they suggest. Choose one of these general subjects and, using the library's resources, do some background reading. (You should find helpful some of the sources listed on pages 469–70 and 471–74.) On either index cards or notebook paper, keep an informal record of the works you consult. As you read,

jot down potential limited topics. After doing some further reading on *one* of the limited topics, devise a working thesis. (Don't, by the way, feel constrained by the point of view expressed in the essay(s) that initially prompted your research.)

a. "Photographs of My Parents" (page 175); "Louise Cox" (page 207); "My First Conk" (page 307); "And Then I Went to School" (page 339); "Black Men and Public Space" (page 373)

   Preservation of cultural differences

   Relations between different racial or ethnic groups

b. "Am I Blue?" (page 213)

   Use of animals in medical research or product testing

   Use of animals in the entertainment industry

   Vegetarianism

c. "Sexism and Language" (page 243); "When Is It Rape?" (page 397); "What Should Be Done About Rock Lyrics?" (page 443)

   Sexist attitudes in children's books

   Gender roles depicted in the mass media

   Sexism on the college campus

d. "Stallone vs. Springsteen" (page 335); "Rambos of the Road" (page 403)

   Causes of aggression

   Educational programs to discourage competition and encourage cooperation

e. "The Faltering Family" (page 364)

   Day care

   "Latchkey" children

   Two-wage families

f. "The Bounty of the Sea" (page 371)

   Effects of pollution on marine life

   The relationship between the greenhouse effect and the destruction of the Amazon rain forest

   Adequacy of current environmental-protection laws

g. "Propaganda Techniques in Today's Advertising" (page 271)

   Political advertising

   Advertising of cigarettes or alcohol

   Advertising on children's television

Selecting a Subject, Using the Library, and Taking Notes

    h. "Why Nothing Is 'Wrong' Anymore" (page 279)

        Ethics and politicians

        Business ethics

        Student ethics

    i. "Low-Cost Drugs for Addicts?" (page 446); "Our Drug Problem" (page 449)

        Federal efforts to reduce the drug trade

        Drug-education programs

        Drug testing of a particular group

    j. "Institution Is Not a Dirty Word" (page 439)

        Government's responsibility toward the handicapped

        Trends in caring for the disabled

        Hospital regulations regarding severely handicapped infants

8. Referring to paragraphs 33–36 of Gallup's essay on pages 364–70, prepare three note cards: a direct quotation, a summary, and a combined note. Assume you are using the Gallup essay to research women's motives for working outside the home.

22 WRITING THE RESEARCH PAPER

AFTER you complete your note-taking, you're ready to begin the writing phase of the research project. When writing the paper, you'll probably find it helpful to follow these steps:

- Refine your working thesis.
- Sort the note cards.
- Organize the evidence by outlining.
- Prepare the Works Cited list.
- Write the first draft.
- Document borrowed material.
- Revise, edit, and proofread.

REFINE YOUR WORKING THESIS

This is a good time to *reexamine your working thesis;* it's undoubtedly evolved since you first started your research. Indeed, now that you're more informed about the topic, you may feel that your original thesis oversimplifies the issue. To clarify your position, begin by sifting through your note cards; your goal is to formulate a position that makes the most sense in light of the research you've done and the information you've gathered. Then, revise your working thesis, keeping in mind the evidence on your note cards. This refined version of your thesis will serve as the starting point for your first draft. Remember, though—as you write the paper, new thoughts may emerge that will cause you to modify your thesis even further. (For more on thesis statements, see Chapter 3.)

SORT THE NOTE CARDS

Keeping your refined thesis in mind, *sort your note cards* into piles by *topic*. If, for example, your thesis is "Lotteries are an inefficient means of raising money for state programs," you might form one pile of note cards on administrative costs, another on types of state programs, a third on the way money is allocated, and so on. Although you can sort by the key terms or headings you previously placed at the tops of cards, it's a good idea to reread the cards. You may find, for example, that a heading needs to be changed because its information better suits some other category. If some cards don't fit into any pile—and this is likely—put them aside. You don't need to use every note card. At this point, though, you should consider which organizational approach (see pages 53–55) will help you sequence your material. Arrange your topic piles to reflect this order.

Once you've arranged your note cards according to the topic headings at the top, sort each topic pile by *subtopic*. For example, the pile of cards about types of state programs might be divided into these three subtopic piles: programs for the elderly, programs for preschool children, programs for the physically disabled. Next, using the patterns of development and organizational approaches discussed, respectively, on pages 45–46 and 53–55, order each set of subtopic cards to match the sequence in which you think you'll discuss those subtopics in your paper. This sorting will make your next step—preparing an outline—much easier.

ORGANIZE THE EVIDENCE BY OUTLINING

Whether or not your instructor requires an *outline*, it's a good idea to prepare one before you begin writing the paper. Because an outline groups and sequences points, it provides a blueprint you can follow when writing. Outlining clarifies what your main ideas are, what your supporting evidence is, and how everything fits together. It reveals where your argument is well supported and where it is weak.

To design your outline, focus first on the paper's body. How can you best explain and support your thesis? For now, don't worry about your introduction or conclusion. General guidelines on outlining are discussed in Chapter 5 (pages 55–57). To apply those guidelines to a research paper, keep the following points in mind:

- Base your outline on your organized piles of note cards.
- Label your *main topic* headings (those on your main pile of cards) with roman numerals (I, II, III, and so on) to indicate the order in which you plan to discuss each topic in the paper.

- Label the *subtopics* grouped under each main topic heading with capital letters (A, B, C). Indent the subtopic entries under their respective main topics, listing them in the order you plan to discuss them.
- Label *supporting points* (ideas noted on your cards) with arabic numerals (1, 2, 3) and indent them under the appropriate subtopics.
- Label *specific details* (facts, quotations, statistics, examples, expert opinions) with lowercase letters (a, b, c) and indent them under the appropriate supporting points. Use shorthand for details. For example, write "Bitner quote here" instead of copying the entire quotation into your outline.
- Where appropriate, map out sections of the paper that will provide background information or define key terms.

Here's how the various outline elements look when they're properly labeled and indented:

I. Main topic
    A. Subtopic
        1. Supporting point
        2. Supporting point
            a. Specific detail
            b. Specific detail
    B. Subtopic
        1. Supporting point
        2. Supporting point
II. Main topic
    A. Subtopic
        1. Supporting point
        2. Supporting point
            a. Specific detail
            b. Specific detail
    B. Subtopic

Your first outline probably won't be a formal full-sentence one; rather, it's more likely to be a *topic* (or phrase) *outline,* like those on pages 293–94, 325, and 429. A topic outline helps you clarify a paper's overall structure. A *full-sentence* outline (see pages 229 and 517–18) or a *combined topic and sentence outline* (see pages 356–57) is better suited to mapping out in detail the development of a paper's ideas. If you're preparing an outline that will be submitted with the paper, find out in advance which kind your instructor prefers.

Before you go any further, it's a good idea to get some feedback on your outline—from an instructor or a critical friend—to make sure others agree that your meaning and organization are logical and clear. Then, based on your readers' reactions, make whatever changes seem necessary.

Writing the Research Paper

Finally, key your note cards to your outline. Label each card according to the section of the paper in which the card will be used: "IA," "IIB2," and so on. Using a different color ink for each main-topic section makes it easier to locate appropriate card stacks when you write the paper later on.

PREPARE THE WORKS CITED LIST: MLA FORMAT

At this point, you should draft a tentative **Works Cited list** (or bibliography) before you write the paper. That way, each time you include borrowed material in your paper, you can easily key that material to the appropriate item on the Works Cited list.

The following discussion focuses on the MLA—Modern Language Association—format for preparing the Works Cited list. The **MLA format** is used widely in the liberal arts. (The system used in the social sciences—that of the American Psychological Association (APA)—is described on pages 513–15. On page 515, you'll also find a description of the format used in the hard sciences and in technical fields.)

As a first step in preparing your Works Cited list, pull out the bibliography cards (or working bibliography) for the sources you think you'll actually refer to in your paper. Alphabetize them by the authors' last names. For now, put any anonymous works at the end.

The Works Cited list, which will appear at the end of your final paper, should include only those works you actually quote, summarize, or otherwise directly refer to in your paper. Don't list other sources, no matter how many you may have read. Placed on its own page, the Works Cited list provides readers with full bibliographic information about the sources you cite in the paper.

Double-space the entries on the Works Cited list, and *don't* add extra space between entries. The first line of each new entry should start at the left margin; if an entry extends beyond one line of type, all subsequent lines should be indented five spaces. The major items in a bibliographic entry (the author's full name, the title, all the information on publication) are separated with periods. (See the sample Works Cited list on pages 525–26.)

The following sample entries will help you prepare an accurate Works Cited list.

Book Sources

Here is the basic format for listing a book in Works Cited:

- Start with the author's name, last name first, then first name and any initial, with a comma between the first and last names. Put a period after the first name or initial. Skip two spaces between the period and the next item in the entry.

- Give the complete book title. If the book has a subtitle, separate it from the title with a colon. Leave a space after the colon. Underline the full title and follow it with a period. Leave two spaces between the period and the next item.
- Next, give the city of publication, followed by a colon. Leave a space between the colon and the next item. If the publisher has more than one location, use the city listed first on the book's title page. If the book is published in the United States, give only the city. If it is published in another country, give the city as well as the country, separating them with a comma.
- Supply the publisher's name, giving only key words and omitting the words *Company, Press, Publishers, Inc.,* and the like. (For example, write *Macmillan* for Macmillan Publishing Company, *St. Martin's* for St. Martin's Press.) In addition, use *UP* to abbreviate the names of university presses (as in *Columbia UP* and *U of California P*). Place a comma and a space after the publisher's name.
- End with the publication date and a period. Supply the most recent year of copyright. Don't use the year of the most recent printing.

Here is a sample entry for a book in the MLA format:

Book With One Author

Yesley, Marjorie G. <u>Political Campaigns: A Retrospective</u>. New York: Vintage, 1979.

For books varying from this basic entry, consult the examples that follow. If you don't spot a sample entry for the type of source you need to document, consult the latest edition of the *MLA Handbook for Writers of Research Papers* for more comprehensive examples.

Several Works by the Same Author

Reedy, George E. <u>The Presidency in Flux</u>. New York: Columbia UP, 1973.

---. <u>The Twilight of the Presidency</u>. New York: World, 1970.

If you use more than one work by the same author, list each book separately. Give the author's name in the first entry only; begin the entries for other books by that author with three hyphens followed by a period. Arrange the works alphabetically by title. In the preceding example, note that *The Presidency in Flux* is alphabetized as if its first letter were *P,* not *T.* The words *A, An,* and *The* are ignored when alphabetizing by title.

Book With Two or Three Authors

Beddoes, Richard, Stan Fischler, and Ira Gitler. <u>Hockey! The Story of the World's Fastest Sport</u>. Toronto: Collier-Macmillan, 1969.

For a book with two or three authors, give all the authors' names but reverse only the first name. List the names in the order shown on the title page.

Book With Four or More Authors

Dansker, Isadora, et al. <u>Geological Formations in New England</u>. Boston: Newtown, 1990.

For a work with four or more authors, give only the first author's name followed by a comma and *et al.* (Latin for "and others").

Revised Edition of a Book

Fiedler, Leslie A. <u>Love and Death in the American Novel</u>. 2nd ed. New York: Dell, 1966.

Indicate which edition you used after the book's title.

Book With an Editor or Translator

Jonson, Ben. <u>Epicoene</u>. Ed. L. A. Beaurline. Lincoln: U of Nebraska P, 1966.

Place the editor's or translator's name after the title, with the identifying abbreviation *Ed.* or *Trans.* before the person's name. Don't reverse the first and last name of the editor or translator.

An Anthology or Compilation of Several Authors

Ghiselin, Brewster, ed. <u>The Creative Process: A Symposium</u>. Berkeley: U of California P, 1952.

If you refer in general to an edited book—rather than to the individual authors whose work it contains—give the editor's name in the author position, followed by a comma and the abbreviation *ed.*

Section of an Anthology or Compilation of Several Authors

Shapero, Harold. "The Musical Mind." <u>The Creative Process: A Symposium</u>. Ed. Brewster Ghiselin. Berkeley: U of California P, 1952. 49-53.

If you use only a section from an anthology, list first the author of that particular selection or chapter. The remaining information should be presented in this order: selection title (in quotation marks), book title (underlined), editor's name (preceded by the abbreviation *Ed.*), publication data, and the selection's page numbers. Don't use *p.* or *page*.

Section or Chapter in a Book by One Author

Canin, Ethan. "The Year of Getting to Know Us." <u>Emperor of the Air</u>. New York: Harper, 1988. 21-43.

If you use only one named section or chapter of a book, give the section's title in quotation marks before the title of the book. At the end, give the section's page numbers. Don't use *p.* or *page*. If you use several sections, don't name each of them; just put the page numbers for all the sections at the end of the entry.

Book by an Institution or Corporation

Commission on Higher Education. <u>Characteristics of Excellence in Higher Education: Standards for Accreditation</u>. Philadelphia: Commission on Higher Education of the Middle States Association of Colleges and Schools, 1982.

Give the name of the institution or corporation in the author position, even if the same institution is the publisher.

Articles in Periodicals

Here is the basic format for listing periodical articles in Works Cited:

- Start with the author's last name, following the guidelines for a book author. If the article is unsigned, begin with its title.
- Give the article's complete title, enclosed in quotation marks, and follow it with a period. Leave two spaces between the period and the next item in the entry.
- Supply the periodical's name, underlining it. Don't place any punctuation after it.
- Give the date of publication. For newspapers and weekly magazines, include the day, month, and year—in that order. Abbreviate the month if it is longer than four letters. For scholarly journals, give the volume number, issue number (if appropriate), and year. In both cases, follow the date with a colon. Leave a space between the colon and the next item.
- Provide page number(s), without using *p.* or *page*. Place a period after the page.

The following sample entries for articles in periodicals are formatted in the MLA style. If you don't spot an entry for the type of source you need to document, consult the *MLA Handbook* for more comprehensive examples.

Article From a Weekly or Biweekly Magazine

"Short Takes." <u>Publishers Weekly</u> 22 Aug. 1986: 20.
Strobe, Talbot. "Why Kohl Is Right." <u>Time</u> 15 May 1989: 26.

Article From a Monthly or Bimonthly Magazine

Steele, Shelby. "The Recoloring of Campus Life: Student Racism, Academic Pluralism, and the End of a Dream." <u>Harper's</u> Feb. 1989: 47-55.

Article From a Daily Newspaper

Bartlett, Sarah. "Why Wall Street's So Topsy-Turvy." <u>New York Times</u> 7 May 1989, natl. ed., sec. 4: 1+.

Use the name of the newspaper as it appears on the masthead, but delete any initial *The*. If the paper's location isn't given in the title, put the town or city in brackets after the title: *Today's Sunbeam* [Salem, NJ]. If the paper is a large daily, indicate the particular edition (late city, early, national, and so on) by abbreviating this information and placing it after the date. For a newspaper with sections, give the appropriate section number or letter, placing a colon between the section and page(s). However, if the section letter appears at the top of the page along with the page number, the abbreviation *sec.* isn't used; instead, the section letter is given along with the page number (see the following example). If a newspaper article runs more than one page, put a plus sign after the first page of the article (see the last example on page 500).

Editorial, Letter to the Editor, or Reply to a Letter

"Patience on Panama."   Editorial.   Philadelphia Inquirer 12 May 1989: A22.

List as you would any signed or unsigned article, but indicate the nature of the piece by adding *Editorial, Letter,* or *Reply to a letter of [letter writer's name]* after the article's title.

Article from a Scholarly Journal

Connors, Robert J.   "Personal Writing Assignment."   College Composition
    and Communication 38 (1987): 166-83.
Juneja, Renu.   "The Trinidad Carnival: Ritual, Performance, Spectacle, and
    Symbol."   Journal of Popular Culture 21.4 (1988): 87-90.

Some journals are paged continuously (the first example); the first issue of each year starts with page one, and each subsequent issue picks up where the previous one left off. For such journals, use numerals to indicate the volume number after the title, and then indicate the year in parentheses. Note that neither *volume* nor *vol.* is used. The article's page(s) appears at the end, separated from the year by a colon. For a journal that pages each issue separately (the second example), use numerals to indicate the volume *and issue* numbers; separate the two with a period, but leave no space after the period.

Nonprint Sources

Television or Radio Program

"Colonial Days."   The United States and the Philippines: In Our Image.   Narr.
    Stanley Karnow.   Part 1 of 3.   PBS.   WHYY-TV, Philadelphia.   8 May
    1989.

List, at the minimum, the program's title (underlined), the network, the local station on which it was seen or heard, the city, and the broadcast date. If, as in the preceding example, the program is one episode in a series, give the episode title first (in quotation marks), then the series title (underlined). Other information might include the director, narrator, and so on.

Movie, Recording, Videotape, Filmstrip, or Slide Program

<u>Field of Dreams</u>. Dir. Phil Alden Robinson. With Kevin Costner. Universal, 1989.

Belushi, James, actor. <u>Wired</u>. Dir. Larry Peerce. Universal, 1989.

List the title (underlined), director, distribution company, and year. The writer, main performers, or producers may be listed after the director and before the company. If the work is a videotape, filmstrip, or slide program, indicate the medium right after the title. If you use the source to discuss the work of a particular individual, begin with that person's name (as in the second example above).

Computer Software

Harvey, Will. <u>Music Construction Set</u>. Computer software. Electronic Arts, 1983. Commodore 64.

List the program's author, if known, then the title (underlined), the designation *Computer software,* the distributor, and the year. Conclude with any other information that helps identify the software, such as the system it runs on.

Personal Interview

Harrow, Morgan. Personal interview. 5 Aug. 1989.

Lecture

Akers, Sharon. "Managing Pension Funds." Workshop. Association of Retirement Communities. Miami, 14 Dec. 1988.

Bateman, Paul. "The Media and the Electoral Process." Lecture. Sociology 202, Kirkwood University. New Castle, 10 Oct. 1989.

Start with the speaker's name, followed by the lecture's title (in quotation marks) if there is one. If not, identify the lecture with an appropriate label such as *Keynote address* or *Lecture.* Then provide the sponsoring organization's name and the date.

WRITE THE FIRST DRAFT

Once you've refined your working thesis, sorted your note cards, constructed an outline, and prepared a preliminary Works Cited page, you're ready to write your first draft. As with the early versions of an essay, don't worry at this stage about grammar, spelling, or style. Just try to get down as much of the paper's basic content and structure as you can.

Chapter 6 offers general guidelines for writing a first draft (pages 63–66). When applying those guidelines to a research paper, keep the following points in mind:

- As you write, refer to your note cards and outline. Don't rely on your memory for the information you've gathered.

- Feel free to deviate from your outline if, as you write, you discover a more effective sequence, realize some material doesn't fit, or see new merit in previously discarded information.
- Include any quotations and summaries in the draft. Rather than recopy, you may tape or staple the appropriate note cards to the page.
- Provide rough documentation (see pages 504–10) for all material borrowed from your sources.
- Use the present tense when quoting or summarizing a source ("Gallup *reports* that..." rather than "Gallup *reported* that...").
- Use the third-person point of view throughout, unless your instructor has indicated that you may use the first person when presenting primary research (see pages 459–60).

There are two contrasting strategies for generating a first draft. One is to *overwrite*, explaining each point as fully as possible, even including alternate explanations and wordings. The other strategy is to *underwrite*. In this approach, you jot down your ideas quickly, leaving gaps where points need to be expanded, making notations like "Insert a quote here." The disadvantage of this strategy is that it simply defers filling in the gaps until a later time, when it might be difficult to recapture your original train of thought. The advantage is that generating material quickly can make a long piece of writing more manageable and less forbidding. Some writers combine the two strategies—writing out parts of the paper fully but only sketching out those sections where getting all the details down would interrupt the flow of thought.

Whichever strategy you use, keep in mind that your draft shouldn't merely string together other people's words and ideas. Rather than simply presenting fact after fact or quotation after quotation, you must *analyze* and *comment on* your research, clearly showing how it supports your thesis. Similarly, when drafting the paper, be sure your language doesn't stay too close to that of your sources. To avoid over-reliance on your sources' language, refer to your note cards as you write, not to the sources themselves. Remember, too, that taking source material and merely changing a word here and there still constitutes *plagiarism*—passing off someone else's thoughts or language as your own. Such a charge is valid even if you acknowledge your source. (For more pointers on steering clear of plagiarism, see pages 477, 488–89, and 504–10.)

Presenting the Results of Primary Research

If your instructor requires you to conduct primary research (see pages 459–60), you might be tempted to include in the draft every bit of information you gathered through any surveys, experiments, or interviews you conducted. Remember, though, your primary purpose is to provide evidence for your thesis, so include only that material which furthers your goal. To preserve the draft's overall unity, you should also avoid the temptation to mass, without commentary, all your primary research in one section of the paper. Instead, insert the material at those places where it supports the points you want to make. Sometimes instructors will ask you to devote one part of the paper to a detailed discussion of the process you used to conduct primary research—everything from your methodology to a detailed interpretation of your results. In such a case, before writing your draft, ask your instructor where you should cover that information. Perhaps it should be placed in a separate introductory section or in an appendix.

DOCUMENT BORROWED MATERIAL: MLA FORMAT

How to Avoid Plagiarism

Copyright law and the ethics of research require that you give credit to those whose words and ideas you borrow; that is, you must provide full and accurate **documentation.** A lack of such documentation results in *plagiarism*—borrowing someone's ideas, facts, and words without properly crediting your source. Faulty documentation undermines your credibility. For one thing, readers may suspect that you're hiding something if you fail to identify your sources clearly. Further, readers planning follow-up research of their own will be perturbed if they have trouble locating your sources. Finally, weak documentation makes it difficult for readers to distinguish your ideas from those of your sources.

To avoid plagiarizing, you must provide documentation in the following situations:

- When you include a *word-for-word quotation* from a source.
- When you *summarize or restate in your own words* ideas or information from a source, *unless* that material is *commonly known* and *accepted* (whether or not you yourself were previously aware of it) *or* is a *matter of* historical or scientific record.
- When you *combine* a *summary* and a *quotation.*

One exception to formal documentation occurs in writing for the general public. For example, you may have noticed that the authors of this book's essays don't use full documentation when they borrow ideas. *Academic writers*, though, *must provide full documentation* for all borrowed information. The next section explains how to do this.

Indicate Author and Page

Both the MLA documentation system described here and the APA system described later in the chapter use the **parenthetic reference,** a brief note in parentheses inserted into the text after borrowed material. The parenthetic reference doesn't provide full bibliographic information, but it provides enough so that readers can turn to the Works Cited list for complete information. If the method of documentation you learned in high school involved footnotes or endnotes, you'll be happy to know that parenthetic documentation, which is currently preferred, is much easier to use and is accepted by most professors. To be on the safe side, though, check with your professors to determine their documentation preferences.

Whenever you use borrowed material, you must, within your paper's text, do two things. First, you must *identify the author*. (Since the Works Cited page is arranged according to authors' last names, readers can refer to that listing for title, publisher, and so on.) Second, you must *specify the page(s)* in your source on which the material appears.

Using Only Parentheses

The simplest way to provide documentation involves the use of *parentheses* for both *author* and *page* references. The examples that follow, based on references to George Gallup's "The Faltering Family" (pages 364–70), illustrate this method. (If you like, turn to Gallup's piece and compare the documentation with the original.)

Another factor contributing to changes in the family has been the "power of feminist philosophy to permeate attitudes . . ." (Gallup 368), as well as modify behavior.

It's clear that "we're confused . . . in our feelings about marriage and the family" (Gallup 369).

Even a brief review of history reveals that the "sexual revolution of the 1960s worked a profound change on our society's family values . . ." (Gallup 365).

In the early 1980s, most women believed that being married and having children would offer them the most satisfying life (Gallup 369).

Take a moment to look again at the preceding examples. Note the following:

What to Provide Within the Parentheses

- Give the author's last name only, even when the author is cited for the first time.
- Write the page number immediately after the author's last name, with no punctuation between. (If the source is only one page, only the author's name is needed.) Provide a full page range of the summary or quotation if it spans more than one page. Don't use the designation *p.* or *page*.

Where to Place the Parentheses

- Immediately *after* the borrowed material, at a natural pause in the sentence, or at the end of the sentence
- Before any internal punctuation (comma, semicolon) or terminal punctuation (period, question mark)

- After an ellipsis at the end of a quotation but before the final period. Note (see the third preceding example) that when there is a parenthetic citation, the period in the sentence follows rather than precedes the ellipsis. (See page 485 for information on when the period precedes the ellipsis.)

Using Parentheses and Attributions

Skilled writers indicate clearly where their ideas stop and those of their sources begin. So, besides providing careful parenthetic documentation, writers often provide **attributions**—nonparenthetical source identifiers like those (underlined) in the following *summary* statements:

<u>George Gallup states that</u> most families find they need dual incomes to meet the escalating costs of raising children--expenses that are, in practice, almost three times greater than parents imagine (368).

<u>In a recent poll,</u> more than half the adolescents surveyed expressed the view that divorce is taken too lightly nowadays (Gallup 369).

A *quotation* should also be inserted smoothly with an attribution. Don't just drop a quotation into your text, as in this example:

Incorrect

"The basic feminist philosophy has filtered down to the grass roots . . ." (Gallup 368).

Instead, provide an attribution for the quoted statement:

Correct

Gallup argues, "The basic feminist philosophy has filtered down to the grass roots . . ." (368).

One researcher points out that "the basic feminist philosophy has filtered down to the grass roots . . ." (Gallup 368).

Glance back at the examples on this page and note the following:

- An attribution may specify the author's name *(George Gallup states that; Gallup argues)*, or it may refer to a source more generally *(In a recent poll; One researcher points out)*.
- The first time an author is referred to in the text, the author's full name is provided; afterwards, only the last name is given.
- When the author's name is provided in the text, the name is *not* repeated in the parentheses. (Later nonparenthetic references to the same author give only the last name.)

Sometimes, to inform readers of an author's area of expertise, you may identify that person by profession (*Pollster* George Gallup). Don't, however, use such personal titles as *Mr.* or *Ms.* Finally, as part of an attribution, you may mention your source's title (In "The Faltering Family," Gallup maintains that . . .). No matter what information you include, try to vary your attributions. In addition to those already mentioned, you might try the following lead-ins, placing them wherever they fit best—at the beginning, middle, or end of the sentence:

As _____ states, . . .
The information compiled by _____ shows . . .
In _____'s opinion, . . .
_____ contends that . . .
_____'s study reveals that . . .

Also, aim for smooth, graceful attributions, avoiding such awkward constructions as these: "According to George Gallup, he says that . . ." and "In the essay by George Gallup, he argues that. . . ."

Special Cases of Authorship

In some situations, providing authorship in the attribution or in the parenthetic citation becomes slightly more complicated. The guidelines that follow will help you deal with special types of authorship.

More Than One Source by the Same Author. When your paper includes references to more than one work by the same author, you must specify the particular work being cited. You do this by providing the *title*, as well as the author's name and the page(s). As with the author's name, the title may be given in *either* the attribution *or* the parenthetic citation. Here are some examples:

In <u>The Language and Thought of the Child</u>, Jean Piaget states that "discussion forms the basis for a logical point of view" (240).

Piaget considers dialog essential to the development of logical thinking (<u>Language and Thought</u> 240).

<u>The Child's Conception of the World</u> shows that young children think that the name of something can never change (Piaget 81).

Young children assume that everything has only one name and that no others are possible (Piaget, <u>Child's Conception</u> 81).

Notice that when a work is named in the attribution, the full title appears; when a title is given in the parenthetic citation, only the first few significant words appear. (However, don't use the ellipsis to indicate that some words have been omitted from a title; the ellipsis is used only when quoting a source.) In the preceding examples, the work is a book, so its title is underlined. If the source is an article or a selection from a compilation, the title is placed in quotation marks.

Two or Three Authors. Supply all the authors' last names in either the attribution or parentheses.

More Than Three Authors. In either the attribution or parentheses, give the last name of the first author followed by *et al.* (which means "and others").

Two or More Authors With the Same Last Names. When you use two or more sources written by authors with the same last names, you must include (in either the attribution or parentheses) each author's first name or initial(s).

A Source With No Author. For a source without a named author, use, in your attribution or parenthetic reference, the title of the work *or* the name of the issuing organization—whichever you used to alphabetize the source on the Works Cited list.

Special Cases of Pagination

Occasionally, a source will have unusual pagination. Here's how to deal with such situations.

A Source With No Page Numbers. The parenthetic citation simply lacks a page number and the Works Cited list indicates "unpaged" with the abbreviation *N. pag.*

Each Volume of a Multivolume Source Paged Separately. Indicate the volume number, then the page number, with a colon between the two (Kahn 3:246). Do not use *vol.* or *v.*

A Nonprint Source (Television Show, Lecture, Interview). In a parenthetic citation, give only the item (title, speaker, person interviewed) you used to alphabetize the source on your Works Cited list. Or provide the identifying information in the attribution, thus eliminating the need for parenthetic information:

In the documentary Financing a College Education, Cheryl Snyder states that. . . .

More About Quotations

On the whole, you should try to state borrowed material in your own words. A string of quotations signals that you haven't sufficiently evaluated and distilled your sources. Use quotations sparingly; draw upon them only when they dramatically illustrate key points you want to make. Also, keep in mind that quotations won't, by themselves, make your case for you. You need to interpret and comment on them, showing how they support your points.

Besides following the guidelines on pages 484–85 for using ellipses and brackets, you should be familiar with the following capitalization and punctuation conventions when quoting.

Capitalization and Punctuation of Short Quotations

The way a short quotation is used in a sentence determines whether it begins with a capital letter and is preceded by a comma.

1. When blending a quotation into the structure of your own sentence, *don't capitalize* the quotation's *first word* and *don't precede it with a comma:*

Gallup observes that "the woman who doesn't hold any sort of outside job but stays at home to care for her children represents a small percentage of wives today" (368).

Even if—as in this case—the material being quoted originally started with a capital letter, you still use lowercase when incorporating the quotation into your own sentence. Quotations often *merge* with your own words in this way when they are introduced, as in the preceding example, by a pronoun *(that, which, who)*—either stated or implied.

2. When an attribution introduces a quotation that can stand alone as a sentence, *do capitalize* the quotation's *first word.* Also, *precede the quotation with a comma:*

According to Gallup, "The woman who doesn't hold any sort of outside job but stays at home to care for her children represents a small percentage of wives today" (368).

Gallup observes, "The woman who doesn't hold any sort of outside job but stays at home to care for her children represents a small percentage of wives today" (368).

3. If, for variety, you *interrupt a full-sentence quotation* with an attribution, *place commas on both sides of the attribution,* and *resume* the quotation with a *lowercase* letter:

"Few women," Gallup comments, "are likely to give up their jobs" (368).

Long Quotations

A quotation extending beyond four typed lines starts on a new line and is indented ten spaces from the left margin throughout its length. Since this so-called **block format** already indicates a quotation, quotation marks are unnecessary. Double-space the block quotation, as you do the rest of your paper. Long quotations, which should be used sparingly, require a lead-in. A lead-in that *isn't* a full sentence is followed by a comma, whereas a lead-in that *is* a full sentence (as in the following example) is followed by a colon:

Gallup cites changed sexual mores as one reason for the decline of marriage:

> Clearly, attitudes have changed a great deal in just three decades. Teenagers have accepted the idea of premarital sex as the norm. In one recent national poll, 52 percent of girls and 66 percent of boys favored having sexual relations in their teens. Ironically, however, 46 percent of the teenagers thought that virginity in their future marital partner was fairly important. (367)

Notice that the page number appears in parentheses, just as in a short quotation. But in a long quotation, the parentheses come two spaces *after* the period that ends the quotation.

Quoting or Summarizing a Source Within a Source

If you quote or summarize a *secondary source* (someone whose ideas come to you only through another source), you need to make this clear. The parenthetic documentation should indicate "as quoted in" with the abbreviation *qtd. in:*

According to Sherman, "Recycling has, in several communities, created unanticipated expenses" (qtd. in Pratt 3).

Sherman explains that recycling can be surprisingly costly (qtd. in Pratt 3).

If the material you're quoting includes a quotation, place single quotation marks around the secondary quotation:

Pratt believes that "recycling efforts will be successful if, as Sherman argues, 'communities launch effective public-education campaigns' " (2).

Note: Your Works Cited list should include the source you actually read (Pratt), rather than the source you refer to secondhand (Sherman).

REVISE, EDIT, AND PROOFREAD THE FIRST DRAFT

After completing your first draft, reward yourself with a break. Set the paper aside for a while, as least for a few hours. When you pick up the draft later, you'll have a fresh, more objective point of view on it. Then, referring to the checklist on pages 94–95 and the first section of the revision checklist that follows, reread your entire draft to get a general sense of how well the paper works. Outlining the draft (see page 94)—*without* referring to the outline that guided the draft's preparation—is a good way to evaluate the paper's overall meaning and structure.

Despite all the work you've done, you may find when you reread the paper that a main point in support of your thesis seems weak. Sometimes a review of your note cards—including those you didn't use for your draft—will uncover appropriate material that you can add to the paper. Other times, though, you may need another trip to the library to gather additional information. Once you're confident that the paper's overall meaning and structure are strong, go ahead and write your introduction and conclusion—if you haven't already done so.

That done, move ahead and evaluate your paper's paragraph development. To focus your revision, use the checklist on pages 96–97, as well as the second section of the revision checklist that follows. As you work, it's a good idea to pay special attention to the way you present evidence in the paragraphs. Does your evidence consist of one quotation after another, or do you express borrowed ideas in your own words? Do you simply insert borrowed material without commentary, or do you interpret the material and show its relevance to the points you want to make?

Before moving to the next stage in the revision process, look closely at the way you introduce borrowed material. If you had prepared the draft without providing many attributions, now is the time to supply them. Then, consulting the checklists on pages 116 and 127, as well as the third section of the revision checklist that follows, go ahead and refine your draft's words and sentences.

Finally, when you start editing and proofreading, allow enough time to verify the accuracy of quoted and summarized material. Check such material against your note cards, and check your documentation against both your bibliography cards and Works Cited list, making sure everything matches. When preparing the final copy of your paper, follow the format guidelines on pages 134–36, using the sample research paper (pages 516–26) as a model. Note that the research paper, when accompanied by an outline, has a separate title page. For a research paper without an outline, the title and other identifying information are usually placed at the top of the paper's first page.

Chapters 7, 8, and 9 discuss techniques for revising and editing an essay draft. The following checklist will help you and those giving you feedback apply those techniques to the research paper.

> ✓ REVISING THE RESEARCH PAPER: A CHECKLIST
>
> *Revise Overall Meaning and Structure*
> ☐ What is the thesis of the research paper? Where is it stated? How could the thesis be expressed more clearly?
> ☐ Where would background material or a definition of terms clarify overall meaning?
> ☐ Where does research evidence (facts, statistics, expert opinion, surveys, and experimental results) seem irrelevant or contradict the thesis? What can be done to correct these problems?

- What principle of organization (chronological, spatial, emphatic, simple-to-complex) does the paper use? How does this organizing principle reinforce the paper's thesis and make it easy for readers to follow the paper's line of reasoning?

Revise Paragraph Development

- In which paragraphs is evidence solid and compelling? Where is it confusing, insufficient, irrelevant, too abstract, inaccurate, nonrepresentative, or predictable? How can these problems be remedied?
- Which paragraphs merely present research, without analyzing and relating it to the thesis? How can the research material be better incorporated into the paper's point of view?
- Which paragraphs simply string together quotations, without interpretative commentary? Where is commentary needed? Which quotations could be eliminated?

Revise Sentences and Words

- Where is more documentation needed to avoid plagiarism? Where do another author's words appear but without quotation marks? Where is a source's language only slightly modified? Which borrowed ideas are summarized but not credited?
- Where would attributions help signal more clearly where a source's ideas begin and stop?
- How could attributions be made more graceful and varied?

Edit and Proofread

- Where is parenthetic documentation lacking required information? Where must an author's name, a title, publication data, or page numbers be added?
- Which parenthetic citations contain punctuation errors? Where should a title be underlined or placed in quotation marks? Where should a comma be added or deleted?
- Where are quotations punctuated incorrectly? Which should start with a capital letter? Which should begin in lowercase? Which should be preceded by a comma? Which should not? Where should a capital letter be deleted? Where is a comma needed to connect the quote to the text? Where should a comma be deleted?
- Where is the format for long quotations incorrect? How can it be corrected?
- Where is the format for the Works Cited list incorrect? Which entries are out of alphabetical order? Which titles should be underlined or placed in quotations? Where should commas or periods be added or deleted? Where should page numbers be added?

APA DOCUMENTATION FORMAT

MLA documentation style is appropriate for research papers written for courses in the humanities, such as your composition course. Researchers in the social sciences and in education use a different citation format, one developed by the American Psychological Association (APA). If you're writing a paper for a course in sociology, psychology, anthropology, economics, or political science, your professor will probably expect **APA-style documentation.** History, philosophy, and religion are sometimes considered humanities, sometimes social sciences, depending on your approach to the topic.

Parenthetic Citations

As in the MLA format, APA citations are enclosed in parentheses within the text and provide the author's last name. The main difference between the two formats is that the APA parenthetic note always includes the year of publication but gives the page number only with a quotation, not with a summary. Also, APA citations are punctuated—with commas between the author's name and the year and between the year and the page. Finally, *p.* or *pp.* appears before the page number(s).

Here are some examples of APA parenthetic citations from an anthropology paper:

APA Format

In Java, "it is 'shock,' not suffering itself, which is feared" (Geertz, 1973, p. 154).

Javanese mourning rituals are designed to mute death's finality (Geertz, 1973).

If the same source were cited in a research paper prepared for a course in the humanities, it would be given in the MLA style:

MLA Format

In Java, "it is 'shock,' not suffering itself, which is feared" (Geertz 154).

Javanese mourning rituals are designed to mute death's finality (Geertz 154).

In the APA format, if you lead into a quotation with an attribution that gives the author's name, the publication year follows the author's name in parentheses, and the page number appears at the end of the quotation:

Hemrick (1988) maintains that only "a massive publicity campaign will convince Americans that psychologists really do help people" (p. 57).

If a work has two authors, cite both authors, joined by an ampersand (&), in the attribution or in the parenthetic citation. If a work has three to five authors, name all authors in the first citation. In subsequent citations, name only the first author followed by *et al.* If there are six or more authors, cite the first author followed by *et al.*

References List

As in the MLA style, an alphabetical list of sources appears at the end of a research paper using APA documentation style. However, whereas the MLA titles this list Works Cited, the APA gives it the heading **References.**

The MLA and APA formats for listing sources include the same basic information, but they present it in different ways. Here are some of the distinguishing features of APA-style entries:

- The publication date is placed in parentheses directly after the author's name and is followed by a period.
- Two or more works by the same author are arranged according to publication date, with the earliest appearing first.
- An author's works published in the same year are differentiated by lowercase letters—(1986a), (1986b)—and are alphabetized by title.
- All authors' names, no matter how many, are given in the reference. When there are two or more authors, use the ampersand instead of *and*.
- All authors' names are inverted. In addition, an author's first and middle names are represented by initials only.
- Only the first letter of a book or article title (and subtitle) and any proper names contained within it are capitalized.
- If an entry extends beyond one line of type, all subsequent lines are indented three spaces.

Here's a sample APA-style reference for a *book with a single author:*

Thompson, W. I. (1976). Evil and world order. New York: Harper.

What about articles listed on the References page? Unlike the MLA, the APA uses no quotation marks around article titles. And, as noted, only the first word of an article's title and subtitle is capitalized. However, as in the MLA style, all major words in the name of the periodical are capitalized and underlined. Finally, inclusive page numbers are required for all types of articles. The page numbers are preceded by *p.* or *pp.* for articles in newspapers, magazines, and anthologies, but not for articles in scholarly journals.

Here are sample APA listings for articles:

Magazine Article

Holden, C. (1985, January). Genes, personality and alcoholism. Psychology Today, pp. 38, 42-44.

Journal Article

Driskill, L. P., & Goldstein, J. R. (1986). Uncertainty: Theory and practice in organizational communication. <u>Journal of Business Communication,</u> <u>23</u>(3), 41-56.

Article in a Book-Length Anthology

Winter, E. H. (1966). Territorial groupings and religion among the Iraqw. In M. Banton (Ed.), <u>Anthropological approaches to the study of religion</u> (pp. 155-174). London: Tavistock.

More information about APA documentation format can be found in the latest edition of the *Publication Manual of the American Psychological Association.*

A NOTE ABOUT OTHER DOCUMENTATION SYSTEMS

Generally, professionals in the hard sciences (biology, chemistry, medicine, physics) and technical fields (computer science and electrical engineering) use neither the MLA nor the APA system of documentation. Rather, using bracketed or superscripted (raised) reference numbers, they key each item of borrowed material to an entry on the References page. The References list, therefore, isn't alphabetized; instead, the numbered sources simply appear in the order in which they are mentioned in the paper.

When you write a paper for a science course, ask your professor whether you should use the MLA, APA, or the system found in most science and technical journals. If your instructor prefers the latter, find out which publication can serve as your model. That way, you won't be unpleasantly surprised by any criticism that you've used an inappropriate system of documentation.

STUDENT RESEARCH PAPER: MLA-STYLE DOCUMENTATION

The sample outline and research paper that follow were written by Brian Courtney for a composition class. In his paper, Brian uses the MLA documentation system. To help you spot various types of sources, quotations, and attributions, we've annotated the paper. Our marginal comments also flag key elements, such as the paper's thesis statement, plan of development, and concluding summary.

Note that the main headings in Brian's outline parallel, to a large degree, the topic sentences of the paper's paragraphs; subheadings generally represent the points that develop those paragraphs. The outline contains no sections corresponding to Brian's introduction and conclusion because he wrote those only after completing the body of his paper. As you read the paper, pay special attention to the way Brian incorporates source material and uses it to support his own ideas.

Although a title page isn't necessary, you may be asked to provide one.

A paper with an outline often has a separate title page.

Title begins about one-third down the page.

Center the title. Double-space between lines of the title and your name.

Course and section, instructor's name, and date, on seperate lines, are double-spaced and centered.

A paper *without* an outline has no title page. Instead, type —on separate lines —your name, the instructor's name, the course number, and the date on the first page. Place this information, double-spaced, one inch from the top of the page, flush with the left margin.

Double-space again and center the title. If the title runs more than one line, double-space between lines.

Double-space between the title and first line of text.

America's Homeless:

How the Government Can Help

by

Brian Courtney

English 101, Section 19

Professor Janko

8 May 1993

Courtney i

Outline

Thesis: The federal government should do more for the homeless.

  I. Homelessness is a major problem in the United States.
      A. There are millions of homeless.
      B. The number of homeless is increasing.
      C. Homeless people are in every region of the country.
 II. There are too few overnight shelters, and these don't solve the problem.
      A. Even if the homeless get enough to eat and have a place to sleep, they still spend most of their time on the street.
      B. Shelters don't teach the homeless the skills they need to change their lives.
III. Some programs, like CORPP and DRC, do teach the homeless how to be independent.
      A. They offer detoxification and rehabilitation programs.
      B. They provide follow-up care.
 IV. Some programs provide troubled homeless people with psychological counseling.
      A. Many of the homeless are teenage runaways.
      B. Many are recovering from disrupted marriages.
      C. Many are mentally disabled.
  V. Some programs provide training in everyday survival skills.
      A. They provide pointers on personal hygiene.
      B. They provide instruction on money management.
          1. They explain how to spend money wisely.
          2. They explain how to save for essentials.
          3. They explain how to apply for government benefits.

Courtney ii

VI. Some programs help the homeless get a job.
   A. Many of the homeless have no jobs.
   B. Many need job and interview training.
   C. Groups like CORPP and DRC have shown that job training can succeed.

VII. The government should help fund programs like CORPP and DRC.
   A. Such programs are expensive.
   B. They can handle only a few clients.
   C. They don't have the resources to expand.

VIII. The government should also raise the minimum wage.
   A. Many of the homeless hold jobs, but their incomes are paltry.
   B. Many don't earn enough to pay for housing.

IX. The government should finance more public housing.
   A. The cost of housing has risen sharply.
   B. There isn't enough federally subsidized low-cost housing.
     1. The government has cut back its funding.
     2. HUD has been corrupt.
   C. There isn't enough affordable private housing.
     1. The number of affordable private units is decreasing.
     2. More rent-controlled units are needed.

Courtney 1

America's Homeless: How the Government Can Help

They rummage through trash cans and solicit spare change. They lie on the floors of public restrooms. Seeking warmth, they huddle over sidewalk steam grates. At the age of thirty, they look fifty-five. "They" are the homeless, and they represent a growing percentage of America's population. Indeed, homelessness has reached such massive proportions that the private sector and local governments can't possibly cope. To help the homeless toward independence, the federal government must support rehabilitation and training programs, raise the minimum wage, and fund more low-cost housing.

Not everyone agrees on the number of Americans who are homeless. Conservative estimates indicate that there are more than 700,000 homeless people in our country (Foscarinis 1233); however, a 1988 estimate numbers the homeless at roughly 3 million (Fabricant and Kelly 99). Although their figures may vary, experts agree that the number continues to increase at an alarming rate. Peter Marcuse, a professor of urban planning at Columbia University, notes that the number of people using New York City shelters was more than three times larger in 1986 than in 1982 (426). One of the federal government's own studies projected that the number of homeless Americans will reach nearly 19 million by the year 2003 (Kozol 73).

As the number of homeless increases, Americans inevitably become more aware of the problem. A nationwide telephone survey done by the New York Times and CBS News on January 6-8, 1992, indicated that nearly 60 percent of Americans now encounter homeless people during the

Courtney 2

course of a typical day. This statistic reverses the results of a similar survey done in 1986; at that time, nearly 60 percent of Americans said they knew about homelessness only through the media and not through personal observations (Steinfels A1).

It's not just city dwellers in the Northeast who come face to face with the homeless. Nowadays the homeless can be found in all regions of America. In the words of investigative reporter Jonathan Kozol,

> The homeless are not just in midtown Manhattan. They are also in the streets of Phoenix, Salt Lake City, Philadelphia, San Antonio, Miami, and St. Paul. They are in the Steel Belt. They are in the Sun Belt. They are in Kansas City and in Seattle. (17)

Clearly, there are too few shelters to accommodate this growing homeless population. Besides, even when the homeless manage to find a shelter that will give them three meals a day and a place to sleep at night, they still spend the bulk of each day wandering the street. Mary Orton, director of a state shelter service, sums up the problem when she says that having "three hots and a cot" (qtd. in Whitman 26) helps, but it doesn't enable the homeless to acquire the skills they need to stay off the street.

Where can the homeless go to learn these crucial life skills? One such place is the Community Occupations Readiness and Placement Program (CORPP), a small nonprofit organization in Philadelphia. As media coverage shows, many of the homeless are addicted to alcohol and drugs. CORPP faces this problem head-on. In a telephone

Courtney 3

interview, Vivian Norton, CORPP's Director of Adult Services, explained that her organization offers detoxification and rehabilitation programs, including intensive follow-ups to ensure that clients remain sober and drug-free. The Diagnostic Rehabilitation Center (DRC), another small grass-roots agency in Philadelphia, offers similar rehabilitative and follow-up service (Whitman 26).

Norton explained that her organization's follow-ups often take the form of psychological counseling. One-to-one sessions help not only recovering addicts but other homeless individuals as well: runaway teenagers, some of whom are pregnant; those trying to recover (emotionally and financially) from separation, divorce, or the death of a spouse). Then, too, there are the mentally disabled who have been released from institutions yet are unable to care for themselves in the outside world. For this group, follow-up often involves referral to community mental health agencies. Norton commented that these various individuals "always find somebody at CORPP to listen."

In addition to receiving psychological support, many of the homeless need instruction in everyday survival skills. CORPP gives pointers on personal hygiene and provides training in money management, teaching clients how to spend money wisely and save it for essentials like apartment security deposits. As Norton pointed out, many homeless are unaware of their eligibility for government benefits, so CORPP gives them the necessary information--showing them, for example, how to apply for and use food stamps.

Job training is another essential, especially because so many homeless are unemployed. A study of Chicago's

Courtney 4

homeless found that one in five had no income at all. Many more had income only from Social Security, welfare, veterans' and other benefits, but not from a steady job (Rossi et al. 1338). At CORPP and DRC, the homeless are given job and interview preparation. The results? CORPP has a job-placement rate ten times that of the national average for rehabilitation programs (Norton); 70 percent of those completing DRC's program now live on their own (Whitman 34).

Unfortunately, programs such as CORPP and DRC are costly to operate and can handle only a limited number of clients. The organizations are barely surviving on donations from private citizens and allocations from local governments. At any given time, CORPP's job-training program can accommodate no more than twenty people (Norton) and DRC's no more than thirty-five (Whitman 31).

It would be logical, given their track records, for CORPP and DRC to expand. Without government assistance, though, they lack the financial resources to grow. Similarly, these successful organizations should serve as models for other grass-roots programs throughout the country. But again, federal support is needed to establish a network of agencies committed to helping the homeless.

Besides funding local programs for the homeless, the government should act to raise the minimum wage. Many of the homeless have jobs, but their incomes are inadequate. A team of researchers headed by Peter Rossi found that the homeless in Chicago had an average income 2.6 times lower than the national poverty level (1338). In The New American Poverty, Michael Harrington describes the problem this way:

Courtney 5

"The minimum wage . . . is so low that men and women can work full time and not be able to provide minimum necessities for their families" (110).

13 Surely one of the most basic necessities is housing. Yet a low wage can't begin to cover the cost of housing, which has risen sharply in recent years. From 1970 to 1980, the median price of a house more than tripled; so did rents. According to Levitan, Belous, and Gallo, "These increases far surpassed the rate of inflation" (170). In the 1980s, additional factors, such as increased interest rates for home loans and several recessions, led to less housing construction and bigger pricetags on houses (Kiesler 1248).

14 There simply isn't enough federally subsidized public housing for all those seeking relief from such inflated costs. In Newark, New Jersey, alone, some 11,000 families are on a waiting list for low-cost public housing (McKillop 20). Yet, instead of increasing federal housing subsidies, the government has cut back. Kozol notes that "from 1981 to 1987 . . . federal funds for building or rehabilitating low-income housing" dropped from 32 to 9 billion (72). In addition, as the media revealed in 1989, widespread corruption in the Department of Housing and Urban Development (HUD) led to millions of these dollars being misspent. It is, then, an understatement to say, as New Jersey State Assemblyman David Schwartz has, that the country suffers from "the absence of an effective [public] housing policy. . ." (109).

15 Private housing has also failed the homeless. Affordable privately owned units are rapidly disappearing (Mathews 58). As an article in the UNESCO Courier explains,

Courtney 6

property owners aren't eager to operate low-rent units when it is much more profitable to rent at the higher rates the market will bear ("World's Homeless" 19).

There seems to be no alternative: The government must take a more active role in resolving the housing crisis. The government's own National Housing Task Force reported that federal efforts to date weren't enough to guarantee acceptable, reasonably priced housing (McQueen 68). Yet, in the wake of the HUD scandal, the government has pulled back from building additional low-income housing. Under such circumstances, there is all the more reason for the government to intervene in some other way. It could, for example, require private owners to set aside a certain percentage of units as rent controlled (with a base rent, established by law, and limited increases). Certainly, owners won't take such action on their own.

No matter what the source of a homeless person's problem, the federal government must increase its support for programs that help. These programs must do more than provide emergency food and shelter; they must also offer drug and alcohol rehabilitation, psychological counseling, instruction in basic survival skills, and job training. Nor should the government stop there. Even a skilled, well-adjusted individual may lack adequate housing unless the government guarantees a decent minimum wage and affordable housing. The government can't continue to walk past the homeless, face averted. In doing so, it walks past millions in need.

Courtney 7

Works Cited

Fabricant, Michael, and Michael Kelly. "The Problem of ⟵ Article from collection
    Homelessness Is Serious." Poverty. Ed. William Dudley.
    St. Paul: Greenhaven, 1988. 98-104

Foscarinis, Maria. "The Politics of Homelessness: A Call to ⟵ Article from a scholarly journal that pages issues continuously
    Action." American Psychologist 46 (1991): 1232-37.

Harrington, Michael. "Uprooted." The New American
    Poverty. New York: Holt, 1984. 95-122. ⟵ Chapter from a book — publisher's name shortened

Kiesler, Charles A. "Homelessness and Public Policy
    Priorities." American Psychologist 45 (1991): 1245-52.

Kozol, Jonathan. "The Homeless and Their Children." New ⟵ Article from a weekly magazine that doesn't page issues continuously
    Yorker 25 Jan. 1988: 65-84.

Levitan, Sar, Richard S. Belous, and Frank Gallo. What's ⟵ Book, revised edition, with three authors
    Happening to the American Family? Rev. ed. Baltimore:
    Johns Hopkins UP, 1988.

Marcuse, Peter. "Why Are They Homeless?" Nation 4 Apr.
    1987: 426-29.

Mathews, Tom. "Homelessness in America: What Can Be
    Done?" Newsweek 21 Mar. 1988: 57-58.

McKillop, Peter. "They Should Never Have Built It."
    Newsweek 4 Jan. 1988: 20.

McQueen, Michael. "Housing Panel Report Recommends ⟵ Article from a newspaper
    Plan to Steer U.S. Funds to States, Localities." Wall
    Street Journal 29 Mar. 1988, natl. ed., sec. A:18.

Norton, Vivian. Telephone interview. 9 Aug. 1989. ⟵ Interview

Rossi, Peter H., et al. "The Urban Homeless: Estimating ⟵ Journal article with more than three authors
    Composition and Size." Science 235 (1987): 1335-41.

Schwartz, David C. "Wanted: A New Housing Policy."
    Journal of Housing 44.3 (1987): 109.

Courtney 8

Steinfels, Peter. "Apathy Is Seen Greeting Agony of
    Homeless." <u>New York Times</u> 20 Jan. 1992, natl. ed.:
    sec A:1.

Whitman, David. "Hope for the Homeless." <u>U.S. News &
    World Report</u> 29 Feb. 1988: 25+.

"The World's Homeless Millions." <u>UNESCO Courier</u> Jan.
    1987: 18-19.

Anonymous article

Commentary

Brian begins his introduction with an evocative description of a typical street person's struggle to survive. These descriptive passages prepare readers for a general statement of the problem of homelessness. This two-sentence statement, starting with " 'They' are the homeless" and ending with "the private sector and local governments can't possibly cope," leads the way to Brian's *thesis:* "To help the homeless toward independence, the federal government must support rehabilitation and training programs, raise the minimum wage, and fund more low-cost housing."

By researching his subject thoroughly, Brian was able to marshal many compelling facts and opinions. He sorted through this complex web of material and arrived at a logical structure that reinforced his thesis. He describes the extent of the problem (paragraphs 2–5), analyzes some of the causes of the problem (6–10, 12–15), and points to solutions (6–9, 16–17). He frequently draws upon *statistics* to establish the severity of the problem and quotes *expert opinion* to demonstrate the need for particular types of programs. Note, too, that Brian writes in the *present tense* and uses the *third-person point of view*—even when discussing material he gathered from an interview.

Beyond being clearly organized and maintaining a consistent point of view, the paper is *unified* and *coherent.* For one thing, Brian makes it easy for readers to follow his line of thought. He often uses *transitions:* "Besides" (5), "Then, too" (7), "In addition" (8), and so forth. In other places, he asks a *question* (for example, at the beginning of the sixth paragraph), or he uses a *bridging sentence* (for instance, at the beginning of the fourth and eighth paragraphs). Moreover, he always provides clear attributions and parenthetic references so that readers know at every point along the way whose idea is being presented. Brian has, in short, prepared a well-written, carefully documented paper.

ACTIVITIES: WRITING THE RESEARCH PAPER

1. Imagine that you've just written a research paper exploring how parents can ease their children's passage through adolescence. Prepare a *Works Cited* list for the following sources, putting all information in the correct MLA format.

   a. "Pictures of the Family," a chapter in Phillipe Arles's book titled *Centuries of Childhood* and subtitled *A Social History of Family Life.* The chapter runs from page 339 to 364. The American edition was translated by Robert Baldick and published by Random House (New York) in 1962.

b. One radio broadcast within a series called *Family Matters,* hosted by Dr. Daniel Gottlieb and produced by Laura Jackson. The broadcast, titled "Understanding Adolescents," was aired on 16 September 1989, on WHYY-FM of Philadelphia, PA, and Wilmington, DE.

c. An article titled "Transitions to Parenthood: His, Hers, and Theirs," by Carolyn Pape Cowan and six coauthors. The article appeared in volume 6, number 4 (1985) of the *Journal of Family Issues* and ran from page 451 to 481.

d. A book and an article by Laurence Steinberg. The book, *Adolescence,* was published in 1985 by Alfred A. Knopf, Publishers (New York). The article, "Bound to Bicker," appeared on pages 62–65 in the September/October 1989 issue of *Psychology Today.*

e. A thirty-page guidebook issued in January 1988 by the U.S. Department of Education. The guidebook was titled *AIDS and the Education of Our Children* and subtitled *A Guide for Parents and Teachers.*

f. An article from pages 1 and 74 of the November 27, 1977 issue of the *New York Times.* The article, by Jon Nordheimer, is titled "The Family in Transition: A Challenge From Within."

g. Chapter 16, "Social and Personality Development in Adolescence," pages 511–46, of *A Child's World: Infancy Through Adolescence,* by Diane E. Papalia and Sally Wendkos Olds. The book, in its fourth edition, was published in 1986 by McGraw-Hill Book Company of New York.

h. A public lecture given at your college the first day of last week. Psychologist Julia Rafsky's topic was "A New Perspective on Adolescence."

2. Assume you're writing a research paper showing that American English reflects stereotyped cultural attitudes toward males and females. You want to include ideas presented in paragraphs 11–19 of Alleen Pace Nilsen's essay "Sexism and Language" (page 243). To practice using attributions, parenthetic citations, and correct punctuation with quoted material, do the following:

a. Choose a statement from these paragraphs to quote. Then write a sentence that includes the quotation, specific attribution, and the appropriate parenthetic citation.

b. Choose an idea to summarize from these paragraphs. Then write a sentence that includes the summary, a general attribution, and the appropriate parenthetic documentation.

c. Find a place in the source where the author quotes another person. Use this quotation as the basis for two sentences:

- One in which you quote the person quoted by the source
- One in which you summarize the ideas of the person quoted by the source

Each sentence should include the appropriate attribution and parenthetic citation.

PART V

THE LITERARY PAPER AND EXAM ESSAY

23
WRITING ABOUT LITERATURE

DOES the idea of writing a **literary analysis** make you anxious? If it does, we'd like to reassure you that in some ways writing a literary analysis is easier than writing other kinds of essays. For one thing, you don't have to root around, trying to figure out what you want to accomplish: Your purpose in any literary analysis is simply to share with readers some insights about an aspect of a poem, play, story, or novel.* Second, in a literary analysis, your thesis and supporting evidence grow directly out of your reading of the text. All you have to do is select the textual evidence that supports your thesis.

By examining both *what* the author says and *how* he or she expresses it, you increase your readers' understanding and appreciation of the work. And, of course, literary analysis rewards you as well. Close textual analysis develops your ability to think critically and independently. Studying literature also strengthens your own writing. As you examine literary works, you become familiar with the strategies that skilled writers use to convey meaning with eloquence and power. Finally, since literature deals with the largest, most timeless issues, literary analysis is one way to learn more about yourself, others, and life in general.

---

*For the sake of simplifying a complex subject, we discuss literary analysis as though it focuses on a single work. In practice, though, a literary analysis often examines two or more works.

ELEMENTS OF LITERARY WORKS

Before you can analyze a literary text, you need to become familiar with literature's key elements. The following list of literary terms will help you understand what to look for when reading and writing about literature.

List of Literary Terms

Theme: a work's controlling idea, the main issue the work addresses (for example, loyalty to an individual versus loyalty to a cause; the destructive power of a lie). Most literary analyses deal with theme, even if the analysis focuses on the methods by which that theme is conveyed.

Plot: the series of events that occurs within the work. Typically, plays and stories hinge on plot much more heavily than poetry, which is often constructed around images and ideas rather than actions.

Structure: a work's form, as determined by plot construction, act and scene divisions, stanza and line breaks, repeated images, patterns of meter and rhyme, and other elements that create discernible patterns. (See also *stanza, image, meter,* and *rhyme.*)

Setting: the time and place in which events unfold (the present, on a hot New York City subway car; a nineteenth-century sailing vessel in the South Pacific).

Character: an individual within a poem, play, story, or novel (Tom Sawyer, Ophelia, Oliver Twist).

Characterization: the way in which the author develops an individual within the work.

Conflict: a struggle between individuals, between an individual and some social or environmental force, or within an individual.

Climax: the most dramatic point in the action, usually near the end of a work and usually involving the resolution of conflict.

Foreshadowing: hints, within the work, of events to come.

Narrator or **speaker:** the individual in the work who relates the story. It's important to remember that the narrator is not the same as the author. The opening of Mark Twain's *Huckleberry Finn* makes this distinction especially clear: "You don't know me, without you have read a book by the name of *The Adventures of Tom Sawyer,* but that ain't no matter. That book was made by Mr. Mark Twain, and he told the truth, mainly." A poorly educated boy named Huck Finn is the narrator; it is *his* captivating but ungrammatical voice that we hear. In contrast, Twain, the author, was a sophisticated middle-aged man whose command of the language was impeccable.

Point of view: the perspective from which a story is told. In the **first-person** ("I") point of view, the narrator tells the story as he or she experienced it ("*I* saw the bird flap its wings"). The first-person narrator either participates in or observes the action. In the **third-person** point of view, the narrator tells the story the way someone else experienced it ("*Dave* saw the bird flap its wings"). The third-person narrator is not involved in the action. He or she may simply report outwardly observable behavior or events, enter the mind of only one character, or enter the minds of several characters. Such a third-person narrator may be *omniscient* (all-knowing) or have only *limited knowledge* of characters and events.

Irony: a discrepancy or incongruity of some kind. *Verbal irony*, which is often tongue-in-cheek, involves a discrepancy between the literal words and what is actually meant ("Here's some news that will make you sad. You received the highest grade in the course"). If the ironic comment is designed to be hurtful or insulting, it qualifies as *sarcasm* ("Congratulations! You failed the final exam."). In *dramatic irony*, the discrepancy is between what the speaker says and what the author means or what the audience knows. The wider the gap between the speaker's words and what can be inferred about the author's attitudes and values, the more ironic the point of view.

Satire: ridicule (either harsh or gentle) of vice or folly, with the purpose of developing awareness—even bringing about reform. Besides using wit, satire often employs irony to attack absurdity, injustice, and evil.

Figure of speech: a non-literal comparison of dissimilar things. The most common figures of speech are **similes,** which use the word *like* or *as* ("*Like* a lightning bolt, the hawk streaked across the sky"); **metaphors,** which state or imply that one thing *is* another ("All the world's a stage"); and **personification,** which gives human attributes to something nonhuman ("The angry clouds unleashed their fury").

Image: a short, vivid description that creates a strong sensory impression ("A black flag writhed in the wind").

Imagery: a combination of images.

Symbol: an object, place, characteristic, or phenomenon that suggests one or more things (usually abstract) in addition to itself (rain as mourning; a lost wedding ring as betrayal). Usually, though, symbols don't convey meaning in pat, unambiguous ways. Rain, for example, may suggest purification as well as mourning; a lost wedding ring may suggest a life-affirming break from a destructive marriage as well as betrayal.

Motif: a recurring word, phrase, image, figure of speech, or symbol that has particular significance.

Meter: a basic, fixed rhythm of accented and unaccented syllables that the lines of a particular poem follow.

Rhyme: a match between two or more words' final sounds (*Cupid, stupid; mark, park*).

Stanza: two or more lines of a poem that are grouped together. A stanza is preceded and followed by some blank space.

Alliteration: repetition of initial consonant sounds (such as the "b" sounds in "A *b*utterfly *b*looms on a *b*uttercup").

Assonance: repetition of vowel sounds (like the "a" sounds in "m*a*d *a*s *a* h*a*tter").

Sonnet: a fourteen-line, single-stanza poem following a strict pattern of meter and rhyme. The Italian, or *Petrarchan*, sonnet consists of two main parts: eight lines in the rhyme pattern *a b b a, a b b a,* followed by six lines in the pattern *c d c, c d c* or *c d e, c d e*. The English, or *Shakespearean*, sonnet consists of twelve lines in the rhyme scheme *a b a b, c d c d, e f e f,* followed by two rhymed lines *g g*. Traditionally, sonnets are love poems that involve some change in tone or outlook near the end.

HOW TO READ A LITERARY WORK

Read to Form a General Impression

The first step in analyzing a literary work is to read it through for an overall impression. Do you like the work? What does the writer seem to be saying? Do you have a strong reaction to the work? Why or why not?

Ask Questions About the Work

One way to focus your initial impressions is to ask yourself questions about the literary work. You could, for example, select from the following checklist those items that interest you the most or those that seem most relevant to the work you're analyzing.

> ☑ **ANALYZING A LITERARY WORK: A CHECKLIST**
>
> - What *themes* appear in the work? How do *structure, plot, characterization, imagery,* and other literary strategies reinforce theme?
> - What gives the work its *structure* or shape? Why might the author have chosen this form? If the work is a poem, how do *meter, rhyme, alliteration, assonance,* and *line breaks* emphasize key ideas? Where does the work divide into parts? What words and images are repeated? What patterns do they form?
> - How is the *plot* developed? Where is there any *foreshadowing*? What are the points of greatest suspense? Which *conflicts* add tension? How are they resolved? Where does the *climax* occur? What does the *resolution* accomplish?
> - What do the various *characters* represent? What motivates them? How is character revealed through dialog, action, commentary, and physical description? In what ways do major characters change? What events and interactions bring about the changes?
> - What is the relationship between *setting* and *action*? To what extent does setting mirror the characters' psychological states?

- Who is the *narrator*? Is the story told in the *first* or *third person*? Is the narrator omniscient or limited in his or her knowledge of characters and events? Is the narrator recalling the past or reporting events as they happen?
- What is the author's own *point of view*? What are the author's implied *values* and *attitudes*? Does the author show any religious, racial, sexual, or other biases? Is there any discrepancy between the author's values and attitudes and those of the narrator? To whom in the work does the author grant the most status and consideration? Who is presented as less worthy of consideration?
- What about the work is *ironical* or surprising? Where is there a discrepancy between what is said and what is meant?
- What role do *figures of speech* play? What *metaphors*, if any, are sustained and developed? Why might the author have used these metaphors?
- What functions as a *symbol*? How can you tell?
- What *flaws* do you find in the work? Which elements fail to contribute to thematic development? Where does the work lose impact because ideas are stated directly rather than implied? Do any of the characters seem lifeless or inconsistent? Are any of them unnecessary to the work's key events and themes?

Reread and Annotate

Focusing on what you consider the most critical questions from the preceding checklist, begin a second, closer reading of the literary work. With pen or pencil in hand, look for answers to your questions, being sure to note telling details and patterns. Underline striking words, images, and ideas. Draw connecting lines between related items. Jot down questions, answers, and comments in the margins. Of course, if you don't own the work, then you can't write in it. In this case, make notes on a sheet of paper or on index cards.

We've marked the accompanying poem to give you an idea of just what annotation involves. The poem is Shakespeare's Sonnet 29, first published in 1609. Notice that the annotations reveal patterns crucial to an interpretation. For example, jotting down the *rhyme scheme* (*a b a b, c d c d*, and so on) leads to the discovery that one change in rhyme corresponds to a turning point in the narrator's thoughts (see line 9). Similarly, the circling or underlining of repeated or contrasting words highlights ideas developed throughout the poem. The words, *I, my,* and *state,* for instance, are emphasized by repetition. The marginal comments also capture possible *themes,* such as love's healing, redemptive power and the futility of self-absorption and envy.

536   The Literary Paper and Exam Essay

Contrast between unhappy self-absorption ("beweep") and joyous love ("haply"), between "outcast state" and "scorn to change my state."

When, in disgrace with Fortune and men's eyes,	a
I all alone beweep my outcast state,	b
And trouble deaf heaven with my bootless cries, *useless*	a
And look upon myself and curse my fate,	b
Wishing me like to one more rich in hope,	c
Featur'd like him, like him with friends possess'd, *good looks*	d
Desiring this man's art, and that man's scope, *talent knowledge*	c
With what I most enjoy contented least;	d
Yet in these thoughts myself almost despising	e
Haply I think on thee, and then my state, *(First time lover is mentioned.)*	b
Like to the lark at break of day arising	e
From sullen earth, sings hymns at heaven's gate	b
For thy sweet love rememb'red such wealth brings	f
That then I scorn to change my state with kings. *don't want*	f

Envy brackets lines 5–7.

Changes to increasing joy.. Turns away from self-absorption. →

Joyous images. New beginning. Healing power of love.

Modify Your Annotations

Your annotations will help you begin to clarify your thoughts about the work. With these ideas in mind, try to read the work again; make further annotations on anything that seems relevant and modify earlier annotations in light of your greater understanding of the work. At this point, you're ready to move into the actual analysis.

WRITE THE LITERARY ANALYSIS

When you prepare a literary analysis, the steps you follow are the same as those for writing an essay. You start with prewriting; next, you identify your thesis, gather evidence, write the draft, and revise; finally, you edit and proofread your paper.

Prewrite

Early in the prewriting stage, you should take a moment to think about your purpose, audience, point of view, and tone. Your **purpose** in writing a literary analysis is to share your insights about the work. Even if your paper criticizes some aspect of the work (perhaps it finds fault with the author's insensitive depiction of the poor), your primary purpose is still to convey your interpretation of the work's meaning and methods. When writing literary analysis, you customarily assume that your *audience* is composed of readers already familiar with the work. This makes your task easier. In the case of a play or story, for example, there's no need to rehash the plot.

As you write, you should adopt an objective, **third-person point of view.** Even though you're expressing your own interpretation of the work, guard against veering off into first-person statements like "In my opinion" and "I feel that." The **tone** of a literary analysis is generally serious and straightforward. However, if your aim is to point out that an author's perspective is narrow or biased or that a work is artistically unworthy of high regard, your tone may also have a critical edge. Be careful, though, to concentrate on the textual evidence in support of your view; don't simply state your objections.

Prewriting actually begins when you annotate the work in light of several key questions you pose about it (see pages 534–35). After refining your initial annotations (see page 536), try to impose a tentative order on your annotations. Ask yourself, "What points do my annotations suggest?" List the most promising of these points on a separate sheet; then link these points to your annotations. There are a number of ways to proceed. You could, for instance, simply list the annotations under the points they support. Or you can number each point and give relevant annotations the same number as that point. Another possibility is to color-code your annotations: Give each point a color; then underline or circle in the same color any annotation related to that point. Finally, prepare a scratch outline of the main points you plan to cover, inserting your annotations in the appropriate spots. (For more on scratch outlines, see pages 32–34 in Chapter 2.)

If you have trouble generating and focusing ideas in this way, experiment with other prewriting strategies. You might, for example, *freewrite* a page or two on what you have highlighted in the literary text, *brainstorm* a list of ideas, or *map out* the work's overall structure (see pages 27–30 in Chapter 2). Mapping is especially helpful when analyzing a poem.

If the work still puzzles you, it may be helpful to consult outside sources. Encyclopedias, biographies of the author, and history books can clarify the context in which the work was written. Such reference books as *The Oxford Companion to American Literature* and *The Oxford Companion to English Literature* offer brief biographies of authors and summaries of their major works. In addition, *Twentieth-Century Short Story Explication: Interpretations, 1900–1975, of Short Fiction* lists books and articles on particular stories; and *Poetry Explication: A Checklist of Interpretation Since 1925 of British and American Poems Past and Present* does the same for individual poems.

Identify Your Thesis

Looking over your scratch list and any supplementary prewriting material or research notes you collected, try to formulate a **working thesis.** As in other kinds of writing, your thesis statement for a literary analysis should include both your *limited subject* (the literary work you'll analyze and what aspect of the work you'll focus on), as well as your *attitude* toward that subject (the claim you'll make about the work's themes, the author's methods, the author's attitudes, and so on).

Here are some effective thesis statements for literary analysis:

In the poem "The Garden of Love," William Blake uses sound and imagery to depict what he considers the deadening effect of organized religion.

The characters in the novel <u>Judgment Day</u> illustrate James Farrell's belief that psychology, not sociology, determines fate.

The figurative language in Marge Piercy's poem "The Longings of Women" reveals much about women's feelings and their struggle for power.

If your instructor asks you to include commentary from professional critics, or if you explore such sources at your own initiative, proceed with caution. To avoid merely adopting others' ideas, try to formulate your thesis about the work *before* you read anyone else's interpretation. Then use others' opinions as added evidence in support of your thesis or as opposing viewpoints that you can counter. (For more on thesis statements, see pages 37–41 in Chapter 3.)

Thesis Statements to Avoid

Guard against a *simplistic* thesis. A statement like "The author shows that people are often hypocritical" doesn't say anything surprising and fails to get at a work's complexity. More likely, the author shares insights about the *nature* of hypocrisy, the *reasons* underlying it, the *forms* it can take, or its immediate and long-term *effects*.

An *overly narrow* thesis is equally misguided. Don't limit your thesis to the time and place in which the work is set. You shouldn't, for example, sum up the theme of Hawthorne's *The Scarlet Letter* with the thesis "Hawthorne examines the intolerance of seventeenth-century Puritan New England." Hawthorne's novel probes the general, or universal, nature of communal intolerance. Puritan New England is simply the setting in which the work's themes are dramatized.

Also, make sure your thesis is *about the work*. Discussion of a particular *social* or *political issue* is relevant only if it sheds light on the work. If you feel a work has a strong feminist theme, it's fine to say so. It's a mistake, however, to stray to a nonliterary thesis such as "Feminism liberates both men and women."

A *biographical thesis* is just as inappropriate as a sociopolitical one. By all means, point out the way a particular work embodies an author's prejudices or beliefs ("Through a series of striking symbols, Yeats pays tribute in 'Easter, 1916' to the valiant struggle for Irish independence"). Don't, however, devise a thesis that passes judgment on the author's personal or psychological shortcomings ("Poe's neurotic attraction to inappropriate women is reflected in the poem 'To

Helen' "). It's usually impossible to infer such personal flaws from the text alone. Perhaps the author had a mother fixation, but that determination belongs in the domain of psychoanalysis, not literary analysis.

Support the Thesis With Evidence

Once you've identified a working thesis, return to the text to make sure that nothing in the text contradicts your theory. Also, keeping your thesis in mind, search for previously overlooked **evidence** (*quotations* and *examples*) that develops your thesis. Consider, too, how *summaries* of portions of the work might support your interpretation.

If you don't find solid textual evidence for your thesis, either drop or modify it. Don't—in an effort to support your thesis—cook up possible relationships among characters, twist metaphors out of shape, or concoct elaborate patterns of symbolism. As Sigmund Freud once remarked, "Sometimes a cigar is just a cigar." Be sure there's plentiful evidence in the work to support your interpretation. The text of Shakespeare's *Romeo and Juliet*, for instance, doesn't support the view that the feud between the lovers' two families represents a power struggle between right-wing and left-wing politics.

Organize the Evidence

When it comes time to **organize your evidence,** look over your scratch list and evaluate the main points, textual evidence, and outside research it contains. Focusing on your thesis, decide which points should be deleted and which new ones should be added. Then identify an effective sequence for your points. That done, check to see if you've placed textual evidence and outside research under the appropriate points. If you plan to refute what others have said about the work, the discussion on pages 417–18 will help you block out the outline's refutation section. What you're aiming for is a solid, well-developed outline that will guide your writing of the first draft. (For more on outlining, see pages 55–58 in Chapter 5.)

When preparing your outline, remember that the patterns of development can help you sequence material. If you're writing in response to an assignment, the assignment itself may suggest certain patterns. Consider these examples:

Comparison-Contrast

In Mark Twain's *Huckleberry Finn*, what traits do the Duke and the Dauphin have in common? In what ways do the two characters differ?

Definition

How does Ralph Waldo Emerson define "forbearance" in his poem of that name?

Process Analysis

Discuss the stages by which Morgan Evans is transformed into a scholar in Emlyn Williams's play *The Corn is Green*.

Notice that, in these assignments, certain words and phrases (*have in common; in what ways . . . differ; define;* and *discuss the stages*) signal which pattern would be particularly appropriate. Often, though, you'll write on a topic of your own choice. For help in deciding which pattern(s) of development you might use in such circumstances, turn to pages 65–66 in Chapter 6.

Write the First Draft

At this point, you're all set to write. As you rough out your first draft, try to include textual evidence (quotations, examples, summaries), as well as any outside commentary you may have gathered. However, if you get bogged down either incorporating all the evidence or making it blend smoothly with your own points, move on. You can go back and smooth out any rough spots later. In general, proceed as you would in a research paper when blending quotations and summaries with your own words (see pages 508–10 in Chapter 22).

When preparing the draft, you should also take into account the following four conventions of literary analysis.

Use the Present Tense

Literary analysis is written in the **present,** not the past, tense:

In "Arrangement in Black and White," Dorothy Parker depicts the self-deception of a racist who is not conscious of her own racism.

The present tense is used because the literary work continues to exist after its completion. Use of the past tense is appropriate only when you refer to a time earlier than that in which the narrator speaks.

Identify Your Text

Even if your only source is the literary work itself, some instructors may want you to identify it by author, title, and publication data in a formal bibliographic note. In such a case, the first time you refer to the work in the paper, place an asterisk after its title. Then, at the bottom of the page, type an asterisk, and, after it, provide full bibliographic information. Here's an example of such a bibliographic footnote:

*Marianne Moore, "To a Steam Roller," The Voice That Is Great Within Us: American Poetry of the Twentieth Century, ed. Hayden Carruth (New York: Bantam, 1985) 126.

(For more about bibliographic footnotes, consult the most recent edition of the *MLA Handbook for Writers of Research Papers*.)

Use Parenthetic References

If you're writing about a very short literary work, your instructor may not require documentation. Usually, however, documentation is expected.

Fiction quotations are followed by the page number(s) in parentheses (89); poetry quotations, by the line number(s) (12–14); and drama quotations, by act, scene, and line numbers (2.1.34–37). The parenthetic reference goes right after the quotation, even if your own sentence continues. When your sentence concludes with the quotation, the final period belongs *after* the parenthetic reference. If you use sources other than the literary text itself, document these as you would quotations or borrowed ideas in a research paper, and provide a Works Cited page. In this case, the literary work you're writing about should also be listed on the Works Cited page, rather than in a bibliographic footnote. (For more on parenthetic documentation and Works Cited listings, see Chapter 22.)

Quote Poetry Appropriately

If you're writing about a short poem, it's a good idea to include the poem's entire text in your paper. When you need to quote fewer than four lines from a poem, you can enclose them in quotation marks and indicate each line break with a slash (/): "But at my back I always hear / Time's winged chariot hurrying near." (Notice that space appears before and after the slash.) Verse quotations of four or more lines should be indented ten spaces from the left margin of your paper and should appear line for line, as in the original source.

Revise Overall Meaning, Structure, and Paragraph Development

After completing your first draft, you'll gain helpful advice by showing it to others. The checklist that follows will help you and your readers apply to literary analysis some of the revision techniques discussed in Chapters 7 and 8.

> ✔ **REVISING A LITERARY ANALYSIS: A CHECKLIST**
>
> *Revise Overall Meaning and Structure*
> - What is the thesis of the analysis? According to the thesis, which elements of the work (such as theme and structure) will be discussed? In what ways, if any, is the thesis simplistic or too narrow? In what ways, if any, does it introduce extraneous social, political, or biographical issues?
> - What main points support the thesis? If any points stray from or contradict the thesis, what changes should be made?
> - How well supported by textual evidence is the essay's thesis? What evidence, crucial to the thesis, needs more attention? What other interpretation, if any, seems better supported by the evidence?

- Which patterns of development (comparison-contrast, process analysis, and so on) help shape the analysis? How do these patterns support the thesis?
- What purpose does the analysis fulfill? Does it simply present a straightforward interpretation of some aspect of the work? Does it point out some flaw in the work? Does it try to convince readers to accept an unconventional interpretation?
- How well does the analysis suit an audience already familiar with the work? How well does it suit an audience that may or may not share the interpretation expressed?
- What tone does the analysis project? Is it too critical or too admiring? Where does the tone come across as insufficiently serious?

Revise Paragraph Development

- What method of organization underlies the sequence of paragraphs? How effective is the sequence?
- Which paragraphs lack sufficient or sufficiently developed textual evidence? Where does textual evidence fail to develop a paragraph's central point? What important evidence, if any, has been overlooked?
- Which paragraphs contain too much textual evidence? Which quotations are longer than necessary?
- Where could textual evidence in a paragraph be more smoothly incorporated into the analysis?
- If any of the paragraphs include outside research (expert commentary, biographical data, historical information), how does this material strengthen the analysis? If any of the paragraphs consider alternative interpretations, are these opposing views refuted? Should they be?

Revise Sentences and Words

- Which words and phrases wrongly suggest that there is only one correct interpretation of the work ("Everyone must agree ...," "Obviously ...")?
- What words give the false impression that it is possible to read an author's mind ("Clearly, Dickinson intends us to see the flowers as ...," "With Willy Loman's suicide, Miller wants to show that ...")?
- Where does the analysis fail to maintain the present tense? Which uses of past tense aren't justified—that is, which don't refer to something that occurred earlier than the narrator's present?
- Where is there inadequate or incorrect documentation?
- Where does language lapse into needless literary jargon?
- If poetry is quoted, where should slash marks indicate line breaks? Where should lines be indented?

Writing About Literature

Edit and Proofread

When editing and proofreading your literary analysis, you should proceed as you would with any other type of essay (see pages 133–36 in Chapter 9). Be sure, though, to check textual quotations with special care. Make sure you quote correctly, use ellipses appropriately, and follow punctuation and capitalization conventions.

PULLING IT ALL TOGETHER

Read to Form a General Impression

By this time, you're familiar with the steps involved in writing a literary analysis, so you're probably ready to apply what you've learned. The following short story was written by Langston Hughes (1902–67), a poet and fiction writer who emerged as a major literary figure during the Harlem Renaissance of the 1920s. Published in 1963, the story first appeared in *Something in Common*, a collection of Hughes's work. Read the story and gather your first impressions. Then follow the suggestions after the story.

LANGSTON HUGHES
EARLY AUTUMN

1   When Bill was very young, they had been in love. Many nights they had spent walking, talking together. Then something not very important had come between them, and they didn't speak. Impulsively, she had married a man she thought she loved. Bill went away, bitter about women.
   Yesterday, walking across Washington Square, she saw him for the first time in years.
   "Bill Walker," she said.
   He stopped. At first he did not recognize her, to him she looked so old.
5   "Mary! Where did you come from?"
   Unconsciously, she lifted her face as though wanting a kiss, but he held out his hand. She took it.
   "I live in New York now," she said.
   "Oh"—smiling politely. Then a little frown came quickly between his eyes.
   "Always wondered what happened to you, Bill."
10 "I'm a lawyer. Nice firm, way downtown."
   "Married yet?"
   "Sure. Two kids."
   "Oh," she said.
   A great many people went past them through the park. People they didn't know. It was late afternoon. Nearly sunset. Cold.
15 "And your husband?" he asked her.
   "We have three children. I work in the bursar's office at Columbia."
   "You're looking very . . ." (he wanted to say *old*) ". . . well," he said.

She understood. Under the trees in Washington Square, she found herself desperately reaching back into the past. She had been older than he then in Ohio. Now she was not young at all. Bill was still young.

"We live on Central Park West," she said. "Come and see us sometime."

"Sure," he replied. "You and your husband must have dinner with my family some night. Any night. Lucille and I'd love to have you."

The leaves fell slowly from the trees in the Square. Fell without wind. Autumn dusk. She felt a little sick.

"We'd love it," she answered.

"You ought to see my kids." He grinned.

Suddenly the lights came on up the whole length of Fifth Avenue, chains of misty brilliance in the blue air.

"There's my bus," she said.

He held out his hand, "Good-by."

"When . . ." she wanted to say, but the bus was ready to pull off. The lights on the avenue blurred, twinkled, blurred. And she was afraid to open her mouth as she entered the bus. Afraid it would be impossible to utter a word.

Suddenly she shrieked very loudly, "Good-by!" But the bus door had closed.

The bus started. People came between them outside, people crossing the street, people they didn't know. Space and people. She lost sight of Bill. Then she remembered she had forgotten to give him her address—or to ask him for his—or tell him that her youngest boy was named Bill, too.

Ask Questions About the Work

Now that you've read Hughes's story, consult the questions on pages 534–35 so you can devise your own set of questions to solidify your first impressions. Here are some questions you might consider:

1. How does *setting* help bring out the theme?

   Answer: Both the time of year, "early autumn," and the time of day, "nearly sunset," suggest that time is running out. The place, a crowded walkway in a big city, highlights the idea of all the people with whom we never make contact—that is, of life's missed connections.

2. From what *point of view* is the story told? How does this relate to the story's meaning?

   Answer: The point of view is the third-person omniscient. This enables the author to show the discrepancy between what characters are thinking and what they are willing or able to communicate.

3. What *words* and *images* are repeated in the course of the story? How do these *motifs* reflect the story's theme?

   Answer: The words *young* and *old* appear a number of times. This repetition helps bring out the theme of aging, of time running out. *Walking* is another repeated word that gives the reader the sense of people's uninterrupted movement through life. The repeated phrase *people they don't know* emphasizes how hard it is for people to genuinely communicate and connect with one another. *Love,* another repeated word, underscores the tragedy of love lost or unfulfilled.

Writing About Literature 545

Reread and Annotate

In light of the questions you develop, reread and annotate Hughes's story. Then consider the writing assignments that follow.

1. Analyze how Hughes develops the theme that it is urgently important for people to "take time out" to communicate with one another.
2. Discuss some strategies that Hughes uses to achieve universality. You might, for example, call attention to the story's impersonal point of view, the lack of descriptive detail about the characters' appearances, and the generality of the information about the characters' lives.
3. Explain how Hughes uses setting to reveal the characters' psychological states and to convey their sense of loss.

STUDENT ESSAY

Which of the preceding assignments appeals to you most? Student Karen Vais decided to write in response to the first assignment. After using questions to focus her initial impressions and guide her annotations, Karen organized her prewriting and began to draft her literary analysis. The final version of her analysis follows. As you read the essay, consider how well Karen addresses both *what* Hughes expresses and *how* he expresses it. What literary devices does Karen discuss? How are these related to the story's theme? Also note that Karen doesn't identify "Early Autumn" with a bibliographic footnote. Because the story was assigned in class and everyone used the same text, she didn't need to provide such a footnote. Similarly, her instructor didn't require parenthetic documentation of quoted material because the story is so brief.

Stopping to Talk

by Karen Vais

1   In his short story "Early Autumn," Langston Hughes dramatizes the   Introduction
idea that hurried movement through life prevents people from forming or
maintaining meaningful relationships. Hughes develops his theme of   Thesis with plan
"walking" versus "talking" through such devices as setting, plot   of development
construction, and dialogue.

2   The story's setting continually reminds the reader that time is   First supporting
running out; it is urgent for people to stop and communicate before it is   paragraph: focus
too late. The meeting between the two characters takes place on a busy   on setting
walkway, where strangers hurry past one another. The season is autumn,
the time is "late afternoon," the temperature is "cold." The end of the
renewed connection between Mary and Bill coincides with the blurring of

the streetlights. The chilly, dark setting suggests the coming of winter, of night, even of death.

Second supporting paragraph: focus on plot

In keeping with the setting, the plot is a series of lost chances for intimacy. When they were young and in love, Bill and Mary used to "walk . . . [and] talk . . . together," but that was years ago. Then "something not very important . . . [came] between them, and they didn't speak." When she says Bill's name, Mary halts Bill's movement through the park, and, for a short time, Bill "Walker" stops walking. But when Mary hurries onto the bus, the renewed connection snaps. Moreover, even their brief meeting in the park is already a thing of the past, having taken place "yesterday."

Third supporting paragraph: focus on dialog

Like their actions, the characters' words illustrate a reluctance to communicate openly. The dialogue consists of little more than platitudes: "I live in New York now. . . . We have three kids. . . . You and your husband must have dinner with my family some night." The narrator's telling comments about what remains <u>unspoken</u> ("he <u>wanted</u> to say . . . ," "she <u>wanted</u> to say . . .") underscore Bill and Mary's separateness. Indeed, Mary fails to share the one piece of information that would have revealed her feelings for Bill Walker--that her youngest son is also named Bill.

Conclusion

The theme of walking vs. talking runs throughout "Early Autumn." "Space and people," Hughes writes, once again come between Bill and Mary, and, as in the past, they go their separate ways. Through the two characters, Hughes seems to be urging each of us to speak--to slow our steps long enough to make emotional contact.

Commentary

Note that Karen states her *thesis* in the opening paragraph; this first sentence addresses the *what* of the story: "the idea that hurried movement through life prevents . . . meaningful relationships." The next sentence addresses the *how*: "Hughes develops his theme . . . through such devices as setting, plot construction, and dialog." This second sentence also announces the essay's *plan of development*. Karen will discuss setting, then plot, then dialog, with one paragraph devoted to each of these literary elements. In the body of the analysis, Karen backs up her thesis with *textual evidence* in the form of summaries and quotations. The quotations are no longer than is necessary to support her points. In the concluding paragraph, Karen repeats her thesis, reinforcing it with Hughes's own words. She ends by pointing out the relevance of the story's theme to the reader's own life.

Writing Assignment on "Early Autumn"

Having seen what one student did with "Early Autumn," look back at the second and third writing assignments on page 545 and select one for your own

Writing About Literature

analysis of Hughes's story. Then, in light of the assignment you select, read the story again, making any adjustments in your annotations. Next, organize your prewriting annotations into a scratch list, identify a working thesis, and organize your ideas into an outline. That done, write your first draft. Before submitting your analysis, take time to revise, edit, and proofread it carefully.

ADDITIONAL SELECTIONS AND WRITING ASSIGNMENTS

The two selections that follow—a poem by Elizabeth Bishop and a short story by Kate Chopin—will give you further practice in analyzing literary texts. No matter which selection you decide to write on, the following guidelines should help you approach the literary analysis with confidence.

Start by reading the text once to gain an overall impression. Then, draw on any of the questions on pages 534–35 to help you focus your first impressions and guide your annotations. When deciding what to write about, you may select a topic of your own, a subject proposed by your instructor, or one of the assignments suggested after the readings. With your topic in mind, reread the selection and evaluate the appropriateness of your earlier annotations. Make whatever changes are needed before moving your annotations into an informal scratch list. Next, review the scratch list so you can formulate a working thesis and prepare an outline of your ideas. Then go ahead and write your first draft, making sure you revise, edit, and proofread thoroughly before handing in your analysis.

ELIZABETH BISHOP

The recipient of a Pulitzer Prize, Elizabeth Bishop (1911–79) is considered one of the country's leading twentieth-century poets. Her sensitivity to life in all its forms, expressed in simple yet powerful images, is reflected in the poem reprinted here. The poem first appeared in 1946 in *North and South,* a collection of Bishop's work.

THE FISH

1 I caught a tremendous fish
and held him beside the boat
half out of water, with my hook
fast in a corner of his mouth.
5 He didn't fight.
He hadn't fought at all.

He hung a grunting weight,
battered and venerable
and homely. Here and there
his brown skin hung in strips   10
like ancient wallpaper,
and its pattern of darker brown
was like wallpaper:
shapes like full-blown roses
stained and lost through age.   15
He was speckled with barnacles,
fine rosettes of lime,
and infested
with tiny white sea lice,
and underneath two or three   20
rags of green weed hung down.
While his gills were breathing in
the terrible oxygen
—the frightening gills,
fresh and crisp with blood,   25
that can cut so badly—
I thought of the coarse white flesh
packed in like feathers,
the big bones and the little bones,
the dramatic reds and blacks   30
of his shiny entrails,
and the pink swim bladder
like a big peony.
I looked into his eyes
which were far larger than mine   35
but shallower, and yellowed,
the irises backed and packed
with tarnished tinfoil
seen through the lenses
of old scratched isinglass.*   40
They shifted a little, but not
to return my stare.
—It was more like the tipping
of an object toward the light.
I admired his sullen face,   45
the mechanism of his jaw,
and then I saw
that from his lower lip
—if you could call it a lip—
grim, wet, and weaponlike,   50
hung five old pieces of fish line,
or four and a wire leader
with the swivel still attached,

*isinglass: mica, a thin, nearly transparent mineral.

with all their five big hooks
55 grown firmly in his mouth.
A green line, frayed at the end
where he broke it, two heavier lines,
and a fine black thread
still crimped from the strain and snap
60 when it broke and got away.
Like medals with their ribbons
frayed and wavering,
a five-haired beard of wisdom
trailing from his aching jaw.
65 I stared and stared
and victory filled up
the little rented boat,
from the pool of bilge
where oil had spread a rainbow
70 around the rusted engine
to the bailer rusted orange,
the sun-cracked thwarts,*
the oarlocks on the strings,
the gunnels**—until everything
75 was rainbow, rainbow, rainbow!
And I let the fish go.

Writing Assignments on "The Fish"

1. The language that Bishop uses to describe the fish is striking. Analyze Bishop's images and figures of speech in the poem, showing what they reveal about the fish and its history. Explain how this history relates to the poet's vision of the sanctity of life.

2. In the biblical story of Noah and the flood, a rainbow is a sign of God's promise never again to threaten the world with destruction. Discuss the symbolism of the rainbow in Bishop's poem. Explain why you think the poem's climax follows the appearance of the rainbow.

3. Discuss the way the narrator's attitude toward the fish changes as the poem unfolds. Consider the foreshadowing that Bishop provides to prepare readers for the change.

KATE CHOPIN

Fiction-writer Kate Chopin (1851–1904) is best known for her novel *The Awakening* (1899). When first published, the novel shocked readers with its frank sensuality and

---

thwarts: the seats of a boat.
**gunnels:* the upper sides of a boat.

the independent spirit of its female protagonist. The story that follows, first published in *Vogue* in 1894, shows a similar defiance of socially prescribed expectations and norms.

THE STORY OF AN HOUR

1   Knowing that Mrs. Mallard was afflicted with a heart trouble, great care was taken to break to her as gently as possible the news of her husband's death.

2   It was her sister Josephine who told her, in broken sentences, veiled hints that revealed in half concealing. Her husband's friend Richards was there, too, near her. It was he who had been in the newspaper office when intelligence of the railroad disaster was received, with Brently Mallard's name leading the list of "killed." He had only taken the time to assure himself of its truth by a second telegram, and had hastened to forestall any less careful, less tender friend in bearing the sad message.

3   She did not hear the story as many women have heard the same, with a paralyzed inability to accept its significance. She wept at once, with sudden, wild abandonment, in her sister's arms. When the storm of grief had spent itself she went away to her room alone. She would have no one follow her.

4   There stood, facing the open window, a comfortable, roomy armchair. Into this she sank, pressed down by a physical exhaustion that haunted her body and seemed to reach into her soul.

5   She could see in the open square before her house the tops of trees that were all aquiver with the new spring life. The delicious breath of rain was in the air. In the street below a peddler was crying his wares. The notes of a distant song which someone was singing reached her faintly, and countless sparrows were twittering in the eaves.

6   There were patches of blue sky showing here and there through the clouds that had met and piled one above the other in the west facing her window.

7   She sat with her head thrown back upon the cushion of the chair, quite motionless, except when a sob came up into her throat and shook her, as a child who has cried itself to sleep continues to sob in its dreams.

8   She was young, with a fair, calm face, whose lines bespoke repression and even a certain strength. But now there was a dull stare in her eyes, whose gaze was fixed away off yonder on one of those patches of blue sky. It was not a glance of reflection, but rather indicated a suspension of intelligent thought.

9   There was something coming to her and she was waiting for it, fearfully. What was it? She did not know; it was too subtle and elusive to name. But she felt it, creeping out of the sky, reaching toward her through the sounds, the scents, the color that filled the air.

10   Now her bosom rose and fell tumultuously. She was beginning to recognize this thing that was approaching to possess her, and she was striving to beat it back with her will—as powerless as her two white slender hands would have been.

11   When she abandoned herself a little whispered word escaped her slightly parted lips. She said it over and over under her breath: "Free, free, free!" The vacant stare and the look of terror that had followed it went from her eyes. They stayed keen and bright. Her pulses beat fast, and the coursing blood warmed and relaxed every inch of her body.

12   She did not stop to ask if it were not a monstrous joy that held her. A clear and exalted perception enabled her to dismiss the suggestion as trivial.

13   She knew that she would weep again when she saw the kind, tender hands folded in death; the face that had never looked save with love upon her, fixed and gray and dead. But she saw beyond that bitter moment a long procession of years to come that would belong to her absolutely. And she opened and spread her arms out to them in welcome.

14   There would be no one to live for during those coming years; she would live for herself. There would be no powerful will bending her in that blind persistence with which men and women believe they have a right to impose a private will upon a fellow creature. A kind intention or a cruel intention made the act seem no less a crime as she looked upon it in that brief moment of illumination.

15   And yet she had loved him—sometimes. Often she had not. What did it matter! What could love, the unsolved mystery, count for in face of this possession of self-assertion which she suddenly recognized as the strongest impulse of her being.

16   "Free! Body and soul free!" she kept whispering.

17   Josephine was kneeling before the closed door with her lips to the keyhole, imploring for admission. "Louise, open the door! I beg; open the door—you will make yourself ill. What are you doing, Louise? For heaven's sake open the door."

18   "Go away. I am not making myself ill." No; she was drinking in a very elixir of life through that open window.

19   Her fancy was running riot along those days ahead of her. Spring days, and summer days, and all sorts of days that would be her own. She breathed a quick prayer that life might be long. It was only yesterday she had thought with a shudder that life might be long.

20   She arose at length and opened the door to her sister's importunities. There was a feverish triumph in her eyes, and she carried herself unwittingly like a goddess of Victory. She clasped her sister's waist, and together they descended the stairs. Richards stood waiting for them at the bottom.

21   Some one was opening the front door with a latchkey. It was Brently Mallard who entered, a little travel-stained, composedly carrying his gripsack and umbrella. He had been far from the scene of accident, and did not even know there had been one. He stood amazed at Josephine's piercing cry; at Richards' quick motion to screen him from the view of his wife.

22   But Richards was too late.

23   When the doctors came they said she had died of heart disease—of joy that kills.

Writing Assignments on "The Story of an Hour"

1. Show how Chopin uses imagery and descriptive detail to contrast the rich possibilities for which Mrs. Mallard yearns with the drab reality of her everyday life.

2. Argue that "The Story of an Hour" dramatizes the theme that domesticity saps a woman's spirit and physical strength.

3. Does Chopin's characterization of Mrs. Mallard justify the story's unexpected and ironic climax? Explain your response.

24
WRITING EXAM ESSAYS

YOU may never consider **exam essays** fun, but once you develop the knack, writing an essay as part of an exam can be as much of a learning experience as writing an essay or report out of class. There are differences, of course. At home, you can "hatch" your essay over several hours, days, or even weeks; you can write and rewrite; you can produce an impressively typed final copy.

Exam essays, though, are different. Time pressure is the name of the game. If you have trouble writing essays at home, the idea of preparing one in a test situation may throw you into a kind of panic. How, you may wonder, can you show what you know in such a short time? Indeed, you may feel that such tests are designed to show you at your worst.

Befuddling students and causing anxiety are not, however, the goals that instructors have in mind when they prepare essay exams. Instructors intend such exams to reveal your understanding of the subject—and to stimulate you to interpret course material in perceptive, new ways. They realize that the writing done under time pressure won't result in a masterpiece; such writing may include misspellings and awkward sentences. However, they *do* expect reasonably complete essay answers: no brief outlines, no rambling lists of unconnected points. Focused, developed, coherent responses are what instructors are looking for. Such expectations are not as unrealistic as they may first seem when you realize that all the writing techniques discussed in this book are applicable when taking essay tests.

Writing Exam Essays

THREE FORMS OF WRITTEN ANSWERS

There are three general types of questions that require written answers—some as short as one or two sentences, others as long as a full, several-paragraph essay.

Short Answers

One kind of question calls for a **short answer** of only a few sentences. Always read the instructions carefully to determine exactly what's expected. Such questions often ask you to identify (or define) a term *and* explain its importance. An instructor may give full credit only if you answer *both* parts of the question. Also, unless the directions indicate that fragmentary responses are acceptable, be prepared to write one to three full sentences.

Here are several examples of short answers for an exam in modern art history.

Directions: Identify and explain the significance of the following:

1. *Composition with Red, Yellow, and Blue*, 1921: Like most of Piet Mondrian's "compositions," this painting consists of horizontal and vertical lines and the primary colors, red, yellow, and blue. The painting also shows Matisse's influence on Mondrian since Matisse believed that art should express a person's spirit through pure form and color rather than depict real objects or scenes.
2. "Concerning the Spiritual in Art": This is an essay written by Wassily Kandinsky in 1912 to justify the abstract painting style he used. Showing Matisse's influence, the essay maintains that pure forms and basic colors convey reality more accurately than true-to-life depictions.
3. The Eiffel Tower Series: Done around 1910 by Robert Delaunay, this is a series of paintings having the Eiffel Tower as subject. Delaunay used a cubist approach, analyzing surface, space, and interesting planes.

Paragraph-length Answers

Questions requiring a **paragraph-length answer** may signal—directly or indirectly—the length of response expected. For example, such questions may indicate "answer in a few sentences," or they may be followed by a paragraph-sized space on the answer sheet. In any case, a successful answer should address the question as completely yet as concisely as possible. Beginning with a strong topic sentence will help you focus your response.

Following is a paragraph-length answer to a question on a political science exam:

Directions: Discuss the meaning of the term *interest group* and comment briefly on the role such groups play in the governing of democratic societies.

An interest group is an "informal" type of political organization; its goal is to influence government policy and see legislation enacted that favors its members. An interest group differs from a political party; the interest group doesn't want to control the government or have an actual share in governing (the whole purpose of a political party). Interest groups are considered "informal" because they are not officially part of the governing process. Still, they exert tremendous power. Democratic governments constantly respond to interest groups by passing new laws and policies. Some examples of interest groups are institutions (the military, the Catholic Church), associations (the American Medical Association, Mothers Against Drunk Driving), and nonassociational groups (car owners, television viewers).

Essay-length Answers

You will frequently be asked to write an **essay-length answer** as part of a longer examination. Occasionally, an exam may consist of a single essay, as in a "test-out" exam at the end of a writing course.

Here is a typical essay question from an exam in an introductory course in linguistics. A response to this question can be found on pages 560–61.

> Account for the differences in American and British English by describing at least *three* major influences that affected the way this country's settlers spoke English. Give as many examples as you can of words derived from these influences.

The rest of this chapter discusses the features of a strong essay response and shows how the writing process can be adapted to a test-taking situation.

HOW TO PREPARE FOR EXAM ESSAYS

Being able to write a good exam essay is the result of a certain type of studying. There are times when cramming is probably unavoidable, but you should try to avoid this last-minute crunch whenever possible. It prevents you from gaining a clear overview of a course and a real understanding of a course's main issues. In contrast, spaced study throughout the semester gives you a sense of the *whys* of the subject, not just the *who, what, where,* and *when*.

As you prepare for an exam essay, you should try to follow these steps:

- In light of the main concepts covered in the course, identify key issues that the exam might logically address.
- With these issues in mind, design several exam essay questions.
- Draft an answer for each anticipated question.
- Commit to memory any facts, quotations, data, lists of reasons, and so forth that you would include in your answers.

Although you may not anticipate the exam's actual questions, preparing some questions and answers can give you practice analyzing and working with the course material. In the process, you'll probably allay some pre-exam jitters as well.

AT THE EXAMINATION

Survey the Entire Test

Look over the entire written-answer section of a test before working on any part of it. Note which sections are worth the highest point value and plan to spend the longest time on those sections. Follow any guidelines that the directions may provide about the length of the response. When "a brief paragraph" is all that is required, don't launch into a full-scale essay.

If you're given a choice about which exam questions to answer, read them all before choosing. Of course, select those you feel best equipped to answer. If it's a toss-up between two, you might quickly sketch out answers to both (see page 557) before deciding which to do. To avoid mistakes, circle questions you plan to answer and cross out those you'll skip. Then give yourself a time limit for writing each response and, within reason, stick with your plan.

Understand the Essay Question

Once you've selected the question you're going to write on, you need to make sure you know what the question is looking for. Examine the question carefully to determine its slant or emphasis. Most essay questions ask you to focus on a specific issue or to bring together material from different parts of a course.

Many questions use **key directional words** that suggest an answer developed according to a particular pattern of development. Here are some key directional words and the patterns they suggest:

Key Directional Words	Pattern of Development
Provide details about . . .	Description
Give the history of . . .	Narration
Trace the development of . . .	
Explain . . .	Illustration
List . . .	
Provide examples of . . .	
Analyze the parts of . . .	Division-classification
Discuss the types of . . .	
Analyze . . .	Process analysis
Explain how . . .	
Show how . . .	

Key Directional Words	Pattern of Development
Discuss advantages and disadvantages of . . . Show similarities and differences between . . .	Comparison-contrast
Account for . . . Analyze . . . Discuss the consequences of . . . Explain the reasons for . . . Explain why . . . Show the influence of . . .	Cause-effect
Clarify . . . Explain the meaning of . . . Identify . . .	Definition
Argue . . . Defend . . . Evaluate . . . Justify . . . Show the failings or merits of . . . Support . . .	Argumentation-persuasion

The following sample questions show the way key directional words imply the approach to take. In each example, the key words are italicized. Note that some essay questions call for two or more patterns of development. The key terms could, for example, indicate that you should *contrast* two things before *arguing* the merits of one.

1. Galileo, now recognized as having made valuable contributions to our understanding of the universe, was twice tried by the Vatican. *Explain the factors* that *caused* the church and the astronomer to fall into what one historian has termed a "fatal collision of opposite philosophies." [Cause-effect]
2. *Define* the superego and *explain how,* according to Freud, the superego develops. [Definition; process analysis]
3. *Explain the difference* between "educational objectives" and "instructional objectives." *Provide specific examples* of each, focusing on the distinction between students' immediate and long-term needs. [Comparison-contrast; illustration]

WRITE THE ESSAY

The steps in the writing process are the same, whether you compose an essay at home or prepare an essay response in a classroom test situation. The main difference is that during a test the process is streamlined. Following are some

Writing Exam Essays

helpful guidelines for handling each writing stage when you prepare an essay as part of an exam.

Prewrite

Prewriting begins when you analyze the essay question and determine your essay's basic approach (see pages 555–56). We suggest that you do your analysis of the question on the exam sheet: Underline key directional terms, circle other crucial words, and put numbers next to points that the question indicates you should cover.

Then, still using your exam page or a piece of scratch paper, make notes for an answer. (Writing on the exam sheet means you won't have several pieces of paper to keep track of.) Jot down main points as well as facts and examples. If you feel blocked, try brainstorming, freewriting, mapping, or another prewriting technique (see pages 25–30) to get yourself going.

What to Avoid. Don't get overinvolved in the prewriting stage; you won't have time to generate pages of notes. Try using words and phrases, not full sentences or paragraphs. Also, don't spend time analyzing your audience (you know it's your instructor) or choosing a tone (exams obviously require a serious, analytic approach).

Identify Your Thesis

Like essays written at home, exam essays should have a **thesis.** Often, the thesis is a statement answering the exam question. For example, in response to a question asking you to "Discuss the origins of apartheid," your thesis might begin, "The South African law of 'separateness,' or apartheid, originated in 1948, a result of a series of factors that...." Similarly, the essay answer to a question asking you to "Discuss the process by which nations are admitted to the European Community..." might start, "Nations are admitted to the European Community through the process of...." Note that these thesis statements are somewhat informal. They state the *subject* of the essay but *not* the writer's *attitude* toward the subject. In a test-taking situation, these less-structured thesis statements are perfectly acceptable. (For more on thesis statements, see Chapter 3.)

Support the Thesis With Evidence

In the prewriting stage, you jotted down material needed to answer the question. At this point, you should review the **evidence** quickly to make sure it's *adequate.* Does it provide sufficient support for your thesis? If not, make some additional quick notes. Also, check that support for your thesis is *unified, specific, accurate,* and *representative* (see pages 46–49 and 66–69).

Organize the Evidence

Before you start writing, devise some kind of **outline.** You may simply sequence your prewriting jottings by placing numbers or letters beside them. Or you can quickly translate the jottings into a brief, informal outline.

However you proceed, go back and review the essay question one more time. If the question has two or three parts, your outline should tackle each one in turn. Suppose a question asks you to "Consider the effects of oil spills on wildlife, ocean ecology, and oil reserves." Your answer should address each of these three areas, with separate paragraphs for each area.

Also, focus again on the question's *key directional words*. If the question asks you to discuss similarities and differences, your outline should draw on one of the two basic *comparison-contrast* formats (see pages 320–21). Since many exam questions call for more than one task (for example, you may be asked both to *define* a theory and to *argue* its merits), you should make sure your outline reflects the appropriate patterns of development.

Many outlines use an *emphatic* approach to organize material ("Discuss which factors are most critical in determining whether a wildlife species will become extinct"). However, when discussing historical or developmental issues (for example, in psychology), you often structure material *chronologically*. In some fields (art history is one) you may choose a *spatial* approach—for instance, if you describe a work of art. Quickly assess the situation to determine which approach would work best, and keep it in mind as you sequence the points in your outline. (Turn to pages 55–57 and 53–55 for more on, respectively, outlining and emphatic, chronological, spatial, and simple-to-complex plans.)

What to Avoid. Don't prepare a formal or many-leveled outline; you'll waste valuable time. A phrase outline with two levels of support should be sufficient in most cases.

Write the Draft

Generally, you won't have time to write a formal introduction, so it's fine to begin the essay with your thesis, perhaps followed by a plan of development (see page 76). Write as many paragraphs as you need to show you have command of the concepts and facts taught in the course. Refer to your outline as you write, but, if inspiration strikes, feel free to add material or deal with a point in a different order.

As you draft your response, you may want to write on every other line or leave several blank spaces at the bottom of the page. That way, you can easily slot in any changes you need to make along the way. Indeed, you shouldn't feel hesitant about crossing out material—a quotation you didn't get quite right, a sentence that reads awkwardly, a fact that should be placed elsewhere. *Do* make these changes, but make them neatly.

When preparing the draft, remember that you'll be graded in part on how *specific, accurate,* and *representative* your evidence is (see pages 47–49 and 66–69). Provide concrete, correct, true-to-type evidence. Make sure, too, that your response is *unified* (see pages 46–47 and 66). Don't include interesting but basically irrelevant information. Stay focused on the question. Using topic sentences to structure your paragraphs will help you stay on track.

Your instructor will need transitions and other markers to understand fully how your points connect to one another. Try to show how your ideas relate by using *signal devices,* such as *first, second, however, for instance,* and *most importantly* (see pages 71–72).

As you near the end of the essay, check the original question. Have you covered everything? Does the question call for a final judgment or evaluative comment? If so, provide it. Also, if you have time, you may want to close with a brief, one- or two-sentence summary.

What to Avoid. Don't write your essay on scrap paper and plan to recopy. You probably won't have enough time. Even if you do, you may, in your haste, leave out words, phrases, or whole sentences. Your first and only draft should be the one written on the exam booklet or paper. Also, unless your instructor specifically requests it, don't waste time recopying the question in your exam booklet.

Instructors find it easier to evaluate what you know if you've used paragraphs. Don't, then, cast your answer as one long paragraph spanning three pages. If you've outlined your ideas, you'll have a clear idea where paragraph breaks should occur. Finally, don't cram your response with everything you know about the subject. Most instructors can detect padded answers in a second. Give focused, intelligent responses, not one rambling paragraph after another.

Revise, Edit, and Proofread

If you've budgeted your time, you should have a few minutes left to review your essay answer. (Don't skip rereading it just so you can leave the room a few minutes early.) Above all, read your response to make sure it answers the question fully. Make any changes that will improve the answer—perhaps add a fact, correct a quotation, tighten a sentence. If you want to add a whole sentence or more, write the material in some nearby blank space and use an arrow to show where it goes. If something is in the wrong place, use an arrow and a brief note to indicate where it should go.

Instructors will accept insertions and deletions—as long as such changes are made with consideration for their sanity. Use a few bold strokes to cross out, not wild spidery scribbles. Use the standard editing marks such as the caret (see page 136) to indicate additions and other changes.

As you reread, check grammar and spelling. Obvious grammatical errors and spelling mistakes—especially if they involve the subject's key terms—may affect your grade. If spelling is a problem for you, request permission to have your dictionary at hand.

SAMPLE ESSAY ANSWER

The essay that follows was written by Andrew Kahan in response to this exam question:

> Account for the differences in American and British English by describing at least three major influences that affected the way this country's settlers spoke English. Give as many examples as you can of words derived from these influences.

1) Maritime pidgin (Portug. infl.)
2) African pidgin (Slaves comm. with each other and with owners)
3) Indian pidgin (words for native plants and animals)

Andrew started by underlining the question's key words. Then he listed in the margin the main points and some of the supporting evidence he planned to include in his answer. That done, he formulated a thesis and began writing his essay. The handwritten annotations reflect the changes Andrew made when he refined his answer before handing in his exam.

American English diverged from British English because those who settled the New World had contact with people that those back in England generally did not. As a result of *this* contact, several pidgin languages developed. A pidgin language, which has its own grammar and vocabulary, comes about when the speakers of two or more unrelated languages communicate ~~for a while~~ over a period of time. Maritime pidgin, African pidgin, and Indian pidgin were three influences that helped shape American English.

By the time the New World began to be settled, sailors and sea merchants of *all* the European nations had traveled widely. A maritime pidgin thus ~~immerged~~ emerged that enabled diverse groups to communicate.* Since Portugal controlled the seas around the time the colonies were settled, maritime pidgin was largely influenced by the Portuguese. Such Portuguese-derived words as "cavort," "palaver," and "savvy" first entered American English in this way.

The New World's trade with Africa also ~~effec~~ affected American English. The slave trade, in particular, took American sailors and merchants all over the African continent. Since the traders mixed up slaves of many tribes to prevent them from becoming unified, the Africans had to rely on *their own* pidgin to communicate with each other. Moreover, slave owners relied on this African-based pidgin to communicate with their slaves.** Since slaves tended to be settled in the heavily populated American coastal areas, elements of the African pidgin readily worked their way into the language of the New World. Words and phrases derived from African pidgins include "caboodle" and "kick the bucket." Other African-based words include "buckaroo" and "goobers," plus words known only in the Deep South, like "cooter" for turtle. African-based slang terms and constructions ("uptight," "put-on," and "hip," meaning "cool" or "in") continue to enter mainstream English from black English even today.

Another *important* influence on American English, in the nation's early days, was contact with Native American culture. As settlers moved inland from coastal areas, they confronted Native Americans, and new pidgins grew up,

* and trade with each other   *** until they mastered English.*

melding English and Indian terms. Indian-based words like "squaw," "tomahawk," and "papoose" entered English. Also, many words for Native American plants and animals have Indian roots: "squash," "raccoon," and "skunk" are just a few. Another possible effect of Native American languages on American English may be the tendency to form noun-noun compounds ("apple butter" and "shade tree"). While such constructions do occur in British English, they are *much* more frequent in American English.

British and American English differ because the latter has been shaped by contact with European languages like Portuguese, as well as by contact with non-European languages--especially those spoken by Africans and Native Americans.

Commentary

Alert to such phrases as *account for* and *influences that affected* in the question, Andrew wrote an essay that describes three *causes* for the divergence of American from British English. The three causes are organized roughly chronologically, beginning with the influence of maritime exploration, moving to the effect of contact with African culture, and concluding with the influence of Native Americans.

Although the essay is developed mainly through a discussion of causes, other patterns of development come into play. The first paragraph *defines* the term "pidgin," while the second, third, and fourth paragraphs draw on *process analysis*; they describe how pidgins developed, as well as how they affected the language spoken by early settlers. Finally, the essay includes numerous *examples*, as the exam question requested. Andrew's response shows a solid knowledge of the material taught in the course and demonstrates his ability to organize the material into a clear, coherent statement.

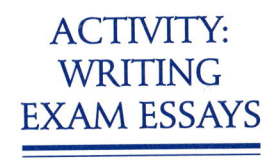

ACTIVITY: WRITING EXAM ESSAYS

In preparation for an exam with essay questions, devise four possible essay questions on the material in one of your courses. For each, do some quick prewriting, determine a thesis, and jot down an outline. Then, for one of the questions, write a full essay answer, giving yourself a time limit of fifteen to twenty-five minutes, whatever is appropriate for the question. Don't forget to edit and proofread your answer.

ACKNOWLEDGMENTS

Adler, Mortimer. "How to Mark a Book." From *Saturday Review,* July 6, 1940. Reprinted by permission of General Media Publishing Group.

Angelou, Maya. "Louise Cox." From *Singin' and Swingin' and Gettin' Merry Like Christmas* by Maya Angelou. Copyright © 1976 by Maya Angelou. Reprinted by permission of Random House, Inc.

Baker, Russell. "The Plot Against People." From the *New York Times,* June 18, 1968. Copyright © 1968 by The New York Times Company. Reprinted by permission.

Bishop, Elizabeth. "The Fish." From *The Complete Poems 1927–1979* by Elizabeth Bishop. Copyright © 1979, 1983 by Alice Helen Methfessel. Reprinted by permission of Farrar, Straus & Giroux, Inc.

Britt, Suzanne. "Neat People vs. Sloppy People." From *Show and Tell* by Suzanne Britt, © 1983. Reprinted by permission of Suzanne Britt.

Ciardi, John. "Dawn Watch." From *Manner of Speaking* (1982). Reprinted by permission of Ciardi Family Publishing Trust and John L. Ciardi.

Cole, K.C. "Entropy." From the *New York Times,* March 18, 1982. Copyright © 1982 by The New York Times Company. Reprinted by permission.

Cousteau, Jacques-Yves. "The Bounty of the Sea." From *The Bounty of the Sea* by Jacques-Yves Cousteau. Reprinted with the permission of The Cousteau Society, © The Cousteau Society.

Gallup, George, Jr. "The Faltering Family." From *Forecast 2000* by George Gallup, Jr., with William Proctor. Copyright © 1984 by George Gallup, Jr., Reprinted by permission of William Morrow & Company, Inc.

Gibbs, Nancy. "When Is It Rape?" From *Time,* June 3, 1991. Copyright 1991 Time Inc. Reprinted by permission.

Gottfried, Martin. "Rambos of the Road." Reprinted by permission of Martin Gottfried.

Greene, Bob. "Unwritten Rules Circumscribe Our Lives." From the *Chicago Tribune,* June 2, 1982. Reprinted by permission of Tribune Media Services.

Greenfield, Meg. "Why Nothing Is 'Wrong' Anymore." From *Newsweek,* July 28, 1986. Copyright © 1986, Newsweek, Inc. All rights reserved. Reprinted by permission.

Hughes, Langston. "Early Autumn." From *Something in Common* by Langston Hughes. Copyright © 1963 by Langston Hughes. Copyright renewed © 1991 by Arnold Rampersad and Ramona Bass. Reprinted by permission of Hill and Wang, a division of Farrar, Straus & Giroux, Inc.

Kingston, Maxine Hong. "Photographs of My Parents." From *The Woman Warrior* by Maxine Hong Kingston. Copyright © 1975, 1976 by Maxine Hong Kingston. Reprinted by permission of Alfred A. Knopf, Inc.

Kupfer, Fern. "Institution Is Not a Dirty Word." From "My Turn" column of *Newsweek*, December 13, 1982. Reprinted by permission of Fern Kupfer.

Lindbergh, Anne Morrow. "The Channelled Whelk." From *Gift from the Sea* by Anne Morrow Lindbergh. Copyright © 1955 by Anne Morrow Lindbergh. Reprinted by permission of Pantheon Books, a division of Random House, Inc.

Malcolm X. "My First Conk." From *The Autobiography of Malcolm X* by Malcolm X, with Alex Haley. Copyright © 1964 by Alex Haley and Malcolm X. Copyright © 1965 by Alex Haley and Betty Shabazz. Reprinted by permission of Random House, Inc.

McClintock, Ann. "Propaganda Techniques in Today's Advertising." Reprinted by permission of Ann McClintock.

Newfield, Jack. "Stallone vs. Springsteen." From *Playboy*, 1986. Reprinted by permission of Jack Newfield. Quoted within essay, thirteen lines from "Born in the U.S.A." by Bruce Springsteen, used by permission of Jon Landau Management.

Nilsen, Alleen Pace. "Sexism as Shown Through the English Vocabulary." From *Sexism and Language* by Alleen Pace Nilsen, Haig Bosmajian, H. Lee Gershuny, and Julia P. Stanley. Copyright 1977 by the National Council of Teachers of English. Reprinted with permission.

Nizer, Louis. "Low-Cost Drugs for Addicts?" From "How About Low-Cost Drugs for Addicts?" by Louis Nizer, from the *New York Times*, June 8, 1986 (op-ed). Copyright © 1986 by The New York Times Company. Reprinted by permission.

Orwell, George. "Shooting an Elephant." From *Shooting an Elephant and Other Essays* by George Orwell, copyright 1950 by Sonia Brownell-Orwell and renewed 1978 by Sonia Pitt-Rivers, reprinted by permission of Harcourt Brace & Company.

Quinn, Carin C. "The Jeaning of America—and the World." Reprinted by permission of *American Heritage* magazine, a division of Forbes Inc., © Forbes Inc., 1978.

Rivers, Caryl. "What Should Be Done About Rock Lyrics?" Reprinted by permission of Caryl Rivers.

Ruth, Beth Johnson. "Our Drug Problem." Reprinted by permission of Beth Johnson Ruth.

Staples, Brent. "Black Men and Public Space." Reprinted by permission of Brent Staples.

Suina, Joseph. "And Then I Went to School." From *Linguistic and Cultural Influences on Learning Mathematics*, Rodney Cocking & Jose Mestre, eds. Reprinted by permission of Lawrence Erlbaum Associates, Inc., and the author.

Theroux, Phyllis. "The Worry Factor." Copyright © 1981 by Phyllis Theroux, from *Night Lights* by Phyllis Theroux. Used by permission of Viking Penguin, a division of Penguin Books USA Inc.

Walker, Alice. "Am I Blue?" From *Living by the Word: Selected Writings 1973–1987*, copyright © 1986 by Alice Walker, reprinted by permission of Harcourt Brace & Company.

White, E.B. "Once More to the Lake." From *Essays of E.B. White* by E.B. White. Copyright 1941 by E.B. White. Reprinted by permission of HarperCollins Publishers.

INDEX

Abstract language, 68, 116, 121
Academic Index, 474
Accurate support in an essay, 49, 225
Activities, *See* Prewriting activities; Revising activities
Adequate support in an essay, 48, 69
Ad hominem argument, 425
Adjectives, 159–60
Adler, Mortimer, 303
　"How to Mark a Book," 303–305
Adverbs, 106, 123
Alliteration, in literary works, 533
"Am I Blue?" (Walker), 214–16
Ambiguity, 223
"America's Homeless: How the Government Can Help" (Courtney), 516–25
Analogy, 318–19
Analyzing your audience, 19–21
　checklist, 21
"And Then I Went to School" (Suina), 339–42
Anecdote, as evidence, 44–45
Angelou, Maya, 207
　"Louise Cox," 207–12
Annotating a literary work, 535–36, 545
Announcement thesis, 39–40
APA documentation format, 513–15
Appeal to authority (fallacy), 425
Argumentation-persuasion, 408–454
　audience in, 409–412, 433
　deductive reasoning, 418, 420–22
　defined, 408–409
　factors in,
　　ethos, 410–13
　　logos, 410–13
　　pathos, 410–13
　goodwill in, 416
　inductive reasoning, 418–20, 434
　　inductive leap, 420
　logical fallacies
　　ad hominem argument, 425
　　appeal to faulty authority, 425
　　bandwagon, 274–75
　　begging the question, 425
　　cardstacking, 274
　　either-or, 425
　　false analogy, 425
　　faulty conclusion, 420, 421–22
　　hasty or sweeping generalization, 225, 419
　　non sequitur thinking, 425
　　post hoc thinking, 351, 425
　　questionable or faulty authority, 425
　　red herring, 425
　　sweeping major premise, 420–21
　organization in, 417–18
　in other patterns of development, 390, 409
　other patterns of development in, 155, 186, 221, 317, 347, 380, 416–17, 434–35
　prewriting activities, 436–37
　prewriting checklist, 412–13
　prewriting for, 152, 412–13
　purpose, 409–11
　refutation of opposition, 417–18, 433–34
　revising, 426–27, 435
　revising activities, 437–39
　revising checklist, 426–27
　strategies for using, 413–26
　student essay and commentary, 427–35
　support in, 414–16
　syllogism, 420–22
　thesis in, 412–14, 433
　tone in, 410–11
　Toulmin logic, 422–24
　Writing assignments with a specific purpose, audience and point of view, 453–54
Articles in bibliography, 479, 500–501
Assertion, in argumentation-persuasion, 413, 417
Assignment boundaries, determining, 19
Assignments with a specific purpose, audience, and point of view, *See* Writing assignments with a specific purpose, audience, and point of view
Assonance, in literary works, 533
Attitude expressed in a thesis, 38–39
Attribution, in research documentation, 506–507

565

Audience
  in argumentation-persuasion, 409–12, 433
  in cause-effect, 347, 349–50
  in comparison-contrast, 316
  in definition, 380
  in description, 154–55
  determining during prewriting, 19, 20–21
  in division-classification, 255, 266
  in illustration, 221–22
  in narration, 186
  in process analysis, 285
  in writing a literary analysis, 537
Authority, questionable appeal to, 425
Authorship, in documentation, 507–508, 514
Author's name in bibliography, 478–80, 514

Background paragraphs, 73, 433
Baker, Russell, 276
  "The Plot Against People," 276–78
Bandwagon propaganda technique, 274–75
"Becoming a Strong Reader," 3–11
Begging the question, 425
Bias in sources, 415–16, 477
Bibliographies, list of common 472–73
Bibliography cards, 478–80
  sample, 479–80
Bibliography form, 479–80
Bibliography, preliminary, 465
Bibliography, working, 475–76, 478–80
Biographical thesis, in literary analysis, 538
Bishop, Elizabeth, 547
  "The Fish," 547–49
"Black Men and Public Space" (Staples), 374–76
Blocked format for quotations, 509–10
Body paragraphs, 63–73
  in argumentation-persuasion, 415–16, 433–34
  in cause-effect, 350–53, 360
  in comparison-contrast, 319–22, 328–29
  in definition, 383–84, 390–91
  in description, 157, 166
  in division-classification, 259–60, 266–68
  in illustration, 224–27, 232–33
  in narration, 188–93, 197–98
  in process analysis, 288–90, 298
  revising, 167, 198–99, 233–34, 361–62, 391–92
Books, in bibliography, 478–80, 497–500
Bound periodicals, 472
"Bounty of the Sea, The" (Cousteau), 371–72
Brainstorming, 25–29
  in argumentation-persuasion, 427–28
  in definition, 386–87
  group, 28–29, 427
Bridging sentences, 72
Britt, Suzanne, 332
  "Neat People vs. Sloppy People," 332–34
Broad thesis, 40

Call numbers, 467–68, 478
Card catalog, 465–69
Card stacking propaganda technique, 274
Causal analysis. *See* Cause-effect
Causal chain, 350–51, 360
Causes, types of, 350–51
Cause-effect, 346–78
  audience in, 347–50
  causal chains, 350–51, 360
  defined, 346
  organization in, 352–54
  in other patterns of development, 165, 197–98, 232, 262, 347, 390
  other patterns of development in, 154, 186, 221, 256, 286, 316–17, 380
  outlining, 353, 356–57
  post hoc thinking, 351
  prewriting activities, 362–63
  prewriting checklist, 348
  prewriting for, 152, 348, 356
  purpose, 347–50, 360
  revising, 354
  revising activities, 363–64
  revising checklist, 354–55
  strategies for using, 349–54
  student essay and commentary, 355–62
  thesis in, 351–52, 353
  tone in, 349–50
  writing assignments with a specific purpose, audience, and point of view, 377–78

CD-ROM indexes, 472, 473–74
"Channelled Whelk" (Lindbergh), 237–41
Checklists
  audience analysis, 21
  literary analysis, 534–35
  outlining, 56–57
  prewriting
    argumentation-persuasion, 412–13
    cause-effect, 348
    comparison-contrast, 317
    definition, 381–82
    description, 156–57
    division-classification, 256–57
    illustration, 223
    narration, 186–87
    process analysis, 286–87
    manuscript format, 134–36
    research paper subject selection, 462
  revising, 94–95, 96–97
    argumentation-persuasion, 426–27
    cause-effect, 354–55
    comparison-contrast, 322–23
    definition, 385–86
    description, 160–61
    division-classification, 260–61
    illustration, 227–28
    literary analysis, 541–42
    narration, 193–94
    process analysis, 291–92
    research paper, 511–12
  revising essay components
    meaning, 94–95
    paragraph development, 96–97
    sentences, 116
  subject selection, 462
  words, 127
Choosing a research paper subject, 462
Chopin, Kate, 549
  "The Story of an Hour," 550–52
Chronological method of organization, 53–54, 66, 71, 189–90
  in cause-effect, 352
  in description, 158
  in division-classification, 267
  in exam essays, 558
  flashback, 189, 197
  flashforward, 189–90
  in illustration, 226
  in narration, 189–90
  in process analysis, 288–89, 298

Index

Ciardi, John, 179
  "Dawn Watch," 179–81
Circular definition, 383
Claims, in argumentation-persuasion, 413, 422–24
Classification. See Division-classification
Clauses, 105–108, 113
Clichés, 124
Climactic emphasis in sentences, 112–13
Climax, in literary works, 532
Clustering, See Mapping
Coherent support, 69–73
Cole, K. C., 394
  "Entropy," 394–96
Colloquial expressions, 118
Combined notes, 489
Commentary for student essays
  argumentation-persuasion, 433–35
  cause-effect, 359–62
  comparison-contrast, 328–30
  definition, 389–92
  description, 165–67
  division-classification, 266–69
  illustration, 282–85
  narration, 197–99
  process analysis, 297–99
  research paper, 527
Common ground, in argumentation, 416
Comparison-contrast, 315–45
  analogy in, 318–19
  audience in, 316
  defined, 315
  organization of, 320–21
    one-side-at-a-time, 320–21
    point-by-point, 320–21
  in other patterns of development, 262, 316–17, 390
  other patterns of development in, 221, 232, 328
  outlining, 325
  prewriting activities, 330–31
  prewriting checklist, 317
  prewriting for, 151, 317, 324
  purpose in, 316–17
  revising, 322–23, 329–30
  revising activities, 331–32
  revising checklist, 322–23
  strategies for using, 318–22
  student essay and commentary, 323–30
  thesis in, 319, 328
  transitions in, 321

writing assignments with a specific purpose, audience, and point of view, 345
Complex sentences, 107–108, 109
Compound-complex sentences, 108
Compound sentences, 106–107
Computerized catalog, in library, 465–66, 473–75
Conclusion (to essay), 76–78, 147
  in argumentation-persuasion, 435
  in cause-effect, 361
  in comparison-contrast, 329
  in definition, 390
  in description, 166
  in division-classification, 260, 266, 268–69
  methods, 76–78
  in process analysis, 290–91
  purpose of, 76
  revision of, 268–69, 299
Concrete language, 68, 120–21, 159–60, 165–66, 190–92
Conflict, 187–88, 532
Conjunctions, coordinating, 106
Conjunctions, correlative, 106
Conjunctions, subordinating, 107–108
Conjunctive adverbs, 106
Connotative language, 119, 155–56, 165, 410–11
Controlling idea. See Thesis
Coordinating conjunction, 106
Correlation, 351
Correlative conjunctions, 106
Courtney, Brian
  "America's Homeless: How the Government Can Help," 516–27
Cousteau, Jacques, 371
  "The Bounty of the Sea," 371–72
Credibility. See Ethos
Cumulative sentence, 110

Deductive reasoning, 418, 420–22
Definition, 379–407
  audience in, 380–84
  circular, 383–84
  defined, 379–80
  etymology, 384
  extended, 380–81, 384
  formal, 382–83, 389
  in other patterns of development, 262, 380, 434
  other patterns of development in, 186, 316, 347, 382, 384

  by negation, 384–85
  prewriting activities, 392–93
  prewriting checklist, 381–82
  prewriting for, 152, 381–82, 386–87
  purpose in, 380, 382
  revising activities, 393
  revising checklist, 385–86
  stipulative, 385
  strategies for using, 382–85
  student essay and commentary, 386–92
  tone in, 380
  writing assignments with a specific purpose, audience, and point of view, 407
Definition by negation, 384–85
Denotative language, 119, 156
Dependent clause, 105–108, 113
Description, 154–84
  audience in, 154–55
  connotative language in, 155–56, 165
  defined, 154
  denotative language in, 156
  details in, 157–59
  dominant impression in, 157, 165
  figurative language in, 159–60, 166
  objective, 156
  organization in, 158–59
  in other patterns of development, 154–55, 198, 262, 389
  other patterns of development in, 165
  prewriting activities, 168
  prewriting checklist, 156–57
  prewriting for, 156–57, 163
  purpose in, 154–55
  revising, 160–61, 167
  revising activities, 168–69
  revising checklist, 160–61
  sensory language, 159–60, 165
  strategies for using, 157–60
  student essay and commentary, 161–68
  subjective, 156–57
  thesis in, 157
  tone in, 156–57
  types of, 155–56
  writing assignments with a specific purpose, audience, and point of view, 183–84
Details as evidence, 44–46, 79, 157–59, 188, 197

Dewey decimal system, 467–68
Diagramming. See Mapping
Dialog, 191, 198
Diction, 116, 117–18
Directional process analysis, 285, 289
Direct quotations, 191, 198
  in note-taking, 484–85
Division-classification, 253–83
  audience in, 254–56
  defined, 253–54
  introduction, 266, 268–69
  organization in, 260, 267,
  in other patterns of development, 255–56
  other patterns of development in, 262, 267
  prewriting activities, 269
  prewriting checklist, 256–57
  prewriting for, 152, 256–57, 262
  principle of, 257–59, 266
  purpose in, 254–56, 266
  revising, 260–61, 268–69
  revising activities, 270
  revising checklist, 260–61
  strategies for using, 257–60
  student essay and commentary, 261–69
  thesis in, 259–60, 266
  tone in, 255, 266, 267
  writing assignments with a specific purpose, audience, and point of view, 283
Documentation
  APA format, 513–15
  MLA format, 504–10, 513–15, 516–26
  scientific format, 515
Dominant impression, 157, 165
Doublespeak, 118
Dramatic emphasis, 102, 225
Dramatic license, 189, 297

"Early Autumn" (Hughes), 543–44
Economy, 102–105
Edition (book), 479, 499
Editing, 133–42, 148
  of exam essays, 559
  of literary analysis, 543
  of research paper, 510–11
"Editing and Proofreading," 133–42
  activities, 142
  checklist, 135–36
Either-or fallacy, 425
Elements of literary works, 532–34
Ellipsis, 485

Emphasis, 102, 112–16, 225
Emphatic method of organization, 54, 66
  in argumentation-persuasion, 416–17
  in cause-effect, 352–54
  in description, 158, 166
  in exam essays, 558
  in first draft, 66
  in illustration, 226, 232
Empty phrases, 102–104
"Entropy" (Cole), 394–96
Error chart, 134
Essays
  argumentation-persuasion, 408–54
  cause-effect, 346–78
  comparison-contrast, 315–45
  definition, 379–407
  description, 154–84
  division-classification, 253–83
  exam essay, 552–67
  illustration, 220–52
  literary analysis, 531–51
  narration, 186–219
  process analysis, 284–314
  reading, 3–11
  research paper, 494–527
  writing, 15–142
  See also Student essays
Essay exam answers, writing, 552–67
Ethos, 410–11, 433
Etymology, 384
Evaluating sources, 415–16, 477–78
Evidence in an essay, 40, 44–51, 146, 221–23, 287
  characteristics of
    accurate, 49, 225
    adequate, 48, 69, 224
    coherent, 69–73
    documented, 40–41, 49–50
    dramatic, 48–49, 225
    relevant, 46–47
    representative, 49
    specific, 47–48, 66–68, 225–26, 283
    unified, 46–47, 66
  See also Supporting paragraphs
Exams, types of answers, 553–54
Exam essays, writing, 552–61
  activity, 561
  sample answer, 559–61
Examples
  characteristics of, 46–50, 52–60, 66–69, 360, 415
  colon with, 605

variety of, 224
See also Evidence
Exemplification. See Illustration
Expert authority, 40, 425
Explaining with illustrations, 222
Extended definition, 380–81, 384
Extended example, 224

Facts, 44, 45, 48, 76, 220, 224, 415
Factual thesis, 40
Fallacies. See Logical fallacies
False analogy (fallacy), 425
"Faltering Family, The" (Gallup), 364–70
Faulty authority (fallacy), 425
Feedback, 91–93, 167, 299, 329, 361, 435
  chart, 92, 435
Figurative language, 119, 123–24, 159–60, 166
Figures of speech, 123–24, 159–60, 166
  analogy, 318–19
  clichés, 24
  in comparison-contrast, 318–19
  in description, 159–66
  in literary works, 533
  metaphor, 124, 160, 533
  mixed, 124
  personification, 124, 160, 533
  simile, 124, 159–60, 166, 533
First draft, writing, 61–87
  activities, 82–87
  of literary analysis, 540–41
  of research paper, 502–10
  on word processor, 146–47
First-person point of view, 23, 192–93, 198, 227, 415
"Fish, The" (Bishop), 547–49
Flashback, 189, 197
Flashforward, 189–90
Foreshadowing, in literary works, 532
Formal definition, 382–83, 389
Formal diction, 116–18
Fragments
  correction strategies, 569–70, 571–73
  practice in correcting, 573–74
  types of, 568–69, 570–71, 596
  used for emphasis, 114–15
Freewriting, 27–28, 195, 228–29

Gallup, George, 364
  "The Faltering Family," 364–70
General periodicals, 471
General Periodicals Index, 474

Index

General subject of any essay, 19, 24–27
Generalizations, hasty or sweeping, 419
Generalized examples, 224
Generating raw material, 27–31, 45–50, 151–52
"Getting Started Through Prewriting," 15–36
Gibbs, Nancy, 397
   "When Is It Rape?" 397–402
Glittering generalities, 272
Goodwill, in argumentation, 416
Gottfried, Martin, 403
   "Rambos of the Road," 403–405
Greene, Bob, 248
   "Unwritten Rules Circumscribe Our Lives," 248–50
Greenfield, Meg, 279
   "Why Nothing Is 'Wrong' Anymore," 279–81
Group brainstorming, 28–29, 427

Hasty generalization (fallacy), 225, 419
"How to Mark a Book" (Adler), 303–306
Hughes, Langston, 543
   "Early Autumn," 543–44
Hypothetical example, 224

"Identifying a Thesis," 37–43
Illustration, 220–52
   audience in, 221–22
   defined, 220
   extended example, 224
   organization in, 226–27, 229, 232
   in other patterns of development, 221, 262, 390
   other patterns of development in, 232
   prewriting activities, 235–36
   prewriting checklist, 223
   prewriting for, 223, 228–29
   purpose in, 221–23
   revising, 227, 233–35
   revising activities, 236–37
   revising checklist, 227–28
   strategies for using, 224–27
   student essay and commentary, 228–34
   tone in, 233
   writing assignments with a specific purpose, audience, and point of view, 252
Imagery, in literary analysis, 533

Immediate cause, 350
Independent clause, 105–108, 113
Index cards, for bibliography, 476, 479–80
   for note-taking, 482–83, 486–87
Indexes, list of common, 472–73
Inductive leap, 420
Inductive reasoning, 418–20, 434
Inference, 419, 434
Informational process analysis, 285, 289, 297
"Institution Is Not a Dirty Word" (Kupfer), 439–41
Instructor feedback, 90–91
Interviews, 459
Introduction to an essay, 74–76, 147
   in cause-effect, 359
   in definition, 384–85, 389
   methods of, 74–76
   in process analysis, 290–91
   purpose of, 74
   revision of, 97, 128, 268–69, 329–30, 435
Inverted word order, 115
Irony, 533

Jargon, 117–18
"Jeaning of America—and the World, The" (Quinn), 310–14
Journals, 17–19, 323–25

Key directional terms, 555–56, 558
Kingston, Maxine Hong, 175
   "Photographs of My Parents," 175–78
Kupfer, Fern, 439
   "Institution Is Not a Dirty Word," 439–41

Ladder of abstraction, 121
Length of papers, 18–19, 458–59
Length of paragraphs, 95–96
Length of sentences, 108–10
Library of Congress Subject Headings, 467–68
Library of Congress system, 467–68
Library research, 31, 40–41, 457–93
   activities, 490–93
   author cards, 467
   bibliographies and indexes, list of, 472–73
   call numbers, 467–68
   card catalog, 466–67
   computerized catalog, 465–66
   computerized periodicals index, 473–75

Dewey decimal system, 467–68
Humanities Index, 472–73
Library of Congress, 467–68
   note-taking, 476–89
   periodicals, 470–75
Readers' Guide to Periodical Literature, 472–73
   reference section, 469–70
Social Sciences Index, 472–73
   subject cards, 467
   title cards, 466–67
   using indexes and bibliographies, 473–75
Limited subject of an essay, 24–32
Limited subject of a research paper, 461–63
Lindbergh, Anne Morrow, 237
   "Channelled Whelk," 237–41
Literary analysis paper, writing, 531–51
   assignments, 546, 549, 551
   quotations in, 541
   sample student essay, 545–56
Literature, elements of, 532–34
Logic, 418–26
   Toulmin, 422–24
Logical fallacies, 424–26
   ad hominem, 425
   appeal to authority, 425
   bandwagon, 274–75
   begging the question, 425
   cardstacking, 274
   either-or, 425
   false analogy, 425
   faulty conclusion, 420, 421–22
   hasty or sweeping generalization, 225, 419
   non sequitur thinking, 424–25
   post hoc thinking, 351, 424
   questionable or faulty authority, 425
   red herring, 425
   sweeping major premise, 420–21
Logos, 410–11
Loose sentences, 110
"Louise Cox" (Angelou), 207–12
"Low-Cost Drugs for Addicts?" (Nizer), 446–48

Magazines, bibliography of, 478–79, 500–501
Major premise, 420–22
Malcolm X, 307
   "My First Conk," 307–309
Manuscript format, 134–36, 512, 516–25

Mapping, in generating raw material, 29, 355–56
Mass-market periodicals, 471
McClintock, Ann, 271
　"Propaganda Techniques in Today's Advertising," 271–75
Meaning, revising for, 88–89, 94–95, 97
Meaning and structure, revision checklist, 94–95
Metaphor, 124, 160, 533
Meter, in poems, 533
Microfilm periodicals, 475
Minor premise, 420–22
MLA format, 476, 497–502, 504–508,
　attributions, 506
　bibliography, 476, 497–502
　used in sample research paper, 516–26
　works cited page, 476, 497–502, 526
Model essays. See Student essays
Model research paper, 516–26
Modifiers, 109
Motif, in literary work, 532
"My First Conk" (Malcolm X), 307–309

Name-calling, 272
Narration
　audience in, 186
　defined, 185
　details in, 190–92
　dialog in, 191, 198
　dramatic license in, 189
　flashback in, 189
　flashforward in, 189–90
　narrative point, 187–89, 197
　organization in, 189–90, 197
　in other patterns of development, 186, 262
　other patterns of development in, 197–98
　point of view in, 192–93
　prewriting activities, 199–200
　prewriting checklist, 186–87
　prewriting for, 186–87, 194–95
　purpose in, 186
　revising, 193, 198–99
　revising activities, 200–201
　revising checklist, 193–94
　sensory description in, 190–91, 198–99
　strategies for using, 187–93
　student essay and commentary, 194–99
　thesis in, 187–88
　tone in, 188, 191
　verb tense in, 192–93
　writing assignments with specific purpose, audience, and point of view, 218–19
Narrative commentary, 189
Narrative point, 187–89, 197
Narrator, 532
Narrowing topics, 24–32, 461–63
Near-quotes, sample notecard, 484
"Neat People vs. Sloppy People" (Britt), 332–34
Newfield, Jack, 332
　"Stallone vs. Springsteen," 335–38
Newspaper articles in bibliography (MLA), 478–79, 500–501
Nexis, 474
Nilsen, Alleen Pace, 243
　"Sexism in the English Language," 243–47
Nizer, Louis, 446
　"Low-Cost Drugs for Addicts?" 446–48
Nominative case, 385–87
Nonrestrictive clauses, 107
Non sequitur thinking, 424–25
Notes, duplicating, 483–84
Note-taking, 476–93
　activities, 490–93
　combined notes, 489
　direct quotations, 484–85
　duplicating, 483–84
　key terms in, 482
　keyed to source, 482
　kinds of notes, 484–89
　near-quotes, 488–89
　on paper, 483
　outlining and writing, 485–91
　over-brief, 483
　page numbers on, 482
　paraphrase, 488
　plagiarism, 477, 486–87, 488–89
　problems with, 476–77
　reading sources, 481
　sample note cards, 483, 486–89
　sorting, 495
　summary, 486
　word-for-word notes, 488
Noun–verb combinations, 123

Objective description, 156
Objectivity of sources, 477–78
Omniscient point of view, 533
"Once More to the Lake" (White), 170–75

One-side-at-a-time organization, 320–21, 418, 433
Onomatopoeia, 165
Opposing viewpoints, 417–18, 434
Organization in an essay, 52–60, 146
　activities, 59–60
　chronological, 53–54, 71, 158, 166, 189–90, 197, 226, 232
　cause-effect, 353–54
　emphatic, 34, 71, 166, 227, 353
　format for, 78–79
　one-side-at-a-time, 320–21
　outlining to achieve, 55–56
　patterns of development, 52–53, 65–67, 226
　point-by-point, 320–21, 328
　simple-to-complex, 55, 227
　spatial, 34, 71, 158, 166, 226
　traditional format, 78–79
Organizations' abbreviations, 621
"Organizing the Evidence," 52–60
Orwell, George, 201
　"Shooting an Elephant," 201–205
"Our Drug Problem" (Ruth), 449–51
Outlining, 55–58, 61
　checklist, 56–57
　in first draft, 61, 63–64
　formal, 55–58, 229, 293–94, 325, 356–57, 429
　research paper, 495–97
　sample, 517–18
　sample, 57–58
　scratch, 32–33, 56, 145
　sentence, 57
　topic, 57

Pagination, 508
Paragraph development, 63–78
　checklist, 96–97
　revising, 95–97
Paragraph length, 95–96
Parallelism, 102, 113–14
Paraphrases, in note-taking, 488
Parentheses
　in APA format, 513
　in MLA format, 504–508
Parenthetic documentation
　APA format, 513–15
　MLA format, 497–502, 504–508
Passive verbs, 122–23, 192
Pathos, 410–11
Patterns of development, 30–31, 42, 45–46, 48, 52–53, 154–454
　in essay exams, 558

to generate raw material, 45–46, 151–52, 262
in literary analysis, 539–40
mixed, 20, 48, 151–52, 154–55, 181–83, 186, 221, 255–56, 285–86, 316–17, 347, 380, 409
to organize the evidence, 52–56
in supporting paragraphs, 65–66
Peer feedback, 91–93, 147
Periodic sentence, 110–12
Periodicals, 470–75, 479, 500–502
Periodical indexes, 470–75
Personalized inventory, 192
Personal experience, 17–18, 44–45, 224, 415
Personification, 124, 160, 533
Persuasion. *See* Argumentation-persuasion
"Photographs of My Parents" (Kingston), 175–79
Plagiarism, 477, 486–87, 488–89
Plain folks propaganda technique, 263
Plan of development, 75, 232, 389,
"Plot Against People, The" (Baker), 276–78
Plot, in literature, 532
Poetry, 533–34, 541, 547–49
Point-by-point organization, 320–21, 328, 418
Point of view, 19, 23–24, 227, 232, 415, 459
in literary analysis, 533
in narration, 192–93, 197
Popular diction level, 117–18
Post hoc thinking, 351, 424
Preliminary research, for research paper, 463–64
Premises, 420–22
Preparing for essay exams, 552–55
Prepositional phrases, 104–105
Present tense, in literary analysis, 540
Prewriting, 15–36, 145
in argumentation-persuasion, 412–13, 428, 436–37
audience in, 20–21
brainstorming, 25–26, 28, 145, 386, 436–37
group brainstorming, 29, 427
in cause-effect, 348–49, 356, 362–63
in comparison-contrast, 317, 324, 330–31
in description, 156, 160–61, 168
in definition, 381–82, 387, 392–93

in division-classification, 256–57, 262, 269
for essay exams, 555–56
freewriting, 27, 195, 228–29, 145
in illustration, 223, 228–29, 235
for literary analysis, 536–37
journal use in, 17–18, 324
mapping, 29, 293, 356
in narration, 186–87, 194–95, 199–200
patterns of development in, 30–31, 151–52, 262
point of view in, 23
in process analysis, 286–87, 293, 300–301
purpose in, 19–20
questioning the subject, 25, 162
tone in, 21–22
on word processor, 145
Prewriting activities
for argumentation-persuasion, 437–38
for cause-effect, 363–64
for comparison-contrast, 331–32
for definition, 393–94
for description, 168
for division-classification, 270
for illustration, 235–36
for narration, 199–200
for process analysis, 300–301
Prewriting checklists
argumentation-persuasion, 412–13
cause-effect, 348
comparison-contrast, 317
definition, 381–82
description, 156–57
division-classification, 256–57
illustration, 223
literary analysis, 334–35
narration, 186–87
process analysis, 286–87
Primary causes, 350–51
Primary research, 459–61, 503
Principle of division-classification, 257–59, 266
Problem-solving, 285
Process
reading, 3–11
in writing, 15–148
Process analysis, 284–314
audience in, 285–88
conclusion, 290–91, 299
defined, 284
directional, 289
informational, 289

introduction in, 290–91
organization in, 288–300
in other patterns of development, 286
other patterns of development in, 154, 255, 298, 380
outlining in, 293–94
prewriting activities, 200
prewriting checklist, 286–87
prewriting in, 152, 286, 293
purpose in, 285–86, 288, 297
revising activities, 201–202
revising checklist, 291–92
signal devices, 289
strategies for using, 287–91
student essay and commentary, 292–300
thesis in, 287–88, 297
tone in, 290, 297
writing assignments with a specific purpose, audience, and point of view, 314
Pronoun *I*, 23
Pronouns
sexism of, 126–27
Proofreading, 136, 543, 559
"Propaganda Techniques in Today's Advertising" (McClintock), 271–75
Propositions in argumentation-persuasion, 413, 417–18
Publication date of book, 467
Publishing information for bibliography, 478–79
Punctuation
in quotations, 509–10
Purpose
in argumentation-persuasion, 409–11
awareness of in outlining, 55–57
blended, 20
in cause-effect, 347–50, 360
in comparison-contrast, 316–17
in definition, 380, 382
in description, 154–55
determining, in prewriting, 19–20
in division-classification, 254–56, 266
in illustration, 221–23
in literary analysis, 536
in narration, 186
in process analysis, 285–88, 297
in research paper, 458
revising for paragraph development, 95

Qualifying a claim (Toulmin logic), 424
Questionable authority (fallacy),425
Question as emphasis, 115
Questioning the subject, 25, 162
Questions for evaluating essays, 6, 153
Quinn, Carin, 310
    "The Jeaning of America—and the World," 310–14
Quotations
    APA, documentation of, 513–15
    attributions for, 506–507
    blocked format, 509–10
    capitalization with, 509, 608
    comma with, 509
    direct, 191, 198, 484–95
    ellipses with, 485
    interrupted, 509
    in literary analysis, 541
    near-quotes, 448–49
    in note-taking, 484–85
    plagiarism, 486–87, 488–89
    in research paper, 509–10
    sample note cards of, 486–88
    single, 488
    source within a source, 510
    word-for-word, 488
Quotation-within-a-quotation, 510

"Rambos of the Road" (Gottfried), 403–405
Random sample, 461
Raw material, generating, 27–32
Readers' Guide to Periodical Literature, 471, 472–73
Reading literary works, 534–36
Reading process, 1–11
    model selection, 6–8
    questions for evaluating essays, 5–6
    steps in effective reading, 4–6, 153
"Reading Process, The," 1–11
Reading research sources, 481
Reasoning. See Logic
Red herring fallacy, 425–26
Redundancy, 102–103
Reference books, list of commonly held, 469–70
Reference section of library, 469–70
"References" list, APA format, 513–15
Refutation of opposition, 417–18, 433–34
Relative clauses, 105, 107
Relevance of sources for research, 477–78

Relevant support in an essay, 46–47, 225
Remote causes, 350–51
Repeated words, synonyms, and pronouns, 72–73
Repetition, for emphasis, 102
Representative support in an essay, 49, 225
Research, conducting
    activities, 490–93
    bibliography, working, 475–76, 478–80
    card catalog, 465–69
    evaluating sources, 477–78
    interviews, 459
    library, 31, 457–93
    note-taking, 476–89
    plagiarism, 477, 486–89, 504
    preliminary, 463–64
    primary, 459–61, 503–504
    Readers' Guide to Periodical Literature, 471–73
    schedule, 464–65
    secondary, 459
    survey, 459–61, 503–504
    working bibliography, 475–76, 478–80
"Research Paper, The," 453–526
Research paper
    activities, 490–93, 527–28
    APA format, 513–15
    attributions in, 506–507
    checklist for subject selection, 462
    checklist, revising, 511–12
    choosing a subject, 462
    documentation of
        APA, 513–15
        authorship, 478–80
        MLA, 476, 497–502, 504–508
    forming a thesis, 464, 494–95
    limiting the subject, 463
    note-taking, 476–93
    outline for, 495–96
    outline, sample, 517–18
    plagiarism, 477, 486–89
    planning research, 458–65
    purpose of, 457–58
    quotations in, 484–89, 506–507, 509–10
    research stages, 458, 494
    revising, editing, proofreading, 510–12
    sample, 516–26
    writing the draft of, 502–10
    works cited page, 497–502
Restrictive clauses, 107

Revising
    in argumentation-persuasion, 426–27, 435
    of body paragraphs, 167, 178–79, 233–34, 361–62, 391–92
    in cause-effect, 354
    in comparison-contrast, 322–23, 329–30
    conclusions, 268–69, 299
    in definition, 385–86
    in description, 160–61, 167
    in division-classification, 260–61, 268–69
    of exam essays, 559
    in illustration, 227, 233–35
    introductions, 97, 128, 268–69, 329–30, 435
    in literary analysis, 541–43
    in narration, 193, 198–99
    overall organization, 94–95
    in process analysis, 291–92
    paragraph development, 95–96
    research paper, 510–12
    sentences, 101–16
    strategies, 88–93
    structure, 94–95
    words, 116–27
    on word processor, 147–48
Revising activities
    argumentation-persuasion, 436–37
    cause-effect, 362–63
    comparison-contrast, 330–31
    definition, 372–73
    description, 168–69
    division-classification, 269
    illustration, 235
    narration, 200–201
    overall meaning and structure, 98–100
    paragraph development, 98–100
    process analysis, 301–302
    words and sentences, 129–32
Revising checklists
    argumentation-persuasion, 426–27
    cause-effect, 354–55
    comparison-contrast, 322–23
    definition, 385–86
    description, 160–61
    division-classification, 260–61
    illustration, 277–78
    narration, 193–94
    paragraph development, 96–97
    process analysis, 291–92
    research paper, 511–12
    sentences, 116
    words, 127

Index

"Revising Overall Meaning, Structure, and Paragraph Development," 88–100
"Revising Sentences and Words," 101–32
Rhetorical questions, 115–16
Rhymes, in poetry, 533
Rivers, Caryl, 443
   "What Should Be Done About Rock Lyrics?" 443–45
Roundabout openings, 104
Ruth, Beth Johnson, 449
   "Our Drug Problem," 449–51

Sample note cards, 483, 486–90
Sample student essay, successive stages of
   brainstorming for, 26
   conclusion of, 142
   final draft, 137–41
   first draft, 80
   freewriting for, 27
   introduction, 97–98, 128
   mapping for, 29
   outline for, 58
   patterns of development in, 30
   prewriting for, 26–30
   questioning subject for, 25
   revising of, 97, 128
   scratch outline for, 32, 33–34
Satire, 533
Schedule, for research paper, 464–65
Scholarly journals in bibliography, 478–80
Scholarly periodicals, 477–78
Scratch outline, 32–33, 56
Sears list of subject headings, 466
Secondary research, 459, 463–90
Second person in process analysis, 289
"Selecting a Subject, Using the Library, and Taking Notes," 457–93
Sensory description, 159–60, 165
Sentence
   patterns, 110–12
   style, 105–108
   variety, 110–12
Sentences
   revising, 101
      checklist, 116
   variety, 105–108
Seriousness, of sources, 477–78
Setting, in literary works, 532
"Sexism and Language" (Nilsen), 243–47

Sexist language, 125–27
"Shooting an Elephant" (Orwell), 201–205
Signal devices, 71–73
   in argumentation-persuasion, 435
   bridging sentences, 72
   in cause-effect, 354, 360–61
   in comparison-contrast, 321–22, 328
   in definition, 392
   in description, 158, 166
   in division-classification, 260, 267
   in exam essay, 558
   in first draft, 71–73
   in illustration, 232–33
   in narration, 190
   in process analysis, 289–90, 298
   transitions, 71–72
   repeated words, synonyms, and pronouns, 72–73
Simile, 124, 159–60, 166, 533
Simple sentence, 105–106
Simple-to-complex approach, 55, 227
Simplistic thesis, 538
Slanted type. See Italics
Social Sciences Index, 472–73
Sonnet, 534
Source within a source, 510
Sources
   conflicting, 477–78
   documenting, 416, 504–26
   evaluating, 415–16, 477–78
Spatial organization
   in description, 158, 166
   in exam essays, 558
   in first draft, 71
   in illustration, 226
   in organizing essay, 54
Specific support in an essay, 47–48, 66–73, 225, 419
Specific word choice, 120–21
"Stallone vs. Springsteen" (Newfield), 332–38
Stanza, in poems, 533
Staples, Brent, 374
   "Black Men and Public Space," 374–76
Statistics, as evidence, 45
Stipulative definition, 385
"Story of an Hour, The" (Chopin), 550–52
Strong verbs, 68, 121–23
Structure, in literature, 532

Student essays and commentary. *See also* Sample student essay, successive stages of
   argumentation-persuasion, 427–35
   cause-effect, 355–62
   comparison-contrast, 323–30
   definition, 386–92
   description, 161–68
   division-classification, 261–69
   exam essay, 559–61
   illustration, 228
   literary analysis, 545–46
   narration, 194–99
   process analysis, 292–99
   research paper, 516–26
Style, revising for, 101–32
Subject cards in card catalog, 466
Subjective description, 156–57
Subordinate clause. *See* Dependent Clause
Subordinating conjunction, 107–108
Suina, Joseph H., 339
   "And Then I Went to School," 339–42
Summaries, in note-taking, 486
Supporting paragraphs in an essay,
   in argumentation-persuasion, 414–15
   in cause-effect, 355–62
   in comparison-contrast, 323–30
   in definition, 382–84
   in description, 161–68
   in division-classification, 261–69
   in exam essays, 559–61
   in illustration, 228–33
   in literary analysis, 539
   in narration, 188–89
   in process analysis, 292–97
Supporting points in research paper, 495–97
"Supporting the Thesis with Evidence," 44–51
Sweeping generalization. *See* Hasty generalization
Syllogism, 420–22
Symbol, in literary works, 533
Surveys, 459–61

Technical terms, 288
Testimonial (propaganda technique), 273
Theme, in literature, 532
Theroux, Phyllis, 7
   "The Worry Factor," 7–9

Thesis
  activities, 41–43
  announcement, 39–40
  in argumentation-persuasion, 413–14
  broad, 40
  in cause-effect, 351–52
  in comparison-contrast, 319, 328
  in definition, 382–84
  in description, 157
  in division-classification, 259–60
  dominant impression, 157
  effective, 38–40
  in exam essays, 557
  factual, 40
  identifying, 37–41, 145
  in illustration, 226
  in literary analysis, 537
  in narration, 187–88
  placement of in essay, 41
  in process analysis, 288
  in research paper, 464, 494–95
  working, 458, 464, 537–38
Third person, 23, 192, 227, 459, 532
Timeliness of sources, 477–78
Title
  in bibliography, 478–79, 498, 500
  card in catalog, 466–67
  of essays, 78
  page, 135–36
Tone
  awareness of in prewriting, 21–22
  in argumentation-persuasion, 410–12
  in cause-effect, 349–50
  in comparison-contrast, 316–17
  in definition, 382
  in description, 155–56
  in division-classification, 254
  in illustration, 221–22, 233
  in literary analysis, 537
  in narration, 186, 190–91
  in prewriting, 21–22
  in process analysis, 285, 290
  relation to audience and purpose, 20–21
  sentences in relation to, 101–102
  words in relation to, 117
Topic, limiting, 24–27
  for research paper, 463
Topic sentences
  in argumentation-persuasion, 433
  in cause-effect, 360
  in comparison-contrast, 326–27
  in definition, 390
  in description, 159

in division-classification, 267
first draft of, 63–65
in illustration, 232
in narration, 190, 197
in process analysis, 292, 298
revising, 95–96
Toulmin logic, 422–24
Transfer (propaganda technique), 272–73
Transitional paragraphs, 73
Transitions. *See* Signal devices
Typical case example, 224

Understanding the boundaries of an assignment, 19
Unified support in an essay, 46–47, 66
Unnecessary clauses, 105
"Unwritten Rules Circumscribe Our Lives" (Greene), 248–50

Verbs
  active, 121–22
  in description, 159
  linking, 121–22
  in narration, 192–93
  passive, 121–22
  strong, 68, 121–23
  to be, 121–22
Vivid language, 68–69, 159–60, 190–92

Walker, Alice, 214
  "Am I Blue?" 214–16
Warrants (in logic), 422–24
Weak phrases, 103–106
"What Should Be Done About Rock Lyrics?" (Rivers), 443–45
"When Is It Rape?" (Gibbs), 397–402
White, E. B., 170
  "Once More to the Lake," 170–75
"Why Nothing Is 'Wrong' Anymore" (Greenfield), 279–81
Word choice
  revising activities, 127
  revising checklist, 129–32
Word-for-word notes, 488
Word-for-word quotations, 504
Word order, 115
Word processing, 143–48
Words
  abstract, 68, 116, 121
  clichés, 124

concrete, 68, 120–21, 159–60, 165–66, 190–92
connotations of, 119, 155–56, 165, 410–11
denotations, 119, 156
diction level, 116, 117–18
figurative, 119, 123–24, 159–66
formal, 116–18
jargon, 117–18
revising, 127
revising activities, 129–32
revising checklist, 127
sexist, 125–27
specific, 120–21
tone and, 117
verbs, 121–22, 159
vivid, 68–69, 159–60, 190–92
Wordy expressions, 103–105
Working bibliography, 475–76, 478–80
  sample cards, 479–80
Working thesis
  in literary paper, 537–38
  in research paper, 458, 464
Works cited page
  APA format, 513–15
  MLA format, 476, 497–502, 526
"Worry Factor, The" (Theroux), 7–9
Writer's block, 62–63
"Writing About Literature," 531–51
Writing assignments with a specific purpose, audience, and point of view
  argumentation-persuasion, 453–54
  cause-effect, 377–78
  comparison-contrast, 345
  definition, 407
  description, 183–84
  division-classification, 283
  illustration, 252
  narration, 218–19
  process analysis, 314
"Writing Exam Essays," 552–67
"Writing on a Word Processor," 143–48
Writing process
  activities
    editing and proofreading, 142
    identifying the thesis, 41–43
    organizing the evidence, 59–60
    prewriting, 34–36
    revising, 98–100, 129–32
    supporting the thesis, 50–51
    writing the first draft, 82–87
  audience in, 20

Index

point of view in, 23
purpose in, 20
stages in, 16
   editing and proofreading, 139–42, 149
   identifying the thesis, 37–43, 145

organizing the evidence, 53–60, 146
prewriting, 15–36, 145
revising, 88–132, 147–48
supporting the thesis, 44–51, 146

writing the first draft, 61–87, 146
"Writing Process, The," 13–148
"Writing the First Draft," 61–87
"Writing the Research Paper," 494–527